Symbol, Atomic Number and Molar Mass of each Element

Element	Symbol	Atomic Number	Molar Mass / g mol^{-1}	Element	Symbol	Atomic Number	Molar Mass / g mol^{-1}
Actinium	Ac	89	227.0278	Mercury	Hg	80	200.59
Aluminium	Al	13	26.98154	Molybdenum	Mo	42	95.94
Americium	Am	95	(243)	Neodymium	Nd	60	144.24
Antimony	Sb	51	121.75	Neon	Ne	10	20.179
Argon	Ar	18	39.948	Neptunium	Np	93	237.0482
Arsenic	As	33	74.9216	Nickel	Ni	28	58.69
Astatine	At	85	(210)	Niobium	Nb	41	92.9064
Barium	Ba	56	137.33	Nitrogen	N	7	14.0067
Berkelium	Bk	97	(247)	Nobelium	No	102	(259)
Beryllium	Be	4	9.01218	Osmium	Os	76	190.2
Bismuth	Bi	83	208.9804	Oxygen	O	8	15.9994
Boron	B	5	10.81	Palladium	Pd	46	106.42
Bromine	Br	35	79.904	Phosphorus	P	15	30.97376
Cadmium	Cd	48	112.41	Platinum	Pt	78	195.08
Caesium	Cs	55	132.9054	Plutonium	Pu	94	(244)
Calcium	Ca	20	40.08	Polonium	Po	84	(209)
Californium	Cf	98	(251)	Potassium	K	19	39.0983
Carbon	C	6	12.011	Praseodymium	Pr	59	140.9077
Cerium	Ce	58	140.12	Promethium	Pm	61	(145)
Chlorine	Cl	17	35.453	Protactinium	Pa	91	231.0359
Chromium	Cr	24	51.996	Radium	Ra	88	226.0254
Cobalt	Co	27	58.9332	Radon	Rn	86	(222)
Copper	Cu	29	63.546	Rhenium	Re	75	186.207
Curium	Cm	96	(247)	Rhodium	Rh	45	102.9055
Dysprosium	Dy	66	162.50	Rubidium	Rb	37	85.4678
Einsteinium	Es	99	(252)	Ruthenium	Ru	44	101.07
Erbium	Er	68	167.26	Samarium	Sm	62	150.36
Europium	Eu	63	151.96	Scandium	Sc	21	44.9559
Fermium	Fm	100	(257)	Selenium	Se	34	78.96
Fluorine	F	9	18.998403	Silicon	Si	14	28.0855
Francium	Fr	87	(223)	Silver	Ag	47	107.868
Gadolinium	Gd	64	157.25	Sodium	Na	11	22.98977
Gallium	Ga	31	69.72	Strontium	Sr	38	87.62
Germanium	Ge	32	72.59	Sulphur	S	16	32.06
Gold	Au	79	196.9665	Tantalum	Ta	73	180.9479
Hafnium	Hf	72	178.49	Technetium	Tc	43	(98)
Helium	He	2	4.00260	Tellurium	Te	52	127.60
Holmium	Ho	67	164.9304	Terbium	Tb	65	158.9254
Hydrogen	H	1	1.0079	Thallium	Tl	81	204.383
Indium	In	49	114.82	Thorium	Th	90	232.0381
Iodine	I	53	126.9045	Thulium	Tm	69	168.9342
Iridium	Ir	77	192.22	Tin	Sn	50	118.69
Iron	Fe	26	55.847	Titanium	Ti	22	47.88
Krypton	Kr	36	83.80	Tungsten	W	74	183.85
Lanthanum	La	57	138.9055	Uranium	U	92	238.0289
Lawrencium	Lr	103	(260)	Vanadium	V	23	50.9415
Lead	Pb	82	207.2	Xenon			
Lithium	Li	3	6.941	Ytterbium			
Lutetium	Lu	71	174.967	Yttrium			
Magnesium	Mg	12	24.305	Zinc			
Manganese	Mn	25	54.9380	Zirconium			
Mendelevium	Md	101	(258)				

These data are based on IUPAC values to be found in Pure and Applied Chemistry, 52 (1980) 2349.

chemistry
FOR SCIENCE AND ENGINEERING

W.G. BRECK
B.Sc., M.Sc. (Queen's), Ph.D. (Cambridge)

R.J.C. BROWN
B.Sc., M.Sc. (Sydney), Ph.D. (Illinois)

J.D. McCOWAN
B.A., Ph.D. (Toronto), Ph.D. (Cambridge)

Department of Chemistry
Queen's University

MCGRAW-HILL RYERSON LIMITED
Toronto   Montréal   New York   St. Louis   San Francisco
Auckland   Bogotá   Guatemala   Hamburg   Johannesburg
Lisbon   London   Madrid   Mexico   New Delhi   Panama
Paris   San Juan   São Paulo   Singapore   Sydney   Tokyo

CHEMISTRY FOR SCIENCE AND ENGINEERING

ISBN   0-07-092372-8

1234567890   D   0987654321

Printed and bound in Canada

Care has been taken to trace ownership of copyright material contained in this text. The publishers will gladly take any information that will enable them to rectify any reference or credit in subsequent editions.

This book was set in Times Roman by
   Dimensions in DesignType Ltd.
The illustrations and cover art were done by
   Samuel Daniel; design by Brian Reynolds.
The editors were Jane Martin, Jane Ryley and
   Clive Powell.
John Deyell Company was printer and binder.

Canadian Cataloguing in Publication Data

Breck, W. G.
Chemistry for science and engineering

Includes index.
ISBN   0-07-092372-8

1. Chemistry.   I. Brown, R.J.C.   II. McCowan, J.D.
III. Title.

QD31.2.B73   540   C81-094292-5

PREFACE

Chemistry is the science of matter, the study of materials from which the world is made, and a means of understanding the laws governing the natural world. It is the basis for manufacturing new materials, and a source of wealth through the products of chemical industry. Chemistry is at the centre of the scientific and technological developments of the last two centuries, developments which have changed the course of history.

Chemistry is a source of endless fascination and reward for an enquiring mind. Some people find enjoyment in preparing new materials, some in discovering the chemical basis for understanding biology, some in using mathematical skills to solve chemical problems, and some in applying chemical techniques in an industrial environment.

The boundaries of chemistry are indistinct. It merges with physics, with biology, with medicine, and with many areas of engineering. This book is written both for people who intend to work in chemistry itself and for those who want a sound basis of chemistry which they can put to use in these related fields.

It is assumed that students using this book are taking concurrent courses in calculus and physics, and have some knowledge of chemistry from their previous studies. Throughout the book, we have avoided making simplifications that can be misleading, although there are many places where simple ideas are used to assist in understanding the topic under discussion. There is a liberal use of examples throughout the book, and in many places the examples extend, as well as illustrate, the material in the text. From the beginning there is an emphasis on chemical industry and on the chemistry of energy supplies, which will give the student a basis for understanding public debates on developments in these areas. Corrosion and the chemistry of water are other ways where the scientific principles are illustrated in practical ways. We have been relatively strict in adhering to the units, symbols and conventions of the Systeme Internationale, which have been agreed to internationally, and are used here in the forms legally adopted in Canada.

The book has evolved over about a decade of teaching at Queen's University. To Brian Hunter, Doug Hutchinson, Ken Russell, Gus Shurvell and John Stone, we owe our thanks for the errors and omissions which each has uncovered in the course of teaching from earlier versions of the manuscript. To Don Heyding we owe this and much more, for he contributed greatly to the chapter on solid state chemistry, and was a constant support to our efforts during his time as Head of Department. To Professor Louis Bodnar of the Department of Chemical Engineering at the University of Waterloo and Professor E.A. Robinson of the Department of Chemistry at the University of Toronto, we owe our thanks for the care and interest with which they read every chapter, and for the many suggestions and improvements which they provided. These teachers and many, many students have made contributions to the development of the book. We hope that future users—lecturers, students, and practising scientists and engineers—will be kind enough to send us their comments so that the process may continue.

Kingston

January 1981

ACKNOWLEDGEMENTS

The authors wish to thank the following organizations and individuals for their support and cooperation in supplying material for publication in the text.

Page 37: photograph courtesy of C.I.L. Inc.; pages 40 and 41: photographs courtesy of Cominco Limited; page 45: photograph courtesy of C.I.L. Inc.; page 47: photograph courtesy of Alberta Gas Ethylene Company Ltd.; page 50: photograph courtesy of Petrosar Limited; page 145: reprinted with permission from *Chemistry* (1970) **43** 27, copyright by the American Chemical Society, with permission of the Society and Dr. Theodore Benfey; pages 438, 439: courtesy of Professor R.D. Heyding, Queen's University; page 560: courtesy of Duracell Products Company; page 572: courtesy of Aluminum Company of Canada Ltd., Figure 22-7 courtesy of Cominco Ltd.; page 606: data in Table 23-2 are reprinted from *Chemical Data* by G.H. Aylward and T.J.V. Findlay with permission of John Wiley and Sons Ltd.; page 621-623: criteria quoted courtesy of the Ontario Ministry of the Environment; page 629: photograph courtesy of Ontario Hydro; page 672: photograph courtesy of Mr. W.N. Burgess of Bowser, British Columbia; page 677: the Thermochemical Tables are either quoted from or derived from the sources listed in Appendix I itself with the permission of the Committee on Data for Science and Technology (CODATA), Paris, Dr. J.B. Pedley of the University of Sussex, the National Bureau of Standards in Washington, and the Thermodynamic Research Center of Texas A M University.

TABLE OF CONTENTS

I SOME BASIC IDEAS

In the early chapters of this book, we review some of the elementary ideas of chemistry. Not everything is covered, but that should not be necessary for students beginning University work. These chapters should be found to contain mostly familiar material which can be covered fairly quickly.

Some will ask, why bother with the simple topics at all? There are two answers. First, different teachers and books use different notations, or conventions, or even definitions in discussing elementary matters, so that confusion and misunderstandings can arise when using a new book. By starting simply, these difficulties can be avoided. Secondly, elementary concepts must be understood very well by every student who hopes to succeed. A student who does not understand simple chemistry is likely to have a lot of trouble studying complicated chemistry. And finally, mistakes in elementary calculations are a common cause of error. Such mistakes, whether due to misunderstanding or carelessness, lead to wrong answers to problems just as surely as other sorts of mistakes, and can be avoided most of the time if care is taken over simple matters.

1-1 ELEMENTS, COMPOUNDS AND MIXTURES

All matter can be classified as a **mixture**, a **compound** or an **element**, and it is as well to be clear about the definitions of these terms.

The simplest type of matter is an **element**, a substance which cannot be broken up into any other stable substances by chemical means, and which cannot be made as the sole product of a chemical reaction between other substances. This is a negative definition, which identifies those substances which are not elements. For example, when limestone is strongly heated, a gas is given off and quicklime is left; from this observation it may be concluded that limestone is not an element. When an electric current is passed through water, bubbles of gas are formed on the surfaces of the electrodes, and these gases can be shown to be hydrogen and oxygen. The two gases produced by electrolysis can be collected and recombined to form water, showing that they are in some way constituents of water. Hence water is not an element.

However, attempts to decompose iron by such means as heating or electrolysis have never led to any new substances, and so it has been postulated that iron is an element.

Because of the difficulty of proving chemically that a given substance is an element, this definition of elements was very important historically. The development of ideas about the structure of atoms in the twentieth century makes it easier to understand what is meant by an element, but it should be kept in mind that the idea of elements, and the discovery of most of the naturally occurring elements, was the work of chemists. Much of this work was done years before the structure of atoms became known. In modern terms, it could be said simply that in an element all the atoms have the same number of electrons and the same nuclear charge. In a sample of an element, all the atoms are chemically the same. Even this last definition is not exact because of the existence of different *isotopes* of the same element, namely, atoms with the same nuclear charge and different nuclear masses.

A **compound** can be defined as a substance containing more than one element, with well-defined physical and chemical properties which differ in essence from the properties of the elements contained in the substance. In many common compounds, the elements are combined in definite proportions by mass, and the ratio of masses is one of the most important characteristics of the compound. For instance, in water the elements are present in the proportions of 8.00 g of oxygen for every 1.00 g of hydrogen. In carbon dioxide, the proportions are 2.67 g of oxygen for every 1.00 g of carbon.

In some compounds, this rule of "definite proportions" does not apply strictly and such compounds show a range of properties. It might be asked whether such materials should be called compounds. This question is a difficult one, and at this stage it is sufficient to note that some important substances such as the oxides of iron (rust) are of this type.

Many elements and compounds can be mixed together without any chemical reaction occurring, and the resulting material is of course called a **mixture**. A simple example is sand mixed with sugar. The mixture retains some of the properties of both sand and sugar, and can be separated into the two components without any chemical decomposition. For instance the sand can be separated from the sugar by washing the mixture with enough water to dissolve the sugar. Another method of separation would be to use a microscope and tweezers.

Some mixtures are *heterogeneous*, and the two substances in the mixture retain their separate physical characteristics. The sand-sugar mixture is an example of this, for a magnifying glass would enable an observer to distinguish the grains of sand from the sugar crystals. Other mixtures are *homogeneous*, and such mixtures are called *solutions*; an example is a solution of sugar in water. Small amounts of sugar can be mixed with water without any recognizable chemical reaction, and yet no amount of examination of the solution with a microscope will allow any observer to see the sugar in solution.

Virtually all materials are mixtures, but most substances encountered in a chemical laboratory consist predominantly of a single element or compound. A bottle labeled "NaCl" from a reputable laboratory or chemical company can be assumed to contain a substance that is almost all sodium chloride.

However, it is likely that there are small amounts of other salts such as potassium chloride and sodium bromide in the bottle as either a homogeneous or heterogeneous mixture, and so the question of *purity* of chemical substances must be considered. Purity is closely allied to the cost of chemicals, as a simple example will show. Ethanol, C_2H_5OH, is a liquid which is used in society for various purposes in various degrees of purity. For instance, an engineer may use 100 000 L of ethanol as a solvent in an industrial process. Cost is of major importance in buying a large amount of material, and moderate amounts of impurities such as water and methanol may be acceptable to the engineer as he or she tries to minimize costs. On the other hand, a scientist carrying out experiments on the molecular structure of ethanol may require a small sample of very high purity, and will be happy to pay a thousand times the price per gram that the engineer pays in order to get a ten gram sample containing the smallest possible amount of impurities.

Purity is a difficult property to measure. There are many situations in science, engineering and commerce where the presence of certain impurities must be checked and measured routinely: mercury in lake water, calcium in boiler feed water, sulphur dioxide in furnace stack gases, and carbon in steel are just a few examples. The measurement of purity is part of the business of *analytical chemistry*.

1-2   CHEMICAL FORMULAE AND VALENCE

In the shorthand notation used by chemists, the elements are denoted by symbols, such as Na for sodium, F for fluorine, and so on. A list of these symbols along with the names of the elements is to be found opposite the inside front cover.

According to the atomic theory of the English chemist John Dalton, chemical compounds contain numbers of atoms of the different elements in the proportions of simple whole numbers. The history of the theory covers a century of careful work in which the relative masses of the atoms were deduced and the ratios of numbers of atoms in compounds were measured. The history will not be followed here, but the conventions used in writing chemical formulae need to be defined.

A chemical formula lists the elements contained in the compound, and the relative numbers of atoms of each element, expressed as a set of whole numbers, and written as subscripts to the symbols for the elements. For instance, calcium carbonate has the formula $CaCO_3$, indicating that the elements calcium, carbon and oxygen are present, and the numbers of atoms of each element present are in the ratios 1:1:3 respectively. However, there are several types of chemical formulae which are used in different situations and for different purposes. These are defined as follows.

Empirical Formula: the relative numbers of atoms of each element in the compound are expressed as the simplest set of whole numbers.

Molecular Formula: the actual number of atoms of each element in a single molecule of the compound is given. This type of formula only makes sense when well-defined molecules exist in the substance.

Structural Formula: the symbols of the elements are arranged on paper and lines are drawn between the symbols to show which atoms are joined by chemical bonds. In addition, a structural formula may indicate the geometrical arrangement of the atoms in a molecule.

Some examples of these three types of formulae are given in Table 1-1. Each type of formula is used commonly, and the student should study the limitations and uses of each of them.

TABLE 1-1 The Different Kinds of Chemical Formulae

Name	Empirical	Molecular	Structural
hydrogen	H	H_2	H—H
water	H_2O	H_2O	$\overset{O}{\diagup \diagdown}$ H H
methane	CH_4	CH_4	H—C—H with H above and H below
hydrogen peroxide	HO	H_2O_2	H—O—O—H (angular)
ethane	CH_3	C_2H_6	H—C—C—H with H's above and below
ethene, commonly called ethylene	CH_3	C_2H_4	C=C with H's
ethanol	C_2H_6O	C_2H_6O or C_2H_5OH	H—C—C—O—H with H's
dimethyl ether	C_2H_6O	C_2H_6O or $(CH_3)_2O$	H—C—O—C—H with H's

The concept of **valence** or **combining power** of an element is a useful guide in writing formulae correctly. Hydrogen and chlorine combine to form hydrogen chloride, with a molecular formula HCl; each atom is combined with one other atom in this molecule, and each is said to have a valence of one. Water has the molecular formula H_2O, and so oxygen has a valence of two. Calcium chloride has the formula $CaCl_2$, and so calcium has a valence of two. Hence we would expect that calcium and oxygen atoms would be present in equal numbers in calcium oxide, since they have equal valence; this expectation is confirmed by the known formula of calcium oxide, CaO.

Methane has the molecular formula CH_4, from which it can be concluded that carbon has a valence of four. The structural formula shown in Table 1-1 indicates the presence of four "single bonds" from the carbon atom to the hydrogen atoms. The carbon atoms in the ethane molecule, C_2H_6, also have a valence of four, with one of the bonds being used to join the two carbon atoms. However, in ethylene, each carbon atom is bonded to only three atoms. The valence of four is retained by showing the bond between the two carbon atoms as a *double bond*. There is good justification for this procedure since the carbon- carbon bonds in ethane and ethylene have different properties.

Some elements show more than one valence. For example, phosphorus forms two different compounds with chlorine, having the formulae PCl_3 and PCl_5, corresponding to phosphorus valencies of 3 and 5 respectively. Carbon forms two common oxides, carbon monoxide CO, and carbon dioxide CO_2, in which carbon shows valencies of 2 and 4 respectively.

1-3 AMOUNT OF SUBSTANCE: THE MOLE

The amount of a substance present must often be specified, and is commonly measured by the mass, or the volume if the substance is a liquid or a gas. Because of thermal expansion, the volume is not a good method of specifying the amount of substance; for gases, the volume is meaningless as a measure of the amount of matter unless both the temperature and pressure are also specified.

The mass of a sample is not of direct significance in chemistry. One gram of iron contains a different number of atoms from one gram of zinc, and therefore contains a different amount of substance. "Amount of substance" is measured in units of *moles*, and is measured by the *number* of atoms, molecules or other specified entities. The mole as a unit is defined as follows:

The mole is the amount of substance which contains as many elementary entities as there are carbon atoms in exactly 12 g of isotopically pure carbon-12. The elementary entities must be specified, and may be atoms, molecules, ions, electrons, other particles, or specified groups of such particles.

The history of this definition is complicated and is not of concern here. Naturally occurring carbon contains two stable isotopes, with masses which are in the approximate ratio of 12:13, the heavier isotope constituting about 1 percent of the total number of carbon atoms. The definition of the mole is based on the lighter, more abundant isotope ^{12}C. The abbreviation of mole is "mol" when used as a unit and the symbol used to denote amount of matter is n.

The mass of an atom of carbon is exceedingly small, and the number of elementary entities in a mole is correspondingly large. This number is known as the *Avogadro number*, or the *Avogadro constant*, and its value is:

$$N_A = 6.022045 \times 10^{23} \text{ mol}^{-1}$$

Since the mole defines a fixed number of elementary entities, the mass of a mole is proportional to the mass of the elementary entities. The masses of the atoms of the elements can therefore be conveniently compared by using the *molar mass* of the elements rather than the masses of individual atoms. The molar mass of an element is often called the *atomic weight* of the element, and historically a scale of relative atomic weights was built up based upon setting the atomic weight of hydrogen equal to unity. The term "atomic weight," and the related term "molecular weight" will be avoided in this book although they are widely used. The term "molar mass" is preferable because it avoids confusion over units in some circumstances. There is a table of molar masses of the elements opposite the inside front cover. The molar mass is shown as having units of grams per mole, but the figures in the table can also be regarded as being relative atomic weights, which are dimensionless. The use of this table to calculate molar masses is a simple but important skill that students must master. Errors in later work can often be traced to mistakes in calculations of this type.

Example 1-1   Calculate the molar mass of hydrogen gas.

The molar mass of hydrogen atoms is 1.0079 g mol^{-1}; this means that the mass of one mole of hydrogen atoms is 1.0079 g. However, hydrogen gas consists of *diatomic* molecules of formula H_2, and hence the molar mass of hydrogen gas is 2.0158 g mol^{-1}.

Example 1-2   Calculate the molar mass of methane, CH_4.

The molar mass of carbon is 12.011 g mol^{-1}, and that of hydrogen is 1.0079 g mol^{-1} and so

$$\text{molar mass of } CH_4 = 12.011 + (4 \times 1.0079)$$
$$= 16.043 \text{ g mol}^{-1}$$

Example 1-3   How many moles of CH_4 are there in 100.0 kg of methane?

$$\text{Molar mass of } CH_4 \text{ is } 16.043 \text{ g mol}^{-1} \text{ and so}$$
$$\text{number of moles} = 100.0 \times 10^3 \text{ g} / 16.043 \text{ g mol}^{-1}$$
$$= 6.233 \times 10^3 \text{ mol of } CH_4$$

Example 1-4   What is the mass of 0.7852 mol of carbon dioxide, CO_2?

$$\text{Molar mass of } CO_2 = 12.011 + (2 \times 15.999)$$
$$= 44.009 \text{ g mol}^{-1}$$
$$\text{Hence the mass} = 44.009 \text{ g mol}^{-1} \times 0.7852 \text{ mol}$$
$$= 34.56 \text{ g}$$

Example 1-5   What mass of carbon is contained in 1.000 g of carbon dioxide?
One mole of CO_2 contains one mole of carbon atoms. Hence 44.009 g of carbon dioxide contains 12.011 g of carbon, and so 1.000 g of carbon dioxide contains 12.011 g / 44.009 g mol^{-1} or 0.2729 g of carbon.

The reverse procedure to that of the last example is a common problem. Given the percentages by mass of the elements present in a compound, it is required to determine the empirical formula. One way of approaching such problems is shown in the next example.

Example 1-6   A compound containing only carbon and hydrogen is analyzed, and found to contain 85.63% carbon and 14.37% hydrogen by mass. What is its empirical formula?
Consider 100.00 g of the compound; this contains 85.63 g of carbon, or

$$\frac{85.63 \text{ g}}{12.011 \text{ g mol}^{-1}} = 7.129 \text{ mol of C atoms.}$$

It also contains 14.37 g of hydrogen, or

$$\frac{14.37 \text{ g}}{1.008 \text{ g mol}^{-1}} = 14.26 \text{ mol of H atoms.}$$

Thus the ratio of the numbers of H and C atoms present in the molecule is 14.26/7.129 or 1.9997. This is sufficiently close to 2 that the empirical formula is written CH_2. Notice that there are a number of different molecules which have this empirical formula, as discussed previously, and further experiments must be carried out to discover the molecular formula of this compound.

Some substances are not composed of molecules, and further consideration of the idea of molar mass may be helpful for such cases. For example, sodium chloride consists of sodium ions Na^+ and chloride ions Cl^- under virtually all conditions and so molecules having the formula NaCl are rarely dealt with. However, it is convenient to deal with a molar mass corresponding to one mole of the formula NaCl; this quantity is known as the *formula molar mass, formal mass,* or *formula weight,* so as to avoid reference to molecules which do not exist. For NaCl, the formula molar mass is 22.99 + 35.45, or 58.44 g mol^{-1}.

1-4   STOICHIOMETRY

In a chemical reaction, the atoms in the reacting substance or substances are rearranged so that the products of the reaction are different compounds from the reactants. The conventional method of representing chemical reactions is by writing *chemical equations* in which the formulae of the reactants are shown on the left hand side and an arrow shows the direction of reaction to give the products, which are written on the right hand side. As a simple example, the combustion of carbon is represented by the equation

$$C + O_2 \rightarrow CO_2$$

The study of chemical equations and the mass relationships implied by them is called *stoichiometry.*

In a chemical reaction the total number of atoms of each element is not altered, and the notation of chemical equations must reflect this by placing equal numbers of atoms of each type on both sides of the equation. For instance, when hydrogen is burned in oxygen, water is produced. This could be shown by the equation

$$H_2 + O_2 \rightarrow H_2O$$

but such an equation would be very misleading, for it suggests that an atom of oxygen disappears in the reaction. The equation is not *balanced*, and if it were used for further calculations, it would lead to error. A correct, balanced equation for this reaction is

$$H_2 + \tfrac{1}{2}O_2 \rightarrow H_2O$$

In this equation, it is stated that for every mole of molecular hydrogen which reacts, half a mole of oxygen molecules is required. An equally valid balanced equation for the same reaction is

$$2\,H_2 + O_2 \rightarrow 2\,H_2O$$

Balanced equations can be used for calculations of the relationships between the masses of products and reactants.

Example 1-7   What mass of oxygen is required to burn 1.0 t of carbon completely to carbon dioxide?
From the equation

$$C + O_2 \rightarrow CO_2$$

the same number of moles of oxygen as carbon is required. But 1.0 t of carbon is 1.0×10^6 g/12 g mol^{-1}, or 8.22×10^4 mol, and so

$$\text{mass of oxygen} = 8.33 \times 10^4 \text{ mol} \times 32 \text{ g mol}^{-1}$$

$$= 2.67 \times 10^6 \text{ g}$$

$$= 2.7 \text{ t}$$

The chemical equation for the last example is very simple but complicated equations can be treated just as easily.

Example 1-8 An essential step in the industrial production of the element iodine is the reaction of sodium iodate with sulphur dioxide:

$$2\,NaIO_3 + 4\,H_2O + 5\,SO_2 \;\rightarrow\; Na_2SO_4 + 4\,H_2SO_4 + I_2$$

What is the mass of SO_2 required to react with 100. g of sodium iodate, and what mass of iodine is produced?

The molar mass of $NaIO_3$ is 197.9 g mol⁻¹, and so 100. g is equal to 0.505 mol. From the stoichiometric coefficients of the equation, 5 mol of SO_2 are needed for every 2 mol of $NaIO_3$, and so

$$\text{amount of } SO_2 \text{ needed} = 0.505 \times \tfrac{5}{2} \text{ mol}$$

$$= 1.262 \text{ mol}$$

$$\text{and mass of } SO_2 \text{ needed} = 1.262 \text{ mol} \times 64.1 \text{ g mol}^{-1}$$

$$= 80.0 \text{ g}$$

Again, from the equation, 1 mol of I_2 is produced from 2 mol of $NaIO_3$, and so:

$$\text{amount of } I_2 \text{ produced} = 0.505 \times \tfrac{1}{2}$$

$$= 0.252 \text{ mol}$$

$$\text{and mass of iodine produced} = 0.252 \text{ mol} \times 253.8 \text{ g mol}^{-1}$$

$$= 64.1 \text{ g}$$

Example 1-9 When heated strongly, calcium carbonate decomposes to give the metal oxide and carbon dioxide gas. What is the ratio of the mass of the oxide to the mass of the calcium carbonate from which it is produced?

The equation for the decomposition is

$$CaCO_3 \;\rightarrow\; CaO + CO_2$$

One mole of $CaCO_3$ yields one mole of CaO, and so the

$$\text{ratio of masses} = \frac{\text{molar mass of CaO}}{\text{molar mass of CaCO}_3}$$

$$= \frac{56.08 \text{ g mol}^{-1}}{100.09 \text{ g mol}^{-1}}$$

$$= 0.560$$

Example 1-10 Chlorine and caustic soda, NaOH, are produced industrially by electrolysis of salt brine, for which the reaction is summarized by the equation

$$2\,NaCl + 2\,H_2O \;\rightarrow\; 2\,NaOH + Cl_2 + H_2$$

In 1969, Canadian production of chlorine was 834 000 t. Estimate the corresponding production of caustic soda.

Two moles of NaOH are produced for every one mole of Cl_2, and so for this amount of reaction

$$\frac{\text{mass of NaOH}}{\text{mass of } Cl_2} = \frac{2 \text{ mol} \times 40.0 \text{ g mol}^{-1}}{1 \text{ mol} \times 71.0 \text{ g mol}^{-1}}$$

$$= 1.13$$

This ratio can be applied to the entire output for 1969, and so production of NaOH $= 1.13 \times 834\,000$ t

$$= 942\,000 \text{ t}$$

Notice that in this case it is not necessary to convert a mass in tons (a nonmetric unit) to number of moles in order to reach the answer.

1-5   ELECTROLYTES IN SOLUTION

There is much to be learned about the chemical properties of solutions by studying their electrical properties. The simplest electrical property is the ability of the solution to conduct an electric current. Water of high purity is a poor conductor of electricity and could even be called an insulator by comparison with metals. When certain compounds are dissolved in water, the electrical resistance is found to drop to a very small fraction of the resistance of pure water. A compound which has this property is called an *electrolyte,* and other compounds which give non-conducting solutions are called non-electrolytes.

When an electrolyte is dissolved in water, *ions* are formed. An ion is a charged atom or molecule, and it is the motion of the ions in the solution that allows the conduction of electricity through the solution. Ions carry an amount of electrical charge which is an integer multiple of the fundamental unit of charge, the charge of the electron. When an electrolyte is added to water, the solution remains electrically neutral, i.e., does not become electrically charged. Both positive and negative ions are produced in the solution, and the total charge on all the positive ions is equal to the total charge on all the negative ions. Positive ions are often called *cations,* and negative ions *anions.*

Some electrolytes produce ions in solution by *dissociation.* In these cases the ions found in solution are simply related to the structure of the electrolyte in its pure form. As a well known example, sodium chloride crystals consist of sodium ions Na^+ and chloride ions Cl^-. Upon dissolution in water these are released to form the aqueous solution:

$$NaCl(c) \xrightarrow[H_2O]{} Na^+(aq) + Cl^-(aq)$$

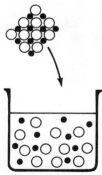

Dissociation of NaCl into Na^+ and Cl^- ions when the crystal is dissolved in water.

In this equation each chemical symbol is followed by an abbreviated description of the state of the chemical species. The description "(c)" means that the NaCl is in the form of crystals, and "(aq)" means that the ions Na^+ and Cl^- are in aqueous solution, i.e., a solution in water. These and similar descriptions will be used throughout this book when the physical state of the chemical substance is not perfectly clear.

The formation of solutions of many salts proceeds by similar dissociation processes. There are other cases, however, where the ions which are found in solution are formed by a chemical reaction between the solute and solvent molecules. Acids provide the simplest examples of this phenomenon. Hydrogen chloride in the pure form is a gas at room temperature, consisting of molecules with the molecular formula HCl. When this gas is dissolved in water, it forms a solution of hydrochloric acid which is a good electrical conductor because it contains hydrogen ions and chloride ions. All evidence points to the fact that the hydrogen ion in aqueous solutions does not conform to the simple structure implied by the chemical formula H^+. Instead, the positively charged hydrogen ion is bonded chemically to one or more water molecules, and its structure is therefore better represented by the chemical formula H_3O^+ or by a formula involving more than one water molecule, $H(H_2O)_n^+$. For the present purposes it is sufficient to use the formula H_3O^+, and this ion is called the *hydrogen ion,* or sometimes the *hydronium ion.* Where the association with water is not relevant, the expression $H^+(aq)$ will also be used, but the symbols $H^+(aq)$ and H_3O^+ refer to exactly the same species.

The process which occurs when HCl gas is dissolved in water can therefore be represented by the chemical equation

$$HCl + H_2O \rightarrow H_3O^+ + Cl^-$$

$$\text{or } HCl(g) \xrightarrow[H_2O]{} H^+(aq) + Cl^-(aq)$$

This is a reaction between the solute and the solvent, water, rather than a dissociation of the solute molecules into ions, and the process is called *ionization.* It is also called *hydrolysis,* since it is a chemical reaction in which water is a reactant.

Ammonia, NH_3, is also a gas at room temperature and moderate pressures, and it too dissolves in water to give an electrically conducting solution. In this case the ions responsible for the conductivity, NH_4^+ and OH^-, are certainly not produced by ionic dissociation of NH_3, but must be formed by a hydrolysis reaction:

$$NH_3(g) + H_2O(l) \rightleftarrows NH_4^+(aq) + OH^-(aq)$$

This is also a case of ionization resulting from hydrolysis. The double arrow symbol used in this equation emphasizes that there is a *chemical equilibrium* involved, and that the reaction can be observed to proceed in either direction depending on the starting point.

Some salts undergo both dissociation and hydrolysis, with important chemical consequences in some cases. For example when sodium carbonate, Na_2CO_3, is dissolved in water, the resulting solution contains significant amounts of the following ions: Na^+, CO_3^{2-}, HCO_3^-, OH^-. The formation of this solution can be described as the dissociation of the salt into its component ions,

$$Na_2CO_3(c) \xrightarrow[H_2O]{} 2\,Na^+(aq) + CO_3^{2-}(aq)$$

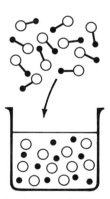

Ionization of HCl into H_3O^+ and Cl^- ions when the gas is dissolved in water.

followed by hydrolysis of the carbonate ion,

$$CO_3^{2-}(aq) + H_2O(l) \rightleftharpoons HCO_3^-(aq) + OH^-(aq)$$

Therefore, when a solution containing large amounts of hydroxide ion, OH^-, is required, it can be made using sodium carbonate as solute instead of using sodium hydroxide, which forms hydroxide ions by dissociation:

$$NaOH \xrightarrow[H_2O]{} Na^+(aq) + OH^-(aq)$$

Electrolytes are often classified as being either *strong* or *weak*. These words are not directly related to the chemical reactivity of the solutions formed, or the concentrations of the solution, but instead, refer to the fraction of the solute which is dissociated or ionized in the solution. A strong electrolyte is completely converted to ions in solution, or very nearly so. Hydrochloric acid is a strong electrolyte and there are virtually no molecules with the molecular formula HCl in its aqueous solutions. All the hydrochloric acid has been converted to hydrogen ions and chloride ions. Ammonia, on the other hand, is a weak electrolyte and the position of the equilibrium

$$NH_3(aq) + H_2O(l) \rightleftharpoons NH_4^+(aq) + OH^-(aq)$$

lies substantially to the left, as suggested by the double arrows. When ammonia is dissolved in water, only a fraction of the molecules are hydrolyzed to ammonium ions and hydroxide ions, and the solution contains a significant fraction of the dissolved ammonia in the form of NH_3 molecules. Although the solution is a conductor of electricity it is not as good a conductor as it would be if the ammonia were completely hydrolyzed.

Water is itself a very weak electrolyte, and is slightly ionized so that in any aqueous solution there are hydrogen ions and hydroxide ions present:

$$2\,H_2O \rightleftharpoons H_3O^+ + OH^-$$

In a *neutral* solution, the concentrations of hydrogen ion and hydroxide ion are equal. In an *acidic* solution the hydrogen ion concentration is increased and the hydroxide ion is decreased compared to a neutral solution. In an acidic solution the hydroxide ion concentration is numerically very small. In a *basic* solution, the hydroxide ion concentration is increased, and the hydrogen ion concentration is very small.

1-6   COMPOSITION AND CONCENTRATION OF SOLUTIONS

Many chemical reactions are carried out in solution, and it is necessary to be able to specify quantitatively the *concentration* or *composition* of a solution. There are a number of different systems used for describing a solution, and the system best suited to a particular purpose depends on the nature of the work in hand.

The **composition** of a solution is defined by the relative amounts of the various substances in the solution. The composition of a solution is not changed by changes of volume when the temperature or pressure on a solution change. There are three commonly used measures of composition, which are

TABLE 1-2   Measures of Composition and Concentration for a Solution of a Solute B in a Liquid Solvent A

For chemical work involving liquid solutions, the volume is generally measured in litres, mass in kilograms, and amount of material in moles.

measure	symbol	definition	units
mass fraction	w	$w_B = \dfrac{\text{mass (B)}}{\text{mass (A)} + \text{mass (B)}}$	none*
mole fraction	x	$x_B = \dfrac{\text{amount (B)}}{\text{amount (A)} + \text{amount (B)}}$	none*
molality	m	$m_B = \dfrac{\text{amount (B)}}{\text{mass (A)}}$	mol kg^{-1}
concentration (or molarity)	[ ] or c	$[B] = c_B = \dfrac{\text{amount (B)}}{\text{volume of solution}}$	mol L^{-1}
formal concentration (or formality)	F	$F_B = \dfrac{\text{amount (B)}}{\text{volume of solution}}$	mol L^{-1}
relative concentration	[ ]$_r$	$[B]_r = c_B/c°$, where $c°$ is a standard state concentration of exactly 1 mol L^{-1}	none

*More precisely, the units of mass fraction are kg of B/kg of solution, and of mole fraction are mol of B/mol of solution. However it is common to omit the units of these quantities.

listed and defined below. Table 1-2 contains a summary of composition and concentration measures and recommended symbols.

Mass fraction   of a substance in a solution is the mass of that substance divided by the total mass of the solution.

Mole fraction   of a substance in a solution is the amount of that substance (in moles) divided by the total amount of solution (in moles).

Molality   of a solution is the amount of solute, in moles, divided by the mass of *solvent,* in kilograms.

The mass fraction is met frequently in engineering and technology, while mole fraction and molality are used in physical chemistry. Mass fraction is often used to specify the compositions of the very dilute aqueous solutions met in environmental studies, in the form "parts per million," ppm, or "parts per billion," ppb.

For a solution containing a number of different substances A, B, C, ... the total mass of solution, m_T, is equal to the sum of the masses of the separate substances:

$$m_T = m_A + m_B + m_C + \ldots\ldots$$

If this equation is divided on both sides by m_T, we get the equation

$$1 = \frac{m_A}{m_T} + \frac{m_B}{m_T} + \frac{m_C}{m_T} + \ldots\ldots$$

which can be rewritten

$$w_A + w_B + w_C + \ldots = 1$$

Hence in a solution, the sum of the mass fractions of all the substances in the solution is equal to one. Of course the solvent must be included in this calculation, and indeed in most ordinary solutions the mass fraction of the solvent is larger than the mass fractions of the solutes. A similar relation holds for the mole fractions of the substances in a solution:

$$x_A + x_B + x_C + \ldots = 1$$

Example 1-12   10.0 g of sodium chloride is dissolved in 250.0 g of water. Calculate the mass fraction and mole fraction of the solute, and the molality of the solution.

(i)   Total mass of solution = 260.0 g

$$\text{so mass fraction of NaCl} = w_{NaCl} = \frac{10.0\,g}{260.0\,g} = 0.0385$$

(ii)   Amount of NaCl $= \dfrac{10.0\,g}{58.44\,g/mol} = 0.171$ mol,

and amount of $H_2O = \dfrac{250.0\,g}{18.01\,g/mol} = 13.88$ mol,

so total amount of solution $= 0.171 + 13.88 = 14.05$ mol

and mole fraction of NaCl $= \dfrac{0.171\,mol}{14.05\,mol} = 1.22 \times 10^{-2}$

(iii)   Molality $= \dfrac{0.171\,mol\ NaCl}{0.2500\,kg\ H_2O} = 0.684$ mol kg^{-1}

Example 1-13   Lead is found to be present in a sample of river water at the level of 2.0 ppm. What mass of lead is contained in 3.0 L of this water?

From the definition of mass fraction,

$$\frac{m_{Pb}}{m_{Pb} + m_{H_2O}} = 2.0 \times 10^{-6}$$

Hence m_{Pb} is very small compared with m_{H_2O}, and so to a good approximation

$$\frac{m_{Pb}}{m_{H_2O}} \approx 2.0 \times 10^{-6}$$

The mass of 3.0 L of water is approximately 3.0 kg, and so

$$m_{Pb} = 2.0 \times 10^{-6} \times 3.0\,kg$$

$$= 6.0 \times 10^{-3}\,g \text{ or } 6.0\,mg$$

Concentration is used to specify the amount of solute in a given volume of solution. It is important to note that concentrations are based upon the volume of the *solution* rather than the volume of solvent used to make up the solution. This means that when the volume of a sample of solution and its concentration are known, the amount of solute in that sample can be calculated directly. Known volumes of solution can be measured out using a *pipette* (for a fixed volume) or a *burette*. Conversely, if a known amount of solute is dissolved in solvent and the resulting solution is diluted to a known volume, then the concentration of the solution can be calculated directly. Special *volumetric flasks* are available for preparing solutions of known concentration in this way. Concentration and formal concentration are defined as follows.

Concentration or *molarity* of a solute in a solution is the amount of that solute present in solution, in moles, divided by the volume of the *solution* in litres.

Formal concentration or *formality* of a solute in a solution is the amount of solute, expressed as number of moles of the solute substance of specified formula divided by the volume of the solution in litres.

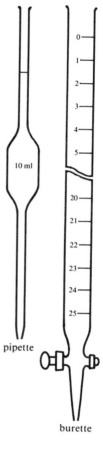

pipette

burette

Example 1-14   A sample of 25.43 g of sucrose, $C_{12}H_{22}O_{11}$, is dissolved in a small amount of water, and the solution is diluted to 250.0 mL in a volumetric flask. Calculate the concentration of the solution.

The molar mass of sucrose is 342.3 g mol⁻¹, and so amount of sucrose

$$= \frac{25.43 \text{ g}}{342.3 \text{ g mol}^{-1}} = 0.07429 \text{ mol}.$$

Hence concentration of sucrose $= \dfrac{0.07429 \text{ mol of solute}}{0.2500 \text{ L of solution}}$

$$= 0.2972 \text{ mol L}^{-1}$$

For a solute which is not an electrolyte, and does not react with the solvent, there is no difference between the concentration of the solution and the formal concentration of the solution. The sucrose solution described in Example 1-14 falls into this category. However, when an electrolyte is dissolved in water, it dissociates to some extent into *ions,* and in such cases it is useful to distinguish between the actual concentration of molecules and ions which are in equilibrium in the solution, and the amount of solute which was used per litre in preparing the solution. For instance, when sodium chloride dissolves in water it dissociates into Na^+ and Cl^- ions. The concentration of undissociated "NaCl" in solution is zero, and the concentrations of Na^+ ions and Cl^- ions are both equal to the number of moles of NaCl which were added per litre of solution.

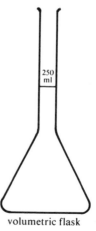

volumetric flask

Example 1-15   A sample of 10.0 g of sodium chloride is dissolved in water, and the solution is diluted to 250.0 mL in a volumetric flask. Calculate the formal concentration of NaCl, and the concentration of Na^+ and Cl^- ions.

$$\text{Amount of NaCl added} = \frac{10.0\,g}{58.44\,g/mol}$$

$$= 0.171\,mol$$

$$\text{hence formality of NaCl in the solution} = \frac{0.171\,mol}{0.2500\,L}$$

$$= 0.684\,mol\,L^{-1}$$

However, because of dissociation, the concentration of NaCl is zero, and the concentration of each of the ions Na^+ and Cl^- is $0.684\,mol\,L^{-1}$.

Example 1-16   A solution of $BaCl_2$ is prepared with a formal concentration of $0.351\,mol\,L^{-1}$. Calculate the concentrations of Ba^{2+} and Cl^- ions.

Since $BaCl_2$ is a strong electrolyte, it dissociates into ions:

$$BaCl_2 \rightarrow Ba^{2+} + 2\,Cl^-$$

One mole of $BaCl_2$ yields one mole of Ba^{2+} ions and two moles of Cl^- ions in solution. Hence

$$[Ba^{2+}] = 0.351\,mol\,L^{-1}$$

$$\text{and } [Cl^-] = 0.702\,mol\,L^{-1}$$

When dealing with weak electrolytes which are not completely dissociated, the concentrations of the ions and undissociated electrolyte can only be calculated using the theory of equilibrium constants, and in these cases it is especially useful to use formal concentration to express the total concentration of electrolyte. For instance, if 0.050 mol of acetic acid is dissolved in water, and the solution is made up to a volume of 100. mL the formal concentration of acetic acid is $0.50\,mol\,L^{-1}$. But because of the ionization of the acid, expressed by the reaction

$$CH_3COOH + H_2O \rightleftharpoons H_3O^+ + CH_3COO^-$$

the concentration of acetic acid molecules, CH_3COOH, is smaller than 0.50 $mol\,L^{-1}$. The actual concentration of acetic acid molecules can be calculated or measured, and is expressed as a molar concentration in units of $mol\,L^{-1}$. From the stoichiometry of the ionization reaction, it is seen that one mole of acetate ion is generated for every mole of acetic acid that ionizes, and hence the sum of the acetic acid concentration and the acetate ion concentration must be equal to the formal concentration of the acetic acid. If the formal concentration of the acid is denoted F_a, then

$$[CH_3COOH] + [CH_3COO^-] = F_a$$

This kind of relationship is called a *mass balance* equation, and expresses the fact that matter is not created or destroyed in chemical processes. This is often expressed by saying that mass is *conserved* in chemical reactions. Mass balance equations will be used later in the book when discussing chemical equilibria.

Despite its usefulness, the concept of formal concentrations is not used by all chemists, and students must be aware of the possibility of confusion when reading other books.

Finally, Table 1-2 contains a quantity called *relative concentration*. This is defined as the concentration of a solute divided by a standard concentration, c°, of exactly 1 mol L^{-1}. The relative concentration is, therefore, numerically equal to the concentration but is dimensionless and has no units. This quantity is used in some calculations on chemical equilibria.

PROBLEMS

1. Calculate the formula molar masses of the following substances: H_2SO_4, NH_3, $CaCO_3$, NH_4NO_3, C_2H_6.

2. Given the molar mass and the empirical formula, determine the molecular formulae of the following substances:

Empirical Formula	Molar Mass (g mol^{-1})
CH_2	56.0
CS_2	76.0
BNH_2	80.4
SCl	135.4

3. An organic substance was analyzed and found to contain 74.03% carbon, 8.70% hydrogen and 17.27% nitrogen, by mass. What is the empirical formula of the substance?

$$[C_5H_7N]$$

4. Balance the following chemical equations:

   (a) $SO_2 + O_2 \rightarrow SO_3$

   (b) $Cl_2 + P \rightarrow PCl_3$

   (c) $KClO_3 \rightarrow KCl + O_2$

   (d) $ZnS + O_2 \rightarrow ZnO + SO_2$

   (e) $CaC_2 + H_2O \rightarrow Ca(OH)_2 + C_2H_2$

   (f) $NH_3 + O_2 \rightarrow NO + H_2O$

   (g) $LiH + BF_3 \rightarrow LiBF_4 + B_2H_6$

   (h) $C_6H_{14} + O_2 \rightarrow CO_2 + H_2O$

5. Natural gas is often contaminated with the poisonous, foul-smelling gas H_2S. After separation from the other gases, H_2S is often converted to sulphur in the following two-stage process:

$$H_2S + O_2 \rightarrow H_2O + SO_2$$

$$H_2S + SO_2 \rightarrow S + H_2O$$

(a) Balance both of these equations.

(b) Write a single balanced equation to represent the overall process.

(c) What mass of sulphur is formed when 32.0 g SO_2 reacts with H_2S?

[48.1 g]

6. A sample of 12.63 g of hydrated magnesium sulphate $MgSO_4.xH_2O$ is heated to 400°C to remove the water of crystallization, and it is found that 6.17 g of anhydrous magnesium sulphate is left. What is the value of x?

[7]

7. The important abrasive material silicon carbide is manufactured from sand (SiO_2) and coke (C), according to the reaction

$$SiO_2 + 3C \rightarrow SiC + 2CO$$

What mass of silicon carbide can be obtained from a tonne of sand and a tonne of coke?

[0.67 t]

8. Air is a solution, the major components of which are nitrogen, oxygen and argon with mole fractions 0.781, 0.210 and 0.009 respectively. Calculate the mass fractions of these components.

[0.756, 0.232, 0.012]

9. What mass of sodium sulphate is contained in 27.3 mL of a 0.250 F solution of sodium sulphate?

[0.969 g]

10. A sample of 8.73 g of potassium iodide is dissolved in 120. g of water. What are the molality and the mole fraction of KI in the solution?

[0.438 mol kg^{-1}, 0.00783]

11. A 2.000 g sample of phosphorus is burned in air, and forms 4.582 g of an oxide. This quantity of the oxide is then found to react with 1.744 g of water to give a compound of phosphorus, oxygen and hydrogen. What are the empirical formulae of the oxide and of the other compound?

12. A sample of an organic compound of mass 4.00 mg was burned in excess oxygen and gave 9.60 mg CO_2 and 1.96 mg H_2O. Calculate the percentages by mass of carbon and hydrogen in the compound. Assuming that the only other element present is oxygen, determine the empirical formula of the compound.

[C_3H_3O]

13. A sample of water contains 410 ppm calcium chloride as the only solute. Calculate the formal concentration of calcium chloride, the molality of calcium chloride, and the concentration of chloride ion.

[0.0037 mol L^{-1}, 0.0037 mol kg^{-1}, 0.0074 mol L^{-1}]

II CHEMICALS IN THE LABORATORY: SOME SIMPLE REACTIONS

A large part of the study of chemistry is concerned with the way in which substances change their nature through chemical reactions. There are many different types of chemical reaction, and they can be described and classified in several different ways. The objective of the present chapter is to describe some of the simpler reactions that are common in the elementary laboratory and in chemical industry. In describing these reactions, some of the terminology of elementary reactions will be introduced and defined, and some reactions will be described which will be suitable examples for study in later chapters. Some of the reactions will be met by the student in the laboratory work early in his or her course of study, or perhaps will have been met in secondary school classes.

The types of reaction that will be discussed in this chapter are the following:

1. decomposition and synthesis;

2. double decomposition, or metathesis;

3. acid-base reactions;

4. reduction-oxidation reactions;

5. electrolysis.

2-1 DECOMPOSITION AND SYNTHESIS

Decomposition is a reaction which breaks up a chemical compound into two or more simpler compounds, or elements. It is usually carried out by heating the compound to a sufficiently high temperature. In this type of reaction, the starting material is often a solid, and one or more of the products is a gas. If, as the decomposition proceeds, the gaseous product is removed from the site of the reaction, the reaction proceeds to completion. Some examples follow.

(i) Metal carbonates decompose when heated, to yield carbon dioxide and the oxide of the metal. The temperature required for decomposition varies with the metal; for the important case of calcium carbonate, a temperature of 1000°C is suitable.

$$CaCO_3(c) \rightarrow CaO(c) + CO_2(g)$$

(ii) A metal oxide that decomposes at a relatively low temperature is mercuric oxide, HgO. When heated in a test tube in a Bunsen burner it decomposes to give oxygen, and a vapour of metallic mercury which condenses at the top of the tube:

$$2\,HgO(c) \rightarrow 2\,Hg(l) + O_2(g)$$

(iii) The usual way of preparing oxygen in the laboratory is by decomposition of potassium chlorate, $KClO_3$, in the presence of manganese dioxide, MnO_2, at a temperature of approximately 270°C:

$$2\,KClO_3(c) \rightarrow 2\,KCl(c) + 3\,O_2(g)$$

The MnO_2 serves as a catalyst which causes the decomposition to take place at a lower temperature, and in a more controlled manner, than would otherwise occur.

(iv) Many salts, when crystallized from aqueous solution, incorporate a definite number of water molecules in the crystal. Examples are copper sulphate pentahydrate, with formula $CuSO_4.5\,H_2O$, and sodium carbonate decahydrate, with formula $Na_2CO_3\,.10\,H_2O$. When a crystalline hydrated salt is heated some or all of the water can be driven off in a decomposition reaction. A good demonstration of this is the case of copper sulphate pentahydrate, for when these blue crystals are heated, the loss of water of crystallization is indicated by the loss of the blue colour:

$$CuSO_4.5\,H_2O(c) \rightarrow CuSO_4.H_2O(c) + 4\,H_2O(g) \rightarrow CuSO_4(c) + 5\,H_2O(g)$$
$$\text{blue} \qquad\qquad \text{white} \qquad\qquad\qquad\qquad \text{white}$$

The reverse of decomposition is *synthesis,* in which two or more compounds or elements combine to give a single compound. An example is the formation of carbon dioxide through the combustion of pure carbon (graphite, charcoal or diamonds),

$$C(c) + O_2(g) \rightarrow CO_2(g)$$

Ammonia, NH_3, can be made by the direct combination of the elements nitrogen and hydrogen in the presence of a catalyst:

$$N_2(g) + 3\,H_2(g) \rightarrow 2\,NH_3(g)$$

Ammonia manufactured in this way is sometimes referred to as synthetic ammonia to distinguish the process from other ways of making ammonia. The word "synthetic" in this context means "manufactured by a process of chemical synthesis," and does not imply that ammonia made in this way differs from ammonia made in some other way.

2-2   DOUBLE DECOMPOSITION, OR METATHESIS

When salts are dissolved in water, they dissociate into ions. The result of mixing the two salts in solution may simply be a solution containing all the ions of the two salts, and then it could not be said that any chemical reaction had occurred. For instance, when sodium nitrate and potassium chloride solutions are mixed, there is no visible reaction, and the resulting solution contains the ions Na^+, K^+, Cl^-, and NO_3^-. *Methathesis* is a reaction between two salts in solution in which the ions exchange partners, and one of the resulting salts is removed from solution by precipitation. Thus, when a solution of silver nitrate (containing Ag^+ and NO_3^- ions) and potassium chloride (containing K^+ and Cl^- ions) are mixed, a chemical reaction between the reactants is immediately obvious, since a white precipitate of silver chloride is formed. Silver chloride is a very insoluble salt, and so the silver ions and chloride ions in the mixed solution spontaneously form solid silver chloride. These ions are therefore removed from the solution, which then contains only the ions K^+ and NO_3^- if equal numbers of moles of the two original salts are mixed. The reaction can be represented by the chemical equation

$$AgNO_3 + KCl \rightarrow AgCl(c) + KNO_3$$

The reaction is driven essentially to completion by removal of one of the products from solution, just as decomposition reactions are driven to completion by the removal of one of the products as a gas.

The potassium and nitrate ions, K^+ and NO_3^-, do not play any important part in the above reaction, and could be replaced by any of a number of other ions without altering the essential character of the chemical reaction which is taking place. They are sometimes referred to as *spectator* ions for this reason, and are often left out of the chemical equation altogether. The above reaction is represented best by the *net ionic* reaction

$$Ag^+(aq) + Cl^-(aq) \rightarrow AgCl(c)$$

If an excess of KCl is added to a solution of $AgNO_3$, then essentially all of the Ag^+ ions will be removed from solution in the form of AgCl. The solution remaining will then contain the ions K^+, Cl^- and NO_3^-. Only a trace of Ag^+ ions will be left in solution.

On the other hand, if an excess of $AgNO_3$ is added to a solution of KCl, essentially all of the Cl^- ions will be removed from solution in the form of AgCl; the solution remaining will contain the ions K^+, Ag^+ and NO_3^-. Only a trace of Cl^- ions will be left in solution.

Example 2-1   A volume of 10.0 mL of 0.100 *F* KCl is added to 50.0 mL of 0.0120 *F* $AgNO_3$. Determine which ions are present in significant concentrations in the solution, and calculate the concentration of each of them.

Amount of K^+ and Cl^- added $= 10.0 \times 10^{-3}$ L $\times 0.100$ mol L^{-1}

$= 1.00 \times 10^{-3}$ mol

$$\text{Amount of } Ag^+ \text{ and } NO_3^- \text{ added } = 50.0 \times 10^{-3} \text{ L} \times 0.0120 \text{ mol L}^{-1}$$
$$= 0.600 \times 10^{-3} \text{ mol}$$

Hence an excess of Cl^- ion over Ag^+ ion is added to the solution, and after the silver ion is removed from the solution by precipitation of $AgCl$, there will be $(1.00 \times 10^{-3} - 0.60 \times 10^{-3})$ or 0.40×10^{-3} mol left in the solution. The amounts of K^+ and NO_3^- in the solution are not affected by the precipitation. Since the total volume of the solution is 60.0 mL, the concentrations of the various ions will be as follows:

$$[K^+] = 1.00 \times 10^{-3} \text{ mol}/60.0 \times 10^{-3} \text{ L} = 0.0167 \text{ mol L}^{-1}$$

$$[NO_3^-] = 0.600 \times 10^{-3} \text{ mol}/60.0 \times 10^{-3} \text{ L} = 0.0100 \text{ mol L}^{-1}$$

$$[Cl^-] = 0.400 \times 10^{-3} \text{ mol}/60.0 \times 10^{-3} \text{ L} = 0.00667 \text{ mol L}^{-1}$$

Example 2-2   A volume of 15.0 mL of 0.10 F KOH is added to 40.0 mL of 0.015 F ferrous chloride, $FeCl_2$, resulting in the precipitation of ferrous hydroxide, $Fe(OH)_2$. Determine which ions are present in significant concentrations in the solution, and calculate the concentration of each of them, assuming the reaction goes to completion.

The reaction is represented by the equation

$$2 \, KOH + FeCl_2 \rightarrow 2 \, KCl + Fe(OH)_2(c)$$

$$\text{or } Fe^{2+}(aq) + 2 \, OH^-(aq) \rightarrow Fe(OH)_2(c)$$

$$\text{Amount of } K^+ \text{ and } OH^- \text{ added } = 15.0 \times 10^{-3} \text{ L} \times 0.10 \text{ mol L}^{-1}$$
$$= 1.5 \times 10^{-3} \text{ mol}$$

$$\text{Amount of } Fe^{2+} \text{ added } = 40.0 \times 10^{-3} \text{ L} \times 0.015 \text{ mol·L}^{-1}$$
$$= 0.60 \times 10^{-3} \text{ mol}$$

$$\text{Amount of } Cl^- \text{ added } = 2 \times 40.0 \times 10^{-3} \text{ L} \times 0.015 \text{ mol L}^{-1}$$
$$= 1.2 \times 10^{-3} \text{ mol}$$

The amount of Cl^- added to the solution includes the factor 2 because the formula unit $FeCl_2$ contains two chlorine atoms. The figures show that in forming the precipitate of $Fe(OH)_2$ the hydroxide ion is in excess. There is sufficient Fe^{2+} to form 0.60×10^{-3} mol of $Fe(OH)_2$ provided that there is 1.20×10^{-3} mol of OH^- in the solution. The actual amount of OH^- present in the solution has been shown to be in excess of this figure by 0.3×10^{-3} mol. The total volume of the solution is 55.0 mL, and so the concentrations of the ions left in the solution are:

$$[K^+] = 1.5 \times 10^{-3} \text{ mol}/55.0 \times 10^{-3} \text{ L} = 0.027 \text{ mol L}^{-1}$$

$$[Cl^-] = 1.2 \times 10^{-3} \text{ mol}/55.0 \times 10^{-3} \text{ L} = 0.022 \text{ mol L}^{-1}$$

$$[OH^-] = 0.3 \times 10^{-3} \text{ mol}/55.0 \times 10^{-3} \text{ L} = 0.005 \text{ mol L}^{-1}$$

2-3   ACID-BASE REACTIONS

Reactions of the acid-base type are carried out very frequently in chemical laboratories, and it is essential that the student grasp the chemistry of these reactions in order to follow the more detailed calculations which are required later in the course study.

According to the Arrhenius definition, an acid is a substance which ionizes in solution to give a hydrogen ion $H^+(aq)$, and a base is a substance which ionizes to give a hydroxide ion $OH^-(aq)$. A reaction between an acid and a base can be summarized as the reaction between $H^+(aq)$ and $OH^-(aq)$ to form water,

$$H^+(aq) + OH^-(aq) \rightarrow H_2O(l)$$

This equation summarizes the essential reaction between a strong acid such as hydrochloric acid and a strong base such as such as sodium hydroxide. It will be recalled from section 1-5 that the word "strong" in this connection means that these substances are strong electrolytes, and are therefore completely ionized in solution. The overall reaction may be written

$$HCl + NaOH \rightarrow NaCl + H_2O$$

for the purposes of calculations, but the essential process is the reaction between hydrogen ions and hydroxide ions. The chloride ions Cl^- and sodium ions Na^+ are spectator ions and after the reaction has taken place they constitute a solution of sodium chloride, which is a strong electrolyte. The acid-base reaction is driven to completion by the combination of $H^+(aq)$ and $OH^-(aq)$ ions to form water, just as metathesis reactions are driven to completion by precipitation of one of the products.

Example 2-3   A volume of 23.4 mL of 0.214 F NaOH is added to 25.0 mL of 0.104 F HCl. Determine which ions are present in significant concentration and calculate the concentration of each of them.

Both NaOH and HCl are strong electrolytes, and are completely ionized in aqueous solution. The amounts of Na^+ and OH^- added are each 5.01×10^{-3} mol, and the amounts of $H^+(aq)$ and Cl^- added are 2.60×10^{-3} mol. Hence, considering the net reaction

$$H^+(aq) + OH^-(aq) \rightarrow H_2O(l)$$

the OH^- ion is present in excess, and the H^+ is completely removed in the reaction. Hence the major ions present in solution are Na^+, OH^- and Cl^-, and their concentrations are as follows:

$[Na^+]$ $= 5.01 \times 10^{-3}$ mol$/48.4 \times 10^{-3}$ L $= 0.104$ mol L^{-1}

$[OH^-]$ $= (5.01 - 2.60) \times 10^{-3}$ mol$/48.4 \times 10^{-3}$ L $= 0.0498$ mol L^{-1}

$[Cl^-]$ $= 2.60 \times 10^{-3}$ mol$/48.4 \times 10^{-3}$ L $= 0.0537$ mol L^{-1}

The concentrations of solutions of acids or bases are usually determined in the laboratory by carrying out a *titration*. A known amount of one reagent in solution is taken in a conical flask, and the other solution is added from a *burette* until an *endpoint* is reached. The endpoint is usually detected with a small amount of an indicator which is added to the flask. The indicator is chosen from a range that are available so as to change colour when equal amounts of the acid and base are contained in the solution in the conical flask. This solution, at the endpoint, is approximately "neutral," but need not be exactly so. The choice of indicator for a particular titration will be discussed in Chapter 20. At the endpoint, equal amounts of acid and base have been added, the volume of the solution added is known, and so the amounts of the reagents are in a known relationship to each other. The principle is illustrated in the following example.

Example 2-4   A volume of 25.0 mL of a solution of sodium hydroxide of unknown concentration was measured into a conical flask using a pipette, and 0.224 F hydrochloric acid was added from a burette. A volume of 36.4 mL of the acid solution had been added when the endpoint was reached. What was the concentration of the sodium hydroxide solution?

$$\text{Amount of HCl added} = 36.4 \times 10^{-3} \text{ L} \times 0.224 \text{ mol L}^{-1}$$

$$= 8.15 \times 10^{-3} \text{ mol}$$

Since the titration was carried to the endpoint, and since one mole of HCl reacts with one mole of NaOH, this is also the amount of sodium hydroxide present in the 25.0 mL sample of solution. Hence the concentration of the NaOH solution

$$= 8.15 \times 10^{-3} \text{ mol}/25.0 \times 10^{-3} \text{ L}$$

$$= 0.326 \text{ mol L}^{-1}$$

An acid does not have to be a strong acid in order to react completely with a strong base. For instance, acetic acid, CH_3COOH, is only weakly ionized in aqueous solution

$$CH_3COOH + H_2O \rightleftarrows H_3O^+ + CH_3COO^-$$

but it reacts essentially completely with an equal number of moles of sodium hydroxide. As in the case of a strong acid, hydrogen ions and hydroxide ions combine to form water. As the hydrogen ions are removed, more acetic acid dissociates to replenish the supply; the new hydrogen ions combine with more hydroxide ions, and so on..The reaction proceeds essentially to completion in this way, despite acetic acid being a weak acid.

$$CH_3COOH + NaOH \rightarrow CH_3COONa + H_2O$$

$$\text{or } CH_3COOH(aq) + OH^-(aq) \rightarrow CH_3COO^-(aq) + H_2O(l)$$

In aqueous solution, sodium acetate CH_3COONa is dissociated completely into sodium ions Na^+ and acetate ions CH_3COO^-. A solution of sodium acetate is not neutral in an acid-base sense, but is slightly basic. The reason for this will be discussed shortly. However, with a suitable indicator, weak acids can be titrated with strong bases, and weak bases with strong acids, to yield accurate values for the concentration. Concentrations measured by titration are best thought of as *formal* concentrations.

There are only a few common acids which are strong acids. Commonly met strong acids are hydrochloric acid HCl, perchloric acid $HClO_4$, nitric acid HNO_3, and the first stage of ionization of sulphuric acid H_2SO_4. Any other acids which are met are likely to be weak acids. In particular organic acids containing the carboxyl group $-COOH$, shown in the margin are nearly all weak acids. For example CH_3COOH, acetic acid and $HCOOH$ formic acid are weak acids.

The commonly used strong bases are all alkali metal hydroxides, such as sodium hydroxide $NaOH$, and potassium hydroxide KOH. Hydroxides which are only slightly soluble, such as calcium hydroxide, also react with an acid as if they were strong bases. The most important weak base is ammonia NH_3, and there are a number of other weak bases which are derived from ammonia by replacement of one or more of the hydrogen atoms by an organic group of atoms:

$$\begin{array}{ccc}
\begin{array}{c} N \\ H \diagup \ | \ \diagdown H \\ H \end{array} &
\begin{array}{c} N \\ H \diagup \ | \ \diagdown CH_3 \\ H \end{array} &
\begin{array}{c} N \\ H \diagup \ | \ \diagdown CH_2-CH_2OH \\ H \end{array} \\
\text{ammonia} & \text{methylamine} & \text{ethanolamine}
\end{array}$$

When ammonia acts as a base by accepting a proton, it forms the ammonium ion NH_4^+. Thus when ammonia is dissolved in water, it hydrolyzes partially to form a basic solution:

$$NH_3(g) + H_2O \rightleftarrows NH_4^+(aq) + OH^-(aq)$$

Such a solution is commonly labelled "NH_4OH" even though the ammonia exists almost entirely in the form of NH_3 molecules. Ammonia can itself react with strong acids to form salts even in the absence of water:

$$HCl(g) + NH_3(g) \rightarrow NH_4Cl(c)$$

The ability of a compound to act as an acid or base cannot be guessed in a naive way from its formula. The presence of an H at the beginning or the end of a chemical formula does not indicate that the compound is an acid, nor does the presence of the pair of letters OH indicate that the compound is a base. As an example, the structural formula for sulphuric acid may be written

$$\begin{array}{c}
O \diagdown \qquad \diagup OH \\
\quad S \\
O \diagup \qquad \diagdown OH
\end{array}$$

and from some points of view it would be better to write the formula of sulphuric acid as $SO_2(OH)_2$. An unwary student seeing this latter formula might be tempted to think that this substance is a base which ionizes to give SO_2^{2+} ions and OH^- ions, which does not fit the observed facts at all.

Some compounds have well defined acidic or basic character without having H or OH in their formulae at all. The most interesting group of compounds to consider is the oxides. Sodium oxide is a very strongly basic compound, which reacts vigorously with water to produce a solution of sodium hydroxide, which is of course basic:

$$Na_2O(c) + H_2O \rightarrow 2NaOH(aq)$$

On the other hand, sulphur trioxide produces sulphuric acid when dissolved in water:

$$SO_3(g) + H_2O \rightarrow H_2SO_4(aq)$$

Thus sodium oxide and sulphur trioxide can be said to be strongly basic and acidic, respectively, and the reaction between them could be regarded as an acid- base reaction even though no hydrogen ions are involved:

$$Na_2O(c) + SO_3(g) \rightarrow Na_2SO_4(c)$$

Some salts act as acids or bases when they are dissolved in water. It was mentioned above that a solution containing only sodium acetate is not neutral in an acid-base sense. The solution is basic because of the production of hydroxide ions by the following hydrolysis reaction involving the acetate ion:

$$CH_3COO^- + H_2O \rightleftharpoons CH_3COOH + OH^-$$

Since acetic acid is a weak acid, it is only slightly ionized in an aqueous solution of reasonable concentration, and so it may be concluded that the acetate ion has the property of being reactive towards any molecule or ion which can donate a hydrogen ion to it.

A water molecule is a potential source of hydrogen ions, and the above reaction can be interpreted as a competition between the acetate ion and the hydroxide ion for attachment of the hydrogen ion. On the left hand side of the reaction the hydrogen ion is attached to the hydroxide ion to form a water molecule, and on the right hand side the hydrogen ion is attached to the acetate ion to form an acetic acid molecule. The position of the equilibrium depends on the relative strengths of the hydroxide ion and acetate ion in attaching the hydrogen ion i.e., their relative strengths as bases. In this case the hydroxide ion is a good deal stronger as a base than the acetate ion and the equilibrium lies fairly strongly to the left. In general, the anion of a weak acid is a base. The weaker the acid, the greater is the affinity of the anion for hydrogen ions, and so the better the anion is able to compete for hydrogen ions in the hydrolysis reaction,

$$A^- + H_2O \rightleftharpoons HA + OH^-$$

Hence, solutions of salts of weak acids are basic in character.

An example of anion hydrolysis of widespread use is the salt sodium carbonate, called *soda ash* in industry. This salt is often used as a base instead of sodium hydroxide, a role which it can fill because of hydrolysis of the carbonate ion:

$$CO_3{}^{2-}(aq) + H_2O \rightleftharpoons HCO_3{}^-(aq) + OH^-(aq)$$

There is a corresponding phenomenon in which some salts produce acidic solutions when dissolved in water. The easiest examples to understand are the ammonium salts, for the ammonium ion in aqueous solution undergoes hydrolysis according to the following equation:

$$NH_4{}^+(aq) \rightleftharpoons NH_3(aq) + H^+(aq)$$

The above argument may be rephrased for this case of acid hydrolysis. Since ammonia is a weak base, it is only slightly ionized in a solution of reasonable concentration, and so it may be concluded that the ammonium ion is reactive towards any molecule or ion from which it can accept a hydrogen ion. In aqueous solution, the water molecules can accept hydrogen ions from the ammonium ions, and so the resulting solution is slightly acidic. To generalize, the cation of a weak base is an acid.

Some metal ions in solution are acidic in nature, and produce solutions containing an excess of hydrogen ions. This can be understood if the structure of the solvated ion is considered. For instance, the chromium ion in solution, $Cr^{3+}(aq)$, has six water molecules bound relatively strongly to the metal ions, and so can be represented by the formula $Cr(H_2O)_6{}^{3+}(aq)$. This ion has 12 hydrogen atoms, and ionization is possible, forming an acidic solution:

$$Cr(H_2O)_6{}^{3+}(aq) \rightleftharpoons Cr(H_2O)_5(OH)^{2+}(aq) + H^+(aq)$$

The last idea that will be mentioned in this introduction to acids and bases is that of *amphoteric* compounds. Some molecules and ions are able to react with both acids and bases, thereby acting as bases or acids depending on the circumstances. The simplest examples of these are the salts of acids with two acidic hydrogens, such as sodium bicarbonate, $NaHCO_3$. The bicarbonate ion in solution is able to accept a proton and to donate a proton, and therefore can act as an acid,

$$HCO_3{}^-(aq) + OH^-(aq) \rightleftharpoons CO_3{}^{2-}(aq) + H_2O$$

or as a base,

$$HCO_3{}^-(aq) + H^+(aq) \rightleftharpoons H_2CO_3(aq) \rightleftharpoons CO_2(g) + 2H_2O(l)$$

Carbonic acid, H_2CO_3, is not very stable in solution, and decomposes into water and gaseous carbon dioxide when formed in substantial amounts. The bicarbonate ion can react with either hydrogen ion or hydroxide ion, and is therefore amphoteric.

An amphoteric salt which is commonly used to *standardize* solutions of bases by titration is potassium hydrogen phthalate, which has the structural formula shown in the margin.

This salt can be dried easily and weighed accurately for use in determining the concentration of a base solution by titration. The procedure is illustrated in the following example.

Example 2-5   A sample of dried potassium hydrogen phthalate of mass 3.944 g was placed in a conical flask and titrated with a solution of NaOH of unknown concentration. Base solution was added from a burette, and 35.5 mL was required to reach the endpoint. Calculate the concentration of the solution of NaOH.

The formula molar mass of potassium hydrogen phthalate, $C_8O_4H_5K$, is 204.2 g mol^{-1}, and so the amount reacted is

$$\frac{3.944 \text{ g}}{204.2 \text{ g mol}^{-1}} = 1.931 \times 10^{-2} \text{ mol.}$$

The net balanced equation for the reaction is

$$OH^- + C_8O_4H_5^- \rightarrow C_8O_4H_4^{2-} + H_2O$$

which shows that one mole of the hydrogen phthalate ion reacts with one mole of NaOH. Hence, since the titration was carried to the endpoint, an amount of 1.931×10^{-2} mol of NaOH must be contained in the volume 35.5 mL. The formal concentration of the NaOH is therefore

$$= \frac{1.931 \times 10^{-2} \text{ mol}}{35.5 \times 10^{-3} \text{ L}}$$

$$= 0.544 \text{ mol L}^{-1}$$

2-4   REDUCTION-OXIDATION REACTIONS

In the original sense of the word, oxidation means a reaction with the element oxygen. For example, combustion in air and corrosion reactions are oxidation reactions:

$$C(c) + O_2 \rightarrow CO_2(g)$$

$$Fe(c) + \tfrac{1}{2}O_2 \rightarrow FeO(c)$$

$$CH_4(g) + 2\,O_2 \rightarrow CO_2(g) + 2\,H_2O(l)$$

$$Mg(c) + \tfrac{1}{2}\,O_2 \rightarrow MgO(c)$$

The burning of carbon in a coal fire, the slow corrosion of iron to give the oxide FeO, the burning of methane in a Bunsen burner flame, and the blinding white light of a piece of burning magnesium ribbon, are all chemical reactions of the same sort: a fuel is oxidized by oxygen in the form of molecules, O_2.

Some oxides can themselves be oxidized by further reaction with oxygen. When carbon is oxidized in a restricted supply of oxygen rather than an excess, the result of the combustion is a mixture of carbon monoxide and carbon dioxide:

$$C(c) + \tfrac{1}{2}\,O_2(g) \rightarrow CO(g)$$

$$C(c) + O_2(g) \rightarrow CO_2(g)$$

The carbon in CO_2 is more highly oxidized than the carbon in CO. In a later chapter, formal methods will be introduced to describe the *oxidation state* of an atom in a compound.

A similar situation is well known in the corrosion of iron. The equation for the oxidation of iron metal to ferrous oxide, FeO, has been given above. Ferrous oxide, FeO, reacts further with oxygen to yield ferric oxide, Fe_2O_3, in which the iron atom shows a valence of three; ferrous oxide has been oxidized to ferric oxide. The charge on the iron atom has been changed from +2 to +3 by oxidation. The oxide ion has a charge of −2 in both compounds.

The substance which causes oxidation to occur is said to be *reduced* in the reaction. Whenever oxidation takes place, there must be a simultaneous reduction. As an example, when an oxide of iron is mixed with carbon and heated, the carbon is oxidized to CO or CO_2, and the iron oxide is reduced to metallic iron. One possible reaction is the following:

$$Fe_2O_3(c) + 3\,C(c) \rightarrow 2\,Fe(l) + 3\,CO(g)$$

Reactions like this take place in blast furnaces in which the temperature is very high, and the metal is produced in the form of a liquid. The iron oxide is the oxidizing agent, and in the reaction is reduced to iron. The carbon is the reducing agent and is oxidized to carbon monoxide. It is the change of the charge associated with an atom which is used in the general definition of the process of oxidation.

The need for a generalized definition of oxidation becomes clear if the following reactions are considered. Ferrous oxide dissolves in hydrochloric acid to form ferrous chloride in solution:

$$FeO + 2\,HCl \rightarrow FeCl_2 + H_2O$$

The solution of ferrous chloride is then reacted with an acidic solution of potassium permanganate, $KMnO_4$, which reacts according to the following equation:

$$5\,FeCl_2 + 8\,HCl + KMnO_4 \rightarrow 5\,FeCl_3 + MnCl_2 + KCl + 4\,H_2O$$

If the solution containing ferric chloride is treated with base, a precipitate of $Fe(OH)_3$ is formed:

$$FeCl_3 + 3\,NaOH \rightarrow Fe(OH)_3 + 3\,NaCl$$

The ferric hydroxide can be filtered, dried and heated to decompose the hydroxide to the oxide:

$$2\,Fe(OH)_3 \rightarrow Fe_2O_3 + 3\,H_2O(g)$$

The net result of these chemical transformations has been to convert ferrous oxide, FeO, to ferric oxide, Fe_2O_3, the same overall reaction that can be done by direct reaction with pure oxygen. And yet the steps outlined are all done without the participation of pure oxygen at all. Hence, it is possible to carry out the process of oxidation without oxygen being directly involved. The step in which the oxidation must have taken place is the reaction with potassium permanganate, in which the ferrous ion Fe^{2+} is converted to ferric ion Fe^{3+}. The permanganate ion is the oxidizing agent, and is itself reduced to the ion Mn^{2+}. **Oxidation** occurs when electrons are lost, **reduction** occurs when electrons are gained. Since electrons are not destroyed in chemical reactions, but only transferred, there must be a reduction process associated with every oxidation process. Hence, reactions of this type are called *reduction-oxidation* reactions; the usual abbreviation of this description is *redox reactions.* The following are, by this definition, examples of redox reactions.

$$Fe(c) + Cl_2(g) \xrightarrow[300K]{} FeCl_2(c) \text{ (iron oxidized, chlorine reduced)}$$

$$2 FeCl_2(g) + Cl_2(g) \xrightarrow[800K]{} 2 FeCl_3(g) \text{ (iron oxidized, chlorine reduced)}$$

$$2 Fe^{3+}(aq) + H_2S(g) \rightarrow 2 Fe^{2+}(aq) + 2 H^+(aq) + S(c)$$
$$\text{(iron reduced, sulphur oxidized)}$$

$$Zn(c) + 2 H^+(aq) \rightarrow Zn^{2+}(aq) + H_2(g)$$
$$\text{(hydrogen reduced, zinc oxidized)}$$

2-5   ELECTROLYSIS

Since redox reactions involve the transfer of electric charge, it is not surprising that there is a close connection between redox reactions and the reactions carried out by the process of *electrolysis.* Electrolysis refers to the process of carrying out reactions by passing an electric current through the reaction mixture. Electrolysis can be used to carry out redox reactions which do not occur spontaneously. Usually the reaction mixture is a solution of an electrolyte in water or in some other solvent, but can also be a molten salt or mixture of salts. The result of electrolysis is usually a simple reaction resulting in decomposition of the solvent, or the solute, or sometimes both.

When water is electrolyzed using platinum *electrodes* to carry the current into the solution, the products of the reaction are hydrogen and oxygen:

$$H_2O \rightarrow H_2(g) + \tfrac{1}{2} O_2(g)$$

This electrolysis is most easily carried out if a salt which does not take part in the electrolysis is added to the water. For instance electrolysis of a solution of sodium sulphate Na_2SO_4 proceeds according to the above reaction, which describes the decomposition of the solvent. The two gases are produced at the electrodes, and may be collected separately as shown in Figure 2-1. The volume of hydrogen which is generated is twice the volume of oxygen, when measured under the same conditions of temperature and pressure, corresponding to the stoichiometry of the decomposition of water. In the next chapter, the electrolytic method of industrial production of chlorine from a solution of sodium chloride is described; this is an example of an electrolysis of a solution in which both the solvent and solute are decomposed. In the electrolysis of a solution of cupric chloride $CuCl_2$, the solute itself is decomposed: copper is deposited as a coating on one electrode, and chlorine gas is evolved at the other electrode.

$$CuCl_2(aq) \rightarrow Cu(c) + Cl_2 (g)$$

Electrolysis reactions take place as two separate electrochemical processes at the two electrodes. Neither of these separate processes can take place without the other, and so they are called *half-reactions.* The electric current carried by the electrodes, and deposited in the solution through the electrode-solution in-

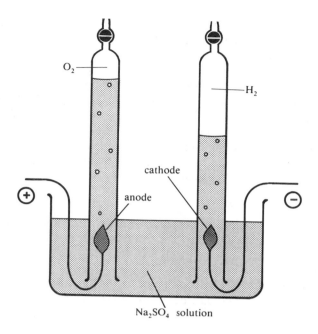

Figure 2-1. Apparatus for the electrolysis of a solution of sodium sulphate using inert platinum electrodes. The gases produced by decomposition of water are collected in inverted burettes for volume measurement.

terface, must be considered as being an essential part of the symbolic representation of the two half reactions. The current is represented in chemical equations by the symbol "e" for each electron. The two half-reactions which take place in the electrolysis of water are:

cathode: $2 H_2O + 2 e \rightarrow H_2(g) + 2 OH^-(aq)$

anode: $H_2O \rightarrow \frac{1}{2} O_2(g) + 2 H^+(aq) + 2 e$

When these two half-reactions are combined, the net process is:

$3 H_2O(l) \rightarrow H_2(g) + \frac{1}{2} O_2(g) + 2 H^+(aq) + 2 OH^-(aq)$

This equation represents not only the decomposition of water into its elements, but also the ionization of water. Of course, if the solution is allowed time to mix, the acidic hydrogen ions will recombine with the basic hydroxide ions to form water. However, the use of appropriate indicators shows that the solution near the electrode producing hydrogen is basic, and the solution near the electrode producing oxygen is acidic.

In the half-reaction which takes place at the cathode, two electrons are added to the water molecule, and by the definition of the last section, this is called a reduction half-reaction. Speaking loosely, it may be said that the water is reduced to hydrogen at the cathode. In all electrochemical cells, the electrode at which reduction takes place is called the cathode, no matter whether the cell is used for electrolysis or as a battery. At the other electrode, the anode, electrons are removed from the water molecules, and so the half-reaction is an oxidation. The electrode at which oxidation takes place is always called the anode. In an electrolysis cell, the cathode is made negative by the external source of current, so as to make a supply of electrons available to the solution;

the anode is made positive by the external source of current, and provides the path through which electrons leave the solution.

The amount of chemical reaction produced by electrolysis is proportional to the amount of charge which passes through the cell. The amount of reaction can be measured by weighing the electrodes, or by measuring the amount of gas evolved, depending on the cell reaction involved. The amount of charge passed through the cell is equal to the current multiplied by the time. The amount of reaction taking place at a given electrode also depends on the number of electrons involved in the half-reaction at that electrode. For instance, one mole of electrons is required to deposit one mole of silver metal from solution, because the reduction half-reaction for silver is

$$Ag^+(aq) + e \rightarrow Ag(c)$$

Two moles of electrons are required to deposit one mole of copper from a solution of a cupric salt since cupric ions Cu^{2+} are doubly charged:

$$Cu^{2+}(aq) + 2e \rightarrow Cu(c)$$

The charge carried by one mole of electrons is one of the basic constants of nature and has been called the *Faraday constant*, after the English electrochemist, Michael Faraday. It is given the symbol F, and has the numerical value

$$F = 96\ 485\ C\ mol^{-1}$$

A more accurate value is given in the table of fundamental constants inside the back cover of the book. With this constant the amounts of chemical reaction in electrolysis cells can be readily calculated. The faraday is also used as a unit of electric charge.

Example 2-6   What mass of copper is deposited at the cathode by the passage of a current of 1.56 A for 500 s through a solution of $CuSO_4$?

$$\text{Amount of charge } = 1.56\ A \times 500\ s$$

$$= 780\ C$$

Since the reduction half-reaction is $Cu^{2+} + 2e \rightarrow Cu$, two electrons are required for each copper atom. Hence

$$\text{amount of Cu deposited } = \frac{780\ C}{2 \times 96\ 485\ C\ mol^{-1}}$$

$$= 4.04 \times 10^{-3}\ mol$$

$$\text{and mass of Cu deposited } = 4.04 \times 10^{-3}\ mol \times 63.5\ g\ mol^{-1}$$

$$= 0.257\ g$$

Example 2-7   If 56.200 g of a pure metal is plated by the passage of one faraday of charge, identify the metal.

The possibility that the metal ion in solution carries a multiple charge must be considered. If the ion were singly charged, the molar mass would be 56.200 g mol^{-1} which lies between iron (55.85) and cobalt (58.93). If the ion were doubly charged, two faradays would be required to electrolyze one mole of metal ions, and so the molar mass would be 112.40 g mol^{-1}, which corresponds exactly to cadmium (112.40). Similarly, if the ion were triply charged, its molar mass would have to be 168.60 g mol^{-1}, which is close to, but not equal to, the molar mass of thulium (168.93). The other possible molar mass is 224.80 g mol^{-1} which is a little lower than the molar mass of radium (226.0). These figures are summarized in the following table.

Assumed Charge on Ion	Molar Mass (g/mol)	Possible Elements
+1	56.200	Fe=55.85, Co 58.93
+2	112.40	Cd=112.40
+3	168.60	Tm=168.93
+4	224.80	Ra=226.0

It is concluded that the metal is cadmium.

Example 2-8 The metal aluminium is produced by electrolytic reduction of the ion Al^{3+} in molten Al_2O_3. An industrial machine produces 600 aluminium soft-drink cans per minute, each of which has a mass of 20 g. What current is required in the electrolysis plant to supply metal for the cans produced by one such machine?

The metal must be produced at a rate of 10 cans/second × 20 g/can or 200 g/s. Since the molar mass of aluminium is 27 g mol^{-1}

$$\text{production rate} = \frac{200 \text{ g s}^{-1}}{27 \text{ g mol}^{-1}}$$

$$= 7.4 \text{ mol s}^{-1}$$

Since the ions are triply charged, three faradays of charge are needed for each mole of metal, $Al^{3+} + 3e \rightarrow Al(c)$, and hence

$$\text{current} = 7.4 \text{ mol s}^{-1} \times 3 \times 96\,485 \text{ C mol}^{-1}$$

$$= 2.14 \times 10^6 \text{ C s}^{-1}$$

$$= 2.14 \times 10^6 \text{ A}$$

PROBLEMS

1. A sample of pure calcium carbonate of mass 3.734 g was heated until evolution of carbon dioxide was complete. What mass of calcium oxide remained?

[2.092 g]

2. A mixture of calcium and magnesium carbonates of mass 1.8403 g was heated until its mass was constant, and the resulting mixture of oxides was found to have a mass of 0.9015 g. What was the composition of the mixture of carbonates, expressed as a mass fraction of calcium carbonate? What was the mass fraction of calcium oxide in the mixture of oxides?

[0.144, 0.0895]

3. When lead dioxide PbO_2 is heated, it decomposes to lead monoxide PbO, and oxygen; similarly, barium peroxide BaO_2 decomposes to barium oxide BaO, and oxygen. A mixture of PbO_2 and BaO_2 of mass 15.070 g was decomposed to yield 13.808 g of a mixture of PbO and BaO. What mass of PbO_2 was present in the original mixture?

[5.87 g]

4. What mass of silver chloride will be precipitated when a solution containing 2.884 g of silver nitrate is added to a solution containing 5.000 g of sodium chloride? Will any sodium chloride remain unreacted? If so, how much?

[2.433 g, yes, 4.008 g]

5. A solution of volume 25.0 mL contains 2.500 g of ammonium sulphate. What volume of 1.20 F $BaCl_2$ solution is needed to precipitate all the sulphate ion from solution as $BaSO_4$? How would you describe the solution remaining after the $BaSO_4$ is removed by filtering?

[15.8 mL, 0.927 M NH_4Cl]

6. Excess hydrochloric acid was added to 10.0 mL of $AgNO_3$ solution, and 1.00 g of $AgCl$ precipitate was formed. What was the concentration of the $AgNO_3$ solution?

[0.698 M]

7. What volume of 0.127 F potassium hydroxide is required to react completely with 10.0 mL of 0.839 F acetic acid, CH_3COOH?

[66.1 mL]

8. Describe the solution left as a result of the titration described in question 7.

[0.110 F potassium acetate]

9. What volume of 0.1873 F NaOH would be required to react completely with 10.0 mL of 0.2070 F H_2SO_4?

[22.1 mL]

10. What volume of 0.150 F NaOH is required to react completely with 10.0 mL of 0.350 F oxalic acid, $(COOH)_2$?

[46.7 mL]

11. 17.4 mL of a KOH solution was required to react completely with 10.0 mL of 0.473 F HCl. What is the concentration of the KOH solution?

[0.272 F]

12. In each of the following acid/base reactions, state which reactant is in excess, and by how many moles it is in excess.

   (a) 0.800 g KOH reacts with 30.0 mL of 0.150 F H_2SO_4

   $[5.3 \times 10^{-3}$ mol KOH$]$

   (b) 0.0080 mole KOH reacts with 15.0 mL of 0.20 F CH_3COOH

   $[5.0 \times 10^{-3}$ mol KOH$]$

   (c) 20.0 g $NaHCO_3$ reacts with 50. mL 5.00 F HCl

   $[12 \times 10^{-3}$ mol HCl$]$

   (d) 20.0 g Na_2CO_3 reacts with 50. mL 5.00 F HCl

   $[64 \times 10^{-3}$ mol $Na_2CO_3]$

13. 0.420 g of $KMnO_4$ is reduced by exactly 40.0 mL of an acidified solution of ferrous ion, Fe^{2+}. What is the concentration of the ferrous ion in that solution?

   $[0.332$ M$]$

14. Oxalic acid has the molecular formula $H_2C_2O_4$, and the structural formula

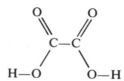

   Oxalic acid can react as an acid; in addition, it is oxidized to CO_2 by $KMnO_4$ in acid solution:

   $$5H_2C_2O_4 + 2KMnO_4 + 6HCl \rightarrow 2MnCl_2 + 2KCl + 10CO_2 + 8H_2O$$

   A 10.0 mL sample of an oxalic acid solution required 35.5 mL of 0.150 F NaOH to react completely. What volume of 0.150 F $KMnO_4$ would be required to react completely with a second 10.0 mL sample of the same oxalic acid solution?

   $[7.10$ mL$]$

15. What mass of copper metal is deposited by electrolytic reduction of a Cu^{2+} solution if 10.0 A is passed through the solution for 1.00 h?

   $[11.9$ g$]$

16. A solution of volume 8.0 mL containing a trace of Zn^{2+} is electrolyzed so as to reduce the Zn^{2+} ions to metallic zinc, and it is found that a current of 100 μA passed for 25 s is required to carry out this reduction. What is the concentration of Zn^{2+} in the solution?

   $[1.6 \times 10^{-6}$ M$]$

III CHEMICALS IN COMMERCE AND INDUSTRY

The maintenance and improvement of society depends on the provision of a multitude of goods and services. In the production of these goods and services, which is called "industry," and in their sale and distribution, which is "commerce," chemistry has a significant part to play. Those who enter a career of science or engineering ought to be aware of the role of chemistry in industry generally, and of the scope of the chemical industry. The subject is too diverse and large for detailed study at this point, but examples from chemical industry serve well to illustrate points in elementary chemistry, as well as indicating to the student some of the chemical processes which are vital to the well-being of society.

There are two main subdivisions of the chemical manufacturing industry, the *heavy chemical* industry, where the output of a single plant may be thousands of tonnes a year, and the *fine chemical* industry, which produces chemicals in much smaller amounts, but in higher states of purity.

There are other industries which depend on chemistry or chemical technology. Mineral processing could be regarded as a heavy chemical industry, and the petroleum industry uses many chemical techniques in processing petroleum into fuels, lubricants, and other products. The pharmaceutical industry depends upon sophisticated organic chemistry to produce medical drugs. The polymer, or plastics, industry is based on chemistry, but is a consumer rather than a producer of chemicals. The same can be said for the paper industry. Modern military operations are heavily dependent on science and engineering, and chemistry is involved in the production of explosives and propellants.

Recently, the effects of industrial activities on the natural environment have become widespread and serious, and this has led to many studies of the pollution problem. The basis of many of these environmental studies is the identification, and measurement of the concentrations of chemicals in the air, water and other natural surroundings, using the techniques of analytical chemistry.

In this chapter the chemistry involved in several heavy chemical manufacturing industries is discussed. The reactions will be used as examples in discussing chemical principles in later parts of the book. A knowledge of the reactions used in heavy chemical manufacture is sometimes useful in understanding the economics of the industry, and the ways in which the markets for different commodities interact.

3-1   SULPHURIC ACID

Sulphuric acid is a simple industrial chemical, produced in immense quantities, and used in a wide variety of other industries. Some industries, such as the phosphate fertilizer industry, use sulphuric acid in very large quantities. Other industries use it in small amounts, but nevertheless depend upon a ready supply at low cost.

The raw material for sulphuric acid manufacture is the element sulphur, which is derived from three sources. Sulphur occurs in the form of mineral deposits of the pure element; the major North American deposits are on the Gulf coast of the United States. Sulphur is also found in the form of the gas H_2S in some natural gas wells. Natural gas containing H_2S is said to be "sour," and the H_2S must be removed before the gas is distributed for use as a fuel. Large amounts of sulphur are produced in Alberta from this source. The third source of sulphur is the gases produced in the operation of smelters for

Figure 3-1 In the upper left corner may be seen the base of a tall stack for disposing of smelter gases at the Copper Cliff refinery of Inco. The duct work shown conducts a portion of these smelter fumes to a C-I-L plant at which SO_2 is removed and converted to sulphuric acid. Some 700 000 t of acid is produced each year at this facility.

sulphide minerals. In the past, these gases have been vented to the atmosphere, causing considerable damage to the environment, particularly through what is known as "acid rain." As part of the effort to control this source of pollution, sulphuric acid plants have been installed at some smelters, using the SO_2 which previously was sent up the stack into the atmosphere. A major part of the sulphuric acid made in Canada is made directly or indirectly from metal sulphides.

There are three major steps in the manufacturing process, the production of SO_2, the conversion of SO_2 to SO_3, and the reaction of SO_3 with water to give H_2SO_4. Starting from sulphur or from H_2S, SO_2 is produced by combustion in air:

$$S + O_2 \rightarrow SO_2$$
$$2\,H_2S + 3\,O_2 \rightarrow 2\,SO_2 + 2\,H_2O$$

Both of these combustion reactions produce a large amount of heat, which is used for the production of steam for use elsewhere in the plant. In mineral smelters, the roasting of the ore in air leads to reactions such as the following:

$$2\,ZnS + 3\,O_2 \rightarrow 2\,ZnO + 2\,SO_2$$

Purification of the SO_2 gas produced in smelters is needed before it is taken to the next step.

The oxidation of SO_2 to SO_3 is one of the prime examples of chemical equilibrium in the gas phase, and is used as such in Chapter 15:

$$SO_2 + \tfrac{1}{2}\,O_2 \rightarrow SO_3$$

The reaction goes almost to completion at low temperatures, but takes place too slowly for the plant to be economical. The reaction proceeds faster at a higher temperature. But if the temperature is raised too much, the SO_3 which is produced has a tendency to dissociate, in the reverse of the reaction shown above, and this reduces the amount of SO_3 which is produced:

$$SO_3 \rightarrow SO_2 + \tfrac{1}{2}\,O_2$$

Put another way, the chemical equilibrium between SO_2, O_2 and SO_3 is shifted towards dissociation of the SO_3 when the temperature is raised. The equilibrium can be shifted back by compression of the reacting mixture to higher pressure. The reaction can also be speeded up by passing the reaction mixture over a *catalyst*, a substance which increases the rate of the reaction without altering the position of the equilibrium. Use of a suitable catalyst increases the rate of the reaction and allows the temperature to be kept low so that the position of equilibrium remains favourable to the production of SO_3. The choice of operating conditions must be a compromise between the requirements of high speed of reaction, and favourable position of the chemical equilibrium. This choice can only be made with a proper understanding of the chemistry of the reaction. The reaction produces enough heat to raise the temperature above the optimum, and the temperature is controlled with large heat exchangers which remove this heat.

The final step in the manufacture is the reaction of SO_3 with water,

$$SO_3 + H_2O \rightarrow H_2SO_4$$

There are practical difficulties in carrying out this apparently simple step. If the SO_3 is brought into contact with water, a mist of sulphuric acid solution is formed which is impossible to handle. This can be avoided by dissolving the SO_3 in either pure H_2SO_4, to form a solution called *oleum*, or in a very concentrated (98%) aqueous solution of H_2SO_4, which can be subsequently diluted. The final products of the manufacturing process are liquid oleum and very concentrated aqueous sulphuric acid, which are shipped by railway tank car, barge, or other bulk carrier.

The prime use for H_2SO_4 is in the production of phosphate fertilizers. Phosphate rock, the largest source of phosphorus in industry, consists primarily of calcium phosphate $Ca_3(PO_4)_2$ which is insoluble in water. In order to make the phosphate ion available for use in the soil by plants, this salt must be converted to one which is soluble in water. Addition of sulphuric acid to phosphate rock results in several chemical reactions, but in simple terms the following reaction takes place, forming a calcium hydrogen phosphate which is soluble in water:

$$Ca_3(PO_4)_2 + 2\,H_2SO_4 + H_2O \rightarrow Ca(H_2PO_4)_2.H_2O + 2\,CaSO_4$$

This is the key reaction in the conversion of phosphate rock to *superphosphate*, perhaps the most important of all artificial fertilizers.

Superphosphate production accounts for more than half of the total annual production of sulphuric acid. Consequently, the economics of the sulphuric acid industry is closely related to the state of the fertilizer industry, and hence to the agricultural markets of the world.

3-2 AMMONIA

The production of ammonia, NH_3, nitric acid, HNO_3, and related chemicals is known collectively as the nitrogen industry, and is basic to two major activities of the twentieth century, the growing of food and the waging of war. Prior to this century, compounds of nitrogen were derived mostly from the salt sodium nitrate, $NaNO_3$, which occurs naturally as a mineral on the west coast of South America. The supply of nitrates to Europe was one of the last jobs of bulk transport which could be done economically by sailing ship. The production of nitrogen compounds for the explosives and fertilizer industries using the plentiful nitrogen in the air was an important problem for chemical technology in the nineteenth century. This problem became critically important for Germany when she entered a major war in 1914 without being able to secure the sea lanes to South America against attack by the British navy. The chemist Fritz Haber had been studying the chemistry of the direct reaction between the elements nitrogen and hydrogen. These studies were at a stage where they could be rapidly developed into a practical large scale process for ammonia production, and in a short time a large plant was installed using the *Haber* process. The production of explosives, and equally important in an extended war, nitrogenous fertilizers, could then proceed despite the British naval blockade. The use of the Haber process extended worldwide after the war ended, and the

Figure 3-2 Western Canada provides both a market for large amounts of fertilizer and the resources to produce it. The Carseland, Alberta plant of Cominco produces 400 000 t of ammonia per year. Much of it is used to produce 480 000 t per year of urea, sold mainly as agricultural and forest grade fertilizer.

nitrogen industries are now entirely based upon the synthetic production of ammonia. Like sulphuric acid, ammonia is a "heavy chemical" and is manufactured in very large amounts. Canadian ammonia plants are situated primarily in Alberta, close to the source of natural gas which is the key raw material.

There are two main parts to the ammonia synthesis process. First, the two elements nitrogen and hydrogen must be prepared in a pure condition. Natural gas is the main source of hydrogen and the nitrogen comes from air. The second step is the synthesis of ammonia from its elements, and is carried out at very high pressure and closely controlled temperature.

In order to obtain nitrogen from air, the oxygen must be removed. This is done by burning a fuel in the air. The fuel is generally natural gas, which may be thought of as pure methane for the present purposes:

$$CH_4 + 2 O_2 \rightarrow CO_2 + 2 H_2O$$

The combustion products are passed through an absorber containing a basic solution, which reacts with the acidic CO_2:

$$CO_2 + H_2O + K_2CO_3 \rightarrow 2 KHCO_3$$

When the water and CO_2 have been removed from the combustion products, the remaining gas is essentially pure nitrogen, with a small amount of the noble gas argon.

Figure 3-3 The remainder of the ammonia from the Cominco facility at Carseland is shipped to this nearby C-I-L plant which produces 220 000 t a year of nitric acid, almost all of which is used to make ammonium nitrate fertilizer in the same plant.

Hydrogen is obtained from methane and steam, in a two stage process. In the first step methane reacts with steam in the presence of a catalyst:

$$CH_4 + H_2O \rightarrow CO + 3\,H_2$$

This reaction is called *steam reforming* of the hydrocarbon. The carbon monoxide is a reducing agent which reacts further with additional steam to produce more hydrogen:

$$CO + H_2O \rightarrow CO_2 + H_2$$

This reaction is called *shift conversion*. The overall reaction between steam and methane is the sum of these two steps,

$$CH_4 + 2\,H_2O \rightarrow CO_2 + 4\,H_2$$

The carbon dioxide is removed from the gas stream by reaction with a basic solution, and only hydrogen remains.

In practice, these two steps can be carried out in the same stream of gas. Excess methane is mixed first with steam, and the reforming and shift conversion reactions are carried out. Then air is added to the gas stream to react with the remaining methane, with the result that nitrogen is added to the gas stream. The carbon dioxide produced by both these reactions is then removed in a single step by reaction with a base, and any water remaining is removed by condensation. The remaining gas stream contains only nitrogen and hydrogen, and by adjustment of the proportions of steam, methane and air, the proportions of hydrogen and nitrogen can be adjusted to the 3:1 ratio needed for ammonia synthesis. Each of these reactions is carried out at a carefully controlled temperature and in the presence of a suitable catalyst.

The synthesis step is chemically very simple, but high level technology is required to put it into practice; the reaction for the synthesis is

$$N_2 + 3\,H_2 \rightarrow 2\,NH_3$$

When nitrogen, hydrogen and ammonia are at equilibrium at low temperatures, the position of equilibrium lies far to the right, thus favouring the formation of ammonia from its elements. However, at low temperatures the reaction is so slow that it takes too long to reach equilibrium for the process to be practical. The reaction can be accelerated by raising the temperature, but this moves the position of equilibrium to the left. At temperatures high enough for the reaction to be reasonably fast, almost all the ammonia is dissociated. The equilibrium can be shifted to the right again by compressing the gas mixture to high pressure, and hence, a large part of the engineering associated with ammonia production is the handling of large amounts of gas at high pressures—up to 1000 times atmospheric pressure in some plants. The key step in the process is the use of a suitable catalyst which makes the reaction reasonably fast without using very high temperatures, or very high pressures. The situation is very similar to that described for the oxidation of sulphur dioxide in the last section. The choice of temperature, pressure and catalyst is made on the basis of minimizing the cost of the final product.

A certain amount of ammonia is used directly as fertilizer. However, large amounts of ammonia are converted to other compounds for fertilizer and other uses, via the nitric acid route. Since natural gas is the key raw material in ammonia production, the dramatic increases in the prices of energy since 1973 are reflected in increases in the cost of nitrogenous fertilizer. These increases may have disastrous effects in the future in parts of the world where there is a shortage of food.

3-3   NITRIC ACID

Before the availability of synthetic ammonia, nitric acid was produced by the reaction of sulphuric acid with a nitrate salt such as sodium nitrate:

$$H_2SO_4 + NaNO_3 \rightarrow NaHSO_4 + HNO_3$$

When the reaction mixture is heated, nitric acid is driven off as a vapour.

Nitric acid is now produced from ammonia by the *Ostwald* process. The first step is the oxidation of ammonia in the presence of a catalyst to produce nitric oxide:

$$4\,NH_3 + 5\,O_2 \rightarrow 4\,NO + 6\,H_2O$$

The nitric oxide is then further oxidized to nitrogen dioxide,

$$NO + \tfrac{1}{2}\,O_2 \rightarrow NO_2$$

which is then reacted with water,

$$3 NO_2 + H_2O \rightarrow 2 HNO_3 + NO$$

This reaction is not as simple as the corresponding step in the sulphuric acid process, since nitric oxide is produced. The nitric oxide is recycled, to be oxidized again in the preceding step.

There are no severe technological problems in the Ostwald process. Given a supply of ammonia, a range of ammonium salts and nitrate salts can be manufactured. Ammonium salts are made by reaction of the base ammonia with the appropriate acid. For example, ammonium sulphate is produced in large amounts using sulphuric acid:

$$2 NH_3 + H_2SO_4 \rightarrow (NH_4)_2SO_4$$

Nitrate salts are made by reaction of nitric acid with base:

$$K_2CO_3 + 2 HNO_3 \rightarrow 2 KNO_3 + CO_2(g) + H_2O$$

The largest production of salts of this type is of ammonium nitrate itself:

$$NH_3 + HNO_3 \rightarrow NH_4NO_3$$

This salt is widely used as a fertilizer for supplying nitrogen to the soil, and as such it is commonly handled in very large amounts. It is also a powerful explosive when heated or detonated, for it decomposes with the release of energy and the formation of a large volume of gas. This curious combination of properties has led to some immense accidental explosions of fertilizer in ships and storage facilities.

3-4 LIMESTONE PRODUCTS: LIME AND SODA ASH

Limestone is a common type of rock. It is used as a building material itself, for the manufacture of cement, and as the raw material for the manufacture of two important heavy chemicals. Chemically, limestone consists of a mixture of calcium carbonate and magnesium carbonate. For the present purposes it will be considered to be pure calcium carbonate, $CaCO_3$.

When limestone is heated to about 1200°C it decomposes to give off CO_2. This process is called *calcining*.

$$CaCO_3 \rightarrow CaO + CO_2$$

The basic oxide which results, CaO, is called *quicklime*, or simply *lime*. Quicklime reacts vigorously with water to produce calcium hydroxide, $Ca(OH)_2$, which is called *slaked lime*. Both forms of lime are sold and used in the building industry for making mortar, and in many other parts of the chemical industry. In terms of tonnage, lime is second only to sulphuric acid as a heavy chemical. Slaked lime is sometimes used in the form of a suspension of fine particles of precipitated calcium hydroxide in water. This suspension is called "milk of lime."

Limestone is also the starting point for the manufacture of the important industrial base *soda ash*, or sodium carbonate, Na_2CO_3. The process is called the

Solvay process, and the overall chemical reaction is given by the following equation:

$$CaCO_3 + 2\,NaCl \rightarrow Na_2CO_3 + CaCl_2$$

Despite the simplicity of this reaction, the process is not straightforward and must be carried in several steps. Solvay plants have fallen into disfavour recently because they produce, as well as the wanted product, a large amount of unsaleable calcium chloride, which is very soluble in water and must be dumped into the drainage system surrounding the plant. The resulting pollution of river systems by chloride ion is no longer acceptable, and to some extent Solvay process soda ash is being replaced by sodium carbonate derived from the mineral *trona*, which has the chemical formula

$$Na_2CO_3.NaHCO_3.2\,H_2O$$

The Solvay process begins with the calcining of limestone to produce CO_2 and lime, which is slaked. The other raw material is a concentrated solution of common salt, NaCl, called *brine*. Brine is obtained from wells which produce naturally salty water, or by dissolving rock salt in water. The brine is used to dissolve ammonia gas, and then the carbon dioxide produced from the limestone. The resulting solution contains a number of ions, and the result of the reaction is determined by solubility considerations. Sodium bicarbonate is precipitated from the solution, and the net reaction can be represented by the following equation:

$$NH_3 + CO_2 + H_2O + NaCl \rightarrow NaHCO_3(c) + NH_4^+(aq) + Cl^-(aq)$$

The sodium bicarbonate is filtered off, and heated to produce sodium carbonate, or soda ash:

$$2\,NaHCO_3 \rightarrow Na_2CO_3 + H_2O + CO_2$$

There are two steps in which materials are recycled. Firstly, the carbon dioxide produced in the last step is returned to be dissolved in more brine. Secondly, the solution of NH_4Cl remaining after the sodium bicarbonate is precipitated is treated with the slaked lime produced from the initial calcined limestone. The resulting acid-base reaction converts the ammonium ion to ammonia gas:

$$2\,NH_4^+(aq) + Ca(OH)_2(c) \rightarrow 2\,NH_3(g) + Ca^{2+}(aq) + 2\,H_2O$$

There is no loss of ammonia in the process, since all the ammonia dissolved in the brine initially is recovered in the last step. The solution remaining after the ammonia is removed contains calcium chloride.

Soda ash is used industrially as a base, and large amounts are used to manufacture soap and glass.

3-5   THE ELECTROLYTIC CHLORINE-ALKALI INDUSTRY

Chlorine and sodium hydroxide, also called *caustic soda,* are produced simultaneously by the electrolysis of brine. The process requires a cheap and

Figure 3-4 The Bécancour, Québec plant of C-I-L utilizes I.C.I. designed diaphragm cells to produce 140 000 t per year of chlorine and a corresponding quantity of alkali. The photograph shows the individual cells, the collectors for the chlorine leaving each cell, and the heavy conductors necessary to carry the large currents.

reliable source of electrical energy, and so this industry is usually associated with large hydroelectric power generators. The process is summarized in the following chemical reaction:

$$NaCl + H_2O \rightarrow NaOH + \tfrac{1}{2}H_2 + \tfrac{1}{2}Cl_2$$

There are two main types of electrolytic cell in use. In the *diaphragm* cell, the anode and cathode are on opposite sides of an asbestos diaphragm which keeps the products separate. At the *anode,* chloride ions are oxidized to chlorine gas:

$$Cl^-(aq) \rightarrow \tfrac{1}{2}Cl_2(g) + e$$

At the *cathode,* water is reduced to hydrogen gas, and hydroxide ions are released in solution:

$$H_2O + e \rightarrow \tfrac{1}{2}H_2(g) + OH^-(aq)$$

The gases chlorine and hydrogen bubble out of the solution. Sodium ions, hydroxide ions, and some chloride ions remain in the solution leaving the cathode compartment. When this solution is evaporated, NaCl precipitates, leaving a solution of caustic soda. Solid caustic soda is isolated by further evaporation.

The second type of electrolytic cell is the *mercury* cell. The half-reaction at the anode is the same as in the diaphragm cell, producing chlorine gas. However, the cathode is made of liquid mercury metal. Instead of water being reduced, sodium ions are reduced to sodium metal, which then dissolves in the mercury. The liquid mercury runs like a river across the bottom of the electrolytic cell, and carries the dissolved sodium off to another tank where it reacts with water:

$$Na + \tfrac{1}{2} H_2O \rightarrow NaOH + \tfrac{1}{2} H_2(g)$$

The overall reaction is the same in the two types of cell. Due to poor industrial "house-keeping" practices, the mercury cell has been responsible for the dumping of large quantities of mercury into the river systems of industrialized nations. Some mercury cells have been closed down, and the loss of mercury from those remaining in operation has been greatly reduced since the discovery of serious mercury pollution in the Great Lakes. However, mercury which has already been released may remain a hazard to man and to wildlife for a long time to come.

Chlorine and caustic soda are both used in a wide variety of industrial chemical operations, as well as in the plastics, soap and paper industries. Since they are produced simultaneously, the markets for these substances are closely linked together. The hydrogen produced as a by-product is used for making ammonia and other chemicals.

3-6 ETHYLENE

Organic chemistry is the chemistry of carbon compounds, of which several million are known. Carbon has the special property of being able to form long chains or rings of carbon atoms bonded together. There are more known compounds of carbon in existence than there are for all the other chemical elements taken together. If a carbon compound contains just carbon and hydrogen it is called a *hydrocarbon*. Although carbon and hydrogen are the most important constituents of most organic compounds they may also contain one or more other atoms such as oxygen, nitrogen, sulphur, phosphorus or a halogen. Many organic molecules are important to living systems and biologically active molecules often also contain metal atoms, for example, haemoglobin (Fe) and chlorophyll (Mg). Indeed, many organic compounds containing carbon-metal bonds are of considerable importance and constitute the basis for a branch of chemistry known as organometallic chemistry.

Organic chemistry is the basis for a large part of the chemical industry. However, despite the importance and variety of the organic chemical industry, only one organic compound, ethylene, is produced in sufficiently large amount to be called a heavy chemical. Ethylene is used in a variety of chemical products, the most important being the polymer polyethylene, industrial grade ethyl alcohol, and ethylene glycol antifreeze.

Oil refineries handle vast amounts of hydrocarbons, which are processed into fuels, lubricants and solvents. These products are usually not refined to a state of high chemical purity, and so the oil refining industry is not regarded as part of the chemical industry. However, there is a growing trend towards the use of materials derived from petroleum for the manufacture of chemicals. Ethylene is the starting point for much of this *petrochemical* industry.

Petroleum consists of a mixture of many different hydrocarbons. The

Figure 3-5 Much ethylene is produced from petroleum, but increasingly it is made by dehydrogenation of ethane extracted from natural gas. This Alberta Gas Ethylene plant at Joffre, Alberta produces 544 000 t per year of ethylene. This ethylene is distributed by pipeline to plants of other companies for the production of polyethylene, polyvinyl chloride, polyvinyl acetate and ethylene glycol. A second ethylene plant of the same size is planned for the Joffre site.

saturated straight chain hydrocarbons of low molar mass have the following molecular formulae.

$$
\begin{array}{c}
\;\;\;\;H \\
\;\;\;\;| \\
H-C-H \\
\;\;\;\;| \\
\;\;\;\;H
\end{array}
$$

methane CH_4

$$
\begin{array}{c}
\;\;H\;\;\;H \\
\;\;|\;\;\;| \\
H-C-C-H \\
\;\;|\;\;\;| \\
\;\;H\;\;\;H
\end{array}
$$

ethane C_2H_6

$$
\begin{array}{c}
\;\;H\;\;\;H\;\;\;H \\
\;\;|\;\;\;|\;\;\;| \\
H-C-C-C-H \\
\;\;|\;\;\;|\;\;\;| \\
\;\;H\;\;\;H\;\;\;H
\end{array}
$$

propane C_3H_8

$$
\begin{array}{c}
\;\;H\;\;\;H\;\;\;H\;\;\;H \\
\;\;|\;\;\;|\;\;\;|\;\;\;| \\
H-C-C-C-C-H \\
\;\;|\;\;\;|\;\;\;|\;\;\;| \\
\;\;H\;\;\;H\;\;\;H\;\;\;H
\end{array}
$$

butane C_4H_{10}

$$
\begin{array}{c}
\;\;H\;\;\;H\;\;\;H\;\;\;H\;\;\;H \\
\;\;|\;\;\;|\;\;\;|\;\;\;|\;\;\;| \\
H-C-C-C-C-C-H \\
\;\;|\;\;\;|\;\;\;|\;\;\;|\;\;\;| \\
\;\;H\;\;\;H\;\;\;H\;\;\;H\;\;\;H
\end{array}
$$

pentane C_5H_{12}

There are also branched chain hydrocarbons, in which the skeleton of carbon atoms is branched. The compounds are systematically named on the basis of the longest chain of carbon atoms which can be found in the molecule, although older non-systematic names remain in common use. Some examples are given below.

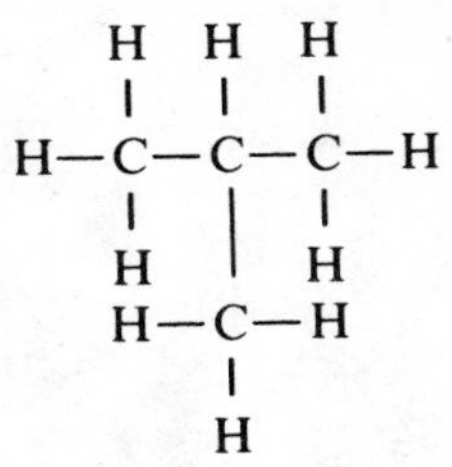

$$
\begin{array}{c}
\overset{\displaystyle H}{|}\ \overset{\displaystyle H}{|}\ \overset{\displaystyle H}{|} \\
H-C-C-C-H \\
\overset{\displaystyle |}{H}\ \ \ \overset{\displaystyle |}{H} \\
H-C-H \\
\overset{\displaystyle |}{H}
\end{array}
$$

methylpropane C_4H_{10}
or isobutane

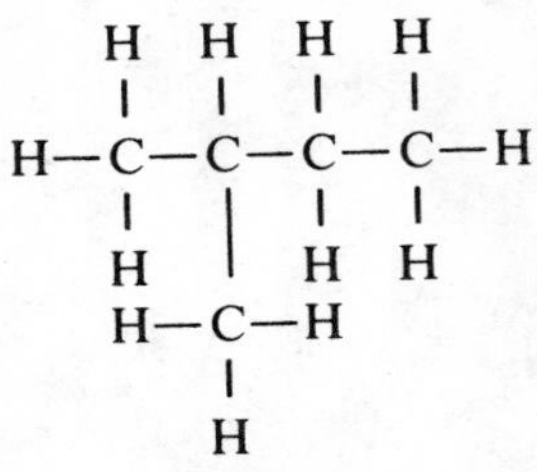

$$
\begin{array}{c}
\overset{\displaystyle H}{|}\ \overset{\displaystyle H}{|}\ \overset{\displaystyle H}{|}\ \overset{\displaystyle H}{|} \\
H-C-C-C-C-H \\
\overset{\displaystyle |}{H}\ \ \ \overset{\displaystyle |}{H}\ \overset{\displaystyle |}{H} \\
H-C-H \\
\overset{\displaystyle |}{H}
\end{array}
$$

methylbutane C_5H_{12}
or isopentane

The branched chain and straight chain hydrocarbons have the same general formula, C_nH_{2n+2}, where n is an integer. Saturated hydrocarbons in which the carbon atoms form a ring have the general formula C_nH_{2n} and are identified by the prefix *cyclo-* in their names.

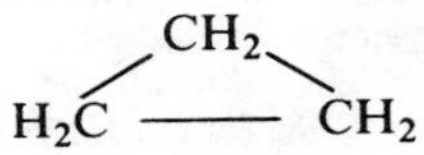

cyclopropane C_3H_6

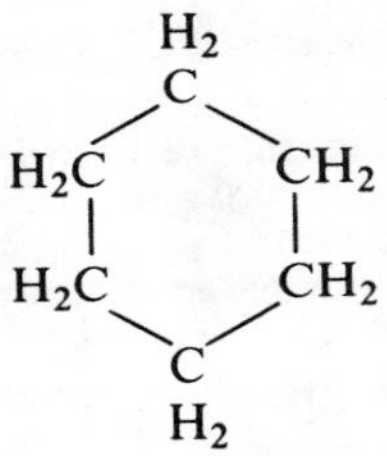

cyclohexane C_6H_{12}

Hydrocarbons in which double bonds occur are called *unsaturated* hydrocarbons, or *olefins*. The two olefins of lowest molar mass are ethene and propene, which are commonly called by their non-systematic names ethylene and propylene.

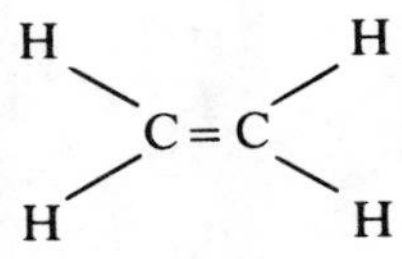

ethene
or ethylene C_2H_4

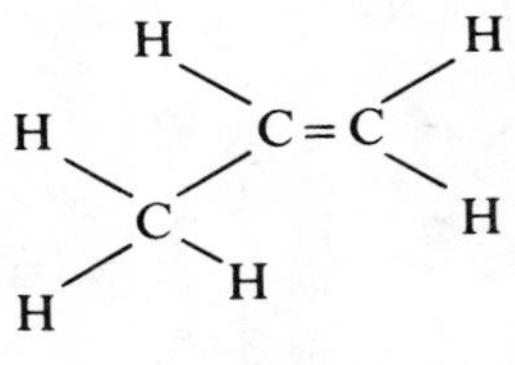

propene
or propylene C_3H_6

Olefins do not occur in any significant concentrations in petroleum or natural gas, and must be manufactured. There are several reactions which can be used for ethylene production, but the process favoured in modern practice is the *cracking* reaction starting from ethane or propane derived from natural gas. The mixture of ethane and propane gas is passed at high speed through a region of high temperature. The resulting decomposition reaction is sometimes known as *pyrolysis*. The saturated hydrocarbons decompose to form the olefins ethylene and propylene:

$$
\begin{array}{c}
\text{H} \quad \text{H} \\
| \quad | \\
\text{H}-\text{C}-\text{C}-\text{H} \\
| \quad | \\
\text{H} \quad \text{H}
\end{array}
\longrightarrow
\begin{array}{c}
\text{H} \qquad \text{H} \\
\diagdown \qquad \diagup \\
\text{C}=\text{C} \\
\diagup \qquad \diagdown \\
\text{H} \qquad \text{H}
\end{array}
+ \text{H}_2
$$

$$
\begin{array}{c}
\text{H} \quad \text{H} \quad \text{H} \\
| \quad | \quad | \\
\text{H}-\text{C}-\text{C}-\text{C}-\text{H} \\
| \quad | \quad | \\
\text{H} \quad \text{H} \quad \text{H}
\end{array}
\longrightarrow
\begin{array}{c}
\text{H} \qquad \text{H} \\
\diagdown \qquad \diagup \\
\text{C}=\text{C} \\
\diagup \qquad \diagdown \\
\text{H} \qquad \text{H}
\end{array}
+ \text{CH}_4
$$

$$
\begin{array}{c}
\text{H} \quad \text{H} \quad \text{H} \\
| \quad | \quad | \\
\text{H}-\text{C}-\text{C}-\text{C}-\text{H} \\
| \quad | \quad | \\
\text{H} \quad \text{H} \quad \text{H}
\end{array}
\longrightarrow
\begin{array}{c}
\text{H} \qquad\qquad \text{H} \\
\diagdown \qquad\qquad \diagup \\
\text{H} \quad \text{C}=\text{C} \\
\diagdown \qquad\qquad \diagdown \\
\text{C} \qquad \text{H} \\
\diagup \diagdown \\
\text{H} \quad \text{H}
\end{array}
+ \text{H}_2
$$

Ethylene and propylene produced in these reactions are separated from the alkanes and hydrogen by condensation. Alkanes and hydrogen are then returned to the natural gas stream to be used as fuel. Cracking reactions are also carried out on higher saturated hydrocarbons, C_{15} and up, in order to convert them to the lower hydrocarbons, C_4 to C_8, for use in gasoline. The process of cracking always produces a large amount of olefins including ethylene, and so oil refineries are large suppliers of ethylene and propylene. The largest use for ethylene is the production of polymer polyethylene. This is formed from ethylene at high pressure in the presence of a catalyst. The unsaturated hydrocarbon molecules are joined together to form very long chains of carbon atoms.

$$
\cdots +
\begin{array}{c}
\text{H} \qquad \text{H} \\
\diagdown \qquad \diagup \\
\text{C}=\text{C} \\
\diagup \qquad \diagdown \\
\text{H} \qquad \text{H}
\end{array}
+
\begin{array}{c}
\text{H} \qquad \text{H} \\
\diagdown \qquad \diagup \\
\text{C}=\text{C} \\
\diagup \qquad \diagdown \\
\text{H} \qquad \text{H}
\end{array}
+ \cdots
$$

$$
\longrightarrow \cdots
\begin{array}{c}
\text{H} \quad \text{H} \quad \text{H} \quad \text{H} \\
| \quad | \quad | \quad | \\
-\text{C}-\text{C}-\text{C}-\text{C}- \\
| \quad | \quad | \quad | \\
\text{H} \quad \text{H} \quad \text{H} \quad \text{H}
\end{array}
\cdots
$$

Polyethylene is used for many practical applications in industry and in everyday life.

Figure 3-6 The Petrosar plant at Sarnia, Ontario produces both aromatics and olefins from naphtha obtained from petroleum. The scale is large, with annual production of 500 000 t of ethene, 270 000 t of propene, 220 000 t of butadiene and butene, 180 000 t of benzene and 160 000 t of toluene and xylene. All production is taken under contract by neighbouring firms to produce polyethylene, polypropylene, styrene, isobutyl alcohol, and several elastomers. The large tower on the right fractionates gasoline. Both fuel oil and gasoline are major 'by-products'.

Ethylene glycol is one example of the great variety of petrochemicals produced from ethylene. The first step in its manufacture is the controlled oxidation of ethylene. Ethylene is fuel, like other hydrocarbons, and burns well with air to form carbon dioxide and water. However, if ethylene and oxygen are reacted at low temperature in the presence of a suitable catalyst, the cyclic compound ethylene oxide is formed instead:

$$\begin{matrix} H \\ \diagdown \\ C \\ \diagup \\ H \end{matrix} = \begin{matrix} H \\ \diagup \\ C \\ \diagdown \\ H \end{matrix} \quad + \quad \tfrac{1}{2}O_2 \quad \longrightarrow \quad \begin{matrix} H_2C \text{——} CH_2 \\ \diagdown \quad \diagup \\ O \end{matrix}$$

Ethylene oxide is a very versatile "intermediate," which can be used to make a number of other products. To make ethylene glycol, it is reacted with water.

$$H-\underset{\underset{\displaystyle O}{\diagup\!\diagdown}}{\overset{\overset{\displaystyle H}{|}}{C}}-\overset{\overset{\displaystyle H}{|}}{C}-H \;+\; \underset{\underset{\displaystyle O}{\diagup\!\diagdown}}{H\quad H} \;\longrightarrow\; \begin{array}{c} H \\ | \\ H-C-O-H \\ | \\ H-C-O-H \\ | \\ H \end{array}$$

ethylene glycol

Ethylene glycol has two −OH groups in each molecule, and it dissolves in water, unlike hydrocarbons which are insoluble. Concentrated solutions of ethylene glycol have much lower freezing points than water, and are used as antifreeze coolants for equipment which is exposed to cold climates.

Ethyl alcohol or ethanol, C_2H_5OH, is used for many industrial purposes in addition to its use in beverages. It is produced in large amounts by fermentation of sucrose and starch, but ethylene is also used to make industrial grade ethanol. Ethylene is reacted with steam in the presence of a catalyst:

$$\underset{\underset{\displaystyle H}{\diagup}}{\overset{\overset{\displaystyle H}{\diagdown}}{}}C=C\underset{\underset{\displaystyle H}{\diagdown}}{\overset{\overset{\displaystyle H}{\diagup}}{}} \;+\; H\underset{\underset{\displaystyle O}{\diagup\!\diagdown}}{\quad}H \;\rightleftharpoons\; H-\overset{\overset{\displaystyle H}{|}}{\underset{\underset{\displaystyle H}{|}}{C}}-\overset{\overset{\displaystyle H}{|}}{\underset{\underset{\displaystyle H}{|}}{C}}-O-H$$

The reaction is reversible and the position of equilibrium is moved to the right by high pressures and low temperatures, and again the choice of operating conditions must be made on the basis of minimizing the cost of the product.

FURTHER READING

Only the briefest sketch of the giant chemical industry can be given in a single short chapter, and further exploration will be of interest to many students. Several books giving broad surveys of the subject are listed below, and for the most part these books are quite readable for a student beginning a university course in chemistry. They will provide a useful understanding of the way in which chemistry is used outside the school or university classroom.

Accounts of current trends in individual parts of the chemical industry, plant openings and closings, government activities, and employment opportunities are to be found in magazines such as "Chemical and Engineering News" published in the U.S., "Chemistry and Industry" and "Chemistry in Britain" published in the United Kingdom, and "Chemistry in Canada." Statistics on national production figures and related data are published regularly in government publications.

Shreve R.N., *The Chemical Process Industries.* (McGraw-Hill, New York, 1967). An authoritative survey of the industry, concentrating on the United States.

Wiseman P., *An Introduction to Industrial Organic Chemistry.* (Applied Science Publishers Ltd, London 1972). A survey of the production of organic chemicals, with emphasis on the British industry.

Thomson R. (Editor), *The Modern Inorganic Chemicals Industry.* (The Chemical Society, London 1977). This is a series of papers given at a British symposium summarising the current situation at the time. It is mostly easy to read, and covers economic and environmental factors as well as purely chemical and engineering matters.

PROBLEMS

1. What mass of sulphur is used in producing one million tonnes of sulphuric acid? What mass of air is used? Assume air to contain 22% oxygen by mass.

    [0.33 Mt, 3.0 Mt]

2. A Solvay plant produced 5.0×10^4 t of soda ash per annum. What mass of calcium chloride must be dumped annually? If the calcium chloride is dumped into a river which is subject to government regulations limiting chloride ion concentration to be less than 150 p.p.m. (parts per million by mass), calculate the minimum average flow rate of water in the river which is required to absorb the calcium chloride. Express the flow rate in cubic metre per second.

    [5.2×10^4 t, 7.1 m^3 s^{-1}]

3. Consider an ammonia synthesis plant, such as the 1200 t per day plant of Canadian Fertilizers Ltd., in Medicine Hat, Alberta. If this plant operates for 300 days per year, calculate the following quantities for one year. You may assume that air has a composition 80% N_2, 20% O_2 by mole.

    (a) Mass of NH_3 produced

    [3.60×10^5 t]

    (b) Mass of N_2 which must be prepared

    [2.97×10^5 t]

    (c) Mass of CH_4 consumed in N_2 production

    [2.12×10^4 t]

    (d) Mass of H_2 which must be prepared

    [6.40×10^4 t]

    (e) Mass of CH_4 consumed in H_2 production

    [1.27×10^5 t]

    (f) Mass of CO_2 which is produced

    [4.08×10^5 t]

(g) Mass of soda ash (Na_2CO_3) required to absorb the CO_2 by conversion to sodium bicarbonate ($NaHCO_3$)

$$[9.82 \times 10^5 \text{ t}]$$

(h) Is there sufficient CO_2 produced to convert the entire NH_3 output of the plant to urea, $\begin{matrix} H_2N \\ H_2N \end{matrix} C{=}O,$ by the reaction

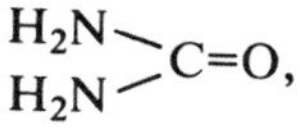

$$2\,NH_3 + CO_2 \rightarrow (H_2N)_2CO + H_2O\ ?$$

$$[\text{No}]$$

(i) In any case, what is the maximum possible output of urea?

$$[5.56 \times 10^5 \text{ t}]$$

(j) If the entire NH_3 output were converted to nitric acid, by the Ostwald process, what mass of acid would be produced?

$$[1.33 \times 10^6 \text{ t}]$$

(k) If the entire NH_3 output were converted to ammonium nitrate, what mass of that salt would be produced?

$$[8.48 \times 10^5 \text{ t}]$$

4. A chlorine plant produces 2.0×10^4 t of chlorine per annum. Calculate the average current in the electrolytic cells. Calculate the masses of sodium hydroxide and of hydrogen which are produced in the process. Calculate the size of the ammonia plant (in tonne per annum) which would convert the electrolytic hydrogen into ammonia, and compare this plant with that described in question 3-3.

$$[1.7 \times 10^6 \text{ A, 23 kt, 564 t, 3.2 kt}]$$

5. Ethylene oxide reacts with a number of hydrogen-containing compounds HX according to the general reaction

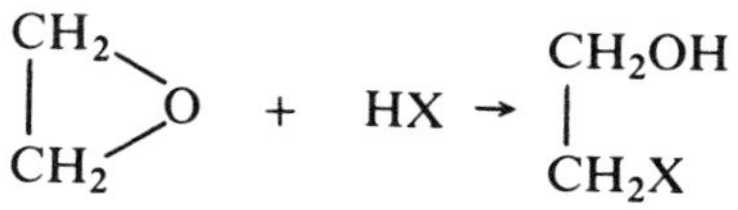

$$\begin{matrix} CH_2 \\ | \quad \rangle O \\ CH_2 \end{matrix} + HX \rightarrow \begin{matrix} CH_2OH \\ | \\ CH_2X \end{matrix}$$

An example is the formation of ethylene glycol in which HX is water. Identify the reactants HX in each of the following reactions:

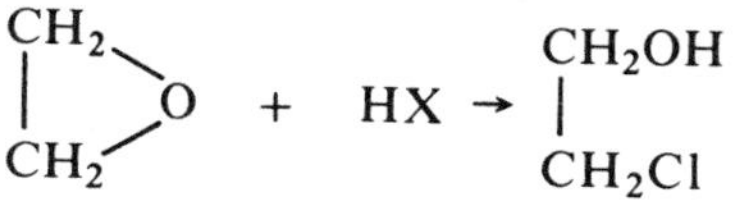

$$\begin{matrix} CH_2 \\ | \quad \rangle O \\ CH_2 \end{matrix} + HX \rightarrow \begin{matrix} CH_2OH \\ | \\ CH_2Cl \end{matrix} \qquad \text{2-chloroethanol}$$

$$\begin{matrix} CH_2 \\ | \quad \rangle O \\ CH_2 \end{matrix} + HX \rightarrow \begin{matrix} CH_2OH \\ | \\ CH_2NH_2 \end{matrix} \qquad \text{ethanolamine}$$

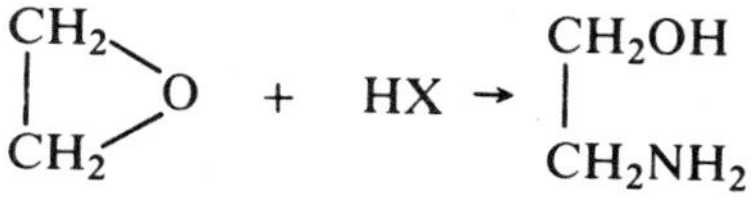

$$\begin{array}{c} CH_2 \\ | \quad\quad O \\ CH_2 \end{array} + HX \rightarrow \begin{array}{c} CH_2OH \\ | \\ CH_2 \\ | \\ O \\ | \\ CH_2 \\ | \\ CH_2OH \end{array} \quad \text{diethyleneglycol}$$

6.   Describe the main movement of ions in the diaphragm cell. Which ions move through the diaphragm, and in which direction?

IV THE PROPERTIES OF GASES

Three physical states of matter, solid, liquid and gas, are commonly met, and most people have a good idea of how to distinguish between them. Precise definitions of each state are difficult to give however. In this chapter we begin the study of one of those states, the gas state. In later chapters the other states, and the relationships between them, will be dealt with and then the whole subject can be seen in perspective.

Gases are met in the laboratory, in the environment, and in industrial processes. A knowledge of their physical properties is essential to all areas of science and technology. To a large degree the physical properties of gases are independent of the chemical properties of the substances present. This is an important fact to grasp, for it allows the development of general gas laws of very wide application. Such generalization of the laws governing basic properties is not possible for liquids or solids. The general laws governing the behaviour of gases were established a long time ago, and the names of the men who formulated these laws are familiar to students of chemistry.

In this chapter, basic measurements related to gases are described, and the properties of ideal gases are defined and discussed. In a later chapter, the way in which real gases deviate from ideal behavior is discussed, but for many gases the deviations are small and the calculations described in the present chapter are sufficiently accurate to be useful.

4-1 THE STATES OF MATTER

Most matter occurs in one of three easily recognized states: solid, liquid and gas. These three ordinary states of matter can be distinguished from one another by considering four properties which can be measured easily and interpreted with common sense. The four properties are the density, compressibility, rigidity and the ability to expand to fill available space.

The density measures the mass of material per unit volume, and the compressibility measures the dependence of density on pressure. Gases have low densities and are easily compressed, while liquids and solids have high densities which are only slightly affected by changes in pressure. Solids are rigid and retain their shapes almost unaltered under external forces, whereas a liquid conforms in shape to its container. A substance in the solid or liquid state has a well defined volume, which is independent of the size of the container, as long as the container is large enough; however, when a gas is placed in a vessel it expands to fill the whole volume available. These properties of the three phases are summarized for comparison in Table 4-1.

The classification given in Table 4-1 is useful but sometimes ambiguous. Some solids are soft and can be deformed easily while others are very hard. Some liquids are viscous and take a long time to adapt themselves to the shape of their container. "Liquid crystals" have the bulk properties of liquids, but in the arrangement of their molecules are like solid crystals. Rubber and similar polymers constitute another class of materials altogether. In Chapter 7 it will be shown that the distinction between the gas and liquid states disappears under certain conditions of temperature and pressure near the critical point. Nevertheless, Table 4-1 is useful as a summary of the properties of the ordinary states of matter.

TABLE 4-1 Properties of Solids, Liquids and Gases

	Gas	Liquid	Solid
Density	Low	High	High
Compressibility	High	Low	Low
Retains shape?	No	No	Yes
Expands to fill available space?	Yes	No	No

4-2 MEASUREMENTS ON GASES

(i) Mass Like any other form of matter, the mass of a gas sample can be determined by weighing, provided that it is contained in a suitable vessel. An accurate balance is needed, for the mass of the gas is generally much less than the mass of the vessel, and must be determined by mass difference. Samples of gas may be collected in two types of sampling bulb, which are shown in Figure 4-1.

A sample of gas may be collected in a bulb with a single connection, provided that the air is first pumped out of the bulb with a vacuum pump. The gas sample can then be introduced through a suitable tubing connection. Gas can also be sampled in a bulb with a double connection by allowing it to flow through the bulb, sweeping out the air which was in the bulb initially; this procedure avoids the need for a vacuum pump.

The buoyancy of the bulb in air must be considered carefully in such determinations. When the bulb is open to the atmosphere, or is filled with air at atmospheric pressure, buoyancy effects are negligible and the measured mass is the mass of the metal or glass used in making the bulb. If the bulb has been

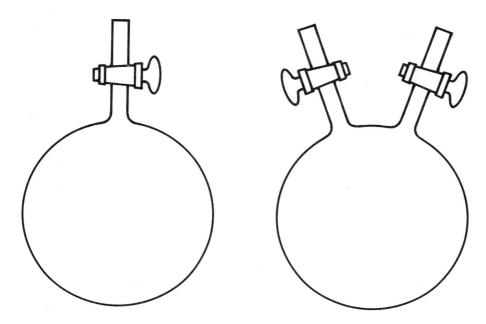

Figure 4-1   Sampling bulbs.

evacuated and sealed, the measured mass is less than the mass of the bulb, the difference being the mass of the air in the bulb. When weighing a sampling bulb, it is often best to fill the bulb with dry nitrogen gas to avoid errors due to moisture in the atmosphere.

0.258 — eva

Example 4-1   A bulb has a mass of 178.510 g when open to the atmosphere, 178.252 g when evacuated, and 178.349 g when filled with a sample of an unknown gas. What is the mass of the unknown sample?

When the unknown gas sample is introduced into the evacuated bulb, the mass of the bulb increases from 178.252 g to 178.349 g, an increase of 0.097 g, and this must be the mass of the unknown sample. Both these measured masses are affected by the buoyancy of the bulb in air, but they are affected equally and so there is no correction to be made after subtraction. The difference between the mass of the open bulb and the mass of the evacuated bulb represents the mass of the air at atmospheric pressure contained within the volume of the bulb.

(ii) Volume   The volume of a cylinder or bulb used for containing gas samples is most easily determined by filling the bulb with water, since the density of water is accurately known. In a large system, it may be necessary to calculate the volume geometrically.

Example 4-2   The cylinder described in Example 1 has a mass of 398.3 g when filled with water at a temperature of 20°C. At this temperature, water has a density of 0.9982 g cm^{-3}. What is the volume of the bulb?

$$\text{The mass of water contained} = 398.3 - 178.252$$

$$= 220.0 \text{ g}$$

$$\text{Hence volume} = 220.0 \text{ g}/0.9982 \text{ g cm}^{-3}$$

$$= 220.4 \text{ cm}^3$$

(iii) Pressure   A gas exerts a force on its surroundings. This can be demonstrated by pumping up a tire with a bicycle pump: a good deal of force must be applied to the pump handle in order to overcome the force exerted by the air on the piston. Experiments show that for a given condition of the gas, the force of the gas on a piston is proportional to the area of the piston, and so the condition of the gas is measured not by the force on the piston, but by the *force per unit area*. This quantity is called the *pressure,* and is measured in units of newtons per square metre, or kilogram metre $^{-1}$ second $^{-2}$. This unit is given a special name, *pascal,* with the abbreviation Pa, after the physicist Blaise Pascal who, with Boyle and Torricelli, established the nature of the atmosphere.

Pressures can be measured in several ways. A common laboratory instrument for this purpose is the *manometer,* which works by balancing the

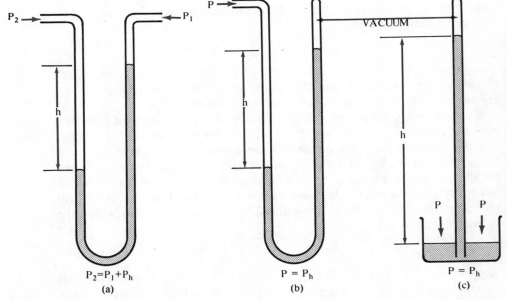

Figure 4-2   Manometers for measuring gas pressure. In each case the hydrostatic pressure is $P_h = \varrho \, g \, h$

pressure of a gas against the hydrostatic pressure of a liquid. Several forms of manometer are shown in Figure 4-2. Reference to a physics textbook will recall for the student that the hydrostatic pressure at a point in a liquid is due to gravity and depends only on the vertical distance h from that point to the plane of the surface of the liquid. If the liquid is of uniform density then the hydrostatic pressure Pa at a distance h below the surface of the liquid is given by

$$P_h = \varrho\, g\, h$$

where ϱ is the density of the liquid, and g is the acceleration due to gravity.

Example 4-3 Calculate the hydrostatic pressure 10.0 m below the surface of Lake Ontario, if the density of water is 998.2 kg m^{-3}, and the acceleration due to gravity is 9.784 m s^{-2}.

The hydrostatic pressure is

$$
\begin{aligned}
P_h &= 998.2 \text{ kg m}^{-3} \times 9.784 \text{ m s}^{-2} \times 10.1 \text{ m} \\
&= 9.766 \times 10^4 \text{ kg m}^{-1} \text{ s}^{-2} \\
&= 9.766 \times 10^4 \text{ N m}^{-2} \\
&= 97.66 \text{ kPa}
\end{aligned}
$$

The manometer uses hydrostatic pressure in an indicator liquid to determine the pressure of a gas. It consists of a U-tube and a scale for reading the vertical distance between the liquid surfaces, as shown in Figure 4-2. It may be a double-ended manometer used for measuring the pressure difference between two vessels, or between one vessel and the atmosphere, or a single-ended manometer in which one side is evacuated and so is at zero pressure. The barometer is a special form of single-ended manometer which is used for measuring atmospheric pressure. Mercury is the most common liquid used in laboratory manometers and has a density of 1.3546 × 10^4 kg m^{-3} at 20°C.

In many engineering applications gas or liquid pressures are quoted as "gauge pressure," which means the difference between the measured pressure and atmospheric pressure. The double-ended manometer, and the Bourdon gauge shown in Figure 4-3, indicate gauge pressure. In this book all pressures

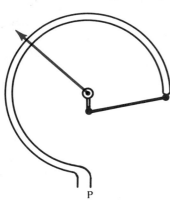

Figure 4-3 The Bourdon pressure gauge when pressure is applied to the bent tube, it straightens out slightly, and a mechanical linkage causes rotation of the pointer.

quoted are absolute pressures; a gauge pressure is converted to absolute pressure by adding the pressure of the atmosphere.

Example 4-4   Calculate the pressure corresponding to a barometric height of 76.00 cm of mercury at 20°C at Kingston, Ontario where the gravitational acceleration is 9.80530 m s^{-2}.

$$P = 13\ 546\ \text{kg m}^{-3} \times 9.80530\ \text{m s}^{-2} \times 0.7600\ \text{m}$$

$$= 100.9 \times 10^3\ \text{kg m}^{-1}\ \text{s}^{-2}$$

$$= 100.9\ \text{kPa}$$

Example 4-5   Calculate the height of the mercury barometer at the same temperature and atmospheric pressure as in Example 4-4 at two other places: Greenwich, England and Brisbane, Australia, where the gravitational accelerations are 9.811 84 m s^{-2} and 9.791 48 m s^{-2} respectively.

The height h′ of the barometer at Greenwich is given by

$$100.9 \times 10^3 = 13\ 546 \times 9.81184 \times h'$$

$$\text{from which}\ h' = 0.7591\ \text{m}$$

$$= 75.91\ \text{cm}$$

The height h″ of the barometer at Brisbane is given by

$$100.9 \times 10^3 = 13\ 546 \times 9.791\ 48 \times h''$$

$$\text{from which}\ h'' = 0.7607\ \text{m}$$

$$= 76.07\ \text{cm}$$

These heights h′ and h″ are measurably different from the height of the barometer at Kingston corresponding to the same pressure.

Pressures of gases are often quoted as an equivalent height of mercury, but this procedure has disadvantages. The value of the gravitational acceleration varies from place to place on the surface of the earth, as shown in Example 4-5, and the density of mercury depends on its temperature. Hence, in basic work, pressures ought to be quoted in the basic unit of force per square meter (or Pascal) rather than the height of a column of mercury. There are situations where other units are convenient and in habitual use. Where habit or convenience is thought preferable to conformity with S.I., the conversion factor for conversion of pressures to units of pascals should be readily available. Some commonly encountered pressure units and associated conversion factors are given in Table 4-2.

The *atmosphere* is approximately the pressure required to support a column of mercury 76 cm high, but is now defined as exactly 101 325 Pa. The *bar* is defined as exactly 100 000 Pa, and the *torr* (after Evangelista Torricelli) is exactly 1/760 atmosphere. The torr is very nearly equal to the hydrostatic pressure of one millimetre of mercury.

TABLE 4-2   Common Pressure Units and Conversion Factors

Unit	To convert pressure in these units to pascals, multiply by:
atmosphere	101 325
bar	100 000
torr	$\dfrac{101\ 325}{760} = 1.333.2$
pounds per square inch	6894.8

Example 4-6   Calculate the absolute pressure in pascals in a vessel equipped with a pressure gauge reading 8.35 p.s.i.g. if the atmospheric pressure is 99.81 kPa.

Expressing all pressures in pascals,

$$\text{pressure} = (8.35\text{ p.s.i.}) \times (6894.8\text{ Pa/p.s.i.}) + 99\ 810\text{ Pa}$$

$$= 157\ 380\text{ Pa}$$

$$= 157.4\text{ kPa}$$

Where data are to be tabulated at a *standard pressure,* it has been agreed that a pressure of 101 325 Pa will be used. This pressure is used so often in chemistry and thermodynamics that a special notation has been defined, $P° = 101\ 325$ Pa. This notation will become familiar through usage, especially in thermochemistry and thermodynamics.

(iv) Temperature   It is convenient to discuss temperature measurement together with measurements on gases because the absolute temperature scale is closely related to the properties of gases. So close is the connection that it is sometimes hard to see the chain of logic used in accurate temperature measurement.

The absolute temperature scale cannot be defined until the second law of thermodynamics has been discussed, and so at this stage a practical temperature scale will be introduced, even though it differs slightly from the absolute scale.

A temperature scale may be defined crudely on the basis of touch. It is common experience that a glass of water with ice in it is colder than a glass of water direct from the tap; that water placed on a fire gets warm, and that water which is boiling is too hot to touch. While this temperature scale is crude, it is sufficiently accurate for finding out which properties of materials are affected by changes in temperature. It can be demonstrated that most solids expand, and that most liquids expand more rapidly than glass when heated. The electrical resistance of a piece of metal wire increases, and that of a suitable semiconductor decreases, when heated. These properties of materials can be used to construct thermometers which are more sensitive and quantitative, and which can be used over a wider range of temperatures, than the thermometer based on the touch of the observer's hand.

Having discovered a property which depends on temperature, it is possible to use that property to establish a temperature scale. This may be done using two *fixed points,* or temperatures which are well defined and reproducible. The two fixed points which are used to define the Celsius temperature scale are the temperature of a mixture of ice and water, and the temperature of boiling water. The lower fixed point is assigned the temperature 0°, and the upper fixed point 100°, on the Celsius scale. The temperatures other than these are measured using a thermometer. The mercury thermometer consists of a bulb of mercury with a small constant diameter capillary tube attached, and the temperature is measured by the height of the column of mercury in the tube. The thermometer is calibrated by marking the height of the column when it is in contact with an ice-water mixture, and again when it is in contact with boiling water. These two points on the capillary are marked on the glass, and are labelled as 0 and 100. The glass tubing between these two marks is then divided into 100 equal *lengths,* using a ruler, and each of these equal lengths is said to represent a temperature change of one degree on this temperature scale. The thermometer constructed and calibrated in this way may be used as a sensitive and reliable way of measuring temperatures, and is used in many laboratory experiments.

Example 4-7   In a certain mercury-in-glass thermometer, the height of the mercury column changes by 252.2 mm when the temperature is changed from 0°C to 100°C. When the temperature of a cup of tea is measured, the mercury column stands 170.0 mm above the 0°C fixed point. What is the temperature of the tea on the mercury-in-glass temperature scale?

The temperature is higher than 0°C by an amount equal to $(170.0/252.2) \times 100°$, or 67.40°. Hence the temperature of the cup of tea is 67.40°C.

After a thermometer is made and calibrated, it will be discovered that the temperature of boiling water, the upper fixed point, is not constant, but varies from day to day. The variations are readily shown to be related to atmospheric pressure, and so the upper fixed point is properly defined as the temperature of boiling water at the agreed-upon standard atmospheric pressure, 101.325 kPa.

A temperature scale can also be defined using a platinum resistance thermometer. The same fixed points at 0° and 100° are used, and the thermometer is calibrated by measuring the electrical resistance of the platinum wire thermometer at these two temperatures. A straight line graph is then drawn passing through the two points of calibration, as shown in Figure 4-4, and can be used to measure intermediate temperatures.

Example 4-8   A platinum resistance thermometer has a resistance of 100.08 Ω at 0°C, and 138.61 Ω at 100°C. When immersed in the cup of tea described in Example 4-7, the resistance is 126.18 Ω. What is the temperature of the cup of tea on the platinum resistance temperature scale?

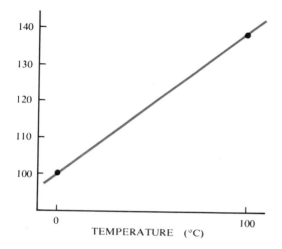

Figure 4-4 The definition of a temperature scale using a platinum resistance thermometer, with linear interpolation between two fixed points.

The temperature is higher than 0°C by

$$\frac{126.18 - 100.08}{138.61 - 100.08} \times 100° = 67.74°$$

Hence the temperature as measured by this thermometer on this temperature scale is 67.74°C.

These two examples illustrate that the simple definition of a temperature scale using two fixed points is not absolute. The mercury-in-glass and platinum resistance thermometers are both very reliable instruments and either could be used to define a temperature scale. These two scales differ slightly, except at fixed points of 0°C and 100°C. Until the definition of the absolute temperature scale using the second law of thermodynamics is discussed in Chapter 16, the mercury-in-glass Celsius temperature scale will be used despite the arbitrary nature of this choice. No serious errors will be introduced by this procedure.

4-3 THE BULK PROPERTIES OF GASES

The behaviour of gases has been the subject of investigation for hundreds of years. The results of these investigations are summarized in two simple statements or laws:

(i) Boyle's Law: for a fixed mass of gas held at a fixed temperature, the product of pressure and volume is a constant:

$$PV = \text{constant, for fixed T and m.}$$

(ii) Charles' Law or Gay-Lussac's Law: for a constant mass of gas held at a constant pressure, the change in volume is proportional to the change in temperature. If the gas is held in a constant volume, the change in pressure is proportional to the change in temperature:

$$\Delta V = \text{constant} \times \Delta T, \text{ for fixed P and m}$$

$$\text{or } \Delta P = \text{constant} \times \Delta T, \text{ for fixed V and m}$$

These laws do not hold exactly, but for most gases the errors are small under ordinary conditions, and for some gases the errors are extremely small. These laws are commonly used for calculations of moderate accuracy.

Boyle's law was established on the basis of experiments carried out by Robert Boyle and Robert Hooke about 1662 using a mechanical air pump. Their work demonstrated the existence of pressure in a gas, and related the pressure of a gas to its volume.

Example 4-9   A tank has a volume of 2.34 m³, and holds gas at a pressure of 700 kPa. What would be the volume of the gas measured at a pressure of 101 kPa at the same temperature?

Since the temperature and amount of gas are both constant, Boyle's law may be used directly, in the form $P_1V_1 = P_2V_2$. The volume of gas is therefore

$$V = 2.34 \text{ m}^3 \times \frac{700 \text{ kPa}}{101 \text{ kPa}}$$

$$= 16.2 \text{ m}^3$$

Boyle's Law can be written in the form

$$P = \text{constant} \times (1/V)$$

and hence the mass per unit volume or density, is proportional to the pressure:

$$\text{density} = \frac{m}{V} = \text{constant} \times P$$

Example 4-10   Air has a density of 1.39 kg m⁻³ at −20°C and sea level. What would be the density of air at the same temperature at the top of Mount Everest, where atmospheric pressure is only 31% of its value at sea-level?

Since the density of a gas is proportional to pressure,

$$\text{density} = 1.39 \text{ kg m}^{-3} \times 0.31$$

$$= 0.43 \text{ kg m}^{-3}$$

Charles' Law describes the thermal expansion of gases. At constant pressure the graph of volume against temperature is a straight line, as shown in Figure 4-5. If the graph is extended to low enough temperatures, deviations from the straight line occur, and eventually the volume of the sample suddenly drops to

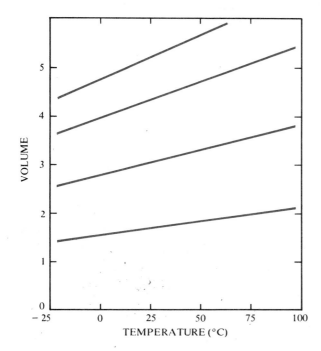

Figure 4-5 Volume plotted against temperature at constant pressure for several gas samples which obey Charles' law. Regardless of the composition or size of the samples, the graphs all intersect the temperature axis near −273°C.

a very small value because the gas condenses to a liquid. Charles' law applies only to the straight portion of the graph.

The remarkable fact about gases is that if the straight lines in Figure 4-5 are extrapolated back to the point where they intersect the temperature axis, the point of intersection is very nearly the same for all gases. The intersection takes place near −273°C, and at this temperature a gas would have zero volume if it continued to obey Charles' law. The temperature −273°C, therefore, is a special temperature which has significance for all gases, and further study through experiments and theory shows that it is not possible to cool *any* substance to a temperature lower than this. This is an *absolute zero* of temperature, rather than an arbitrary zero such as the temperature of a mixture of ice and water. Accurate measurements show that the absolute zero occurs 273.15° below the zero of the Celsius temperature scale.

A new scale can be defined having its zero at this absolute zero and having units of the same size as the degree on the Celsius scale. This temperature scale is called the absolute or Kelvin temperature scale; the unit of temperature is called the *kelvin* and is denoted by the symbol K. On this temperature scale, water freezes at a temperature of 273.15 K and boils at a temperature of 373.15 K at standard pressure. The relationship between a Celsius temperature t_c and the corresponding absolute temperature T is

$$T = t_c + 273.15$$

Charles' law may now be restated by saying that the volume is proportional to the absolute temperature T. Viewed mathematically, the use of the new absolute temperature scale means that the zero for the temperature scale has been moved to the point where the graphs in Figure 4-5 intersect the axis; this means that the equation relating V and T becomes a simple proportionality.

Example 4-11   A tank contains gas at a pressure of 300 kPa at 0°C. What would be the pressure if the temperature were raised to 100°C?

The two temperatures are (0 + 273) K and (100 + 273) K, respectively, and so the pressure at the higher temperature is

$$P = 300\,kPa \times \frac{373\,K}{273\,K}$$
$$= 410\,kPa$$

Example 4-12   The density of air at room temperature and ordinary pressure is 1.18 kg m^{-3}. What is the density of air leaving a heat exchanger at a temperature of 300°C, at the same pressure?

Consider 1.18 kg of air, which occupies 1.00 m^3 at room temperature, 25°C say. At 300°C, it would occupy a volume of

$$1.00 \times \frac{300 + 273}{25 + 273} = 1.92\,m^3$$

Hence the density is

$$\frac{1.18\,kg}{1.92\,m^3} = 0.615\,kg\,m^{-3}$$

A third law or principle bearing on the bulk properties of gases is *Avogadro's Principle*, which states that under the same conditions of temperature and pressure, equal volumes of different gases contain equal numbers of molecules.

Avogadro's Principle was proposed in 1811, as a result of experiments on the volumes of gases undergoing chemical reaction. This chapter is not concerned with chemical reactions, but Avogadro's Principle is closely related to the bulk properties of gases. For example, if equal volumes of two different gases contain equal numbers of molecules (at the same temperature and pressure), then the masses of these equal volumes must be proportional to the masses of the two different molecules. Hence the density of a gas must be proportional to the molar mass of the gas, since a mole of any gas has a fixed number of molecules. This prediction is confirmed in Figure 4-6 in which the densities of a series of gases at atmospheric pressure and 0°C are plotted against molar mass. A number of different chemical types of material are represented, such as acids, bases, oxidants, fuels, and noble gases, but clearly the density is determined only by the molar mass.

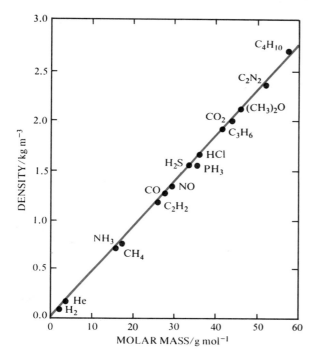

Figure 4-6 Density of gases at standard pressure and 0°C as a function of molar mass.

Example 4-13 When nitrogen, oxygen, carbon dioxide and water are removed from air, the residual gas is found to have a density of about 1.8 kg m^{-3} under the conditions of Figure 4-6, and can be shown to be an almost pure, chemically inert element. Which element is it?

Reading from the graph, the molar mass is approximately 40. Inspection of the periodic table shows that the gas must be argon; the element fluorine, with molecular formula F_2, is a gas of approximately the right molar mass, but is not chemically inert.

4-4   THE IDEAL GAS EQUATION OF STATE

A gas which obeys Boyle's law and Charles' law exactly is called an *ideal* gas. No real gas is ideal, but several gases deviate only slightly from ideal behaviour and for many purposes it is sufficiently accurate to treat all gases as if they were ideal. The laws of Boyle, Charles and Avogadro can be combined in a single equation which can be used for all calculations of the bulk properties of ideal gases. This equation connects the pressure, volume, temperature, and amount of gas present, and is called an *equation of state*. For an ideal gas the equation of state is

$$PV = nRT$$

where n is the amount of gas and R is a constant called the *universal gas constant*. This equation includes the three laws describing the bulk properties of ideal gases. The value of the gas constant can be calculated from the well-known fact that one mole of gas at standard pressure and 0°C ("STP") occupies a volume of about 22.4 L. Rearranging the equation,

$$R = \frac{PV}{nT}$$

$$= \frac{101325 \text{ N m}^{-2} \times 22.4 \times 10^{-3} \text{ m}^3}{1.00 \text{ mol} \times 273.2 \text{ K}}$$

$$= 8.31 \text{ N} \cdot \text{m K}^{-1} \text{ mol}^{-1}$$

$$= 8.31 \text{ J K}^{-1} \text{ mol}^{-1}$$

The accepted value of the gas constant is 8.31441 J K^{-1} mol^{-1}. As in all mathematical equations involving physical quantities, care must be taken with the units, and it is an advantage to use a single set of units for all calculations. In this book, S.I. units are used; pressures are in pascals and volumes in cubic metres. When gas pressures are expressed in atmospheres and volumes in litres, the value of the gas constant and its units are changed to

$$R = 0.082\,056 \text{ litre atmosphere kelvin}^{-1} \text{ mole}^{-1}$$

Calculations with the ideal gas equation of state in S.I. units are illustrated in the following examples.

Example 4-14   What is the pressure of 1.00 g of nitrogen in a 1.20 L flask at 20.2°C?

Since nitrogen molecules are diatomic, the molar mass of nitrogen is 28.0 g mol^{-1}. The known quantities are therefore

$$n = \frac{1.00 \text{ g}}{28.0 \text{ g mol}^{-1}} = 0.0357 \text{ mol}$$

$$V = 1.20 \text{ L} = 1.20 \times 10^{-3} \text{ m}^3$$

$$T = 20.2 + 273.2 = 293.4 \text{ K}$$

$$\text{Hence P} = \frac{0.0357 \text{ mol} \times 8.314 \text{ J K}^{-1} \text{ mol}^{-1} \times 293.4 \text{ K}}{1.20 \times 10^{-3} \text{ m}^3}$$

$$= 7.26 \times 10^4 \text{ N m}^{-2}$$

$$= 72.6 \text{ kPa}$$

Example 4-15   What volume of oxygen is produced by the decomposition of 15.0 g of KClO$_3$, if the oxygen is stored at 23.0°C and a pressure of 98.0 kPa?

The decomposition reaction is

$$KClO_3(c) \rightarrow KCl(c) + \tfrac{3}{2} O_2(g)$$

Molar mass of KClO$_3$ is 122.54 g mol^{-1}, and so the amount of oxygen produced is

$$n = \frac{3}{2} \times \frac{15.0 \text{ g}}{122.54 \text{ g mol}^{-1}}$$

$$= 0.184 \text{ mol}$$

Hence $V = \dfrac{0.184 \text{ mol} \times 8.314 \text{ J K}^{-1} \text{ mol}^{-1} \times 296.2 \text{ K}}{98.0 \times 10^3 \text{ Pa}}$

$\qquad = 4.62 \times 10^{-3} \text{ m}^3$

$\qquad = 4.62 \text{ L}$

Example 4-16 The vapour of an organic liquid is found to have a density of 4.73 g L^{-1} at 100°C and 750 torr. What is its molar mass?

$$\text{The pressure is P} = 101325 \times \frac{750}{760} \text{ Pa}$$

$$= 1.00 \times 10^5 \text{ Pa}$$

Hence the amount of vapour in one litre is

$$n = \frac{1.00 \times 10^5 \text{ Pa} \times 1.00 \times 10^{-3} \text{m}^{-3}}{8.314 \text{ J K}^{-1} \text{ mol}^{-1} \times 373 \text{ K}}$$

$$= 3.23 \times 10^{-2} \text{ mol}$$

The molar mass is

$$M = \frac{4.73 \text{ g}}{3.23 \times 10^{-2} \text{ mol}} = 146 \text{ g mol}^{-1}$$

4-5 MIXTURES OF IDEAL GASES

It is often necessary to deal with gases consisting of a mixture of two or more chemically different substances. For example, air is a mixture of oxygen, nitrogen and small amounts of other gases. The properties of gas mixtures were investigated by Dalton, who found that in many gas mixtures each gas acts independently of the other gases present.

A pressure gauge such as a manometer or Bourdon gauge indicates the total pressure P_T of a gas mixture. The *partial pressure* P_A of a gas in a gas mixture is *defined* as the product of the total pressure P_T and the mole fraction y_A of the gas in the mixture :

$$P_A \equiv y_A P_T$$

with similar equations for the other components B, C, . . . in the mixture. Since the sum of the mole fractions of all the gases in a gas mixture is unity,

$$y_A + y_B + y_C + \ldots = 1$$

therefore the sum of the partial pressures is equal to the total pressure, no matter what the properties of the gas mixture :

$$P_A + P_B + P_C + \ldots = P_T$$

Dalton's law states that the partial pressure of a gas in a mixture of gases is equal to the pressure which that gas would exert if it were the only gas present, under the same conditions of volume and temperature. A mixture of gases which obeys this law exactly is called an *ideal mixture*. Dalton's law is obeyed approximately by many gas mixtures, and is useful for calculating the bulk properties of such mixtures because of its simplicity.

Consider an ideal mixture of ideal gases A, B, C, . . . and let n_A, n_B, n_C, . . . be the amounts of each gas present. If n_A moles of gas A are contained in volume V at temperature T, the pressure is $n_A RT/V$. This pressure will be denoted P_A^* the star means that this quantity refers to the pure substance.

$$P_A^* = n_A \, RT/V, \qquad P_B^* = n_B \, RT/V, \ldots \ldots$$

Dalton's law states that the partial pressures P_A, P_B, . . . are equal to P_A^*, P_B^*, . . . respectively:

$$P_A = P_A^* \qquad P_B = P_B^* \ldots$$

Since the total pressure is the sum of the partial pressures,

$$\begin{aligned} P_T &= P_A + P_B + \ldots \ldots \\ &= P_A^* + P_B^* + \ldots \ldots \\ &= n_A RT/V + n_B RT/V + \ldots \ldots \\ &= (n_A + n_B + \ldots \ldots) \, RT/V \\ &= n_T RT/V \end{aligned}$$

where $n_T = n_A + n_B + \ldots$ is the total number of moles in the gas mixture. Therefore an ideal mixture of ideal gases obeys the ideal gas equation, a fact which is hardly surprising.

Example 4-17 A 2.00 L tank containing oxygen at a pressure of 100 kPa is connected to a 0.10 L tank containing helium at a pressure of 3.00 MPa, and the gases are allowed to mix. What is the final pressure assuming that the temperature is held constant?

When the two tanks are connected, the volume occupied by oxygen increases from 2.0 L to 2.1 L and the volume occupied by helium increases from 0.1 L to 2.1 L. The total pressure is the sum of the partial pressures, and by Dalton's law the partial pressure of each gas is the pressure it would exert if it were the only gas present. Applying Boyle's law to each gas separately,

$$\text{Pressure of oxygen} = 100 \times \frac{2.0}{2.1} \text{ kPa}$$

$$= 95 \text{ kPa}$$

$$\text{pressure of helium} = 3000 \times \frac{0.10}{2.1} \text{ kPa}$$

$$= 143 \text{ kPa}$$

$$\text{Hence total pressure} = 95 + 143$$

$$= 238 \text{ kPa}$$

Example 4-18   A mixture of 8.00 g of CH_4 and 9.00 g of C_2H_6 is stored at a total pressure of 500 kPa. What is the partial pressure of each component present?

The molar mass of CH_4 is 16.0 g and that of C_2H_6 is 30.00 g, and so the amount of each component present is:

$$n_{CH_4} = \frac{8.00 \text{ g}}{16.0 \text{ g mol}^{-1}} = 0.500 \text{ mol}$$

$$n_{C_2H_6} = \frac{9.00 \text{ g}}{30.00 \text{ g mol}^{-1}} = 0.300 \text{ mol}$$

$$n_T = 0.500 + 0.300 = 0.800 \text{ mol}$$

Hence the mole fraction of each component is

$$y_{CH_4} = \frac{0.500}{0.800} = 0.625$$

$$y_{C_2H_6} = \frac{0.300}{0.800} = 0.375$$

and the partial pressures are

$$P_{CH_4} = 0.625 \times 500 = 312 \text{ kPa}$$

$$P_{C_2H_6} = 0.375 \times 500 = 188 \text{ kPa}$$

PROBLEMS

1. A 3.00 L cylinder of argon at 27°C is compressed and heated to a final volume of 1.00 L and a final temperature of 327°C. What is the ratio of the final pressure to the initial pressure?

[6.00]

2. At a certain pressure, the volume of a fixed amount of nitrogen is 22.40 L at 0.0°C; at the same pressure, the same sample of nitrogen occupies 30.63 L at 100.0°C. Use this information to calculate the "absolute zero" on the Celsius scale.

[−272°C]

3. A cylinder holding nitrogen at 14 MPa at 20°C is in danger of exploding if the pressure rises above 30 MPa. What is the maximum temperature at which this cylinder could be safely stored?

[355°C]

4. What is the pressure exerted by 1.00 kg of oxygen in a volume of 20.0 L at a temperature of 27°C?

[3.90 MPa]

5. A sample of gas is contained in a 1.5 L vessel at a pressure of 4.0 torr, and a temperature of 100°C. How many moles of gas are there in the vessel?

$[2.6 \times 10^{-4} \text{ mol}]$

6. An engineer wishes to store 1.0 t of ethane at a pressure of 1.0 MPa at a temperature of 20°C. What is the volume of the tank that he needs?

[81 m^3]

7. A 0.1080 L vessel contains 142.0 mg of nitrogen at a pressure of 790.1 torr. Calculate the temperature.

[269.9 K]

8. How could one tell that nitrogen was diatomic from knowing the experimentally measured density of nitrogen gas at some particular pressure and temperature? What assumptions enter such a deduction?

9. One of the oxides of nitrogen is a gas with a density of 1.41 kg m^{-3} at a temperature of 127°C and a pressure of 101 kPa. What is the molecular formula of the gas?

[NO_2]

10. Carbon monoxide is an air pollutant resulting from automobile exhausts. For a concentration of 10.0 mg per cubic metre at room temperature calculate (a) the partial pressure and (b) the mole fraction of carbon monoxide in the atmosphere.

[0.89 Pa; 0.88 × 10^{-5}]

11. Sulphur dioxide is an air pollutant resulting from burning coal in power generating stations. For a concentration of 0.10 g/m^3 at room temperature, calculate (a) the partial pressure and (b) the mole fraction, of sulphur dioxide in the atmosphere.

[3.9 Pa; 3.8 × 10^{-5}]

12. What is the density of silicon tetrafluoride at standard atmospheric pressure and 100°C?

[3.40 kg m^{-3}]

13. What is the density of air at standard atmospheric pressure and 27°C, assuming a composition of 21.0 mole % oxygen, and 78.0 mole % nitrogen and 1.0 mole % argon?

[1.18 kg m^{-3}]

14. What volume of ammonia measured at 20°C and 100.0 kPa must be dissolved in 50.0 g of water to make a 1.00 molal solution?

[1.22 litre]

15. A very good vacuum system is able to produce a pressure as low as 10^{-10} torr inside a glass vessel. How many molecules of residual gas are present in 1 mL at this pressure and room temperature?

[3.2 × 10^7]

16. Two bulbs, A and B, each have a volume of 1.0 L, and are connected by a length of thin flexible tubing and a valve, as shown.

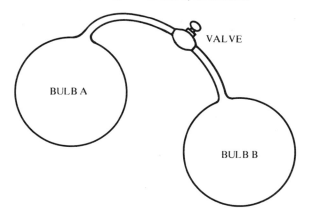

The bulbs each contain 0.050 mol of helium initially, at a temperature of 27°C. Then, with the valve open, bulb A is cooled with liquid nitrogen to a temperature of 77 K, and bulb B is maintained at 27°C; the valve is closed, and bulb A is returned to 27°C.

Calculate (a) the initial pressure in each bulb;   [125 kPa]
              (b) the final pressure in bulb A;   [199 kPa]   74
              (c) the final pressure in bulb B;   [51 kPa]

17. In a certain diesel engine, air is taken into the cylinder at 1.0 atmosphere and 27°C, and compressed rapidly into 1/10 of its original volume; the pressure is found to be 25 atmosphere after the compression. Calculate the temperature of the air after the compression.

[750 K]

18. Consider two identical tanks at room temperature, one containing phosphine PH_3, the other containing hydrogen sulphide H_2S at the same pressure. Which is the heavier tank? Which tank contains more molecules? Which tank contains more atoms?

19. What volume of acetylene C_2H_2 is produced from the reaction of 10.0 g of calcium carbide CaC_2 with excess water? The volume is to be measured at 27°C and 100 kPa.

[3.89 L]

20. A sample of 100 mL of oxygen at a pressure of 750 torr is mixed with a sample of 200 mL of nitrogen at the same temperature, and a pressure of 500 torr; the mixture is placed in a vessel with a volume of 150 mL, without change of temperature. Calculate the partial pressure of each gas and the total pressure in the final state.

[500 torr, 667 torr, 1167 torr]

21. A sample of 0.768 g of graphite (carbon) is completely burned in a steel vessel containing 210 mL of oxygen at a pressure of 1.20 MPa and a temperature of 27°C. Calculate the mole fraction of each gas and the total pressure after combustion. Assume that all gases are ideal, and that the temperature rise due to combustion is 1.0°C.

$$[y_{CO_2} = 0.633, y_{O_2} = 0.367, 1.20 \text{ MPa}]$$

22. Natural gas is usually processed to remove propane and butane, so that these may be sold as bottled fuels. If the ratio of propane to butane in a natural gas supply, on a mole basis, is 63:37, what mass of each is produced annually if they total 14.6% of an annual natural gas production of 9.9×10^{10} m^3 at 100 kPa and 290 K?

$$[1.66 \times 10^{10} \text{ kg}, 1.29 \times 10^{10} \text{ kg}]$$

23. (a) At a height of 20 km, the density of air is 0.092 kg m^{-3} and the temperature is 220 K. Assuming that air is 20% oxygen, 80% nitrogen by mole, calculate the pressure 20 km above the earth's surface.

(b) Calculate the minimum volume of a helium filled atmospheric research balloon operating at an altitude of 20 km if the masses of the equipment and the balloon total 400 kg. What is the diameter of such a balloon, assuming it to be approximately spherical? Assume that internal pressure equals external pressure.

$$[5040 \text{ m}^3; 21 \text{ m}]$$

V THERMOCHEMISTRY

Many chemical reactions generate heat, and some reactions absorb heat. The study of the heat associated with chemical reations is called *thermochemistry*. Thermochemistry is part of a broader subject called *thermodynamics,* which is the study of the relationships among heat, work and the properties of matter.

Thermodynamics is based on three assumptions, the "laws" of thermodynamics. These laws, like other laws of science, are statements of apparently universal relationships. Their validity is based on their being consistent with every experimental test and observation. Every prediction based upon the laws has been confirmed by subsequent measurements. Thermodynamics makes no assumptions about the nature of atoms and molecules, and indeed does not even mention their existence. Statistical mechanics, on the other hand, attempts to describe the properties of substances by applying the laws of mechanics to atoms and molecules which form substances; comparison of the measured quantities of classical thermodynamics with the calculated results of statistical mechanics provides a test for the validity of the latter and leads to new understanding of the nature of substances, and of the atoms and molecules of which substances are made.

5-1 THE LANGUAGE OF THERMODYNAMICS

Because the assumptions of thermodynamics are few, they must be stated carefully. Unambiguous vocabulary and definitions are required.

The material being considered is called the *system*. It may be as simple as 5 g of argon gas or as complicated as an entire engine. Everything outside of the system is part of the *surroundings*. Together the system and the surroundings make up the *universe*. The system and its surroundings may interact, particularly by transfers of energy, and thermodynamics is much concerned with the measurement and control of such transfers.

The *state* of a system is defined by the properties of the system. In very simple systems, temperature, pressure and composition may be sufficient to define the state fully, but the more complex the system, the more variables must be specified to determine the state uniquely. When any of the properties of a system change, the state of the system changes and the system is said to have undergone a *process*. The full description of a process must specify the initial state and the final state of the system, and information about how the process was carried out. Many of the processes of interest are chemical processes, in which the chemical arrangement of the materials present changes. It is assumed in what follows, however, that no material flows into or out of the system during a process. Some of the factors related to a process may be controlled by the experimenter. If the system is placed in thermal contact with a *thermostat* which maintains a constant temperature during the process, the process is said to be *isothermal*. It should be noted that the final temperature of a system may be equal to the initial temperature without the process being isothermal. If a system is thermally insulated so that its temperature is not affected by the temperature of the surroundings, then any process taking place in the system is said to be *adiabatic*. It should be appreciated that the temperature of a system is usually altered as a result of an adiabatic process.

Energy is a concept which is important to all areas of science. Thermodynamics is concerned with two forms of energy, *heat* and *work*. In thermodynamics, heat and work have meaning only in relation to a process, and refer to the energy which enters a system from its surroundings or leaves a system to enter its surroundings. There are many ways of classifying energy which is *in* a system, such as the kinetic energy of gas molecules or the gravitational potential of a mass, but never is any of the energy within a system correctly described as heat or work. These terms are reserved exclusively for energy entering or leaving a system during a process.

The amount of heat is represented algebraically by the symbol q, and work by the symbol w. By convention, they are the heat and work *added* to a system during a process, and so have positive values when heat or work enters the system and negative values when heat and work leave the system. This sign convention is that of the Système Internationale and is used throughout this book. Although it is the convention most commonly found in recent thermodynamic publications, beware of the fact that some books use a different convention.

Work is done if the point of application of a force moves through a distance, according to the elementary definition. In chemical systems, work is usually associated with the compression or expansion of a system or with the movement of an electrical charge through a difference of potential.

The definition of a temperature scale was discussed in the last chapter. When a hot object is placed in contact with a cold object, changes may be observed in the properties of both. These changes result from changes in their temperatures, which in turn result from the flow of *heat* from the hot object to the cold.

It is common knowledge nowadays that a hot object may be used to produce work using a device such as a steam engine. As the work is produced, the hot object becomes cooler, and eventually loses its power to produce work, when its temperature is reduced to the temperature of its surroundings. The hot object may also be cooled by being placed in contact with a cold object, in which case the hot object loses its power to produce work without having produced any work. Thus it may be seen that heat which is transferred by thermal conduction is closely related to work.

The relationship between heat and work was first demonstrated correctly by James Joule in the years 1843 to 1848. He carried out four different experiments in which the temperature of a system consisting of some water was raised by doing work adiabatically on the system, in four different ways. It was shown that the amount of work required to raise the temperature by a certain amount was the same no matter how that work was done. Furthermore, the temperature rise in a given experiment was proportional to the amount of work done. For any given experiment, the same temperature change could have been achieved by breaking open the adiabatic enclosure and transferring heat to the system via thermal conduction from a hotter body. Hence an amount of heat transferred by thermal conduction may be measured by the amount of work which must be done adiabatically in order to produce the same temperature rise. It is not necessary to specify how the work is to be done since Joule showed that for a given system inside an adiabatic enclosure, different methods of doing the same amount of work produce equal rises in the temperature. As was explained earlier, the symbol q is used to denote the amount of heat transferred into a system during a process.

The SI unit of heat and work is the *joule,* symbol J. In many chemistry books heat is measured in units of *calories.* The calorie is an older unit of heat, originally defined as the amount of heat required to raise the temperature of one gram of water by one degree Celsius. The calorie has been redefined several times, and it is now defined as being precisely 4.184 J. The calorie is unnecessary as a unit of heat, and will not be used in this book.

When heat is added to a system, the temperature increase ΔT, and the amount of heat added q, are linearly related. The constant of proportionality is called the *heat capacity* of the system, C, and measures the amount of heat required to raise the temperature by one kelvin:

$$q = C\Delta T \tag{1}$$

The unit of heat capacity is joule/kelvin or $J \ K^{-1}$. For a system containing only one substance, the heat capacity of the system is proportional to the amount of matter in the system:

$$C = n \ C_m$$

where n is the amount of substance present in units of moles and C_m is the *molar heat capacity* of the substance forming the system, with units $J \ K^{-1} \ mol^{-1}$. Different substances have different molar heat capacities, and these are tabulated for a range of chemical compounds in Appendix I. The value of the heat capacity of a substance depends upon the conditions under which the system is maintained during the process of heating. The two most common conditions, constant pressure and constant volume, are discussed later. The heat capacities quoted in Appendix I are constant pressure molar heat capacities, as indicated by the subscript p in the symbol C_{pm}°.

Molar heat capacities may vary with the pressure and temperature of the system. The values quoted in Appendix I refer to standard pressure of 101.325 kPa (indicated by a superscript $^{\circ}$) and a temperature of 25°C. These molar heat capacities may be used over a reasonable range of temperature, but for accurate work over a wide range of temperature and pressure, C_{pm}° cannot be treated as a constant, and more detailed heat capacity data must be used.

Example 5-1   Calculate the heat required to raise the temperature of 10.0 g of liquid water from 20.0°C to 70.0°C.

$$\text{Amount of water} = \frac{10.0\ g}{18.0\ g\ mol^{-1}} = 0.555\ mol$$

From Appendix I, molar heat capacity of H_2O (l) = 75.3 J K^{-1} mol^{-1}

and so the heat capacity of water = 0.555 mol × 75.3 J K^{-1} mol^{-1}

$$= 41.8\ J\ K^{-1}$$

The temperature change is ΔT = 70.0°C − 20.0°C

$$= 50.0\ K$$

Hence heat required = 41.8 J K^{-1} × 50.0 K

$$= 2090\ J = 2.09\ kJ$$

5-2   THE FIRST LAW OF THERMODYNAMICS

Since work and heat have been shown to be equivalent, it is convenient to regard them as different forms of energy. Energy can be exchanged between a system and its surroundings both as work and as heat, depending on the process which is carried out. The first law of thermodynamics is a statement of conservation of energy:

In ordinary processes, energy is not created or destroyed.

In recent times the phrase "energy conservation" has come to have a special meaning in common language. To conserve energy means to perform some function using less energy than had been done before. In thermodynamics, "conservation of energy" means that although energy may change from one form to another in a process, the total amount of energy is a constant.

"Ordinary processes" in thermodynamics excludes nuclear fission or other processes in which mass is converted to energy according to the Einstein formula $E = mc^2$. When thermodynamics is applied to a nuclear power station, such processes are considered simply as a source of heat.

If work w is done on a system and heat q is added to the system, the total amount of energy added to the system is q+w. The first law asserts that the energy has not been destroyed but is stored within the system. The quantity q+w must therefore measure the change in the energy which is contained within the system. It is convenient to define a quantity called the *internal energy,* which is denoted by the sumbol U. The change in U in a process is denoted ΔU. The above statement of the first law can then be re-stated in symbols:

$$\Delta U = q + w \tag{2}$$

It should be recalled that q and w are algebraic quantities with associated signs which must be carefully handled in calculations using the above equation.

Equation (2) allows calculation of *changes* in the internal energy of the system, but no "absolute zero" of internal energy can be determined. This situation might be worrying to the student at first, but it will be found that the lack of an absolute zero of energy does not prevent the calculation of amounts of heat and work in thermodynamic processes.

Example 5-2 A sample of air is compressed adiabatically and then passed through a cooler; 4.0 kJ of work is done during the compression, and 3.0 kJ of heat is removed from the air in the cooler. Calculate q, w, and ΔU.

The system to be considered is the air. Since heat is removed from the system, q is negative:

$$q = -3.0 \, kJ$$

Since work must be done on the system in order to compress it, w is positive:

$$w = +4.0 \, kJ$$
$$\text{Hence } \Delta U = q + w$$
$$= (-3.0) + (+4.0)$$
$$= +1.0 \, kJ$$

Example 5-3 Some gasoline mixed with air is burned in a small engine; the combustion mixture expands against the piston, doing 25 J of work, while 90 J of heat is lost by cooling. Calculate q, w, and ΔU for the combustion mixture.

The sign of q is negative since heat is lost from the system:

$$q = -90 \, J$$

The sign of w is negative since work is done by the system on the surroundings, by moving the piston:

$$w = -25 \, J$$
$$\text{Hence } \Delta U = (-90) + (-25)$$
$$= -115 \, J$$

In certain circumstances, chemical reactions are carried out in sealed containers which have fixed volume and no mechanism for doing work by electrical or other means. For such a process, no work is done. Even though the pressure inside the container may change considerably during the process, no work is done since the forces which keep the volume of the container constant do not move through any distance.

$$\text{Hence } w = 0, \text{ and so q and } \Delta U \text{ must be equal:}$$
$$\Delta U = q \quad \text{for a constant volume process} \tag{3}$$

Many chemical processes are carried out in contact with the atmosphere, or else in equipment where the pressure is maintained constant by pumps. The volume of the products of a chemical process need not be equal to the volume of the reactants at the same pressure. In such a case, a change in the volume of the system as a result of the process must result in work associated with the expansion or contraction of the system against the constant external pressure.

The work can be calculated by imagining that the process is carried out in the device shown in Figure 5-1. The system is contained in a cylinder equipped with a frictionless gas-tight piston. The cylinder is housed in a bell-jar from which all the air has been removed, so that the only pressure on the system is that due to the force of gravity on the piston. Weights may be added to the piston to raise the pressure in the system to any desired value. Since the mass of the piston together with any added weights is constant, the system within the cylinder is under constant *external* pressure during any process, as would be the case if the process were carried out in contact with the atmosphere. The work done in any expansion or contraction of the system can now be calculated in terms of the volume change and the external pressure. Again, it will be assumed that no electrochemical process takes place.

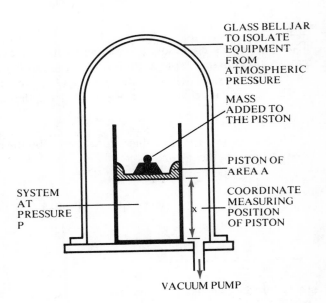

Figure 5-1 Hypothetical frictionless piston and cylinder in a vacuum, containing a system under a known external pressure. The external pressure is equal to the total weight of the piston and added mass divided by the area of the piston. At equilibrium the pressure of the system, P, is equal to the external pressure.

If the pressure exerted by the piston on the system is P and the cross- sectional area of the piston is A, the total force exerted by the piston is PA. If the position of the piston is measured by the coordinate x as shown in the figure, the work done in a change of volume is given by the product of the force PA and the distance through which that force moves, Δx:

$$W = - PA. \, \Delta x$$

The sign is important in this equation; a negative value of Δx corresponds to a compression of the system, in which case work is done by the surroundings on the system and w is positive. Now the volume change of the system, ΔV, is equal to $A\Delta x$ and so w is given by $-P.A\Delta x$, or $-P\Delta V$. Hence the change in the internal energy, ΔU, in this case is given by the equation

$$\Delta U = q - P\Delta V \qquad \text{under constant external pressure} \qquad (4)$$

It is important to realize that this equation remains true even if the *internal* pressure of the system varies greatly during the process. Suppose, for instance, that the system contained within the cylinder consists of a mixture of methane and oxygen, and that the process to be considered is the combustion reaction

$$CH_4(g) + 2\,O_2(g) \rightarrow CO_2(g) + 2\,H_2O(l)$$

This reaction proceeds to completion very rapidly under some conditions, leading to an explosion; when the reaction is initiated, the temperature and pressure inside the cylinder of Figure 5-1 suddenly increase and the piston starts to move upwards with a high acceleration. After a short time, heat is transferred from the system to the walls of the cylinder and piston, and water starts to condense. After the process is complete, the volume of the system is *less* than it was originally, since the number of moles of gas has been reduced to a third of its initial value and the volume of the liquid water is negligible. Hence the piston finally comes to rest *below* its starting point, even though it started its movement in the upwards direction due to the high initial internal pressure of the system. Clearly, the total work done by the piston on the system can be calculated from the initial and final positions of the piston, and has nothing to do with the fluctuations of the internal pressure while the process is in progress.

Example 5-4   The heat required to melt ice at $P°$ is 6.010 kJ mol^{-1}. Calculate ΔU for the melting of one mole of ice, at 0°C and standard atmospheric pressure. The density of ice is 916.8 kg m^{-3} and the density of water is 999.8 kg m^{-3} under these conditions.

$$\text{The molar volume of ice} = \frac{18.02 \times 10^{-3} \text{ kg mol}^{-1}}{916.8 \text{ kg m}^{-3}}$$

$$= 1.966 \times 10^{-5} \text{ m}^3 \text{ mol}^{-1}$$

$$\text{and molar volume of water} = \frac{18.02 \times 10^{-3} \text{ kg mol}^{-1}}{999.8 \text{ kg m}^{-3}}$$

Hence the volume change in melting one mole of ice is

$$\Delta V = (1.802 - 1.966) \times 10^{-5} \text{ m}^3$$

$$= -1.64 \times 10^{-6} \text{ m}^3$$

$$\text{and so } P\Delta V = 101\ 325 \text{ Nm}^{-2} \times (-1.64 \times 10^{-6} \text{ m}^3)$$

$$= -0.166 \text{ Nm} = -0.166 \text{ J}$$

Since $q = +6.010\,kJ$,

$$\Delta U = 6.010\,kJ - (-0.166 \times 10^{-3}\,kJ)$$

$$= 6.010\,kJ$$

In this example the volume change in the process is very small, $P\Delta V$ is very small compared to q, and q is practically the same as ΔU. However, this is not the case in the following example.

Example 5-5 The heat required to boil water at $P°$ is 40.88 kJ mol^{-1}. Calculate ΔU for the boiling of one mole of water at 100°C and standard pressure. The density of water is 958.4 kg m^{-3} and the density of steam is 0.5782 kg m^{-3} under these conditions.

$$\text{The molar volume of water} = \frac{18.02 \times 10^{-3}\,kg\,mol^{-1}}{958.4\,kg\,m^{-3}}$$

$$= 1.880 \times 10^{-5}\,m^3\,mol^{-1}$$

$$\text{and molar volume of steam} = \frac{18.02 \times 10^{-5}\,kg\,mol^{-1}}{0.5782\,kg\,m^{-3}}$$

$$= 3.177 \times 10^{-2}\,m^3\,mol^{-1}$$

Hence the volume change in boiling one mole of water is

$$\Delta V = 3.117 \times 10^{-2} - 1.880 \times 10^{-5}$$

$$= +3.115 \times 10^{-2}\,m^3$$

$$\text{and so} \quad P\Delta V = 101\,325\,Nm^{-2} \times 3.115 \times 10^{-2}\,m^3$$

$$= 3.16 \times 10^3\,J$$

Since $q = 40.88\,kJ$,

$$\Delta U = 40.88\,kJ - 3.16\,kJ$$

$$= 37.72\,kJ$$

In this example, ΔV is much larger than in the previous example, and hence $P\Delta V$ is much larger too. Where $P\Delta V$ is large, q and ΔU must differ significantly. ΔV will be large wherever the amount of *gas* changes in a process. The volume of a mole of gas is typically a thousand times greater than that of a mole of a liquid or solid. As seen in the previous examples, only changes in the amount of gas are significant in determining ΔV. Where there are no gases among either the reactants or the products, as in example 5-4, or where there is the same amount of gas in the products as in the reactants, ΔV can be taken to be zero.

5-3 THE ENTHALPY H

It has been seen in the previous section that the internal energy U cannot be used directly to calculate the heat q associated with a process which is carried out under constant external pressure. Since such processes are common and important in chemistry and in the chemical industry, another function has been defined which is more convenient to use under these conditions. This new function is called the *enthalpy* and is given the symbol H. The enthalpy is very closely related to the internal energy. The equation which defines the enthalpy of a system is

$$H \equiv U + PV \tag{5}$$

For any process whatever, the enthalpy change is

$$\Delta H = \Delta U + \Delta(PV)$$

$$= \Delta U + (P_{final}V_{final} - P_{initial}V_{initial})$$

For a process which is carried out under a constant external pressure P, the initial pressure $P_{initial}$ and the final P_{final} are both equal to P, and so

$$\Delta H = \Delta U + P(V_{final} - V_{initial})$$

$$= \Delta U + P\Delta V$$

For a non-electrochemical process carried out under constant external pressure, ΔU is equal to $q - P \Delta V$ according to equation (4) and so for such a process the enthalpy change is

$$\Delta H = (q - P\Delta V) + P\Delta V$$

i.e. $\qquad \Delta H = q \qquad$ under constant external pressure $\qquad$ (6)

It is the simplicity of this relationship which makes the enthalpy so useful in the calculations of thermochemistry. The value of ΔH for a chemical reaction is called the *heat of reaction* or *enthalpy of reaction*.

As examples, the heats of melting and of boiling of water, which were quoted in Examples 5-4 and 5-5 can be thought of as ΔH values since melting and boiling are processes which are carried out at atmospheric pressure. If these processes are written as elementary chemical reactions, the associated ΔH values are written as follows:

$$H_2O(c) \rightarrow H_2O(l) \qquad \Delta H = +6.010 \text{ kJ at } 0°C, 101 \text{ kPa}$$

$$H_2O(l) \rightarrow H_2O(g) \qquad \Delta H = +40.88 \text{ kJ at } 100°C, 101 \text{ kPa}$$

5-4 STATE FUNCTIONS IN THERMODYNAMICS

Consider a system in a well defined *state*. The state of a system is defined by giving the temperature, pressure, the physical state (i.e., solid, liquid or gas), chemical composition and any other variables which are found to be relevant. The amount of material in the system is assumed to be fixed, although chemical reactions may take place within the system, changing the chemical form of the material present.

Consider a process which changes the state of the system from its initial state A to some other state B, and let it be called "Process 1." Then consider another process—perhaps quite a complicated one—by which the same system is converted back to its initial state A, and let this process be called "Process 2." Finally, consider a third process, "Process 3," which, like Process 1, converts the system from A to B but in a different way. Let ΔU_1, ΔU_2 and ΔU_3 be the changes in the internal energy of the system when these three processes are carried out. Figure 5-2 shows the relationship between these states and processes, and gives a practical example in which a mixture of hydrogen and oxygen is first burned, the resulting water is decomposed by electrolysis to yield the initial elements again, and finally the elements are recombined in a fuel cell which generates some electricity as well as heat.

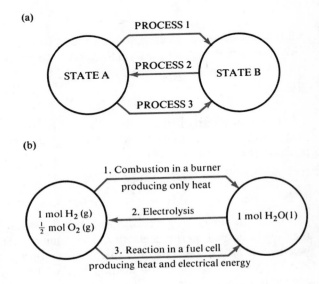

Figure 5-2   Process carrying a system between two states: a) the general case; b) a practical example.

It is a result of the first law of thermodynamics that $\Delta U_1 = -\Delta U_2 = \Delta U_3$. In order to see why this is so, consider the situation after Process 1 and Process 2 have been carried out. The system has been returned to its inital state, A, and the total change in internal energy due to the two-step process is $\Delta U_1 + \Delta U_2$. If this quantity were positive, it would mean that energy had been absorbed by the system in a two-step process which made no detectable change in the state of the system. On the other hand, if this quantity were negative, it would mean that energy had been given out by the system to the surroundings without there being any change in the state of the system. Neither of these phenomena has ever been observed. Energy does not disappear or appear but is conserved, according to the first law of thermodynamics. Hence it must be concluded that $\Delta U_1 + \Delta U_2 = 0$.

By an identical argument, it can be seen that $\Delta U_2 + \Delta U_3 = 0$, and so ΔU_1 and ΔU_3 must be equal to each other.

It then follows that *all* processes which convert the system from state A to state B must have the same value of ΔU. In other words, the value of ΔU for a process is determined by the initial and final states of the system, and is not affected by the way in which the process is carried out. A function which has this property is called a *state function*. The internal energy U is a state function. By contrast, q and w are *not* state functions. Although the sum of q and w equals the change in a state function ΔU, the manner in which ΔU is distributed between q and w varies with the path taken from state A to state B. From its definition in terms of U, P and V, the enthalpy H is also a state function.

5-5   HESS'S LAW AND THERMOCHEMISTRY

When a chemical reaction is carried out under constant external pressure, the heat involved is equal to the change in the enthalpy of the system. It follows that the heat is equal to the change in a state function; if a chemical reaction can be carried out in several steps, the heat of the overall reaction is equal to the sum of the heats of the individual steps, a law known as *Hess's law*.

Several points follow from the properties of state functions. For the process

$$H_2(g) + \tfrac{1}{2} O_2(g) \rightarrow H_2O(g),$$

the enthalpy change ΔH_1 is -241.8 kJ, and so for the reverse process

$$H_2O(g) \rightarrow H_2(g) + \tfrac{1}{2} O_2(g)$$

the enthalpy change ΔH_2 is $+241.8$ kJ. This can be seen by considering the two step process

$$H_2 + \tfrac{1}{2}O_2 \xrightarrow{\Delta H_1} H_2O \xrightarrow{\Delta H_2} H_2 + \tfrac{1}{2}O_2$$

Since the overall process involves no change in the state of the system, the overall enthalpy change, $\Delta H_1 + \Delta H_2$, must be zero and hence $\Delta H_1 = -\Delta H_2$.

Similarly the enthalpy change for the process

$$2 H_2(g) + O_2(g) \rightarrow 2 H_2O(g)$$

is $2 \times (-241.8$ kJ$)$, or -483.6 kJ.

As a simple example of the addition of two different reactions, consider the steam reforming reaction between methane and steam:

$$CH_4(g) + H_2O(g) \rightarrow CO(g) + 3 H_2(g) \qquad \Delta H = +206.1 \text{ kJ}$$

The carbon monoxide may be further reacted with steam to produce more hydrogen, in the shift conversion reaction:

$$CO(g) + H_2O(g) \rightarrow CO_2(g) + H_2(g) \qquad \Delta H = -41.2 \text{ kJ}$$

These two reactions may be combined by adding them together, and the enthalpy of the overall reaction is equal to the algebraic sum of the enthalpies of the individual reactions:

$$CH_4(g) + 2 H_2O(g) \rightarrow CO_2(g) + 4 H_2(g)$$
$$\Delta H = (+206.1) + (-41.2) = +164.9 \text{ kJ}$$

The enthalpy of the overall reaction is $+164.9$ kJ, regardless of how the reaction is carried out in the laboratory or industrial plant. In some plants the steam reforming and shift conversion reactions are carried out in two entirely separate steps, while in others the two steps are not clearly separated at all. The first law of thermodynamics guarantees the design engineer that the total enthalpy change of the overall process is +164.9 kJ, no matter how he might carry out intermediate steps of the process.

In more complicated cases, the individual reactions may have to be multiplied by a factor, or reversed, and the enthalpies of reaction must be multiplied by the same factor, or changed in sign.

Example 5-6 Calculate the enthalpy change of the reaction

$$C(graphite) + \tfrac{1}{2} O_2 \rightarrow CO(g)$$

given the following data:

$$C + O_2 \rightarrow CO_2 \qquad \Delta H = -393.5 \text{ kJ}$$
$$2\,CO + O_2 \rightarrow 2\,CO_2 \qquad \Delta H = -566.0 \text{ kJ}$$

Reversing the second of these reactions and multiplying by one half gives the equation

$$CO_2 \rightarrow CO + \tfrac{1}{2} O_2$$

The enthalpy of this reaction is obtained by multiplying the given ΔH by $(-\tfrac{1}{2})$:

$$\Delta H = (-\tfrac{1}{2}) \times (-566.0) = +283.0 \text{ kJ}$$

The required reaction is now obtained by adding this reaction to the first of the given reactions:

$$C + O_2 \rightarrow CO_2 \qquad \Delta H = -393.5 \text{ kJ}$$
$$CO_2 \rightarrow CO + \tfrac{1}{2} O_2 \qquad \Delta H = +283.0 \text{ kJ}$$

$$\overline{C + \tfrac{1}{2} O_2 \rightarrow CO \qquad \Delta H = (-393.5) + (+283.0)}$$
$$= -110.5 \text{ kJ}$$

Hess's law allows the determination of the ΔH values of many reactions which are very difficult or impossible to carry out under controlled conditions in the laboratory. It is very difficult to burn carbon in oxygen in such a way that pure carbon monoxide is produced; there is always some carbon dioxide formed as well as the monoxide. However, it is easy to burn carbon so as to produce pure carbon dioxide, by using an excess of oxygen, and carbon monoxide which has been purified chemically can be burned with oxygen to form carbon dioxide. The ΔH values of both of these reactions can be measured, and combined as in Example 5-6 in order to obtain ΔH for the formation of carbon monoxide from its elements, the reaction which is difficult to measure directly.

When a ΔH value is quoted for a reaction, it refers to a particular temperature and pressure. Usually ΔH values are quoted for a pressure equal to the standard state pressure $P^\circ = 101.325$ kPa, and the ΔH value is then written with a superscript zero, ΔH°. The temperature is specified as a subscript. For a reaction at a temperature of 350 K, and standard state pressure, the enthalpy change is written ΔH°_{350}. Many standard state ΔH values are quoted at a temperature of 25°C, and are written ΔH°_{298}; if no subscript is shown, it may be assumed that the ΔH value is given for a temperature of 25°C. Students should note that the "standard temperature" used in thermodynamics is 25°C, whereas the "standard temperature" used in elementary discussions of gases, and given the abbreviation "S.T.P.," is 0°C.

The precise meaning of ΔH°_{298} is as follows: it is the enthalpy for the process in which the reactants, in separate containers at 25.00°C and at pressures of 101.325 kPa, are converted to the products, also in separate containers at 25.00°C and at pressures of 101.325 kPa. Reactants and products are in the states, or phases, specified in the chemical reaction written to describe the process. The process involves mixing the reactants, the chemical reaction itself, and then separation of the reaction products from each other into separate containers. For simplicity, ΔH°_{298} may be regarded as the heat required to convert the reactants at partial pressures of 101.325 kPa and 25°C to the products at partial pressures of 101.325 kPa and 25°C; this is only an approximation however.

If heat leaves a system and enters the surroundings when a reaction is carried out isothermally, the reaction is said to be *exothermic*. If an exothermic reaction is carried out adiabatically, the temperature of the system rises. In the absence of electrochemical work, a negative value of ΔH indicates that a reaction is exothermic.

The opposite kind of reaction is called *endothermic*. When an endothermic reaction is carried out isothermally, heat is transferred *to* the system from the surroundings. In the absence of electrochemical work, ΔH is positive for an endothermic reaction.

5-6 ENTHALPY OF FORMATION

The ΔH° value for the reaction in which one mole of a compound is formed directly from its elements in their most stable form under the standard state conditions is called the *enthalpy of formation* of the compound, and is given a special symbol, ΔH°_f. A table of heats of formation of chemical compounds is the basic tool of thermochemistry, for it allows the calculation of the ΔH° value for any reaction between compounds which are listed in the table. Appendix I contains a table of ΔH°_f value for a temperature of 25°C. The procedure for this calculation is developed in the following example.

Example 5-7   Calculate ΔH°_{298} for the calcining of calcite, $CaCO_3$.
    The reaction for calcining calcite is expressed by the equation

$$CaCO_3(c) \rightarrow CaO(c) + CO_2(g)$$

Suppose that this reaction were carried out by first decomposing limestone into its elements:

$$CaCO_3(c) \rightarrow Ca\,(c) + C(graphite) + \tfrac{3}{2}\,O_2(g)$$

This reaction is the reverse of the reaction in which calcite is formed from its elements, and so the enthalpy change of this reaction is equal to $-\Delta H^\circ_f(CaCO_3)$.

The next step is the synthesis of the products from the elements obtained by decomposition of the reactant limestone:

$$C(graphite) + O_2(g) \rightarrow CO_2(g)$$

$$Ca(c) + \tfrac{1}{2} O_2(g) \rightarrow CaO(c)$$

The ΔH of the first of these two reactions is ΔH_f° for CO_2 and ΔH for the second is ΔH_f° for CaO. Hence the enthalpy change of the calcining reaction is given by

$$\Delta H_{298}^\circ = \Delta H_f^\circ(CaO) + \Delta H_f^\circ(CO_2) - \Delta H_f^\circ(CaCO_3)$$

Insertion of numerical values from the table in Appendix 1 gives

$$\Delta H_{298}^\circ = (-635.1) + (-393.5) - (-1206.9)$$

$$= +178.3 \text{ kJ}$$

It will be noticed that the table contains two values for the enthalpy of formation of $CaCO_3$. These refer to two different crystal structures of $CaCO_3$ which differ, slightly but measurably, in their enthalpy of formation. It will also be noticed that ΔH_f° values are listed for more than one physical state of some compounds. Examination of a case such as water, for which values are listed for the liquid and gas states, shows that the difference in ΔH_f° values is much larger than in cases where two solid states differing only in crystal structure are compared. In either case, however, the lesson is the same. Precise work requires that the state of the reactants and products be specified exactly.

When an element in its most stable form takes part in a reaction, its enthalpy of formation is zero by definition. When a compound occurs in a reaction statement with a stoichiometric coefficient other than one, that coefficient must be applied to the enthalpy of formation. All of these points are illustrated in the example which follows.

Example 5-8   Calculate ΔH° for the oxidation of ammonia to nitric oxide at 25°C.

$$4\,NH_3(g) + 5\,O_2(g) \rightarrow 4\,NO(g) + 6\,H_2O(g)$$

This process can be carried out in the following steps:

$$4\,NH_3 \rightarrow 2\,N_2 + 6\,H_2 \qquad \Delta H = -4\Delta H_f^\circ(NH_3)$$

$$6\,H_2 + 3\,O_2 \rightarrow 6\,H_2O(g) \qquad \Delta H = 6\Delta H_f^\circ(H_2O(g))$$

$$2\,O_2 + 2\,N_2 \rightarrow 4\,NO \qquad \Delta H = 4\Delta H_f^\circ(NO)$$

These three individual reactions can be added together to obtain the specified reaction for oxidation of ammonia, and so the required ΔH is the sum of the ΔH's of the individual reactions:

$$\Delta H° = 4\Delta H_f°(NO) + 6 \ \Delta H_f°(H_2O(g)) - 4 \ \Delta H_f°(NH_3)$$

$$= 4(+90.2) + 6(-241.8) - 4(-46)$$

$$= -906 \ kJ$$

The value $-906 \ kJ$ refers to the reaction as it is written in the question; it will be noticed that in the reaction four moles of ammonia are oxidized, and so the enthalpy of oxidation per mole of ammonia can be given as

$$\Delta H° = -906 \ kJ/4 \ mol \ NH_3$$

$$= -227 \ kJ \ mol^{-1}$$

The procedure for using enthalpies of formation for calculating the enthalpy of a reaction can be summarized in the following general formula. When the reaction is written in the generalized form

$$a \ A + b \ B \rightarrow c \ C + d \ D$$

the enthalpy of reaction is given by

$$\Delta H° = c\Delta H_f°(C) + d\Delta H_f°(D) - a\Delta H_f°(A) - b\Delta H_f°(B) \tag{7}$$

When the enthalpies of formation are taken from a table such as that in Appendix I, the $\Delta H°$ value refers to a temperature of 25°C. If the enthalpy of reaction at some other temperature is required further calculation is needed.

5-7 ENTHALPY OF REACTION AT DIFFERENT TEMPERATURES

The enthalpy of a reaction at a temperature other than 25°C is calculated using the fact that the enthalpy is a state function. The temperature of the reactants is first changed to 25°C by heating (or cooling) the reactants at constant pressure; the heat required for this first step is calculated from the heat capacities of the reactants at constant pressure, and the temperature change. Next, the chemical reaction is carried out at 25°C, the enthalpy of reaction being calculated from the heats of formation at 25°C. Finally, the products of the reaction are cooled (or heated) back to the initial temperature. The ΔH for the reaction carried out at the initial temperature is the sum of the ΔH values for the three steps. The procedure is illustrated in the following example.

Example 5-9 Calculate the enthalpy of oxidation of SO_2 to SO_3 at a temperature of 525°C, or 798 K.

The enthalpy of reaction at 798 K can be calculated using standard thermochemical data by considering the following three step process:

$$798 \ K: \quad SO_2 \ + \tfrac{1}{2}O_2 \qquad \qquad SO_3$$

$$298 \ K: \quad SO_2 \ + \tfrac{1}{2}O_2 \ \xrightarrow[\Delta H_{298}°]{} \ SO_3$$

The overall result of this process is the same as if the reaction were carried out at 798 K, and hence the enthalpy must be the same. The enthalpies of the individual steps are calculated as follows, using heat capacities and heats of formation from Appendix 1.

Enthalpy of cooling SO_2 = 1 mol × 39.7 J K^{-1} mol^{-1} × (298 − 798) K

$$= -19.85 \text{ kJ}$$

Enthalpy of cooling O_2 = $\frac{1}{2}$ mol × 29.4 J K^{-1} mol^{-1} × (298 − 798) K

$$= -7.35 \text{ kJ}$$

Enthalpy of reaction at 298 K = (−395.8 kJ) − (−296.6 kJ) − (0)

$$= -99.2 \text{ kJ}$$

Enthalpy of heating SO_3 = 1 mol × 50.6 J K^{-1} mol^{-1} × (798 − 298) K

$$= +25.3 \text{ kJ}$$

The required enthalpy of reaction at 798 K is the sum of these four contributions:

$$\Delta H^{\circ}_{798} = (-19.85) + (-7.35) + (-99.2) + (+25.3)$$

$$= -101.1 \text{ kJ}$$

In this example it should be noticed that the element oxygen makes no contribution in the calculation of the heat of reaction ΔH°_{298}, but must be included in the calculation of the heat involved in cooling the reactants.

Care is needed in combining the enthalpy changes for heating and cooling with the enthalpy of reaction ΔH°_{298} since heats of formation are quoted in *kilojoules,* whereas the heat capacity data are quoted in *joules* per kelvin. It will be noticed that the enthalpy changes of heating and cooling are of opposite sign, are of comparable magnitude to each other, and are a good deal smaller than the enthalpy of reaction ΔH°_{298}. Hence it may be expected that in most cases the heat of reaction ΔH°_{T} will not differ greatly from ΔH°_{298}. This guideline provides a useful check on mistakes in arithmetic.

5-8   MEASUREMENT OF ENTHALPIES OF REACTION

The enthalpy of a chemical reaction can be measured in a device called a *calorimeter.* If the heat of reaction is to be measured accurately, a great deal of skill is required in the construction and operation of the calorimeter.

The heat of a reaction which involves only solids and liquids can be measured simply and with modest accuracy in the calorimeter shown in Figure 5-3. The calorimeter is carefully insulated to prevent heat loss, and sometimes the calorimeter is built into a Dewar flask for that purpose. The top of the calorimeter is open to the atmosphere, so the external pressure on the reaction system is constant and the heat measured is an enthalpy change. The *chemical system* is contained in the innermost container. Everything else inside the insulation is called the *calorimeter* and consists of the stirrer, thermometer, con-

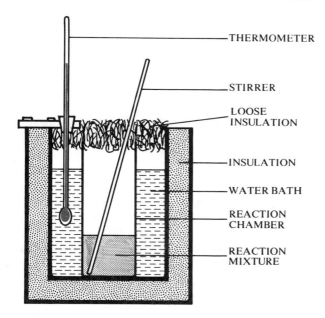

THERMOMETER

STIRRER

LOOSE
INSULATION

INSULATION

WATER BATH

REACTION
CHAMBER

REACTION
MIXTURE

Figure 5-3 A simple calorimeter for measurement at constant pressure.

tainers and the water in the outer container. The heat capacity of the calorimeter C_c, is measured in a separate experiment, and must be accurately known.

The chemical reactants are placed in the inner container, and before mixing are allowed time to come to the temperature of the calorimeter, T_1. The reaction is initiated by mixing the reactants, and when it is complete the final temperature T_2 is measured.

Both the calorimeter and the chemical system begin at T_1 and end at T_2. Since the calorimeter is in thermal contact with the chemical system but is insulated from all other matter, it can change temperature only by gaining heat from (or losing heat to) the chemical system. If T_2 is greater than T_1, the system must have transferred heat to the calorimeter whereas a drop in temperature means the converse. Since an increase in system temperature ($T_2 > T_1$) results in a heat flow *out* of the system ($q < 0$) to the calorimeter, the relationship is

$$q = -C_c(T_2 - T_1)$$

This q is ΔH for the process

$$\text{reactants } (T_1) \rightarrow \text{products } (T_2).$$

The value of ΔH°_{298} for the reaction at 25°C is obtained from the steps specified in the following diagram. It is necessary to know the total heat capacity of the reactants, C_1, and of the products, C_2.

$$\text{reactants (25°C)} \xrightarrow{\Delta H^\circ_{298}} \text{products (25°C)}$$
$$\Delta H_a \downarrow \qquad\qquad\qquad \uparrow \Delta H_c$$
$$\text{reactants } (T_1) \xrightarrow{\Delta H_b} \text{products } (T_2)$$

Since the enthalpy is a state function,

$$\Delta H^\circ_{298} = \Delta H_a + \Delta H_b + \Delta H_c$$
$$= C_1(T_1 - 25\,°C) - C_c(T_2 - T_1) + C_2(25\,°C - T_2) \qquad (8)$$

For convenience, this formula is written with the temperatures in degrees Celsius, since in practice the temperatures T_1 and T_2 are close to room temperature and are read from a thermometer calibrated in degrees Celsius.

Many ΔH°_f values are obtained from heats of combustion. Combustion reactions require a large excess of oxygen gas in order that the reaction shall proceed smoothly to completion, and this makes the constant pressure calorimeter unsuitable for these measurements. Instead, a constant volume calorimeter is used in which the combustible sample is placed in contact with pure oxygen at high pressure. Figure 5-4 illustrates a simple form of such a constant volume calorimeter. The chemical system occupies a strongly built container or "bomb" which contains the combustible sample, oxygen at a pressure of about 3 MPa, and a wire fuse which is heated electrically to set fire to the sample. The rest of the calorimeter operates in the same way as in the constant pressure calorimeter, and the analysis of the data proceeds in a similar way. However, the analysis differs in two aspects. Firstly, since the reaction is carried out at constant volume, the heat leaving the system is equal to a change in internal energy rather than the enthalpy. Secondly, the pressure in the chemical system differs considerably from the standard state pressure, $P^\circ = 101.325$ kPa.

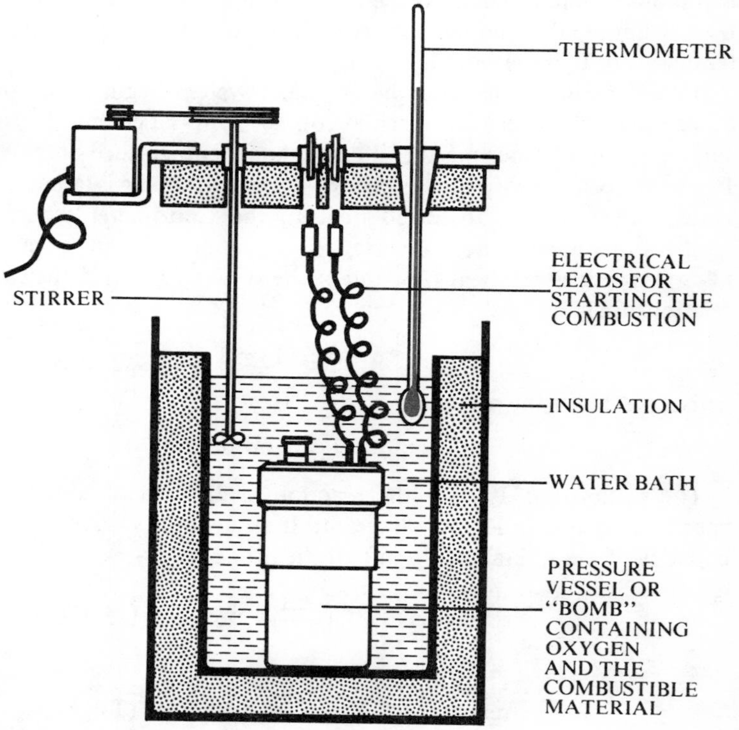

Figure 5-4 Bomb calorimeter for measurement of heat of combustion.

The value of $\Delta U°$ for the reaction at 25°C and standard state pressure is obtained from the following diagram, using the fact that the internal energy is a state function. The initial pressure in the chemical system is denoted by P_1, and the final pressure by P_2.

$$\text{reactants (25°C, P°)} \xrightarrow{\Delta U^\circ_{298}} \text{products (25°C, P°)}$$

$$\Delta U_a \downarrow \qquad\qquad \uparrow \Delta U_c$$

$$\text{reactants (T}_1\text{, P}_1\text{)} \xrightarrow{\Delta U_b} \text{products (T}_2\text{, P}_2\text{)}$$

As before, the value of ΔU_b is obtained from the heat capacity of the calorimeter system and the temperature change:

$$\Delta U_b = -C_c(T_2 - T_1)$$

The values of ΔU_a and ΔU_b can be estimated from the heat capacities of the reactants and products, as before:

$$\Delta U_a \approx C_1(T_1 - 25°C)$$

$$\Delta U_c \approx C_2(25°C - T_2)$$

However, there are corrections to be made in very precise work to allow for the changes of pressure of the chemical system, the dissolving of gases in liquids, and the evaporation of liquids. Furthermore the heat capacities C_1 and C_2 are not so easily defined as in the constant pressure calorimeter. The gases are constrained to be at constant volume, while solids and liquids are not. These difficulties are not of great importance despite their complexity, because ΔU_a and ΔU_c are generally small compared to ΔU_b. Since $\Delta U° = \Delta U_a + \Delta U_b + \Delta U_c$, the following equation is approximately true:

$$\Delta U^\circ_{298} \approx C_1(T_1 - 25°C) - C_c(T_2 - T_1) + C_2(25°C - T_2)$$

The enthalpy change for the chemical reaction is calculated from $\Delta U°$ using the equation of state of gases. From the definition of enthalpy,

$$\Delta H = \Delta(U + PV)$$
$$= \Delta U + \Delta(PV)$$

and so $\qquad\qquad \Delta H° = \Delta U° + P°\Delta V$

The volume change in the chemical reaction when carried out under constant external pressure is very nearly equal to the change in the volume of the gases involved in the reaction, since the volume of the solids and liquids is very small compared to that of the gases. Since the temperature and pressure are the same before and after the reaction, the volume change is due entirely to the change in the number of moles of gas in the reaction, Δn_g, and so

$$\Delta V = \Delta n_g.RT/P°$$

Combining the last two equations,

$$\Delta H° = \Delta U° + \Delta n_g.RT \qquad\qquad (9)$$

This equation is the last step in the determination of the enthalpy change of a combustion reaction; from this value the enthalpy change of formation of the sample can be calculated using Hess' law. The whole procedure is illustrated in the next example.

Example 5-10   A sample of 1.00 g of octane, C_8H_{18}, is placed in a constant volume calorimeter of volume 100. mL and heat capacity 10.90 kJ K^{-1}. The pressure vessel is filled with oxygen to a pressure of 3.0 MPa and the octane is then ignited. The temperature rises from 23.90°C to 28.20°C. Calculate $\Delta U°$ and $\Delta H°$ for combustion of one mole of octane.

The combustion reaction is given by the following balanced reaction:

$$C_8H_{18}(l) + 12\tfrac{1}{2}O_2(g) \rightarrow 8\,CO_2(g) + 9\,H_2O(l)$$

First it should be checked that there is sufficient oxygen present to burn all of the octane. The molar mass of octane is 114.2 g mol^{-1} and so the amount of octane present is (1.00/114.2) mol or 8.757×10^{-3} mol. The amount of oxygen present is calculated from the equation of state,

$$n_{O_2} = \frac{3.0 \times 10^{+6} \times 100 \times 10^{-6}}{8.314 \times 297.0}$$

$$= 0.1215 \text{ mol}$$

Hence there is sufficient oxygen for complete combustion, and the amount of oxygen left after the combustion is

$$0.1215 - 12.5 \times 8.757 \times 10^{-3} = 1.20 \times 10^{-2} \text{ mol}.$$

The amount of carbon dioxide produced is $8 \times 8.757 \times 10^{-3}$ or 7.01×10^{-2} mol, and the amount of water produced is $9 \times 8.757 \times 10^{-3}$ or 7.88×10^{-2} mol. The heat capacity of the reactants is

$$C_1 = 8.757 \times 10^{-3} \text{ mol} \times 276 \text{ J K}^{-1} \text{ mol}^{-1} + 0.1215 \text{ mol} \times 21.2 \text{ J K}^{-1} \text{ mol}^{-1}$$

$$= 4.99 \text{ J K}^{-1}$$

and the heat capacity of the products and the remaining oxygen is

$$C_2 = 7.88 \times 10^{-2} \times 75.3 + 7.01 \times 10^{-2} \times 30.3 + 1.20 \times 10^{-2} \times 21.2$$

$$= 8.31 \text{ J K}^{-1}$$

Hence, using the notation of the previous discussion, the internal energy change for changing the temperature of the reactants from 25°C to the initial temperature of the reaction is

$$\Delta U_a = 4.99 \text{ J K}^{-1} \times (23.90 - 25.00) \text{ K}$$

$$= -5.5 \text{ J},$$

the internal energy change of the combustion process which took place in the calorimeter is

$$\Delta U_b = -10.90 \times 10^3 \text{ J K}^{-1} \times (28.20 - 23.90) \text{ K}$$

$$= -4.69 \times 10^4 \text{ J},$$

and the internal energy change for bringing the products back to 25°C is

$$\Delta U_c = 8.31 \text{ J K}^{-1} \times (25.00-28.20) \text{ K}$$
$$= -26.6 \text{ J}.$$

The overall internal energy is the sum of these three contributions. It can be seen that ΔU_a and ΔU_c are very small compared to the heat of the reaction:

$$\Delta U^\circ_{298} = (-5.5) + (-4.69\times10^4) + (-26.6) = -4.69\times10^4 \text{ J}$$

Hence for one mole of octane,

$$\Delta U^\circ_{298} = -4.69 \times 10^4 \text{ J}/8.757 \times 10^{-3} \text{ mol}$$
$$= -5.35 \times 10^3 \text{ kJ mol}^{-1}$$

For the reaction as written above, the change in the number of moles of gas per mole of octane is

$$\Delta n_g = 8 - 12.5 = -4.5$$

and so the enthalpy change is

$$\Delta H^\circ_{298} = -5.35 \times 10^3 + (-4.5) \times 8.314 \times 298 \times 10^{-3}$$
$$= -5.36 \times 10^3 \text{ kJ mol}^{-1}$$

It should be noted that in this calculation care must be taken to avoid adding a quantity in *kilojoules* to a quantity in *joules*.

FURTHER READING

Thermochemistry and the first law of thermodynamics are discussed in many books. The student should be aware of the possibilities of confusion because of the existence of different sign conventions for q and w, and the persistent use of the calorie as a unit of heat. An authoritative account is the book by Kenneth Denbigh, "The Principles of Chemical Equilibrium" (Cambridge University Press, 1971).

A discussion of thermochemical measurements is given by A. J. Head, "Combustion and Reaction Calorimetry", Chapter 3 of "Chemical Thermodynamics" Volume 1, Specialist Periodical Reports, The Chemical Society.

PROBLEMS

1. Use the thermochemical tables to calculate the following enthalpy changes. Assume that the temperature is 298 K unless otherwise stated.
   (a) The heat lost by 200 t of iron cooling from 900 K to 300 K.
   $[5.4 \times 10^{10} \text{ J}]$
   (b) The value of ΔH° for making one mole of slaked lime from quicklime and water, $CaO(c) + H_2O(l) \rightarrow Ca(OH)_2(c)$ $[-65.2 \text{ kJ}]$
   (c) The value of the molar heat of hydration of anhydrous copper(II) sulphate, using the reaction $CuSO_4(c) + 5H_2O(g) \rightarrow CuSO_4.5 H_2O(c)$
   $[-300 \text{ kJ mol}^{-1}]$
   (d) The ΔH for production of 1000 t of soda ash by the Solvay process, from rock salt and limestone. $[+9.6 \times 10^8 \text{kJ}]$

(e) The ΔH for production of one mole of ethylene by pyrolysis of ethane.

[136.2 kJ]

2. Estimate ΔU for each of the processes described in the previous question.

[same; same; -288 kJ mol^{-1}; same; $+133.7$ kJ]

3. Use the thermochemical tables to calculate the following,
   (a) The ΔH for calcining limestone at a temperature of 1200°C.

[+176.0 kJ mol^{-1}]

   (b) The ΔH for ammonia synthesis at 500°C.

[-56.7 kJ mol^{-1}]

   (c) The ΔH for the manufacture of calcium carbide (used as a source of acetylene), from quicklime and coke at a temperature of 2000°C:
   $CaO(c) + 3C(c) \rightarrow CaC_2(c) + CO(g)$

[+511.1 kJ mol^{-1}]

4. Calculate the heat required to dissociate a nitrogen molecule into two atoms at 298.15 K and at 500 K, in both cases at 101.325 kPa.

[945.36 kJ; 947.88 kJ]

5. The "heat of total cracking" of hydrocarbons, ΔH_{TC}, is defined as ΔH at 298.15 K and 101.325 kPa for the process below.
   $$C_nH_m(g) + (2n - \tfrac{1}{2})\,H_2(g) \rightarrow n\,CH_4(g)$$
   Given that ΔH_{TC} is -65.2 kJ for C_2H_6 and -87.4 kJ for C_3H_8, calculate ΔH for
   $$CH_4(g) + C_3H_8(g) \rightarrow 2C_2H_6(g)$$

[43.0 kJ]

6. A 500.0 g lot of methanol at 101 kPa is cooled from 350.0 K (where it is a vapour), past the boiling point (337.8 K) where it condenses, to 300.0 K. How much heat is emitted?

[618 kJ]

7. Calculate ΔH and ΔU for the thermal decomposition of silver sulfate at 600 K and 101 kPa according to the following equation
   $$Ag_2SO_4(c) \rightarrow 2Ag(c) + SO_2(g) + O_2(g)$$

[415.3 kJ; 405.3 kJ]

8. 10.0 g of ice at 0°C is added to 500.0 g of water at 50°C in an insulated container. What is the final temperature? The latent heat of fusion of ice is 6.010 kJ mol^{-1}.

[47.5°C]

9. Calculate the "latent heat of evaporation", in kJ mol^{-1}, of benzene, both at 298.15 K and at its boiling point of 353.25 K. In making the second calculation, assume that Cp values are constant over this range of temperature.

[33.9 kJ; 31.1 kJ]

10. In a solvent recovery operation following an industrial process, hot benzene vapour enters a condenser at 240°C and leaves it as a liquid at 35°C. If the unit handles 2700 kg of benzene per hour, what is the rate of heat removal by the condenser in kJ s^{-1}

[470 kJ s^{-1}]

11. The heat of combustion of solid benzoic acid, C_6H_5COOH, is −3226.7 kJ mol^{-1}; the products of combustion are $CO_2(g)$ and $H_2O(l)$ only. What is the ΔH_f° of benzoic acid?

[−385.4 kJ mol^{-1}]

12. Consider a constant pressure calorimeter. Show that, if the heat capacity of the reactants is approximately equal to that of the products ($C_1 \approx C_2$), then the heat of the reaction is

$$\Delta H \approx (C_1 + C_c)(T_1 - T_2)$$

13. A constant pressure calorimeter consists of an insulated beaker of mass 92.0 g, made of glass with a heat capacity of 0.75 J K^{-1} g^{-1}. The beaker contains 100. mL of 1.00 M HCl at a steady temperature of 22.6°C, and 100. mL of 1.00 M NaOH at a temperature of 23.4°C is added. The final temperature after the reaction is complete is 29.3°C. What is the ΔH per mole for this neutralisation reaction? Assume that the heat capacities of all solutions are equal to that of the same volumes of water.

[57.0 kJ mol^{-1}]

14. A sample of 0.7340 g of benzoic acid is placed in a constant volume calorimeter of volume 120 mL. The pressure vessel is filled with oxygen to a pressure of 3.0 MPa, and the benzoic acid is ignited, causing the calorimeter temperature to rise from 22.03°C to 25.21°C. Calculate the heat capacity of the calorimeter system. The heat capacity of benzoic acid is 146.8 J K^{-1} mol^{-1}. (Benzoic acid is a standard substance used for calibrating calorimeters).

[6.10 kJ K^{-1}]

VI ENERGY SOURCES

The provision and distribution of energy in convenient and economical forms are essential services in the operation of present day society. The application of energy allows such an increase in the productivity of a person's labour in a factory or on a farm that it is impossible to compete in the market place without using energy in the production of goods. This has led to great industrial expansion in the manufacturing nations during the twentieth century, an expansion which has been based in part on the assumption that energy supplies are unlimited and cheap. During the last quarter of the twentieth century, this assumption will no longer be a good basis for planning, and great changes in society may be forced upon the western world as a result of this "energy crisis."

The "production" of energy is not production at all, but rather the conversion of energy into a form which can be distributed economically and used conveniently by the consumer. A store of energy in nature is called a *primary source* of energy. The most important primary sources are petroleum, natural gas, coal, and falling water. Wood is a primary source which has been decreasing in importance, while uranium is the primary source upon which nuclear energy is based, and is of growing significance. By far the largest part of the energy derived from primary sources comes from the use of petroleum, natural gas and coal as fuels; energy from these sources is released as a result of the chemical reactions which take place in combustion. Chemistry enters into energy considerations in another way, for the primary hydrocarbon fuels are also the raw materials for the manufacture of important industrial chemicals such as ammonia (for fertilizer) and ethylene (for plastics) which in the long run may be more valuable to man than the energy derived from the combustion of the fuel.

Energy from a primary source usually requires some form of processing before it is made available to the consumer at the point of use. The source as used by the consumer is called a *secondary source* of energy. The five most common secondary sources are solid fuels such as coal and coke, natural gas, gasoline and diesel fuel, heavy fuel oils, and electricity. The transformation of primary sources into secondary sources is itself an important industry, and one in which chemistry plays a major role.

There are several specialized secondary sources which are of chemical interest. The use of electrochemical cells, more commonly known as batteries, depends upon carrying out an oxidation-reduction reaction in an apparatus in which the transfer of electrons takes place through an external circuit. Electrochemistry is basic to the design and construction of batteries, and will be discussed in Chapter 22. Explosives form another secondary source, very small in terms of the amount of energy produced, but very prominent in the public eye because of the use of explosives in military operations.

6-1 FUELS

Fuels provide from eighty to ninety percent of the energy of most industrialized countries. The combustion reactions are mostly simple and provide an excellent opportunity to apply the principles of thermochemistry in an area of great public interest. The use of thermochemistry enables an engineer to determine the amount of energy which can be obtained from combustion of a fuel, and hence to determine the economic value of that fuel. Organizations which buy and sell large quantities of fuel carry out many measurements of the heat of combustion as quality control checks on contracts for the supply of fuel. The *heat of combustion* is the enthalpy of the reaction in which one mole, or one gram, of fuel is completely oxidized, the reaction products being $CO_2(g)$ and $H_2O(l)$ in most cases. The heat of combustion is measured in a constant volume calorimeter and may be used as a good estimate of the heat which is obtainable by burning the fuel in a full-scale furnace. It may be assumed that the combustion reaction in the furnace proceeds to completion unless the furnace is not working properly.

The heats of combustion and boiling points of a number of fuels in pure form are given in Table 6-1, and data for a number of commercial fuels are

TABLE 6-1   Properties of Fuels

Name	Formula	State	Heat of Combustion[1] kJ mol^{-1}	kJ g^{-1}	Boiling Point K
carbon	C	c	− 393.5	− 32.7	−
hydrogen	H_2	g	− 285.8	−141.8	20
methane	CH_4	g	− 890.3	− 55.5	112
ethane	C_2H_6	g	−1559.9	− 51.9	185
propane	C_3H_8	g	−2220.0	− 50.3	231
butane	C_4H_{10}	g	−2878.5	− 49.5	273
methylpropane	C_4H_{10}	g	−2871.6	− 49.4	261
hexane	C_6H_{14}	l	−4163.1	− 48.3	342
octane	C_8H_{18}	l	−5470.7	− 47.9	398
acetylene	C_2H_2	g	−1299.6	− 49.9	189
ethylene	C_2H_4	g	−1411.0	− 50.3	169
methanol	CH_3OH	l	− 726.6	− 22.6	338
ethanol	C_2H_5OH	l	−1366.9	− 29.7	352

[1]Enthalpy for reaction with O_2 to yield $CO_2(g)$ and $H_2O(l)$. Values given are for 1 mol of fuel and 1 g of fuel respectively.

TABLE 6-2   Enthalpies of Combustion of Commercial Fuels

Coal values vary widely from mine to mine. Crude petroleum values are less variable but still show substantial variations. In all cases the values shown below are mean Canadian values as calculated by Statistics Canada. Individual values will vary from these means, particularly in the case of coals.

Coal	$GJ\ t^{-1}$	
Anthracite	29.5	
Bituminous	29.3	
Sub-bituminous	19.8	
Lignite	15.3	
Petroleum and		
Petroleum Products	$GJ\ t^{-1}$	$GJ\ m^{-3}$
Crude Oil	46	27.2
Motor Gasoline C_4–C_{12}	48	34.7
Kerosene C_9–C_{15}	47	37.7
Diesel and Light Fuel Oil C_{12}–C_{20}	47	38.7
Heavy Fuel Oil	45	41.7
Aviation Turbofuel C_9–C_{16}	46	35.9
L.P.G. C_3–C_4	50	27.2
Natural Gas		$kJ\ m^{-3}$
Natural Gas C_1–C_2		37.0

Footnotes

Gas volumes are measured at 101 325 Pa and 15°C. Conversion of old units to S.I. units can be achieved using the following factors:

$$1\ \text{B.T.U.} = 1.054615\ \text{kJ}$$
$$1\ \text{barrel} = 35\ \text{imperial gallons} = 0.15891\ m^3$$
$$1\ \text{short ton} = 2000\ \text{pounds} = 0.9070\ t$$
$$1\ \text{long ton} = 2240\ \text{pounds} = 1.0158\ t$$

Note in comparing the combustion energies of petroleum products, the densities vary significantly. Typically fuel oil has a density of $870\ kg\ m^{-3}$, motor gasoline of $740\ kg\ m^{-3}$ and L.P.G. of $540\ kg\ m^{-3}$.

given in Table 6-2. Since atmospheric oxygen is readily available without cost, the heats of combustion are quoted for a given amount of fuel only. When considering applications in which the oxidizer must be carried as well as the fuel, the heats of combustion per gram of combustion mixture must be calculated in comparing figures.

The simplest fuel is carbon, which burns to CO_2. Carbon is readily available as a major component of coal, coke and charcoal, and the heats of combustion of these fuels are generally close to 30 kJ/g. World consumption of coal is of the order of 10^9 tonne/year, and accounts for about a quarter of the total energy consumed. Coal is classified in four *ranks* on the basis of the moisture content, the content of volatile organic compounds, and the content of carbon. The four ranks are, in order of decreasing "quality," anthracite, bituminous coal, sub-bituminous coal and lignite. A further consideration in determining the value of coal is the content of sulphur, for this is released to the atmosphere in the form of sulphur dioxide when the coal is burned; further oxidation of the SO_2 to SO_3 then occurs in the atmosphere, and the sulphur is returned to the ground in the form of sulphuric acid dissolved in rainwater. Coal which is to be burned in large amounts in a populated area must be carefully monitored for its sulphur content as well as for its heat of combustion. Emission of oxides of sulphur in stack gases is closely controlled by government regulations.

Hydrogen is a simple fuel, which yields only water when it burns. It is not used as a fuel at present except for some special applications in welding, and in rockets. There is considerable danger from explosion when hydrogen is mixed with oxygen. Recently there have been proposals to use hydrogen pipelines rather than electrical transmission lines for the transport of energy over long distances, and in future, hydrogen may become an important secondary energy source.

All other major fuels are saturated hydrocarbons, with chemical formulae which can be written C_nH_{2n+2}. Natural gas consists of methane mixed with some ethane and smaller amounts of propane and butane. Higher hydrocarbons with $n \geq 5$ occur in deposits of liquid petroleum.

Natural gas is prepared for market in three steps. First, any propane and butane is removed by condensation, for sale separately as "liquefied petroleum gas," or LPG. These gases have higher molar heats of combustion (see Table 6-1), and higher heats of combustion per unit volume, than methane or ethane. LPG is used as a fuel in applications where volume is restricted, and as a raw material in the chemical industry. Second, water is removed by contact with a dehydrating agent. Third, hydrogen sulphide, H_2S, is removed; since this gas is acidic in aqueous solution, it can be removed from natural gas by passing the gas through a basic solution. The most commonly used base in North American practice is ethanolamine:

$$HOCH_2CH_2NH_2(aq) + H_2S \rightarrow HOCH_2CH_2NH_3{}^+(aq) + HS^-(aq)$$

The H_2S is removed from the solution subsequently by heating, which reverses the above reaction. The H_2S is then oxidized to SO_2, as has been described in the section on sulphuric acid. If there is no immediate market for the SO_2, pure sulphur is produced for storage by reaction of the SO_2 with more H_2S, as described in Problem 1-5.

After these processing steps, natural gas consists of a mixture of ethane and methane with practically no impurities, and is therefore a very "clean" fuel. The heat of combustion of the gas depends on the amount of ethane in the mixture; where large amounts of ethane are present, it may be separated for further conversion to ethylene or to other chemicals.

The refining of petroleum into commercial fuels and other products is an immense industry, upon which every aspect of modern society depends. A large part of the refining process consists of separating petroleum into its different chemical constituents by distillation processes, without carrying out any chemical reaction. This type of operation requires knowledge of the hydrocarbons present in the petroleum feedstock, and of the way these complex solutions behave when distilled. The other important chemical process is the *cracking* reaction, in which heavy hydrocarbons are heated or pyrolyzed so that they decompose into simpler hydrocarbons. The use of cracking reactions is essential to the economical production of gasoline from a wide variety of petroleums. A typical reaction is shown:

$$
\begin{array}{ccc}
\underset{\text{n-pentane}}{
\begin{array}{c}
\text{H H H H H} \\
\text{| | | | |} \\
\text{H--C--C--C--C--C--H} \\
\text{| | | | |} \\
\text{H H H H H}
\end{array}}
\rightarrow
\underset{\text{propylene}}{
\begin{array}{c}
\text{H H \quad H} \\
\text{| | \quad /} \\
\text{H--C--C=C} \\
\text{| \quad \quad \textbackslash} \\
\text{H \quad \quad H}
\end{array}}
+
\underset{\text{ethane}}{
\begin{array}{c}
\text{H H} \\
\text{| |} \\
\text{H--C--C--H} \\
\text{| |} \\
\text{H H}
\end{array}}
\end{array}
$$

As a result of the constancy of the valence of the carbon atom, cracking reactions produce *olefins,* molecules containing carbon-carbon double bonds. The simplest cracking reaction is the conversion of ethane to ethylene, which has already been discussed.

The mixture of light hydrocarbons which is separated from petroleum by distillation is called "straight run gasoline," and consists mostly of straight chain molecules. These gasolines are found to have low "octane" rating and cannot be used in high compression engines because of "knocking" due to unsatisfactory combustion properties. High octane gasolines have significant amounts of branched chain hydrocarbons in them. Cracking reactions produce branched chain saturated molecules as well as olefins, and hence the cracking process is essential to the production of fuels for modern high compression engines. For many years it has been the practice to add tetraethyl lead,

$$
\begin{array}{c}
\text{C}_2\text{H}_5 \\
| \\
\text{H}_5\text{C}_2 - \text{Pb} - \text{C}_2\text{H}_5 \\
| \\
\text{C}_2\text{H}_5
\end{array}
$$

to motor gasoline as a way of reducing knocking. This compound is exceedingly toxic, however, and leads to the deposit of lead salts along highways, and so lead-free gasoline has been introduced.

The composition of some commercial fuels in terms of the saturated hydrocarbon formula C_nH_{2n+2}, together with their heats of combustion in commercial and SI units are summarized in Table 6-2. Table 6-1 shows that the heat of combustion of the pure hydrocarbons per unit mass is approximately 48 kJ g^{-1} for all values of n above 3. Hence any mixture of hydrocarbons has a heat of combustion of approximately this value. This very important conclusion is borne out by the figures in Table 6-2, which show that the heat of combustion per unit mass or per barrel is approximately the same for a wide range of different hydrocarbon fuels.

Other fuels are of less importance except for specialized purposes. The alcohols, methanol and ethanol, are used in circumstances where hydrocarbon fuels are in short supply, but it is seen from Table 6-1 that their heat of combustion is considerably lower than that of the hydrocarbons. Ethylene is too valuable a chemical to be burned as a fuel, but acetylene is used for welding metals. The heat of combustion of acetylene is not unusually large, but the flame temperature produced by burning a mixture of pure oxygen and acetylene is higher than that of most other gas mixtures.

6-2 EXPLOSIVES

The main characteristics of an explosive reaction are the sudden release of energy, and the formation of a shock wave due to the sudden expansion of gases. The destructive effects of an explosion are caused by the shock wave, and may be applied in mining, construction, and military operations. The shock wave is usually associated with the sudden release of a large amount of gas in the reaction, but if the energy release is fast enough and large enough, the Charles' law expansion of gases in the vicinity of the reaction may be sufficient to produce a shock wave even without additional gas being produced.

Much effort has been applied to the development of nuclear explosions for military purposes, but the application of nuclear explosions in civil engineering projects has been prevented by political and environmental difficulties. Hence all practical explosives are chemical in nature, and may be studied using chemical principles. The manufacture of explosives is a branch of the chemical industry.

Fuels which normally burn smoothly under controlled conditions may become explosive when mixed with air in certain proportions. Hydrogen and gasoline vapour are notoriously dangerous in this regard, and have caused many explosions and fires due to careless handling. Finely powdered coal dust, and wheat dust in grain elevators, have been known to explode when present in air due to rapid combustion reactions. In reactions such as these, the change in volume is small, and may even be negative:

$$H_2(g) + \tfrac{1}{2} O_2(g) \rightarrow H_2O(g)$$

Hence the formation of a shock wave in such cases must be due to the thermal expansion caused by the heat released.

All explosives give rise to the production of considerable heat, the explosion process being invariably exothermic. The process usually, but not always, leads to combustion products, such as carbon dioxide and water. For solid or liquid explosives, the oxygen required to form these compounds cannot come from the air, as in a combustion, because the explosion process is too rapid for this to be possible. The internal availability of oxygen is therefore a characteristic of all but a few explosives.

Explosives can be classified as detonating agents and as non-initiating high explosives. It is advantageous if the main explosive used is not easily set off, so that it can be manufactured, transported and stored with relative safety. The explosion of such materials can be initiated with a very small quantity of a detonating agent. Detonators do not need the properties of high explosives to shatter or move material, nor is their price so important since they are used in small quantities. Lead azide, $Pb(N_3)_2$; mercury fulminate, $Hg(OCN)_2$; and diazodinitrophenol or DDNP, $C_6H_2O_5N_4$ are among the most common.

High explosives may be pure materials like trinitrotoluene or TNT, $C_7H_5O_6N_3$ but they are more commonly mixtures. This is done either to provide more oxygen to a good explosive that is improved if more oxygen is available, or to stabilize a good explosive which is too dangerous to use pure. The addition of ammonium nitrate to TNT to give the explosive amatol is an example of the first, while the addition of inert clays to nitroglycerine to give the explosive dynamite is an example of the second.

Explosives are judged and classified by several criteria for which specialized names have arisen. The *heat of explosion* is the total heat produced per unit mass of explosive, and corresponds to ΔH for the explosion process. *Detonation velocity* is the rate at which the explosion races through the charge. It depends both on the chemical mechanism by which successive layers are ignited and on the efficiency with which the heat produced is confined. The latter depends in turn on the physical shape and dimensions of the explosive charge, and the manner in which it is confined. *Brisance* is a measure of the shattering ability of an explosive and is measured empirically by the amount of sand crushed by a given charge fired under carefully set conditions. The brisance of all modern high explosives is large, whereas for detonators it is not an important characteristic. Brisance is increased by high detonation velocities and, to some extent, by high heats of explosion. *Volume change* also contributes to brisance and is simply the increase in volume per unit mass of explosive, standardized to some stated temperature and pressure. *Explosive strength* is an empirically defined and measured quantity involving the movement of a suspended mortar in which a charge is fired under specific conditions. Explosive strength reflects all of the above characteristics.

Sensitivity is a measure of the ease with which an explosion is initiated. The relative sensitivity of explosives depends on the stimuli being considered, friction, heat, electric spark and impact all being important. Ideally, high explosives are insensitive to all of these sources, and can be exploded only by a detonator. Detonators must, on the other hand, be moderately sensitive to one of these sources at least, although clearly, sensitivity to heat or to the friction inevitable in handling would make an explosive useless for practical purposes. *Stability* is a very different property, referring to the ability of the compound to remain unchanged over long periods of time. An unstable explosive may become inactive in storage, or worse perhaps, become too sensitive.

The oldest known explosive is a mixture of inorganic materials called "black powder" or "gunpowder." The explosion reaction can be represented by the following equation:

$$2\,NaNO_3 + S + 3\,C \rightarrow Na_2S(c) + N_2(g) + 3\,CO_2(g)$$

This reaction is highly exothermic, and produces a large volume of gas entirely from solids. Black powder is no longer used as widely as it was formerly, having been replaced for blasting purposes by high explosives based on the salt ammonium nitrate and organic nitro compounds.

The explosive decomposition of ammonium nitrate can be described by the reaction

$$NH_4NO_3(c) \rightarrow N_2(g) + \tfrac{1}{2}O_2(g) + 2\,H_2O(g)$$

The solid salt decomposes yielding only gaseous products; the water is in the form of a gas because of the high temperature produced in the explosion. It has been mentioned before that ammonium nitrate is used as a fertilizer. It is common practice to store large amounts of fertilizer in heaps, and to transport it in bulk by ship. Careless handling has on occasion caused immense explosions in fertilizer facilities containing thousands of tonnes of ammonium nitrate fertilizer.

The explosive decomposition of ammonium nitrate produces half a mole of molecular oxygen among its products, per mole of salt. This oxygen can be used to oxidize a suitable fuel by mixing the fuel with the salt. The oxidation of the fuel leads to a great increase in the amount of energy released in the explosion. Aluminium powder is sometimes used, since the oxidation reaction

$$2 \, Al(c) + \tfrac{3}{2} O_2(g) \rightarrow Al_2O_3(c)$$

is exceedingly exothermic. For blasting purposes, the ammonium nitrate is mixed with fuel oil, and has largely replaced dynamite in the mining industry.

Most other explosives are organic compounds containing the nitro group, $-NO_2$. Two examples are nitroglycerine, which decomposes according to the reaction

$$
\begin{array}{c}
H \\
| \\
H-C-O-NO_2 \\
| \\
2 \; H-C-O-NO_2 \rightarrow 6 \; CO_2 + 5 \; H_2O + 3 \; N_2 + \tfrac{1}{2} O_2 \\
| \\
H-C-O-NO_2 \\
| \\
H
\end{array}
$$

and trinitrotoluene, which has the structure,

Nitroglycerine is an oily liquid which is uncontrollably explosive when pure. However, when mixed with a fine clay it is less sensitive and in this form it is used as an industrial explosive called dynamite. Dynamite was the first of the modern industrial explosives, and the profits from its invention and manufacture are used to finance the annual Nobel prizes in science and other fields.

Trinitrotoluene, commonly known as TNT, is typical of a class of explosive compounds in which nitro groups replace hydrogen atoms around a benzene ring. The products of the explosive reactions include CO_2, CO, C_2H_2, H_2 and

TABLE 6-3   Some Properties of Commercial Explosives

Name	Formula	Heat of Explosion[1] kJ g^{-1}	Volume Change[2] mL g^{-1}	Brisance
Lead Azide	$Pb(N_3)_2$	1.5	—	18
Diazodinitrophenol (DDNP)	$C_6H_2(NO_2)_2(N_2O)$	3.4	—	46
Mercury Fulminate	$Hg(OCN)_2$	1.8	—	22
Trinitrotoluene (TNT)	$C_6H_2(NO_2)_3(CH_3)$	3.9	730	48
Ammonium Nitrate	NH_4NO_3	1.4	980	—
Nitroglycerine	$C_3H_5(NO_2)_3$	6.2	720	59
Pentaerythrityl tetranitrate (PETN)	$C(CH_2ONO_2)_4$	5.8	790	61
Amatol	50:50 mixture of TNT and ammonium nitrate	4.1	860	39
Cyclonite (RDX)	$(CH_2)_3(NNO_2)_3$	5.4	910	59
Black Powder	74:16:10 mixture of KNO_3, charcoal, and sulphur	2.8	280	8

Footnotes

[1]Heat of Explosion is the enthalpy of reaction.
[2]Water is a gas at the high temperature of the explosion. The volume is standardized to 298 K and 101 kPa.

N_2, and the decomposition cannot be represented by a single chemical equation.

Some simple properties of explosives are listed in Table 6-3. The volume change per gram due to production of gas is seen to be very large, since a gram of most of these materials occupies only about 1 cm^3. The energy released per gram of explosive is rather small, being roughly a tenth of the energy released in the combustion of the same mass of a fuel. However, rate of energy release in an explosion is very much greater than in a combustion reaction. It is the rapid rate of energy release and expansion that produces the shock wave and its associated destruction.

It will have been noticed that all important explosives are compounds of nitrogen, and can only be manufactured from nitric acid or nitrate salts. It is for this reason that the Haber process for producing synthetic ammonia and the Ostwald process for nitric acid were of such historical importance.

The technology of explosives is very complex, since all manufacturing, handling and storage operations are hazardous. No explosive should be made or handled except in accordance with established practice.

6-3   ENERGY SUPPLIES IN THE FUTURE

In recent years the supply of energy in the industrialized countries has become a matter of public debate, and the phrase "the energy crisis" has been coined to describe the confusion surrounding this debate. The future of energy supplies used to be regarded as stable and within the control of the countries which require the energy, but it has become apparent that this is no longer the situation.

We have seen in this chapter that the major part of the world's energy comes from three primary sources, coal, petroleum and natural gas, which are found as geological deposits in various parts of the world. At one time coal was the most important primary source of energy. It was burned in fireplaces for heating, and in the furnaces of boilers to make steam to drive factories, locomotives, steamships and electric generating stations. This was a satisfactory situation politically because the industrial countries of Europe and North America had ample supplies of coal within their boundaries, and so were not dependent on imports from foreign countries for their energy supplies. Gradually, however, coal was replaced as a primary source by the liquid and gaseous hydrocarbon fuels. A furnace can be fired more conveniently by oil or gas than by coal, and the prices of hydrocarbon fuels remained low as long as supplies remained plentiful. The development of the internal combustion engine changed the transportation industry from a coal-using to a petroleum-using industry. The introduction of the cheap and popular private car ensured the rapid growth of the consumption of petroleum for transportation.

During most of the twentieth century, the economic life of industrial countries has depended on sources of hydrocarbon fuels which are cheap, reliable and able to supply a demand that was doubling every ten years. At the same time there has been a realization that geological deposits of hydrocarbons are limited in extent, and that the rate of consumption is now higher than the rate of discovery. The supply of energy has become a major item of international trade and politics, particularly as the United States and the U.S.S.R. become increasingly less able to meet their requirements from their own domestic sources. Since Japan and most European nations have long been major importers, the oil trade has become a seller's market and prices have escalated rapidly.

Examination of the pattern of energy sources in different countries shows that each, naturally, exploits its own resources. Hydroelectricity is important in Canada and Norway, natural gas in Canada, the Netherlands and the United States, and coal in Germany and the United Kingdom. Nevertheless, petroleum is the largest single energy source in every industrial country, always providing over 40% of national energy and, in countries with few native sources, as much as 90%.

How these patterns will change in the twenty-first century is difficult to predict. One strategy favours keeping existing technology as unchanged as possible, and finding alternative sources of liquid hydrocarbons, such as tar sands and heavy oils in Canada, oil shales in the United States, and Fisher-Tropsch synthesis of liquid hydrocarbons from coal as is done in South Africa. An alternative strategy is based on the belief that the present generation of automobile engines, diesel equipment and the like is the product of an abundance of inexpensive liquid hydrocarbons, and now that oil is no longer cheap, a new generation of equipment using different secondary sources should be developed. These include electricity, stored probably in a new generation of rechargeable batteries; methanol, which is a renewable source which can be manufactured from vegetation; and hydrogen, produced from coal and steam or from electrolysis of water using nuclear power. New primary sources are also of interest, particularly those that are renewable. Solar energy is being utilized increasingly. Wind generation of electricity is being actively developed in several countries, and wave energy is popular in the United Kingdom. Many of these sources tend to be suited to a more decentralized system of energy production than has been appropriate in the past. Research and development into these and many competing possibilities is a major challenge to science and technology. Those systems which become established must, of course, be reliable technically, but environmental protection, national security and economics must also be considered.

Overlying all of these futuristic considerations is the issue of conservation. There is every reason to believe that most industrial countries could reduce their consumption drastically without reducing their living standards. In particular, each resident of Canada and the United States uses approximately 70% and 90% more energy, respectively, than residents of such prosperous countries as Australia, Denmark, France, Germany and Sweden. Analysis of usage figures show that this arises from such sources as inefficient transportation, especially the use of large automobiles to move a single person. While variations in climate and transportation distances complicate national comparisons, there seems to be little doubt that Canada and the United States could maintain and improve their standard of living while reducing their per capita consumption of energy. Moreover, almost every study, whether from industry or government sources, has indicated that the cheapest way of bringing supply and demand together is to reduce demand.

The eventual decisions on energy sources for the twenty-first century and beyond will arise from a period of major research and development. The outcome may well vary from country to country, just as present patterns differ from country to country. These differences reflect cultural and geographical factors, as well as the availability of primary sources. The Scandinavian countries and Canada require much energy for heating buildings. Canada and the United States use a large fraction of their total for transportation, partly because distances within those countries are great and partly because there is much travel by automobile and aircraft, both inefficient when energy per passenger mile is considered. The large petroleum and petrochemical industry of the Netherlands, which has grown there for geographic and commercial reasons, makes that country a major user of petroleum for industry simply because of the requirements for operating the refineries themselves. These few illustrations are included to demonstrate the close relationship between the details of energy consumption in a country and the culture and commerce of that country. Any abrupt change, such as a disruption of the traditional energy sources, is capable of creating deep social unrest.

FURTHER READING

Quarterly Report on Energy Supply-Demand in Canada. Statistics Canada 57-003, Ottawa. Quarterly.

Crude Petroleum and Natural Gas Production. Statistics Canada 26-006, Ottawa. Monthly.

These excellent reports on Canadian energy statistics have their counterparts in most industrial countries, such as those published by H.M.S.O. in the United Kingdom, or by the Superintendent of Documents in the United States.

Energy Statistics. Organization for Economic Cooperation and Development, Paris. Annual. This is a fine source of information on all the major countries of western Europe, Canada, United States, Japan and Australia.

Energy in Transition. Secretariat for Future Studies, Government of Sweden. Stockholm, 1977. This publication deals with energy conservation and policies in the nation which leads the world in this field.

Energy and Power (W. H. Freeman and Company, San Francisco 1971) Scientific American prepared this highly readable primer on energy sources.

PROBLEMS

1. Write balanced equations for combustion of the following fuels: CH_4, C_3H_8, C_8H_{18}, C_2H_2, C_2H_5OH

2. Using only the data listed in Table 6-1, calculate the value of ΔH_f for CO_2, $H_2O(l)$, CH_4, C_3H_8, C_2H_2, CH_3OH

3. A sample of natural gas, known to contain only methane and ethane, was burned under controlled conditions, and was found to produce 15.80 g of water, and 410.0 kJ of heat. What was the composition of the gas, expressed as mole fraction of ethane?

[0.222]

4. A small tank has a capacity of 2.0 L, and has been constructed to hold a pressure of 0.70 MPa. Calculate the total heat of combustion of the fuel in the tank if it is:
   (a) methane at a pressure of 0.70 MPa

[0.50 MJ]

   (b) propane at a pressure of 0.70 MPa

[1.2 MJ]

   (c) fuel oil of density 730 kg m^{-3}

[70. MJ]

   (d) charcoal of density 1800 kg m^{-3}

[118 MJ]

5. Suppose the tank in question 3 were filled with trinitrotoluene, which has a density of 1654 kg m^{-3}. Calculate the total heat of explosion, and compare with the combustion of fuels.

[13 MJ]

6. Ammonium nitrate explodes to give excess oxygen, whereas trinitrotoluene explodes to give, in a simplified view, carbon and carbon monoxide.

$$2\,NH_4NO_3(c) \rightarrow 2\,N_2(g) + 4\,H_2O(g) + O_2(g)$$

$$2\,C_6H_2(CH_3)(NO_2)_3(c) \rightarrow 3\,N_2(g) + 5\,H_2O(g) + 7\,CO(g) + 7\,C(c)$$

Amatol is a mixture of these two substances. What is the minimum percentage, by mass, of ammonium nitrate which amatol must contain in order that all of the carbon and carbon monoxide is converted to carbon dioxide?   [79%]

7. Wood has returned to favour as a domestic heat source, since it is a renewable resource. A full cord (piled hardwood 2.4 m × 1.2 m × 1.2 m) of hard maple has a combustion energy of 30 GJ. If the price of fuel oil is p per litre, at what price per cord is maple competitive?

[780 p]

8. Calculate the total heat of combustion available from the fuel in each of the following cases:

(a) a household storage tank containing 900 L of light fuel oil, density 730 kg m^{-3}.   [31 GJ]

(b) an automotive fuel tank of 50 L of motor gasoline, density 0.70 g cm^{-3}
[1.7 GJ]

(c) a hiker's fuel cartridge containing 250 g of butane   [12.4 MJ]

(d) a motor camper's fuel supply of 4.5 kg of propane   [230 MJ]

(e) a cowboy's can of "sterno" containing 300 g ethanol   [8.9 MJ]

9. How many tonnes of coal per day are needed to operate an electrical generating station of 2000 MW output if the conversion factor of the station is 40%? If the waste heat is rejected to a nearby lake by passing lake water through heat exchangers in which the water is heated 10 K, what is the flow of water in m^3 day^{-1}? Density of water is 1000 kg m^{-3}.
[1.5×10^4 t/day; 6.2×10^6 m^3/day]

10. Petroleum consists of compounds of hydrogen, carbon, and to a small extent sulphur. How many kilograms of oxygen are needed for the total combustion to CO_2, H_2O and SO_2 of a kilogram of petroleum analyzed at 85.89 mass % carbon, 11.11 mass % hydrogen and 3.00 mass % sulphur? How many kilograms of dry air are required, taking air to be 76.85% nitrogen and 23.15% oxygen by mass? Calculate the mass of each gas produced in the combustion of 1 kg of the above fuel oil. What is the total mass of gas produced? If the flue temperature is 400 K, what is the volume of this gas at atmospheric pressure? Remember the nitrogen.
[3.200 kg of O_2; 13.82 kg of air; 14.82 kg of products; 16.6 m^3]

11. (a) In an industrial process, natural gas is burned using dry air as the oxidizer. Taking natural gas as being 100% methane, and dry air as being 79 mol % N_2 and 21 mol % O_2, calculate the minimum volume of air (298 K, 10^5 Pa) necessary for the complete combustion of 1000 m^3 of natural gas to $CO_2(g)$ and $H_2O(g)$. How much heat is produced?

(b) While the above calculation correctly determines the heat produced when both products and reagents are at 298 K, the normal case is more likely to be flue gases leaving at around 500 K. If the methane and air are at 300 K and the CO_2 and H_2O at 500 K, what fraction of the heat produced escapes via the chimney?

(c) A further loss in real cases comes about because of incomplete combustion. If use of the stoichiometric minimum quantity of air calculated in question (a) resulted in only 80% of the carbon going to CO2, and the remaining 20% to CO, what fraction of the heat calculated in question (a) is obtained? Ignore loss to the chimney. Assume all hydrogen goes to H2O(g) and unused oxygen remains as O2.

(d) Suppose that in order to achieve complete combustion, four times the minimum amount of air calculated in question (a) must be used. When so operated, how does the heat lost to the chimney compare with what would otherwise be lost through incomplete combustion, calculated in question (c)?

[(a) 9500 m^3; -32.4×10^6 kJ,   (b) 0.081
(c) 0.93,   (d) 0.28 lost vs 0.07 lost]

12. A bituminous coal from British Columbia was found to be 7.4% by mass moisture, 32.1% volatile hydrocarbons, 53.4% carbon, 1.0% sulphur and 6.1% incombustible materials. Taking the hydrocarbons, for model purposes, to be benzene, C_6H_6 (it is actually a very large group of chemicals), calculate the heat available per tonne from burning such a coal to $CO_2(g)$ and $H_2O(g)$ at 298 K. Allow for the vaporization of the moisture in the coal. Repeat the calculation for an Ontario lignite which is 46.7% by mass moisture, 30.2% volatile matter, 16.0% carbon, 1.0% sulphur and 6.1% noncombustible material.

[30.3 GJ; 16.3 GJ]

13. A fuel sometimes considered as a replacement for gasoline is hydrazine, N_2H_4, if an inexpensive way could be found for its manufacture. Cost is not the only problem but hydrazine does have the virtues of being liquid at ordinary temperatures (m.p. 275 K, b.p. 387 K) and of burning to non-polluting products. Calculate the heat available from the combustion of 50 L of hydrazine and compare it with the motor gasoline calculation of question 6-8(b). The density of liquid hydrazine is 1010 kg m^{-3}. Assume that the only process is

$$N_2H_4(l) + O_2(g) \rightarrow N_2(g) + 2H_2O(l)$$

[0.98 GJ vs. 1.7 GJ]

VII GASES AND LIQUIDS

In Chapter 4 the bulk properties of ideal gases were discussed and the ideal gas equation of state was introduced as a means of calculating these properties in a routine way. No real gas is ideal under all conditions, although all gases approach ideality at sufficiently low densities and sufficiently high temperatures. All gases condense to liquids if cooled to low enough temperatures. The formation of a liquid, in which the molecules are close together, is evidence of the existence of forces of attraction between molecules. The same forces which cause condensation are responsible for the deviations of the bulk properties of real gases from ideal behaviour.

In an ideal gas the molecules do not interact with each other, and it is possible to calculate certain properties of the gas from the laws of motion of the molecules. The properties so calculated apply to many real gases in which the deviations from ideality are small. In addition, it is possible to understand how intermolecular forces modify the bulk properties of real gases, using the kinetic theory of ideal gases as a basis.

7-1 THE KINETIC THEORY OF GASES

The similarities in the bulk properties of most gases are so striking that it is reasonable to suppose that only those properties that substances have in common are important in determining their behaviour in the gas state. The theory of gases is based upon Dalton's hypothesis that all materials are made of discrete particles, which will be called molecules even though in some cases a molecule consists of a single atom. The molecules are real objects which obey Newton's laws of motion, even though they are exceedingly tiny so that the motion of a single molecule cannot be seen by even the most powerful microscope.

Since liquids and solids are relatively incompressible, the molecules must be packed together in close contact with each other in these states. By contrast, a gas has a much lower density and is easily compressed, so the molecules must be widely separated from each other. A given molecule spends most of its time travelling in a straight line, only altering its velocity as a result of collisions with other molecules or with the walls of the vessel containing the gas.

The calculation of the properties of the gas from this model appears at first to be quite impossible. There are so many molecules in a sample of gas that we cannot write down Newton's equations of motion for each molecule individually, for that would take too much time and too much paper. The solution of all these equations of motion, about 10^{23} of them, would be more difficult still. Furthermore, the results of the calculation would be an apparently interminable list of positions and velocities, including details of all the collisions between molecules, and collisions of molecules with the walls. Such an immense list of numbers is in sharp contrast to the simplicity of the ideal gas equation of state, and would be quite useless without further calculations. Therefore, any molecular model for the properties of a gas must be essentially *statistical* in nature. The measured properties of a gas reflect the *average* behaviour of the molecules and so suitable averages of the velocities and positions of all the molecules must be calculated from the detailed list.

It is found that in a gas of low density with weak interactions between the molecules, the process of averaging makes it unnecessary to follow the motion of every molecule in detail. The greatest complication, the collisions between molecules, is found to have no effect on the results, and this greatly simplifies the calculation.

When a gas is cooled or compressed, its density increases, the molecules are closer together on average, and the effects of the intermolecular forces become important. The gas deviates from the ideal equation of state, the deviations increasing as the density increases and the temperature falls. Eventually the gas condenses to a liquid, and the molecules are held in contact with each other by intermolecular forces. The properties of the liquid are quite different from those of the gas, although it is the same molecules and the same intermolecular forces which govern the properties of both states of matter. Theories of dense gases and liquids are much more complicated than the theory of ideal gases, and have to take into account the different intermolecular forces for different chemical substances.

Progress has been made recently in calculating the properties of dense gases and liquids by solving the equations of motion of the molecules using large and fast computers. In these "computer model" calculations, a sample containing several hundred molecules is considered. The intermolecular forces are assumed to be known as a function of the distance between molecules, and the equations of motion for all the molecules are solved numerically so that the motion for all the molecules is known over a period of time. The density of the sample is set equal to that of a real gas or liquid, which means that the volume of the sample containing only a few hundred molecules is very small. However, molecules reaching the edge of the sample are treated mathematically in such a way that the sample behaves as if it were very large. In this way the problem of solving an immense number of equations of motion is avoided. When the motion of the molecules in the sample is known, the properties of the gas or liquid are calculated by carrying out the appropriate averages.

In this section, the theory of ideal gases is treated as a first step in understanding the relationship between molecular properties and the bulk and thermodynamic properties of materials. The implications of Boyle's law and Charles' law for molecular motion in gases are examined, and an important new principle, the *principle of equipartition of energy,* is demonstrated. The thermodynamic internal energy of an ideal gas is investigated and used to calculate the heat capacity of ideal monatomic gases numerically.

In order to proceed with this *statistical* approach to gases, it is necessary to assume that the motion of individual molecules is *random,* even though the motion of each molecule is governed by Newton's laws of motion. If a molecule were chosen at some instant of time, it is as likely to be moving in one direction as any other direction, and its speed may be low, medium or high compared with the speeds of other molecules. It may be found anywhere within the walls of the vessel containing the gas, and its next collision with another molecule may take place at any time in the near future. This assumption of randomness greatly simplifies the calculations.

The pressure exerted by the gas on the walls of the vessel is a result of the momentum change of the molecules as they collide with the walls. Pressure is a force per unit area, and since force is equal to the rate of change of momentum, pressure is equal to the total rate of change of the momentum of the molecules colliding with unit area of the wall. The pressure of a gas seems to an observer to be constant in time, but according to the theory it is the result of an enormous number of individual collisions of molecules with the wall. The pressure might be expected to fluctuate in time due to the randomness of the collisions, but ordinarily the fluctuations are too small to be covered. The fluctuations may be observed in very small systems.

For a gas at equilibrium all the bulk properties of the gas are constant in time. Hence any quantity which is added up for all the molecules is constant in time because of the enormous number of molecules present. Consider a single molecule in a gas containing N identical molecules in a cubic container with edges of length L. The corners of this cubic box of gas are labelled with letters as shown in Figure 7-1. The position of the molecule under consideration is

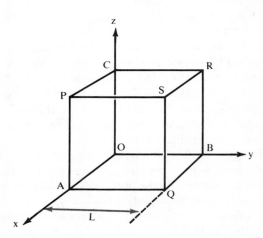

Figure 7-1.   The cubic box of gas used in developing the kinetic theory of gases.

specified by the coordinates x, y, z, and the velocity vector is specified by its three components u, v, and w along the x, y, and z axes respectively. The force on the molecule is specified by its three components F, G, and H along the same axes. These quantities are all functions of time since the molecule is moving at high speed and is colliding with the walls and with other molecules.

The distance of the molecule from the origin is $r = \sqrt{x^2+y^2+z^2}$, and the rate of change of r^2 is given by

$$\frac{d}{dt}(r^2) = 2\left(x\frac{dx}{dt} + y\frac{dy}{dt} + z\frac{dz}{dt}\right)$$

which can be rewritten

$$\frac{1}{2}\frac{d}{dt}(r^2) = xu + yv + zw$$

If this equation is differentiated again, we obtain

$$\frac{1}{2}\frac{d^2}{dt^2}(r^2) = \left(\frac{dx}{dt}u + \frac{dy}{dt}v + \frac{dz}{dt}w\right) + \left(x\frac{du}{dt} + y\frac{dv}{dt} + z\frac{dw}{dt}\right)$$

$$= (u^2 + v^2 + w^2) + \frac{1}{m}(xF + yG + zH)$$

where Newton's law of motion has been used to calculate the acceleration along each axis, and m is the mass of a molecule. If the corresponding equations for all the molecules in the gas are added up, we obtain

$$\frac{1}{2}\frac{d^2}{dt^2}(\Sigma r^2) = \Sigma(u^2 + v^2 + w^2) + \frac{1}{m}\Sigma(xF + yG + zH)$$

where the Σ sign means summation over all the molecules in the gas.

Now Σr^2 is the sum of the squares of the distances of all the molecules in the gas from the origin, and is constant in time because the gas is not in motion as a whole. In other words, the mean squared distance of the molecules from the origin is independent of time. Hence any time derivative of the quantity $\Sigma(r^2)$ is zero. In particular the left hand side of the last equation is zero:

$$0 = \Sigma(u^2 + v^2 + w^2) + \frac{1}{m}\Sigma(xF + yG + zH)$$

Rearranging the equation,

$$-\Sigma(xF + yG + zH) = \Sigma m(u^2 + v^2 + w^2)$$

The right hand side of this equation is equal to the total kinetic energy of all the molecules, except for a factor of $\frac{1}{2}$, and so this equation can be rewritten

$$-\Sigma(xF + yG + zH) = 2 \times \text{total kinetic energy} \qquad (1)$$

The left hand side of this equation is now considered in detail. For most of the time, any given molecule is moving freely through space, and the components of force, F, G and H, are zero. A molecule contributes to the summation on the left hand side only when it is involved in a collision with another molecule or with the walls.

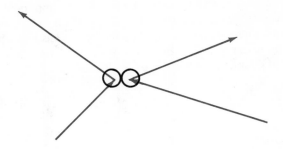

Figure 7-2 A representation of the collision between two molecules. The molecules are supposed to be extremely small and so when they collide, their centres are at almost the same place. It is also assumed that the molecules do not interact at all until they collide.

The collisions between molecules contribute nothing to the summation and can be ignored under certain circumstances. Suppose that molecule No. 1 collides with molecule No. 2, as shown in Figure 7-2. At the moment of collision the molecules exert equal and opposite forces on each other, and if the molecules are extremely small, they are at the same point in space, to a good approximation. These statements can be expressed mathematically by the equations

$$x_1 = x_2 \qquad\qquad y_1 = y_2 \qquad\qquad z_1 = z_2$$
$$F_1 = -F_2 \qquad\qquad G_1 = -G_2 \qquad\qquad H_1 = -H_2$$

and hence the total contribution of these two molecules in this collision to the left hand side of equation (1) is zero:

$$x_1F_1 + y_1G_1 + z_1H_1 + x_2F_2 + y_2G_2 + z_2H_2 = 0$$

The same result is true for all pairs of molecules which collide: the contributions of the two molecules cancel out.

Hence we conclude that collisions between molecules can be ignored as long as the molecules are sufficiently small. However, if the molecules exert forces on each other when their centres are separated by an appreciable distance, this proof is not valid, and then collisions between molecules have an effect on the bulk properties of the gas and the gas will not obey the ideal gas equation of state.

We next consider the collisions of the gas with the walls of the vessel, which is assumed to be that shown in Figure 7-1. The quantity $\Sigma(xF)$ is calculated first, and it must be recalled that only molecules colliding with the walls are being considered. First, notice that for all molecules colliding with the wall OBRC, $x = 0$, and so these molecules make no contribution to the summation. Second, the average force exerted by a wall on the molecules is perpendicular to that wall, and so the average value of F is zero for molecules colliding with the walls OAPC, CPSR, RSQB, and BQAO. This means that molecules colliding with these four walls make no contribution to $\Sigma(xF)$. Hence the only molecules to contribute to $\Sigma(xF)$ are those colliding with the wall APSQ. For all these molecules $x = L$, and so

$$\Sigma(xF) = L\Sigma F$$

But ΣF is the total force exerted by the wall on the molecules and so is equal to the pressure multiplied by the area. Hence

$$\Sigma(xF) = L \times (-P \times L^2)$$
$$= -PV$$

where V is the volume of the box. The negative sign indicates that the force on the molecules is directed along the negative x-axis. It is left as an exercise for the student to write out the argument to show that

$$\Sigma(yG) = \Sigma(zH) = -PV.$$

Collecting these three results together, the left hand side of equation (1) is equal to $-(-PV - PV - PV)$, and hence the equation can be rewritten

$$3PV = 2 \times \text{total kinetic energy}$$

or
$$PV = \tfrac{2}{3} \times \text{total kinetic energy} \qquad (2)$$

Hence we have deduced from our assumptions and the laws of mechanics that the product PV is related by a simple equation to the total kinetic energy of the molecules. Boyle's law is a rule which at first sight demonstrates the variation of pressure with volume, but once the relationship given in equation (2) is known the most interesting part of Boyle's law is the stipulation about temperature. Constancy of the temperature implies that the quantity PV is constant and hence, from theory supporting equation (2), the total kinetic energy of the molecules is constant. In other words, the total kinetic energy of the molecules is a function only of the temperature, and is independent of the pressure.

Charles' law can then be used to find out what is the functional relationship between temperature and kinetic energy. Since PV is proportional to temperature for an ideal gas, the total kinetic energy of the molecules is also proportional to the temperature. For one mole,

$$\text{total kinetic energy} = \tfrac{3}{2}PV = \tfrac{3}{2}RT \qquad (3)$$

where the ideal gas equation of state has been used.

Avogadro's hypothesis states that equal volumes of chemically different gases at the same temperature and pressure contain the same number of molecules. For the two chemically different samples of gas the product PV is the same, and hence the total kinetic energy of the molecules in one sample is the same as the total kinetic energy of the molecules in the other sample. Hence the average kinetic energy of the molecules in one sample must be the same as the average kinetic energy of the molecules in the other, even though the two samples are chemically different, and the molecules have different masses. This means that on the average, light molecules move faster than heavy molecules. This result is one aspect of a very general law of statistical physics called the *principle of equipartition of energy*.

The kinetic theory can be used to determine how fast the molecules in a gas are travelling. Because of collisions, the speed of a given molecule changes rapidly in a random way. Therefore, only an average speed can be determined.

For one mole of gas containing Avogadro's number of molecules, N_a, the total kinetic energy is $3RT/2$ from equation (3), and so the average kinetic energy of a single molecule is $3RT/2N_a$. The average kinetic energy of a molecule is equal to one half times the molecular mass times the average value of the square of the speed, and so

$$\tfrac{1}{2} m \langle v^2 \rangle = \frac{3RT}{2N_a}$$

Therefore

$$\langle v^2 \rangle = \frac{3RT}{mN_a} = \frac{3RT}{M}$$

where $M = mN_a$ is the molar mass and $\langle ... \rangle$ means the average value of the quantity inside the angular brackets. The square root of this equation gives the "root mean square" value of the speed of the molecule:

$$v_{rms} = \sqrt{\langle v^2 \rangle} = \sqrt{\frac{3RT}{M}} \tag{4}$$

The root mean square speed is approximately equal to the average or mean speed.

Example 7-1   Calculate the root mean square speed of an oxygen molecule at room temperature.

Taking $M = 0.032 \text{ kg mol}^{-1}$ and $T = 300 \text{ K}$,

$$v_{rms} = \sqrt{\frac{3 \times 8.314 \text{ J K}^{-1} \text{ mol}^{-1} \times 300 \text{ K}}{0.032 \text{ kg mol}^{-1}}}$$

$$= 483 \text{ m s}^{-1}$$

It should be noticed that the units in this equation are only correct if the molar mass is given in kilogram per mole. The inverse dependence of v_{rms} on the molar mass reflects the earlier noted fact that in a mixture of gases the lighter molecules move faster than the heavier molecules, on the average. This fact is used in the separation of isotopes of uranium by diffusion of gaseous uranium hexafluoride, UF_6, through porous barriers. The rate of diffusion of a gas through the tiny holes in the porous barrier is proportional to the root mean square speed of the molecules. Since the molar masses of $^{238}UF_6$ and $^{235}UF_6$ differ only slightly, the rates of diffusion differ only slightly, and significant separation can only be achieved by repeating the diffusion process many times.

The theory given in this section is known as the kinetic theory of gases. It originated primarily from the work of James Clerk Maxwell in Scotland and Ludwig Boltzmann in Germany. The theory goes on to calculate many other properties of gases in satisfactory agreement with experiment. The kinetic theory was one of the highlights of nineteenth century physics, and was particularly important because it was the origin of the use of *statistical mechanics* in describing the properties of materials in terms of the properties of the molecules of which the materials are composed. In the next section the kinetic theory is applied to the discussion of the heat capacities of gases.

7-2 THE HEAT CAPACITY OF A GAS

Gases are by far the most important materials used in the conversion of heat into mechanical work, and their thermodynamic properties are of great practical importance.

In monatomic gases, each molecule contains only one atom, and so has no way to store energy internally, apart from the electronic energy of the atoms which does not concern us here. Hence the thermodynamic internal energy U can be identified as the total kinetic energy of motion of the molecules. For one mole of a monatomic gas, therefore, the molar internal energy U_m can be written down explicitly using equation (3):

$$U_m = \tfrac{3}{2}RT \tag{5}$$

From this equation, we draw the very important conclusion that the internal energy of an ideal monatomic gas depends only on the temperature of the gas. For gases with diatomic or more complicated molecules, energy can be stored in the molecules in the form of vibrational or rotational energy, and the internal energy of the gas is larger than is indicated by equation (5). However, the energy stored within the molecules of a gas is not affected by the volume of the gas, and depends only on the temperature. Hence for all ideal gases, the internal energy depends only on the temperature of the gas and not on the pressure or volume. For any such gas, equation (5) gives the *translational* internal energy, or in other words the energy associated with the motion of the molecules through space.

From equation (5) the heat capacity of a monatomic gas can be calculated. If heat is added to a gas at constant volume, so that the temperature is raised by an amount ΔT, the internal energy changes by an amount $\Delta U_m = (3/2) R\Delta T$. The amount of heat required is $C_{vm}\Delta T$ by definition, and no work is done. Hence

$$\Delta U_m = \tfrac{3}{2}R\Delta T = C_{vm}\Delta T$$

and

$$C_{vm} = \tfrac{3}{2}R = 12.47 \text{ J K}^{-1}\text{ mol}^{-1} \tag{6}$$

Heat capacities of gases are often needed for conditions of constant pressure rather than constant volume, and the heat capacities given in Appendix I are C_{pm} values rather than C_{vm}. The value of C_{pm} is different from that of C_{vm} because energy has to be supplied to do the work of expansion against the constant external pressure as well as raising the temperature of the gas. We can calculate the value of C_{pm} from that of C_{vm} using the thermodynamic cycle shown in Figure 7-3. One mole of gas is heated from a temperature T to a slightly higher temperature T' by two different paths. In the first path the gas is heated at constant pressure, and the internal energy change is denoted ΔU_1. In the second path, the gas is heated from T to T' at constant volume, and then the volume of the gas is altered isothermally so that the final pressure is equal to the initial pressure. The change in internal energy in the second path is

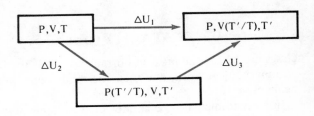

Figure 7-3 Thermodynamic cycle used to relate the heat capacity at constant volume to that at constant pressure.

equal to the sum of the internal energy changes for the two steps along this path, $\Delta U_2 + \Delta U_3$. Since these two paths have identical initial and final states, and the first law of thermodynamics assures us that the internal energy is a state function,

$$\Delta U_1 = \Delta U_2 + \Delta U_3$$

If the gas is ideal, then $\Delta U_3 = 0$ because there is no temperature change in this step. Furthermore, $\Delta U_2 = C_{vm}(T' - T)$ since the volume is constant in this step.

For the constant pressure path the change in internal energy is

$$\Delta U_1 = \text{heat} + \text{work}$$

$$= C_{pm}(T' - T) - P\Delta V \qquad \text{by equation (4) of Chapter 5}$$

$$= C_{pm}(T' - T) - P\left(\frac{VT'}{T} - V\right)$$

$$= C_{pm}(T' - T) - \frac{PV}{T}(T' - T)$$

$$= (C_{pm} - R)(T' - T)$$

Substituting these values for ΔU_1, ΔU_2 and ΔU_3 in the previous equation,

$$(C_{pm} - R)(T' - T) = C_{vm}(T' - T) + 0$$

from which it follows that

$$C_{pm} = C_{vm} + R \qquad (7)$$

This result is true for all ideal gases, and is a good approximation for most ordinary gases. For monatomic gases equations (6) and (7) can be combined to show that

$$C_{pm} = \tfrac{5}{2}R = 20.78 \text{ J K}^{-1} \text{ mol}^{-1} \qquad (8)$$

Appendix I lists the C_{pm} values for a number of gases. For the noble gases, which are monatomic, the heat capacity is given accurately by equation (8). Diatomic and polyatomic molecules have larger heat capacities because energy can be stored in the vibrational and rotational motion of the molecules. From the heat capacity of mercury vapour, it may be concluded that the vapour consists of single mercury atoms rather than molecules such as Hg_2.

Example 7-2 Calculate the molar heat capacity at constant volume for ethylene.

From Appendix I C_{pm} for ethylene is 43.6 J K^{-1} mol^{-1}. The heat capacity at constant volume is

$$C_{vm} = C_{pm} - R$$
$$= 43.6 - 8.3$$
$$= 35.3 \text{ J K}^{-1} \text{ mol}^{-1}$$

7-3 EQUATIONS OF STATE FOR REAL GASES

Real gases do not obey the ideal gas equation exactly, particularly at high pressure and low temperature. Under some circumstances the deviations from ideal behaviour are large enough to be important for accurate laboratory or industrial calculations. In such circumstances the ideal gas equation of state must be modified in a way which reflects the properties of each individual gas. There have been many attempts at modifications with the objective of describing the properties of a variety of gases over the widest possible range of conditions. Two of these equations of state will be described in this section. These equations do not "explain" the deviations from ideal behaviour, nor are they exactly obeyed by any gas. However, they are an improvement over the ideal gas equation of state as a way of calculating the bulk properties of real gases.

The Van der Waals equation is the best known non-ideal equation of state. It was proposed by the Dutch physical chemist J. D. Van der Waals in 1873. The equation is usually written in the form

$$(P + \frac{n^2 a}{V^2})(V - nb) = nRT \tag{9a}$$

but it is sometimes more convenient to use the molar volume $V_m = V/n$:

$$(P + \frac{a}{V_m^2})(V_m - b) = RT \tag{9b}$$

The constants a and b are chosen for each individual gas so as to fit the measured properties of the gas as closely as possible. The equation has a pressure factor and a volume factor on the left hand side, and so has the same form as the ideal gas equation. However, both factors contain correction terms. The correction $n^2 a/V^2$ in the pressure factor accounts for the forces of attraction between the molecules of the gas, which act when the molecules are close together. The correction nb in the volume factor is related to the volume of the molecules regarded as spheres which occupy space. Table 7-1 lists values of a and b for a number of gases for use in the Van der Waals equation. It should be noted that the values of a and b vary from gas to gas, and reflect the properties of each individual gas. By contrast the gas constant R is a universal constant of nature which applies to all gases.

TABLE 7-1   Parameters for the Van der Waals and Redlich-Kwong Equations of State

Gas	Van der Waals		Redlich-Kwong	
	a	b	a'	b'
He	0.00344	23.6	0.00795	18.4
H_2	0.0245	26.5	0.1428	20.7
Ne	0.0211	16.9	0.142	13.2
N_2	0.137	38.7	1.56	30.2
O_2	0.138	31.7	1.74	24.7
Cl_2	0.658	56.2	13.6	43.9
NH_3	0.424	37.3	8.66	29.1
SO_2	0.686	56.8	14.4	44.4
CO_2	0.366	42.8	6.47	33.4
H_2O	0.552	30.4	14.25	23.7
CH_4	0.229	42.9	3.21	33.5
C_2H_6	0.557	65.0	9.87	50.8
C_2H_4	0.455	57.4	7.76	44.8
C_2H_2	0.452	52.2	8.05	40.8
Units:	a: $N\ m^4\ mol^{-2}$		a': $N\ m^4\ K^{\frac{1}{2}}\ mol^{-2}$	
	b: $10^{-6}\ m^3\ mol^{-1}$ or $mL\ mol^{-1}$		b': $10^{-6}\ m^3\ mol^{-1}$ or $mL\ mol^{-1}$	

Example 7-3   What is the pressure in a tank containing 0.500 kg of carbon dioxide in a volume of 4.00 L at a temperature of 27°C? Use both the ideal and the Van der Waals equations of state.

The amount of CO_2 in the tank is 500 g/ 44.0 g mol^{-1}, or 11.4 mol. Hence the molar volume of the gas under these conditions is

$$V_m = 4.00 \times 10^{-3}\ m^3\ /\ 11.4\ mol$$

$$= 3.51 \times 10^{-4}\ m^3\ mol^{-1}$$

From the ideal gas equation of state, the pressure is

$$P = RT/V_m = \frac{8.314\ J\ K^{-1}\ mol^{-1} \times 300\ K}{3.51 \times 10^{-4} m^3\ mol^{-1}}$$

$$= 7.11 \times 10^6\ Pa = 7.11\ MPa$$

Using the Van der Waals equation of state with the values a = 0.366 N m^4 mol^{-2} and b = 42.8 × 10^{-6} m^3 mol^{-1} taken from Table 7-1,

$$P = \frac{8.314 \text{ J K}^{-1}\text{mol}^{-1} \times 300 \text{ K}}{(3.51 - 0.428) \times 10^{-4} \text{ m}^3 \text{ mol}^{-1}} - \frac{0.366 \text{ N m}^4 \text{ mol}^{-2}}{(3.51 \times 10^{-4})^2 \text{ m}^6 \text{ mol}^{-2}}$$

$$= 5.12 \times 10^6 \text{ Pa} = 5.12 \text{ MPa}.$$

The units of the various quantities in Van der Waals equation require a little careful study.

The Van der Waals equation is important because it was the first non-ideal equation of state, is simple to deal with algebraically, and correctly describes the qualitative features of the behaviour of real gases. However, it is not numerically accurate under all conditions and a number of equations have been suggested which are more satisfactory numerically. The simplest of these equations is that proposed by O. Redlich and J.N.S. Kwong, two American chemical engineers. The Redlich-Kwong equation is:

$$\left(P + \frac{a'}{T^{\frac{1}{2}} V_m (V_m + b')} \right)(V_m - b') = RT \qquad (10)$$

The constants a' and b' must be determined for each gas, like the corresponding constants in the Van der Waals equation. The form of the equation is similar to that of the Van der Waals equation, but the correction term in the pressure factor is different. The form of the equation was chosen to give good agreement with experiment without using more than two adjustable parameters, and there is no theoretical basis for it. Values of a' and b' for use in this equation are given in Table 7-1.

Example 7-4   Repeat the calculation of Example 7-3 using the Redlich-Kwong equation.

From Table 7-1, $a' = 6.47 \text{ N m}^4 \text{ K}^{\frac{1}{2}} \text{mol}^{-2}$ and $b' = 33.4 \times 10^{-6} \text{ m}^3 \text{ mol}^{-1}$, and so the pressure is given by

$$P = \frac{8.314 \times 300.}{(3.51 - 0.334) \times 10^{-4}} - \frac{6.47}{\sqrt{300} \times 3.51 \times 10^{-4} \times (3.51 + 0.334) \times 10^{-4}}$$

$$= 5.08 \times 10^6 \text{ Pa} = 5.08 \text{ MPa}.$$

The units of the various quantities in this equation need careful study, and great care is needed in adding or subtracting quantities with different powers of 10, as usually happens in the quantities $V_m + b'$ and $V_m - b'$. The answer to this example does not differ greatly from that obtained using Van der Waals equation, and both non-ideal equations are in much better agreement with experiment than the ideal equation. The Redlich-Kwong equation is noticeably more accurate than the Van der Waals equation in the vicinity of the critical point, which will be defined shortly.

7-4   THE PROPERTIES OF LIQUIDS

In comparison with a gas, a liquid has a high density, and is relatively incompressible. For a given amount of material the volume is small, and almost independent of the external pressure on the sample. A liquid is also coherent, and retains its characteristic density even if the volume of the container is larger than the volume of the sample. All these properties indicate that the molecules in a liquid are held in close contact by intermolecular forces. The molecules may be considered to be in almost continuous collision with each other, whereas in a gas the molecules collide relatively infrequently, and spend most of their time travelling in straight lines.

In the discussion of the kinetic theory of gases, it was shown that the bulk properties of gases are only slightly affected by the collisions between molecules, and so the bulk properties are almost independent of the properties of the molecules (apart from the molar mass of course). The reverse is true for liquids. Since the molecules are in close contact with their neighbours, the interactions between the molecules are very important in determining the properties of liquids. Notwithstanding this, many liquids have properties in common, and general rules describing their behaviour have been formulated.

When a liquid is heated, it can be converted to a gas (sometimes called a vapour) by *boiling* or by *evaporation*. Since the vapour consists of the same molecules which form the liquid, the properties of the liquid are correlated with those properties which are specific to that substance, namely the deviations from ideal behaviour. Another way of expressing this is that the deviations from ideal behaviour as measured by the Van der Waals or Redlich-Kwong (or similar) constants for the particular substance reflect the way the molecules interact with each other during collisions; in the liquid it is the same interactions between the molecules which are dominant in determining the properties of the liquid.

When a liquid is heated in an open vessel, the temperature of the liquid rises until the liquid starts to boil. While a pure liquid is boiling the temperature is constant. The *boiling point* temperature is a characteristic of each chemical substance, as long as the atmospheric pressure is constant. However, the boiling point measured in the laboratory varies with the weather due to variations in the atmospheric pressure. Standard boiling point data are quoted at the standard pressure of 101.325 kPa.

When a liquid is cooled by removal of heat, the temperature drops until the process of *freezing* begins. Once a small amount of solid is formed by freezing, further removal of heat converts more liquid to solid but the temperature remains fixed at the *freezing point* temperature, again with the proviso that the liquid be pure. Addition of heat to a mixture of solid and liquid at the freezing point causes melting of some of the solid, but no change in the temperature of the mixture. The freezing point temperature is a characteristic property of each chemical substance. When a liquid is cooled initially, it is often possible to lower the temperature below the freezing point of the liquid. This is particularly true of liquids which are very pure and free from dust. This phenomenon is called *supercooling*. Supercooled liquids can sometimes be maintained for long periods of time at temperatures of several degrees or more below the freezing point. Crystallization can be induced by adding a small "seed" crystal, by scratching the container, or by lowering the temperature further at one point in the liquid.

The processes of freezing and evaporation of a pure liquid are somewhat more complicated than is apparent from observation of freezing or boiling in an open vessel. In order to investigate these phenomena fully it is necessary to take a pure system isolated from the atmosphere in a closed container such as the apparatus shown in Figure 7-4. The liquid must be chemically pure, and even dissolved gases such as oxygen from the atmosphere must be removed.

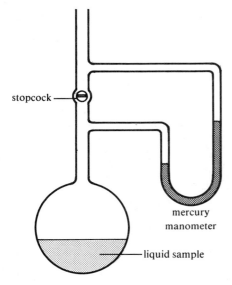

stopcock

mercury
manometer

liquid sample

Figure 7-4 Apparatus for measuring the vapour pressure of a liquid.

All the air is removed from the space above the liquid by means of a vacuum pump. During this evacuation, the liquid sample is frozen at a very low temperature to prevent evaporation. Then the stopcock is closed, and the liquid sample is warmed up to the temperature of interest. It is found that the mercury manometer indicates that there is a pressure in the bulb due to evaporation of the liquid in the bulb. The measured pressure is a function of the temperature of the liquid, but is independent of the amount of liquid present (as long as there is some there), and of the volume available to the vapour above the liquid. The pressure is called the *vapour pressure* of the liquid at that temperature. The vapour pressure has a characteristic value for each substance at each temperature. The vapour pressure rises rapidly with temperature. Figure 7-5 shows the vapour pressures of several substances as functions of temperature, and the mathematical form of these curves will be discussed in detail in a later chapter.

Careful measurements show that solids also have vapour pressures. Figure 7-5 shows that liquids have very small vapour pressures at low temperatures, and the vapour pressures of solids are usually very small indeed. The conversion of a solid directly to the vapour state without the presence of liquid is called *sublimation,* and is an important process for some substances. Under at-

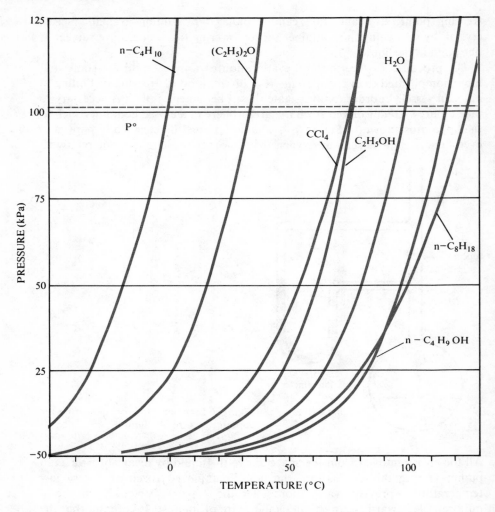

Figure 7-5 The vapour pressure of several compounds as a function of temperature. The dotted line shows the value of standard pressure, 101.325 kPa.

mospheric pressure, solid carbon dioxide evaporates without melting, and so is a convenient refrigerant called *dry ice*. On a cold sunny day in late winter when snow is lying on the ground, no appreciable melting of the snow takes place, but substantial amounts of snow are removed by evaporation under the influence of the radiation from the sun.

The process of boiling can be described in terms of the vapour pressure curves given in Figure 7-5. Normally boiling takes place when heat is applied to the bottom of an open container of liquid. When a bubble is formed on the bottom of the vessel, the fate of the bubble is determined by the pressure of the gas inside it. The gas consists mainly of the vapour formed from the liquid, together with some oxygen and nitrogen from the air which was dissolved in the liquid. The bubble is subjected to the pressure of the atmosphere, plus a small contribution from the hydrostatic pressure and surface tension effects. If the gas pressure inside the bubble is larger than the external pressure it will expand and rise to the surface of the liquid, otherwise it will collapse and disappear. Hence, boiling takes place at the temperature at which the vapour pressure of the liquid is equal to the pressure of the atmosphere. The standard boiling points of the liquids in Figure 7-5 may be read from the vapour pressure curves at the points where each curve crosses the horizontal line at a pressure of 101.325 kPa. Atmospheric pressure varies from day to day due to changes in weather conditions, and so the boiling point also varies, in a way that depends on the slope of vapour pressure curve in Figure 7-5.

Energy is required to evaporate a solid or liquid, or to melt a solid to a liquid. Energy absorbed in changes of state is called *latent heat,* since it is usually supplied in the form of heat which produces no change in temperature. Examples of latent heat calculations have been discussed in Chapter 5, and some data on latent heats are contained in the thermochemical tables in Appendix I. Like all enthalpy changes, latent heats are almost independent of temperature; the temperature dependence of a latent heat can be calculated if the heat capacities of the two states of the material are known.

It can be shown that the principle of equipartition of energy mentioned in Section 7-1 applies to the molecules in a liquid as well as to molecules in a gas. This is so even though the nature of the motion of a molecule in a liquid is quite different from that in a gas. Hence, at equal temperatures, the average kinetic energy of translation of a molecule in a liquid is the same as that of a molecule in the gas state, namely $3RT/2N_a$. Hence the latent heat of vaporization which is absorbed when the molecule leaves the liquid and becomes part of the gas makes no difference to the *kinetic energy* of the molecule, and so must be equal to the change in the *potential energy* of the molecules. The potential energy of the molecules in a liquid is due to the interactions of the molecules with each other, and so the latent heat of vaporization of a liquid is a measure of the energy of the intermolecular interactions. The absorption of latent heat in the process of vaporization does not make the molecules move any faster on the average. The latent heat of melting is much smaller than the latent heat of vaporization because there is only a small change in the total energy of the intermolecular interactions when a solid is melted.

The latent heat of vaporization is employed in the ordinary refrigerator or heat pump. The working fluid is compressed to a pressure at which it is a liquid at a temperature somewhat above room temperature. The latent heat associated with this *condensation* is released and must be removed to the surroundings (the room) using a *heat exchanger,* often called the *condenser.* The compressed liquid is then allowed to expand through a small hole to a region of low pressure. At this low pressure the stable state of the working fluid is the gas state, and so evaporation takes place. The latent heat required for the evaporation is supplied from the inside of the refrigerator; evaporation takes place in another heat exchanger, called the *evaporator,* placed inside the refrigerator. After evaporation, the vapour is recompressed and the cycle is repeated.

A moderately efficient cooler can be made by allowing water to evaporate from a cloth which acts as a wick. This will not work if the humidity is high,

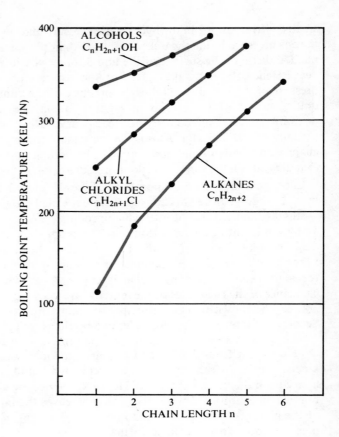

Figure 7-6 The boiling points of three series of organic straight chain compounds, the alkanes, alkyl chlorides, and alcohols, plotted as a function of chain length.

but under desert conditions food and water can be kept cool by this method. Water can be kept cool in a canvas bag through which it seeps slowly and evaporates. The latent heat of vaporization is removed from the water in the bag, which is thereby kept cool.

Boiling points generally increase with molar mass for a series of similar molecules, as shown in Figure 7-6 for the alkanes, alkyl chlorides and alcohols. For the hydrides of the non-metals, the boiling point is a periodic property. Figure 7-7 shows the boiling points of the series CH_4, NH_3, H_2O, HF and the noble gas Ne, and of the corresponding series of compounds for the second, third and fourth rows of the periodic table. The similarity of the trends in the various rows is apparent, but clearly the first row compounds NH_3, H_2O and HF are anomalous because of some effect which does not influence the properties of the other compounds. This effect is *hydrogen bonding,* which is found to occur in molecules containing hydrogen bonded to nitrogen, oxygen or fluorine. The effect of hydrogen bonding can also be recognized in Figure 7-6, which shows that alcohols have higher boiling points than the corresponding alkyl chlorides. Increased boiling point suggests that the energy of the intermolecular interactions is increased, and hence the heat of vaporization of hydrogen bonded liquids ought to be abnormally high, as is indeed the case.

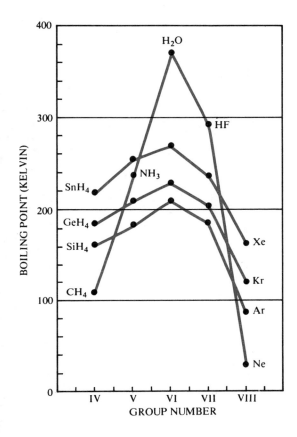

Figure 7-7 The boiling points of the hydrides of the non-metals and of the noble gases plotted against the group number of the non-metal in the periodic table. Compounds belonging to the same row of the periodic table are joined together by lines.

For many liquids the ratio of the latent heat of vaporization to the boiling point temperature has roughly the same value, lying between 75 and 90 J K^{-1} mol^{-1}. This empirical rule is known as *Trouton's Rule,* and can be expressed as the following equation:

$$\frac{\Delta H_{vap}}{T_b} \approx 75 \text{ to } 90 \text{ J K}^{-1} \text{ mol}^{-1}$$

Thus a liquid with a high boiling point can be expected to have a high latent heat of vaporization too. For hydrogen bonded liquids, the latent heat of vaporization is even larger than Trouton's rule would predict, and the ratio $\Delta H_{vap}/T_b$ can be as large as 120 J K^{-1} mol^{-1}. Some values of this ratio for various liquids are given in Table 7-2.

7-5 THE CRITICAL POINT

When a liquid is heated, its vapour pressure rises steeply, as shown by the graphs in Figure 7-5, and hence the density of the vapour or gas in equilibrium with the liquid increases. At the same time the density of the liquid decreases because of thermal expansion. Therefore the densities of the liquid and of the

TABLE 7-2   The Trouton's Law Ratio for Various Liquids

Liquid	T_b K	$\Delta H_{vap}/T_b$ J K^{-1} mol^{-1}
He	4.2	20
H_2	20	44
N_2	77	72
O_2	90	76
CH_4	112	73
C_2H_6	185	79
C_6H_6	353	98
NH_3	240	97
H_2O	373	109
CH_3OH	338	112
C_2H_5OH	351	122
CH_3Cl	249	86
C_2H_5Cl	286	84

vapour in equilibrium with it tend to approach each other at high temperatures.

Consider a strong closed vessel of fixed volume containing some pure liquid. The space above the liquid has been previously evacuated so that it contains only the vapour of the liquid at the vapour pressure corresponding to the temperature of the system. Consider what happens when the temperature of the system is increased. The vapour pressure increases and so some of the liquid must evaporate to provide the increase. At the same time thermal expansion reduces the density of the liquid. As the temperature is raised further, these trends continue. Of course, if there isn't very much liquid in the container to start with, the liquid may eventually all evaporate in a simple way; as the temperature increases the meniscus or surface of the liquid falls lower and lower in the vessel until it reaches the bottom. However if more liquid is added to the vessel it is possible to bring the system to a state where the meniscus disappears in a different way. It is possible for the densities of the liquid and gas phases to become equal before the liquid has all evaporated, and then the difference between the two phases of the system vanishes. The surface separating the liquid from the gas can be seen to disappear, at a temperature called the *critical temperature* T_c. At temperatures above the critical temperature, the system exists in only one phase, which can be described as a very dense gas. The pressure of the system at the critical point has a unique value for a given substance, called the *critical pressure* P_c.

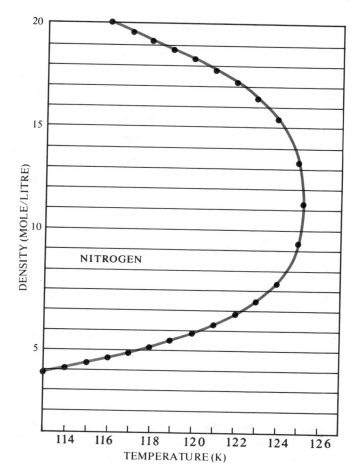

Figure 7-8 The densities of the liquid and vapour phases of a substance in equilibrium at the vapour pressure, plotted as a function of temperature. The two densities become equal at the critical temperature, T_c.

Figure 7-8 shows the way in which the densities of the liquid and gas phases approach each other at the critical temperature. Just below the critical temperature, the two densities vary rapidly with temperature, as the liquid density drops and the gas density rises. The two curves join smoothly at the critical point with a vertical tangent. From the density of the system at the critical point, the *critical volume* per mole of the system, V_c, can be calculated.

The bulk properties of the gas phase are very sensitive to changes in temperature and pressure in the vicinity of the critical point, and it is essential to use an equation of state such as the Van der Waals equation or the Redlich-Kwong equation when calculating the properties of a gas in this region. The constants a and b, or a′ and b′, in these equations which are tabulated in Table 7-1 are chosen so that the equations yield correct values for the critical pressure and critical temperature. Of these two equations, the Redlich-Kwong equation is the more accurate in predicting the bulk properties of gases in the vicinity of the critical point.

The critical point parameters P_c, V_c and T_c reflect the intermolecular interactions in each substance, and so there is a great variation in these

TABLE 7-3   Critical Point Data for Various Substances

Substance	T_c K	P_c MPa	$P_c V_c / RT_c$	T_b / T_c
He	5.2	0.229	0.307	0.79
H_2	33.0	1.294	0.309	0.61
Ne	44.4	2.73	0.308	0.61
N_2	126.2	3.39	0.291	0.61
O_2	154.8	5.08	0.308	0.58
Cl_2	417	7.71	0.276	0.57
NH_3	405	11.30	0.243	0.59
SO_2	431	7.88	0.269	0.61
CO_2	304	7.38	0.274	—
H_2O	647	22.12	0.243	0.58
CH_4	190.6	7.88	0.269	0.59
C_2H_6	305.4	4.88	0.284	0.60
C_2H_4	282.6	5.12	0.278	0.60
C_2H_2	308.4	6.14	0.271	0.61

parameters between substances. Table 7-3 lists critical point data for a number of common substances. There are two empirical rules about the critical parameters which can be added to Trouton's rule as a summary of the properties of many liquids.

The first rule is that the ratio of the boiling point temperature to the critical temperature, T_b/T_c, is close to 0.6 for many liquids. This rule seems to hold true even for a strongly hydrogen-bonded liquid like water. Thus if the boiling point of a liquid is known, its critical temperature can be estimated from this rule.

The second rule is that the quantity $P_c V_c/RT_c$ lies in the range 0.25 to 0.30 for many liquids. If the substance were to obey the ideal gas law at the critical point, this quantity would of course be one. For a substance obeying the Van der Waals equation, $P_c V_c/RT_c$ would be 0.375, and for a substance obeying the Redlich-Kwong equation, 0.334. It should be noted from Figure 7-8 that the critical density, and hence the critical volume, is hard to determine experimentally.

7-6   PHASE DIAGRAMS FOR PURE SUBSTANCES

It is possible to summarize information about the freezing. and evaporation of liquids in a single diagram called the *phase diagram*. There are a number of

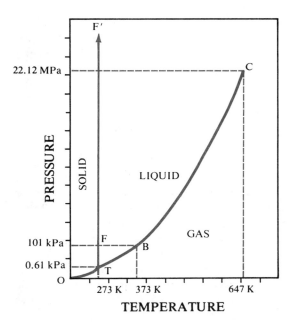

Figure 7-9 The phase diagram for water. In order to display the phenomena around the point T properly, both the temperature and pressure scales have been distorted. Numerical values are given so that the various points can be identified.

different sorts of phase diagrams which are used in various different circumstances, but we are concerned here with the phase diagrams used to describe the properties of a pure substance, sometimes called a single *component*. Phase diagrams are very useful in interpreting and predicting the behaviour of substances when the conditions of temperature, pressure or volume are changed.

The phase diagram for water is shown in Figure 7-9, and consists of three lines labelled OT, TBC and OFF′. The three lines separate the diagram into three regions labelled solid, liquid and gas. The diagram is not to scale along either axis, because the large range of pressures involved makes it impossible to show the details around the point T on a diagram drawn to scale. The diagram is a description of the phases occurring in pure water, contained in a sealed vessel from which all air and other substances have been removed.

The line TBC is the graph of the vapour pressure of water as a function of temperature, and a section of this curve has already been met in Figure 7-5. When liquid water is in equilibrium with water vapour, the state of the system is represented by a point on the line TBC at the appropriate temperature. The pressure in the system is fixed and equal to the vapour pressure no matter what the volume of the vessel. If the volume of the vessel is increased, then more water evaporates so that the pressure is maintained. Indeed, if the volume of the vessel becomes very large, the water will all evaporate and the liquid phase will disappear. If the volume is increased still further, then the pressure drops in accordance with the equation of state for water vapour. The state of the system is then represented by a point on the phase diagram below the line TBC in the region labelled "gas." The exact position of the point in the diagram is fixed by the temperature and pressure of the water vapour.

If the system is compressed, on the other hand, water vapour condenses to form liquid water. The pressure remains equal to the vapour pressure as long as some vapour remains. Eventually, as the volume is reduced, all the vapour is condensed. Further reduction of the volume results in a rapid rise in the pressure, since liquid water is rather incompressible. The state of the system is now represented by a point in the phase diagram above the line TBC, in the region labelled "liquid."

Thus the line TBC represents states of the system when both liquid and gas phases are present. The point B represents the standard boiling point of water, at which the vapour presure is equal to the standard pressure of 101.325 kPa. The point C represents the critical point, at which the gas and liquid states become identical in their properties. The line TBC which separates the gas and liquid regions ends at C. It is therefore possible to convert the system from the gas state to the liquid state without crossing the two-phase boundary line TBC, by heating the gas above the critical temperature T_c, compressing it to a pressure above P_c, cooling it back to a lower temperature and finally reducing the pressure.

If a system consisting of liquid water and water vapour is cooled to the vicinity of 0°C, the water begins to freeze and form ice. It is therefore possible to have solid, liquid and gas phases present simultaneously. While three phases are present, the temperature and pressure are both fixed at the values given for the point T. This point is called the *triple point* because three phases are present at once, and has a characteristic temperature and pressure for each substance.

If the temperature is lowered further, the liquid water is completely frozen, and a small amount of vapour is still present. The state of the system is then represented by a point on the curve OT, which is a graph of the vapour pressure of ice. Sublimation is the conversion of solid directly to vapour across the line OT.

The line TFF′ represents the melting of ice to form liquid water. When ice is heated at a pressure of 101 kPa, as happens for ice in contact with the atmosphere, it is converted to water by melting at the point F, which represents a mixture of ice and liquid water at this pressure. As long as there is some ice and some water present, the temperature is fixed, and has been defined as zero on the Celsius scale. The point F, then, represents the freezing point of water, or the melting point of ice, at atmospheric pressure. By contrast the triple point T is the freezing point of water, or melting point of ice, under its own vapour pressure. The temperature of the triple point need not be the same as that of the freezing point, and for water the triple point temperature is +0.01°C. Hence in the case of water the line TFF′ slopes slightly to the left.

The slope of the line TFF′ for a given substance depends on the relative volumes per mole of the liquid and solid phases. Ice is less dense than water. When ice in equilibrium with water is subjected to an increase of pressure, Le Chatelier's principle of equilibrium predicts that some ice will melt, since water occupies less volume than ice under the same conditions. Therefore, for water, an increase of pressure at constant temperature moves the system from the solid state to the liquid state, and so the line TFF′ must slope to the left. For the great majority of substances the liquid contracts when it freezes, and correspondingly, the line TFF′ slopes to the right.

The line TFF' continues on up to very high pressures. At very high pressures ordinary ice changes to other forms of ice which have different crystal structures, which do not concern us at this stage. The important point to know is that there is no critical point terminating the line TFF'.

It has been found experimentally that, for a given system, there is an upper limit to the number of phases that can exist in equilibrium, and an upper limit to the number of variables such as temperature, pressure and composition that can change while still maintaining equilibrium among phases. These restrictions have also been proved from the laws of thermodynamics, and are an important aid in the study of phase diagrams. The restrictions are summarized in a single equation:

$$F = C - P + 2$$

This equation is called the *phase rule*. In the equation, P represents the number of phases present, C the number of components, or different chemical substances present in the system, and F is the number of variables that can be varied independently, sometimes called the number of degrees of freedom. The phase rule has nothing to do with the amount of each phase present.

The phase rule is most useful in dealing with the phase diagrams for mixtures, in which C is 2 or more, but it is instructive to see how the rule applies to the case of a pure substance, and correctly describes the behaviour that has already been discussed. For a pure substance, there is only one component, and so C = 1 and the phase rule becomes

$$F = 3 - P$$

We have seen that water can exist as a liquid over a range of temperatures, and at each temperature, over a range of pressures too. Therefore, there are two degrees of freedom for the system in this state. In the phase rule, P = 1 for a single phase, and so F must be 2, in agreement with observation.

At any given pressure, ice exists in equilibrium with water at only one temperature, the melting point. The pressure may be chosen at will, but once the pressure is chosen, the temperature is fixed if ice and water are to be present simultaneously and at equilibrium. The same situation applies to the equilibrium between water and water vapour, and to the equilibrium between ice and water vapour. For these three cases, the point representing the state of the system lies along one of the lines TFF', TBC or OT in Figure 7-9. In each case only one variable can be chosen independently. In the phase rule, P = 2 since there are two phases, and hence F = 1, showing that there is one degree of freedom, in agreement with observation.

Finally, at the triple point T neither the temperature nor the pressure can be varied without one of the phases disappearing. The state of the system is entirely determined by the nature of the substance forming the system. Since there are three phases, P = 3 and so F = 0, indicating that there are no degrees of freedom.

FURTHER READING

Further discussion of the material in this chapter is to be found in books such as "Physical Chemistry" by P. W. Atkins (Oxford University Press, 1978), and in more specialized books on kinetic theory and the properties of gases. A set of collected readings on the history of the theory of gases is the three volume set "Kinetic Theory" by S. G. Brush (Pergamon Press, 1965).

J. V. Sengers and A. L. Sengers describe an interesting demonstration of critical point phenomena in an article in the journal *Chemical and Engineering News*, Volume 46, No. 25, page 104, 1968. O. Redlich and J.N.S. Kwong describe their equation in an article in *Chemical Reviews*, Volume 44, page 233, published in 1949.

PROBLEMS

1. Calculate the total kinetic energy of molecular translational motion per mole of nitrogen at 25°C.

   [3.72 kJ mol^{-1}]

2. Calculate the root mean square molecular speed of a nitrogen molecule at 25°C.

   [515 m s^{-1}]

3. How much heat per mole is required to raise the temperature of nitrogen gas from 20°C to 100°C
   (a) at constant pressure, and
   (b) at constant volume?

   [2.34 kJ mol^{-1}, 1.68 kJ mol^{-1}]

4. Calculate the ratio C_p/C_v for three monatomic gases, three diatomic gases, three triatomic gases, and three tetratomic gases from the data in Appendix 1. Do not include gases that contain hydrogen atoms. Comment upon your results as fully as you can.

5. Calculate the ratio of the root mean square molecular speeds of two UF_6 molecules in the gas phase, one containing the uranium isotope ^{235}U and the other the isotope ^{238}U. Note that there is only one naturally abundant fluorine isotope, ^{19}F.

   [1.0043]

6. A bulb contains 0.200 mol of pure nitrogen gas at a temperature of 300 K. The gas is heated to 400 K using an electrical heater without any change in volume.
   (a) How much energy is needed to heat the gas?
   (b) What fraction of the energy added is converted to the kinetic energy of translational motion of the molecules.
   (c) What happens to the rest of the energy which was added?

   [420 J, 0.594]

7. A container of volume 4.40 L contains 68.0 g of ammonia at a temperature of 330 K.
   (a) Calculate the pressure using the ideal gas equation.
   (b) Calculate the pressure using Van der Waals' equation.
   (c) Calculate the pressure using the Redlich-Kwong equation.

   [2.49 MPa, 2.23 MPa, 2.18 MPa]

8. A 0.1000 L vessel contains 142.0 mg of carbon dioxide at a pressure of 790.1 torr. Calculate the temperature of the vessel using Van der Waals' equation.

   [393.3 K]

9. A 42 L commercial cylinder contains 11 kg of oxygen when full. Use the Redlich-Kwong equation to calculate the pressure in such a cylinder at a temperature of 20°C.

   [19 MPa]

10. Use the data in Figure 7-5 to estimate the boiling point of water high on a mountain where the atmospheric pressure is 60 kPa.

    [86°C]

11. For CO_2 the triple point occurs at a pressure of 0.518 MPa and a temperature of 216.6 K. Solid CO_2, or "dry ice," in contact with the atmosphere maintains a temperature of approximately 195 K. Use these data together with critical point data from Table 7-3 to draw a sketch of the phase diagram for CO_2. Explain why dry ice remains dry as it evaporates. Explain how you would prepare a sample of liquid CO_2.

VIII PERIODICITY IN THE PROPERTIES OF THE ELEMENTS

In thermodynamics and in the properties of gases, we have been concerned primarily with similarities among all materials. We have emphasized, for example, that all systems undergoing a process are subject to the first law and that all materials, in their gaseous state, approach at low pressure the behaviour predicted by the ideal gas equation of state.

Chemistry is equally concerned, of course, with understanding the *differences* among materials. Why do materials have such widely differing boiling points, or optical properties or reactivities with oxygen? Consideration of these and countless other properties long ago led chemists to realize that there were many cases where several elements exhibited marked similarities to one another in nearly all of their properties. Some sort of rule was sought which could rationalize these similarities.

Döbereiner expressed his faith in a rationalization based partly on atomic weights as early as 1817, and many chemists sought to find one. As the number of discovered elements increased and the accuracy of determinations of the molar mass of elements improved, the basis for doing so became ever stronger. Mendeleev, in 1869, published the first organization including all of the essential features of the modern periodic table, but others had contributed greatly to the development, notably Newlands in 1866 and Meyer in 1868. All three deserve substantial, perhaps equal, credit. Von Spronsen, whose book is listed at the end of this chapter, has produced a concise and highly readable history of this development.

What Newlands, Meyer and Mendeleev proposed was that if the elements were ordered by molar mass, many properties of the elements and their compounds recurred in a predictable way along the series. Where a gap existed, Mendeleev correctly predicted the existence of a then unknown element having properties appropriate to that place.

In fact, the regularity of the repeating patterns generated by considering molar mass is excellent but not perfect. Three adjacent pairs of elements, each with closely similar molar masses, must be transposed in order for there to be complete regularity. Such deviations suggest that an even more fundamental basis exists for ordering the elements. This is the quantity known as the atomic number, described in Section 9-7.

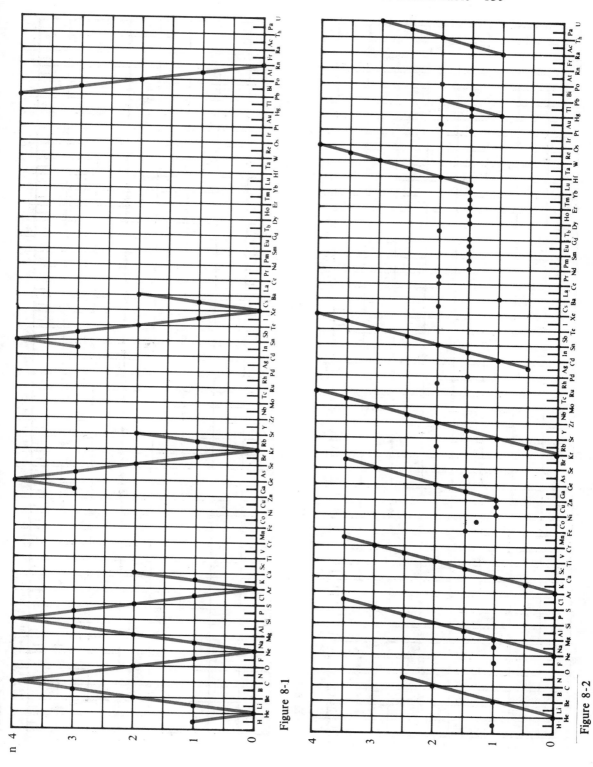

Figure 8-1

Figure 8-2

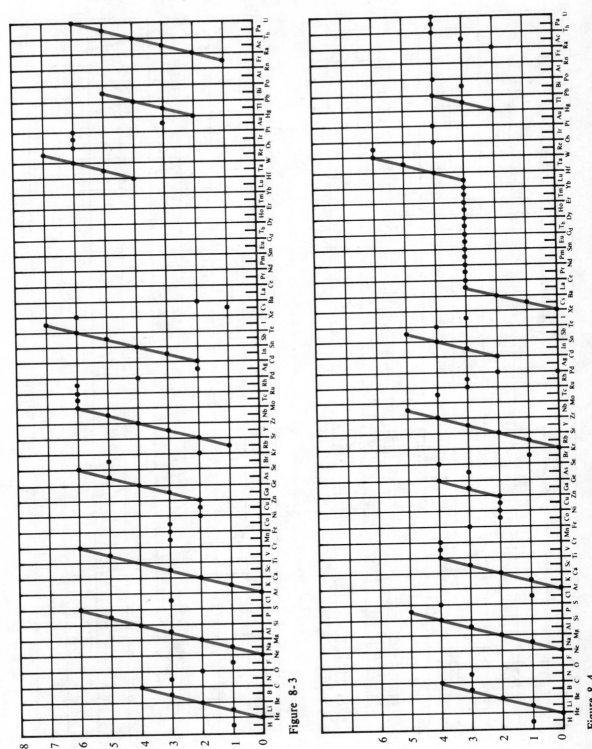

Figure 8-3

Figure 8-4

Returning to the way in which properties vary periodically, consider the compounds which each element forms with hydrogen. In some cases, more than one compound may form, as in H_2O and H_2O_2 or PH_3 and P_2H_4. Focus in each case on the compound having the highest ratio of hydrogen to the element (H_2O and PH_3 in the examples above). In Figure 8-1, the elements are arranged in order of increasing atomic number and the hydrogen to element ratio in the ''highest'' hydride is plotted for each. It is clear that in this one property, there is a repeating sequence of behaviour in the elements. The elements lithium, sodium, potassium, rubidium and caesium not only have the same ratio but each occurs at the same point in the repeating sequences. The same could be said of calcium, strontium, beryllium and magnesium as a group. There is a basis for organization here but more properties must be examined, both to reinforce our tentative conclusions based on the hydrides and to extend our organization to other elements, such as those from scandium to zinc, which do not have well characterized hydrides.

Figures 8-2, 8-3 and 8-4 illustrate the analogous property for the formation of oxides, fluorides and chlorides respectively. The periodicity is similar but there are instructive differences. An elementary one is that n for hydrides, fluorides and chlorides is usually double what it is for oxides. There are more subtle differences too. The elements which we shall call the d-block elements, from scandium to zinc and from yttrium to cadmium,stand apart in that their hydrides are of variable composition. For oxides, fluorides and chlorides, however, the early members of each d-block series show a continuation of the trends seen in the elements preceding them. The later members usually form a compound, although they are erratic in their values of n. One feature common to all four plots is the spacing of the sloping lines. The spacing is 8, 8, 10, 8, 10, 8, 14, 10, 8. Remember that the elements are placed in order of increasing atomic number which is almost, although not quite, the order of increasing molar mass.

If the elements are written from left to right, in order of increasing atomic number, beginning a new row as each new cycle of properties begins so that similar elements lie one below the other, we obtain the organization shown in Figure 8-5.

H																															He
Li	Be																									B	C	N	O	F	Ne
Na	Mg																									Al	Si	P	S	Cl	Ar
K	Ca															Sc	Ti	V	Cr	Mn	Fe	Co	Ni	Cu	Zn	Ga	Ge	As	Se	Br	Kr
Rb	Sr															Y	Zr	Nb	Mo	Tc	Ru	Rh	Pd	Ag	Cd	In	Sn	Sb	Te	I	Xe
Cs	Ba	La	Ce	Pr	Nd	Pm	Sm	Eu	Gd	Tb	Dy	Ho	Er	Tm	Yb	L	Hf	Ta	W	Re	Os	Ir	Pt	Au	Hg	Tl	Pb	Bi	Po	At	Rn
Fr	Ra	Ac	Th	Pa	U	Np	Pu	Am	Cm	Bk	Cf	Es	Fm	Md	No	Lr															

Figure 8-5

The construction of this table ensures that it has two properties. The first is that the behaviour of the elements in a horizontal row will change steadily and predictably along the row, although some rows will exhibit different trends in different sections of the row. For example, the row from potassium to krypton contains a section from scandium to zinc having quite different properties from those of the remaining eight elements. The next row, from rubidium to xenon, shows an identical two part pattern.

The second property implicit in our construction is that elements in vertical columns are similar in their properties. Fluorine, chlorine, bromine and iodine are so similar, for example, that they are often referred to collectively as the *halogens*. Helium, neon and the other elements of the last column are unreactive (only xenon and krypton are known to form compounds, and then only a few) and have low boiling points, giving rise to their collective name, the *noble gases*. It is convenient to have such collective names for elements having many properties in common. Some of the most useful of these names are shown in Figures 8-6 and 8-7. The terms s-block, p-block, d-block and f-block elements arise from the treatment of atomic structure presented in the next chapter. The terms shown in Figure 8-7 are much older, but most are still in common usage. It is particularly useful to refer to the s-block and p-block elements combined as the *representative elements*.

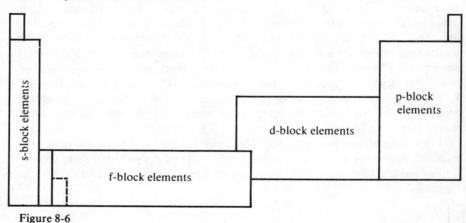

Figure 8-6

The exact elements to which these terms apply are not uniformly agreed upon in all cases. Scandium and yttrium are sometimes included with the transition metals and sometimes not. Zinc, cadmium and mercury are sometimes excluded both from the transition elements and from the d-block elements. Lanthanum fits the position below yttrium on all counts, but it is rarely thought of as a d-block element. Discussion of these points is continued in the next chapter, where a background of atomic theory will better permit our assigning these borderline cases to one or other groups. Note in Figure 8-6, however, that we assign lutetium to both d-block and f-block elements, that we have included zinc, cadmium, mercury, scandium and yttrium among the d-block elements but have excluded all of these from the transition elements, that lanthanum is included (naturally) as one of the lanthanides but not as one of the f-block elements and that actinium, in total analogy with lanthanum, is

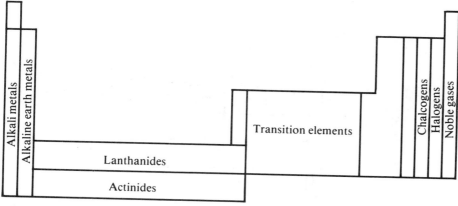

Figure 8-7

included in the actinides but not in the f-block. Each of these decisions should be examined by the reader after the next chapter, since each will help to fix in the mind the electronic configurations of the elements in their ground states and common oxidation states as well as the basis of the various groupings shown in Figures 8-6 and 8-7.

There is yet another way of referring collectively to the elements of a column. Titanium, zirconium and hafnium behave, in some respects, like carbon, silicon, germanium, tin and lead. In particular, it can be seen in Figures 8-3 and 8-4 that all exhibit a value of 4 for n in their fluorides and chlorides. Thus these elements are frequently called group IV elements, and the two sets are differentiated as IVa and IVb. Unfortunately, there is as yet no international agreement as to which is IVa and which IVb. For example, the carbon group is designated IVb in most of the world but IVa in the United States. A few texts in the United States increase the confusion by adapting an intermediate convention, naming the scandium group IIIa, and the boron group IIIb but using the normal American convention for the remainder of the d-block and p-block elements. In this text, the a and b designations are avoided altogether. The reader should note the important fact that there are similarities in valence between the elements of the scandium and boron groups, between the elements of the titanium and carbon groups, and to a decreasing extent, between the elements of the following columns.

Sc_2O_3	B_2O_3
Na_3ScF_6	Na_3AlF_6
$ScCl_3$	$AlCl_3$
YPO_4	$AlPO_4$
$TiCl_4$	CCl_4
TiO_2	SiO_2
CH_3TiCl_3	CH_3SiCl_3
K_2ZrO_3	K_2CO_3

8-1 FORMS OF THE PERIODIC TABLE

The particular form of the periodic table shown in Figure 8-5 is but one of the many that have been suggested during the last century. Three others are shown in Figures 8-8, 8-9 and 8-10. Each attempts to overcome some disadvantage of the Figure 8-5 version. While Figure 8-5 shows vertical relationships well, it could be misleading horizontally. The large gap between beryllium and boron, and between magnesium and aluminium, is unfortunate, since the trends in elemental properties are fairly uniform across these rows, with never more than a small discontinuity at this point. Such a difficulty is reduced by drawing

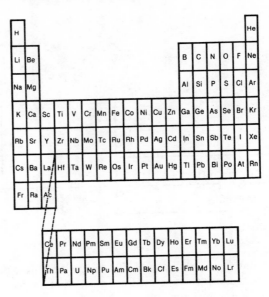

Figure 8-8

the lanthanides and actinides separately, as shown in Figure 8-8. This is by far the most common way of portraying the periodic table, but the gap between beryllium and boron does remain. It can be eliminated, however, by drawing the d-block elements separately, as in Figure 8-9. This is in many ways the

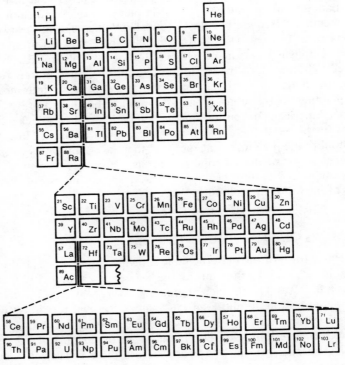

Figure 8-9

most satisfying form. More complex forms such as the spiral in Figure 8-10 do offer some additional advantages in accurate portrayal, in this case the continuity from one row to the next. However, while such forms are intriguing to examine, they are difficult to use in practice. Type is normally set, and read, vertically on a page. Moreover, the restarting of each row at the alkali metals is not without meaning, as is apparent in the next chapter, and the periodic table in Figure 8-9 is the form used in this text.

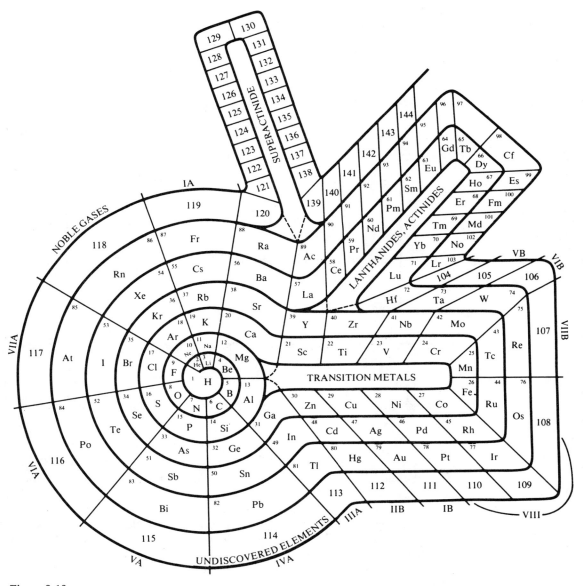

Figure 8-10

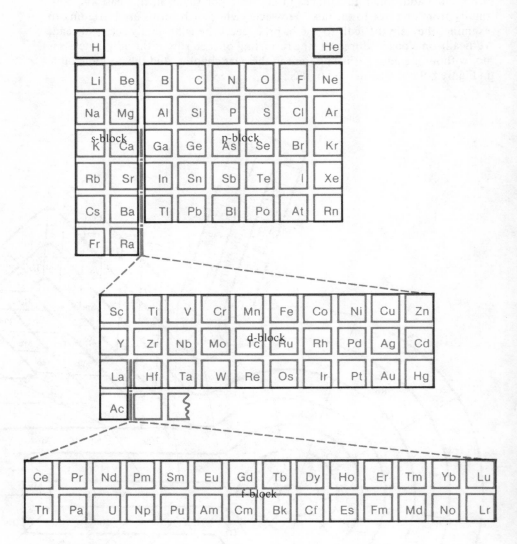

Figure 8-11

Figure 8-11 shows that this form of the table involves a three way division into the representative elements (s-block plus p-block), the d-block elements and the f-block elements. While this terminology has its basis in the work on atomic structure in the next chapter, the lengths of the rows can be seen to be related to the lengths of the cycles in properties. The s-block plus p- block total eight elements per row, while the d-block has ten and the f-block fourteen. These numbers, while emerging here on the basis of empiricism and direct observation, will take on added significance when atomic structure has been examined.

8-2 THE DIAGONAL BOUNDARIES FOR MANY PROPERTIES

A reasonable periodicity, corresponding always to that which we have already observed, can be found for numerous chemical and physical properties. In textbooks and papers published in the very late nineteenth and early twentieth centuries, a significant periodicity was noted for melting point and boiling point (of both the elements and various classes of their compounds), volume change on fusion, molar volume in the solid state at the melting point, heat of formation of oxides and of sulphides, and many others.

The properties which are portrayed in Figures 8-1 to 8-4 have integral values, and while the variation in these values across a row is obvious, there is no scope for variation down each column. Indeed we constructed the table by placing in a vertical column elements having identical values of n.

However, for properties such as melting point, the elements in a column will have similar values but not, of course, identical values. Thus for such properties there will be a trend within the columns as well as within the rows. Invariably, the trend from top to bottom within the columns is the same as that from right to left within the rows, as in Figure 8-12. Rationalization of this link will come with our later considerations of atomic structure but it has most to do with the tendency of atom, in any of a wide variety of circumstances, to gain or lose electrons. The elements to the left and bottom of the table lose them most readily. The elements to the top and right gain them most readily. It is worth illustrating this extremely important point with a couple of examples.

One example is the "acidity" or "basicity" of the oxides of each element when dissolved in water. Consideration of a single row shows the periodic trend. Sodium oxide, Na_2O, dissolves in water to give a very basic solution. Conventionally we think of this in terms of the formation of sodium hydroxide. Magnesium oxide, MgO, also produces a basic aqueous solution. Aluminium oxide, Al_2O_3, produces a neutral solution; silica, SiO_2, a very weakly acidic solution; P_2O_5, SO_3 and Cl_2O_7 progressively stronger acidic solutions. As with the bases, we think of these as forming acids, namely silicic acid (H_4SiO_4), phosphoric acid (H_3PO_4), sulphuric acid (H_2SO_4) and perchloric acid ($HClO_4$). This same trend from basicity to acidity occurs in every row, with the d-block elements again exhibiting differences. Figure 8-12 shows the pattern, although it should be noted that choosing the borderline between weak acids (shown as acids) and very weak acids (shown as neutral) is highly arbitrary and the analysis is further complicated by differences in solubility among the oxides.

Notice that the combination of trends across the rows with trends down the columns leads to a situation where the lower left hand elements (e.g. caesium) exhibit one extreme in properties whereas the upper right hand elements, excluding noble gases, exhibit the opposite extreme. This is a common pattern.

Other features of this figure are also common to most other properties that one might examine. The d-block elements are usually similar, with only very little variation along each row. The same is even truer of the f-block elements, especially the series from lanthanum to lutetium. On the other hand, strong trends exist across the rows of s-block and p-block elements.

The noble gases usually stand apart because, except for some compounds of

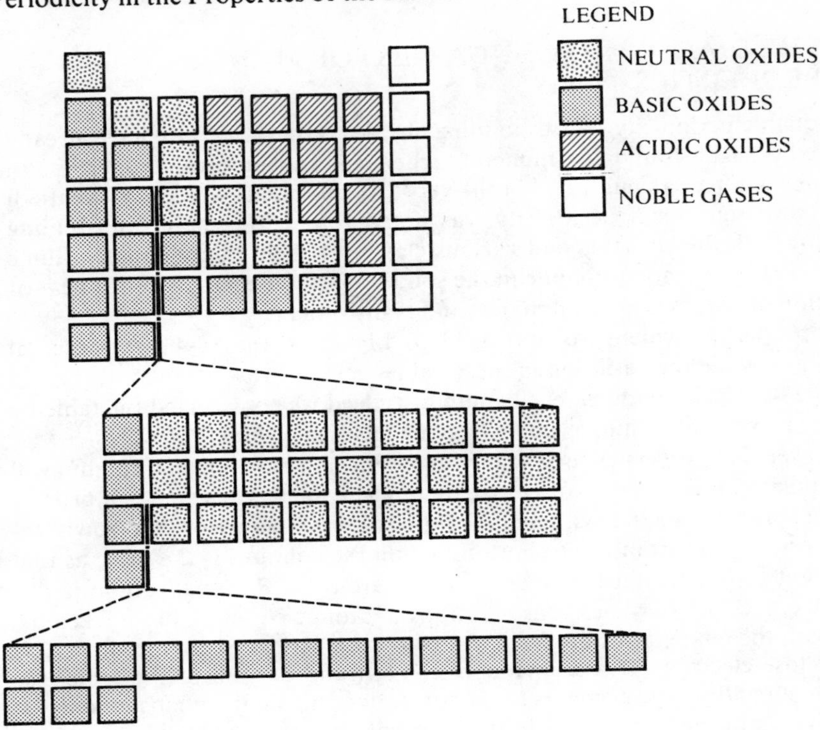

Figure 8-12

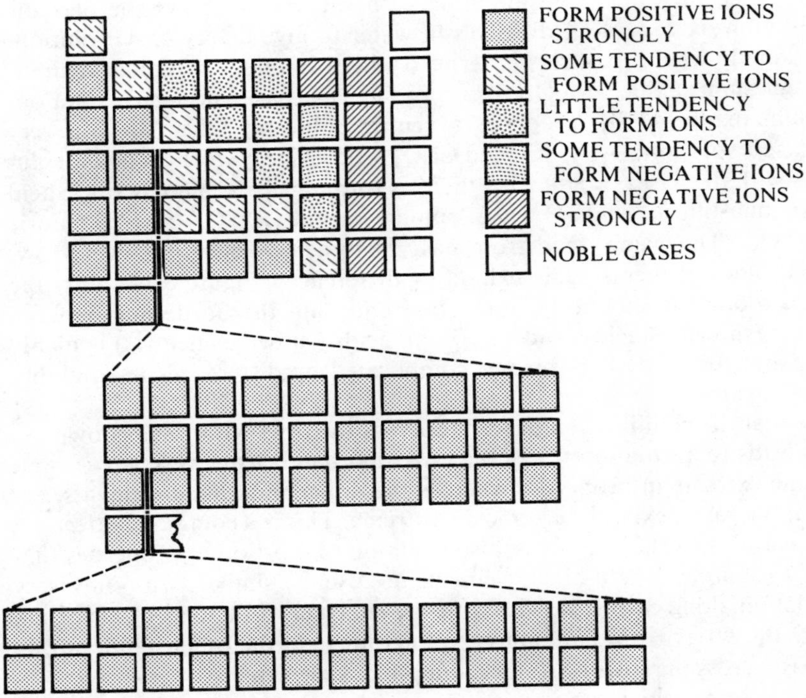

Figure 8-13

xenon and krypton, they form no compounds to discuss. When, however, the property measured is one by which they can be judged on the same basis as other elements (Figures 8-1 to 8-4 and ionization energies in the next chapter), they exhibit the same trends.

Many elements form ionic crystals. Ions result from a complete (or substantial) transfer of one or more electrons from one atom to another, creating a cation (positively charged) and an anion (negatively charged). In Figure 8-13, those elements which tend to form negative ions, those which tend to form positive ions and those which do not tend to form ions at all are indicated. A clear pattern emerges. Notice again in the s- and p-blocks that the combination of trends across the rows with the trend down each column leads to a situation in which the lower left hand elements exhibit one extreme in properties whereas the upper right hand elements, excluding noble gases, exhibit the opposite extreme.

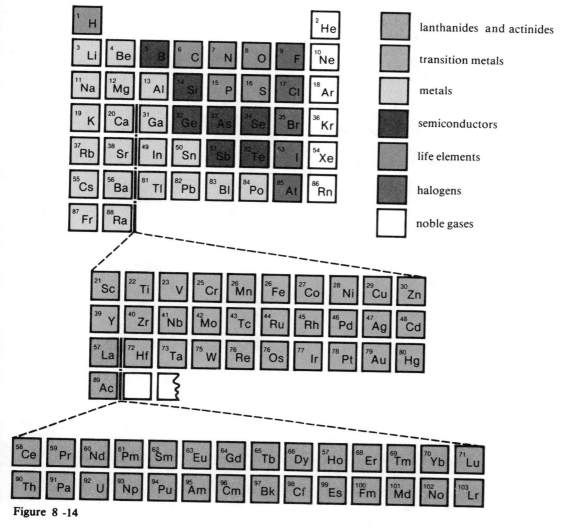

Figure 8-14

8-3 USING THE PERIODIC TABLE

While the table was created by organizing the elements in accordance with their properties, its utility lies in doing the reverse, predicting the properties of an element from its position within the table. Such an approach is a very basic one in science. It should be possible for anyone with only limited experience in chemistry to predict the approximate properties of a previously unfamiliar element by locating it within the table. A richer ability to predict comes, of course, with experience, particularly laboratory experience in such fields as qualitative analysis. Almost every chapter of this book provides details of the properties of one or more groups. The facts below serve only as a brief introduction. For this purpose the elements are grouped as shown in Figure 8-14, a division that is arbitrary but efficient. Note that this arbitrary new organization differs from those in Figures 8-6 and 8-7 in the centre of the table and reflects the strong effect in this area of the diagonal trends discussed in the previous section. The end groups of elements (alkali metals and noble gases) are very much more uniform in their properties than are the elements of groups IV and V. Carbon does have the same formal valency as lead, as shown in Figures 8-1 to 8-4, but it is very different material chemically as Figures 8-13 and 8-14 suggested.

8-4 THE METALS

Sixty-eight of the ninety-two elements shown in the table are metals, characterized by high electrical and thermal conductivity, a lustrous appearance and a tendency to exist as positive ions in compounds. All except

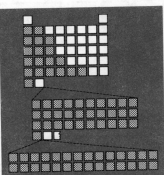

the metals

mercury are solids at normal temperatures and all have high boiling points. Most are dense, opaque, malleable and ductile. Within such a large collection of elements, however, there are still significant variations and subdivisions.

The **lanthanides** are probably the least significant elements, technically and economically, within the table. They are exceptionally similar to one another in their properties, so much so that their identification and their separation one from the other are extremely difficult. Both the elements and their compounds exhibit this similarity.

The lanthanides are usually found in a valence state of three, typified by such compounds as La_2O_3 and LaF_3, but there are a few examples of a valence state of two, and more than a few examples of a state of four. Among the last

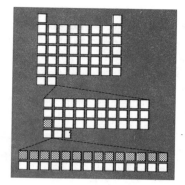

the lanthanides

is cerium, where cerium (IV) nitrate is widely used as an oxidizing agent in analytical and organic chemistry.

Although the lanthanides are sometimes called the rare earths, almost all of them are in fact relatively abundant, more abundant than such better known elements as antimony, cadmium and gold. They exist, however, widely dispersed as minor components in many minerals. Since such minerals usually contain small amounts of several of the lanthanides, the difficulties in separating them one from another limit their availability.

Although the elemental lanthanide metals can be prepared electrochemically, they react slowly with oxygen and rapidly with water, even at normal temperatures, so there is no significant technical application for the metals themselves.

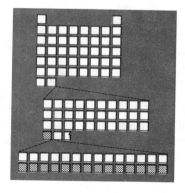

the actinides

The **actinides** are also similar to one another in their chemical and physical properties, although not so markedly so as the lanthanides. They also appear to have a richer and more varied chemistry, with uranium for example having four known valence states besides zero. All of the actinides form a great variety of compounds, including many inter-metallic compounds (e.g. USn_3, $NpAl_4$, Pu_3Pb) and some organometallic compounds (e.g. $Th(C_5H_5)_3Cl$, $U(C_5H_5)_3(CH_3)$), which are of growing interest as potential catalysts.

Of the actinides, only thorium and uranium are naturally occurring, and none has a stable isotope. Thus both thorium and uranium ores are radioactive, although the only naturally occurring isotope of thorium, ^{232}Th, has a half life greater than 10^{10} years so that radioactivity is small and thorium ores can be handled safely. Thorium is more abundant than uranium, but uranium is much the more important economically at this time because of its use as a fuel in the nuclear generation of electricity. The most abundant isotope of uranium (^{238}U, 99.28%) is not the basis of this use. Rather it is ^{235}U, only 0.71% of natural uranium, which is readily used as a fission fuel. Most reactors designed in Europe, Russia and the United States require fuel in which the ^{235}U content has been enriched, but Canadian reactors use natural uranium. The fuel rods are made of the oxide of uranium (IV), UO_2.

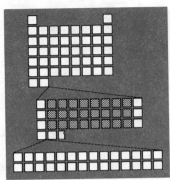

the transition metals

If the lanthanides and actinides have only a few specialized applications, the **transition metals** are by contrast the most widely used. Iron has been the most important structural metal for centuries, particularly alloyed with small amounts of other elements to make steels. Copper is widely used as tubing, sheeting and plate, and enjoys widespread use as well in brasses and bronzes, alloys in which zinc and tin are the other components. Nickel, chromium and manganese are all important in plating or in imparting corrosion resistance to alloys. The mining of ores containing iron, copper, nickel and the others is one of the world's major industries.

Transition metals have a number of important characteristics which, looking ahead a chapter for a moment, are all associated in large part with the partially filled d-shells which are the truly distinguishing characteristic of these elements. These include a multiplicity of valence states, the paramagnetism and ferromagnetism exhibited by many compounds of transition metals, the catalytic activity of both the metals and their compounds, and the bright colours of many of the compounds.

The transition metals form an exceptionally large number of compounds, one contributing factor being the ability to exist in many valence states. Manganese for example exists in every valence state from 0 to 7, although only 2 and 4 give rise to a very large range of compounds. Typical would be $K_5Mn(CN)_6$, $MnCO_3$, $K_3Mn(CN)_6$, MnO_2, K_3MnO_4, K_2MnO_4 and $KMnO_4$. The transition metals also form a very large variety of organometallic compounds (e.g. $(C_5H_5)_2Ti(CH_3)_2$, $(CH_3)_3NbCl_2$, $C_2H_5Mn(CO)_5$, $(C_5H_5)_2Fe$, $PtBr(CH_3)(PR_3)_2$ and $(CH_3)Au(PR_3)$). The cyclopentadienyl group, C_5H_5, many different trialkyl phosphine groups, denoted generally by PR_3, and carbonyl groups, CO, are particularly common in transition metal compounds. The carbonyl group is also present in a novel group of transition metal compounds called cluster compounds which involve small numbers of metal

$Os_3(CO)_{12}$ $Fe_3S_2(CO)_9$ $Ir_4(CO)_{12}$

atoms, bonded together by metal to metal bonds as well as by carbonyl 'bridges,' arranged in geometrically elegant molecules.

Transition metal compounds are often, although by no means always, deeply coloured. The colour depends in fact upon both the metal ion and the atoms which form its immediate environment. Well known examples are the blue of copper (II) ions surrounded by water, and the deep purple of manganese (VII) ions surrounded by four oxygens as in the permanganate ion, MnO_4^- .

Of great technical importance is the activity of transition metals as catalysts, both in metallic form and in compounds. Catalysts are materials which increase the rate of a process without themselves being consumed. Since the rates are often increased by orders of magnitude, the plant size needed to achieve a given production is reduced accordingly. Their greatest value, however, lies in their selectivity, their ability to speed one particular process to the exclusion of any number of other processes which would or could compete. Chemical industry could not exist without them, and almost all are based on transition elements.

The mining and processing of the ores of these elements is an enormous enterprise and specialized processes and techniques have developed for each. The steel-making industry is an obvious example. These techniques are too many and too varied for even a brief summary to be attempted here.

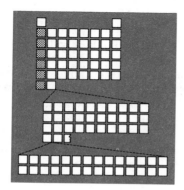

the alkali metals

The **alkali metals** are soft, low melting metals which react readily with oxygen and violently with water, and so are not extensively used in elemental form. They do, however, form numerous compounds, most of which are very

Element	Melting Point/K	Boiling Point/K	Density/G ml^{-1}
Li	459	1500	.33
Na	371	1150	.97
K	335	1030	.87
Rb	312	970	1.53
Cs	302	940	1.87

soluble in water. Aqueous solutions of alkali metal compounds are usually excellent conductors of electricity, evidence of the tendency of these metals to form ionic compounds, in which the metal atoms given up an electron to have a charge of +1.

Unless colour is conferred by the anion, alkali metal compounds are usually colourless, appearing white in powdered form. Particularly common examples are NaCl, NaOH, KOH, NaNO$_3$ and K$_2$O. Only a few organic compounds of alkali metals are known but the simple alkyls of lithium, such as CH$_3$Li, are important synthetic reagents in organic and organometallic chemistry.

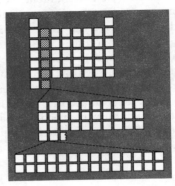

the alkaline earths

The **alkaline earths** are distinctly different from the alkali metals. As metals, they have very much higher melting points, boiling points and densities. These metals are much less subject to chemical attack and magnesium is used as a structural metal, particularly in aircraft where its low density is of value. Be, Mg and Ba are all used in alloys. Probably the most important compounds within this group, from an economic standpoint, are the CaO derivatives which form the basis of lime, mortar and cement. These elements form a wide range of inorganic compounds, but few organometallic compounds. An important exception is the group of "Grignard Reagents," of nominal formula RMgX where R is an alkyl group like methyl or ethyl and X is any halogen. These are important reagents in synthetic chemistry.

Element	Melting Point/K	Boiling Point/K	Density/g ml^{-1}
Be	1620	1770	1.8
Mg	920	1380	1.7
Ca	1080	1440	1.6
Sr	1070	1420	2.5
Ba	1120	1410	3.5

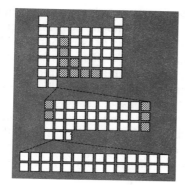

the remaining metals

The remaining metals have little in common except that all are indeed metals, and none fits into any of the five classes so far described. Remaining metals is, of course, merely a classification of use in this chapter and is not a title, like 'alkali metals,' which has meaning elsewhere. The elements to the left of the transition metals, scandium, and yttrium, and those just to the right, zinc, cadmium and mercury, might be expected to *be* transition metals, but their electronic structure is such, as we shall see, that they do not in fact exhibit the properties associated with the transition elements.

Zinc is the most important commercially of these five. Coated on steel it provides the corrosion resistant form known as galvanized steel. Alloyed with copper, it forms the extremely useful series of alloys known as the brasses. Alloyed with copper and tin, it forms the bronzes.

Zinc forms a wide range of inorganic compounds, many of which have commercial uses. The oxide and sulphide are used as pigments, and the chloride as a wood preservative. The range of organometallic compounds is much smaller, and the utility of most of these is limited by their extreme reactivity. Dimethyl zinc, for example, is pyrophoric.

Cadmium and its compounds are analogous to those of zinc. Like zinc the metal is used as a corrosion resistant coating and as an electrode in batteries, notably the nickel/cadmium or nicad battery. The oxide and sulphide are pigments. Inorganic compounds are numerous but organic compounds are few and of little commercial importance.

Mercury is unique in being the only metallic element which is a liquid at ordinary temperatures. This leads to a number of applications in swtiches, in thermometers and in barometers. Like zinc and cadmium, mercury forms a wide range of inorganic compounds and relatively few organic compounds. The latter include dimethyl mercury, $(CH_3)_2Hg$, and methyl mercury ion, CH_3Hg^+, which have gained notoriety as toxic pollutants arising from certain industrial chemical processes. Mercury enters fresh water in inorganic forms but interacts with organisms there to produce the toxic organomercury compounds. The liquid nature of mercury leads to the ready formation of a large class of materials known as amalgams. These are alloys of mercury with one or more other metals. Gold and silver amalgams have long been used to fill cavities in teeth. Alkali metal amalgams are powerful reductants.

Aluminium is a very important structural metal, much used both as sheet and as extruded bars and girders. Although more costly than steel, its low density and natural resistance to corrosion makes its higher price well worthwhile in many applications. It is the third most abundant element, after oxygen and silicon, and occurs in an extremely wide range of compounds with these two elements, compounds called aluminosilicates. However, deposits of compounds which can be used as commercial sources of aluminium are less common. Aluminium is produced commercially by electrolysis and the quantities of electricity needed are extremely large. This has led to smelters being located near large hydroelectric sites, particularly in remote areas of Canada, Norway and Ghana where the source of electricity is far removed from other markets, and on-site use makes particular sense. As with zinc, the organometallic compounds are few and reactive, with trialkyl aluminium compounds being pyrophoric. A wide range of inorganic compounds exists however, particularly the complex aluminates and aluminosilicates.

Tin has been a commercially important metal since ancient times. It is a component of such important alloys as the bronzes (with copper and zinc) and the solders (with lead). Coated on steel, it improves corrosion resistance, and is widely used in making containers popularly although not completely accurately referred to as "tin" cans. It forms a wide range of inorganic compounds in both the +2 and +4 valence states, such as $SnCl_2$ and $SnCl_4$.

Lead is also a commercially important metal with a long history. Because it is low melting and rather soft, it can be easily worked with primitive tools and equipment. Bullets for small calibre weapons are usually molded from lead. Lead sheet is sometimes used as a corrosion-proof sealer which can be readily hammered and shaped to close joints in roofs and other architectural features, although this use is in decline. Like zinc it forms compounds in both the +2 and +4 valence state and like zinc it forms a limited range of organometallic compounds which are, by and large, unreactive. One of them, tetraethyl lead, is commercially important as an "antiknock additive" to gasoline, although like the alkyl mercury compounds it is highly toxic. The lead acid battery is a very economical storage cell and a major user of lead.

8-5   THE NON-METALS

The non-metals form a majority of the representative elements of the periodic table, but they include several elements of unique importance. Whereas the metals exhibit many properties in common, the non-metals grouping includes

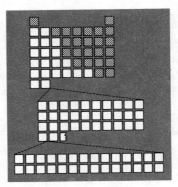

the non-metals

elements having a wide variety of properties, ranging from elements on the border of being nearly like metals to elements having a strong tendency to acquire electrons, and including as well the noble gases which are largely unreactive in any way.

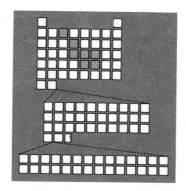

the semiconductors

All of the metals are excellent conductors of electricity. Most of the non-metals are insulators but lying along the boundary of the metals region of the periodic table are seven elements which are **semi-conductors**. Their distinctive characteristic is that whereas they are modest conductors of electricity at ambient temperatures, they have a large conductivity at higher temperatures. Incidentally, this is the reverse of the situation with metals, where conductivity decreases somewhat at higher temperatures. The semi-conducting elements, especially silicon, and their compounds, especially GaAs, form the basis of modern integrated circuits. The electrical conductivity of these materials can be altered drastically by inclusion of trace amounts of atoms of similar size but different valence.

Silicon is the second most abundant element in the earth's crust, exceeded only by oxygen. Almost invariably it occurs in the form of silicates, in which each silicon atom is found at the centre of a tetrahedron of oxygen atoms. The variety of such compounds is impressive, and with the exception of the limestones, almost all common minerals are silicates including the clays, the feldspars and the micas, as well as silica itself SiO_2, which is the major component of sand.

Elemental silicon is a lustrous silvery material but it is not metallic. Reduction of silica to silicon is difficult, and commercial uses of the elemental material are few, the major one being the manufacture of semi-conductors, and the silicon "chips" which are the basis of microelectonics. If the occasional boron atom is included in a silicon crystal, a lattice position is created which is deficient in one valence electron, a condition described as a 'positive hole.' Such a 'doped' crystal is called a 'p-type semi-conductor.' On the other hand, if a silicon or germanium lattice is doped with a small amount of pentavalent arsenic atoms, there is an excess of negative charge in the valence levels and an 'n-type semi-conductor' is created. It should be noted that there is overall neutrality of charge in both types. What is important is that the valence electrons have the mobility on which conductivity depends, with conduction primarily by movement of holes in p-type and by movement of electrons in n-type. The junction between a p-type and an n-type semi-conductor is at the heart of individual diodes and transistors, and of course of integrated circuits as well. Another useful device based on silicon is the thermistor which utilizes the large change in resistance which a semi-conductor exhibits when temperature changes. Thermistors are a very sensitive way to monitor temperature, and can be made smaller than a pin head. Semi-conductors also have importance in the direct conversion of solar radiation to electricity.

Silicones are polymers involving alternating silicon and oxygen in the backbone and short organic groups such as methyl, CH_3, on the silicon atoms. They are prepared by hydrolysis of alkyl silicon chlorides. They are used extensively as waterproof coatings, especially where some penetration by air, often called 'breathing,' is desirable as in footwear. Chemically stable and inert, silicones make high quality insulators, greases and lubricants. Silicone rubbers are also chemically inert, and maintain their resilient quality over a wide range of temperature.

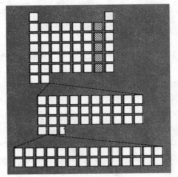

the halogens

The four naturally occurring **halogens** are important in almost all areas of chemistry. Both as elements and in their compounds they show a clear similarity of properties, but with an equally clear trend from fluorine to iodine.

In their elemental form, all exist as diatomic molecules and all are coloured. At ordinary temperatures and pressures, fluorine and chlorine are gases, bromine a liquid and iodine a solid. Fluorine is obtained from the mineral fluorspar, CaF_2, and cryolite, Na_3AlF_6. Chlorine is produced in large quantities by the chlorine-alkali industry at the anode in the electrolysis of aqueous solutions of NaCl. Bromine is extracted from sea water by displacing it with chlorine gas, oxidizing Br^- to Br_2. Iodine occurs in sodium iodate, $NaIO_3$, along with sodium nitrate deposits (e.g., in Chile). In the sea the iodine concentration is very low but is concentrated by certain marine organisms, such as kelp and sponges.

Element	Colour	Stable	Melting Point/K	Boiling Point/K
F	yellow	F_2	50	85
Cl	yellow-green	Cl_2	170	238
Br	red-brown	Br_2	266	332
I	violet-black	I_2	386	457

The chemical reactions of the elemental halogens can also be graded. One such important trend is in their strength as oxidants. F_2 has a strong tendency to acquire electrons and become fluoride ion. The substance which gives up those electrons is said to be oxidized and the substance which acquires them is said to be an oxidizing agent or oxidant. All of the halogens are effective oxidants, grading from fluorine, which is almost the strongest oxidant known, to iodine, which is a moderate oxidant used in analytical work. F_2 is capable of oxidizing the halide ions below it in the table (Cl^-, Br^-, I^-) to the respective halogens (Cl_2, Br_2, I_2). Similarly Cl_2 is capable of oxidizing Br^- to Br_2 and I^- to I_2 and Br_2 is capable of oxidizing I^- to I_2. Of course other oxidants can be used which will oxidize some of the halides and not others. This provides a good means of separating halide ions in solution. For example, in a solution of both Br^- and I^-, the I^- is oxidized by Fe^{3+} but the Br^- remains unchanged. The I_2 can then be removed by shaking or extracting with CCl_4, in which I_2 is very soluble. The Br^- is much more soluble in water, and most of it remains in the aqueous layer.

It has already been observed in discussing Figures 8-1 to 8-4 that some elements combine with another element in more than one ratio. They are said to have more than one 'oxidation state,' a term introduced in Section 2-2 and explained more fully in Section 22-2.

oxidation state	+ 7	+5	+4	+3	+1
examples	$HClO_4$	$HClO_3$	ClO_2	$HClO_2$	$HClO$
	Cl_2O_7	HIO_3	BrO_2	$HBrO_2$	Cl_2O
	H_5IO_6	I_2O_5		IF_3	Br_2O
	IF_7	BrF_5		ClF_3	HIO
	I_2O_7	IF_5			

Although the halogens exhibit a wide range of oxidation states in their compounds with oxygen and with other halogens, they almost invariably exhibit a state of -1 in the very large and important set of compounds formed with metals. Except for some of the halides of Ag^+, Hg_2^{2+} and Pb^{2+}, these are almost all soluble in water. The halide ions are important constituents of ocean water, with chloride the most abundant of all. In dry locations, however, huge naturally occurring deposits of these minerals are found, with NaCl being of particular commercial importance in providing the industrial source of both chlorine and sodium hydroxide.

The hydrogen halides, HX, are all colourless, pungent gases which fume in air and dissolve readily in water to form acids, all of which are strong acids except HF. An aqueous solution of HCl is known to the chemist as hydrochloric acid but is often called muriatic acid commercially. The others are less important commercially but HF has a unique use arising from its ability to dissolve or 'etch' glass.

$$SiO_2(c) + 6HF(aq) \rightleftharpoons 2H^+(aq) + SiF_6^{2-}(aq) + 2H_2O(l)$$

There are few oxygen compounds of fluorine but the other halogens form a variety of oxides all of which are acidic in aqueous solution and many of which are important oxidizing agents. Perchloric acid, $HClO_4$, and its potassium salt,

$KClO_4$, are powerful oxidants, the former being dangerously explosive if not in dilute aqueous solution. Ammonium perchlorate, NH_4ClO_4, is explosive and used as a propellant. Among the other oxides, the most used is hypochlorous acid, HClO, formed by the action of chlorine on water. It is much used in bleaching and in the purification of water supplies.

$$Cl_2(aq) + H_2O(l) \rightleftarrows HClO(aq) + H^+(aq) + Cl^-(aq)$$

The halogens also form several compounds with themselves where again chlorine, bromine and iodine exhibit a variety of oxidation states. These compounds do not have much commercial importance but they are interesting and provide useful tests of theories of molecular structure.

Chlorine forms many organic compounds. Materials such as carbon tetrachloride, CCl_4; chloroform, $CHCl_3$; trichloroethylene, C_2HCl_3 and 1,1,1-trichloroethane, CH_3CCl_3 are among the most important of laboratory and industrial solvents although some are suspected carcinogens and are less used now for that reason. Partially fluorinated, partially chlorinated derivatives of methane and ethane, such as CF_2Cl_2 are important heat transfer fluids and refrigerants. Many polymers contain halogens including polyvinylchloride (PVC) and polytetrafluoroethylene (PTFE).

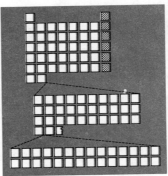

the noble gases

The **noble gases** are sometimes called the inert gases or the rare gases, although argon constitutes 1% of the earth's atmosphere and is certainly not rare. All, however, are noble, forming few compounds. Those compounds which have been prepared are mainly xenon compounds, the remainder being of krypton. Typical are XeF_2, XeF_4, XeF_6, $XeOF_4$, XeF_8, Na_4XeO_6 and XeO_4. Notice that in XeO_4 and XeF_8 xenon has a valence state of eight.

Element	Melting Point/K	Boiling Point/K
He	1	4.3
Ne	24.5	27.3
Ar	84.0	87.5
Kr	116	120
Xe	161	166

All of the noble gases exist as monatomic gases at ordinary conditions with even the heaviest boiling more than 100 K below room temperature. Helium, which is obtained mainly from natural gas wells in western Canada and elsewhere, is the only safe gas suitable for filling large dirigibles and balloons. Hydrogen has only half the density, but explodes readily in contact with air should any flame or spark be present, and its use in dirigibles resulted in several spectacular disasters in the age of airships. Helium, a noble gas, does not suffer this great disadvantage. Argon, by far the most abundant of the noble gases, is easily prepared by fractional distillation of the atmosphere. It is a favourite inert "blanket" material for highly reactive laboratory and industrial chemicals which must be kept isolated from air.

The elements remaining to be described are carbon, hydrogen, oxygen, nitrogen, sulphur and phosphorus. While these form a diverse group indeed, it is notable that they are the key elements in living matter, and in organic chemistry and biochemistry.

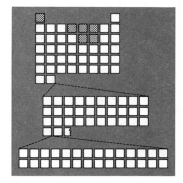

the life elements

Carbon is the basis of the organic world. Besides being the basis of all living organisms, its architectural potential has been utilized by man in the development of a remarkably diverse stock of tailor-made materials required in his technology. What is the explanation for this unique role of carbon not possessed even by its immediate relative, silicon? Mainly it is in the strength of the bonds which carbon forms with other carbon atoms, and with nitrogen, oxygen and hydrogen. Bond energies are defined precisely in Section 11-4. They are a measure of the energy required to separate two atoms bonded together in a molecule. Average lengths and energies for certain types of bonds are listed in Table 8-2. It can be seen that the single C-C bond is much stronger, at 347 kJ mol^{-1}, than the analogue for its near neighbour silicon. The Si-Si bond has an energy of only 176 kJ mol^{-1}. This is a major factor in determining the fact that C-C bonds have no great tendency to produce C-O bonds (335 kJ mol^{-1}) in the presence of oxygen whereas silicon is normally found bonded to oxygen, the Si-O bond being very strong at 369 kJ mol^{-1}. The strength of the carbon-carbon bond is certainly a key to its ability to produce such a great variety of stable structures, and the strength of the bonds which carbon forms with other elements greatly enhances this variety, leading to great classes of compounds such as hydrocarbons (C and H), alcohols, carbohydrates and lipids (all C, H and O) and amino acids and proteins (all C, H, O and N).

In elemental form, carbon exists in different crystalline forms or allotropes. Diamond is the high temperature, very high pressure allotrope, formed by severe compression at temperatures high enough to permit the mobility necessary for the transformation to occur. The density is high for such a light

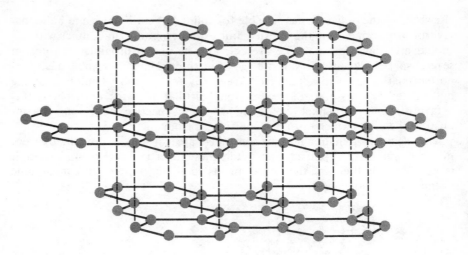

element, at 3.5 g mL^{-1}. Each atom is bonded to four neighbouring atoms, the result being an extremely rigid and strong array of interlocking tetrahedra. All electrons are 'localized' and incapable of travelling through the solid so that diamond is not an electrical conductor. In the empirical scale of hardness known as Moh's scale, diamond represents the extreme in hardness with a value of 10. This hardness is consistent with the ordered nature of the tetrahedral network, the dense compact nature of the structure and the strength of the carbon-carbon bond. The C-C distance is 0.154 nm. The melting point of diamond, at 3800 K, is the highest of any element.

Well formed diamonds are prized on the market for their refractive optical properties as well as hardness, but the price is largely a consequence of a controlled scarcity. Small chips and imperfect crystals are set in bits for drilling hard materials. Some diamonds are produced synthetically; in comparison with natural diamonds they are often smaller, black or coloured, and have sharp edges which make them useful for abrasion in drill bits. Related uses for diamonds include cutting glass, making grindstones, and providing hard stylus tips for record players.

Graphite is the stable allotrope of carbon at normal pressures, but for kinetic or rate reasons, diamond does not in fact convert to graphite unless the temperature is raised above 1800 K. Graphite can be converted to diamond at pressures greater than 10^5 bar at which pressures diamond is the stable form. It is not surprising that graphite has a lower density (2.26 g mL^{-1}) than has diamond. Furthermore the bonding and structure are quite different. Graphite crystallizes in flat sheets of carbon atoms arranged in a hexagonal pattern with bond angles of 120°. The hexagonal bonding is covalent and the bond length (0.142 nm) is approximately equal to the bond length in benzene. Each C atom is surrounded in the sheet by only 3 neighbours so that some electrons not employed in the single covalent bonding of the atoms in the hexagons, are free to form a delocalized population which has the required mobility along the sheets of carbon atoms, to produce electrical and thermal conductivity. In this respect graphite resembles a 'two-dimensional metal.' Even the metallic lustre is present when the surface is smooth. The bonding between the sheets is very

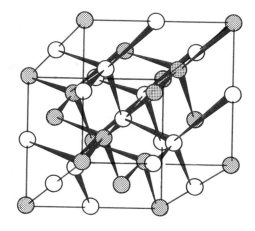

weak, and the separation of the sheets, 0.335 nm, is correspondingly large. There is room between the layers of carbon atoms for the occlusion of gas and this is thought to provide a fluid medium for the movement of one sheet relative to the next. This property makes graphite valuable as a good lubricant where chemical inertness is essential. A suspension of graphite in water is the lubricant known as "aquadag"; suspended in oil it is "oildag." The same property of slip between planes accounts also for the greasy feel of graphite and for its ability to smear or mark when used as the core of a so-called "lead" pencil. Other important uses for graphite are as renewable electrodes in electrochemical cells such as are used in the production of aluminium, and as a moderator for neutrons in atomic reactors.

What is called amorphous carbon may be microcrystalline graphite in particles too small to permit identification of structure. Charcoal is made by the destructive distillation of wood, sugar or other organic matter. After the volatiles are expelled, a finely divided porous residue, mainly of carbon, remains. Charcoal has long been used as a solid fuel and reducing agent in chemistry and metallurgy as well as an adsorbent for gases and chemical substances which produce any unwanted odour or colour. Soot, lamp black, or carbon black is a valuable commodity for making black paints and inks as well as a filler for incorporating in rubber tires to reduce wear. Carbon black is produced by burning natural gas in a limited air supply and condensing the product on a cold metal surface. A useful recycling process disposes of old automobile tires by burning with limited air to recover the carbon black from both the rubber and filler.

Hydrocarbons are compounds of carbon and hydrogen. They are stable and comparatively unreactive. This group exhibits a diversity of structure which includes small, compact molecules, long chains, branched chains, and closed rings.

The alkanes, for which an older name is paraffins, are hydrocarbons of general empirical formula C_nH_{2n+2} which are said to be *saturated* hydrocarbons, signifying that each carbon is bonded to four other atoms, either carbons or hydrogens, and hence that no more hydrogen can be added. Alkanes, like most classes of organic compounds, encompass an entire series of closely related compounds, each differing from the previous by the addition of one more CH_2 unit. Such series are called *homologous series*. The simplest member of the alkane series is methane, CH_4, the next ethane, C_2H_6, and so on. These materials have already been encountered as fuels in Table 6-1. Their structures are discussed in Chapter 11. The C-C bond distance in ethane is 0.154 nm, the same as in diamond. At ordinary temperatures and pressures, methane, ethane, propane and butane are all gases but butane and propane are commonly compressed and sold as liquid fuels. Chains of 5 to about 18 carbon atoms are liquid, and longer chains produce solids. The source of supply of most of the alkanes is from petroleum refining.

number of carbons	name	formula	state at 300 K and 100 kPa	melting point/K	boiling point/K
1	methane	CH_4	gas	90	112
2	ethane	C_2H_6	gas	101	185
3	propane	C_3H_8	gas	86	231
4	butane	C_4H_{10}	gas	138	273
5	pentane	C_5H_{12}	liquid	142	309
6	hexane	C_6H_{14}	liquid	179	342
7	heptane	C_7H_{16}	liquid	182	371
8	octane	C_8H_{18}	liquid	216	398

For alkanes with four or more carbons, it will be seen that the molecule can be assembled in more than one way. Where a molecule can be broken up and assembled again in a different structure, the various configurations possible are known as structural isomers. This is discussed more fully in Section 11-1.

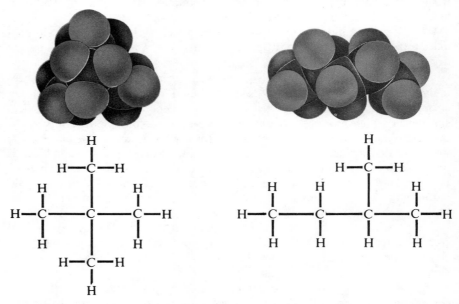

The possible isomers of butane and pentane are shown. One small but important area in which this distinction is important is in engine gasolines, where the branched isomers are found to 'knock' less than the straight chain isomers. A

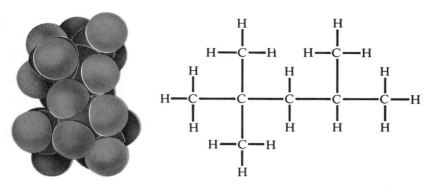

2, 2, 4-trimethylpentane

knock in an engine is an undesirably rapid explosion which is not in time with the controlled explosion initiated by the spark. Knocking wears the engine and reduces fuel efficiency. At one time the best fuel for prevention of knocking was 2,2,4-trimethyl pentane, known commercially as iso-octane. By com-

parison n-heptane was very poor. These two fuels were thought to set upper and lower limits, so that suitable mixtures of the two could be made to match the knocking characteristics of an unknown gasoline, with n-heptane rated 0% and pure iso-octane 100%. The octane number of the gasoline of interest is determined by the percentage of iso-octane in the matching mixture. Fuels have been produced since which have octane numbers greater than 100. Performance is related to the degree of branching in the molecule. It is therefore advantageous in the refinery process to break down (crack) long chains and reform the fragments into molecules with more branching. A cheaper way to reduce knocking is to add tetraethyl lead, $(C_2H_5)_4$ Pb, but this has been shown to create high levels of lead on highway verges and in busy metropolitan areas, constituting an environmental hazard.

There are important series of compounds containing a carbon-carbon 'double bond,' called alkenes, and containing a carbon-carbon 'triple bond,' called

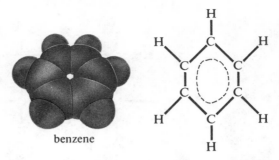

benzene

alkynes. The simplest and most important alkene is called ethene or ethylene, C_2H_4, and the simplest and most important alkyne is ethyne or acetylene, C_2H_2. The thermodynamic and theoretical consideration of double and triple bonds occurs in Chapters 11 and 12 but it can be noted here that a molecule having either double or triple bonds necessarily has fewer hydrogens per carbon than the alkane with the same number of carbons. Consequently, alkenes and alkynes are said to be *unsaturated*. Also important among the hydrocarbons are compounds with flat, six member rings of carbons. The simplest of these is benzene, C_6H_6, but there are numerous derivatives, such as those which substitute at one or more ring positions like toluene, $C_6H_5CH_3$, and those that involve multiple rings, like naphthalene, $C_{10}H_8$. Benzene, toluene and the various xylenes are important industrial and laboratory solvents.

Many classes of organic compounds contain oxygen. These include the proteins and carbohydrates, the alcohols (ROH), the ethers (ROR'), the aldehydes (RCHO), the ketones (RCOR'), the carboxylic acids (RCOOH) and the esters (RCOOR').

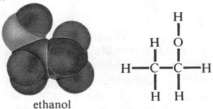

ethanol

Nitrogen is present in the nucleic acids, the basis of genetic information in life forms, and in such classes of organic compounds as the amines and amides, and amino acids. Phosphorus is present in adenosine triphosphate (ATP) and adenosine diphosphate (ADP), the compounds which provide the basis of energy storage and transfer within living cells. Sulphur is less obviously involved in the life elements classification than the other elements above, but the extensive organosulphur chemistry does include many compounds of biological importance including the "sulfa drugs" and the penicillins.

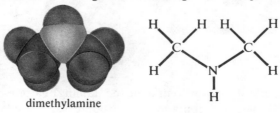

dimethylamine

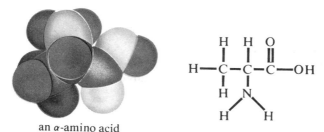

$$H-\underset{\underset{H}{|}}{\overset{\overset{H}{|}}{C}}-\underset{\underset{N}{|}}{\overset{\overset{H}{|}}{C}}-\overset{\overset{O}{\parallel}}{C}-OH$$

an α-amino acid

Carbon, hydrogen, oxygen, nitrogen, phosphorus and sulphur have important inorganic chemistry as well. Oxygen is the most abundant of all elements. It combines with hydrogen to form water, the most ubiquitous and important compound in biological and in environmental chemistry. It is present in many of the most important anions, like the nitrates, the sulphates, and the phosphates. It is combined with silicon in the silicates, the abundance and importance of which has already been mentioned. Last, but not least, it forms twenty percent of the atmosphere, as the diatomic molecule O_2.

Almost all of the remaining eighty percent of the atmosphere is nitrogen, again as a diatomic molecule, N_2. Among the most important nitrogen compounds commercially are ammonia and ammonium nitrate, the latter important both as a fertilizer and as an explosive.

Phosphorus is an abundant element too, found mainly in phosphate minerals. The important fertilizer superphosphate is manufactured from the mineral $Ca_3(PO_4)_2$, which is also the most common source of elemental phosphorus, prepared by reacting the phosphate with coke in the presence of silica.

$$2Ca_3(PO_4)_2 + 6SiO_2 + 10C \rightarrow P_4 + 10CO + 6CaSiO_3$$

Elemental phosphorus exists in two quite different forms. While it is not unique in this (consider for example carbon as diamond and graphite) the two allotropes of phosphorus are remarkably different. 'White phosphorus' is a white, waxy pyrophoric solid of extreme toxicity even to skin contact. 'Red phosphorus' is a red crystalline material, harder and much less reactive. It is unaffected by lengthy exposure to the atmosphere and is not particularly toxic. In forming compounds the usual valence states of phosphorus are +3 and, much more commonly, +5 as in the phosphates. The organic 'phosphines,' such as triphenyl phosphine, $(C_6H_5)_3P$, are analogues of the amines and are important 'ligands,' forming a wide variety of compounds with transition metals and acting as important modifiers of the reactivity and catalytic properties of those metals.

Sulphur in its elemental form is produced mainly from removal of the hydrogen sulphide impurity in natural gas, as in Alberta, or from large deposits of the element itself, as in the Texas and Louisiana Gulf coasts. The most important sulphur compound commercially is sulphuric acid which is produced in several ways, an important one being the utilization of SO_2 in the smelter fumes from treatment of metal sulphide ores. Sulphur is also present in most coals, and much SO_2 enters the atmosphere wherever coal is burned in large quantities such as thermal electric generating stations. This SO_2 dissolves in rain, is oxidized, and falls into natural water courses, the so-called 'acid rain.' This is one of the most serious environmental problems of the day.

FURTHER READING

Von Spronsen, J.W., The Periodic System of the Chemical Elements, Elsevier, London, 1969. This is a highly readable and interesting account of the historical development of the table and of the many attempts over the course of the last century to devise better forms.

Sanderson, R.T., Chemical Periodicity, Reinhold, New York, 1960. This book analyzes the trends observed for many properties of the elements and their compounds.

Trotman-Dickenson, A.F., editor, Comprehensive Inorganic Chemistry, Pergamon Press, London, 1973. This five volume set provides an extensive description of the chemistry of all of the elements.

PROBLEMS

1. Figures 8-3 and 8-4 indicate that 7 fluorines but only 3 chlorines can be bonded to I, 7 fluorines but only 6 chlorines to W, and 6 fluorines but only 4 chlorines to S. Many such pairs can be found. Suggest one factor that might give rise to these differences. Predict what this would mean for bromides and iodides and then consult a modern inorganic textbook to find the maximum ratio n/m which has been found for X_mBr_n and X_mI_n. What determines which elements, X, reflect this factor and which do not?

2. Figure 8-14 shows those elements which are metals. Discuss the relationship between this distribution and those shown in Figures 8-12 and 8-13.

3. For the first fifty elements, consult density data in order to calculate and plot the molar volume of the material as a liquid or solid at 25°C or, in the case of materials which are gases at 25°C, at the boiling point. Plot as a function of atomic number and compare the periodicity with that observed in plots in this chapter.

4. Hydrogen is sometimes placed at the head of both the lithium group and the fluorine group. What justification can you produce for each on the basis of the chemistry of hydrogen?

5. Use the data in Appendix 1 to look for periodic trends in properties such as ΔH_f° of hydrides or oxides of the elements. Look, too, for trends in the columns (e.g. CH_4, SiH_4, GeH_4, etc.). Compare these trends with those in Figures 8-12 and 8-13. Are the trends roughly the same?

IX THE NATURE OF ATOMS

When John Dalton proposed his theory of the atomic nature of substances in 1803, his major concern was with the properties of gases, the masses of atoms, the ratios of the number of atoms which combine together (i.e. the valences of the atoms), and the concept of elements consisting only of atoms which were all of the same type. He had no knowledge of the internal workings of atoms and no way of finding out about those internal workings, and postulated that atoms are indivisible. That atoms have been subsequently broken down into smaller parts did not affect the value of his work, since none of the experiments of his time disagreed with his postulate. By including the indivisibility idea in his theory, he was able to concentrate on the relative masses and valences of the atoms, which proved to be the foundation of modern chemistry.

Almost a hundred years were to pass before experiments indicated that atoms are made of even smaller particles, assembled in a complicated way. The structure of atoms was determined primarily by physicists at the beginning of the twentieth century, and the amount of chemical evidence used in the development of the new theories was insignificant. However, the nature of atoms is so basic to the modern understanding of chemistry, and to the science of materials, that it forms an essential part of the introduction to chemistry.

Atoms are so small that the conventional measuring equipment in an elementary laboratory cannot be used in any simple way to measure the diameter or mass of a single atom. The magnitudes to be measured are very much smaller than the smallest distance which can be measured with a ruler, or the smallest mass which can be detected on a balance. Upon reflection, this is not surprising, for the measuring equipment is itself made of atoms, and so the calibrated scale on which the diameter or mass of the atom is to be read must be much larger than the atom, or else the atomic nature of matter must have been obvious to everyone long ago. In many experiments on the structure of atoms, either a beam of light or a beam of high energy sub-atomic particles is bounced off the atoms which are to be studied. By applying existing knowledge of optics and mechanics to measurements on the reflected beams, the nature of atoms can be discovered. In other experiments, atoms absorb energy, which is then emitted in the form of light which in turn yields information about atoms.

9-1   EXPERIMENTS WITH PARTICLES

When a particle is moving at a moderate speed through space, Newton's laws of motion are obeyed, so that mass multiplied by acceleration is equal to the force at all times. This law apparently applies equally to sub-atomic particles in free space, billiard balls and planets, making it possible to determine the mass or kinetic energy of these objects by applying suitable forces. If an atomic or sub-atomic particle does not carry an electric charge, it is impossible to apply a measured force to it. Therefore, the majority of measurements have been made on charged particles, either positive or negative ions, or electrons. Force can be applied to a charged particle by means of an electric field which acts directly on the charge, or by means of a magnetic field, which produces a force on a charged particle in motion. The properties of the sub-atomic particles were defined and measured in three important experiments carried out between 1897 and 1909, in which Newton's laws of mechanics were applied to measurements of the motion of charged particles in fields controlled by laboratory apparatus.

(i)   The Charge/Mass Ratio of the Electron.   In 1897 J. J. Thomson at the University of Cambridge carried out a series of experiments in which the ratio of charge (e) to mass (m) of electrons was measured. Electrons had already been identified as the negatively charged particles constituting "cathode rays," which can be produced by applying a high voltage between metal electrodes in an evacuated tube containing only a small amount of residual gas. The electrons released from the cathode (or negative electrode) are accelerated to the anode (or positive electrode). In Thomson's experiment the electrons were confined to a narrow beam by a series of slits and then deflected by electric and magnetic fields applied at right angles to the path of the beam. The deflection of the beam was measured using a fluorescent screen. Thomson carried out two different experiments using independent methods, and showed that the two results were consistent. He also showed that his results were the same no matter what the chemical composition of the residual gas in the tube.

In the first experiment he measured the current carried by the electrons, the rate of rise of temperature of the anode, and the radius of curvature of the path of the electrons in an externally applied magnetic field.

In the second experiment, two measurements were made, the sideways deflection of the beam of electrons due to a known electric field at right angles to the path, and the strength of the magnetic field which, when applied at right angles to both the beam and the electric field, reduced this deflection to zero.

The numerical value of e/m determined in these experiments was approximately 1×10^{11} C/kg. The currently accepted value is 1.7588×10^{11} C/kg. The experiments showed that electrons behave like charged particles, and obey the ordinary laws of mechanics, when they travel through a vacuum. The experiments were astonishing to many people because they showed that matter could exist in particles smaller than atoms.

(ii) The Charge on the Electron.   About 1900 R. A. Millikan at the University of Chicago was carrying out experiments on the motion of very small oil droplets in air. Acting on such a droplet is the force of gravity and, if the droplet is moving, an opposing force due to the viscosity of the air. Millikan found that an electric field exerted an additional force on droplets, showing that droplets generally carry an electric charge. Using a microscope to follow the motion of individual droplets, he was able to determine the charge on each droplet. The charges were usually very small, of the order of magnitude of the charge on a single ion, which can be estimated from the Faraday law of electrolysis and the Avogadro constant. Upon examination, the droplet charges which Millikan measured were found to be multiples of a single charge. This charge was interpreted as being the charge on a single electron, and was published by Millikan in 1909 as 1.59×10^{-19} C. The accepted value of e at present is 1.60210×10^{-19} C. Using the value of e/m determined by the methods of J. J. Thomson, the mass of the electron could be calculated, and so it became known that the electron had only about 1/1800 of the mass of a hydrogen atom. This showed in turn that the mass of an atom is associated almost entirely with the positively charged part, and that the electrons contribute only a small fraction of the total mass.

(iii) α-Particle Scattering by Atoms.   The phenomenon of radioactivity was discovered at the end of the nineteenth century, and provided several important methods of studying atoms, both directly, and by providing a source of energetic particles which could be "bounced" off other atoms. The most significant of these early experiments was carried out by H. Geiger and E. Marsden in collaboration with Ernest Rutherford at the University of Manchester about 1911. It had been shown that an *α-particle* is massive compared to an electron and carries a great deal of momentum as well as kinetic energy. In this experiment, a beam of α-particles was directed at a very thin foil of metallic gold. Many particles passed through the foil undeflected, but some were deflected by collisions with the atoms in the foil, a process called *scattering*. A fluorescent screen was used to determine the relative numbers of scattered particles at different angles of deflection. It was shown that while most of the scattered α-particles were deflected through small angles, some were deflected through large angles, their motion being almost reversed. Rutherford found that he could explain the relative numbers of α-particles scattered through different angles by applying classical mechanics to collisions between the α-particles and exceedingly small, heavy particles in the atoms of the gold foil. The force of repulsion between the α-particle and the postulated particle in each gold atom was shown to be electrostatic in nature, varying in proportion to the inverse square of the distance between the particles. The new kind of particle, the *nucleus* of the atom, was shown to be no bigger than 10^{-14} m in diameter, and carried a positive charge about a hundred times bigger than the charge on the electron, in the case of gold.

These three experiments carried out by Thomson, Millikan and Rutherford provided the basis for the modern view of the structure of the atom: there is a very small, positively charged nucleus which carries virtually all the mass of the atom, surrounded by a number of negatively charged electrons sufficient

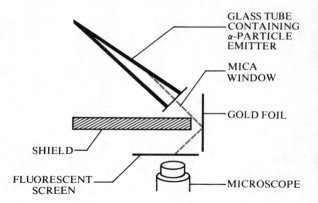

GLASS TUBE
CONTAINING
α-PARTICLE
EMITTER

MICA
WINDOW

GOLD FOIL

SHIELD

FLUORESCENT
SCREEN

MICROSCOPE

Figure 9-1   Apparatus used by Rutherford, Geiger and Marsden in discovering the large-angle scattering of α-particles by a gold foil.

to balance the charge on the nucleus. The atom is electrically neutral as a whole, but may be converted to a positive ion by removing an electron, or to a negative ion by adding an electron. As suggested by Dalton, all the atoms of an element are chemically similar, since an element is characterized by its number of electrons, equal to the charge on the nucleus. However, it is found that the mass of the nucleus of an atom of a given element may take one of several values, the existence of *isotopes,* and so all atoms of a given element need not have identical mass. The "nuclear model" of the atom is the basis for subsequent developments in chemistry and physics. However, the details of the arrangement and motion of the electrons around the nucleus are more complicated, and more important for chemistry than the model suggests so far. The study of the electrons is largely carried out by means of experiments using the light emitted by atoms under certain conditions.

9-2   EXPERIMENTS WITH LIGHT

The nature of light has been the subject of speculation and experiment for hundreds of years, and it would be foolish to claim that the story has ended. The question is of special importance because so many experiments involve light in some way. In chemistry, for example, most knowledge of molecular properties is obtained by studying the interaction of light with chemical systems. There have been several stages in the development of present ideas. Isaac Newton believed that light consisted of a stream of particles despite his familiarity with some interference effects, but a little later the theory of the Dutch scientist Christian Huygens that light consists of a wave motion found universal acceptance. The wave theory of light is important because it provides a method of classifying light according to wavelength. Precise methods for measuring the wavelength were developed, and invisible light in the infrared (long wavelength) and ultraviolet (short wavelength) regions of the spectrum was discovered. It was found that eyes are sensitive to only a very narrow region of the total spectrum of radiation. The wave theory became firmly established when James Clerk Maxwell, working at King's College, London, in about 1865, developed the mathematical theory of electricity and magnetism, predicted the existence of electro-magnetic waves, and showed that the calculated speed of these waves should be equal to the measured speed of light. A little later Heinrich Hertz in Germany detected long-wavelength "radio" waves from an electric spark, in agreement with Maxwell's prediction, thus confirming the concept of an electromagnetic spectrum extending to wavelengths both greater and smaller in magnitude than those of visible light. The extent of the electromagnetic spectrum, with modern classifications as to region, is shown in Figure 9-2.

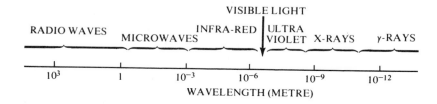

Figure 9-2   Regions of the electromagnetic spectrum, on a logarithmic scale of wavelength.

An instrument capable of classifying light according to wavelength is called a *spectroscope;* if it is able to make its classification so that wavelengths can be measured it is a *spectrometer,* and if it can in addition measure the intensity of light of each wavelength it is called a *spectrophotometer.* These descriptions of spectroscopic instruments are based upon the wave theory of light. Ironically, the development of spectroscopic instruments provided a great deal of experimental evidence which showed that the wave theory of light is "incorrect," or at any rate incomplete. Experiments in three areas of physics provided the basis for the development of the quantum theory of light.

(i) Furnace Radiation.   A simple source of light is a hot object which glows red. The light becomes "white light" if the temperature is increased. Even at temperatures below "red heat," radiation can be felt by hand, indicating that infrared light is being emitted. At the end of the nineteenth century, a number of scientists studied the light emitted by hot objects, measuring the relative intensities of light of different wavelengths using spectrophotometers. The spectral characteristics of the light depend to some extent on the colour of the object being studied, but it was found that the light leaving a small hole in the side of a furnace was independent of the materials used to build the furnace. The light emitted by furnaces was studied very carefully and was referred to as "black body radiation" or "furnace radiation." The study of furnace radiation led to the quantum theory of radiation, in which it is supposed that light consists of particles rather than waves. The paradox is that in reaching this conclusion scientists used instuments which measure the *wavelength* of the light!

The radiation from a hot furnace contains light of all wavelengths. The intensity of radiation is low at both very long and very short wavelengths, and is a maximum at some intermediate wavelength. If the temperature of the furnace is changed, both the total intensity of the radiation and the relative distribution of intensity among different wavelengths change.

In the following, the intensity is discussed as a function of frequency rather than wavelength, but it should be remembered that when dealing with light waves (infrared, visible or ultraviolet) it is wavelength rather than frequency which is measured. The speed of light in vacuo is $c = 3.00 \times 10^8$ m/s, and so if λ is the wavelength of a certain light wave, the frequency, ν, of that light is given by $\nu = c/\lambda$. Frequency is measured in cycles per second or *hertz*. The distribution of intensity of furnace radiation as a function of frequency is shown in Figure 9-3 for several different temperatures of the furnace. There are two experimental facts about these curves.

(a) The total intensity of radiation from a furnace, I(T), is proportional to the fourth power of the temperature,

$$I(T) = aT^4,$$

where the constant a is called Stefan's constant. The total intensity is measured by the area under the appropriate curve in Figure 9-3.

(b) The frequency at which the maximum intensity occurs, ν_{max}, is proportional to the temperature,

$$\nu_{max} = bT,$$

where the constant b is called Wien's constant.

All attempts to explain the form of these curves on the basis of the electromagnetic theory of light were unsuccessful. The problem was solved when Max Planck, at the University of Berlin, described the phenomenon in terms of a "quantum" of energy. He developed this theory fully, but it was so strange to his way of thinking that it has been said that he did not fully believe the theory himself. Planck assumed that the light of frequency ν in furnace radiation was associated with an oscillator of the same frequency. But instead of being able to contain any amount of energy, the oscillator could absorb or emit only discrete, or quantized, amounts of energy $h\nu$, $2h\nu$, $3h\nu$, . . . where h is a constant. The quantity h was introduced as a method of developing the theory and it was thought that when the mathematical limit $h \to 0$ was taken, the correct description would appear. Planck found, however, that the proper fit to experimental facts could only be obtained if h were given a definite non-zero value. The fundamental constant h is called the Planck constant and has the value of 6.6×10^{-34} J s.

In addition to h the theory contained the Boltzmann constant k, which may be thought of as the gas constant R divided by the Avogadro constant N_a, k = R/N_a. From the measured values of the two radiation constants a and b, the two fundamental constants h and k were determined. Knowing the Boltzmann constant and the gas constant, the Avogadro constant was calculated. Faraday's constant, equal to the charge carried by one mole of univalent ions, was known accurately from electrochemistry and so, knowing the Avogadro constant, Planck was able to calculate the charge on an electron.

Planck's theory of furnace radiation was a turning point in science, for it

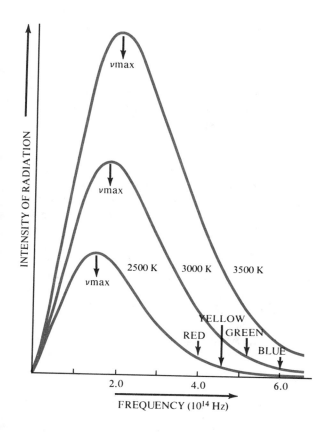

Figure 9-3 Distribution of the intensity of radiation leaving a furnace as a function of frequency, for three different furnace temperatures.

correctly described an important phenomenon, gave the values of four fundamental constants accurately and laid the foundation for the development of further quantum ideas. The theory was first publicly described on December 14, 1900, which can be regarded as the birthday of quantum physics.

(ii) The Photoelectric Effect. When light shines on a metal, electrons may be emitted from the surface into the surrounding space, as long as the wavelength is shorter than a certain threshold value. A number of experiments on this phenomenon were carried out about the turn of the century. It was found that the kinetic energy of the electrons emitted from a metal into a vacuum was proportional to the frequency of the light and independent of the intensity of the light, while the emitted current (i.e. the number of emitted electrons) was proportional to the intensity of the light beam. Albert Einstein, while working in the Swiss Patent Office, proposed in 1905 that the light beam be considered as a stream of particles, or "photons," each of which carried an energy $h\nu$. Upon reaching the metal, the photon may be reflected unchanged if the metal acts as a mirror, or it may be absorbed in which case the photon is totally destroyed and its energy converted to the kinetic energy of an electron. If this energy is greater than the energy binding the electron to the metal then the electron may be emitted. The kinetic energy of the electron outside the metal should be equal to the energy of the photon which was destroyed, less the binding energy ϕ, which depends upon the chemical nature of the metal:

$$\tfrac{1}{2}mv^2 = h\nu - \phi$$

The kinetic energy of the emitted electron can be measured electrostatically provided that the charge on the electron is known. Originally the ratio h/e was the quantity determined, and the value obtained was consistent with existing measurements of h and e. The experiment was much refined by Millikan who published a full verification of the equation and an accurate value for h in 1916.

(iii) The Compton Effect.   The concept of light as a photon stream received further support in 1923 when A. H. Compton at Washington University in St. Louis proposed an explanation for a curious effect in the scattering of X-rays from paraffin wax. It was found that X-rays may be scattered by the paraffin with a small increase in wavelength. This phenomenon is surprising because, while light is often scattered as it passes through materials, there is generally no change of wavelength caused by the scattering process. The geometry of the experiments is shown in Figure 9-4. The increase in wavelength was found to be proportional to $\sin^2 \theta/2$. Compton proposed that this was the result of a collision of a photon with a nearly stationary electron. Using the theory of relativity, the linear momentum of a photon was shown to be h/λ. By applying the principles of conservation of energy and conservation of linear momentum, Compton showed that there must be an increase in wavelength (i.e. decrease in frequency ν) of the scattered photon, because some of the momentum of the photon is carried off by the electron after the collision. The wavelength shift calculated in this way agreed with the observed shift, both in magnitude and its dependence on the scattering angle θ.

These three phenomena showed that while light can be classified according to its wavelength, it often interacts with matter in a way consistent with the existence of discrete particles or photons having energy $h\nu$ and momentum h/λ. The possibility of light behaving in two distinct ways is called the *wave-particle*

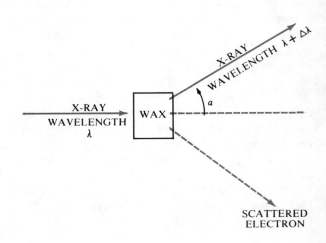

Figure 9-4   Compton scattering of X-rays.

duality. It was later postulated by Louis de Broglie that electrons can also show wave-like properties in certain circumstances, despite the particle-like properties demonstrated by J. J. Thomson, and this postulate has been verified by experimental observations.

9-3   SPECTRA OF ATOMS: HYDROGEN

Most of the experimental information about the electronic structure of atoms has been obtained by studying the light emitted by "excited" atoms using a spectrometer. The spectra of atoms are remarkable because unlike the continuous spectrum of light emitted by a furnace, an atomic spectrum consists of a large number of exceedingly sharp "lines." For instance, the spectrum of the light from an electrical discharge through hydrogen gas is compared with the black body spectrum in Figure 9-5. The electrical energy of the discharge is sufficient to dissociate the hydrogen molecules into atoms, and to excite the atoms to states of high internal energy. Light is emitted when the excited atoms spontaneously revert to their normal lowest energy, or "ground" state.

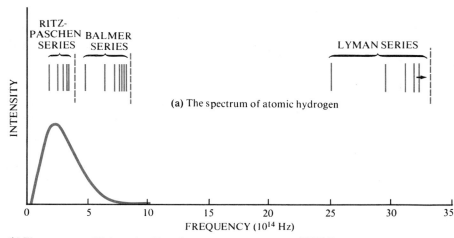

(a) The spectrum of atomic hydrogen

(b) The spectrum of light emitted by a furnace at a temperature of 3500 K

Figure 9-5 The spectrum of atomic hydrogen compared with the spectrum of furnace radiation.

To early workers in this field, the existence of sharp lines seemed to indicate the presence of "oscillators" inside the atom, with a separate oscillator frequency giving rise to each spectral line. Such an idea appeared to be at variance with the Rutherford "Solar-System" concept of the atom, which suggested instead the existence of electrons moving in planetary orbits around the nucleus. Thus, there seemed to be no reason why the simplest atom, hydrogen, should show so many different frequencies of oscillation when it consisted of only two particles, an electron and a nucleus. The complexity of the spectrum of a given element was found to be related to the position of the element in the periodic table. The simplest spectra are found for hydrogen and the alkali metals. By contrast, transition metals show exceedingly complex spectra with thousands of lines in the visible part of the spectrum, and more in the infrared and ultraviolet.

Two elementary facts about atomic spectra are of importance in technology. Firstly, Figure 9-5 shows that the furnace spectrum for a temperature of 3500 K has hardly any intensity at frequencies higher than the visible region, and yet the atomic spectrum of hydrogen extends far into the ultraviolet, high energy, part of the spectrum. It is thus impossible to generate any appreciable amount of ultraviolet light by means of an incandescent object such as a hot tungsten wire. If ultraviolet light is required, a source using excited atoms such as a mercury vapour lamp must be used. Secondly, in chemical analysis the presence or absence of a given element in a sample can be detected with very high sensitivity by spectroscopic analysis of the light emitted when the atoms in the sample are excited by an electrical discharge or a flame. There is little overlap of the spectral lines of different elements and so a determination of the elements present can be made by comparison with the known atomic spectra. Indeed, even in qualitative analytical chemistry, elements can be identified by the colour induced in a flame by a drop of solution. Different elements cause different colours in flame tests because the spectra of the atoms are different.

In this section the optical spectrum of atomic hydrogen will be analyzed. This is the simplest spectrum, and the theoretical analysis given by Niels Bohr in 1913 marked the first application of quantum ideas to the structure of matter.

The spectrum of atomic hydrogen, shown in Figure 9-5, consists of several groups or "series" of lines which are bunched together at the high frequency end, reaching a stage where the spacing between the lines becomes vanishingly small, at the *series limit*. Several series limits are shown, for the Lyman series in the ultraviolet region, the Balmer series in the visible region, and the Ritz-Paschen series in the infrared region. The key to understanding the hydrogen atom structure was careful measurement of the wavelengths of the lines, carried out by a number of workers at the end of the nineteenth century. Rydberg and others showed that the wavelengths of the lines fitted with remarkable precision to the following empirical formula:

$$\frac{1}{\lambda} = R_H \left(\frac{1}{n_1{}^2} - \frac{1}{n_2{}^2} \right) \tag{1}$$

where R_H is a constant having the value 1.096788×10^7 m^{-1}, and n_1 and n_2 are positive integers. Each series of lines is characterized by a particular value of n_1, and each line within a series corresponds to a value of n_2 greater than n_1. For the Lyman series $n_1 = 1$, $n_2 = 2, 3, 4, \ldots$, for the Balmer series $n_1 = 2$, $n_2 = 3, 4, 5, \ldots$, and so on.

The accuracy of the fit of the experimental data to this equation should be emphasized. The equation predicts the wavelength of lines as accurately as those wavelengths could be measured at the time of Rydberg. For example, the longest wavelength member of the Balmer series has a wavelength of 656.460 nm. From the formula, with $n_1 = 2$, $n_2 = 3$,

$$\frac{1}{\lambda} = 1.096788 \times 10^7 \left(\frac{1}{4} - \frac{1}{9} \right)$$

yielding $\lambda = 656.463$ nm. The error in this case is 3 parts in 600 000, far better than the precision of fit of most measurements to empirical formulae. The Rydberg formula is an exact description of some property of the hydrogen atom.

When an electric charge is accelerated, Maxwell's theory of electrodynamics predicts that an electromagnetic wave is emitted. This principle is used in a radio transmitter. The transmitter creates oscillations of electric charge in a suitable antenna so as to radiate waves at the frequency of oscillation. An electromagnetic wave carries energy with it, and so the transmitter has to supply the energy required to maintain the oscillation.

A hydrogen atom consists of two charged particles, a positively charged nucleus and a single negatively charged electron, which are involved in some sort of accelerated motion because of the electrostatic force between the charges. The acceleration of the charged particles within the atom should therefore produce radiation, which would carry energy with it. Hence the atom should lose energy continuously, causing the electron to spiral into the nucleus. This kind of instability is contrary to all observations on atoms, and so the classical theory of electrodynamics was unable to account for the properties of hydrogen atoms. The problem of describing atomic structure was therefore a major concern of physics and chemistry at the beginning of the twentieth century.

Bohr proposed a solution to the problem of the hydrogen atom using several hypotheses which led to agreement with the observed facts, even though, as with Planck's theory of furnace radiation, the hypotheses appeared radical at the time.

First Hypothesis: Certain discrete energy states of the atom are stable and do not lose energy by continuous radiation of light.

Second Hypothesis: Light is emitted or absorbed when an atom passes from one of these discrete energy states to another; the frequency (ν) and wavelength (λ) of the light are given by the Planck relationship

$$E_2 - E_1 = h\nu = hc/\lambda \tag{2}$$

where E_1, E_2 are the energies of the two discrete energy states.

The first hypothesis amounts to a declaration by Bohr that he is ignoring what he cannot explain. The second hypothesis applies Planck's hypothesis and the principle of conservation of energy to atoms. The energy of the photon is hc/λ, and when an atom absorbs or emits a photon, the energy of the photon must be compensated by an equal change in the energy of the atom.

These two hypotheses allow the construction of an *energy level diagram* for the hydrogen atom, in which the energy of every line in the spectrum is represented as the difference between two energy levels. The form of the energy level diagram is fixed by comparing the Rydberg formula, equation (1), with the second hypothesis, equation (2):

$$\frac{1}{\lambda} = \frac{R_H}{n_1^2} - \frac{R_H}{n_2^2} = \frac{E_2}{hc} - \frac{E_1}{hc}$$

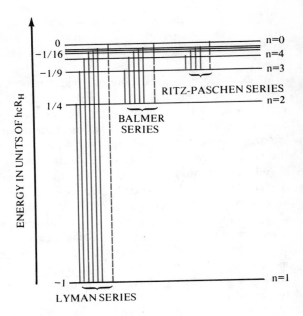

Figure 9-6   The energy levels of the hydrogen atom. Several series of transitions between levels are shown, corresponding to various series of spectral lines. The series limits are shown by dotted lines.

This identity suggests that the energy levels are $E_1 = -hcR_H/n_1^2$ and $E_2 = -hcR_H/n_2^2$. For any integer n, there is an energy level with energy

$$E_n = -\frac{hcR_H}{n^2} \tag{3}$$

The integer n is called a *quantum number,* and can be used to catalogue the energy levels. Figure 9-6 shows the energy level diagram for the hydrogen atom corresponding to equation (3), with the various series of spectral lines shown as *transitions* between energy levels.

Example 9-1   Calculate the numerical value and units for the quantity hcR_H.

Using the accepted values of h and c from the table of fundamental constants on the inside back cover.

$$hcR_H = 6.6262 \times 10^{-34}\ \text{J s}$$
$$\times\ 2.9979 \times 10^8\ \text{m s}^{-1}$$
$$\times\ 1.096788 \times 10^7\ \text{m}^{-1}$$
$$=\ 2.1788 \times 10^{-18}\ \text{J}$$

The spectrum does not by itself prove that the n = 1 level lies lowest in energy, for the same set of levels turned upside down would yield the same spectrum. However, a wealth of other evidence shows that Figure 9-6 is the correct order of energies.

The spectrum does not fix the origin of the energy scale. Every line in a spectrum is related to two energy levels, and the wavelength is determined by the difference, so that the origin of the energy scale is arbitrary. In the diagram the zero of energy is placed at the n = ∞ limit, but it would be equally valid to place the zero of energy anywhere else, and it is sometimes put at the n = 1 energy level.

The concept of an energy level diagram was a great simplification of atomic spectroscopy, for it meant that the thousands of spectral lines of a given spectrum could be described in terms of a much smaller set of energy levels. Furthermore, wavelengths of lines not yet observed could be predicted with great accuracy. The energy level concept is valid for all atoms, molecules and other spectroscopic systems, and is an aspect of Bohr's theory of the hydrogen atom spectrum which remains valid in modern quantum theory.

Example 9-2   Calculate the wavelength of the transition n = 33 to n = 34 in the hydrogen atom spectrum. In what spectral region does this transition lie?

From the Rydberg formula,

$$\frac{1}{\lambda} = 1.096788 \times 10^7 \left(\frac{1}{33^2} - \frac{1}{34^2} \right)$$

$$= 5.8373 \times 10^2 \text{ m}^{-1}$$

Hence $\lambda = 1.7131$ mm, and the transition is in the microwave spectral region.

Example 9-3   The series limit of the Balmer series of the hydrogen atom spectrum occurs at a wavelength of 364.5 nm, and the first line of the Lyman series occurs at 121.5 nm. Calculate the wavelength of the series limit of the Lyman series.

Referring to Figure 9-6, the energy of the Lyman series limit is the sum of the energy of the Balmer series limit and the energy of the first Lyman line:

$$\Delta E_{1 \to \infty} = \Delta E_{1 \to 2} + \Delta E_{2 \to \infty}$$

Writing this equation in terms of wavelengths,

$$\frac{hc}{\lambda} = \frac{hc}{364.5 \times 10^{-9}} + \frac{hc}{121.5 \times 10^{-9}}$$

Hence $\frac{1}{\lambda} = \frac{1}{10^{-9}} \left(\frac{1}{364.5} + \frac{1}{121.5} \right) = 1.097 \times 10^7 \text{ m}^{-1}$

and so $\lambda = 9.116 \times 10^{-8}$ m $= 91.16$ nm

9-4   THE MECHANICS OF THE HYDROGEN ATOM

The energy level diagram is the most important concept in understanding spectroscopy, but it does not help directly in understanding the laws governing the motion of electrons in atoms. In this section, Bohr's discussion of the mechanics of a hydrogen atom is summarized and the relation between the

Rydberg constant and other constants demonstrated. The treatment is not quite straightforward, and those without a taste for algebra may wish to omit the first part and begin their reading with equations (13) and (14).

In the Rutherford model of the hydrogen atom a single electron moves in an orbit around a single heavy nucleus, under the influence of the force of electrostatic attraction. Since the electrostatic force between two charges is inversely proportional to the square of the distance between them, it is similar to the gravitational attraction between celestial bodies, and the electron orbit should be circular or elliptical like a planetary orbit. For an electron of charge $-e$ moving with a speed v in a circular orbit of radius r around a nucleus of charge $+e$, the acceleration towards the centre is v^2/r, and application of Newton's law of motion gives:

mass × acceleration = electrostatic force.

$$m \times \frac{v^2}{r} = \frac{e^2}{4\pi\varepsilon_0 r^2} \tag{4}$$

In this equation, ε_0 represents the permittivity of free space and has the value $8.8542 \times 10^{-12} C^2 J^{-1} m^{-1}$. The permittivity of free space is the constant of proportionality which is part of the inverse square law of electrostatic force in the SI system of units. The kinetic energy of the electron is $\frac{1}{2}mv^2$, and using equation (4),

$$E_k = \tfrac{1}{2}mv^2 = \frac{e^2}{8\pi\varepsilon_0 r}$$

The potential energy of the electron in the electrostatic field is

$$E_p = -\frac{e^2}{4\pi\varepsilon_0 r}$$

and so the total energy is

$$E = E_k + E_p = \left(\frac{1}{8} - \frac{1}{4}\right)\frac{e^2}{\pi\varepsilon_0 r} = -\frac{e^2}{8\pi\varepsilon_0 r} \tag{5}$$

Notice that the state of zero energy is that of an electron at rest infinitely far from the nucleus.

The frequency of rotation of the electron in its orbit, f, is equal to the speed divided by the circumference of the orbit. Calculating the speed from equation (4),

$$f = \frac{v}{2\pi r} = \frac{1}{2\pi r}\left(\frac{e^2}{4\pi\varepsilon_0 mr}\right)^{\frac{1}{2}} \tag{6}$$

According to classical electrodynamics, the electron should radiate electromagnetic waves of frequency equal to f. The energy carried by the waves must be supplied by the atom and, by equation (5), as E becomes lower (that is, more negative) the radius r must get smaller. This is inconsistent with the observed fact that the properties of atoms are constant in time, and it is at this point that quantum ideas must be introduced.

It was concluded from Bohr's first two postulates that there are quantized energy levels for the electron in the hydrogen atom. Comparison of equation (3) with equation (5) shows that the radius of a stable orbit, r_n, must be "quantized," being proportional to the square of the quantum number n. This is expressed in the equation

$$r_n = n^2 a_0 \tag{7}$$

where a_0 is the radius of the n = 1 orbit. From equations (5) and (7) the energy of the electron is

$$E_n = -\left(\frac{e^2}{8\pi\varepsilon_0 a_0}\right)\frac{1}{n^2} \tag{8}$$

and from equations (6) and (7), the frequency of rotation in this orbit is

$$f_n = \frac{1}{2\pi a_0}\left(\frac{e^2}{4\pi\varepsilon_0 m a_0}\right)^{\frac{1}{2}}\frac{1}{n^3} \tag{9}$$

The frequency of the light emitted in a quantum jump from level n + 1 to level n is, by equation (8),

$$\nu_{n+1\to n} = (E_{n+1} - E_n)/h$$

$$= \frac{e^2}{8\pi\varepsilon_0 a_0 h}\left(\frac{1}{n^2} - \frac{1}{(n+1)^2}\right)$$

$$= \frac{e^2}{8\pi\varepsilon_0 a_0 h} \cdot \frac{2n+1}{n^2(n+1)^2} \tag{10}$$

The frequency f given by (9) is not equal to the quantum frequency ν given by (10). Classical mechanics has led to incorrect conclusions when applied to the very small particles found in atoms. And yet classical mechanics is not wrong on the macroscopic scale and Bohr saw that for very large orbits with large quantum numbers the classical and quantum frequencies ought to be equal. This **third hypothesis** is called the "correspondence principle."

For large values of n, the quantum frequency from (10) can be approximated by

$$\nu_{n+1\to n} \approx \frac{e^2}{8\pi\varepsilon_0 a_0 h} \cdot \frac{2n}{n^4}$$

$$= \frac{e^2}{4\pi\varepsilon_0 a_0 h} \cdot \frac{1}{n^3} \tag{11}$$

Comparing equations (9) and (11), the coefficients of $1/n^3$ must be equal, according to the correspondence principle:

$$\frac{e^2}{4\pi\varepsilon_0 a_0 h} = \frac{1}{2\pi a_0}\left(\frac{e^2}{4\pi\varepsilon_0 m a_0}\right)^{\frac{1}{2}}$$

which can be solved for a_0:

$$a_0 = \frac{\varepsilon_0 h^2}{\pi e^2 m} \tag{12}$$

This gives the radius of the first Bohr orbit in terms of the fundamental constants ε_0, h, e and m. From (8) and (12), the quantized energy levels are

$$E_n = -\frac{me^4}{8\varepsilon_o^2h^2} \cdot \frac{1}{n^2} \tag{13}$$

and by comparison with (3), the value of the Rydberg constant is:

$$R_H = \frac{me^4}{8\varepsilon_o^2h^3c} \tag{14}$$

Example 9-4   Calculate the numerical value and units of R_H from the fundamental constants.

Using accepted values of the constants,

$$R_H = \frac{9.10953 \times 10^{-31} \times (1.60219 \times 10^{-19})^4}{8 \times (8.85419\times10^{-12})^2 \times (6.62618\times10^{-34})^3 \times 2.99793\times10^8}$$

$$= 1.09737 \times 10^7$$

The units are

$$\frac{kg \ C^4}{(C^2J^{-1} \ m^{-1})^2 \ (J \ s)^3 \ (m \ s^{-1})}$$

$$= \frac{kg}{m^{-1} \ J \ s^2}$$

$$= m^{-1} \qquad \text{since } J = kg \ m^2 \ s^{-2}$$

It is seen that this result is very close to the measured value of R_H. A correction is needed because the centre of mass of the atom does not lie exactly at the nucleus; this correction alters the calculated value by the factor $m_p/(m_p + m_e)$ = 0.9994556, giving a corrected value of $R_H = 1.09677 \times 10^7 m^{-1}$ which agrees with the experimental value within the limits of accuracy of the mass of the electron.

The additional postulate of the correspondence principle allowed the accurate calculation of the Rydberg constant from other physical constants and was a triumph for Bohr. It should be noted that if the correspondence principle were not true, doubt would be cast on the conclusions of J.J. Thomson who applied classical mechanics to the motion of electrons along paths which extend over laboratory scale distances. It is only in the very confined space in an atom that quantum mechanics becomes important. How big, then, is a hydrogen atom, for which the new theory is required? The distance a_o is the radius of the smallest orbit, and gives a measure of the size of atoms in general. From Equation (12),

$$a_o = \frac{8.85419\times10^{-12} \times (6.62618\times10^{-34})^2}{3.14159 \times (1.60219\times10^{-19})^2 \times 9.10953\times10^{-31}}$$

$$= 5.2918 \times 10^{-11} \ m$$

$$= 0.0529 \ nm$$

It is not possible to verify this number experimentally but it gives a measure of the order of magnitude of the distances involved in the study of atoms and molecules.

The integer n is an example of a quantum number, being a number used to classify the allowed energy states of the system. In this case, the quantum number determines the energy of the atom, through equation (13). In atomic and molecular physics various types of quantum numbers are used to describe allowed states, and not all quantum numbers affect the energy. The quantum number n that was introduced for the hydrogen atom is called the *principal quantum number,* and is found to be important in describing the states of electrons in atoms which are more complicated than hydrogen.

The quantization of the energy and the radius of the orbit has a further important result. The *angular momentum* of the electron is the product of the radius and the linear momentum, L = mvr, for a circular orbit. The angular momentum of an electron in a circular orbit is quantized in a very simple way. From equations (4), (7) and (12),

$$L = m \left(\frac{e^2}{4\pi\varepsilon_o mr} \right)^{\frac{1}{2}}$$

$$= \left(\frac{me^2 r}{4\pi\varepsilon_o} \right)^{\frac{1}{2}}$$

$$= \left(\frac{me^2 n^2 \varepsilon_o h^2}{4\pi\varepsilon_o \pi e^2 m} \right)^{\frac{1}{2}}$$

$$= n \left(\frac{h}{2\pi} \right) \tag{15}$$

Thus the angular momentum appears to take only integral multiples of $h/2\pi$. i.e. is also quantized. The quantity $h/2\pi$ occurs often in quantum mechanics, and is often represented by the symbol $\hbar$. When elliptical orbits and the wave properties of electrons are taken into account, this result must be modified. A new quantum number, called the *orbital quantum number l,* must be introduced and the angular momentum is fixed by *l* through the formula

$$L = \sqrt{l(l + 1)} \left(\frac{h}{2\pi} \right) \tag{16}$$

The orbital quantum number takes only non-negative integer values, and must be smaller than the principal quantum number n. The following combinations of n and *l* are therefore allowed:

n	*l*
1	0
2	0 or 1
3	0, 1 or 2
4	0, 1, 2 or 3
etc.	etc.

The orbital quantum number has no effect on the energy of a hydrogen atom, but relates to the shape of the orbit. For instance, an atom in the state (n = 2, *l* = 0) has the same energy as an atom in the state (n = 2, *l* = 1). This is true only for hydrogen. The orbital quantum number is needed to classify the energy levels in all other atoms, and it is found that the dependence of electron energy on the orbital quantum number in heavier atoms is important in explaining their chemical properties and the form of the periodic table.

9-5   THE SODIUM ATOM SPECTRUM

The spectra of atoms other than hydrogen are very complex, except for the alkali metals of group I of the periodic table. The spectrum of the sodium atom is typical of the latter, and will be discussed in detail in order to demonstrate some basic facts about the behaviour of electrons in atoms. The spectrum is shown in Figure 9-7. The visible spectrum of sodium atoms is dominated by a yellow line at a wave length of 590 nm (a frequency of 5.09×10^{14} Hz), which is very intense and causes the characteristic yellow colour of a sodium lamp. The same yellow colour is seen when common salt is sprinkled into a bunsen burner flame. However, the most interesting features of the spectrum are found in the infrared and ultraviolet parts of the spectrum. Three series limits are shown, which are very similar in appearance to the series limits found in the hydrogen atom spectrum. There is a crowding together of spectral lines on the low frequency side of the limit with a characteristic spacing of the lines close to the limit. The occurrence of several series limits suggests that the whole spectrum can be analyzed into series, and this has been done in the four bands above the full spectrum in Figure 9-7.

There are four series shown. The *principal* series is so-called because the lines are the most intense; the series starts with the previously mentioned line in the yellow part of the spectrum, and extends into the ultraviolet. The lines which approach the next series limit, at a frequency of 7.35×10^{14} Hz, belong to two separate series having the same series limit. The lines of one of these

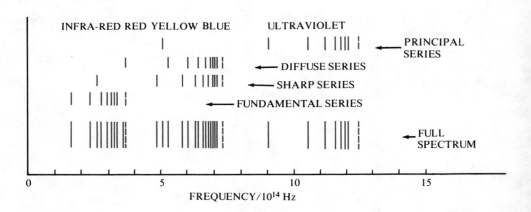

Figure 9-7   The spectrum of the sodium atom, shown plotted against frequency. The full spectrum is shown at the bottom, and the four main series of lines which contribute to the full spectrum are shown separately above it. In the visible region the most prominent line is the first line of the principal series, in the yellow part of the spectrum.

series appeared to early observers to be not so sharp as the lines of the other series, and so the two series were labelled *sharp* and *diffuse* respectively. The series limit for these two series lies in the near ultraviolet, just beyond the limit of visibility for human eyes. The fourth series was called *fundamental* by the early observers, who apparently believed that these were the lowest frequency lines which occurred. However, other series of lines have since been observed with lower frequencies, and the name "fundamental" is no longer of any significance.

The first step in understanding this spectrum is to apply the first two of Bohr's postulates to the sodium atom. It is assumed that certain energy levels, or states, of the atom are stable, and that the spectrum results from transitions between these states in a way governed by Planck's law, $h\nu = E_2 - E_1$. The energy level diagram derived from the spectrum is shown in Figure 9-8. The unit of energy is hcR_H, the same as was used for the hydrogen atom energy level diagram in Figure 9-6.

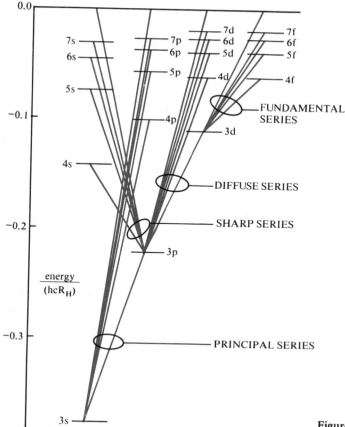

Figure 9-8   The energy levels of the sodium atom, with the four major series of transitions shown.

Instead of the single column of energy levels shown in Figure 9-6 it is seen that the energy levels are arrayed in several columns, and that each series of spectral lines results from transitions from a single energy level to the levels of an adjacent column. It is natural to classify the energy levels according to the name of the associated series of lines in the spectrum, giving rise to the following abbreviated notation for the energy levels:

> s - sharp series
>
> p - principal series
>
> d - diffuse series
>
> f - fundamental series

There are other columns of energy levels which would be placed to the right of the diagram, and these columns are given the symbols g, h, . . . in alphabetical order; these energy levels are not very important and need not be considered further here.

More detailed analysis shows that each column of energy levels corresponds to a single value of the orbital quantum number, l. In the diagram the columns are arranged from left to right in order of increasing angular momentum:

l value	symbol
0	s
1	p
2	d
3	f
4	g
etc.	etc.

The hydrogen atom energy levels could be classified according to a single-quantum number, but for sodium (and all other atoms) it is necessary to introduce the orbital quantum number. All of the observed transitions are between energy levels in adjacent columns, which corresponds to a change of $+1$ or -1 in the orbital quantum number. Rules such as this are called *selection rules*.

Within each column the energy levels are identified by a number, the principal quantum number. These numbers are arranged in order, but do not start at one, as in the case of hydrogen. There are two reasons for this. The first reason is that this diagram is incomplete, the 1s, 2s and 2p levels having been left out; the energies of these levels can only be obtained by examining the X-ray spectrum of sodium atoms, which will be discussed in the next section. These levels are occupied by electrons which are not affected by light in the ultraviolet part of the spectrum. The second reason is that since l must be less than n, certain levels do not occur. For instance in the f column, $l = 3$, and so the smallest associated value of n is 4; the 1f, 2f and 3f levels do not exist.

Closer examination of the diagram shows that while the 3s and 3p and 3d levels are separated by considerable amounts of energy, the corresponding levels for higher principal quantum numbers are close together. In addition, it is found that the energies for large n are almost the same as the energies of the hydrogen atom having the same value of n. This suggests that there is a strong similarity between the structures of the hydrogen and sodium atoms. Each atom consists of an electron or electrons moving around a positively charged ion. There is a proton and electron in the case of hydrogen, but for sodium there is a more highly charged nucleus surrounded by a group of tightly bound electrons. Referring back to equation (7) for the radius of a stable orbit in a hydrogen atom we see that, for large values of the principal quantum number, the orbit is very large since $r = n^2 a_0$. For instance, when n = 7, the radius of the orbit is 49 times the radius of the first orbit, or about 2.6 nm. An electron in such a large orbit would continue in practically the same orbit if the proton of the hydrogen atom were replaced with a Na^+ ion, which has a radius of about 0.1 nm. The charge on the Na^+ ion is the same as the charge on the proton, so that the allowed energy levels of the Na and H atoms are very similar for large principal quantum numbers.

This result leads to the conclusion that the series limits in all spectra of atoms and molecules correspond to the process of *ionization*. The outermost electron is excited to higher and higher energy levels, and in these highly excited states the electron is moving in large orbits about the positively charged ion. The orbit is very large for high values of the principal quantum number, and so the energy of the electron is almost independent of the structure of the ion at the centre of the orbit. This accounts for the very similar appearance of the spacing of lines approaching a series limit, for all atoms.

There are many numerical relationships between the wavelengths of observed spectral lines. For instance, the energies of the series limits of the principal and sharp series must differ by the energy of the 3s → 3p transition. In Figure 9-8 the energy of the ionized atom is assigned as zero, and so the wavelength of the series limit of the principal series, λ_p, is given by:

$$\frac{hc}{\lambda_p} = 0 - E_{3s} = -E_{3s}$$

and for the series limit of the sharp series the wavelength, λ_s, is given by

$$\frac{hc}{\lambda_s} = 0 - E_{3p} = -E_{3p}$$

The wavelength of the strong yellow spectral line corresponding to the 3s → 3p transition, λ_y, is given by

$$\frac{hc}{\lambda_y} = E_{3p} - E_{3s}$$

and so we see that the following relationship must hold:

$$\frac{1}{\lambda_p} = \frac{1}{\lambda_s} + \frac{1}{\lambda_y}$$

From measurements on the spectrum,

$$\lambda_y = 589.7 \text{ nm}$$

$$\lambda_s = 408.3 \text{ nm}$$

Hence we can calculate the wavelength of the series limit of the principal series:

$$\frac{1}{\lambda_p} = \frac{1}{589.7 \times 10^{-9}} + \frac{1}{408.3 \times 10^{-9}}$$

$$= 4.145 \times 10^6 \, m^{-1}$$

hence $\lambda_p = 241.3 \times 10^{-9} \, m = 241.3 \, nm$

This agrees exactly with the measured value of the wavelength of the principal series limit. Such exact agreement gives us confidence that the energy level diagram gives a proper explanation of the observed spectral lines.

Example 9-5   The first line of the diffuse series of the sodium atom spectrum lies at a wavelength of 818.3 nm. Calculate the wavelength of the fundamental series limit from data given in the text.

Referring to Figure 9-8, it is seen that the information needed to solve this problem is the wavelength of the sharp (or the diffuse) series limit, which was given previously as 408.3 nm. This allows the calculation of the energy of the 3p level.

The wavelength of the fundamental series limit is calculated by subtraction of inverse wavelengths; the factor hc required to convert the inverse wave length to energy units can be ignored:

$$\frac{1}{\lambda} = \left(\frac{1}{408.3} - \frac{1}{818.3} \right) \times \frac{1}{10^{-9}}$$

and so $\lambda = 814.9 \times 10^{-9}$

$$= 814.9 \, nm$$

Notice that this series limit lies very close to the first line of the diffuse series, but at slightly shorter wavelength (higher frequency); this result should be compared with the spectrum shown in Figure 9-7.

9-6   X-RAY SPECTRA

When electrons are accelerated to high kinetic energy by an electric field, and allowed to strike a metallic target, it is found that very short wavelength radiation is emitted. This radiation is called "X-rays," and is used in medical and engineering practice since it is able to penetrate materials which are opaque to ordinary light. X-rays can be analyzed into different wavelengths, using a suitable spectrograph, and it is found that the resulting X-ray spectrum of an element is almost as useful as the optical spectra discussed in the last section.

The X-ray spectrum of any sample is made up of contributions from every chemical element contained within the sample. There is a characteristic spectrum for each element, consisting of a number of fairly sharp lines, but instead of being very complicated like the optical spectra, the X-ray spectra consist of a relatively small number of lines. The spectra of adjacent elements in the periodic table are very similar, except that the spectral lines are found at shorter wavelengths in elements of higher molar mass.

The existence of sharp lines in the X-ray spectrum of an atom indicates that sharply defined energy levels occur for the tightly bound electrons, as well as for the outer electrons which are responsible for the optical spectrum. The energy levels are traditionally classified according to the series of X-ray lines with which they are associated. For every element, the group of X-ray lines of shortest wavelength is called the K series; the next group of lines, generally at wavelengths about 10 times as long as the K series wavelengths, are called the L series. For heavier elements further series of lines are found.

When an atom is struck by an energetic electron, an electron may be removed from the atom leaving the atom ionized. If the electron which was removed was an inner electron, the ion is left in a highly excited state, and it can lower its energy by allowing an outer electron to take the place of the inner electron which was removed. The excess energy is removed in the form of an X-ray photon. The process may be understood by reference to the full energy level diagram for sodium in Figure 9-9.

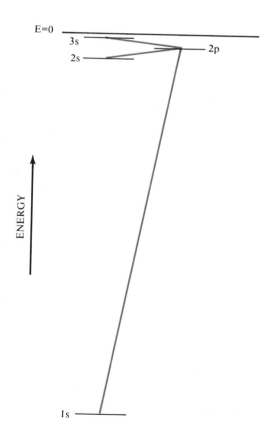

Figure 9-9   The occupied energy levels of the sodium atom, with the X-ray transitions shown.

If a 1s electron is removed from the sodium atom, a 2p electron may make a transition to the 1s energy level, emitting an X-ray photon of wavelength 1.19 nm. If a 2s electron is removed, a 2p electron may make a transition to the 2s level, giving rise to radiation of wavelength 37.6 nm. If a 2p electron is removed, a 3s electron may make a transition to the 2p level, giving rise to radiation of wavelength 40.7 nm. It should be noticed that the observed transitions are between levels in adjacent columns, i.e. between levels whose orbital quantum numbers differ by unity. This is the same selection rule that applies to the optical transitions shown in Figure 9-8.

Given this type of information, it is possible to locate all the quantized energy levels within an atom. It should be understood that all sharply defined spectral transitions are caused by rearrangements of electrons among the energy levels of an atom. The optical spectra, involving small energy differences, are due to rearrangements of the outer or valence electrons of the atom, whereas the X-ray spectra are due to rearrangements of the more strongly bound inner electrons. In order to show the relationships between the optical and X-ray spectra, it can be imagined that the whole of the diagram of the optical levels in Figure 9-8 is fitted between zero level and the 3s level in Figure 9-9. The 1s, 2s, 2p and 3s levels are occupied by electrons; the optical spectra result from transitions of the electron from the 3s level, and the X-ray spectra result from rearrangement of electrons amongst the levels which are normally occupied.

The discovery by Moseley that the K series X-ray wavelengths change gradually with atomic molar mass had a great influence on the understanding of atomic structure. Consider the central group of elements of the third row of the periodic table, scandium to zinc, arranged in order of increasing atomic molar mass; this would place nickel in front of cobalt. The K series of X-ray lines for these elements consists of two lines, corresponding to the transitions

Figure 9-10   The K series X-ray spectra for the first row transition metals, arranged in order of increasing molar mass.

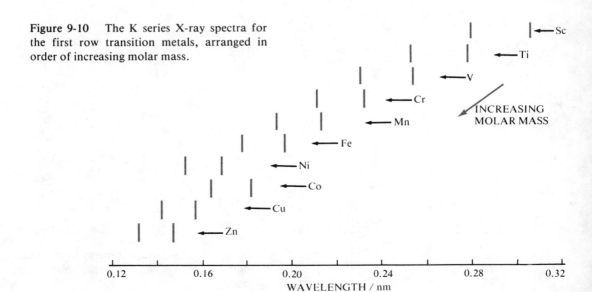

2p → 1s and 3p → 1s; the spectra are shown diagramatically in Figure 9-10. The steady progression of the lines to shorter wavelength as the molar mass increases is apparent, except for the case of nickel and cobalt. However, since the progression is perfectly regular if these two metals are interchanged, it is concluded that there must be a numbering of the elements which is more fundamental than the order of the atomic molar masses. This more fundamental *atomic number* of each element is based upon the electric charge on the nucleus of an atom of the element. The atomic numbers of the elements can be assigned with confidence on the basis of X-ray spectra arranged as in Figure 9-10.

Moseley discovered a simple functional dependence describing the progression of X-ray wavelengths. The square root of the inverse of the wavelength of the K series lines is proportional to the atomic number. The spectra of Figure 9-10 have been plotted in this way in Figure 9-11, and it can be seen that the points fit very closely on two straight lines. The straight lines can be extended to include the K series X-ray lines of other elements, and so for a wide range of atomic numbers, each line has an equation

$$\frac{1}{\sqrt{\lambda}} = aZ + b \qquad (17)$$

where Z is the atomic number of the element, λ is the wavelength of one of the K series lines and a and b are constants. The number b is small, since the straight lines in Figure 9-11 pass close to the origin.

The experimental straight lines can be explained on the basis of the Bohr model assuming that Z measures the charge on the atomic nucleus. Suppose that we have an ion consisting of a nucleus of charge $+Ze$, and a single electron. The Bohr model can be applied, starting from the equation

$$m\,\frac{v^2}{r} = \frac{Ze^2}{4\pi\varepsilon_0 r^2}$$

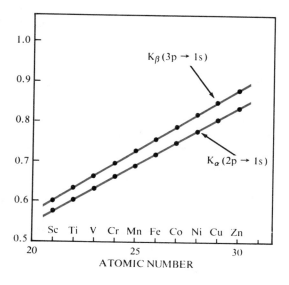

Figure 9-11   The wavelengths of the X-ray spectra of Figure 9-10 plotted against atomic number. Atomic numbers were originally deduced from the regularity of this graph, which is summarized in the Moseley law.

instead of equation (4). Calculation of the quantized energy levels using the quantization condition expressed in equation (15) gives the same result as for the hydrogen atom except for a factor of Z^2:

$$E_n = -Z^2 \cdot \frac{me^4}{8\varepsilon_o^2 h^2} \cdot \frac{1}{n^2} \tag{18}$$

This result should be compared with equation (13). Thus the 1s electron in such an atom lies lower in energy, by the factor Z^2, than the 1s electron in hydrogen. This result is also approximately true in a neutral atom: the 1s energy is approximately proportional to the square of the atomic number or nuclear charge. The 1s electrons lie, on the average, much closer to the nucleus than the outer electrons and so their energy is determined mostly by the electrostatic field of the nucleus.

The wavelength of a K series X-ray is equal to the difference between the 1s energy level and a 2p or higher level. From Figure 9-8 it is clear that the energy of the 2p level is very close to zero, compared with the 1s level, and so to a good approximation, the K series wavelengths are given by

$$h\nu = \frac{hc}{\lambda} \approx 0 - E_{1s}$$

$$\approx \text{constant} \times Z^2$$

Taking the square root of this equation leads to equation (17).

SUMMARY AND FURTHER READING

This chapter describes the structure of atoms as seen by physicists in the period 1890 to 1920. The properties of the electron as a particle were defined by the work of J.J. Thomson and Millikan. The particle nature of photons of light was proposed by Planck and Einstein, and the quantum theory of light provided the basis upon which Bohr described the spectra of atoms. Rutherford and his coworkers demonstrated the existence of a nucleus at the centre of each atom, and Moseley used X-ray spectra to provide a proper numbering of the elements on the basis of nuclear charge.

This work is described in many books on chemistry and atomic physics, and the student will find it useful to read more than one book. In addition, the writings of the original workers are readily available in libraries. The keen student will learn much by reading the original authors. These scientists wrote well, and much of their work is not complicated mathematically. The diagrams of their apparatus are of great interest, and show that while some experiments were simple, other experiments used complicated equipment, at the forefront of the technology of the day. Some books which are of interest are listed below.

Neils Bohr, Collected Works. (North Holland, Amsterdam, 1972). Four volumes of writings including letters. It is not difficult to locate the work on atomic structure.

Collected Papers of Lord Rutherford of Nelson. (George Allen and Unwin, London 1962). Three volumes. The 1920 Bakerian Lecture at the Royal Society, which is printed at the beginning of the third volume, is of particular interest.

Nobel Prize Lectures in Physics 1922-1941. (Elsevier, 1965). Bohr's lecture in 1922 and Millikan's lecture in 1923 are relevant.

PROBLEMS

1. Calculate the energy (in joule) of a mole of photons of:
    (a) red light of wavelength 700 nm,   [170.9 kJ]
    (b) violet light of wavelength 400 nm,   [299.1 kJ]
    (c) far ultraviolet light of wavelength 100 nm,   [1.196 MJ]
    (d) X-radiation of wavelength 0.1 nm.   [1.196 GJ]

2. The wavelength of the principal series limit of the rubidium atom spectrum is 296.8 nm. Calculate the ionization energy of rubidium.

    $[403.0 \text{ kJ mol}^{-1}]$

3. The shortest wavelength X-ray line (K_β) emitted by lanthanum metal upon electron bombardment has a wavelength of 31.8 pm, and the corresponding wavelength emitted by tungsten is 17.8 pm. After careful purification, a lanthanide metal was found to emit an X-ray line of wavelength 25.6 pm, and nothing shorter. Identify the unknown metal.   [Eu]

4. A piece of steel was analyzed for its elements by measuring the wavelengths of its characteristic X-rays. Strong radiation was found at the following wavelengths (in nanometres):
    0.229, 0.208, 0.194, 0.175, 0.166, 0.149
    What elements are present in the steel? What commercial name would you use to describe the steel?

5. The longest wavelength line of the principal series of the spectrum of the lithium atom lies at a wavelength of 671 nm, the longest wavelength line of the sharp series at 813 nm and the sharp series limit at 350. nm. Calculate:
    (a) the ionization energy of lithium, and
    (b) the difference in energy between the 2s and 3s levels.
    Express your energies in kJ mol^{-1} $[520 \text{ kJ mol}^{-1}; 325 \text{ kJ mol}^{-1}]$

6. What relationship would you expect between the constant a in the Moseley law (equation (18)) and the Rydberg constant? Is this relationship confirmed by the X-ray data given in question 3?

7. Show that, for an ion with an atomic number Z and only a single electron, the radii of the Bohr orbits are given by $r_n = n^2 a_o / Z$. (Hint: see the discussion leading to equation (17)).

X THE ELECTRONIC STRUCTURE OF ATOMS

In the last chapter the experimental and theoretical background for understanding the nature of atoms was explained. It was shown that the atom consists of a heavy nucleus carrying all of the positive charge, and a number of very light negatively charged electrons. The nucleus carries a total charge equal to the total charge on the electrons. It is an integer multiple of the electronic charge, the integer being the atomic number which is characteristic of the element and is related to its place in the periodic table.

The most important feature of the electronic properties of atoms is the existence of quantized energy levels. Higher energy levels are unoccupied, and the outer electrons can jump from one level to another with the emission or absorption of photons of light. The unoccupied energy levels are relatively close together in energy, and the transitions between them correspond to photons of light in the infrared, visible, or ultraviolet parts of the spectrum. Lower energy levels are fully occupied and are involved in the X-ray spectrum instead of the optical spectrum. These occupied levels can be observed by bombarding the atom with electrons or photons energetic enough to remove one of the electrons occupying the level in question; a higher energy electron then jumps to the vacancy left in that level and an X-ray of characteristic wavelength is emitted. Light is absorbed or emitted by the atom whenever the electrons jump from one level to another, at a wavelength given by the Planck condition

$$\frac{hc}{\lambda} = \Delta E$$

where ΔE is the change in the energy of the atom and h is Planck's constant. By studying the wavelengths of the lines in the spectrum of an atom, the energy levels of the atom can be determined. These energy levels are classified and labelled using quantum numbers introduced for that purpose. One quantum number is adequate to classify the energy levels of the hydrogen atom, but two quantum numbers are required for other atoms.

In this chapter these concepts will be used to develop the theory of the *electronic configurations* of the atoms, which accounts for many of the simple facts about valence and the periodic nature of the chemical properties of the elements.

10-1   THE PRINCIPAL AND ORBITAL QUANTUM NUMBERS

The principal quantum number, n, in any atom corresponds to the quantum number introduced to describe the spectrum and energy levels of the hydrogen atom, and plays the major role in determining the energy of an electron. In the hydrogen atom, the energy is exactly proportional to $1/n^2$, but in other atoms the dependence of energy on n is more complicated and does not follow any simple formula exactly. In the elementary Bohr theory of quantized circular orbits described in the last chapter, the quantum number n is a measure of the angular momentum of the electron in its orbit. This feature of the elementary theory is unsatisfactory. It results from the initial simplifying assumption that the orbits are circular, and from inadequacies of the Bohr approach in which the theory of mechanics and electrodynamics was modified by the addition of the quantum postulates. The theory of Bohr was superseded by the *wave theory of quantum mechanics* introduced by de Broglie and Schrödinger in 1925-26, and in the newer theory the principal quantum number is given a different interpretation.

The motion of a particle moving in an orbit under the influence of a centre of attraction can be divided into *radial* motion and *angular* motion. The potential energy of the particle depends only on its distance from the centre, and so is associated with the radial motion alone. The kinetic energy, however, is associated with both radial motion and angular motion. The division of the kinetic energy into the radial and angular parts depends upon the shape of the orbit.

In wave mechanics, there is no well-defined orbit for the electron; instead, a pattern of waves define the space where the electrons are most likely to be found. However, the total energy of an electron in this theory still contains both radial and angular contributions. The principal quantum number n determines the nature of the radial motion, and the orbital quantum number l determines the angular momentum of the electron as it moves around the nucleus. In order to fix the total energy, both n and l must be specified. The numbers n and l are not entirely independent. The principal quantum number takes integer values n = 1, 2, 3, . . . , and the orbital quantum number takes values $l =$ 0, 1, 2, . . . , n −1, with the upper limit being determined by the principal quantum number. Apart from the restriction $0 \leqslant l < n$, n and l can independently take any integer values. It has become usual to use spectroscopic notation when referring to the various values of l: s for $l = 0$, p for $l = 1$, and so on, as described in the last chapter. This notation is always used in writing electronic configurations: the symbol 3d refers to an energy level with n = 3 and $l = 2$.

10-2   TWO MORE QUANTUM NUMBERS

The description of the behaviour of electrons in atoms is not complete without considering two further quantum numbers, the magnetic quantum number and the spin quantum number. Both are related to the *vector* properties of angular momentum. The direction of the vector representing the angular momentum of a particle in an orbit is perpendicular to that orbit, as shown in Figure 10-1.

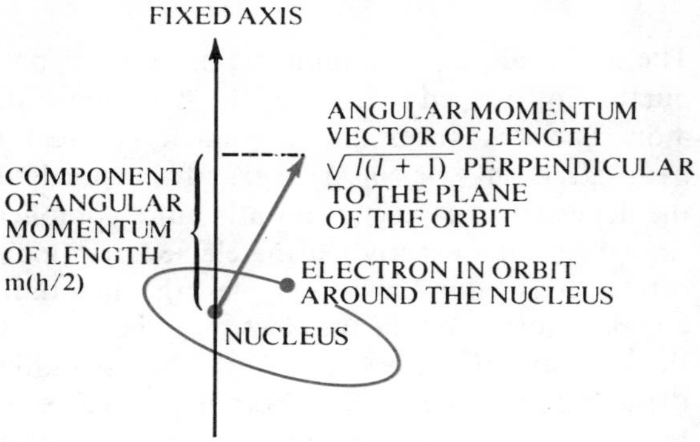

Figure 10-1 The angular momentum vector and its component along a fixed axis. The orbital quantum number l defines the length of the angular momentum vector, and the magnetic quantum number m defines its component along the axis.

A familiar toy which makes use of the properties of angular momentum is a top, consisting of a wheel spinning rapidly about an axis. The angular momentum vector of the top is directed along the axis of the wheel.

Because of its vectorial nature, angular momentum is not completely specified by the quantum number l, which only defines the length of the vector, $\sqrt{l(l+1)}\hbar$. Two further quantities are needed in order to fix a vector; these can be the components of the vector along two different directions in space. Two results of quantum theory will be quoted here. The first is that it is only possible to measure *one* component of the angular momentum vector. If an attempt is made simultaneously to fix a second component, it is found that the first component is altered. This limitation on measurements is a fundamental one, contained in a theorem of quantum mechanics called the Heisenberg *uncertainty principle*. The second result of quantum theory is that the one component of angular momentum that can be measured is quantized, and takes only values equal to $m\hbar$ where m is an integer called the *magnetic quantum number*. It is easy to see that there is a limitation on the values that m can take. The component of a vector along any direction can never be longer than the vector itself, and so m must be a positive or negative integer which is smaller in magnitude than $\sqrt{l(l+1)}$; m can take the following values:

symbol	l	$\sqrt{l(l+1)}$	m
s	0	0.000	0
p	1	1.414	$-1, 0, +1$
d	2	2.449	$-2, -1, 0, +1, +2$
f	3	3.464	$-3, -2, -1, 0, +1, +2, +3$

In general, m can take the values $-l, -l+1, \ldots -1, 0, +1 \ldots l-1, l$, a total of $2l+1$ different values for each value of l. The energy of the atom is independent of the value of m, unless the atom is in a strong magnetic field. In a strong magnetic field, small energy effects can be observed in the spectrum of atoms which are related to the value of m. For this reason, m is called the *magnetic quantum number*.

If the strong yellow line in the spectrum of the sodium atom, due to the $3p \rightarrow 3s$ transition, is examined with a spectrometer of high resolving power, it is found that two lines of slightly different wavelength, 588.9 nm and 589.5 nm can be seen. Other lines in the spectrum are also split, and in the case of the diffuse series, each line is split into three. Analysis of these small splittings in various atoms led to the discovery that an electron behaves as if it were in a state of internal motion, or *spin*, in addition to its motion in an orbit around the nucleus. This internal motion is associated with an angular momentum of spin which is quantized, by the laws of quantum mechanics. The amount of spin angular momentum of an electron is fixed and characteristic, like the mass and charge; the quantum number is equal to 1/2, leading to a spin angular momentum equal to $\sqrt{(\frac{1}{2})(\frac{1}{2} + 1)}\hbar$. The quantum number m_s which defines the component of the spin angular momentum vector along a fixed direction can take the values of $+\frac{1}{2}$ or $-\frac{1}{2}$. These two possible "spin" states of the electron are often referred to in chemical jargon as "spin up" ($m_s = +\frac{1}{2}$) and "spin down" ($m_s = -\frac{1}{2}$) states.

10-3 ELECTRONIC CONFIGURATIONS OF ATOMS

Four quantum numbers have been introduced for the classification of energy levels:

principal quantum number	$n = 1, 2, 3, \ldots$
orbital quantum number	$l = 0, 1, 2, \ldots n{-}1$
magnetic quantum number	$m = -l, \ldots -1, 0, +1, \ldots +l$
spin quantum number	$m_s = \pm\frac{1}{2}$

These quantum numbers will now be used to describe the electronic structure of atoms. The procedure for doing this, the "aufbau" principle, was outlined first by Bohr in 1922. The word "aufbau" means "building-up" or "construction" in German, and the principle provides the rules for putting the nucleus of charge Z together with the proper number of electrons to form a given atom or ion.

The electrons are assigned to quantized energy levels within the atom. If the atom is in its lowest energy state, the electrons are assigned to the lowest energy level or levels, consistent with a certain restriction. The energy of each level is determined by the quantum numbers n and *l*; the other two quantum numbers, m and m_s, do not influence the energy of the levels (except for certain small effects) but they have a direct influence on the number of electrons which can occupy an energy level.

The distribution of electrons among the energy levels is governed by the *exclusion principle,* proposed by Wolfgang Pauli of University of Hamburg in 1925. The exclusion principle states that no two electrons may have the same set of values of the four quantum numbers n, *l*, m, m_s. It is difficult to provide a simple justification for this principle, for it is derived from the symmetry properties of wave functions.

The role of the exclusion principle in the aufbau process can be seen by considering the three atoms hydrogen, helium and lithium, with atomic numbers $Z = 1, 2$ and 3. For hydrogen, the single electron is placed in the lowest energy or 1s level, with either spin "up" or "down": the quantum numbers are

n	l	m	m_s
1	0	0	$\pm\frac{1}{2}$

For helium there are two electrons, and both can be fitted into the 1s level as long as the spin of one electron is up, and the other is down:

1	0	0	$+\frac{1}{2}$
1	0	0	$-\frac{1}{2}$

The spins are forced to take opposite values of m_s, and are said to be *paired*. For lithium, the third electron cannot be fitted into the 1s level without duplicating one of the previous sets of quantum numbers, and so in forming the lithium atom in its lowest energy state the third electron is placed in the 2s level:

1	0	0	$+\frac{1}{2}$
1	0	0	$-\frac{1}{2}$
2	0	0	$\pm\frac{1}{2}$

Just as for hydrogen, it does not matter whether the spin of the third electron is up or down. It might be asked, why did the third electron go into the 2s level instead of the 2p level? The answer to this question is contained in Figure 9-8: for any particular value of the principal quantum number, the s level lies lowest, then comes the p, then the d, and so on.

This model for the structure of atoms is consistent with the known properties of these elements, and explains the great difference in properties between helium and lithium. In helium, both electrons are tightly bound to a nucleus of charge +2. In lithium the two 1s electrons are tightly bound to a nucleus of charge +3, but the third electron is placed in the 2s level because of the exclusion principle. This third electron is farther away from the nucleus and thus much less tightly bound than the 1s electrons in helium (or in lithium) and so it can be moved to another energy level, or even be removed from the atom entirely, with only a relatively small input of energy.

Atoms in which an outer electron is not tightly bound readily undergo reactions in which a positive ion is formed, the electron being used to form a corresponding negative ion. In such a reaction, the atom forming the positive ion is oxidized, as in the reaction of lithium with chlorine:

$$Li(c) + \tfrac{1}{2}Cl_2(g) \rightarrow LiCl(c)$$

Lithium chloride is a solid material containing Li^+ ions and Cl^- ions. The Li^+ ion has two tightly bound electrons in the 1s level, and is therefore chemically inert, like the helium atom. However, despite this inertness the Li^+ ion in aqueous solution produces some chemical effects because it is electrically charged. The Li^+ ion is strongly hydrated in aqueous solution and interacts with other ions which are chemically reactive.

The procedure of listing all four quantum numbers for every electron is too

TABLE 10-1   Configurations of the Elements

#	El	Configuration	#	El	Configuration	#	El	Configuration
1	H	$1s^1$	35	Br	$(Ar)4s^23d^{10}4p^5$	69	Tm	$(Xe)6s^24f^{13}$
2	He	$1s^2$	36	Kr	$(Ar)4s^23d^{10}4p^6$	70	Yb	$(Xe)6s^24f^{14}$
3	Li	$(He)2s^1$	37	Rb	$(Kr)5s^1$	71	Lu	$(Xe)6s^24f^{14}5d^1$
4	Be	$(He)2s^2$	38	Sr	$(Kr)5s^2$	72	Hf	$(Xe)6s^24f^{14}5d^2$
5	B	$(He)2s^22p^1$	39	Y	$(Kr)5s^24d$	73	Ta	$(Xe)6s^24f^{14}5d^3$
6	C	$(He)2s^22p^2$	40	Zr	$(Kr)5s^24d^2$	74	W	$(Xe)6s^24f^{14}5d^4$
7	N	$(He)2s^22p^3$	41	Nb	$(Kr)5s^14d^4$	75	Re	$(Xe)6s^24f^{14}5d^5$
8	O	$(He)2s^22p^4$	42	Mo	$(Kr)5s^14d^5$	76	Os	$(Xe)6s^24f^{14}5d^6$
9	F	$(He)2s^22p^5$	43	Tc	$(Kr)5s^14d^6$	77	Ir	$(Xe)6s^24f^{14}5d^7$
10	Ne	$(He)2s^22p^6$	44	Ru	$(Kr)5s^14d^7$	78	Pt	$(Xe)6s^14f^{14}5d^9$
11	Na	$(Ne)3s^1$	45	Rh	$(Kr)5s^14d^8$	79	Au	$(Xe)6s^14f^{14}5d^{10}$
12	Mg	$(Ne)3s^2$	46	Pd	$(Kr)4d^{10}$	80	Hg	$(Xe)6s^24f^{14}5d^{10}$
13	Al	$(Ne)3s^23p^1$	47	Ag	$(Kr)5s^14d^{10}$	81	Tl	$(Xe)6s^24f^{14}5d^{10}6p^1$
14	Si	$(Ne)3s^23p^2$	48	Cd	$(Kr)5s^24d^{10}$	82	Pb	$(Xe)6s^24f^{14}5d^{10}6p^2$
15	P	$(Ne)3s^23p^3$	49	In	$(Kr)5s^24d^{10}5p$	83	Bi	$(Xe)6s^24f^{14}5d^{10}6p^3$
16	S	$(Ne)3s^23p^4$	50	Sn	$(Kr)5s^24d^{10}5p^2$	84	Po	$(Xe)6s^24f^{14}5d^{10}6p^4$
17	Cl	$(Ne)3s^23p^5$	51	Sb	$(Kr)5s^24d^{10}5p^3$	85	At	$(Xe)6s^24f^{14}5d^{10}6p^5$
18	Ar	$(Ne)3s^23p^6$	52	Te	$(Kr)5s^24d^{10}5p^4$	86	Rn	$(Xe)6s^24f^{14}5d^{10}6p^6$
19	K	$(Ar)4s^1$	53	I	$(Kr)5s^24d^{10}5p^5$	87	Fr	$(Rn)7s$
20	Ca	$(Ar)4s^2$	54	Xe	$(Kr)5s^24d^{10}5p^6$	88	Ra	$(Rn)7s^2$
21	Sc	$(Ar)4s^23d$	55	Cs	$(Xe)6s^1$	89	Ac	$(Rn)7s^26d$
22	Ti	$(Ar)4s^23d^2$	56	Ba	$(Xe)6s^2$	90	Th	$(Rn)7s^26d^2$
23	V	$(Ar)4s^23d^3$	57	La	$(Xe)6s^25d$	91	Pa	$(Rn)7s^25f^26d^1$
24	Cr	$(Ar)4s^13d^5$	58	Ce	$(Xe)6s^24f^2$	92	U	$(Rn)7s^25f^36d^1$
25	Mn	$(Ar)4s^23d^5$	59	Pr	$(Xe)6s^24f^3$	93	Np	$(Rn)7s^25f^46d^1$
26	Fe	$(Ar)4s^23d^6$	60	Nd	$(Xe)6s^24f^4$	94	Pu	$(Rn)7s^25f^6$
27	Co	$(Ar)4s^23d^7$	61	Pm	$(Xe)6s^24f^5$	95	Am	$(Rn)7s^25f^7$
28	Ni	$(Ar)4s^23d^8$	62	Sm	$(Xe)6s^24f^6$	96	Cm	$(Rn)7s^25f^76d^1$
29	Cu	$(Ar)4s^13d^{10}$	63	Eu	$(Xe)6s^24f^7$	97	Bk	$(Rn)7s^25f^9$
30	Zn	$(Ar)4s^23d^{10}$	64	Gd	$(Xe)6s^24f^75d^1$	98	Cf	$(Rn)7s^25f^{10}$
31	Ga	$(Ar)4s^23d^{10}4p^1$	65	Tb	$(Xe)6s^24f^9$	99	Es	$(Rn)7s^25f^{11}$
32	Ge	$(Ar)4s^23d^{10}4p^2$	66	Dy	$(Xe)6s^24f^{10}$	100	Fm	$(Rn)7s^25f^{12}$
33	As	$(Ar)4s^23d^{10}4p^3$	67	Ho	$(Xe)6s^24f^{11}$	101	Md	$(Rn)7s^25f^{13}$
34	Se	$(Ar)4s^23d^{10}4p^4$	68	Er	$(Xe)6s^24f^{12}$	102	No	$(Rn)7s^25f^{14}$
						103	Lw	$(Rn)7s^25f^{14}6d^1$

clumsy for continuing this discussion up to heavy elements, and so a new system of notation is needed. It is sufficient for many purposes to list the number of electrons in each quantum level. Such a list is called a *configuration*. In writing down a configuration, the symbol for the n and *l* values is written down and the number of electrons in that level is written as a superscript. Hydrogen has the configuration $1s^1$, helium $1s^2$, and lithium $1s^2 2s^1$. The configurations of the elements written in this form are listed in Table 10-1.

From the discussion of the structure of the lithium atom, it is clear that in all atoms except H and He there is a group of electrons inside a number of outer, or valence electrons. Because chemical interaction between atoms will be concerned with the interaction of these outer electrons, the inner electrons are not directly concerned in the chemistry of the atoms, and so there is no need to repeat the detailed configuration of this core. The configuration of the core always corresponds to the configuration of one of the noble gases helium, neon, argon, krypton or xenon, and so the symbol for the corresponding noble gas is used to represent the electronic configuration of the core. Thus lithium is listed as having the configuration $(He)2s^1$.

The beryllium atom has the configuration $(He)2s^2$. There are two electrons in the 2s level, and these two electrons must have their spins paired. Beryllium has a valence of two in its compounds.

Boron is the lightest atom in which there is an electron in a p level. It might be expected that this element would form ions with a charge of +1, having the configuration $(He)2s^2$, but this is not so. The valence of boron is three in its characteristic compounds, although these compounds are regarded as being molecular rather than ionic. This might be taken as a warning that one cannot always predict chemical properties of elements using only the electronic configuration of the atoms. It might be noted in passing that the metal thallium, which lies below boron in the periodic table, forms ions of charge +1 *and* ions of charge +3 in its compounds.

Following boron, the 2p shell is progressively filled. Carbon, $(He)2s^2 2p^2$, shows a characteristic valence of four corresponding to four valence electrons. The next three elements show a new phenomenon, for the characteristic valence starts to drop: nitrogen has a valence of three, oxygen two and fluorine one. These valences correspond to the number of *vacancies* in the 2p level. The 2p level can hold a total of six electrons, corresponding to all possible combinations of $m = -1, 0, +1$ and $m_s = +\frac{1}{2}, -\frac{1}{2}$, and so if x is the total number of electrons in the valence shell s and p levels, the number of additional electrons which can be added to the atom without violating the exclusion principle is $8-x$. For $x = 1, 2, 3$ or 4, the commonest valence of the atom is equal to x, and for $x = 5, 6$ or 7 the commonest valence of the atom is equal to $8-x$, the number of vacancies in the 2p level. Nitrogen, oxygen and fluorine form negative ions with charges of -3, -2 and -1 respectively. This series of elements is completed with the element neon, having a closed 2p shell $(x = 8)$. Neon does not appear to form any chemical compounds, and its commonest valence may therefore be regarded as zero.

After neon, the next element is sodium, for which one electron must be placed in the 3s level. The arrangement of energy levels in sodium has already been discussed in detail. The configurations of the elements from sodium up to argon follow exactly the pattern set for the elements from lithium to neon, except that the core corresponds to the structure of neon rather than of helium, and the valence shell corresponds to a principal quantum number of three rather than two.

At this stage a major triumph of the quantum theory of atoms can be grasped. It is a consequence of the aufbau principle, the exclusion principle, and the properties of the quantum numbers, that elements in the same column of the periodic table would be expected to be chemically similar. In other words, the quantum theory provides a natural explanation of periodicity in the properties of chemical elements. Lithium and sodium are chemically very similar elements, and it is easy to understand why; the atoms of these elements have similar electronic structures (a single electron outside a closed shell). The same argument accounts for the chemical similarity of beryllium and magnesium, fluorine and chlorine and so on.

The numerical sizes of the various blocks of the periodic table can now be understood on the basis of quantum numbers and their properties. Recalling that the magnetic quantum number m can take any of the $2l + 1$ integer values from $+l$ to $-l$, and that an electron spin can be "up" or "down," it is easy to see that it takes 2 electrons to fill an s level, 6 to fill a p level, 10 to fill a d level and 14 to fill an f level. Looking at the diagrammatic periodic table in Figure 10-2, the areas of the table where these various types of level are filled can be identified.

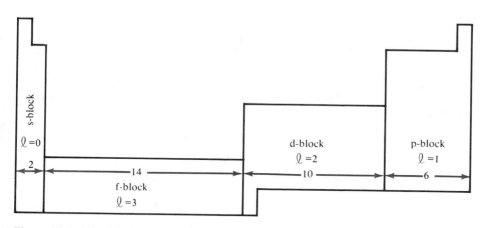

Figure 10-2 The blocks of the periodic table classified according to the orbital quantum number.

There are some curious features about the periodic table. The most obvious anomaly is that the d- and f-blocks lie between the s-block and the p-block, whereas they might have been expected to lie to the right of the p-block. If one examines a full periodic table, it is found that the element with atomic number 19 which follows argon, namely potassium, is listed as group I, under lithium and sodium. It is chemically similar to lithium and sodium, and has a similar optical spectrum. This means that its atomic configuration is $(Ar)4s^1$ rather than $(Ar)3d^1$. The reason for this anomaly can be grasped by reference to the sodium atom energy level diagram in Figure 9-8. The 3d level is higher in energy than the 4s, and so the 4s level is filled first. Similarly, the 5s level lies below the 4d and the 6s below the 5d, and so for all the rows of the periodic table the ns level is filled before the (n − 1)d level. As a result potassium belongs to the s-block. The energy levels of Figure 9-8 are only valid for the electrons in sodium atoms, but the *relative* positions of the s, p and d levels are practically the same for all the neutral atoms having atomic numbers a few units greater than the atomic number of a noble gas.

The configurations of the d-block elements following calcium show several irregularities, as can be seen from examination of Table 10-1. The number of d electrons increases through the values 1, 2 and 3, and then jumps to 5; there is another jump 8 to 10 at the end of the row. These anomalies indicate that the 4s and 3d levels lie close together, and while the total number of electrons in these two levels increases smoothly, it is sometimes energetically favourable to transfer an electron from the 4s level to the 3d level when the next element is considered. This indicates an irregularity in the aufbau principle: the energies of the 4s and 3d levels depend to some extent on the number of electrons contained in each level, and on the interactions among these electrons. The electronic configuration which occurs is the one that has the lowest total energy.

The electronic configurations of the neutral metal atoms are anomalous in some ways, but since the atoms themselves are rarely involved in chemical reactions, the configurations of the ions are of more interest. The metals of group I form ions of charge +1, those of Group II form ions of charge +2, but most d-block metals form several ions of different charges. This ability to form several different ions is the basis for the greater variety of different compounds and reactions which occur with these metals. The electronic configurations of d-block ions form a simple series because when the ions are formed it is the 4s electrons which are removed first. The electronic configurations of the divalent ions of the 3d transition metals show a regular increase in the number of d electrons:

21	Sc^{2+}	(does not occur)	26	Fe^{2+}	$(Ar)3d^6$
22	Ti^{2+}	$(Ar)3d^2$	27	Co^{2+}	$(Ar)3d^7$
23	V^{2+}	$(Ar)3d^3$	28	Ni^{2+}	$(Ar)3d^8$
24	Cr^{2+}	$(Ar)3d^4$	29	Cu^{2+}	$(Ar)3d^9$
25	Mn^{2+}	$(Ar)3d^5$	30	Zn^{2+}	$(Ar)3d^{10}$

These configurations illustrate a general rule. When forming ions of d-block elements, the highest s electrons are removed before the d electrons. When forming ions of f-block elements, the highest s electrons (and d electrons if any) are removed before the f electrons. This rule represents a second irregularity in the aufbau principle.

It is notable that most d-block ions do not have closed shells, whereas s- and p-block ions always have closed shells, examples being Na^+, Mg^{2+} and Cl^-. An atom or ion which does not have a closed shell is usually magnetic, because of the properties of angular momentum involving charged particles. All magnetic materials involve d-block or f-block elements.

Non-closed shell ions commonly form coloured compounds. A closed shell ion such as Na^+ requires a great deal of energy to excite the outermost electrons, in the 2p level, to the 3s level, and so the spectral lines of these ions lie in the ultraviolet region of the electromagnetic spectrum. On the other hand, when the outer electrons do not form a closed shell, there are generally unoccupied energy levels not very far above the highest occupied level, and so there are spectral lines in the lower energy region of the spectrum, i.e. the visible or infrared.

Following the filling of the 3d level, the 4p level is filled, up to the noble gas krypton. The next 18 elements follow in the same order. The first two elements are formed using the 5s level, and then the 4d elements are formed, followed by the 5p elements. It should be noticed that the 4f level is available for filling after the 4d, but the 5p level is filled first.

The next row of the periodic table is more complex, and involves the 4f level. In this row three different principal quantum numbers occur, in the 6s, 5d, 4f and 6p levels. Table 10-1 shows that electrons are placed in the 4f level before the 5d level is systematically filled; this leads to the existence of the group of 14 f-block elements, often called lanthanides since they follow the element lanthanum. As the 4f level is filled, there are irregularities in the order of filling, as some electrons are transferred to the 5d level. However, just as for the d-block metals, the neutral atoms of the lanthanides are not of much chemical interest. These elements are metals which form ions, the most important having charges of +3 and +4. In forming the ions from the neutral atoms, the 6s and 5d electrons (if any) are removed first, and when this is done, the sequence of configurations becomes regular.

The lanthanide metals are very similar to each other in their chemical properties. For instance they all form trivalent chlorides, of formulae $LaCl_3$, $CeCl_3$, $PrCl_3$, etc., which all have very similar values of their molar heats of formation, solubility in water, and other properties. The problem of chemically separating these very similar elements from one another in naturally occurring ores is an old problem in chemistry. The problem is important for the next row of f-block elements, the actinides, where chemical separations of the elements are essential to the nuclear energy industry. The reason for the great similarities amongst the fourteen lanthanide elements can be found in the Bohr theory of the radii of the quantized orbits. Although the 4f electrons which are being added are the highest energy electrons, they are not the outermost electrons of the atom, and it is the outermost electrons which determine the chemical behaviour of an atom or ion. In the Ce^{3+} ion, for which the full configuration can be written

$$(Kr)5s^24d^{10}5p^64f^1$$

the 4f electron is situated inside the eight electrons in the 5s and 5p levels, and so is shielded from the influence of other molecules or ions. The chemical behaviour of the Pr^{3+} ion, with configuration

$$(Kr)5s^24d^{10}5p^64f^2$$

is practically the same, since this ion appears from the outside to have the same configuration, $5s^25p^6$.

After the 4f level is filled, this level plays no further part in the electronic configurations. The elements following form a normal d-block series, and then a normal p-block series, up to the noble gas radon. The next row of the periodic table is very similar. Elements with atomic numbers greater than 92 have been manufactured artificially, and their chemistry is entirely analogous to the chemistry of the lanthanides.

10-4 A CLOSER LOOK AT ELECTRONIC CONFIGURATIONS

For some purposes it is not sufficient to give the electronic configuration in terms of the principal and orbital quantum numbers only, and information about the magnetic and spin quantum numbers must be given. In such discussions it is not necessary to consider the inner shell electrons. Only the valence shell electrons need be considered and a pictorial representation of the distribution of these electrons is often used.

The notation makes use of arrows and *orbital boxes*, and will be demonstrated by reference to the carbon atom, with valence shell configuration $2s^2 2p^2$. There is one possible value of the magnetic quantum number for the 2s level, and three for the 2p level, and so these levels are shown as two separate groups of boxes in Figure 10-3.

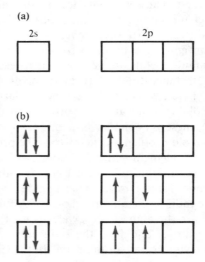

Figure 10-3 (a). Orbital box diagram for the 2s and 2p electrons. (b) Three orbital box diagrams representing different arrangements of four electrons in the configuration $2s^2 2p^2$.

The three boxes of the 2p level could be labelled -1, 0 and $+1$ respectively, corresponding to the values of the magnetic quantum number; however for some purposes, another labelling is more useful and so no label at all is indicated here. The presence of an electron in a level is indicated by placing an arrow in one of the boxes, pointing either up or down to indicate the spin quantum number $m_s = +\frac{1}{2}$ or $-\frac{1}{2}$. According to the Pauli exclusion principle, only two arrows may be placed in any one box; if two arrows are in the same box they must point in opposite directions.

In writing the valence shell configuration of the carbon atom, there is no choice in the placement of the arrows representing the 2s electrons, but there are many ways of drawing the arrows for the 2p electrons. Some of these choices are indicated in Figure 10-3.

To analyze these and other possibilities would lead too far into the theory of atoms, but several simple facts are useful to remember. These three diagrams all refer to the configuration $2s^2 2p^2$, but because of interactions between electrons in the atom, these three diagrams are associated with slightly different energy levels of the atom as a whole. The total energy of an atom is not completely specified by the electronic configuration. If the valence electrons can be distributed amongst the orbital boxes in more than one way, then there are several closely spaced energy levels corresponding to that configuration. For a closed shell configuration there is only one way of placing the arrows in the boxes, and so there is only one energy level for such a configuration.

It is sometimes important in chemistry to be able to determine which of several possible arrow diagrams for a given configuration leads to the lowest energy. Almost all atoms and ions conform to a rule given by the German physicist F. Hund on the basis of the experimental study of atomic spectra. The rule states that the lowest energy level corresponds to an arrow diagram in which as many arrows as possible are parallel. According to this rule, the ground state of the carbon atom corresponds to the third of the diagrams in Figure 10-3.

10-5 IONIZATION ENERGY AND ELECTRON AFFINITY

The smallest amount of energy which is required to remove an electron from an atom in its ground state is called the *ionization energy* of the atom, denoted by the symbol E_I. In the conventional notation of chemical reactions, the ionization energy is the energy required for the reaction

$$A(g) \rightarrow A^+(g) + e^-.$$

The ionization energy of an atom is closely related to its electronic structure, and so is related to the position of the element in the periodic table. Ionization energy can also be defined for molecules, and for ions both positive and negative. The ionization energy of a singly charged positive ion is called the *second ionization energy* of the corresponding atom: the ionization energy of Ca^+ is the second ionization energy of Ca. Ionization energies are sometimes referred to as ionization potentials and quoted in units of volts or electron volts. In this book ionization energies are quoted in kilojoules per mole (kJ/mol).

Only in the case of hydrogen can the ionization energy be calculated from simple theory. For all other atoms, complicated quantum calculations are required to obtain reasonable accuracy.

Example 10-1 Calculate the ionization energy of the hydrogen atom using Bohr's theory, and check the units.

The ionization energy is given by equation (9-13) with n=1, since n=1 refers to the ground state of the atom and removal of the electron corresponds to setting n=∞, an infinitely large orbit. Hence using accepted values of the fundamental constants,

$$E_I = \frac{9.1095 \times 10^{-31} \times (1.6022 \times 10^{-19})^4}{8 \times (8.854 \times 10^{-12})^2 \times (6.626 \times 10^{-34})^2}$$

$$= 2.179 \times 10^{-18} \text{ J}$$

For one mole of hydrogen atoms,

$$E_I = 2.179 \times 10^{-18} \text{J} \times 6.023 \times 10^{23} \text{ mol}^{-1}$$

$$= 1.313 \times 10^3 \text{ kJ mol}^{-1}$$

The units of ionization energy calculated from this formula are:

$$\frac{\text{kilogram} \times (\text{coulomb})^4 \times \text{mole}^{-1}}{(\text{joule}^{-1} \text{ coulomb}^2 \text{ metre}^{-1})^2 \times (\text{joule second})^2}$$

$$= \text{kilogram metre}^2 \text{ second}^{-2} \text{ mole}^{-1}$$

$$= \text{joule mole}^{-1}$$

The ionization energies of many elements have been determined accurately by measuring the wavelengths of series limits in their atomic spectra. In discussing the spectrum of the sodium atom, it was shown that the series limit of the principal series corresponds to the process of removing the valence electron altogether, leaving the Na^+ ion. The energy hc/λ corresponding to the series limit is the energy required to remove this electron, and therefore is the ionization energy of sodium.

Example 10-2 Calculate the ionization energy of sodium from the information given in Section 9-5.

The series limit of the principal series of spectral lines in the sodium atom spectrum corresponds to the removal of the 3s electron from the atom. The wavelength of the series limit is 241.3 nm, and the ionization energy is the energy associated with a photon of this wavelength:

$$E_I = hc/\lambda = 6.626 \times 10^{-34} \times 2.998 \times 10^8 / 241.3 \times 10^{-9}$$

$$= 8.232 \times 10^{-19} \text{ J}$$

Expressed as the energy per mole of atoms, this is

$$E_I = 8.232 \times 10^{-19} \times 6.023 \times 10^{23}$$

$$= 495.8 \text{ kJ mol}^{-1}$$

There are other methods of measuring ionization energies. Perhaps the most direct is to bombard the atom with electrons of known kinetic energy; if the energy of the electrons is high enough, electrons will be "knocked off" the

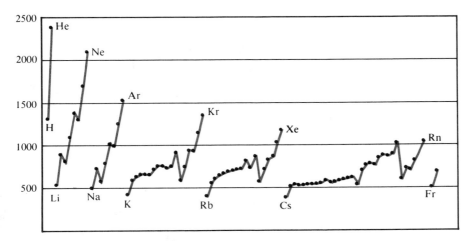

Figure 10-4   The first ionization energies of the elements plotted against atomic number.

atom, leaving an ion which can be detected in various ways. The minimum energy required to produce ions is equal to the ionization energy. This method can also be used to measure the ionization energy of molecules.

The first ionization energies of all the elements have been measured, and the results are summarized in Figure 10-4, in which the ionization energy is plotted as a function of atomic number.

The group I metals have the lowest ionization energies and the noble gases have the highest values within each row. The d-block and f-block elements do not show strong trends in ionization energy, but the values for the light elements are readily interpreted in terms of the theory of electronic configurations.

As the nuclear charge increases, the energy of the given type of level, e.g. the 2p level, becomes more negative and the energy required to remove an electron from that level increases. Hence there is a general increase in ionization energy across each row of the periodic table. This trend can be seen in the sequences from H to He, Li to Ne, Na to Ar; the trend is not quite so obvious in the other rows of the periodic table. When the limit of the six electrons in a p level is reached at the atomic number of a noble gas, the next electron is placed in an s level of the next higher principal quantum number; this s level is at a higher energy than the p level of the preceding rare gas, and so there is a drop in the ionization energy at the beginning of a new row of the periodic table.

Closer examination of the sequences Li–Ne and Na–Ar shows that there are two small decreases along each of these otherwise rising segments of the graph. The first small decrease in ionization energy follows the filling of the 2s (or 3s) level. The second follows "half-completion" of the 2p (or 3p) level and results from the same effects involved in Hund's rule. The first row electronic configurations and the changes in ionization energy are summarized and correlated in Figure 10-5.

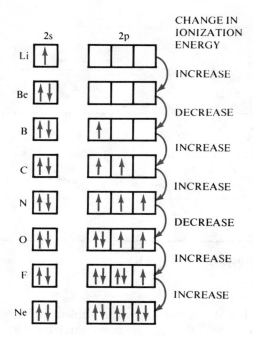

Figure 10-5   The changes in first ionization energy across the first row of the periodic table, correlated with the changes in the electronic configurations of the elements.

There is a general trend towards lower ionization energy in consecutive rows of the periodic table. For instance, carbon is generally considered to be a non-metal, whereas tin and lead which belong to the same group are metals. Metallic character of an element is associated with a low value of the ionization energy of the atoms of that element.

Examination of consecutive ionization energies of atoms provides additional evidence in support of features of atomic structure which have been discussed in this and the previous chapter. Table 10-2 shows the 1st, 2nd, 3rd, . . . ionization energies of the lightest elements, arranged in rows reading from right to left. Beneath each row of ionization energies are the differences between the successive values. The table is arranged so that each column refers to the same electron in all the atoms or ions. For instance, the ionization energy in the first column is the energy required to remove the last electron from each atom, the second column refers to the second last electron, and so on. There is a great deal of data in this table, but it is worth careful examination. Reading down any column of energies in Table 10-2, the ionization energy for a given electron increases with atomic number. This shows the effect of increased nuclear charge on the binding energies of all the electrons.

Reading across the rows of Table 10-2, it is particularly revealing to examine the differences between adjacent ionization energies, given as the second row for each element. The largest differences occur between the second and third columns, corresponding to the very large differences in binding energies of the first (n=1) and second (n=2) shells of electrons. A similar but less marked effect is seen at the boundary between the n=2 and n=3 shells towards the right hand side of the table. The change in ionization energies between the 2s and 2p

TABLE 10-2 The ionization energies of the lightest elements. The consecutive ionization energies of each element are arranged in order beginning at the right hand end. The first column contains the last ionization energy. The second row for each element contains the differences of the entries in the row above.

```
H    1312

He   5252   2373
        2879

Li   11819  7300   520
        4519  6780

Be   21013  14853  1758   900
        6160  13095  858

B    32836  25033  3661   2428   801
        7803  21372  1233   1627

C    47290  37843  6225   4620   2353   1087
        9447  31618  1605   2269   1266

N    64376  53284  9448   7477   4579   2858   1404
        11092 43836  1971   2898   1721   1454

O    84099  71354  13330  10993  7471   5303   3393   1314
        12745 58024  2337   3522   2168   1910   2079

F    106370 90343  17874  15169  11026  8421   6048   3377   1682
        16027 72469  2705   4143   2605   2373   2671   1695

Ne   115400 23080  20000  15240  12200  9380   6130   3965   2081
        92320 3080   4760   3040   2820   3250   2165   1884

Na   28930  25510  20120  16640  13380  9546   6930   4565   496
        3420   5390   3480   3260   3834   2616   2365   4069

Mg   31670  25664  21750  18030  13634  10550  7550   1451   738
        6006   3914   3720   4396   3084   3000   6099   713

Al   31870  27527  23340  18383  14850  11581  2746   1817   578
        4343   4187   4957   3533   3269   8835   929    1239

Si   33960  29300  23789  19800  16096  4357   3230   1577   787
        4660   5511   3989   3704   11739  1127   1653   790
```

electrons is noticeable, for the column of differences at that boundary are all larger than the adjacent differences.

Finally, the effect of Hund's rule can be detected, for the differences corresponding to the half-filled 2p shell are consistently larger than the adjacent columns of differences. The first three 2p electrons go into separate orbitals, as shown in Figure 10-5. The fourth 2p electron has no further empty 2p orbital available, and must be placed with opposite spin in an orbital already occupied. Thus the fourth electron does not have the opportunity for taking advantage of the extra stability (or lowering of energy) described by Hund's rule and so its ionization energy is decreased. This decrease is reflected in the magnitude of the differences in the central column of the 2p block of Table 10-2, as well as in the decrease of first ionization energy between nitrogen and oxygen shown in Figure 10-5.

The ionization energy of a negative ion is called the *electron affinity*, E_A, of the neutral atom. The electron affinity is the energy required for the reaction

$$A^-(g) \rightarrow A(g) + e^-$$

Some data on electron affinities of non-metals are given in Table 10-3. The figures are small, less than any of the ionization energies of the elements. This shows that the extra electron in a negative ion is loosely bound, and can be removed with a relatively small amount of energy.

TABLE 10-3   Electron Affinity Values for Some Atoms

Units: kilojoule/mole

H 73							He (−20)
Li 60	Be (−240)	B 23	C 122	N 0 ± 20	O 140	F 322	Ne (−30)
Na 53	Mg (−230)	Al 44	Si 120	P 74	S 200	Cl 349	Ar (−35)
K 48	Ca (−150)	Ga 36	Ge 120	As 77	Se 195	Br 325	Kr (−40)
Rb 47	Sr (−170)	In 35	Sn 120	Sb 100	Te 190	I 295	
Cs 45	Ba (−50)	Tl 50	Pb 100	Bi 100			

Source: E. C. M. Chen and W. E. Wentworth, J. Chem. Ed. Volume 52, page 486 (1975).

The electron affinities of the elements are a periodic property, although the variations are not large. The most notable periodic feature is the relatively large value for the halogen near the end of each row. This shows that these of all atoms form the most stable negative ions in the gas phase. A negative value of the electron affinity indicates that the negative ion A^- is unstable and would spontaneously form the neutral atom and an electron. The negative values in the table were obtained from theoretical calculations.

PROBLEMS

1. How many electrons are there in each of the following atoms and ions?

   Zn, Al^{3+}, Cs^+, Br^-, Ni^{3+}, O^{2-}, Ne, OH^-, NH_4^+, SO_4^{2-}.

2. How many s electrons are there in the following atoms and ions in their ground states?

   Sr^{2+}, Li, S, Br, Cd^{2+}, Cl^-, Hg, Ti^{2+}.

3. How many p electrons are there in each of the atoms and ions in question 2 in their ground states?

4. Using only a periodic table for reference, write the ground state electronic configuration for each of the following atoms:

   Be, Si, Br, Sr, In, Xe, Ti, Nb, Bi.

5. Using only a periodic table for reference, write the ground state electronic configuration for each of the following ions:

   Na^+, Cl^-, K^+, Al^{3+}, S^{2-}, Ti^{2+}, Fe^{3+}, Cu^+.

6. Use a periodic table to write down the order in which the energy levels are filled in the aufbau process:

   1s, 2s, 2p, . . .

7. Identify the trivalent cations that have the following outer electron configurations.

   $2s^2 2p^6$, $3s^2 3p^6$, $3s^2 3p^6 3d^2$, $3s^2 3p^6 3d^{10}$, $5s^2 4d^{10} 5p^6 4f$, $6s^2 5d^{10} 6p^6 5f^5$.

8. Use the orbital box diagrams and Hund's rule to determine the number of unpaired electrons in the atoms and ions listed in questions 4 and 7.

9. How many arrow diagrams can be drawn for the configuration $2s^2 2p^2$? For $2s^2 2p^3$?   [15; 20]

10. Calculate the energy required for the following reaction:

$$Na(g) + Cl(g) \rightarrow Na^+(g) + Cl^-(g)$$

[147 kJ mol^{-1}]

11. Show that the entries in the first column of Table 10-2 are consistent with equation (9-18), and calculate the entries for the elements Ne to Si.

12. Is there any evidence of the effects of shell structure and Hund's rule in the electron affinity data in Table 10-3?

13. Draw box diagrams for the elements from potassium to zinc, and from caesium to lutetium, basing your diagrams on the electronic configurations in Table 10-1. Some of the electronic configurations of these elements appear to be affected by Hund's rule. Which ones?

XI MOLECULAR STRUCTURE

In chemistry, atoms are the fundamental building blocks from which matter is made, yet isolated atoms are rarely met. Atoms are usually combined together in some way, often as molecules.

A molecule is a stable group of atoms which are joined together by chemical bonds. A molecule moves and reacts chemically as a single unit, and in many substances the properties of single molecules are dominant in determining the properties of the bulk material. This is because the energy of interaction between two molecules is generally small compared with the energy of the chemical bonds holding the atoms of the molecule together. A knowledge of the properties of the molecules of a substance often allows prediction of the bulk properties and chemical behaviour of that substance.

Information about molecules is obtained by many experimental techniques. The empirical formula is determined by chemical analysis. The molecular molar mass can be determined by measuring the density of the vapour of the substance, or by one of the methods based on the properties of solutions to be described in Chapter 18. From these two pieces of information the molecular formula is found. Information about the way in which the atoms in a molecule are bonded together is obtained from study of chemical reactions, from thermochemistry, from spectroscopic experiments of various sorts, and from X-ray diffraction, neutron diffraction, and electron diffraction. Of course, the more different sorts of experimental information are gathered about a molecule, the more detailed and accurate is the picture of the molecular structure which results.

In this chapter, the geometry of molecules and the energy associated with chemical bonds are discussed. It is convenient to include polyatomic ions such as the sulphate ion in the discussion of molecular geometry, even though the word "molecule" usually means a group of atoms which are electrically neutral.

11-1 STRUCTURAL ISOMERISM

The most basic structural property of a molecule is the arrangement of the chemical bonds between the atoms. Different arrangements of the chemical bonds lead to different substances. For example, there are two substances with the molecular formula C_2H_6O, which have entirely different physical and chemical properties. One compound, dimethyl ether, boils at a temperature of $-23°C$ and does not react with acids; the other compound, ethanol, boils at a temperature of $78°C$ and reacts with nitric acid to yield an explosive substance called ethyl nitrate. The differences between these two compounds can be explained on the basis of the arrangement of chemical bonds in the molecules, as shown

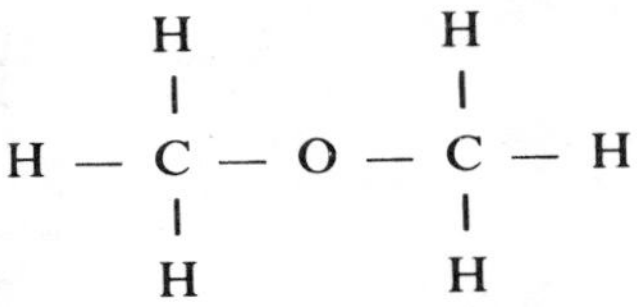

dimethyl ether 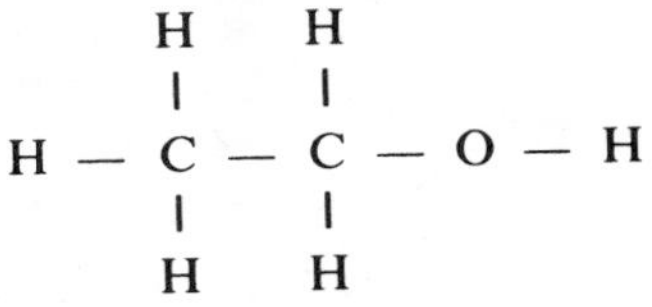   ethanol

When two compounds have the same molecular formula, but have different arrangements of the atoms and bonds in the molecules, they are called *isomers*. In the present case, the two molecules have different numbers of the different types of bond:

dimethyl ether: 6 C-H bonds   ethanol: 5 C-H bonds

2 C-O bonds   1 C-O bond

1 C-C bond

1 O-H bond

When two isomers differ in this way, they are different chemical compounds, and are called *structural isomers*, or sometimes *functional isomers* since these two molecules have different functional groups of atoms.

It is also possible for two structural isomers to have equal numbers of the various different types of bond, and yet represent two different substances with different chemical structures. For example, butane and methylpropane both have the molecular formula C_4H_{10}, and both have 3 C-C bonds and 10 C-H bonds

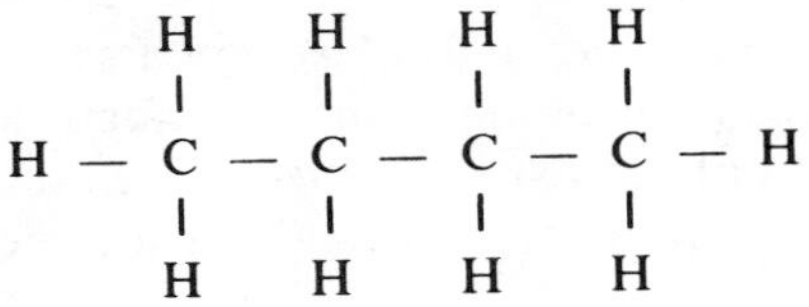

butane

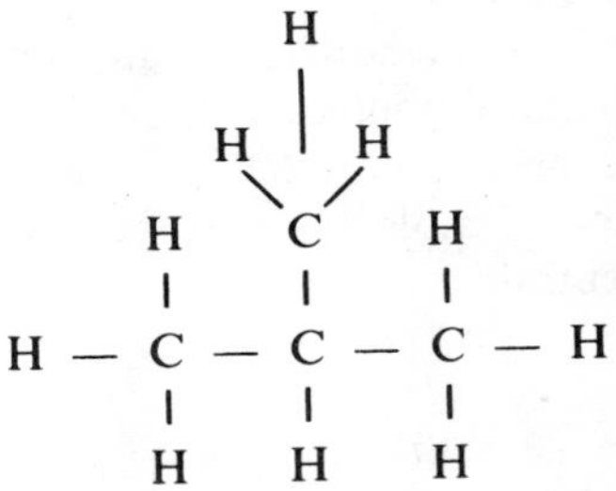

methyl propane

These are two different compounds because the central carbon atom in methyl propane is bonded to three other carbon atoms whereas the four carbon atoms in butane are bonded together in a chain. However, the differences between them are not so marked as the differences between dimethyl ether and ethanol.

11-2   THE SHAPES OF SMALL MOLECULES

Molecules are real objects, and like other real objects they have shape and size, and other geometrical properties. The constituent parts of a molecule are the nuclei of the atoms within the molecule, and the electrons which are moving under the influence of the electrostatic field of the nuclei and of each other. The nuclei constitute most of the mass of a molecule, just as for atoms. In speaking of the geometry of a molecule, the electrons are generally ignored and attention is focused on the relative positions of the nuclei of the atoms. An *inter-atomic distance* or *bond length* is the distance between the nuclei of the two atoms specified. A *bond angle* is the angle between the two imaginary lines joining the nuclei of atoms concerned. For instance, the bond angle in the H_2O molecule is the angle between two imaginary lines from the oxygen nucleus to the hydrogen nuclei.

The shape of a large, complicated molecule is difficult to specify, but generally a large molecule consists of smaller pieces each of which has an easily described geometry. For most purposes, it is sufficient to become familiar with a few typical shapes, which occur again and again in the structure of complicated molecules. These simple shapes will be classified and discussed for a series of compounds in which a central atom is bonded to several identical atoms, for these compounds can be used as prototypes for other molecules of similar structure. There are seven commonly occurring shapes, and other shapes are found only in a small number of cases. Figure 11-1 shows seven common shapes of molecules.

(i) **The CO_2 Structure.** In carbon dioxide, the two oxygen atoms and the carbon atom are collinear. The carbon-oxygen bond lengths are equal, and the O-C-O bond angle is 180°.

(ii) **The H_2O Structure.** In the water molecule, the three atoms are not collinear, and so the H-O-H bond angle is not equal to 180°. The two O-H bond lengths are equal. The bond angle in water is 104.5°, but a range of bond angles is found in similar molecules. The essential difference between the CO_2 and the H_2O structures is that in the former case the bond angle is 180° and the atoms in the molecule are collinear, whereas in the latter case, the bond angle is less than 180°, and the molecule is bent.

(iii) **The BF_3 Structure.** In the boron trifluoride molecule, the four atoms are coplanar, and the three fluorine atoms are arranged in an equilateral triangle with the boron atom in the middle. The bond lengths are all the same, and the F-B-F bond angles are 120°

(iv) **The NH_3 Structure.** In the NH_3 molecule, the three hydrogen atoms form an equilateral triangle; the nitrogen atom is symmetrically placed with respect to this triangle, but lies above the plane of the triangle. The N-H bond lengths are equal, and the H-N-H bond angles are equal but less than 120°.

218   Molecular Structure

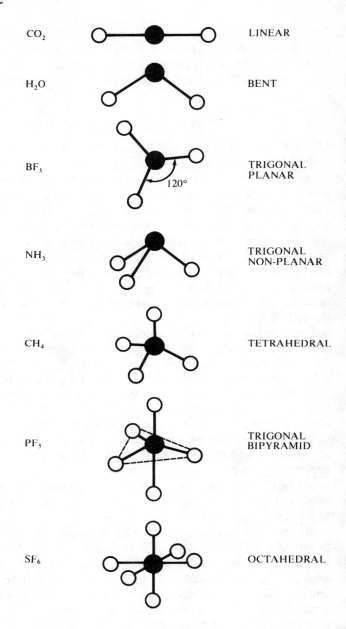

CO_2		LINEAR
H_2O		BENT
BF_3	120°	TRIGONAL PLANAR
NH_3		TRIGONAL NON-PLANAR
CH_4		TETRAHEDRAL
PF_5		TRIGONAL BIPYRAMID
SF_6		OCTAHEDRAL

Figure 11-1 The seven common shapes of small molecules.

(v) **The CH_4 Structure.** The structure of the methane molecule is probably the most important of all the simple shapes, since it is the basic shape used in building up the molecules of organic chemistry. The four hydrogen atoms are at the corners of a regular tetrahedron, and the H-C-H angles are all equal to 109.46°.

The tetrahedron is not commonly met in everyday life, and so it will be described briefly. The easiest approach to a tetrahedron is to consider a cube, and place a star at each *alternate* corner of the cube. If the stars are connected by lines a regular tetrahedron results.

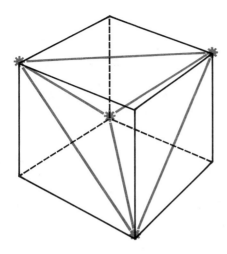

Figure 11-2 A tetrahedron inscribed in a cube. The corners of the tetrahedron are defined by placing a star on alternate corners of the cube.

A cube is a very symmetrical figure. Each face is a square and all the diagonals of these squares are equal, so the four faces of the tetrahedron are equilateral triangles. The centre of the cube is equidistant from the four corners of the tetrahedron and is therefore also the centre of the tetrahedron. In the methane molecule, the carbon atom lies at the centre of the tetrahedron and the hydrogen atoms lie at the corners. Calculations on the geometry of the tetrahedron are not difficult to make if use is made of the cube on which the tetrahedron is based.

Example 11-1   What is the ratio of the C-H bond length to the H-H distance in methane?

The H-H distance is equal to the length of the diagonal of one of the square faces of the cube in Figure 11-2. If L is the length of the edge of the cube, the H-H distance is $\sqrt{2}\,$L.

The C-H distance is equal to half the length of the diagonal of the whole cube, since the carbon atom lies at the centre of the cube. Hence the C-H distance is $\frac{1}{2}\sqrt{3}\,$L. The ratio required is therefore $\frac{1}{2}\sqrt{3}\,/\,\sqrt{2}$ or $\frac{1}{2}\sqrt{3/2}$.

(vi)The PF$_5$ Structure. Phosphorus pentafluoride is not a commonly encountered substance, but it forms an interesting link in the sequence of molecular shapes.

The five fluorine atoms in this molecule are not in identical situations in the molecule. Three fluorine atoms are arranged in an equilateral triangle, and the phosphorus atom lies at the centre; the other two fluorine atoms are symmetrically placed above and below the triangle.

In the drawing in Figure 11-1 the equilateral triangle is indicated with a dotted line, which does not imply chemical bonding. The three atoms forming the equilateral triangle are referred to as *equatorial* atoms, and the other two are referred to as *axial* since they define a unique axis for the molecule. There are two P-F bond lengths in this molecule, which can be designated as axial and equatorial bond lengths. In molecules having this structure, the axial bond length is longer than the equatorial bond length. There are also two different F-P-F bond angles, one being 120° and the other being 90°.

The PF_5 structure is sometimes called a *trigonal bipyramid*, since the solid figure formed by joining all the fluorine atoms can be thought of as two triangular pyramids which are joined so as to share a triangular face.

(vii) **The SF_6 Structure.** In the sulphur hexafluoride molecule, all the S-F bond lengths are equal, and all the F-S-F bond angles are 90°. The fluorine atoms are placed symmetrically on the positive and negative, x, y and z axes of a Cartesian system centred at the sulphur atom.

This structure is often described as *octahedral*, since the solid figure formed by joining all the fluorine atoms is a regular figure having eight equilateral triangular faces. It can also be described as a square bipyramid.

It is helpful to make models of these molecules, to be kept close at hand when dealing with molecular geometry. Simple models can be made using a cork and toothpicks or pieces of wire.

Once these basic shapes have been described the shapes of many other molecules can be predicted using the periodic properties of the elements. If any atom in a molecule is replaced by another atom belonging to the same group of the periodic table, the shape of the molecule is often unaffected. For example, if the carbon atom in methane is replaced by a silicon atom which also lies in Group IV, the resulting molecule, having formula SiH_4 and named silane, has the same tetrahedral shape as CH_4. Similarly, if all the hydrogen atoms in CH_4 are replaced by fluorine atoms, belonging to group VII, the resulting molecule CF_4, carbon tetrafluoride, is also tetrahedral. The application of this rule means that a lot of structural information can be predicted using the periodic table. Some common classes of molecules which have the shapes previously described are listed below.

Linear:	Group II metal halides, such as $HgCl_2$ and BeF_2. Molecules of these salts are obtainable as vapours at moderate temperatures.
Bent:	Group VI hydrides, halides and dioxides, some examples being H_2S, SCl_2, SO_2 O_3 (ozone).
trigonal planar:	Group VI trioxides such as SO_3. The carbonate ion CO_3^{2-} and nitrate ion NO_3^-.
trigonal non-planar:	Group V trihalides and hydrides, such as PH_3, $AsCl_3$, SbF_3, $BiCl_3$.
tetrahedral:	The hydrides and halides of Group IV elements. The sulphate ion SO_4^{2-} and perchlorate ion ClO_4^-.
trigonal bi-pyramid	The pentahalides of Group V elements.
Octahedral:	Group VI hexafluorides. Hexafluorides of a number of d-block and f-block metals, such as MoF_6, PtF_6 and UF_6. Hexahalide ions of a number of d-block elements such as $NiCl_6^{4-}$, $CoCl_6^{3-}$.

With a little practice it should be possible to predict the likely structure of an unknown molecule from a knowledge of these classifications. It should be no surprise that the H_2Se molecule is bent, that the CCl_4 molecule is tetrahedral, and the WF_6 molecule is octahedral, because these compounds can be readily fitted into one of the above classifications.

It is possible to extend the predictions further by noting that when two molecules are isoelectronic, i.e. have the same number of electrons, they generally have the same structure. For example, the carbonate and nitrate ions have equal numbers of electrons and have the trigonal planar structure. The sulphur trioxide molecule SO_3 has the same number of *valence* electrons as the carbonate and nitrate ions and is also trigonal planar. The sulphate and perchlorate ions are isoelectronic and are both tetrahedral. The structure of the BF_4^- ion may be predicted to be tetrahedral since this ion is isoelectronic with the tetrahedral molecule CF_4.

11-3   THE GEOMETRY OF ORGANIC MOLECULES

There are five characteristic shapes which occur in organic molecules. These are combinations of the shapes already described, but the bonding patterns around carbon atoms are so important in organic chemistry that they should be summarized and considered in a separate section. The five basic shapes are shown in Figure 11-3, and are labelled with the formulae of the prototype molecules.

(i) **the CH_4 structure**. This has already been described. This is the basic tetrahedral geometry which is found whenever a carbon atom is bonded to four other atoms by single bonds.

(ii) **The C_2H_6 structure**. The ethane molecule consists of two methyl groups bonded together by a carbon-carbon bond. The arrangement of atoms about each carbon atom is tetrahedral and the two tetrahedra share an apex or corner. In the lowest energy configuration of the molecule the relative orientation of the two methyl groups is such that the hydrogen atoms of one methyl group lie in between the hydrogen atoms of the other when viewed along the C-C axis. This is indicated by the sketch in Figure 11-3. This configuration of the molecule is called the *staggered* configuration, and will be discussed further when the relative motion of the two methyl groups is considered in a later section.

(iii) **The C_2H_4 structure**. In ethylene the six atoms are coplanar. The C-H bond lengths are all equal, and the four H-C-C bond angles all have the same value of approximately $120°$. Thus each end of the molecule displays almost trigonal planar bonding, and the two ends of the molecule are coplanar with each other.

(iv) **The C_2H_2 structure**. In acetylene the four atoms are collinear, and the two C-H bond lengths are equal. Each end of the molecule shows the collinear bonding that was met in the CO_2 molecule.

(v) **The C_6H_6 structure**. In the benzene molecule all twelve atoms are coplanar. All the C-C bonds are equal in length, all the C-H bonds are equal in length, and all the angles between adjacent bonds are equal to $120°$ exactly. The shape of the molecule is that of a regular hexagon.

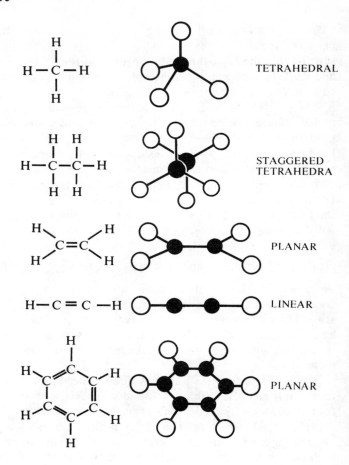

Figure 11-3 The five basic shapes found in organic molecules.

Other compounds can be made from these basic hydrocarbons by substituting other atoms for some of the hydrogen atoms. Generally, substitution has very little effect on the geometry of the rest of the molecule. For instance, if one of the hydrogen atoms in methane is replaced by a chlorine atom, methyl chloride CH_3Cl is obtained. In CH_3Cl the atoms around the carbon atom are arranged tetrahedrally, with the three C-H distances being equal, but different from the C-Cl distance.

Ethane is related to methane by the substitution of a methyl group CH_3 for one of the hydrogen atoms in CH_4. Each carbon atom is still bonded to four other atoms by single bonds, and the characteristic tetrahedral arrangement of the bonds is retained. Further substitution of methyl groups for hydrogen atoms leads to higher hydrocarbons having the formula C_nH_{2n+2}. The branched and straight chain isomers are formed by substitution at different positions in the parent molecule.

In molecules containing a carbon-carbon double bond,

$$\diagup C = C \diagdown$$

the atoms in the vicinity of the double bond are coplanar, as in ethylene itself. Again, the hydrogen atoms can be replaced by other atoms, leading to new compounds in which the same geometry is retained. Chloroethylene, for example, has the planar structure shown opposite.

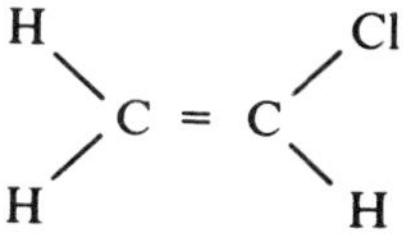

$$
\begin{array}{ccc}
H & & Cl \\
\diagdown & & \diagup \\
 & C = C & \\
\diagup & & \diagdown \\
H & & H
\end{array}
$$

If two chlorine atoms are substituted for hydrogen atoms in ethylene, a new form of isomerism is shown, for there are three different compounds formed, corresponding to the three ways of making the substitution. First, both chlorine atoms may be bonded to the same carbon atom

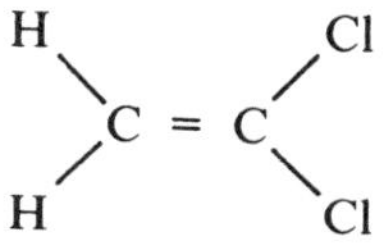

$$
\begin{array}{ccc}
H & & Cl \\
\diagdown & & \diagup \\
 & C = C & \\
\diagup & & \diagdown \\
H & & Cl
\end{array}
$$

1,1-dichloroethylene

Secondly, the two chlorine atoms may be bonded to different carbon atoms. Because the atoms adjacent to the double bond are required to be coplanar, this can be done in two different ways, corresponding to two different compounds

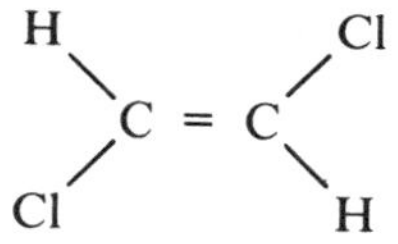

$$
\begin{array}{ccc}
H & & Cl \\
\diagdown & & \diagup \\
 & C = C & \\
\diagup & & \diagdown \\
Cl & & H
\end{array}
\qquad
\begin{array}{ccc}
Cl & & Cl \\
\diagdown & & \diagup \\
 & C = C & \\
\diagup & & \diagdown \\
H & & H
\end{array}
$$

trans-1,2-dichloroethylene 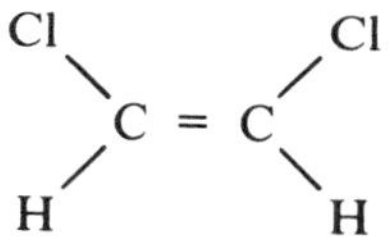   *cis*-1,2-dichloroethylene

Because these molecules are planar, the structural formulae written on paper give an accurate representation of the geometrical relationships within the molecule, unlike the situation for the tetrahedral arrangement of four bonds around a carbon atom. Furthermore, once formed these molecules retain their form since rotation about the central bond, which would convert one to the other, cannot take place since the molecules are always planar. The designations *trans* and *cis* are used to mean "on opposite sides" and "on the same side" respectively, and refer to the relative positions of the atoms which have been substituted for hydrogen in the parent compound, ethylene.

The presence of the 1,1- and 1,2- compounds is an example of structural isomerism, of the type that has been met before. However, the existence of the two 1,2- compounds is a case of a new form of isomerism, called *geometrical isomerism*. There are the same number of bonds of the same types between exactly the same atoms in the two molecules. The difference between them can only be described by considering the geometrical relationships between the atoms in the two molecules. Geometrical isomerism, or different geometrical relationships between the atoms, leads to the existence of distinct chemical compounds, just as surely as structural isomerism. The *cis* and *trans* isomers of 1,2-dichloroethylene can be separated in pure form and are stable compounds; they have different boiling points (60.3°C and 47.5°C, respectively), and other chemical and physical properties differ as well.

Planar geometry is found whenever a carbon atom is involved in a double bond. A common case is the *carbonyl* group, $\mathrm{C} = \mathrm{O}$, in which an oxygen atom is double bonded to carbon. Thus, in formaldehyde, CH_2O, and acetic acid, CH_3COOH, the geometry around the carbon atom carrying the double bond is planar.

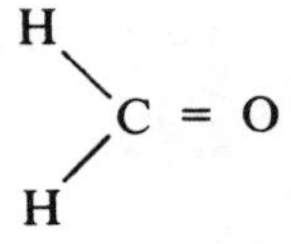

formaldehyde 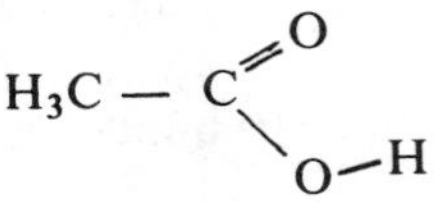   acetic acid

The *carboxyl* group, $-COOH$, is the source of hydrogen ions in most organic acids. When an oxygen atom is bonded to two other atoms by single bonds, the angle between the bonds at the oxygen atom is less than 180°, as in the water molecule. This situation also occurs in alcohols,

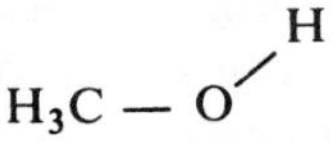

methanol

and in ethers, compounds in which the oxygen atom is bonded to two carbon atoms

dimethyl ether

Triple bonds are not common in organic chemistry, but they are found in the molecule ethyne, more commonly known as acetylene, and its derivatives. The arrangement of the atoms in these molecules is characteristically linear.

The structure of benzene, C_6H_6, is difficult to represent by a conventional structural formula. The shape of the molecule shown in Figure 11-3 shows that the carbon-carbon bonds are all exactly the same. The carbon atoms could be joined in a ring consisting of alternating double and single bonds. This structure could then be written in two ways.

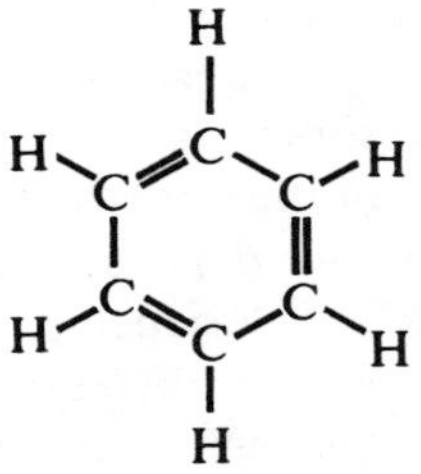

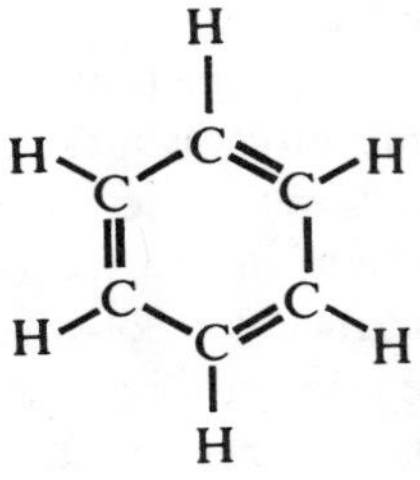

Either one of these structures suggests that there are two different kinds of carbon-carbon bond, but since there are two equivalent structures it is impossible to decide whether a given bond is a double bond or a single bond. Hence the structural formula of benzene is often represented by a dotted circle inside the ring of carbon atoms. Since there is no ambiguity, often the symbols for the carbon atoms (and sometimes the hydrogen atoms too) are omitted in drawing the benzene ring.

    The planarity of the benzene molecule is consistent with the presence of double bonds between the carbon atoms, but the equality of the carbon-carbon bond lengths shows that the bonds all have a character in between purely double and single bonds. This intermediate character of the carbon-carbon bonds is confirmed by the measured distance between the carbon atoms, which lies about halfway between the bond distances measured for ordinary C-C single bonds and C=C double bonds. This is discussed in connection with Figure 11-5.

    Benzene forms the basis for a large class of compounds, called *aromatic* compounds, in which some of the hydrogen atoms around the ring are replaced by other atoms or groups of atoms. In all such molecules, the hexagonal ring of carbon atoms is planar, and the atoms bonded to the ring carbon atoms lie in the plane of the ring. When writing the formula for an aromatic molecule such as chlorobenzene, it is common to omit the hydrogen atoms of the benzene ring which have not been substituted:

chlorobenzene

    When there are two or more substituent atoms around a benzene ring, there are several possible structural isomers. These isomers are named either by a systematic procedure in which the carbon atoms around the ring are numbered from 1 to 6, or by a system of prefixes which remains in common use. For example, the structural isomers with the formula $C_6H_4Cl_2$ are three in number:

1,2-dichlorobenzene
or *ortho*-dichlorobenzene

1,3-dichlorobenzene
or *meta*-dichlorobenzene

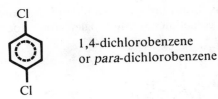

1,4-dichlorobenzene
or *para*-dichlorobenzene

The geometrical properties of a complicated organic molecule are almost impossible to represent easily with pencil and paper. Great familiarity with these basic shapes is needed in order to be able to visualize the relationships in space which are implied by a given structural formula. However the basic geometrical shapes associated with the various ways in which carbon atoms may be bonded are sufficiently constant from molecule to molecule that kits of "parts" are available commercially which enable one to build a scale model of many molecules according to their structural formulae. Such models are essential to the building of an accurate mental picture of organic molecules containing more than a few atoms, and are used regularly in research in organic chemistry.

11-4   THE PROPERTIES OF CHEMICAL BONDS

A line or lines between the symbols for the atoms in a molecule is a convenient way of showing chemical bonds, but the true nature or these bonds is not easy to describe. In this section, two of the properties of chemical bonds, their length and their energy, are described. These properties are important because they are approximately the same in many different molecules containing the same type of bond.

The *bond length* is the distance between the nuclei of atoms joined by the bond. The length of a bond of a given type is found experimentally to be approximately the same from molecule to molecule, and as examples the lengths of the C-H and C-Cl bonds in a number of closely related molecules are given in Table 11-1. The lengths given in the last two columns of the table are approximately constant, and so it is useful to assume that the length of the C-H bond is about 0.108 nm in all molecules, and that of the C-Cl bond is about

Table 11-1   C-H and C-Cl Bond Lengths

Molecule	C-H Bond Length (nm)	C-Cl Bond Length (nm)
CH_4	0.1091	—
CH_3Cl	0.111	0.1784
CH_2Cl_2	0.1068	0.1772
$CHCl_3$	0.1073	0.1767
CCl_4	—	0.1766
C_2H_6	0.1107	—
C_2Cl_6	—	0.174

Table 11-2 Average Bond Lengths and Bond Energies

Bond	Length nm	Energy kJ mol^{-1}
H – H	0.074	436
H – F	0.092	567
H – Cl	0.127	432
H – Br	0.141	366
H – I	0.161	298
F – F	0.142	157
Cl – Cl	0.199	243
O – O	0.148	146
O = O	0.121	498
O – H	0.096	464
O – F	0.142	184
O – Cl	0.170	205
S – S	0.205	264
S – H	0.135	339
S – Cl	0.199	276
N – N	0.145	163
N ≡ N	0.110	945
N – H	0.101	389
N – Cl	0.175	201
P – H	0.144	318
P – Cl	0.203	318
C – C	0.154	347
C = C	0.134	599
C ≡ C	0.120	829
C – H	0.108	414
C – O	0.143	335
C = O	{ 0.122 { 0.116	{ 686 in ketones { 804 in CO_2
C – F	0.138	441
C – Cl	0.177	326
C – Br	0.194	276
C – I	0.214	240
C – N	0.147	285
C ≡ N	0.116	866
Si – Si	0.232	176
Si – H	0.148	295
Si – O	0.163	369
Si – Cl	0.202	359

0.175 nm. Rules as simple as this are bound to be in significant error sometimes, but in the absence of other information these values may be assumed to be approximately correct. Average values of bond lengths for a number of different bond types are listed in Table 11-2. These values may be used to estimate the size of molecules without carrying out the complicated experiments required to determine the facts experimentally.

Chemical reactions between molecular substances may be considered as a rearrangement of the bonds in the molecules concerned. Atoms are conserved in chemical reactions, but the chemical bonds are changed or rearranged. For example, in the reaction between hydrogen and oxygen,

$$2H_2 + O_2 \rightarrow 2H_2O$$

the effect of the reaction is that two H-H bonds and one O=O bond are broken and four O-H bonds are formed. This reaction results in the release of a large amount of energy, and it is natural to associate this energy release with the change in the number and type of the chemical bonds which takes place in the reaction. Energy in molecules appears to be associated with the bonds holding the atoms together, rather than the atoms themselves. Thermochemical data can be used to show that a given type of bond has approximately the same energy associated with it in many different molecules. Although the energy associated with a given type of bond varies somewhat from molecule to molecule, just like the bond length, it is possible to determine a set of *bond energies* which describe the thermochemistry of chemical bonds in a reasonably accurate way. Bond energies for individual molecules are very small and so bond energies are usually quoted for one mole of chemical bonds, with units kilojoules/mole. Table 11-2 contains a list of bond energies as well as bond lengths.

The bond energy is defined as the energy per mole required to break the specified bond when *all* of the bonds in the molecule are broken. The energy required to break a molecule completely apart into atoms is therefore the sum of the bond energies of all the bonds. Bond energies must be measured for molecules in the gas phase. In the gas phase the average energy of interaction between the molecules is very small, and the energy required to convert a sample of substance into gaseous atoms consists only of the energy of the chemical bonds within each molecule with no contribution from the intermolecular interactions.

Bond energies are determined, then, by considering the enthalpy change for a process in which isolated molecules in the gas phase are broken up into isolated atoms, also in the gas phase. It is impossible to carry out such reactions in the controlled conditions of a calorimeter, even for simple molecules, and the table of bond energies is constructed by piecing together evidence from spectroscopic and thermodynamic experiments.

The energy required to break a diatomic molecule into atoms can be measured spectroscopically with great accuracy, and is equal by definition to the bond energy for that molecule. The energies of bonds such as H$-$H, Cl$-$Cl, and H$-$Cl are determined in this way. For diatomic molecules of the elements, such as H_2, the process of dissociation yields two atoms,

$$H_2(g) \rightarrow 2H(g)$$

and so the bond energy is equal to twice the enthalpy change of formation of the atoms of the element in the gas phase. Reference to Table 11-2 and Appendix I shows that the H$-$H bond energy, 436 kJ mol^{-1}, is exactly twice the ΔH_f° value for H(g). This must be so because for the above reaction,

$$\begin{aligned} \Delta H &= 2\Delta H_f^\circ(H(g)) - \Delta H_f^\circ(H_2(g)) \\ &= 2\Delta H_f^\circ(H(g)) \end{aligned}$$

since $H_2(g)$ represents the element in its standard state and has zero enthalpy change of formation, $\Delta H_f{}^\circ(H_2(g)) = 0$.

The bond energy for a diatomic molecule such as HCl can most conveniently be determined by thermochemistry when the heats of formation of the atoms of the elements are known. For the bond energy is the enthalpy change for the reaction:

$$HCl(g) \rightarrow H(g) + Cl(g)$$
$$\Delta H = \Delta H_f^\circ(H(g)) + \Delta H_f^\circ(Cl(g)) - \Delta H_f^\circ(HCl(g))$$
$$= (+218.00) + (+121.290) - (-92.307)$$
$$= +431.60 \text{ kJ mol}^{-1}$$

This figure calculated from the enthalpies of formation in Appendix I is in agreement with the value given for the H—Cl bond energy in Table 11-2, namely 432 kJ mol⁻¹.

For polyatomic molecules containing only one kind of chemical bond, the bond energy can be calculated thermochemically by a similar method, considering the hypothetical reaction in which the molecule is completely dissociated into atoms. For example the bond energy in methane is calculated by the following method.

In the following reaction, methane is dissociated into atoms. Four moles of C—H bonds are broken, and so the bond energy of one mole of C—H bonds is one quarter of the energy of this reaction.

$$CH_4(g) \rightarrow C(g) + 4H(g)$$
$$\Delta H = \Delta H_f^\circ(C(g)) + 4\Delta H_f^\circ(H(g)) - \Delta H_f^\circ(CH_4(g))$$
$$= 716.7 + 4(218.0) - (-76.8)$$
$$= 1661.6 \text{ kJ}$$

Hence the C—H bond energy in this molecule is 1661.6 kJ per 4 mol of bonds, or 415.4 kJ mol⁻¹. This value differs slightly from the value in Table 11-2, which is an average value calculated for C—H bonds in numerous molecules.

The bond energy of C—C bond may be calculated using the value of the C—H bond energy and the enthalpy of formation of ethane.

$$C_2H_6(g) \rightarrow 2C(g) + 6H(g)$$
$$\Delta H = 2\Delta H_f^\circ(C(g)) + 6\Delta H_f^\circ(H(g)) - \Delta H_f^\circ(C_2H_6(g))$$
$$= 2(716.7) + 6(217.5) - (-84.5)$$
$$= 2822.9 \text{ kJ}$$

Now while one can say precisely that the total energy required to break one C—C bond and six C—H bonds is 2822.9 kJ mol⁻¹, one cannot say precisely how this energy is distributed among those seven bonds. There are, however, two pieces of evidence which allow a very reasonable guess to be made. First, all spectroscopic and chemical evidence indicates that the six hydrogens in ethane are all equivalent. Secondly, making an assumption that C—H bonds are very similar in all molecules seems to lead to reasonable and self-consistent results. Measurements made on a wide range of compounds have produced a widely accepted mean value for C—H bonds of 414 kJ mol⁻¹, slightly below the value calculated above for methane. If one assumes that each C—H bond in ethane contributes this much to the total bond energy of the molecule, then the

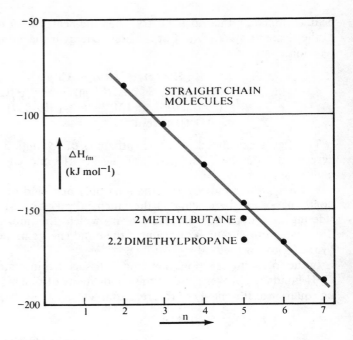

Figure 11-4 Enthalpy of formation of hydrocarbons, C_nH_{2n+2}, plotted as a function of chain length.

C$-$C bond energy can be calculated by the difference

$$E_{C-C} = 2822.9 - 6 \times 414$$

$$= 339 \text{ kJ mol}^{-1}$$

The constancy of bond energies in a series of molecules can be demonstrated using the heats of formation of the hydrocarbons of formula C_nH_{2n+2}. The heats of formation of these compounds in the gas phase are plotted against chain length in Figure 11-4, in which it is shown that for the straight chain hydrocarbons, the heat of formation is a linear function of n.

The reaction in which the molecule C_nH_{2n+2} is formed from the elements carbon and hydrogen in their standard states can be written in two stages. First the elements are converted into atoms in the gas phase,

$$nC(c) \rightarrow nC(g) \qquad\qquad \Delta H = n \, \Delta H_f^\circ (C(g))$$

$$(n+1) H_2(g) \rightarrow (2n+2) H(g) \qquad \Delta H = (2n+2) \, \Delta H_f^\circ (H(g))$$

and then these atoms are reacted to form the hydrocarbon in the gas phase:

$$nC(g) + (2n+2) H(g) \rightarrow C_nH_{2n+2}(g)$$

The heats of the first two reactions are multiples of the heats of formation of the atoms in the gas phase, and are obtained from the thermochemical tables. The heat of the third reaction can be expressed in terms of the average bond energies E_{C-C} and E_{C-H}. Since C_nH_{2n+2} has $(n-1)$ C$-$C bonds and $(2n+2)$ C$-$H bonds, the heat of the third reaction is given by the approximate equation

$$\Delta H \approx -(n-1)E_{C-C} - (2n+2) E_{C-H}$$

The signs in this equation are negative since heat is given out by the system when bonds are formed. Hence the heat of the overall reaction,

$$nC(c) + (n+1) H_2(g) \rightarrow C_nH_{2n+2}(g)$$

which is the heat of formation of $C_nH_{2n+2}(g)$, is the sum of these three contributions,

$$\Delta H_f^\circ(C_nH_{2n+2}(g)) \approx n \Delta H_f^\circ(C(g)) + (2n+2) \Delta H_f^\circ(H(g))$$

$$-(n-1)E_{C-C} -(2n+2)E_{C-H}$$

As long as the bond energies are constant, this equation predicts that $\Delta H_f^\circ(C_nH_{2n+2})$ is a linear function of n. For an increase of 1 in the value of n, ΔH_f° should change by the amount

$$\Delta H_f^\circ(C(g)) +2 \Delta H_f^\circ(H(g)) - E_{C-C} - 2E_{C-H}$$

Inserting values from Appendix I and Table 11-2, this quantity is

$$(+716.7) + 2 (218) - 347 -2 (414) = -22.3 \text{ kJ mol}^{-1}$$

From the graph, the actual heat of formation changes by -20.6 kJ mol^{-1}. This is satisfactory agreement for an approximate theory. However, it will be noticed that the heats of formation of the two structural isomers of pentane do not lie on the graph despite having the same number of the same types of bonds.

It must always be recalled that calculations using bond energies are approximate, while calculations using heats of formation are reliable because the first law of thermodynamics guarantees the conservation of energy. A particularly important case of variation of bond energies is the carbon-oxygen double bond, which has a value in CO_2 markedly different from the average value used for the C=O bond in aldehydes, ketones and carboxylic acids.

Example 11-2 Calculate the heat of combustion of ethanol using bond energies.

The combustion reaction is assumed to produce CO_2 and water in the gas phase:

$$C_2H_5OH(g) + 3O_2(g) \rightarrow 2CO_2(g) + 3H_2O(g)$$

In carrying out this reaction, the following bonds are broken:

		bond energy
3	O=O	1494
1	C-C	347
1	C-O	335
1	O-H	464
5	C-H	2070
	Total	+4710 kJ

In forming the product molecules from these atoms, the following bonds are formed:

4	C=O	-3216	(for the CO_2 molecule)
6	O–H	-2784	
		-6000 kJ	

Hence the molar heat of combustion of ethanol is estimated as the sum of these two values:

$$\Delta H = -6000 + 4710$$
$$= -1290 \text{ kJ mol}^{-1}$$

The measured heat of combustion listed in Table 6-1 is $-1366.9 \text{ kJ mol}^{-1}$.

The constancy of bond energies has interesting implications in the study of hydrocarbon fuels. For gaseous fuels such as methane, ethane and propane, equal volumes of these gases under the same conditions of temperature and pressure contain equal numbers of molecules by Avogadro's Principle. Hence the most energetic gaseous fuel, volume for volume, is that fuel with the greatest number of bonds in each molecule, namely propane. A tank of propane with a suitable burner is often used when a mobile source of heat is required. For stationary applications where large volumes of gas can be brought in by pipeline, the preferred gaseous fuel is methane, since it is available in large quantities at moderate prices as the major component of natural gas.

In some liquid fuel applications, such as aircraft engines, the weight of the fuel rather than the volume is important. Table 6-1 shows that for all hydrocarbon fuels the heat of combustion per unit mass is about 48 kJ g^{-1}. The molar heat of formation of these compounds is a linear function of chain length, as shown in Figure 11-4, and the molar heat of combustion is therefore also a linear function of chain length. The molar mass is proportional to the chain length and so the heat of combustion per unit mass of liquid hydrocarbons is approximately constant. This is a useful fact to remember because it enables an engineer to estimate the heat content of a hydrocarbon fuel on a mass basis without any detailed knowledge of its chemical composition. The heats of combustion of commercial fuels listed in Table 6-2 conform to this rule.

From Table 11-2, it can be seen that the bond lengths and bond energies of double and triple bonds between two given atoms are different from those of a single bond. The best example of this is the carbon-carbon bond, for which the bond lengths and bond energies have been measured in a great many molecules. As the *bond order* increases from 1 to 2 to 3 (i.e. single bond to double bond to triple bond) the bond energy becomes greater and the bond length becomes shorter. These trends are consistent with the intuitive idea that a double bond is "stronger" than a single bond, and a triple bond is "stronger" than a double bond. The dependence of the carbon-carbon bond length on bond order is well enough defined that a measured bond length in a molecule may be used as a reliable indicator of the bond order for the bond joining those two carbon atoms. Occasionally, cases of non-integer bond order occur. The carbon- carbon distance in benzene is 0.140 nm, which lies in between the bond lengths for single and double bonds, 0.154 and 0.134 nm respectively. This value is consistent with the previous discussion of the bonding in benzene, for each carbon-

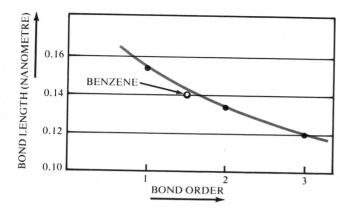

Figure 11-5 Carbon-carbon bond lengths plotted against bond order.

carbon bond is intermediate in character between a single and a double bond. Taking a strict average, the bond order in benzene is 1.5, and it is seen in Figure 11-5 that this point lies near a smooth curve joining the points for integer values of the bond order.

11-5 INTERNAL MOTION IN MOLECULES

In the preceding sections the relative positions of atoms in molecules have been discussed on the assumption that the atoms are at rest relative to each other. This assumption is not strictly true for any molecule, and in some molecules there are internal motions which are fast and which affect the characteristics of the molecule as a whole.

The simplest internal motion is vibration. This type of motion occurs in all molecules at all temperatures, and can be best understood by considering the simplest molecule, namely a diatomic molecule containing two atoms.

Suppose that two atoms of hydrogen are brought together slowly, and that the energy of interaction between the two atoms can be measured continuously as a function of the distance between them. When the atoms are infinitely far apart, the energy of interaction, E, is zero. As the atoms approach, however, E becomes negative because the chemical bond between them begins to form. The energy, E, continues to fall until the distance between the atoms equals the H-H bond length. At this point, E equals the H-H bond energy except for a small correction. If the distance between the two atoms decreases further, strong electrostatic repulsions between the nuclei cause E to increase quickly to become positive. The qualitative form of the function E(r) is shown in Figure 11-6.

When the atoms are separated by a distance equal to the bond length, the molecule is in its lowest energy configuration. If the atoms were placed at any other distance and allowed to move under the influence of the force between them, they would undergo an oscillation or vibration in which the interatomic distance fluctuates about the bond length, or average interatomic distance. This motion is an example of *simple harmonic motion*. The energy of interaction E(r) provides the potential energy of the motion. To a very good approximation, the graph of the potential energy E(r) is a parabola near the

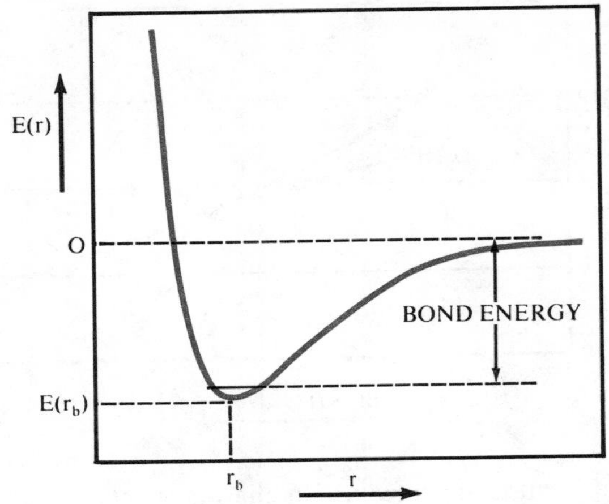

Figure 11-6 The energy of interaction of two atoms forming a covalent bond. The lowest vibrational energy level is shown, and the bond energy identified. The dotted curve shows a parabola which has the same shape as the energy curve in the region of the minimum.

minimum, because even though $E(r)$ is not exactly quadratic, it may be expanded in a Taylor series about the bond length, r_b:

$$E(r) = E(r_b) + (r - r_b)\, E'(r_b) + \tfrac{1}{2}\, (r - r_b)^2 E''(r_b) + \ldots$$

The first derivative evaluated at the bond distance, $E'(r_b)$, is zero because that defines the minimum of the potential energy. The third and higher derivative terms may be ignored as small quantities as long as r does not deviate too far from r_b. Hence to a good approximation

$$E(r) = E(r_b) + \tfrac{1}{2}k\, (r - r_b)^2$$

where $k = E''(r_b)$ is called the *force constant,* by analogy with the force constant of an ordinary spring which relates the force exerted by the spring to its compression or extension. This equation defines a parabola, and it is a result of classical mechanics that such a potential energy function is associated with simple harmonic motion. The frequency of the motion in cycles per second, or hertz, is given by

$$\nu = \frac{1}{2\pi}\,\sqrt{\frac{k}{m_r}}$$

where m_r is the *reduced mass* for this molecule. The reduced mass for a diatomic molecule is defined by

$$\frac{1}{m_r} = \frac{1}{m_1} + \frac{1}{m_2}$$

where m_1 and m_2 are the masses of the two atoms forming the molecule.

As in all mechanics on an atomic or molecular scale, quantum effects must be considered. It is found from quantum mechanics that there are only certain energy levels which are allowed for this molecular oscillator. This result is consistent with previous experience, that energy in a quantum system is restricted to a set of certain special quantized levels which are characteristic of the system. In the case of a vibrating molecule, the vibrational energy is allowed to take one of the values

$$\tfrac{1}{2}h\nu, \tfrac{3}{2}h\nu, \tfrac{5}{2}h\nu, \tfrac{7}{2}h\nu, \ldots$$

where h is Planck's constant and ν is the vibrational frequency. It is notable that this set does not include the value zero, so that a quantum oscillator can never be completely at rest; the lowest possible energy is $(1/2)h\nu$, and it is this energy, called the *zero point energy*, which is responsible for the vibrational correction shown in Figure 11-6. The bond energy is given by

$$\begin{aligned} B.E. &= -E(r_b) - \tfrac{1}{2}h\nu \\ &= -E(r_b) - \frac{h}{4\pi}\sqrt{\frac{k}{m_r}} \end{aligned}$$

in which it should be remembered that $E(r_b)$ is a negative number. For most molecules, the vibrational correction is less than five per cent of $E(r_b)$, and the deviations of r away from r_b are small compared with r_b. For the hydrogen molecule, the vibration frequency ν is 1.32×10^{14} Hz, and the zero point energy is

$$\tfrac{1}{2}h\nu \times N_A = \tfrac{1}{2} \times 6.626 \times 10^{-34} \text{ J s} \times 1.32 \times 10^{14} \text{ s}^{-1} \times 6.022 \times 10^{23} \text{ mol}^{-1}$$

$$= 26.4 \text{ kJ mol}^{-1}$$

The vibrational energy levels given for this molecular oscillator are the basis for an important type of spectroscopy. Since the energy levels are equally spaced, all the transitions between adjacent energy levels involve the same energy difference:

$$E = \tfrac{3}{2}h\nu - \tfrac{1}{2}h\nu = \tfrac{5}{2}h\nu - \tfrac{3}{2}h\nu = \ldots = h\nu$$

Recalling the Planck assumption that the energy of a photon is equal to h multiplied by the frequency of the light, it is seen that light can cause transitions between adjacent energy levels by absorption of a photon, whenever the frequency of the light is equal to the frequency of vibration of the molecule. For all molecules, this frequency lies in the infra-red part of the electromagnetic spectrum.

The frequency of vibration is determined by the masses of the atoms in the molecule, and by the force constant k. Since these quantities are different for different subtances, there is a characteristic vibrational frequency for each different substance. The vibrational frequency can be determined by either *infrared* spectroscopy or *Raman* spectroscopy depending upon the circumstances. These spectroscopic techniques are powerful methods for identifying chemical substances.

In molecules containing more than two atoms, all the atoms are involved in vibrational motion, but more complicated motions are also possible. Two cases will be discussed: inversion and internal rotation.

Consider the ammonia molecule, NH_3, which is pyramidal in shape. There is a type of motion in which the three hydrogen atoms remain equidistant from each other, and the nitrogen atom moves towards the plane of the hydrogen atoms. This motion is shown in Figure 11-7. The motion is similar to the open-

Figure 11-7 The process of inversion of an ammonia molecule. A stable configuration of the molecule is shown on the left. In the process of inversion the hydrogen atoms move up and the nitrogen atom moves down, until the other stable configuration of the molecule, shown on the right, is reached.

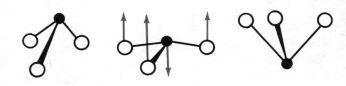

ing of an umbrella. The amplitude of the motion for vibrations is generally small, but for this umbrella motion in ammonia, the nitrogen atom moves right through the plane of the hydrogen atoms to the other side, until the molecule reaches a configuration equivalent to the initial configuration.

The energy of the molecule is higher when it is planar than when it is non-planar. The most stable configuration is non-planar, and so the molecule is said to be non-planar. But the molecule is in the process of constantly turning "inside-out" and "outside-in" like an umbrella in a windstorm. This type of motion is called *inversion,* and can occur whenever there is a non-planar configuration of three bonds about an atom.

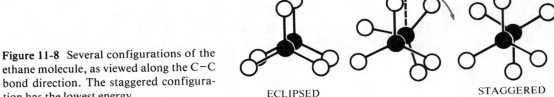

Figure 11-8 Several configurations of the ethane molecule, as viewed along the C−C bond direction. The staggered configuration has the lowest energy.

ECLIPSED   STAGGERED

The molecule of ethane, C_2H_6, can be considered to be two methyl groups joined together by a carbon-carbon single bond. Each carbon atom is surrounded by a tetrahedron of other atoms, but this does not specify the relative orientations of the two methyl groups. Figure 11-8 shows several relative orientations, looking along the carbon-carbon bond.

When the two sets of hydrogen atoms appear to be lined up, as in the left hand diagram, the configuration of the molecule is described as *eclipsed*; the front set of atoms lies in front of the rear set. When one set of hydrogen atoms is twisted through an angle of 60° relative to the other set, the configuration of the molecule is described as *staggered*. Other intermediate angles of twist are also possible.

The difference in energy between the eclipsed and staggered configurations is about 20 kJ mol⁻¹, and is therefore small compared with bond energies. The staggered configuration has the lower energy. The molecule is in a state of internal rotational motion, in which the configuration is staggered for most of the time, but one end of the molecule twists through an angle of 120° relative to the other end in a series of jumps. The rate of jumping is very rapid, and it is impossible to fix one end of the molecule with respect to the other.

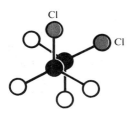 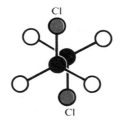

Figure 11-9 Two configurations of the molecule of 1, 2-dichloroethane. Internal rotation about the C−C bond converts each of these into the other many times per second, and it is not possible to separate two compounds corresponding to these two configurations.

The occurence of internal rotation has an important chemical consequence. If one hydrogen atom bonded to each carbon atom is substituted by a chlorine atom to form 1, 2-dichloroethane, it might be thought that two isomers could be formed, as in 1, 2-dichloroethylene. The two possible configurations of the staggered forms can be pictured as in Figure 11-9.

In the first of these the chlorine atoms are twisted through 180°, and in the second, they are twisted through 60°, relative to each other. It is, however, not possible to isolate two different compounds corresponding to these two configurations, because each configuration is rapidly converted to the other by internal rotation. Hence there is a very important distinction between double bonds and single bonds: internal rotation about single bonds is generally allowed, but no internal rotation about double bonds is possible.

In hydrocarbons containing five or more carbon atoms in a chain, the molecule does not have a well defined shape at all, because of internal rotation about each carbon-carbon single bond. In polymers, each molecule may contain hundreds or thousands of carbon atoms, and because of internal rotation, the molecules can take a nearly random shape; the intertwining of these flexible molecules gives polymers some special properties not available in other materials. Despite the randomness due to internal rotation, the bond lengths and bond angles around each carbon atom are typical of hydrocarbon molecules.

11-6 OPTICAL ISOMERISM

The tetrahedral arrangement of four single bonds about a carbon atom has a remarkable consequence. If four different atoms (or groups of atoms) are bonded to a carbon atom, it is found that there are two different ways of arranging the four atoms. The student should build himself or herself a simple model to show this result. An example to consider is CHFClBr, in which three of the hydrogen atoms in methane are replaced by three different halogen atoms. The two molecules may be represented by these two molecular formulae:

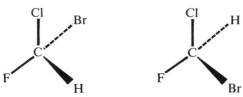

In both cases the carbon, fluorine and chlorine atoms are shown lying in the plane of the paper. In the molecule on the left the hydrogen atom is in front of the paper and the bromine atom is behind the paper. In the molecule on the right, the positions of the bromine and hydrogen atoms are reversed. Careful examination of these formulae, or of models based on the drawings, will show that these two molecules are different from each other, and that each is the *mirror image* of the other. Furthermore, there are no other ways of arranging the four atoms around the carbon atom. These two molecules are called *optical isomers* or *enantiomers*.

An object which is different from its mirror image is called *chiral,* a word based on the Greek word for a hand because the commonest example of a chiral object and its mirror image is a pair of hands. A chiral object and its mirror image can be classified as "left-handed" and "right-handed" respectively. This is done for screw threads on bolts, probably the commonest chiral object in ordinary use, and for the propellers on ships and aircraft. An object which is identical to its mirror image is called *achiral.*

A chiral molecule and its mirror image have very similar properties. The two isomers have the same solubility in common solvents, the same melting points, and the same boiling points. They undergo identical chemical reactions in many cases. As a result, it is generally difficult to separate the two isomers when they are mixed together.

When a simple chemical reaction results in a substance having molecules which are chiral, the two isomers are generally formed in equal amounts, and the result of the reaction is a mixture of the two isomers. As an example, propanoic acid reacts with bromine, the result being the replacement of a hydrogen atom on the central carbon atom by a bromine atom:

$$CH_3-\underset{\underset{\displaystyle H}{|}}{\overset{\overset{\displaystyle H}{|}}{C}}-C\overset{\displaystyle O}{\underset{\displaystyle OH}{\diagdown}} \quad + \ Br_2 \ \rightarrow \ CH_3-\underset{\underset{\displaystyle H}{|}}{\overset{\overset{\displaystyle Br}{|}}{C}}-C\overset{\displaystyle O}{\underset{\displaystyle OH}{\diagdown}} \quad + HBr$$

propanoic acid 2-bromopropanoic acid

The central carbon atom in 2-bromopropanoic acid has four different atoms or groups bonded to it, and so the molecule is chiral and has two optical isomers. The molecule of propanoic acid is achiral; the two hydrogen atoms bonded to the central carbon atom are equivalent, and there is equal probability that either one will be replaced by a bromine atom. Replacement of one of those hydrogen atoms by a bromine atom leads to formation of one of the optical isomers of 2-bromopropanoic acid, and replacement of the other hydrogen atom leads to formation of the other isomer. The mixture of equal amounts of the two isomers is called a *racemic* mixture.

Chiral molecules are produced by some chemical reactions in biological systems. The simplest example of this is lactic acid, with the following structural formula.

$$CH_3 - \underset{\underset{\displaystyle OH}{|}}{\overset{\overset{\displaystyle H}{|}}{C}} - C\underset{\displaystyle OH}{\overset{\displaystyle \nearrow O}{}}$$

lactic acid

This molecule is chiral since the central atom has four different atoms or groups bonded to it. This acid is formed in milk which has turned sour because of fermentation, and it is found that lactic acid formed in this way contains only one of the two possible molecules; it is a pure isomer. Lactic acid is also produced in muscles as they work, and causes soreness if allowed to accumulate; the lactic acid produced in muscles is also found to be a pure isomer, and it is the *opposite* isomer from that produced in sour milk. It is generally true that if a chiral molecule is produced by chemical reaction in a living organism, only one of the optical isomers is produced; a different organism may produce the other isomer of the same molecule.

Even though the physical properties of two optical isomers are almost identical, there is one physical property which can be used to distinguish between them: two optical isomers differ in their interaction with *polarized light.* Light is an electromagnetic wave, in which there are electric and magnetic fields. The electric field, the magnetic field and the direction of motion of the wave are at right angles to each other, and the direction of the electric field is called the direction of *polarization.* When such a wave passes through air, empty space or some such achiral medium, the direction of polarization is constant, but if the wave is passed through a chiral medium such as a solution of one optical isomer of a chiral substance, the plane of polarization becomes rotated as the wave passes through the solution. The rotation of the plane of polarized light is shown in Figure 11-10.

The name "optical isomer" resulted historically from this effect, called *optical activity.* The angle through which the polarization direction is rotated is proportional to the concentration of the solution and the length of path of the light through the solution. If the solution is replaced by a solution of the other optical isomer, of the same concentration, it is found that the angle of rotation is equal, but the rotation takes place in the opposite direction. If a solution of a racemic mixture of the two isomers is used, the observed rotation is the resultant of two equal and opposite effects, namely zero.

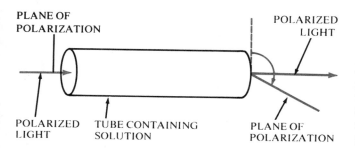

PLANE OF
POLARIZATION

POLARIZED
LIGHT

POLARIZED
LIGHT

TUBE CONTAINING
SOLUTION

PLANE OF
POLARIZATION

Figure 11-10 Rotation of the plane of polarization of polarized light passing through a solution of optically active molecules. An instrument designed to measure the angle of rotation is called a polarimeter.

Ordinary light contains electromagnetic waves of all possible polarizations, and cannot be used to measure optical rotations due to chiral molecules in solutions. However a special prism called a Nicol prism, or a piece of Polaroid film, may be used to select light of known polarization from ordinary light, and the angle of rotation can be measured using a second Nicol prism or Polaroid film.

FURTHER READING

Molecular structure is a popular subject for discussion, and many books will provide useful background. Following is a small selection of books dealing with the factual aspects of structure.

P.J. Wheatley, *The Determination of Molecular Structure.* (Oxford, 1968). A book about experimental methods.

R.J. Gillespie, *Molecular Geometry.* (Van Nostrand Reinhold, 1972). An extensive discussion covering material in this chapter and the next.

L Pauling and R. Hayward. *The Architecture of Molecules.* (Freeman, 1964). A book of drawings of models of molecules and crystals.

PROBLEMS

1. Draw formulae for the structural isomers of :
   (a) pentane C_5H_{12}
   (b) hexane C_6H_{14}
   (c) trichlorobenzene $C_6H_3Cl_3$

2. Classify the following pairs of molecules as being either structural isomers, or identical molecules:

   (a) $CH_3 - O - CH_2 - CH_3$ $\qquad$ $CH_3 - CH_2 - O - CH_3$

   (b) $CH_3 - O - CH_2 - CH_3$ $\qquad$ $H - O - CH_2 - CH_2 - CH_3$

   (c) $CH_3 - O - CH_2 - CH_2$ $\qquad$ $CH_3 - O - CH - CH_3$
   $\qquad\qquad\qquad\qquad |$ $\qquad\qquad\qquad\qquad\qquad |$
   $\qquad\qquad\qquad\qquad CH_3$ $\qquad\qquad\qquad\qquad\qquad CH_3$

   (d)
   $$\begin{array}{cc} H & H \\ | & | \\ H - C - C - Br \\ | & | \\ H & H \end{array} \qquad \begin{array}{cc} H & Br \\ | & | \\ H - C - C - H \\ | & | \\ H & H \end{array}$$

   (e)
   $$\begin{array}{cc} H & CH_3 \\ \diagdown & \diagup \\ C = C \\ \diagup & \diagdown \\ H & H \end{array} \qquad \begin{array}{cc} H & H \\ \diagdown & \diagup \\ C = C \\ \diagup & \diagdown \\ H & CH_3 \end{array}$$

$$
\begin{array}{cc}
\text{H H} & \text{H H}\\
\text{| |} & \text{| |}\\
\text{(f) H } - \text{ C } - \text{ C } - \text{ Br} \qquad & \text{Br } - \text{ C } - \text{ C } - \text{ H}\\
\text{| |} & \text{| |}\\
\text{H H} & \text{H H}
\end{array}
$$

3. Use the periodic table and known molecular structures to predict the shapes of the following molecules and molecular ions.

BiH_3, PuF_6, $SeCl_2$, BrO_4^-, PCl_3, NH_4^+, CH_3^+

4. Show that the H-C-H bond angle in methane is 109°28′. Hint: use the diagram in Figure 11-2.

5. What is the distance between the hydrogen atoms in methane? (See Table 11-1).   [0.178 nm]

6. Use bond lengths to estimate the distance between the hydrogen atoms in each of the following locations in the ethylene molecule:
(a) 1,1   (b) *cis*-1,2   (c) *trans*-1,2

[0.187; 0.242; 0.306 nm]

7. Use bond energies to calculate ΔH_{fm} of $H_2O(g)$, and compare your result with the thermodynamic value.

[−243 kJ mol⁻¹]

8. Use bond energies to calculate ΔH for the conversion of ethane to ethylene.
$$C_2H_6 \rightarrow C_2H_4 + H_2 \qquad [+140 \text{ kJ}]$$
Repeat your calculation using ΔH_{fm} data from Appendix I, and compare the results.   [+136.2 kJ]

9. Phosphorus vapour contains P_4 molecules in which the phosphorus atoms are at the corners of a tetrahedron. Calculate the P-P bond energy by considering reaction
$$P_4(g) + 6H_2(g) \rightarrow 4PH_3(g)$$
[194 kJ mol⁻¹]

10. Calculate the molar heat of formation of trichloroethylene in the gas phase using bond energies and any other necessary thermochemical data.
[+24 kJ mol⁻¹]

11. The energy difference between adjacent vibrational energy levels in the N_2 molecule corresponds to light of wavelength 4.24 μm. Calculate the energy difference in kJ mol⁻¹ and compare this value with (a) the bond energy of the molecule, and (b) the average kinetic energy of motion of the molecule at room temperature.

[28.2 kJ mol⁻¹]

12. Which of the following molecules might show optical activity?

$$CH_2Cl_2, \quad CH_3CHBrCl, \quad CH_3 - \underset{\underset{OH}{|}}{\overset{\overset{H}{|}}{C}} - C \equiv N, \quad \underset{\underset{H}{/}}{\overset{\overset{H}{\backslash}}{C}} = \underset{\underset{Cl'}{\backslash}}{\overset{\overset{H}{/}}{C}}$$

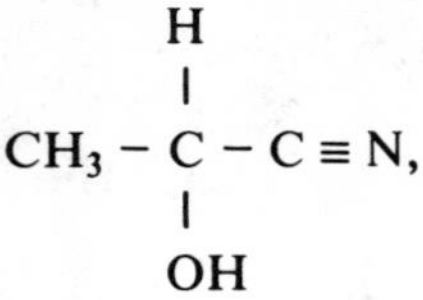

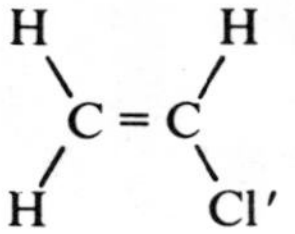

$$CH_3CHBrCH_2CH_3, \quad \underset{\underset{Br}{|}}{\overset{\overset{H}{|}}{N}} - Cl$$

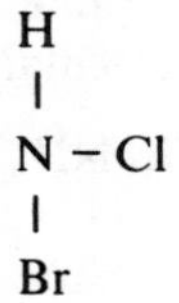

13. Use the data in Appendix I to calculate the S-F bond energy in SF_6.

[327 kJ mol^{-1}]

14. Use the data in Appendix I and a value for O-H bond energy from Table 11-2 to determine the O-O bond energy in hydrogen peroxide, H_2O_2.

[142 kJ mol^{-1}]

XII CHEMICAL BONDING IN MOLECULES

In the last chapter, the structure of molecules was discussed. Experimentally determined quantities such as bond lengths and angles, and bond energies, formed the basis of the discussion, and no attempt was made to explain the data presented in terms of any theory. Such collections of experimental results are very important in science, for they allow trends to be seen, and suggest new measurements which ought to be made to extend the scope of existing knowledge. But it is also important that models and theories be considered in the light of the observed facts, for in this way the theories are tested against what is known from experimental work. Theories which are not consistent with experimental results must be modified or rejected.

Theories of chemical bonding are not easy to deal with at an introductory level. All the elementary theories are incomplete, either because they deal with only part of the available data, or because they are inconsistent with some of the known facts. On the other hand the more sophisticated theories are mathematically complicated even when applied to single atoms or simple molecules. In addition, accounting for the properties of atoms or molecules requires a great deal of numerical computing if accurate results are required, and in most calculations approximations are made which must be considered very carefully. Finally, simple concepts of the chemical bond are usually lost in the pursuit of numerical accuracy, and it is difficult to interpret the results of calculations in terms of the language and concepts of the more elementary theories.

Despite these difficulties, a start must be made. Theories of chemical bonding play a vital role in chemistry at all levels, and the more complex theories are likely to be used more commonly in the future as computing methods improve.

12-1 THE LEWIS THEORY OF COVALENT BONDING

The theory of chemical bonding based upon the electronic configurations of atoms was proposed by the American chemist G. N. Lewis in 1916, and a similar theory of *ionic bonding* was discussed by the German chemist W. Kossel at about the same time. The theory is valuable because it gives an account of the way in which *covalent bonds* are formed, and gives a natural explanation of the way in which the valencies of the elements vary across the periodic table. A development of the theory extends the concept of an acid-base reaction to cover cases where hydrogen ions are not involved.

The outer shell of electrons in an atom is called the *valence shell*. In s-block and p-block elements the valence shell has the highest value of the principal quantum number of all the occupied levels. In d-block and f-block metals, it is the d and f electrons which influence the chemistry of the element, and these are generally discussed separately from the other elements. In the Lewis theory, the valence shell electrons are represented by dots drawn around the symbol for the element, one dot for each electron. No distinction is made between s and p electrons. The dots are generally drawn in pairs, and the two dots within a pair may be considered to have opposite spin. Thus the symbols for the first two rows of elements with their valence electrons are drawn as follows.

$$H\cdot \qquad He\!:$$

$$Li\cdot \quad Be\!: \quad \cdot B\!: \quad \cdot\overset{\displaystyle\cdot}{C}\!: \quad \cdot\overset{\displaystyle\cdot}{N}\!: \quad \cdot\overset{\displaystyle\cdot}{\underset{\displaystyle\cdot}{O}}\!: \quad :\overset{\displaystyle\cdot}{\underset{\displaystyle\cdot}{F}}\!: \quad :\overset{\displaystyle\cdot\cdot}{\underset{\displaystyle\cdot\cdot}{Ne}}\!:$$

The essential feature of any covalent bond is the sharing of valence electrons between the atoms which are bonded together. This idea was the basis for Lewis' theory of bonding, and remains part of all modern theories. Hydrogen forms the simplest molecule, containing two electrons, and the Lewis structure is written as follows:

$$H\!:\!H$$

This indicates that the two electrons are shared between the two atoms. A bond involving just one pair of electrons is defined as a single bond. The valence shell of a hydrogen atom can hold a maximum of two electrons, according to the exclusion principle, and in sharing the pair of bonding electrons each atom appears to have "filled" its valence shell. This feature of covalent bonding governs the maximum valence that an atom shows in forming molecules, and suggests that hydrogen cannot have a valence greater than one in covalent compounds.

The halogens, in Group VII, commonly have a valence of one, which can be readily explained by the sharing of a single pair of electrons in the Lewis structures of the diatomic molecules of the elements:

$$:\overset{\displaystyle\cdot\cdot}{\underset{\displaystyle\cdot\cdot}{F}}\!:\!\overset{\displaystyle\cdot\cdot}{\underset{\displaystyle\cdot\cdot}{F}}\!: \qquad\qquad :\overset{\displaystyle\cdot\cdot}{\underset{\displaystyle\cdot\cdot}{Br}}\!:\!\overset{\displaystyle\cdot\cdot}{\underset{\displaystyle\cdot\cdot}{Br}}\!:$$

and of the hydrogen halides:

$$H\!:\!\overset{\displaystyle\cdot\cdot}{\underset{\displaystyle\cdot\cdot}{F}}\!: \qquad\qquad H\!:\!\overset{\displaystyle\cdot\cdot}{\underset{\displaystyle\cdot\cdot}{Br}}\!:$$

In all of these molecules the halogen atom completes the "octet" of s and p electrons by sharing the pair of bonding electrons, and the hydrogen atom fills its valence shell similarly. In each case the bond between the atoms is a single bond.

Group VI elements show a valence of two, as shown in the hydrides, H_2O and its analogues:

The two electrons obtained through sharing bonding electrons with the hydrogen atoms are sufficient to complete the octet of s and p electrons in the valence shell of the central atom in each case. Oxygen as an element forms the diatomic molecule O_2, and in this molecule four electrons must be shared for the octet to be completed:

$$\overset{\text{\Large ..}}{\underset{\text{\Large ..}}{O}} \overset{\text{\Large ..}}{::} \overset{\text{\Large ..}}{\underset{\text{\Large ..}}{O}}$$

This structure corresponds to the double-bonded formula O=O. Evidence for the presence of a double bond in this molecule is to be found in the value of the bond length in the O_2 molecule, 0.121 nm, which is significantly shorter than 0.148 nm, the average oxygen-oxygen single bond length (Table 11-2).

Group V elements commonly show a valence of three. Examples are the hydrides ammonia NH_3 and phosphine PH_3:

$$\begin{array}{c} \text{\Large ..} \\ H\text{\Large :}N\text{\Large :}H \\ \text{\Large ..} \\ H \end{array} \qquad \begin{array}{c} \text{\Large ..} \\ H\text{\Large :}P\text{\Large :}H \\ \text{\Large ..} \\ H \end{array}$$

In the molecule of the element nitrogen, N_2, there is a triple bond in which six valence electrons are shared by the two atoms, and again each atom has eight electrons associated with it:

$$\text{\Large :}N\text{\Large :::}N\text{\Large :}$$

Again, the bond length in N_2 is considerably shorter than the N-N single bond length (Table 11-2).

The Group IV elements carbon and silicon show a valence of four in most situations, as in the molecules of methane and silane:

$$\begin{array}{c} H \\ \text{\Large ..} \\ H\text{\Large :}C\text{\Large :}H \\ \text{\Large ..} \\ H \end{array} \qquad \begin{array}{c} H \\ \text{\Large ..} \\ H\text{\Large :}Si\text{\Large :}H \\ \text{\Large ..} \\ H \end{array}$$

The boron atom has three valence electrons, and generally shows a valence of three. This means that there are six electrons rather than eight associated with the boron atom. Molecules in which this occurs are sometimes called *electron-deficient* molecules, and they serve as a warning that there is nothing to *require* an octet of electrons around each atom in a molecule. The molecule of boron trifluoride is an example of such a molecule.

Some Group II metals form halides and other compounds which are molecular in nature rather than ionic, and the valence of the metal atom in the molecules is two. These are also electron-deficient molecules. Examples are the halides of beryllium, zinc, cadmium and mercury, and organo-metallic compounds such as dimethyl mercury.

Double and triple bonds were introduced in Section 1-2 as a method of maintaining the valence of an element constant, and evidence for the reality of multiple bonds is to be found in the bond lengths and bond energies of these bonds in Table 11-2, as compared with the values for single bonds. In terms of Lewis structures, constancy of valency means that the number of electrons around an atom is constant, and usually equal to eight in light non-metallic elements. Lewis structures for some molecules containing multiple bonds are given below.

In the Lewis structures of many molecules, two kinds of electrons can be distinguished. Those which are shared between atoms are called *bonding electrons* or *bonding pairs,* and those which are not are called *lone pairs.* Lone pair electrons on atoms which are on the "outside" of a molecule are sometimes omitted when they are not directly concerned in the bonding within the molecule. For example the essence of the bonding in carbon tetrachloride is adequately expressed by the following structure in which the lone pairs on the chlorine atoms are omitted.

$$
\begin{array}{c}
\text{Cl} \\
\text{Cl} \;\overset{..}{:}\text{C}\overset{..}{:}\; \text{Cl} \\
\text{Cl}
\end{array}
$$

Omission of lone pairs in such a case is often desirable because it makes the structure clearer and easier to understand. However, lone pairs on atoms in the centre of a molecule should never be omitted because they usually have a strong influence on the geometrical shape of the molecule, and on its chemical properties. Examples are the lone pair on the nitrogen atom in the ammonia molecule, and the two lone pairs on the oxygen atom in the water molecule.

For elements of the second row of the periodic table, Li to Ne, eight electrons fill the valence shell, and so the octet rule gives an upper limit to the valence that an atom can show. Carbon, nitrogen, oxygen and fluorine generally have valencies of four, three, two and one respectively. However, this limitation does not apply to the non-metals of the third row, and higher valencies are found. For instance phosphorus trifluoride, PF_3, reacts with fluorine to form phosphorus pentafluoride, PF_5, which has the following Lewis structure.

All five valence electrons of the phosphorus atom are shared with the fluorine atoms. The valence of the phosphorus is five in this molecule, and there are ten electrons around the central atom. This is sometimes called an *expanded valence shell,* and is found in atoms of the second and lower rows of the periodic table. In the second row, the principal quantum number of the valence shell is 3. The 3d and 4s levels are empty, but their energies are not much greater than the 3p level which is occupied. Thus it is possible to increase the valence of these atoms by using empty levels to accommodate more electrons than the quota of eight dictated by the exclusion principle on the basis of the 3s and 3p levels alone. Comparing the Lewis structure of PF_5 with that of PF_3,

All five valence electrons of the phosphorus atom are shared with the fluorine atoms.

it can be seen that the lone pair on the phosphorus atom has been split up and used to form two new covalent bonds, by sharing these electrons with each of two additional fluorine atoms. Thus when valence shell expansion occurs, the valence of an atom increases by two. In support of this, Group VI elements show valencies of 4 and 6 in addition to the usual 2, and Group VII elements show valencies of 3, 5, and 7 in addition to the usual 1. Some examples in which the Lewis structures show the central atom surrounded by 10, 12, or 14 electrons are shown below.

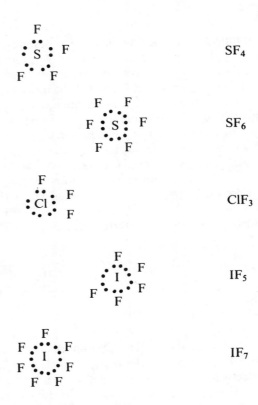

For many years it was thought that the noble gases neon, argon, krypton, xenon and radon could not form chemical compounds because the atoms already had a filled octet of electrons. This has been shown not to be so, and a number of compounds of xenon have been prepared. Some of the earliest work in this field was done in 1961 by N. Bartlett working at the University of British Columbia. Since the octet rule is not obeyed in certain compounds of the heavier elements of Groups VI and VII, it is not surprising that a heavy element of Group VIII also breaks the rule. Examples of compounds that have been prepared are the fluorides of xenon.

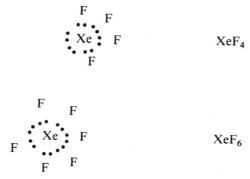

Lewis structures can be written for polyatomic ions, by adding or subtracting electrons to match the charge on the ion. The hydroxide ion, OH^-, has a total of eight valence electrons, six from the oxygen atom, one from the hydrogen atom, and one to produce the negative charge on the ion:

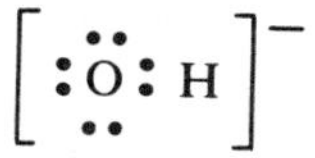

$$\left[\, :\overset{\,\cdot\cdot}{\underset{\cdot\cdot}{O}}\!:H \, \right]^-$$

The ionic charge is indicated by placing the structure inside square brackets, with the charge shown as a superscript outside the brackets. The hydrogen ion H_3O^+ has the following structure,

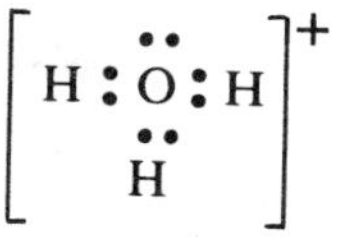

$$\left[\, H:\overset{\,\cdot\cdot}{\underset{\underset{\displaystyle H}{\cdot\cdot}}{O}}\!:H \, \right]^+$$

and can be thought of as a hydrogen nucleus, or proton, H^+, bonded to the water molecule by sharing one of the two available lone pairs on the latter. However, it should be recalled from Section 1-5 that the structure of the hydrogen ion $H^+(aq)$ is more complex in structure than the formula H_3O^+ suggests.

12-2 RESONANCE

Lines drawn between atoms are a surprisingly good way of representing the properties of chemical bonds and the valencies of atoms, but there are cases where bonds cannot be shown in this simple way. Benzene is such a case, and was discussed in Section 11-3. It is necessary to draw two separate structures for the benzene ring if conventional double and single bonds are to be used, and suppose that both structures contribute in some mysterious way to the "real" structure of the molecule. The same approach must be taken in drawing Lewis structures for the benzene molecule, and both the following Lewis structures must be considered:

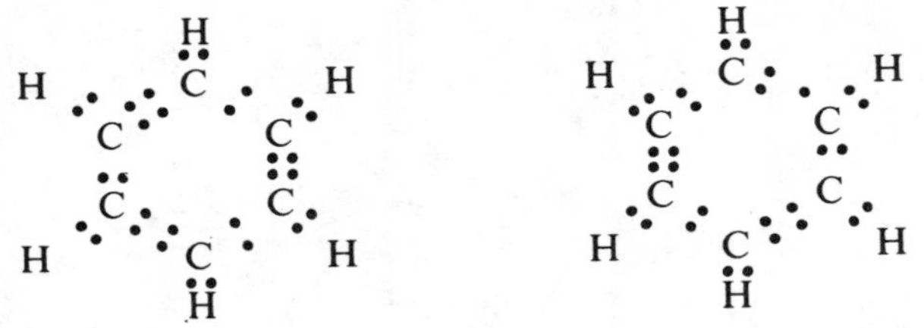

These structures should be compared with the structures using chemical bonds given in Section 11-3. It is not possible to draw a single conventional Lewis structure to describe the properties of benzene. This apparent deficiency in the theory is corrected by introducing the concept of *resonance*. When it is possible to write more than one reasonable Lewis structure for a molecule, the actual structure is to be regarded as a combination of all the possible Lewis structures. The combination is sometimes called a *resonance hybrid*, and the individual Lewis structures are called *resonance forms*. The resonance forms are often shown using conventional bonds rather than using dots for the electrons, and a double-headed arrow is used to indicate that several resonance forms are contributing to a resonance hybrid:

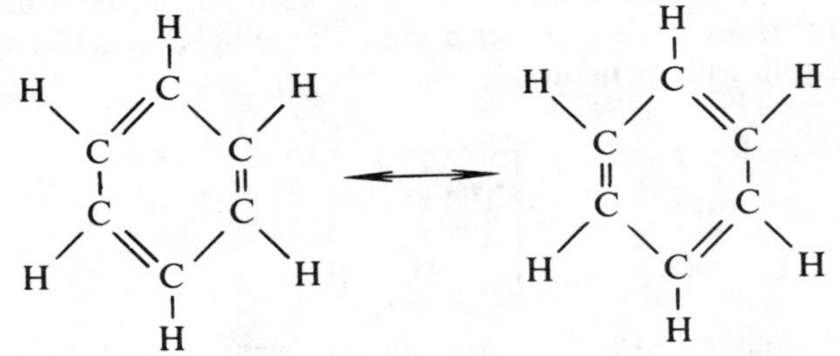

The double-headed arrow must be interpreted very carefully, for it is easy to misunderstand its meaning. The arrow does not indicate a chemical equilibrium between two different molecules. It does not mean that the molecule spends part of the time in one form and part of the time in the other form. It does not indicate that the nuclei move in any way, as happens in the cases of internal rotation and inversion which were discussed in the last chapter. In the ammonia and ethane molecules, the nuclei change their relative positions due to inversion and internal rotation respectively, but the benzene ring is a regular hexagon with all the carbon-carbon distance equal at all times. Resonance refers only to the electrons, and is a concept introduced into the theory of Lewis structures so that the theory can be applied to molecules which would otherwise be outside its range of validity.

The proper procedure for combining resonance forms can only be described properly using the mathematical theory of linear vector spaces, and the wave theory of quantum mechanics. However, a pictorial analogy can be found in the animal world.* A rhinoceros could be described as a resonance hybrid between a dragon and a unicorn. Both dragons and unicorns are imaginary, just as the molecules C_6H_6 with alternating double and single bonds around the ring are imaginary and have never been found. The rhinoceros, however, has some of the properties of a dragon, and some of the properties of a unicorn. The rhinoceros is the real animal, but the imaginary animals may be used to help us to think about the real animal. The imaginary molecules have simple structures which can be adequately represented by the simple procedures of Lewis structures, and the real molecule with all its complexities can be thought of as having some of the properties of both the simple, imaginary structures. If a rhinoceros is photographed many times, the pictures always show a rhinoceros, never a dragon or a unicorn. When the properties of the benzene molecule are measured the results are always those appropriate to a benzene molecule, and the molecules with alternating double and single bonds are never observed.

When resonance occurs, it is generally found that the energy of the molecule is lower than would be expected on the basis of a single resonance form or Lewis structure, and known average bond energies. The extent of the lowering can be calculated using the enthalpy of formation of the compound, and the table of bond energies, and is known as the *resonance energy.*

Example 12-1   Calculate the resonance energy of benzene.

The heat of formation of a single resonance form of benzene will be calculated using the following two step process:

$$6C(c) + 3H_2(g) \xrightarrow{\Delta H_a} 6C(g) + 6H(g) \xrightarrow{\Delta H_b}$$

The enthalpy of the first step, ΔH_a, is obtained from the enthalpies of formation of the atoms of carbon and hydrogen in the gas phase:

$$\Delta H_a = 6 \times 716.7 + 6 \times 218$$
$$= 5608 \text{ kJ}$$

---

*The reference for this analogy is to be found in the reading list at the end of the chapter.

In the second step, three C-C bonds, three C=C bonds and six C-H bonds are formed, and so ΔH_b can be estimated using bond energies:

$$\Delta H_b = -3 \times 347 - 3 \times 599 - 6 \times 414$$

$$= -5322 \text{ kJ}$$

Hence the estimated value for ΔH_f° for a single resonance form of benzene is the sum of these contributions:

$$\Delta H_f^{\circ}(C_6H_6(g)) = +5608 - 5322$$

$$= +286 \text{ kJ mol}^{-1}$$

The value of ΔH_f° for benzene taken from Appendix I is $+83$ kJ mol^{-1}, which is about 200 kJ mol^{-1} lower than the value calculated above. Hence the resonance energy for benzene is about 200 kJ mol^{-1}.

Since resonance apparently makes a molecule more stable, as reflected in a lower enthalpy of formation, resonance must be considered whenever more than one Lewis structure can reasonably be drawn for a molecule. In a number of simple molecules, a single Lewis structure would suggest an unsymmetrical structure for the molecule, but when other resonance forms are considered the molecule can be predicted to be symmetrical, in agreement with experimental observations. An example is the nitrate ion NO_3^-. The following Lewis structure satisfies the octet rule for all atoms but suggests that one of the nitrogen-oxygen bonds is shorter than the other two bonds:

However two other equally good structures can be written in which the double bond is placed in the other two positions. These three structures are resonance forms which contribute equally to the "real" structure of the NO_3^- ion, and so the three bonds should be of equal length, just as all the carbon-carbon bonds in benzene are of equal length:

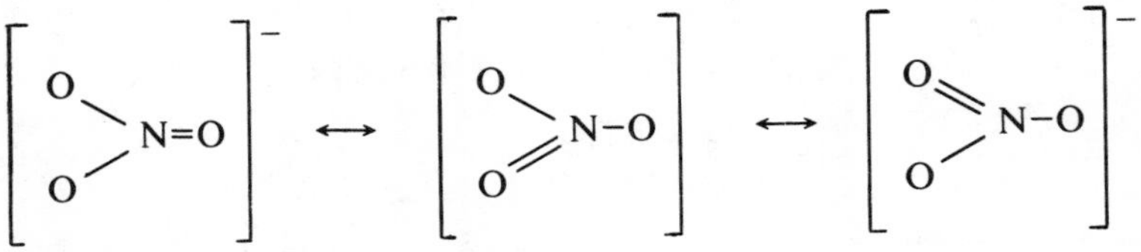

The NO_3^- ion is in fact symmetrical and the three bonds are equal in length.

Another example is the SO_2 molecule. The following structures satisfy the octet rule for all the atoms.

and can therefore be regarded as resonance forms of the SO_2 molecule. Hence the two sulphur oxygen bonds should be of equal length, in agreement with observation.

Three resonance forms for the SO_3 molecule can be written, and the Lewis structure for one of them is:

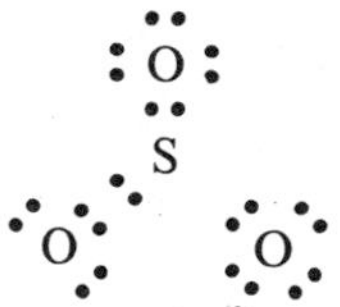

The resonance between the three forms which are equivalent except for permutation of the bonds produces three bonds of equal length:

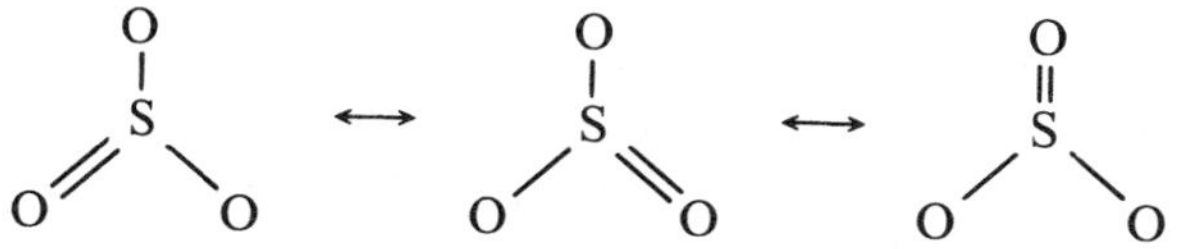

A complication in considering the structure of SO_3 is that sulphur lies in the third row of the periodic table, and so the possibility of having more than eight electrons around the sulphur atom must be considered. Therefore, the following Lewis structure

and the two other equivalent resonance forms must be considered as potentially contributing to the structure of SO_3. These three resonance forms would not contribute equally with the first three structures, of course, since they are not equivalent structurally. Finally, the single symmetric structure

is also a possible contributing resonance form.

These examples suggest that it is rare to find simple molecules which are unsymmetrical. If a Lewis structure indicates that two bonds are not the same, it is possible that another structure can be drawn which interchanges the positions of the two bonds, and then resonance between the two structures will make the two bonds equal in length and in other properties.

12-3   MOLECULAR GEOMETRY

The shape of a molecule is determined by energy considerations. The atoms take up relative positions such that the energy of the molecule is as low as possible. The electrons are the major factor determining the energy and hence the shape of a given molecule, for it is the electrons which provide the "glue" that holds the atoms together in the form of a molecule. The observed shapes of simple molecules can be understood on the basis of the Lewis structure theory of chemical bonding with the addition of a set of assumptions or rules. The theory was originally proposed by N. V. Sidgwick and H. E. Powell, and has been extended by R. J. Gillespie of McMaster University in Canada. The theory is now commonly called the *valence shell electron pair repulsion* theory, often shortened to VSEPR. The theory is extraordinarily successful in accounting for the observed shapes of molecules, considering the simplicity of the approach.

Three of the assumptions or rules upon which the VSEPR theory is based are as follows, and a fourth rule will be given shortly.

(i)   The electron pair associated with a chemical bond is localized in the neighbourhood of the bond.

(ii)   Each lone pair of electrons is localized.

(iii)   The electron pairs around each atom in a molecule are arranged in space so that the distances between pairs are maximized. In this context, a group of electrons consisting of two or three pairs of electrons associated with a double or triple bond behaves like a single pair.

The theory considers only the *valence shell* electrons in the molecule. The electrons are considered in pairs, and the pairs, or multiple pairs in the case of multiple bonds, are arranged in space as if there is a *repulsion* between them, according to the third of the rules. The name of the theory is clumsy, but it is very descriptive and once memorized makes the theory easy to apply. It is natural to expect that the bonds in a molecule keep out of each other's way, but the theory regards lone pairs as being at least as important as the bonding pairs in determining the arrangement of the chemical bonds in space. This feature of the theory is responsible for bringing the predictions of molecular shape into agreement with the observed shapes which were summarized in the last chapter.

The repulsion between the electrons partly is due to electrostatic forces between the electrons, but is primarily a result of the application of the Pauli exclusion principle. In Chapter 9 the exclusion principle was introduced as a restriction on the occupancy of energy levels. However, this is only one aspect of certain symmetry properties of wavefunctions which have other, more subtle, effects. One of these effects is to force the motion of two electrons with the same spin to be correlated in such a way that they occupy the same space. The electrons in an adjacent pair must also have their spins paired. The spin-up electron in one pair must therefore avoid the spin-up electron in the other pair, and the same is true for the other, spin-down, electrons. Electrons with opposite spin, such as the two electrons within a pair, have no such restriction placed upon them by the symmetry of the wavefunction, although of course any two electrons repel each other because they carry the same charge. As a result of the correlation required by the exclusion principle, different electron pairs occupy different regions of space. Exceptions to this rule are the sets of two or three electron pairs forming double or triple bonds. In these cases, electron correlation has its own effect within the region of the multiple bond, but this need not concern us here.

The student with a mind for mathematical rigour, or a desire to find underlying physical reasons for the phenomena of nature, may well feel that this kind of theory, and the quasi-explanation that has been offered in support of its rules, is unacceptable intellectually as a basis for understanding the properties of molecules, and of matter. It is quite right to seek better theories. But any theory should be judged not on its appearance of complexity, but on its ability to make predictions which are in agreement with experimental observations. In the search for better theories, it should not be forgotten that the VSEPR theory is very successful from this point of view, for it accurately describes molecular geometry for a very wide range of molecules, using very simple ideas. Indeed, it is an important intellectual challenge to understand why the VSEPR theory works so well!

The theory is of most use in understanding, rationalizing, and predicting the occurrence of the seven common shapes of simple molecules, which are shown in Figure 11-1. Attention is focussed mainly on the electronic structure around the central atom, particularly the number of electron pairs, for the geometrical arrangement of these pairs is determined by their number. The geometrical arrangements which result from maximizing the distances between pairs according to the third assumption of the theory are shown in Figure 12-1 as points on the surface of a sphere. Two pairs are placed at the opposite ends of a diameter, three pairs form an equilateral triangle, four pairs a tetrahedron, five pairs a trigonal bipyramid, and six pairs an octahedron. There is no easily recognizable arrangement for seven pairs.

To determine the geometry of a molecule, a Lewis structure for the molecule is first written down. The number of electron pairs around the central atom can then be counted, and the molecular geometry determined. The procedure is illustrated for representative cases in Tables 12-1 and 12-2. Table 12-1 shows cases in which there are no lone pairs on the central atom, and in these cases,

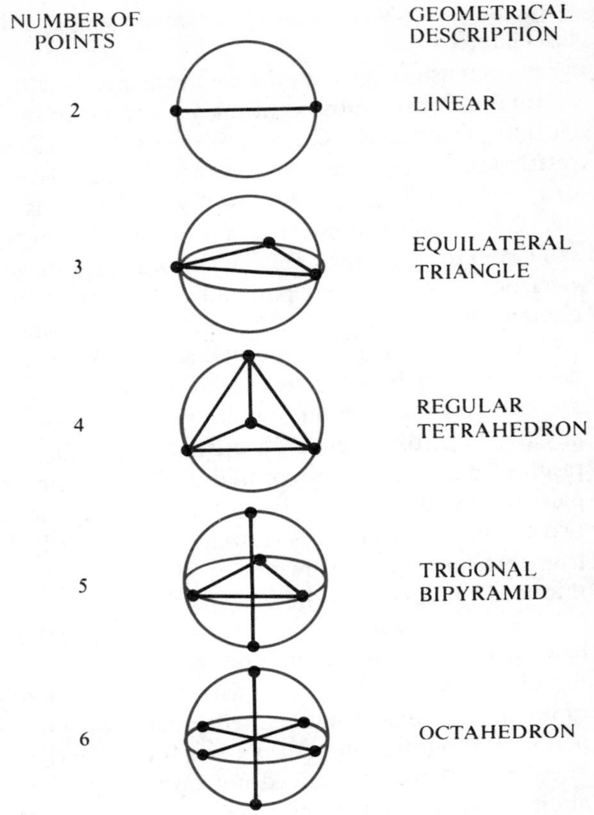

Figure 12-1 The positions of points placed on the surface of a sphere so that their distances apart are a maximum. The relative positions of these points determine the placing of groups of electrons around the central atom in a molecule.

the arrangement of the outer atoms is given directly by the diagrams in Figure 12-1. In Table 12-1 the central atom is indicated by the letter A, and the outer atoms by the letter X. The theory still applies, with only slight modification, if the outer atoms X are different elements. Several cases are given in which there are multiple bonds, and it can be seen that the associated electrons are treated as a single group for the purposes of determining the geometry, although some distortion of the bond angles is expected. For instance, the Cl-B-Cl bond angle in BCl_3 is exactly 120°, and the chlorine atoms form an equilateral triangle. In formaldehyde, CH_2O, the H-C-H angle is 125.8°, but despite this slight distortion, the formaldehyde molecule is planar and the molecular geometry is essentially trigonal, or triangular.

Table 12-2 shows some cases of molecules in which there are lone pairs on the central atom. In Table 12-2, the letters A and X are used to indicate the central and outer atoms respectively, and the letter E indicates a lone pair of electrons. The effect of a lone pair can be seen in the simplest case, NH_3. The nitrogen atom is surrounded by four pairs of electrons, of which one is a lone pair. The four pairs are arranged tetrahedrally, and so the three N-H bonds are non-planar, in agreement with observation. Since one of the four pairs of electrons is different from the other three groups, the tetrahedral arrangement is

TABLE 12-1 Shapes of Molecules Without Lone Pairs on the Central Atom

Bonding Pattern	Example	Lewis Structure	Shape
Two bonds AX_2	$HgCl_2$ CO_2	Cl:Hg:Cl O::C::O	Linear
Three bonds AX_3	BCl_3	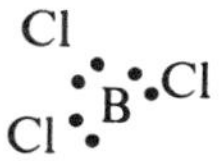 Cl Cl:B.Cl Cl	trigonal planar
	CH_2O	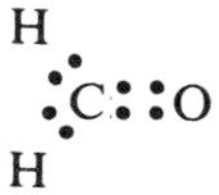 H :C::O H	
Four bonds AX_4	CH_4	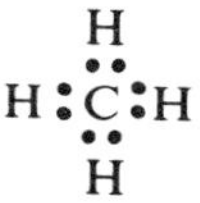 H H:C:H H	tetrahedral
	Cl Cl–P=O Cl	Cl Cl:P::O Cl	
Five bonds AX_5	PF_5	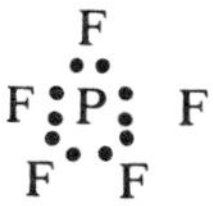 F F:P: F F F	trigonal bipyramidal
Six bonds AX_6	SF_6	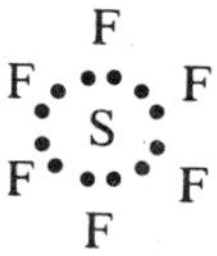 F F. S .F F. .F F	octahedral

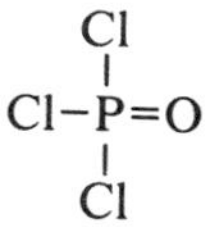

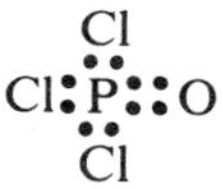

somewhat distorted from the regular tetrahedron. The H-N-H bond angle is 107.3° instead of the value 109.5° found in methane. The bent molecules H_2O and SCl_2 result from having two lone pairs among four groups of electrons. The bond angles in these molecules are somewhat further from the tetrahedral value, being 104.5° in H_2O and 98° in SCl_2.

The bond angles which are observed in many molecules suggest that a lone pair of electrons occupies more space around the central atom than does a bonding pair. Thus in ammonia, the hydrogen atoms are closer together than they would be in a regular tetrahedron, apparently as a result of the larger space required by the lone pair on the nitrogen atom. A possible reason for the larger size of lone pair electrons is that there is a positively charged nucleus in the vicinity of a bonding pair, which attracts the negatively charged electrons

TABLE 12-2   Shapes of Molecules with Lone Pairs on the Central Atom

Bonding Pattern	Example	Lewis Structure	Shape
Two bonds, Two lone pairs AX_2E_2	H_2O SCl_2		bent
Three bonds, One lone pair AX_3E	NH_3 PCl_3	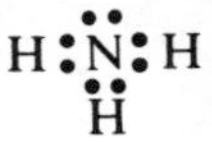	trigonal non-planar
Four bonds, One lone pair AX_4E	SF_4	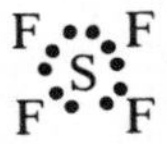	distorted pyramid
Three bonds, Two lone pairs AX_3E_2	ClF_3	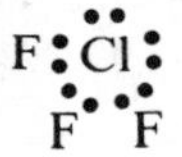	T-shaped
Five bonds, One lone pair AX_5E	BrF_5	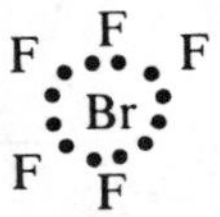	square pyramidal
Four bonds, Two lone pairs AX_4E_2	ICl_4^-	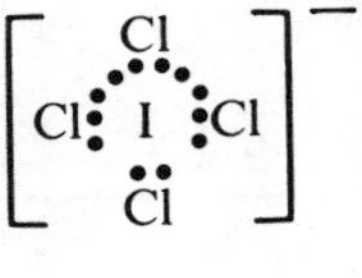	square

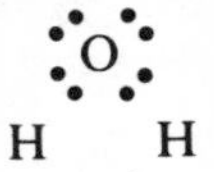

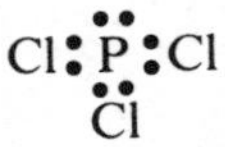

and confines them in space to some extent. These observations are summarized in a *fourth rule* of the VSEPR theory:

(iv) A lone pair of electrons takes up more space than a bonding pair.

This fourth rule is used to determine the geometry of molecules with five pairs of electrons around the central atom, and two examples are shown in Table 12-2. In the molecule of sulphur tetrafluoride, SF_4, there are four bonding pairs and one lone pair. The molecular geometry is based upon the trigonal bipyramid, in which there are two non-equivalent types of site, the equatorial and axial sites. There is therefore a choice of two sites for the lone pair, and

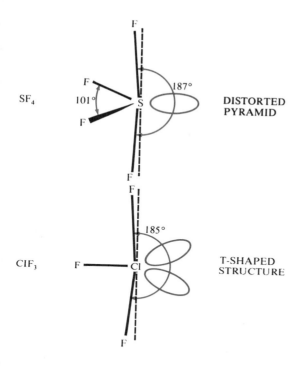

SF$_4$ 101°   187°   DISTORTED PYRAMID

ClF$_3$ F ⎯ Cl   185°   T-SHAPED STRUCTURE

Figure 12-2 The observed structures of two molecules in which there are lone pairs among the five pairs of electrons around the central atom. The axis of the trigonal bipyramid to which the structure is related is shown by a dotted line, and the positions of the lone pairs are shown according to the predictions of VSEPR theory, although they have not been observed experimentally.

the choice is made on the basis of the amount of space available at each site. The axial sites are adjacent to three equatorial sites at angles of 90°, while the equatorial sites are adjacent to only two axial sites at angles of 90° and the other equatorial sites are further away at angles of 120° and can be ignored. Hence the equatorial sites are less crowded by neighbours than the axial sites, and the lone pair is therefore assigned to the equatorial rather than the axial site. The resulting geometry is described as a distorted pyramid and is illustrated in Figure 12-2. The bond angles are distorted away from the ideal values of 180° and 120°, in a direction consistent with the lone pair taking as much room as it can.

When two out of five pairs of electrons around the central atom are lone pairs, both are placed in equatorial sites, and the resulting molecular geometry is planar and T-shaped. An example is the molecule ClF$_3$, which is also shown in Table 12-2 and Figure 12-2. Again the bond angles are distorted away from the ideal values.

Table 12-2 and Figure 12-3 show molecules in which the central atom is surrounded by six pairs of electrons, of which one or two are lone pairs. In the first case, the molecule of BrF$_5$ adopts the shape of a square pyramid. The four fluorine atoms forming the square base lie slightly above the bromine atom because of the extra space required by the lone pair. In the case of the anion ICl$_4^-$ there are two lone pairs to be accommodated, and they are placed on opposite sides of the molecule, resulting in a square planar shape.

Finally, it has been assumed in this discussion that the electronic structure can be adequately represented by a single Lewis structure. However, cases in

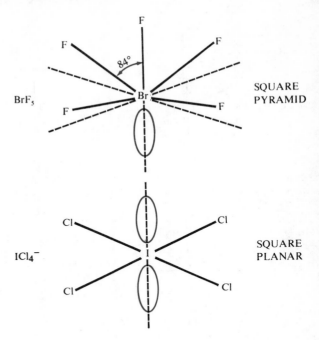

BrF₅

SQUARE PYRAMID

ICl₄⁻

SQUARE PLANAR

Figure 12-3 The observed structures of two molecules in which there are six pairs of electrons around the central atom, including lone pairs. The axes of the octahedra on which the molecular structure is based are shown by dotted lines, and the positions of the lone pairs on the basis of VSEPR are also shown.

which several resonance forms must be considered can also be included in the theory. Generally there is no difficulty in doing this because different resonance forms have the same number of groups of electrons around the central atom, and the effect of resonance is simply to make the molecule more symmetrical. For instance in sulphur dioxide, the two resonance structures

both lead to a VSEPR prediction that the molecule is bent. Each structure taken individually suggests that the two bond lengths are unequal in length, however, and only by considering the structures to make equal contributions can the theory match the observation that the bonds are equal in length. The observed bond angle is 119.5°.

12-4   ELECTRON PAIR DONORS AND ACCEPTORS

A covalent bond exists whenever a pair of electrons is shared between two atoms in a molecule, according to the Lewis theory of bonding. In the cases discussed so far, the electrons forming a covalent bond have been contributed by both the atoms joined by the bond. In methane, for instance, the carbon atom contributes one electron to each of four bonds, and each hydrogen atom contributes one electron to the bond joining it to the carbon atom. However, this need not be so, and there are interesting cases where the electron pair constituting a covalent bond comes entirely from one atom. Such an atom is called an *electron donor,* and the atom to which it is joined by such a bond is called an *electron acceptor.* Bonds of this type are sometimes called *dative* bonds, or *coordinate* bonds.

Consider the molecule boron trifluoride, BF_3. There are only six valence electrons around the boron atom, and so the boron atom in this molecule can accept a pair of electrons from an atom in another molecule or ion to form a dative covalent bond. A suitable atom is one containing at least one lone pair of electrons which can be donated. For example the fluoride ion, F^-, reacts with BF_3 in aqueous solution to form the tetrafluoroborate ion, BF_4^-:

$$BF_3 + F^- \rightarrow BF_4^-$$

The Lewis structure of the product is

$$\left[\begin{array}{c} F \\ \overset{\bullet\bullet}{F \!:\! B \!:\! F} \\ \underset{\bullet\bullet}{} \\ F \end{array} \right]^-$$

The BF_4^- ion is isoelectronic with the methane molecule, and is tetrahedral in shape with four identical bonds.

The ammonia molecule has a lone pair of electrons on the nitrogen atom, and is a common electron donor. It reacts with BF_3 for instance to form an *adduct* molecule, $BF_3.NH_3$:

$$BF_3 + NH_3 \rightarrow \begin{array}{c} F \quad H \\ | \quad | \\ F\!-\!B\!-\!N\!-\!H \\ | \quad | \\ F \quad H \end{array}$$

When a coordinate bond is formed, the valencies of the atoms involved may appear to be incorrect. In BF_4^- and in $BF_3.NH_3$ the boron and nitrogen atoms are joined to four other atoms by single bonds, although their normal valencies are 3. This inconsistency can be avoided in two ways. The first way is to use an arrow for the coordinate bond to show the direction of donation of the electron pair. The molecular formula of $BF_3.NH_3$ using this convention is written

$$\begin{array}{c} F \quad H \\ | \quad | \\ F\!-\!B\!\leftarrow\!N\!-\!H \\ | \quad | \\ F \quad H \end{array}$$

The second way is to show the *formal charges* on the atoms. The formal charge on an atom in a Lewis structure is calculated by formally assigning one electron from each bonding pair to each of the atoms joined by that bond. Lone pairs are of course assigned fully to the atom which carries them. The formal charge on each atom is equal to the number of valence electrons in the neutral atom minus the number of electrons assigned formally in this way for the given Lewis structure.

For instance in the Lewis structure given for the BF_4^- ion, there are four bonding pairs of electrons. The boron atom is formally assigned four bonding electrons and since the neutral boron atom has three valence electrons, the formal charge on boron is $3-4 = -1$. Each fluorine atom is assigned one bonding electron, which with the three fluorine lone pairs make a total of seven electrons, equal to the number of valence electrons on the neutral boron atom. Hence the formal charge on each fluorine atom is zero. Formal charges are indicated by signs in circles near the atoms involved:

$$
\begin{array}{c}
\text{F} \\
| \quad \ominus \\
\text{F}-\text{B}-\text{F} \\
| \\
\text{F}
\end{array}
$$

The sum of the formal charges is equal to the total charge on an ion. It may be helpful to note that the B^- ion would have four electrons, making it isoelectronic with the carbon atom which has a valence of four. The molecular formula of $BF_3 . NH_3$ can be written

$$
\begin{array}{c}
\text{F} \quad \text{H} \\
\ominus| \quad |\oplus \\
\text{F}-\text{B}-\text{N}-\text{H} \\
| \quad | \\
\text{F} \quad \text{H}
\end{array}
$$

in which nitrogen is formally assigned 4 electrons while the neutral nitrogen atom has 5 electrons, making the formal charge on nitrogen in this structure equal to $5-4 = +1$.

The water molecule has two lone pairs on the oxygen atom and so can act as an electron donor. The structure of the H_3O^+ ion can be thought of as the result of formation of a coordinate bond between a water molecule and a proton:

$$
\text{H}_2\text{O} + \text{H}^+ \rightarrow
\begin{array}{c}
\oplus \\
\text{H}-\text{O}-\text{H} \\
| \\
\text{H}
\end{array}
$$

The hydroxide ion OH^- carries three lone pairs on the oxygen atom and so can act as a donor. In the reaction between a hydroxide ion and a hydrogen ion, an electron pair is donated from the OH^- ion to the H^+ ion to form the water molecule:

$$
\text{H}^+ + :\!\overset{\displaystyle ..}{\underset{\displaystyle ..}{\text{O}}}\!:\!\text{H}^- \rightarrow \overset{\displaystyle ..}{\underset{\displaystyle ..}{:\!\text{O}\!:}}
$$
$$
\qquad\qquad\quad \text{H} \quad \text{H}
$$

The reaction of an ammonia molecule with a hydrogen ion to form the ammonium ion is similar:

$$NH_3 + H^+ \rightarrow H\!-\!\overset{\displaystyle H}{\underset{\displaystyle H}{\overset{|}{\underset{|}{N}}}}\!-\!H \;\oplus$$

From the examples given it should be possible to see the connection between the donation of an electron pair and the reaction between an acid and a base. Ammonia has been called a base because it is a proton acceptor, but the electronic basis for this reaction is the donation of a lone pair of electrons from the ammonia molecule to the electron acceptor, the H^+ ion. Hence an electron pair donor is often called a *Lewis base,* and an electron pair acceptor is called a *Lewis acid.* An atom, ion or molecule that is capable of acting as an electron donor in forming a coordinate bond is often called a *ligand.* Ligands are Lewis bases, and form coordinate bonds to Lewis acids. The study of this phenomenon is called *coordination chemistry.*

The formation of a hydrated ion in aqueous solution is an acid-base reaction from this point of view. A metal ion in aqueous solution has a number of water molecules closely associated with it, and in most cases either four or six water molecules are bonded to the metal ion by reasonably strong coordinate bonds. The metal ion has lost some or all of its valence electrons, and therefore in most cases is an electron acceptor, or Lewis acid. The water molecules act as electron donors, or Lewis bases, or ligands, and the structure can be represented by formulae such as the following, for the hydrated cupric ion, $Cu(H_2O)_6^{2+}$:

$$\left[\begin{array}{c} H_2O \\ H_2O \rightarrow Cu \leftarrow OH_2 \\ H_2O \end{array} \right]^{2+}$$

The arrangement of the ligand molecules is a regular octahedron in some ions, but is distorted in others.

Ammonia is a stronger base than water, and therefore a better electron donor. When ammonia is added to the solution, some of the water molecules bonded to the Cu^{2+} ion are replaced by ammonia molecules, to form ions such as $Cu(H_2O)_5(NH_3)^{2+}$:

$$\left[\begin{array}{c} H_2O \\ H_2O \rightarrow Cu \leftarrow NH_3 \\ H_2O \end{array} \right]^{2+}$$

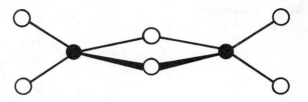

Figure 12-4 The molecular structure of Al_2Cl_6. The plane containing the bridging chlorine atoms is perpendicular to that containing the terminal chlorine atoms.

An interesting case in which a molecule acts as both a Lewis acid and a Lewis base simultaneously is aluminium trichloride. By analogy with BCl_3, this molecule would be expected to have the molecular formula $AlCl_3$ and to be planar. However, the molecular formula is found to be Al_2Cl_6, and the molecular geometry is a bridged structure, shown in Figure 12-4. The Lewis structure for this molecule can be written

in which the bridging chlorine atoms act as Lewis bases, donating lone pair electrons to the metal atoms, which act as Lewis acids. There is an octet of electrons around the aluminium atoms, and the configuration of chlorine atoms around each aluminium atom is tetrahedral rather than trigonal planar.

12-5   ELECTRONEGATIVITY

Covalent bonding exists when an electron pair is shared between two atoms in a molecule. If the two atoms in a diatomic molecule are the same, the bonding electrons are shared equally between the two atoms and there is no net electric charge on either atom. However, if the two atoms in a diatomic molecule are different, the bonding electrons are generally not shared equally and electric charge is transferred from one atom to the other. The extent to which charge is transferred depends on the relative ability of the two atoms to attract electrons from neighbouring atoms. If the two atoms are very similar in this respect, the amount of charge transferred is small, much less than the charge on an electron. If one atom is much more "electron-attracting" than the other, then a large net charge is transferred, and it would be reasonable in such a case to regard the molecule as a pair of ions held together by electrostatic attraction, although such a description is not wholly accurate. For instance, a molecule of sodium chloride in the gas phase at high temperature might be represented by the formula Na^+Cl^- to show the extent and direction of transfer of electronic charge.

The transfer of electrons from one atom to another within a molecule is not difficult to understand qualitatively, but it is difficult to measure in an accurate and meaningful way. Despite this difficulty, the development of the concept of *electronegativity* was one of the most important events in chemistry. The definition of electronegativity has been the subject of a great deal of research over almost fifty years, but the original work of Linus Pauling at the California Institute of Technology remains central to the discussion.

Pauling based his definition of electronegativity on bond energy data, such as the data in Table 11-2. Consider two atoms of different elements A and B which form diatomic molecules A_2, B_2 and AB. If the atoms A and B are of equal "electron-attracting" power, then there should be zero energy involved in the formation of the molecule AB from the molecules A_2 and B_2, since the change in the type of bond should not change the electron distribution between the atoms. Hence for atoms of equal "electronegativity" the enthalpy change of the reaction

$$A_2 + B_2 \rightarrow 2\,AB$$

should be zero. Expressing the enthalpy of reaction in terms of bond energies,

$$\Delta H = E_{A-A} + E_{B-B} - 2\,E_{A-B}$$

If this ΔH is zero, then the bond energy E_{A-B} must be the average of the bond energies E_{A-A} and E_{B-B}:

$$E_{A-B} = \tfrac{1}{2}(E_{A-A} + E_{B-B})$$

Pauling found that the bond energy E_{A-B} is nearly always larger than the value given by this formula, and found that the excess in bond energy could be correlated with the extent of transfer of electronic charge from one atom to another. He defined his scale of electronegativity in terms of this excess bond energy. Each element was assigned an *electronegativity,* denoted by the symbol x, which measures the ability of the atom to attract electrons in a molecule. The electronegativities were determined from an assumed formula involving the energies of the bonds A−A, B−B and A−B, and the difference in electronegativities, $x_a - x_b$. It was found that a better scale of electronegativities was obtained if the excess bond energy was related to the *geometric mean* rather than the arithmetic mean suggested in the above argument, and the formula used in developing the Pauling scale of electronegativities, with bond energies in kilojoules per mole, is the following:

$$E_{A-B} = \sqrt{E_{A-A} \cdot E_{B-B}} + 125\,(x_A - x_B)^2$$

As an example consider the HCl molecule in the gas phase. The bond energies for the molecules H_2, Cl_2 and HCl are listed in Table 11-2, and can be substituted in the above formula:

$$432 = \sqrt{436 \times 243} + 125(x_H - x_{Cl})^2$$

from which the difference in electronegatives can be calculated:

$$\left| x_H - x_{Cl} \right| = 0.92$$

TABLE 12-3   Pauling electronegativities of the s- and p-block elements.

						H
						2.1
Li	Be	B	C	N	O	F
1.0	1.5	2	2.5	3.0	3.5	4.0
Na	Mg	Al	Si	P	S	Cl
0.9	1.2	1.5	1.8	2.1	2.5	3.0
K	Ca	Ga	Ge	As	Se	Br
0.8	1.0	1.6	1.8	2.0	2.4	2.8
Rb	Sr	In	Sn	Sb	Te	I
0.8	1.0	1.7	1.8	1.9	2.1	2.5
Cs	Ba	Tl	Pb	Bi	Po	At
0.7	0.9	1.8	1.8	1.9	2.0	2.2

Notice that this calculation leads to a value for the magnitude but not the sign of the electronegativity difference. Table 12-3 lists electronegativity values for the s- and p-block elements. The electronegativities listed for hydrogen and chlorine are 2.1 and 3.0, which are consistent with the above calculations. Pauling's procedure for determining electronegativities is by calculation and comparison of differences based upon bond energies.

A number of different approaches to the concept of electronegativity have been given since Pauling's original work. These newer approaches are useful, and provide checks on each other's calculations. R. S. Mulliken showed that the ability of an atom to attract electrons in a chemical bond is related to the average value of the ionization energy and the electron affinity of the atom, and gave a scale of electronegativity based upon the quantity $(E_I + E_A)/2$. This scale differs in principle from Pauling's scale because it relates to the properties of each atom individually, determined in totally independent experiments, instead of being related to the properties of atoms combined chemically in molecules. Another important electronegativity scale is that of A. L. Allred and E. G. Rochow which is based upon theoretical calculations of the force on an electron in the vicinity of an atom in a molecule.

While there are minor differences between the various electronegativity scales, there is agreement between them on the electronegativity values for most elements, and on the trends in electronegativity values across the periodic table. This agreement between such widely differing theories is evidence of the validity of electronegativity as a description of the chemical properties of the elements. In more sophisticated treatments of the subject, elements in different oxidation states are assigned different electronegativities. An atom in a high oxidation state has a higher attraction for electrons than the same atom in a lower oxidation state, and therefore a higher electronegativity. This refinement of the theory will not be considered further at this stage, and the values in Table 12-3 should be considered as average values.

Study of Table 12-3 shows that the metals at the left hand side of the periodic table have low electronegativities, and the non-metals at the right hand side of the table have high electronegativities. It follows from Mulliken's definition that electroelectronegativity is a periodic property of the elements, since both ionization energy and electron affinity are periodic. The low values of the electronegativities of the metals corresponds to the strong tendency of metals to form positive ions, whereas non-metals tend to form negative ions. Electronegativities decrease down each column of the periodic table, which is a reflection of the trend from non-metals to metals going down the columns, at least for the p-block elements.

When a chemical bond is formed between two atoms of different elements, the bonding electrons are not shared equally between the two atoms. The more electronegative atom acquires an excess of electrons and carries a net negative charge. The amount of charge transferred from one atom to the other is a measure of the *ionic character* of the bond, and depends on the difference Δx between the electronegativities of the two elements. If Δx is greater than about 2.0, the bond may be assumed to be almost entirely ionic. Thus the diatomic molecules of the alkali halides such as NaCl, which are found in the vapour of the salt at high temperature, are highly ionic in nature except perhaps for the iodides. These molecules may be regarded as a pair of ions held together by electrostatic attraction, and can be represented by a formula such as Na^+Cl^-. In such a molecule, each ion is in the strong electric field of the other, and both ions are somewhat distorted from their spherical shape.

If the electronegativity difference x is smaller than about 0.5, the amount of charge transferred is small and the bonding electrons are shared approximately equally between the two atoms. For intermediate values of Δx, somewhat less than a full electronic charge is transferred. For the hydrogen chloride molecule, Δx is 0.9. The chlorine atom carries a negative charge, the hydrogen atom a positive charge, and the formula $H^{\delta+}Cl^{\delta-}$ is sometimes written to show the distribution of charge.

The HCl molecule is a *polar* molecule, and has an electric *dipole moment*, because even though the molecule is electrically neutral, there is a separation of charges within the molecule which generates an electric field in the space surrounding it. The electric field of the molecule caused by the dipole moment can interact with other molecules, and with laboratory equipment designed to detect such fields.

In the case of the water molecule, the electronegativity difference is 1.4. The oxygen atom carries a negative charge and the hydrogen atoms positive charges. A structural formula which represents this charge distribution is:

$$2\delta_-$$
$$O$$
$$\delta^+ H \qquad H \; \delta^+$$

The water molecule has a dipole moment caused by this charge distribution, because the centre of negative charge in the molecule lies at a different point from the centre of positive charge, the molecule being bent. This is not the case in the CO_2 molecule. In CO_2 the electronegativity difference is 1.0, so the C=O bonds are moderately polar. However, because of the shape of the molecule, the centre of the negative charges on the oxygen atoms lies at the centre of the positively charged carbon atom, and so the molecule has no dipole moment. It is common for highly symmetrical molecules to have a zero dipole moment despite the presence of fairly polar bonds in the molecule, the zero dipole moment being the result of the molecular symmetry.

The phenomenon of *hydrogen bonding* is closely connected with the presence of highly electronegative atoms. It was shown in Chapter 7 that some hydrogen-containing compounds have unusually high boiling points and latent heats of vaporization, and this was ascribed to a specific interaction called hydrogen bonding. Hydrogen bonding can be represented as X—H . . . . . Y in which the hydrogen atom is bonded to an atom X by a covalent bond, but interacts strongly with another atom Y, which may of course be the same element as X. In the cases discussed in Chapter 7, the atoms X and Y are in different molecules. The hydrogen bonding energy, generally in the range 10-40 kJ mol^{-1}, is therefore reflected as an enhanced intermolecular interaction energy, and so influences the process of vaporization of the liquid. For methanol, the molecules are linked together by chains of hydrogen bonds. In water, the molecules form more complicated networks of hydrogen bonds in which there are two hydrogen bonds per molecule.

Cases are also known in which the atoms X and Y which are joined by the hydrogen bond lie in the same molecule, an example being 2-hydroxy-benzaldehyde. In such a case the existence of hydrogen bonding is generally detected by spectroscopic measurements, for the hydrogen bonding does not directly affect the intermolecular interactions, and the boiling points of such compounds are not unusual in comparison with similar molecules in which hydrogen bonding does not take place.

By and large, hydrogen bonding is found to occur only when the atoms X and Y are fluorine, oxygen or nitrogen, although weaker hydrogen bonding may occur involving sulphur and chlorine. Examination of Table 12-3 shows that these elements all have high electronegativities, which suggests that electronegativity is an important factor in determining the strength of a hydrogen bond. A strongly electronegative atom X acquires a negative charge and makes the hydrogen atom bonded to it positive. Therefore the X-H bond is polar:

$$X^{\delta-}\!\!-\!\!H^{\delta+}$$

The positively charged hydrogen atom can then interact electrostatically with another atom Y if the latter carries a negative charge, which is most likely if the atom Y is highly electronegative.

This electrostatic picture of the hydrogen bond is rather oversimplified, and undoubtedly other factors are involved than simply the charges on the atoms. Hydrogen bonding has fairly well defined directional characteristics, which would not be expected if the interaction were purely electrostatic. The atoms of fluorine, oxygen and nitrogen carry lone pairs of electrons which may be involved in the formation of the hydrogen bond through the resonance structure

$$X^{\ominus} \: H—Y^{\oplus}$$

in which the lone pair of electrons on the atom Y are shared in a coordinate bond to the hydrogen atom. However, the electronegativity of the atoms X and Y is a major factor in determining whether a strong hydrogen bond is formed.

12-6 THE WAVE THEORY OF ELECTRONS

The Lewis theory of chemical bonding is successful in explaining certain facts about the structure and reactivity of molecules, but is is far from being a complete theory of the behaviour of molecules and is quite inadequate as a description of the behaviour of electrons generally. Much more is required of a satisfactory theory because chemical bonding is only one aspect of the behaviour of electrons in matter.

The most striking experimental fact about the electronic structure of matter is the existence of quantized energy levels. The best evidence for the existence of these discrete levels is that the spectra of atoms and molecules contain discrete spectral lines. Although there is good evidence that electrons behave as if they are very small particles, discrete energy levels do not occur in the mechanics of particles as described by the laws of Newton. It was this contradiction which puzzled theoretical physicists in the first quarter of the twentieth century, and in finding a solution to this problem the foundations were laid for the quantum theory of chemical bonding. The theory has turned out to be complicated in nature. Quantitative results can only be obtained by application of powerful computers, which have only recently become readily available, and often the results of calculations are difficult to interpret in terms of the language used to describe the results of chemical experiments. However, the results of quantum calculations have come to play a large part in the development of chemical ideas, and with the extension of computing facilities this trend will continue.

The solution to the problem of the existence of quantized energy levels came with the hypothesis by Louis de Broglie at the University of Paris in 1925 that particles could under some circumstances display the properties associated with waves. It had been shown by the work of Planck and Einstein that light waves could sometimes display particle-like properties, and so the ambiguity in the nature of matter was not new to theoretical science when de Broglie made his proposal. But because electrons had become firmly established as one of the fundamental particles of nature, it was difficult to accept the suggestion that electrons can behave like waves. It is still difficult to comprehend the dual nature of electrons. Once the basic ideas of quantum theory are grasped, the theory of chemical bonding is not difficult to follow, at least qualitatively.

Quantized energy levels are observed experimentally only when electrons are confined to a small region of space. Electrons which are bound to a nucleus in an atom, or to several nuclei in a molecule, produce discrete optical or X-ray

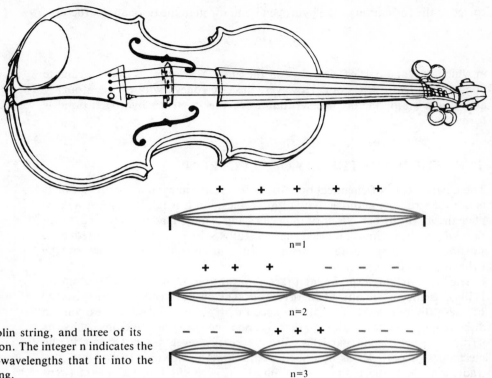

Figure 12-5 A violin string, and three of its modes of vibration. The integer n indicates the number of half-wavelengths that fit into the length of the string.

spectra, showing the existence of discrete energy levels, but electrons which are free to travel through space as in a cathode ray tube can take any energy, and obey Newton's laws of motion when they interact with external fields. Waves have very similar properties. When a wave travels through a medium far from any surfaces or edges, there are no restrictions on the wavelength of the wave. On the surface of a lake or ocean are found waves of short, medium and long wavelengths depending on the conditions which generated the waves. On the other hand, waves in a medium with restrictions at its edges or surfaces have well defined wavelengths which are related mathematically to the conditions at the boundary of the medium. The simplest example to study is a string in a violin. The string is supported at both ends, and can only vibrate in such a way that the ends of the string remain at rest. There is more than one way in which this condition can be met, and several of these "modes" of vibration are shown in Figure 12-5. The ends of the violin string will be at rest as long as the half-wavelength of the wave, or an integer multiple of it, is equal to the length of the string. This is an example of "quantization."

In the first mode of vibration shown in Figure 12-5, the half-wavelength is equal to the length of the string, and in the second, the wavelength is equal to the length of the string. This can be expressed by the equation

$$n\frac{\lambda}{2} = L$$

where λ is the wavelength, L is the length of the string, and n is an integer which is 1,2 or 3 in the examples shown in the figure. The modes of vibration can be classified, listed, or named by means of the integer n, which serves the purpose of a quantum number. The vibration mode for which n=1 is called the fundamental, and modes with higher values of n are called overtones or harmonics, and in musical terms give octaves above the fundamental note. The note of the fundamental, i.e. its frequency, depends on the density of the string and its tension as well as the length, but the wavelengths of the different modes of vibration are determined only by the conditions at the ends of the string. These conditions are called *boundary conditions*.

In the fundamental mode of vibration shown in Figure 12-5, the displacement of the string is in the same direction everywhere, and there is no point where the displacement of the string is zero at all times, except at the ends. The character of this mode is indicated by placing a number of + signs along the string. In the first harmonic, or n=2 mode, the left hand end of the string moves in the opposite direction to the right end at all times. When the left hand end moves up, the right hand end moves down, and vice versa. This is indicated by placing + signs on the left hand half of the string, and − signs on the right hand end. The midpoint of the string does not move at all in this mode, and is the dividing point between the two halves which are moving in opposite directions. Points at which the displacement is zero at all times are called *nodes*. The n=2 mode has one node, the n=3 mode has two nodes, and so on.

Another musical instrument is the drum, in which the tuned element is a skin stretched across the top of a rigid frame. The fundamental note of a drum is related to the density of the skin, the tension in it, and the size and shape of the frame. There is much to be learned from a study of the patterns of vibration of a circular drum, and some of these patterns are shown in Figure 12-6. These show vibrations in a two dimensional flexible skin which is fixed to a circular frame. The displacement of the skin is in a direction perpendicular to the plane of the skin as indicated by + and − signs, which have the same meaning as in Figure 12-5. The patterns of these vibrational modes are more complicated than those of a violin string, and can be most conveniently described by considering the shapes of the nodal lines which separate regions with opposite phase.

The fundamental mode of vibration is shown in diagram (a) which can be compared directly with the fundamental of a violin string in Figure 12-5. The displacement is zero at the edge of the skin, and a maximum at the centre. There is no nodal line for this mode. Diagram (b) shows a mode in which there is a circular nodal line; a cross-section through the skin oscillating in this mode would be rather like the n=3 mode of the violin string, with the centre of the skin having opposite displacement to that of the outer part of the skin.

Diagrams (c) and (d) show two modes which are identical in form, with the second rotated 90° with respect to the first. These are mathematically independent modes of vibration, but they have the same shape and it is sufficient to describe one of them. There is a nodal line along a diameter of the circle, and the displacement is of opposite phase on opposite sides of this line. Diagrams (e) and (f) show two modes which are similarly related, by a rotation of 45°

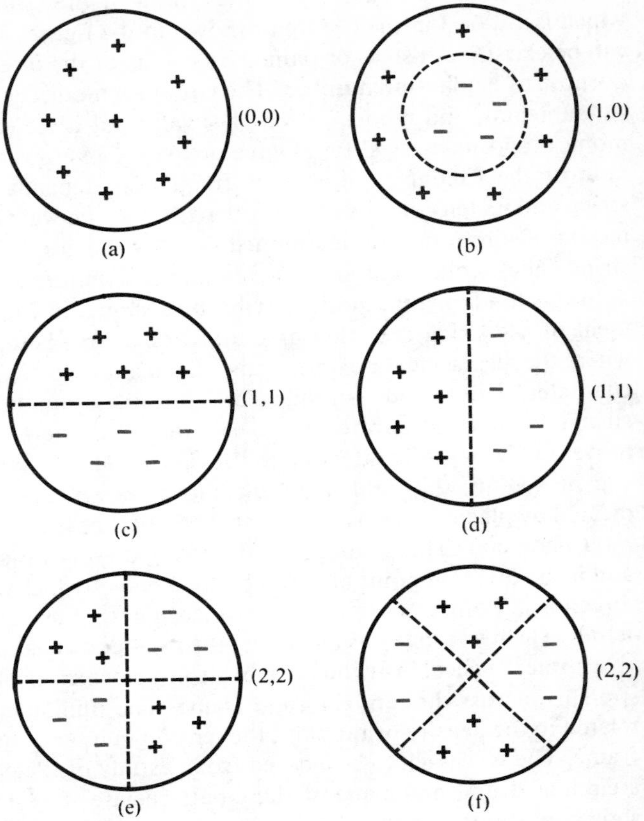

Figure 12-6 The modes of vibration of a circular drum skin. Each mode is labelled with a pair of integers which give first the total number of nodal lines, and then the number of angular nodal lines. The nodes are shown by dotted lines.

These modes have two nodal lines which are at right angles, and separate the 90° segments which have opposite phase.

The circular nodal line shown in diagram (b) is called a *radial* node, because it describes a node of constant radius. The other nodes lie along diameters of the circle which are defined by the angle measured around the circle, and such nodal lines are called *angular nodes.* There are modes of higher frequency which have both angular and radial nodes.

The vibrational modes of violin strings and drums which have been described can be thought of as standing wave patterns resulting from the superposition of wave trains moving in opposite directions. The opposed wave trains result from the reflection or other interaction of the wave trains with the boundaries of the vibrating string or skin. On a string the two wave trains are moving in opposition along the string. On a circular drum the two wave trains can move in and out between the centre and the circumference, resulting in a pattern of radial nodes, or else they can move in a circular manner in opposite directions around the circle, resulting in angular nodes. Thus angular nodes are associated with angular wave motion, and radial nodes with radial wave motion.

The nodes of a vibrational mode can be used to classify the type of the vibration. For a violin string, the number of nodes is equal to (n−1), where n is the number of half-wavelengths in the length of the string. Hence the number of nodes is as useful as n itself in classifying the different modes of vibration. For a circular drum, the radial and angular nodes must be counted separately when describing a particular mode. This is best done by specifying the total number of nodal lines, and the number of angular nodal lines, and in Figure 12-2 each mode has been labelled in this way. This method of labelling corresponds most closely to the quantum numbers n and *l* introduced in Chapter 9; the angular momentum quantum number *l* is closely related to the number of angular nodes in the associated mode.

Particles such as electrons move in three-dimensional space, and so the associated wave motion and standing wave patterns must also be three dimensional in nature.

In de Broglie's hypothesis a particle is assumed to have associated wavemotion, which governs the behaviour of the particle. The wavelength of the wave is related to the momentum of the particle, mv, through the relation

$$\lambda = \frac{h}{mv}$$

where h is Planck's constant. The wave motion interacts with the surroundings of the particle as they are expressed by the potential energy of the particle at different points in space, and shows the effects of reflection, refraction and interference which are observed with more familiar waves, such as the waves on the surface of water, or light waves. If the de Broglie wavelength λ is very small compared with the length over which the potential energy changes significantly, then the particle will be found to obey Newton's laws of motion. This is the situation for an electron in a picture tube of a television set, or cathode ray oscilloscope.

Example 12-2   Calculate the de Broglie wavelength for an electron which has been accelerated through a potential difference of 5 kV, and is moving freely through a vacuum inside a television picture tube.

The kinetic energy of the electron after passing through the potential difference is equal to the change in its potential energy, which is equal to the charge multiplied by the potential difference:

$$\text{kinetic energy} = \tfrac{1}{2}mv^2 = 1.60 \times 10^{-19}\,C \times 5000\,V$$

$$= 8.00 \times 10^{-15}\,J$$

and from this the momentum can be calculated:

$$\text{momentum} = mv = \sqrt{\tfrac{1}{2}mv^2 \times 2m}$$

$$= \sqrt{8.00 \times 10^{-15}J \times 2 \times 9.1 \times 10^{-31}\,kg}$$

$$= 1.2 \times 10^{-22}\,kg\ m\ s^{-1}$$

Hence the de Broglie wavelength is

$$\lambda = \frac{6.6 \times 10^{-34} \text{ J s}}{1.2 \times 10^{-22} \text{ kg m s}^{-1}}$$

$$= 5.5 \times 10^{-12} \text{ m}$$

This wavelength is extremely short, far smaller than the length of the apparatus used to accelerate the electron, or any laboratory apparatus used to deflect the electron. Hence the behaviour of the electron follows the ordinary Newtonian laws of mechanics.

Example 12-3   Calculate the de Broglie wavelength of an electron in the first (n=1) Bohr orbit in a hydrogen atom, and compare it with the radius of the orbit.

The speed of the electron in its orbit can be calculated from equation 4 of Chapter 9.

$$v = \sqrt{\frac{e^2}{4\pi\varepsilon_o \, mr}}$$

Hence the linear momentum of the electron is

$$mv = \sqrt{\frac{me^2}{4\pi\varepsilon_o \, r}}$$

Hence the de Broglie wavelength is

$$\lambda = \frac{h}{mv} = h\sqrt{\frac{4\pi\varepsilon_o \, r}{me^2}}$$

The radius of the first Bohr orbit is equal to a_o, which was calculated in Chapter 9 to be 0.0529 nm. Substituting this value, and the values of the other fundamental constants,

$$\lambda = 6.62 \times 10^{-34} \sqrt{\frac{4\pi \times 8.85 \times 10^{-12} \times 0.0529 \times 10^{-9}}{9.11 \times 10^{-31} \times (1.60 \times 10^{-19})^2}}$$

$$= 0.332 \times 10^{-9} \text{ m}$$

$$= 0.332 \text{ nm}$$

This is equal to the circumference of the orbit.

The last example shows that for an electron in a hydrogen atom, the de Broglie wavelength is comparable to the size of the atom itself, and so the behaviour of the electron is expected to be affected by the presence of a standing wave pattern in the wave motion associated with the electron. This is just what is observed: the quantization that arises naturally in connection with a standing wave pattern corresponds to the quantization of the associated energy levels of the electron, and as a result a spectrum consisting of sharp lines results from transitions between the quantized energy levels. The existence of the quantization can only be understood by abandoning the strict concepts of Newtonian mechanics, and concentrating instead on the properties of standing wave patterns.

In complicated cases, the properties of standing wave patterns can only be determined by solving a *differential equation* subject to certain *boundary conditions*. The differential equation which governs the wave motion associated with particles was first proposed by Erwin Schrödinger in 1926, and is universally known as the *Schrödinger equation*. This equation is often written in the form

$$-\frac{\hbar^2}{2m}\left(\frac{d^2\psi}{dx^2} + \frac{d^2\psi}{dy^2} + \frac{d^2\psi}{dz^2}\right) + V(x,y,z)\psi = E\psi$$

In this equation, ψ represents the amplitude of the quantum mechanical wave, which can be compared with the displacement of the violin string or the vibrating skin of the drum. The **wavefunction**, ψ, is a function of position in space, and so can be written $\psi(x,y,z)$, and can be differentiated with respect to these variables. The quantity V is the potential energy of the electron at the position (x,y,z) in space. The quantity E is the total energy of the electron, consisting of both kinetic and potential energy, and represents the energy which is associated with a particular standing wave pattern. The quantity $\hbar$ is Planck's constant h divided by 2π.

The boundary conditions, or conditions of "good behaviour," to be applied in solving the Schrödinger equation are very much a matter of common sense. The wavefunction ψ is required to be a continuous, differentiable function which has a unique value at each point in space. In addition, the integral of the square of the wavefunction, $\psi^2(x,y,z)$, over all space must exist and be finite; this condition is required for the interpretation of the physical meaning of the wavefunction, to be described below.

The wave theory of the behaviour of particles is not a theory which is derived from some more fundamental postulates, and hence the Schrödinger equation cannot be "proved" in the ordinary sense of that word. The equation is itself one of the basic postulates of the quantum theory. However, it is possible to demonstrate the nature of the terms in the equation, and why their form is reasonable. The total energy of a particle is the sum of the potential and kinetic energies, and so

$$\tfrac{1}{2}mv^2 + V = E$$

The kinetic energy can be rewritten in terms of the momentum mv, so that the momentum can be replaced by a factor involving the de Broglie wavelength:

$$\frac{(mv)^2}{2m} + V = E$$

Substituting from the formula for the de Broglie wavelength, $mv = h/\lambda$, we get

$$\frac{h^2}{2\,m\,\lambda^2} + V = E$$

Now a wavemotion having a wavelength λ has an amplitude which varies through space with a repetition length of λ, and the variation can be described by a sine function. Hence such a wavefunction contains the factor $\sin(2\pi x/\lambda)$. If this function is differentiated twice with respect to x, we find

$$\frac{d^2}{dx^2} \sin(2\pi x/\lambda) = -\frac{(2\pi)^2}{\lambda^2} \sin(2\pi x/\lambda)$$

For any such wavefunction ψ, the factor $1/\lambda^2$ can be replaced by the factor

$$\frac{1}{\lambda^2} = -\frac{1}{(2\pi)^2\psi} \frac{d^2\psi}{dx^2}$$

Making this substitution in the energy equation above, and multiplying by ψ, we get

$$-\frac{h^2}{2m(2\pi)^2} \frac{d^2\psi}{dx^2} + V\psi = E\psi$$

The Schrödinger equation differs from this only in that it allows the wave to be travelling in any direction in three-dimensional space instead of restricting the wave to travel along the x-axis.

The procedures for solving the Schrödinger equation in any given situation are in general difficult and tedious, and will not be dealt with here. However, the nature of the solutions will be discussed for some cases of chemical interest.

Once a solution of the Schrödinger equation has been found which is consistent with the boundary conditions, it remains to interpret the wavefunction physically. It is part of the postulates of wave mechanics that the square of the wave function gives a measure of the probability of finding the particle in the vicinity of the point at which the wavefunction is evaluated. In regions of space where the wavefunction is numerically largest, whether positive or negative, the particle is most likely to be found. In regions where the wavefunction is close to zero, the particle is least likely to be found. With the square of the wavefunction being associated with a probability density it is clear that the sum of the probabilities associated with all regions of space must be equal to unity. This condition is expressed mathematically by the equation

$$\int \psi^2 \, dxdydz = 1$$

where the integral of the function ψ^2 is to be taken over all space.

Solutions of the Schrödinger equation for electrons in atoms and molecules are often called *atomic orbitals,* and *molecular orbitals* respectively. Atomic orbitals in the wave theory of atoms replace the strictly defined orbits deduced by Bohr. An atomic orbital contains all the information about the electron in the atom that can be obtained by experiment, information which can be calculated by appropriate mathematical procedures. The behaviour of the electron is governed by the standing wave pattern which the atomic orbital describes. Its precise orbit cannot be defined, for if the electron in a quantum state were to be *required* to follow a particular path in space, the natural standing wave pattern which is associated with that particular quantum state of the atom would be distorted, and the atom would no longer be in a single state of quantized energy. The lack of localized orbits of the electrons in an atom is a result of a general principle of quantum theory, called the *Heisenberg uncertainty principle.*

12-7   ATOMIC ORBITALS

The orbitals for electrons in atoms are basic to the theory of chemical bonding. They are mathematical functions of position (x,y,z) in three dimensional space, obtained by solving the Schrödinger equation with the function V replaced by the potential energy function for an electron in the atom. Usually the nucleus of the atom is placed at the origin of the coordinate system. For the simplest atom, hydrogen, the potential energy is

$$V(x,y,z) = -\frac{e^2}{4\pi\varepsilon_0\sqrt{x^2+y^2+z^2}}$$

where ε_0 is the permittivity of free space. When this function is substituted into the Schrödinger equation, a set of solutions to the equation can be found which satisfy the conditions of "good behaviour." The corresponding energy levels obtained in the solution of the equation are found to be exactly the energy levels calculated by Bohr with his simple model, which are also those obtained by experiment. However, at this point it is the orbitals, or wavefunctions, which are of interest rather than the energies.

It is convenient to express the wave functions in terms of a set of coordinates different from the cartesian coordinates x,y, and z. The new coordinates, called *spherical polar coordinates,* are particularly suitable for dealing with mathematical problems involving motion around a single point in space. The radius r is the distance of the electron from the nucleus at the origin, the angle ϕ represents longitude on the surface of a sphere, and the angle θ represents

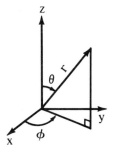

Spherical polar coordinates

latitude measured from the north pole. The orbital functions are found to be of the form

$$\psi(r,\theta,\phi) = R(r)Y(\theta,\phi)$$

where R is the *radial* part of the wavefunction, and Y is a function of the two angles. The exact mathematical forms of these functions do not matter here, but the form of the solutions, in which the radial and angular parts of the orbital function are separate factors is of great importance. The reason for this is that the angular function Y determines the *shape* of the orbital function, while the radial function R determines primarily the *size* of the electron distribution. Now it is the shape of the orbitals which is of the greatest importance in determining the way in which atoms are bonded together, and so the understanding of the formation of chemical bonds depends mostly on understanding the function Y. Furthermore, the angular functions Y are the same in all atoms, while the radial functions vary from atom to atom, and so the discussion of the shapes of the hydrogen atom orbitals can be applied to other atoms. The radial functions are primarily important in determining the sizes and the energies of atoms, and must be considered carefully in a fuller discussion of atomic structure.

In the course of the mathematical solution of the Schrödinger equation it becomes apparent that three quantum numbers are required to classify the orbitals. The quantum numbers arise from the application of the boundary conditions. The three quantum numbers are usually denoted by the symbols n, *l* and m. These quantum numbers were mentioned in the chapters on atomic structure. The principal quantum number, n, is the most important in determining the energy of a state of the atom. The number *l* measures the amount of angular momentum of the electron, and plays a minor role in determining the energy. The number m is related to the orientation of the angular momentum vector, and has no effect on the energy at all. The relations between the values of these three numbers has been explained previously:

$$n = 1,2,3,4, \ldots$$

$$l = 0,1,2, \ldots ,(n-1). \quad \text{(n values)}$$

$$m = -l, \ldots ,+l. \quad (2l+1 \text{ values})$$

The value of the orbital quantum number *l* is so important that special symbols are given to designate the value:

l value	symbol
0	s
1	p
2	d
3	f

From the allowed values of m, it may be concluded that for given n and *l*, there are 2*l*+1 orbitals. Therefore, for a given value of n, there is one s orbital, three p orbitals, five d orbitals, and so on, bearing in mind that *l* cannot be larger than n−1.

In the wavefunction for the s orbitals, the angular function Y turns out to be a constant. The wavefunctions are independent of the angles θ and ϕ, and vary only with the distance from the nucleus, r. These orbitals are analogous to the (0,0) and (1,0) modes of vibration of the drum shown in Figure 12-6, in which the amplitude of the vibration depends only on the distance from the centre of the drum. It should be remembered however that the orbital wavefunctions are functions of position in a three-dimensional space, rather than the two- dimensional drum. Figure 12-7 shows graphically the functions $\psi(r)$ for the 1s and 2s orbitals of the hydrogen atom. The 1s wavefunction decreases exponentially from a finite value at the centre of the atom, and has no nodes. The 2s wavefunction also decreases rapidly, is zero at a nodal surface of radius r = $2a_o$, and is negative for larger values of r. The nature of the wavefunction is therefore similar to that of the (1,0) vibrational mode of the drum in Figure 12-6. The opposite signs of the wavefunction mean that the standing wave pattern has opposite phases at large r and small r.

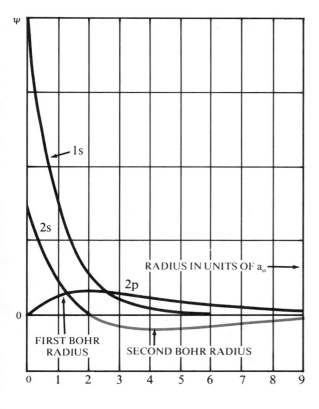

Figure 12-7 The radial dependence of the wavefunctions for the 1s, 2s and 2p states of the hydrogen atom.

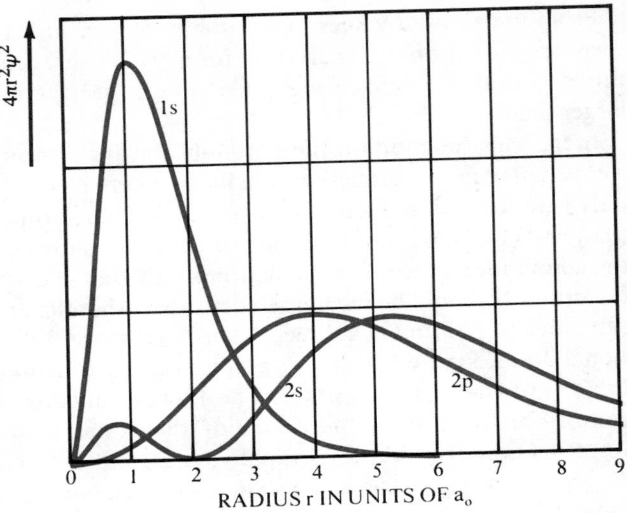

Figure 12-8 The radial distribution functions for the 1s, 2s and 2p states of the hydrogen atom. The graphs give the relative probability of finding the electron between r and r+dr from the nucleus.

The wavefunctions are smooth functions of the radius, and there is no sharply defined radius for the orbit of the electron, as there is in the Bohr model. The position of the electron cannot be precisely located at any instant, but the probability distribution for its location can be calculated from the wavefunction by squaring it. The probability that the electron is found in a given small volume element dV at the position (x,y,z) is equal to the square of the wavefunction multiplied by the magnitude of the volume element:

$$\text{probability} = \psi(x,y,z)^2 dV$$

For the spherically symmetric s orbitals, the most useful shape for the volume element dV is a spherical shell of radius r and thickness dr. The volume of such a shell is

$$dV = 4\pi r^2 dr$$

since the area of the shell is $4\pi r^2$. Hence the probability that the electron is found at a distance between r and r + dr from the nucleus is

$$\text{probability} = 4\pi r^2 \psi(r)^2 dr$$

This probability is called the *radial distribution function,* and is shown in Figure 12-8.

The graphs of Figure 12-8 must be interpreted with great care, for they can be misleading. For instance, Figure 12-7 shows that the 1s and 2s orbitals have their maximum values at the nucleus (r = 0), and hence that the electron density per unit volume is a maximum there. On the other hand the radial distribution functions shown in Figure 12-8 are zero at the origin, and from an initial glance it might be thought that the electron density is therefore zero at the nucleus, a conclusion which is wrong. The correct interpretation of Figure 12-8 is that the volume of the spherical shell used to calculate the radial distribution function, $4\pi r^2 dr$, varies with the radius, and approaches zero at the origin. The most likely radius for the electron to be found is a_0 for the 1s orbital, and $5.24a_0$ for the 2s orbital, which may be compared with the Bohr radii for these states, a_0 and $4a_0$. The node in the orbital wavefunction for the 2s state shows up as zero electron density at a radius of $2a_0$.

These electron distribution functions are very diffuse, when compared with the precisely defined Bohr orbits. The 1s distribution is relatively compact, but even in this state significant electron density extends from the nucleus out to about $3a_0$. The 2s orbital is more diffuse, and the major part of the electron density extends out to at least $9a_0$. In all cases the electron density falls smoothly to zero at infinite distance from the nucleus and there is no definite radius beyond which the electron density is zero, although at large distances it is very small.

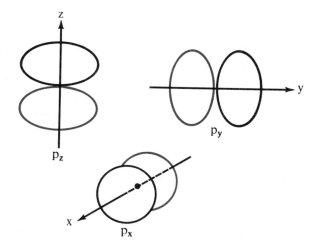

Figure 12-9 Sketches showing the angular dependence of the p_x, p_y and p_z wavefunctions. The negative parts of the function are shown coloured.

The 2p orbitals have two features which require discussion, the radial dependence of the wavefunction, and the angular dependence. Figure 12-7 shows the radial dependence of ψ and Figure 12-8 shows the corresponding radial density distribution. The wavefunction is zero at the origin, in contrast to the s wavefunctions, and has its maximum radial density at a slightly smaller radius than the 2s orbital. The angular dependence of the 2p orbital, and indeed of all p orbitals, is shown in Figure 12-9. It is difficult to show these functions accurately on a diagram in a way that exhibits their three-dimensional character, and the drawings in this figure are qualitative. The most important feature is that each of these three wavefunctions has two regions of opposite sign, separated by a nodal plane passing through the origin. These functions may usefully be compared with the (1,1) modes of vibration of the drum shown in Figure 12-6. There are three functions, which are identical in shape but differ in orientation. The three functions are labelled $2p_x$, $2p_y$ and $2p_z$ to show their orientation along the three axes; these labels also reflect the mathematical form of the wavefunctions, but that is not of concern here. These three functions do not correspond exactly to the three states $m = -1, 0$ and $+1$ which were mentioned previously, but are closely related to them mathematically, and are an equivalent set of functions in an algebraic sense.

12-8 MOLECULAR ORBITALS IN DIATOMIC MOLECULES

Electrons in molecules obey the same laws as electrons in atoms, and their behaviour is described similarly by wavefunctions. The wavefunctions for an electron in a molecule are called *molecular orbitals*. The electrons in a molecule are responsible for binding the atoms of the molecule together, and the discussion of the quantum theory of chemical bonding amounts to a study of the properties of molecular orbitals and their associated energy levels.

Calculations of accurate wavefunctions and energy levels in molecules require the use of a large computer, and are beyond this book. Yet worthwhile understanding can be obtained by simple considerations of the ways in which atomic orbitals combine, and of the effects of molecular symmetry on the properties of the molecular orbitals.

An important consideration in the study of the electronic structure of molecules is the symmetry of the molecule, or more precisely, the symmetry of the geometrical arrangement of the nuclei of the atoms which make up the molecule. Just as the symmetry of the frame of the drum shown in Figure 12-6 is evident in the patterns of vibration of the drum, so the symmetry of the nuclear framework of a molecule influences the standing wave patterns which are described by the molecular orbitals. The study of the influence of molecular symmetry on the molecular orbitals can only properly be carried out using *group theory*, which is again beyond the scope of this book, but some simple ideas will be used in the discussion.

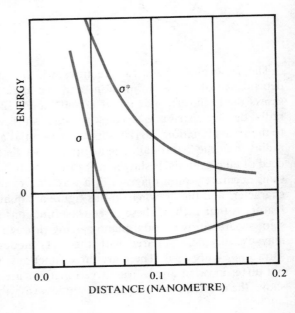

Figure 12-10 The dependence of the energies of the bonding σ and the antibonding σ^* states of the H_2^+ molecule on internuclear distance.

The theory of the chemical bond is best approached by considering first the primitive molecule H_2^+, which consist of two protons and a single electron. Although of little significance itself, the simplicity of this molecule makes it easy to examine the behaviour of electrons in molecules. Its molecular orbitals show many of the features of molecular orbitals in more complex molecules.

The molecular energies of H_2^+ corresponding to the lowest two electronic quantum states are shown in Figure 12-10. The first striking feature of this figure is that the molecular energy depends upon the distance between the two protons. This dependence was met previously in Figure 11-6. The quantized energy of the electron depends on the inter-proton distance because the potential energy of the electron in the Schrödinger equation depends on the position of the electron relative to *both* protons, and the molecular energy includes the potential energy of electrostatic repulsion of the two protons, which increases rapidly at small inter-proton distance. The lower curve, labelled σ, leads to the formation of a stable molecule, since the energy of the molecule is a minimum when the inter-proton distance is about $2a_0$. This electronic state of the molecule is therefore described as a *bonding* state. The upper curve, labelled σ^*, has no minimum, but decreases continuously towards larger values of the inter-proton distance. For a molecule in the σ^* state, the energy would be a minimum with the two protons infinitely far apart, and hence the molecule would dissociate into a hydrogen atom and a hydrogen ion. The electronic state is therefore called an *antibonding* state; the superscript star is attached to indicate an anti-bonding state.

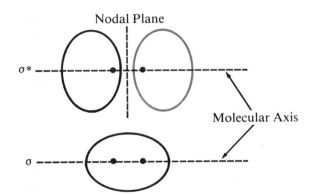

Figure 12-11 Sketches showing the bonding and antibonding molecular orbital wavefunctions for the H_2^+ molecule.

Figure 12-11 shows sketches of the σ and σ^* molecular orbitals in H_2^+ near the equilibrium interproton distance, from which their general characteristics can be drawn. Both orbitals are cylindrically symmetric about the molecular axis, and the orbitals in three dimensions can be generated by rotating these drawings about the molecular axis indicated. For diatomic molecules, the Greek symbol σ is used to refer to molecular orbitals of cylindrical type, in analogy with the use of s for atomic orbitals.

The σ orbital is ellipsoidal in shape, like an atomic s orbital which has been extended along the molecular axis. On the other hand the σ^* orbital has a nodal plane separating positive and negative parts of the wavefunction, and is

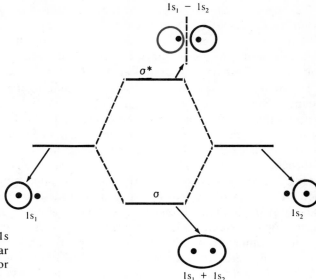

Figure 12-12 The overlap of hydrogen atom 1s atomic orbitals to form the σ and σ^* molecular orbitals, and the associated energy levels for one particular internuclear distance.

reminiscent of the shape of an atomic p orbital. As a result of this nodal plane, the wavefunction is numerically small in the region between the two protons, and therefore the electron density is small in this region. The σ orbital has no such nodal plane; the wavefunction is largest at the centre of the molecule between the two protons, and so the electron density is a maximum at the centre of the chemical bond. It is the concentration of negative charge density associated with the electrons in between the positively charged nuclei which leads to the lowering of energy shown in Figure 12-10 and the formation of a chemical bond.

The orbitals for the H_2^+ molecule can be calculated exactly by solving the Schrödinger equation with the appropriate potential energy function, but for more complicated molecules such calculations are more difficult for both mathematical and financial reasons. Hence approximations are necessary, and in any case are instructive in suggesting the essential features of the detailed calculations. The most useful approximation is called the *linear combination of atomic orbitals,* abbreviated to LCAO, and is readily illustrated using H_2^+ as an example. The lowest two orbitals for this molecule, shown in Figure 12-11, are closely related to the 1s state of the hydrogen atom, and can be approximated by the sum and difference, respectively, of 1s orbitals centred at the two protons. Designating the atomic orbitals on the two different protons as $1s_1$ and $1s_2$, the approximate molecular orbitals are written $1s_1 + 1s_2$ for the σ orbital, and $1s_1 - 1s_2$ for the σ^* orbital. The formation of these approximate molecular orbitals and their relative energies for one particular inter-proton distance are shown in Figure 12-12. It will be seen that when two similar atomic orbitals *overlap* in space, two molecular orbitals are formed, one of which is higher, and the other lower, in energy. The molecular orbital which is higher in energy is also generally anti-bonding in character.

In the H_2 molecule there are two electrons, which form the single covalent bond H – H. According to the Pauli principle, both these electrons can be accommodated in the σ orbital with opposite spins, and hence the electronic structure of the H_2 molecule is written $1\sigma^2$, where the superscript indicates the number of electrons in the molecular orbital, and the prefix "1" is a principal quantum number which identifies the orbitals of each type in order of increasing energy.

This theory helps to understand the fact that the helium diatomic molecule He_2 is not stable. The helium atom contains two electrons, and so the He_2 molecule would contain four electrons. By the Pauli principle, only two of these can be placed in the σ orbital, and the other two must be placed in the σ^* orbital. The energy of the molecule would be slightly greater than the energy of the two separated atoms, for the increase in energy of the σ^* orbital is numerically greater than the decrease in energy of the σ orbital. Hence such a molecule would dissociate at once.

Other well known diatomic molecules are those of the non-metals F_2, O_2 and N_2. The atoms of these elements contain 2p electrons as well as 1s and 2s electrons, and discussion of their bonding requires consideration of the ways in which p orbitals can overlap. There are three p orbitals, directed along the axes of a cartesian coordinate system. In discussing diatomic molecules, it is usual to take the z axis along the molecular axis. The p_z orbital therefore is cylindrical about the molecular axis, and the p_x and p_y orbitals are of a different *type*, or *species*, from the p_z orbital. A basic rule of molecular quantum mechanics is that orbitals of different types do not combine together, and so the overlap of the p orbitals can be considered in two parts.

The $2p_z$ and 2s atomic orbitals are both of σ type, and in a diatomic molecule, these orbitals on both atoms combine to form σ type molecular orbitals, both bonding and antibonding, as shown in Figure 12-13. There are

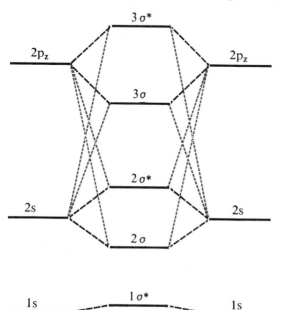

Figure 12-13 The energy levels of the σ and σ^* molecular orbitals for the diatomic molecules of the nonmetallic elements. The dashed lines show the molecular orbitals to which each atomic orbital makes a major contribution. The lighter dotted lines indicate contributions which are permitted by symmetry, but which have only minor influence on the character of the molecular orbitals.

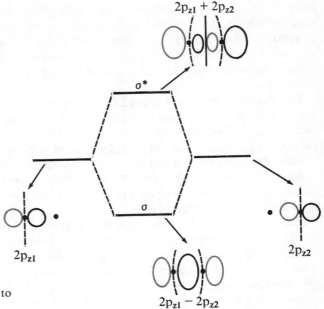

Figure 12-14 Overlap of $2p_z$ atomic orbitals to form σ and σ^* molecular orbitals.

four atomic orbitals involved, and so there are four molecular orbitals formed, labelled 2σ, $2\sigma^*$, 3σ and $3\sigma^*$. The molecular orbitals derived from the 1s orbitals are also shown so that the numbering system is clear, but these molecular orbitals take no part in the chemical bonding. The four atomic orbitals are connected by dashed lines to the atomic orbitals which make the major contribution to each molecular orbital. Thus the 2σ and $2\sigma^*$ orbitals are constructed primarily out of the 2s atomic orbitals in the manner shown in Figure 12-12, and the 3σ and $3\sigma^*$ molecular orbitals are most closely related to the $2p_z$ orbitals, as shown in Figure 12-14. However, the dotted lines in Figure 12-13 show that the 2σ and $2\sigma^*$ orbitals are influenced somewhat by the $2p_z$ atomic orbitals as well as the 2s atomic orbitals, and similarly for the upper pair of molecular orbitals. The mixing together of different atomic orbitals *on the same atom* is called *hybridization*.

The p_x and p_y atomic orbitals are directed at right angles to the axis of our diatomic molecule, and when they interact with each other they form molecular orbitals of a different type, called π orbitals. The Greek letter π is chosen as a name for these orbitals in analogy to the letter p used for the atomic orbitals from which they form. Both bonding and antibonding molecular orbitals of π type are formed, and correspond to the sum and difference of the atomic orbitals, as shown in Figure 12-15. As in the case of the σ molecular orbitals, the bonding π orbital has large electron density in the region between the two nuclei, and the antibonding π^* orbital has an additional nodal plane perpendicular to the bond, and so the electron density between the nuclei is small.

In Figure 12-15 only the p_x orbitals are considered, and so there is another pair of π molecular orbitals related to the p_y atomic orbitals. There is no dif-

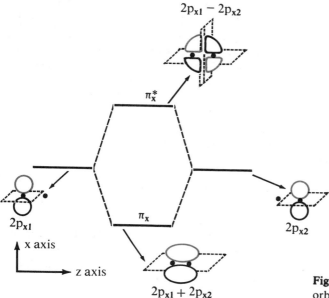

Figure 12-15 Overlap of $2p_x$ (or $2p_y$) atomic orbitals to form π and π^* molecular orbitals.

ference in the shapes of the π_x and π_y orbitals, except that the π_y orbital is rotated by 90° with respect to the π_x orbital. Since the two wavefunctions have the same shape, they also have the same energy. The same is true of the antibonding π_x^* and π_y^* orbitals. Hence the π and π^* energy levels are *doubly degenerate,* and each energy level corresponds to two orbitals.

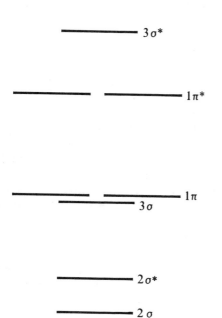

Figure 12-16 The valence shell molecular orbital energy levels for the diatomic molecules of the first row nonmetallic elements.

The relative positions of the π and π^* energy levels in the diatomic molecules of the non-metals F_2, and O_2 and N_2 are shown in Figure 12-16, and this diagram can be used to discuss the electronic structure and bonding in these molecules. The π levels are shown as two states at the same level to show their degeneracy. The 3σ and 1π are shown close together, and are inverted in several molecules, but this does not affect the argument which is to follow.

The fluorine molecule F_2 has 14 valence electrons from the 2s and 2p atomic levels of the fluorine atoms, and these 14 electrons are to be placed in the diagram in Figure 12-16 in a manner consistent with the Pauli principle, each orbital containing two electrons. All levels are filled except the top one, and so the electronic configuration can be written

$$F_2: (2\sigma)^2(2\sigma^*)^2(1\pi)^4(3\sigma)^2(1\pi^*)^4$$

The character of the bonding can be judged by counting the number of electrons in the bonding and antibonding orbitals. There are 8 bonding electrons and 6 antibonding electrons, making a net 2 electrons which are responsible for the chemical bonding. A pair of electrons is counted as a single bond, and so the molecular orbital picture is consistent with a single bond between the fluorine atoms.

Oxygen has 12 valence electrons, and so has the configuration:

$$O_2: (2\sigma)^2(2\sigma^*)^2(1\pi)^4(3\sigma)^2(1\pi^*)^2$$

In this molecule, there is therefore a net total of 4 electrons contributing to the bonding, and so the atoms are shown in the molecular formula as being joined by a double bond, O=O.

Nitrogen has 10 valence electrons, and the $1\pi^*$ orbital is empty. The configuration is:

$$N_2: (2\sigma)^2(2\sigma^*)^2(1\pi)^4(3\sigma)^2$$

There are 8 bonding electrons, and 2 antibonding electrons, making a net total of 6 bonding electrons, which form a triple bond. This agrees with the formula N≡N. Therefore, for these three diatomic molecules, the molecular orbital theory gives a satisfactory account of the usual valence of these non-metals.

The vast majority of molecules have an even number of electrons, and these electrons have their spins paired. This results from the application of the Pauli exclusion principle. Generally molecules with paired spins have no magnetic dipole moment, and interact only weakly with magnetic fields. However, in a few molecules there is opportunity for electron spins to become unpaired, leading to a non-zero magnetic dipole moment for the molecule, and oxygen is just such a case. This is readily understood if the electronic configuration of the molecule is drawn in the form of orbital "boxes," which were introduced in Section 10-4, and Hund's rule is applied to determine the spin orientations. This is done in Figure 12-17. Since the two electrons of highest energy are plac-

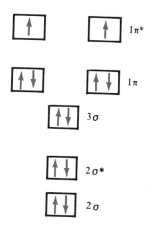

Figure 12-17 The filling of the molecular orbital energy levels in the oxygen molecule O_2, in accordance with Hund's rule. The highest energy pair of electrons is in a doubly degenerate π^* energy level, and are placed one in each state with parallel spins.

ed in the doubly degenerate $1\pi^*$ level, there are two boxes of equal energy available to contain these two electrons, and by Hund's rule the two electrons are placed one in each box, and their spins are parallel. As a result the oxygen molecule has a magnetic dipole moment, and so oxygen is a *paramagnetic* substance. By comparison, nitrogen and fluorine and the great majority of other substances are *diamagnetic*. This property of oxygen has been known for a long time, and it was one of the great successes of molecular orbital theory that this property was accounted for in a simple way.

12-9   MOLECULAR ORBITALS IN HYDRIDE MOLECULES

We must now extend the molecular orbital theory beyond the diatomic molecules of the elements, and this can be done in several ways. The hydrides of the non-metals are a class of molecules which illustrate many of the principles that are needed in the theory of more complicated molecules, and so we will consider the molecules HF, H_2O, and CH_4.

In these molecules, the hydrogen atom has only a 1s electron, whereas the other atom has 1s, 2s and 2p electrons. The 1s electron of the hydrogen atom lies at about the same energy as the highest occupied atomic orbitals on the other atom, the 2s and 2p orbitals. The major interactions in forming molecular orbitals is between orbitals of approximately equal energy, and so the orbitals of interest are formed by overlap of hydrogen 1s orbitals, or linear combinations of them, with the 2s and 2p orbitals of the other atom. As always, molecular symmetry has a further influence in determining which orbitals are permitted to combine.

The HF molecule is diatomic, like the diatomic molecules H_2 and F_2, and so the molecular orbitals are classified into σ and π types. The hydrogen 1s orbital is of σ type in the context of the molecular symmetry, and so can combine with the $2s_F$ and $2p_{zF}$ orbitals of the fluorine atom. The $2p_{xF}$ and $2p_{yF}$ orbitals are of π type, and so do not take part in the bonding because there are no hydrogen orbitals of π type except at very high energy. The molecular orbital

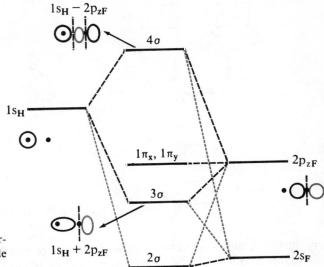

Figure 12-18 The valence shell molecular orbital energy levels in the hydrogen fluoride molecule.

energy levels for HF are shown in Figure 12-18. The 2σ orbital consists primarily of the $2s_F$ fluorine atomic orbital, and does not contribute greatly to the bonding. The two 1π orbitals are the $2p_{xF}$ and $2p_{yF}$ orbitals which are only slightly altered in shape by the presence of the hydrogen atom. The main contributor to the chemical bonding is the 3σ orbital formed from the overlap of the $1s_H$ and $2p_{zF}$ orbitals, with a small contribution from the $2s_F$ orbital as indicated by the dotted lines. The 4σ molecular orbital is the corresponding antibonding orbital.

The 3σ orbital does not have equal contributions from the $1s_H$ and $2p_{zF}$ orbitals, since these atoms are different and have different energy levels. The fluorine $2p_{zF}$ orbital is lower in energy than the hydrogen $1s_H$ level, and as a result the main contributor to the 3σ level is the fluorine orbital. Hence in this orbital the electronic charge density lies more towards the fluorine atom than the hydrogen atom, which is in agreement with the relative electronegativities of these two elements.

There are 8 valence electrons in the HF molecule, and these are placed in the lowest energy orbitals as indicated by the following configuration:

$$\text{HF: } (2\sigma)^2(3\sigma)^2(1\pi)^4$$

The chemical bond is due primarily to the 3σ orbital, and the 2σ and 1π orbitals contain the three pairs of non-bonding or "lone pair" electrons.

The water molecule is of bent shape, and so has different symmetry from the linear molecules that we have been considering. The first step in constructing molecular orbitals is to set up a system of axes, and to classify the atomic orbitals in the context of the molecular symmetry. The z axis is chosen to be the bisector of the H−O−H angle, and the y axis is chosen perpendicular to the plane of the molecule and passing through the oxygen atom. The atomic or-

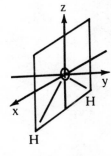

A water molecule lying in the xz plane of a system of axes.

TABLE 12-4 Atomic orbitals classified under the symmetry of the water molecule, particularly with reference to the planes of symmetry.

	Atomic orbital	xz plane	yz plane	type
oxygen:	2s	S	S	a_1
	$2p_x$	S	A	b_2
	$2p_y$	A	S	b_1
	$2p_z$	S	S	a_1
hydrogen:	$1s_1 + 1s_2$	S	S	a_1
	$1s_1 - 1s_2$	S	A	b_2

In this table S means symmetric and A means antisymmetric. The labels in the last column are drived from group theoretical arguments, and can be regarded simply as names at this stage.

bitals are classified according to their properties when reflected in the symmetry planes of the molecule, which are the xz plane (the plane of the molecule) and the yz plane (which is perpendicular to the plane of the molecule and bisects the H−O−H angle), and this is done in Table 12-4.

The oxygen orbitals $2s_O$ and $2p_{zO}$ are symmetric with respect to both planes, and are labelled a_1. The $2p_{xO}$ orbital, which is directed in the plane of the molecule, is antisymmetric across the yz plane, for this plane is the nodal plane of the orbital. The $2p_{yO}$ orbital is antisymmetric across the zx plane. These orbitals are given the labels b_2 and b_1 respectively. Thus the relevant oxygen atomic orbitals are of three types, a_1, b_1 and b_2. The labels used for these different types are derived from group theory.

The individual hydrogen orbitals do not have any special symmetry with regard to these planes of the water molecule, but linear combinations of them can be formed which do have well defined symmetry properties. These linear combinations are the sum $1s_1 + 1s_2$ and the difference $1s_1 - 1s_2$, which are classified as types a_1 and b_2 respectively. The sum orbital is symmetric with respect to both planes, and the difference orbital changes sign across the yz plane.

Once the classification of the atomic orbitals is complete, the molecular orbitals can be constructed by taking linear combinations of atomic orbitals of the same type. The simplest orbital is the b_1 orbital, for only the oxygen $2p_{yO}$ orbital is of this type. There are no hydrogen atomic orbitals of this type, and hence this orbital is a non-bonding orbital. Next to be considered is the b_2 molecular orbital, which consists of the oxygen $2p_{xO}$ orbital overlapping with the difference combination of the hydrogen 1s orbitals. Both bonding and antibonding orbitals exist, which are respectively the sum and difference of the oxygen orbital with the difference of the hydrogen orbitals.

The final type of molecular orbital is the a_1 type, and there are three atomic orbitals of this type listed in Table 12-4. Hence three molecular orbitals of a_1 type are expected, formed from the oxygen $2s_O$ and $2p_{zO}$ orbitals and the sum of the hydrogen 1s orbitals. The character of these three orbitals is best seen by forming first hybrid orbitals $2s + 2p_z$ and $2s - 2p_z$ on the oxygen atom. The

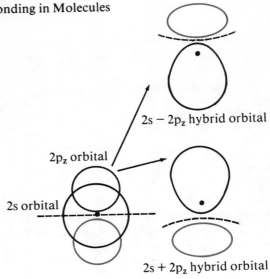

Figure 12-19 The formation of sp hybrid orbitals by mixing s and p orbitals on the same atom.

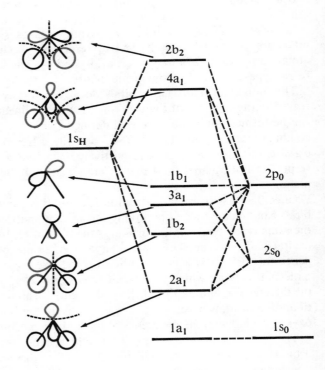

Figure 12-20 The molecular orbital energy levels in the water molecule.

resulting hybrid orbitals are shown in Figure 12-19. These two hybrid orbitals are of the same shape, are highly directional, and point in opposite directions. Since one s and one p orbital are involved in forming the hybrid orbital, the latter is referred to as an *sp hybrid* orbital. In the water molecule, one of these hybrid orbitals points along the z axis away from the hydrogen atoms, and the other points in the other direction, into the space between the two hydrogen atoms. The latter hybrid orbital can overlap with the sum of the hydrogen 1s orbitals, which is also of a_1 symmetry, to form both bonding and antibonding molecular orbitals.

Figure 12-20 shows the arrangement of the energy levels in the water molecule, and the characteristics of the corresponding molecular orbitals. The lowest level, $1a_1$, is simply the 1s level of the oxygen atom, which plays no part in the bonding. The $2a_1$ orbital is the bonding combination of the sp hybrid oxygen orbital with the sum of the hydrogen orbitals, and the $4a_1$ level is the corresponding antibonding level. The $1b_2$ orbital is a bonding orbital consisting of the oxygen $2p_x$ orbital overlapping with the difference of the hydrogen orbitals; the $2b_2$ orbital is the corresponding antibonding orbital. The $3a_1$ orbital is the sp hybrid which points away from the hydrogen atoms, and therefore is a non-bonding orbital. Finally, the $1b_1$ orbital is the oxygen $2p_y$ orbital which points at right angles to the plane of the molecule, and plays no part in the bonding of the molecule. There are 8 valence electrons in the water molecule, and the configuration of the molecule is therefore:

$$H_2O: (2a_1)^2(1b_2)^2(3a_1)^2(1b_1)^2$$

There are four bonding electrons, which account for the two single bonds in the molecule, and four electrons in non-bonding orbitals, corresponding to the two lone pairs.

The molecular orbital picture of water which has been outlined differs somewhat from the Lewis structure of this molecule. The molecular orbitals do not belong to individual bonds in this description, although it is possible to generate orbitals for individual bonds by mathematical transformations of the orbitals which have been described here. The lone pairs of electrons in the molecule are those in the $3a_1$ and $1b_1$ orbitals, which are of different shapes and different energies. This result is in contrast to the Lewis structure/VSEPR picture of the water molecule which places the lone pairs in two equivalent positions arranged tetrahedrally about the oxygen atom. There is nothing in the present description to suggest equivalence of the lone pairs or tetrahedral geometry. Spectroscopic studies of the water molecule support the prediction that there are four energy levels occupied by the valence electrons, and that the two lone pairs are not equal in energy.

Finally we turn our attention to the methane molecule, CH_4. The shape of this molecule is that of a regular tetrahedron of hydrogen atoms about the central carbon atom. The bonding is the result of the interaction of the 2s and 2p orbitals on the carbon atom with the 1s orbitals on the hydrogen atoms. This is a very symmetric molecule, and the characteristics of the molecular orbitals are dominated by the symmetry of the molecule. As for water, the first step in understanding the molecular orbitals is to define a set of axes, and to classify

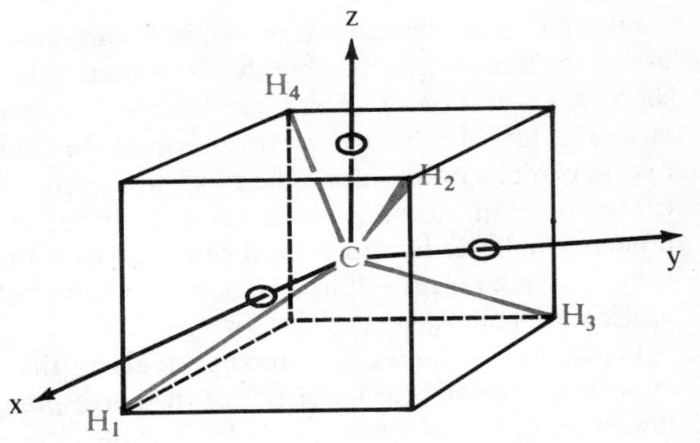

Figure 12-21 The relationship of the tetrahedral CH_4 molecule to a cube, and to a set of cartesian axes which are used to define the p orbitals. The hydrogen atoms have been numbered for the purposes of setting up linear combinations of definite symmetry.

TABLE 12-5 Atomic orbitals classified under the symmetry of the methane molecule.

	Atomic orbital	type
carbon:	2s	a
	$2p_x$ $2p_y$ $2p_z$	t_2
hydrogen:	$1s_1 + 1s_2 + 1s_3 + 1s_4$	a
	$1s_1 + 1s_2 - 1s_3 - 1s_4$ $-1s_1 + 1s_2 + 1s_3 - 1s_4$ $-1s_1 + 1s_2 - 1s_3 + 1s_4$	t_2

the atomic orbitals under the symmetry of the molecule. The regular tetrahedron is closely related to the cube, as has been pointed out previously. The hydrogen atoms can be regarded as being placed at the alternate corners of a cube, and then the cartesian x, y and z axes are placed so that they pass through the carbon atom at the centre of the cube, and the centres of the cube faces. This geometry is shown in Figure 12-21. The atomic orbitals on the carbon and hydrogen atoms are then classified according to their relationships under the symmetry of the tetrahedron. This classification is shown in Table 12-5.

The carbon atomic orbitals can be classified by consideration of rotations of the molecule through angles of 120° about the C-H bonds, for these rotations leave the molecule itself unchanged. The $2s_C$ orbital is unaffected by these rotations, and is classified as being of type a. The three 2p orbitals have the property that the rotation of 120° about the C—H bonds converts one into another. For instance, if the molecule is rotated about the C—H_2 axis in Figure 12-21, the $2p_x$ orbital is converted into the $2p_y$, the $2p_y$ is converted into the $2p_z$, and the $2p_z$ is converted into the $2p_x$. Thus these three orbitals are inextricably involved with each other by the symmetry of the molecule, and are in a sense forced to be equivalent to each other. The result of this is that they are forced to have the same energy, and so are associated with a triply degenerate energy level. These three orbitals are therefore grouped together in the table, and given the type name t_2, which indicates a triply degenerate type of orbital.

The individual hydrogen 1s orbitals do not have any special symmetry in this molecule, but linear combinations can be written down easily which do have definite symmetry. These linear combinations are indicated in Table 12-5. The a type combination of hydrogen orbitals matches the carbon 2s orbital, and the three t_2 combinations can be seen to match the shapes of the carbon 2p orbitals.

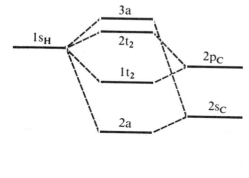

Figure 12-22 The molecular orbital energy levels for the methane molecule. It should not be forgotten that each t_2 energy level is triply degenerate, and can hold six electrons.

Once the atomic orbitals have been classified in this way, the construction of the molecular orbitals is straight-forward. There are molecular orbitals of type a constructed as linear combinations of the carbon 2s orbital and the sum of the hydrogen 1s orbitals; both bonding and antibonding combinations are formed. Then there are three triply degenerate t_2 type orbitals formed by taking a linear combination of a 2p orbital on the carbon atom with the appropriate linear combination of hydrogen orbitals of the same type. Again, both bonding and antibonding molecular orbitals are formed. The resulting energy level diagram is shown in Figure 12-22. The 1a level is the 1s orbital of the carbon atom, which takes no part in the bonding. The 2a and $1t_2$ are the bonding molecular orbitals of the two different types, and the upper two levels are the corresponding antibonding orbitals. The t_2 levels are triply degenerate, and can contain six electrons without violating the exclusion principle. There are 8 valence electrons in the methane molecule, and the electronic configuration is as follows:

$$CH_4: (2a)^2(1t_2)^6$$

As in the case of the water molecule, this molecular orbital picture seems to be at variance with the Lewis structure for the methane molecule. The Lewis structure suggests that there are four pairs of electrons with identical properties. The electronic structure of methane is often presented as four equivalent hybridized orbitals which each describe one of the four equivalent C—H bonds. Such a picture is certainly consistent with the Lewis structure, but can be misleading when the spectroscopic properties of the methane molecule are considered. There is evidence that there are two energy levels associated with the valence electrons in the methane molecule, not one. While the four C—H bonds in the molecule are equivalent to each other, the four pairs of electrons are not equivalent. Again, it is possible to rearrange the orbitals by hybridization so as to obtain four equivalent orbitals, but these rearranged orbitals do not give a correct account of some of the properties of the molecule.

FURTHER READING

The theory of chemical bonding is not easy to understand, because there is no one theory on which the student can focus his or her attention. There is the Lewis theory, which puts dots on paper to represent electrons in a way which is known to be incorrect. By rights such a simple minded theory should have been discarded long ago, and yet the Lewis theory remains part of the language of chemistry because it is so useful. The wave theory of chemical bonding was first formulated in the late 1920s, but a good simplified version of the theory is hard to find. There are several simplified approaches, but when compared with each other, these approaches sometimes seem to be contradictory.

In this difficult situation, the best that any student can do is to learn as much as possible of the language and ideas of the various theories at this stage. Later there will be opportunity to study the theory properly, and to apply the ideas to a number of different chemical problems.

The following books may be of assistance.

Chemical Bonds, by H. B. Gray (W. A. Benjamin, 1973). A readable and useful book at the elementary level.

The Organic Chemist's Book of Orbitals, by W. J. Jorgensen and L. Salem (Academic Press, 1973). This book contains computer-drawn sketches of molecular orbitals in a number of molecules, which might be useful to consult in conjunction with this chapter.

The PMO Theory of Organic Chemistry, by M. J. S. Dewar and R. C. Dougherty (Plenum Publishing Co. 1975). This is an advanced book, but Chapter 1 is very relevant.

Basic Principles of Organic Chemistry, by J. D. Roberts and M. C. Caserio (W. A. Benjamin, 1965). There is a useful discussion of chemical bonding in most introductory books on organic chemistry. This one is the source of the rhinoceros analogy used in the discussion of resonance.

PROBLEMS

1. For each of the following molecules and molecular ions draw a reasonable Lewis structure and predict the shape of the molecule on the basis of the VSEPR theory:

$$H_2S, COCl_2, SbCl_3, SnCl_2, ClO_4^-,$$
$$SO_3, CHCl_3, NOBr, HCN, H_5IO_6 \text{ or}$$
$$IO(OH)_5, SO_3^{2-}, XeF_2, XeF_4.$$

2. Consider the series of molecules and ions $PCl_3, PCl_4^+, PCl_5, PCl_6^-$. All the members of this series exist either in the vapour phase or as ions in the solid phase. Draw the Lewis structure and discuss the shape of each member of the series.

3. In the molecule of nitromethane, CH_3NO_2, the two nitrogen-oxygen distances are equal. Draw the Lewis structures for this molecule, and show that resonance must be considered in order to explain the observed bond distances.

4. Show that there is a resonance structure for CF_4 in which one F atom carries a negative formal charge, one F atom carries a positive formal charge, and there is one double bond. Make sure that your resonance structure obeys the octet rule.

5. Calculate formal charges for all the atoms in the structure of Al_2Cl_6.

6. Discuss the assignment of formal charges in the cases of molecules such as SO_2 and NO_3^- in which resonance must be considered.

7. Prove that the sum of the formal charges on all the atoms in an ion (or neutral molecule) is equal to the charge on the ion (or zero).

8. Aluminium hydroxide is insoluble in water, but dissolves in a solution which is either acidic or basic. This is an example of amphoteric behaviour. The reactions can be represented as follows:

$$Al(OH)_3 \, (s) + 3 \, H^+ \, (aq) \rightarrow Al^{3+} \, (aq) + 3 \, H_2O$$
$$Al(OH)_3 \, (s) + OH^- \, (aq) \rightarrow Al(OH)_4 \, (aq)$$

Discuss these reactions from the point of view of the Lewis theory of acids and bases.

9. Use electronegativity data to estimate the bond energy for a sulphur-carbon single bond. Estimate the enthalpy of formation of methanethiol, CH_3SH, the sulphur analogue of methanol.

[303 kJ mol^{-1}, -16 kJ mol^{-1}]

10. Estimate the bond length of the H_2^+ molecule and compare it to the bond length in H_2. Do these figures conform to the usual relationship between bond length and bond order? Would you expect the bond length in the molecular ion O_2^+ to be longer or shorter than in O_2?

11. Is it possible to form hydrogen bonded rings of methanol molecules instead of linear chains? Suggest a structure for the hydrogen bonded dimer of acetic acid.

12. The molecule of acetylene C_2H_2 is linear, and the orbitals in this molecule are classified in the same way as the orbitals in the diatomic molecules like F_2. Set up a system of axes, and classify the atomic orbitals on the carbon and hydrogen atoms as either σ or π. Hence construct molecular orbitals, and the electronic configuration for acetylene.

13. In planar molecules like ethylene, orbitals which are symmetric with respect to the plane of the molecule are classified as σ, and those which are antisymmetric are classified as π.

   The ethylene molecule consists of two CH_2 "fragments" each of which has the same shape as the water molecule, and therefore the same types of molecular orbitals. Construct molecular orbitals for the ethylene molecule by considering overlap of these CH_2 molecular orbitals. Use these orbitals to explain the nature of the double bond and suggest why internal rotation does not occur in ethylene.

XIII STRUCTURE AND BONDING IN CRYSTALS

The properties of liquids and gases have been described in Chapters Four and Seven, and the relationship between the bulk properties and molecular properties have been investigated. In this chapter we turn to the properties of crystals, and the way in which crystal properties are determined by the arrangement of the atoms and molecules of which they are composed.

Two aspects of crystals will be studied in this chapter. The first is the geometry of crystals, and the second is the nature of the forces which hold crystals together and determine their properties. Crystal geometry is a good deal more complicated than molecular geometry because crystals consist of an essentially infinite number of atoms or molecules arranged in a regular way, and it is not easy to see the various aspects of the crystal structure which are implied by its regularity. The full description of crystal geometry requires extensive use of symmetry arguments and other mathematical techniques which are beyond the scope of this book, but a start can be made on the procedures used for the description of crystal structures.

13-1 THE GEOMETRY OF CRYSTALS

The most remarkable visible property of crystals is their geometrical shape. A visit to a museum display of minerals, which is highly to be recommended, will show the great diversity of shapes which are found in natural crystals, and the striking nature of the regularity of these shapes. Crystals generally have flat surfaces, and these surfaces are arranged in definite relationships to each other. A given mineral may be found in all sorts of shapes and sizes of crystals, but for this mineral the faces are found to have characteristic forms or shapes, and the angles between the faces are constant and characteristic. The shapes of crystals have been studied for a long time, and a system of classification of crystals has been developed independently of knowledge of the arrangements of the atoms or molecules in the crystal.

It was suggested by the French crystallographer René Haüy at the end of the eighteenth century that crystals are composed of fundamental units arranged in a perfectly regular array, and that the constant angles between faces are a property of this regularity. Haüy called his fundamental unit a "molecule intégrante," and in modern language it is called the *unit cell*. This view of crystal structure is essentially correct: the characteristic properties of a crystal are related to the regularity of the arrangement of the atoms, ions or molecules of which the crystal is composed. This suggests that crystals are exactly opposite to gases. In a gas, the molecules are widely separated from each other, and have random positions and velocities at any instant. In a crystal, on the other hand, the molecules are in close contact with each other, each molecule is placed in a definite position in relation to its neighbours, and the motion of each molecule must be highly correlated with that of its neighbours.

The study of the atomic or molecular arrrangements in crystals is called *crystallography*, and has become a highly developed part of science since the application of X-ray diffraction and neutron diffraction methods in conjunction with powerful large-scale computers. The basis of crystallography is the geometry of regular patterns or arrays. In order to fix our ideas, consider the simple example of an array in two dimensions shown in Figure 13-1. The array consists of a pattern which is repeated regularly across the page, and would extend forever in all directions if the page did not come to an end at the edges. A

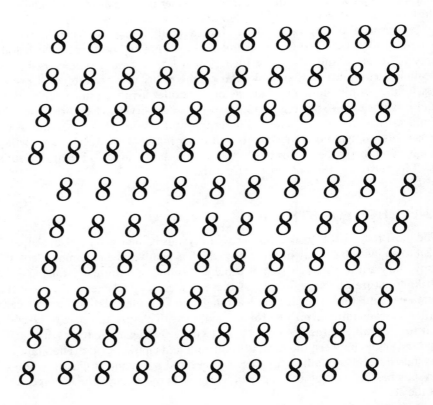

Figure 13-1 A regular array in which a pattern is repeated. The array is assumed to continue in all directions in the plane of the page without any boundaries.

picture of a crystal, much magnified, would resemble this diagram. There would be a drawing representing an atom or group of atoms, and this drawing would be repeated regularly in all directions throughout three-dimensional space.

The full drawing of the array in Figure 13-1 is unnecessarily detailed as a description of the array, for it repeats the same information more than is necessary to define the array. Crystallographers have developed methods for simplifying such a diagram, and reducing description of arrays to the minimum amount of information. The first step in the simplification is the definition of the *lattice*. Suppose a piece of tracing paper is placed over Figure 13-1 and a point is marked on the tracing paper for each repeated figure, at a fixed place on each figure. It does not matter which point on the repeated figure is chosen, but the same point on each figure must be used in drawing the lattice on the tracing paper. When this has been done, the tracing paper carries a set of points which describes the way in which the repeating figures in the array are placed in relation to each other. Given the lattice of points on the tracing paper, and *one* drawing of the repeated figure, the entire array of Figure 13-1 can be easily reconstructed. Figure 13-2 shows the lattice which describes

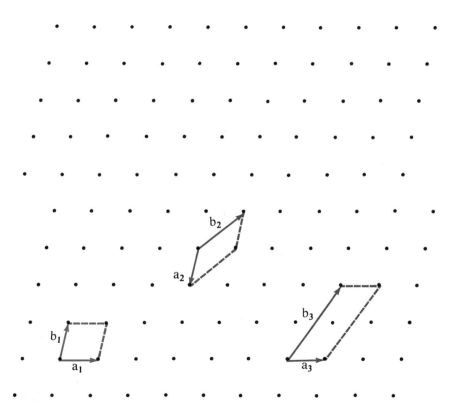

Figure 13-2 The lattice for the array shown in Figure 13-1.

the array in Figure 13-1, and the reader should check the relationship between these two figures with a piece of tracing paper.

The two essential features of the array in Figure 13-1 are that if any one of the repeated figures is examined, it is identical to every other figure in the array, and its *surroundings* are identical to the surroundings of every other figure in the array. The process of representing the array by (a) the drawing of just one of the repeated figures, and (b) the drawing of the lattice, shows these two features of the array separately. The repetition of the figure means that it is only necessary to draw it once, and the lattice carries with it the property that the surroundings of a given point are identical to the surroundings of any other point.

The drawing of the lattice shown in Figure 13-2 can itself be simplified, for it is not necessary to draw the whole lattice to specify and describe it precisely. Suppose one point in the lattice is chosen. Let a and b be two vectors from that point to two other points of the lattice. The vectors a and b must not be collinear, and normally they are chosen to refer to points which are close to the reference point. Then *all* points of the lattice can be represented by position vectors r which are linear combinations of the two vectors a and b:

$$r = xa + yb \tag{1}$$

where x and y are integers or rational fractions. There is a variety of pairs of vectors a and b which can be used to generate the lattice in this way, some of which are shown superimposed on the lattice in Figure 13-2. Any one pair of vectors can be used in equation (1) to express the positions of all points of the lattice with respect to the original point chosen: a_1 and b_1, or a_2 and b_2, or a_1 and b_3. Such a pair of vectors defines a parallelogram. If this parallelogram is no bigger than any other parallelogram defined by lattice vectors, then it constitutes a *primitive unit cell* for the lattice. A primitive unit cell has one lattice point associated with it, which may be placed anywhere in relation to the cell but is often placed at a corner of the cell. In Figure 13-2, the pair of vectors a_1 and b_1 defines a primitive unit cell, and so does the pair a_2 and b_2. The pair of vectors a_1 and b_3 define a parallelogram which has twice the area of the other two parallelograms which have been defined, and is not a primitive cell, although with the two associated lattice points it can be used to define the entire lattice just as well as the primitive cells.

If a and b are two vectors which define a primitive cell, the entire lattice can be reconstructed using equation (1) with x and y taking integer values. From the lattice and the repeated figure, the original array can be reconstructed. Hence the original array is completely defined by specifying the unit cell (by giving the vectors a and b) and the figure which is repeated.

In some cases it is desirable to use a unit cell which is not primitive. Although a primitive unit cell is the simplest way of defining a lattice, it sometimes happens that the lattice has elements of symmetry which the primitive unit cell does not have. Since symmetry has such profound importance in studying the properties of crystals, it is highly desirable that the unit cell which is used to specify the lattice has the same symmetry as the lattice as a whole. The lattice shown in Figure 13-3 is obviously rectangular in nature, with a characteristic angle of exactly 90° between certain lattice vec-

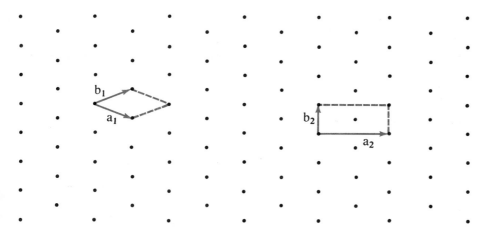

Figure 13-3 The centred rectangular lattice. The unit cell defined by the vectors a_1, b_1 is a primitive cell, but does not reflect the rectangular symmetry of the lattice. It is usual to use the non-primitive unit cell defined by a_2, b_2 in such a case, in order that the lattice symmetry be obvious.

tors. The lattice vectors a_1, b_1 in the figure define a primitive unit cell which is certainly a valid way of specifying the lattice, but does not directly show the existence of the right angles in the full lattice. In such a case it is conventional to choose a non-primitive unit cell such as that defined by the vectors a_2, b_2 which shows clearly the overall symmetry of the lattice. This unit cell contains two lattice points, and it is necessary to specify the positions of both of these points within the unit cell, or at least their relative positions, in order to define the lattice. For the lattice shown in Figure 13-3, if one point is placed at the origin of the cell, the other is in the centre of the cell. Hence this lattice is called the "centred rectangular lattice."

Crystals are three dimensional arrays of atoms, ions or molecules, and three dimensional lattices are required for their description. The unit cell of a three dimensional lattice requires three lattice vectors a, b and c for its specification. In many cases these vectors are chosen so that the unit cell is primitive, but for most of the simple crystal structures there is a good deal of symmetry in the crystal, and the symmetry in the associated lattice can only be displayed by using a non-primitive unit cell which itself has the symmetry of the crystal. It can

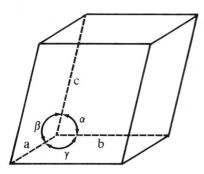

Figure 13-4 The lengths and angles which specify the size and shape of the unit cell.

TABLE 13-1   The Seven Crystal Systems

System	Unit Cell Lengths	Unit Cell Angles
Cubic	$a=b=c$	$\alpha=\beta=\gamma=90°$
Tetragonal	$a=b\neq c$	$\alpha=\beta=\gamma=90°$
Orthorhombic	$a\neq b\neq c$	$\alpha=\beta=\gamma=90°$
Monoclinic	$a\neq b\neq c$	$\alpha=\gamma=90°$, $\beta\neq90°$
Triclinic	$a\neq b\neq c$	$\alpha\neq\beta\neq\gamma\neq90°$
Rhombohedral	$a=b=c$	$\alpha=\beta=\gamma\neq90°$
Hexagonal	$a=b\neq c$	$\alpha=\beta=90°$, $\gamma=120°$

be shown from a study of the symmetry of lattices that there are only fourteen distinct lattices which can be constructed in three dimensional space. These fourteen lattices are called Bravais lattices after the physicist who first catalogued them. The lattices can be classified into seven *crystal systems*, according to the shape of the unit cell and its symmetry. In this account, symmetry considerations will be ignored. The shape of the unit cell is governed by the lengths of vectors *a*, *b* and *c*, and the angles between them, α, β and γ, which are defined in Figure 13-4.

There are seven crystal systems, and the characteristic properties of the corresponding unit cells are listed in Table 13-1. The first five systems listed represent progressive steps in the destruction of the symmetry of the cube. First the lengths of the edges are made unequal in steps while the angles remain right angles, and then the angles are changed from 90° in two steps. The sixth, rhombohedral, system can be considered as a cube which has been distorted by being stretched or compressed along a diagonal through its centre. The seventh, hexagonal, system has the property that when several unit cells are packed together side by side, the corners of the cells form regular hexagons because the angle γ is equal to 120°.

The unit cells of the fourteen Bravais lattices are shown in Table 13-2, classified according to crystal system. The simplest lattices are the seven primitive lattices with a single lattice point per unit cell. In the drawings of the unit cells, a lattice point is shown at all eight corners of the cell in order to help in visualizing the lattice, but seven of these eight lattice points belong to neighbouring unit cells. The non-primitive lattices shown in Table 13-2 are body-centred, end-centred and face-centred unit cells in certain systems, in which additional lattice points are found at the centre of the cell, or at the centre of certain faces of the cell. Again, it should be noticed that in the face- centred and end-centred cells, more points are shown than properly belong to a single unit cell.

With this discussion of lattices and unit cells as a basis, we can now turn to the description of some crystal structures.

**TABLE 13-2   The Unit Cells of the Fourteen Bravais Lattices,
Classified According to Crystal System**

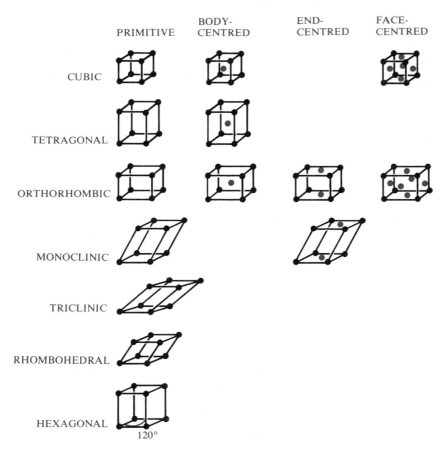

13-2   THE CRYSTAL STRUCTURES OF THE METALS

The three common crystal structures of the metals are the *cubic close-packed* (CCP) structure, the *body-centred cubic* (BCC) structure, and the *hexagonal close-packed* (HCP) structure. Some of the properties of these structures are summarized in Table 13-3, and the metals which crystallize in these structures are indicated in the periodic table in Figure 13-5. There are no very strong periodic trends in the occurrence of these crystal structures although metals in the same column of the table generally have the same structure. The majority of the common and important metals are cubic, either body-centred or face-centred, but the important metals magnesium, zinc, titanium and zirconium are hexagonal. The mechanical properties of a metal such as its Young's modulus, hardness, and behaviour when machined, are not directly related to its crystal structure, although the crystal structure plays a part in determining the nature of the defects in the metal which do influence these properties.

TABLE 13-3 The Three Common Crystal Structures of the Metals

Common Name	Lattice	Atoms per Lattice Point	Atoms per Unit Cell	Coordination Number	Close Packed?
Cubic Close-Packed (CCP)	Face-Centred Cubic	1	4	12	Yes
Body Centred Cubic (BCC)	Body-Centred Cubic	1	2	8	No
Hexagonal Close-Packed (HCP)	Primitive Hexagonal	2	2	12	Yes

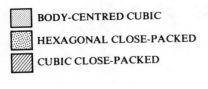

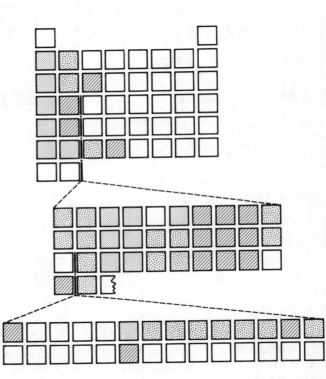

Figure 13-5 Periodicity in the occurrence of the three commonest crystal structures of the metals, at ordinary temperatures and pressures. It should be noted that many metals adopt different structures at high temperatures or pressures.

In the body-centred cubic structure, one atom is associated with each lattice point of the body-centred cubic lattice. The structure can be pictured by placing an atom at each lattice point of the unit cell of the body-centred cubic lattice shown in Table 13-2. There are two atoms per unit cell, and each atom has eight nearest neighbour atoms. The atom at the centre of the unit cell has as neighbours the eight atoms at the corners of the unit cell. The atoms at the corners of the unit cell also have eight nearest neighbours, namely the atoms at the centres of the eight unit cells which meet at that corner. Every atom in the crystal has the same surroundings, since they are all associated one-to-one with a lattice point, and every lattice point has the same surroundings.

The commonest metal which crystallizes in the body-centred cubic structure is iron, but several other d-block metals, including vanadium and chromium, and the Group I alkali metals also are found to have this structure.

The density of a metal as measured in the laboratory must be equal to the average density of the unit cell of the crystal structure. Hence knowing the density of the metal, the mass of an atom of the metal, and number of atoms per unit cell, the size of the unit cell can be calculated. The argument is shown in the following example.

Example 13-1 The density of iron is 7870 kg m^{-3}. Calculate the size of the unit cell, given that the structure is body-centred cubic.

Since the molar mass of iron is 55.8 g mol^{-1}, the mass of the unit cell is

$$\text{mass} = \frac{55.8 \text{ g mol}^{-1}}{6.02 \times 10^{23} \text{ atom mol}^{-1}} \times 2 \text{ atom/unit cell}$$

$$= 1.85 \times 10^{-22} \text{ gram/unit cell}$$

Since the average density of the unit cell is equal to 7870 kg mol^{-1}, the volume of the unit cell is

$$\text{volume} = \frac{1.85 \times 10^{-22} \text{ g}}{7.870 \times 10^{6} \text{ g m}^{-3}}$$

$$= 2.35 \times 10^{-29} \text{ m}^3$$

Since the unit cell is cubic, the length of the unit cell edge is

$$\text{length} = (2.35 \times 10^{-29})^{\frac{1}{3}}$$

$$= 2.86 \times 10^{-10} \text{ m}$$

$$= 0.286 \text{ nm}$$

This reasoning can be carried further to obtain the diameter of the atoms of iron in the metallic state. In order to do this each atom is supposed to be a hard sphere situated at the lattice site, and packed as close together as possible consistent with the lattice, so that each atom is in contact with its nearest neighbours. In the case of the BCC lattice the distance between nearest neighbour atoms is equal to the distance from the centre of the unit cell to a corner of the unit cell, or half the length of the body diagonal of the cell.

Example 13-2 Calculate the radius of the iron atom in the metallic state (the "metallic radius" of iron).

The total length of the body diagonal of the unit cell is $\sqrt{3}$ times the length of the edge of the cube, by Pythagoras' theorem, and the distance between nearest neighbours is half of this. Hence distance between nearest neighbours $= \frac{1}{2}\sqrt{3} \times 0.286$ nm

$$= 0.248 \text{ nm}$$

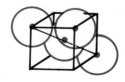

The distance between the centres of two equal spheres in contact is equal to twice the radius of the spheres, and so the radius of the iron atoms is half of 0.248 nm, or 0.124 nm.

The arguments used in these two examples have been used in several other ways in crystallography. The length of the edge of the unit cell can be measured to high accuracy by means of X-ray diffraction, and these measurements can be used to obtain accurate values of the Avogadro constant, using crystals of known structure. If the detailed structure of a crystal is not known, a knowledge of the size of the unit cell and of the measured density of the crystal allows calculation of the number of atoms in the unit cell, which is useful information in determining the detailed structure.

The body-centred cubic structure does not produce the highest packing density. When we try to pack spheres together in three dimensions so as to take up the smallest possible space, the hexagonal close-packed and cubic close-packed structures are generated naturally, and this close-packing of spheres will therefore be discussed before describing the structures formally.

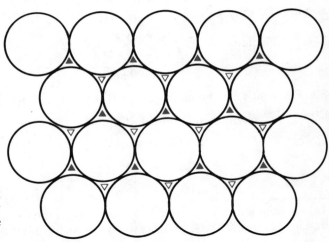

Figure 13-6 The close-packing of spheres in a plane. The small triangular symbols identify the two types of triangular site on which the second layer of spheres may be placed.

The first stage of building a close-packed structure is to build a close-packed layer of spheres in a plane. This is done by packing the spheres in a line, and then extending the packing out into the plane as shown in Figure 13-6. Each sphere is in contact with six adjacent spheres, and the occurrence of equilateral triangles and regular hexagons is apparent. Each trio of spheres in contact defines an equilateral triangle. These triangles are alternately pointing in opposite directions, as indicated by the symbols △ and ▼ placed in the centre of each triangle. When the second layer of spheres is placed on top of the first, there are two possible sites to place the first sphere, since in close packing each sphere of the second layer lies on top of one or other of these triangular sites, in contact with three spheres of the first layer. Once the site of the first sphere of the second layer is chosen, all the spheres of the second layer lie on sites of the same type. The situation after the second layer has been added is shown in

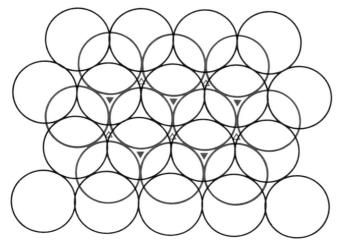

Figure 13-7 The close packing of two planar layers of spheres in a plane. The first, lower, layer is shown by dotted circles, and the second layer is shown by full circles. The small triangular symbols identify the two types of triangular site in the second layer, on which the spheres of the third layer may be placed.

Figure 13-7. Again, there are two types of site on which the third layer can be placed, and these are identified by the symbols △ and ▼ in Figure 13-7. These two choices of site lead to two different structures, the hexagonal close-packed and cubic close-packed structures.

If the spheres of the third layer are placed on the sites labelled ▼, they lie directly above the spheres of the first layer. This choice of site for the third layer leads to the hexagonal close-packed structure. Since the atoms of the third layer of spheres lie directly above the atoms of the first layer, only the second layer is displaced, and the stacking of layers can be represented by the sequence of letters

$$.\,.\,.\,.\,.\,A\ B\ A\ B\ A\ B\ A\ B\ A\ B\ A\ B\,.\,.\,.\,.\,.$$

where each letter represents a layer in the crystal.

Each sphere in this structure has twelve nearest neighbours which it touches, six arranged hexagonally in the same plane, three in the plane below, and three in the plane above. This structure is called close-packed, because it is impossible to pack spheres into any structure of higher density, and hexagonal because it retains the hexagonal symmetry of the individual close-packed planes, such as that shown in Figure 13-6.

The unit cell of the hexagonal close-packed structure is shown in Figure 13-8. The lengths of the a and b vectors are equal, because of the hexagonal symmetry. For hexagonal close-packing of spheres, the c/a ratio is equal to $\sqrt{8/3} = 1.633$. Most metals which crystallize in this structure have c/a ratios which are slightly different from this value, but are nevertheless described as having the HCP structure. There are two atoms associated with each lattice point, and neither of them is placed at the corner of the unit cell in Figure 13-8. The positions of the atoms (or spheres) with respect to the origin of the unit cell are given by the vectors

$$\tfrac{1}{3}\,a + \tfrac{2}{3}\,b + \tfrac{3}{4}\,c$$

$$\tfrac{2}{3}\,a + \tfrac{1}{3}\,b + \tfrac{1}{4}\,c$$

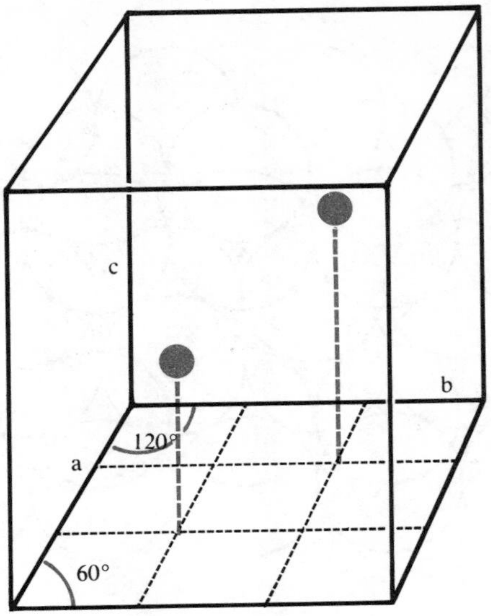

Figure 13-8 The unit cell of the hexagonal close-packed structure. Although the hexagonal lattice is a primitive one, with one lattice point per unit cell, there are two atoms (or spheres) for every lattice point in this structure. Neither atom is placed at the origin of the cell in this representation of the structure.

A projection of this unit cell and the atoms within it can be seen in the diagram of Figure 13-7 if the parallelogram formed by joining four adjacent △ symbols is drawn.

If the spheres of the third layer, in building up the close-packed structure, are placed over the sites labelled △ in Figure 13-7, instead of the sites labelled ▼, the cubic close-packed structure results rather than the hexagonal close-packed structure. In this case the spheres of the third layer do not lie above spheres of either the first or second layers. The sequence of letters representing the stacking of the layers is therefore

. . . . . A B C A B C A B C A B C A B C . . . . .

◌ LAYER A
◯ LAYER B
◯ LAYER C

Figure 13-9 The face-centred cubic unit cell as it appears in the cubic close-packing of spheres. This view is perpendicular to the close-packed planes, as in Figures 13-6 and 13-7. This direction lies along the body diagonal of the cubic unit cell, passing through opposite corners and the centre of the cell.

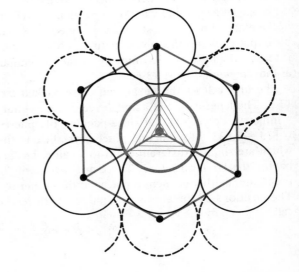

The way in which a cubic structure results from this packing sequence is not obvious. In Figure 13-9, parts of three close-packed planes with the appropriate stacking sequence are drawn so as to show that the centres of the spheres lie on the lattice points of the face-centred cubic unit cell shown in Table 13-2. There is one sphere per lattice point, and since there are four lattice points per unit cell in the representation in Table 13-2, there are four spheres or atoms in the cubic unit cell of this structure. The close-packed cubic structure can be generated by placing an atom at each lattice point in the face-centred cubic lattice, and in many books this structure is called the face-centred cubic structure.

It is difficult for a reader to grasp fully the nature of these crystal structures without examining models of them, or even better, building models of them. These are three dimensional structures, and very difficult to represent realistically on paper.

Example 13-3 Copper has a density of 8930 kg m^{-3}, and crystallizes in the cubic close-packed structure. Calculate the length of the edge of the unit cell.

Following the procedure used in Example 13-1, the mass of the unit cell is

$$\text{mass} = \frac{63.55 \text{ g mol}^{-1}}{6.02 \times 10^{23} \text{ atom mol}^{-1}} \times 4 \text{ atom/unit cell}$$

$$= 4.22 \times 10^{-22} \text{ g/unit cell}$$

Hence the volume of the unit cell is

$$\text{volume} = \frac{4.22 \times 10^{-22} \text{ g/unit cell}}{8.930 \times 10^{6} \text{ g m}^{-3}}$$

$$= 4.72 \times 10^{-29} \text{ m}^3/\text{unit cell}$$

and the length of the edge of this cubic unit cell is

$$\text{length} = (4.72 \times 10^{-29})^{\frac{1}{3}}$$

$$= 3.61 \times 10^{-10} \text{ m}$$

$$= 0.361 \text{ nm}$$

Example 13-4 Calculate the atomic radius in metallic copper from the size of the unit cell.

From study of the drawing in Figure 13-9, or better still from examination of a model of the cubic close-packed structure, it can be seen that the nearest neighbour atoms are in contact across the face diagonal of the cubic unit cell. The length of the face diagonal is $\sqrt{2} \times 0.361$ nm or 0.510 nm, and this distance is equal to the length of four atomic radii. Hence the radius of the copper atom in metallic copper is a quarter of this length, or 0.127 nm.

When a metal is heated, or subjected to very high pressure, it may change its crystal structure from that indicated in Figure 13-5 to some other structure. For example, when iron is heated to high temperatures, it changes from the BCC structure to the CCP structure, then changes back to the BCC structure, before it finally melts. A change of crystal structure is an example of a *change of phase*.

13-3   THE STRUCTURES OF IONIC CRYSTALS

Ionic crystals are found in a much wider variety of crystal structures than the metals, and only a few of these structures can be described here. The principles used in specifying ionic crystal structures are the same as those introduced for the metallic structures, but with the additional feature that there are two types of ions whose positions must be specified, the anions and the cations. The close-packing of spheres, which was useful in understanding the properties of two of the metallic structures, can also be used in the description of several of the important ionic structures.

Ionic compounds can be classified according to the stoichiometric proportions of the cations and anions as 1:1, 1:2, etc, and compounds within each classification often have crystallographic features in common. The 1:1 salts are simplest to describe, and that is where we will start. Four structures account for a large number of the 1:1 salts, and will be described in some detail. These structures are named after well known salts or minerals. The four structures are *sodium chloride* structure, the *caesium chloride* structure, the *zinc blende* structure, and the *wurtzite* structure. The minerals zinc blende and wurtzite both consist of zinc sulphide, ZnS, but they have different crystal structures and are therefore different phases of this compound.

The caesium chloride structure is shown in Figure 13-10. It is a cubic structure, and is based upon the primitive cubic lattice. The structure can be developed from the lattice by placing the cation (caesium ion) at the lattice point, and the anion (chloride ion) at points displaced by the vector

$$\tfrac{1}{2}\,a + \tfrac{1}{2}\,b + \tfrac{1}{2}\,c$$

from the lattice point. Thus in Figure 13-10 the cations occupy the corners of the unit cell, and the anion is situated at the centre of the unit cell. Each ion is

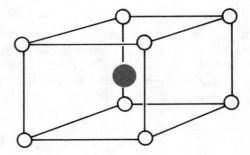

Figure 13-10 The unit cell of the caesium chloride structure. One of the ions is placed at the lattice point at the corner of the cell, and the other ion is placed at the centre of the cell.

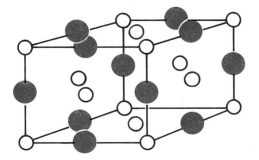

Figure 13-11 The cubic unit cell of the sodium chloride structure. Each ion forms a cubic close-packed structure, and the other ion is situated in the octahedral holes.

surrounded by a cube of eight ions of opposite charge. If the anions and cations are considered separately, each forms a primitive cubic lattice.

The sodium chloride structure is shown in Figure 13-11. It is generated in the same way as the caesium chloride structure by associating a pair of ions with a lattice point, but in this case the lattice concerned is the face-centred cubic lattice. In the figure, the cations have been placed at the lattice points, and the anions are at points displaced by the vector $\frac{1}{2}$ a from the lattice points. Each ion is surrounded by an octahedron of six ions of the opposite charge, and both the cations and anions form cubic close-packed structures. In the cubic close-packing of spheres discussed in the last section, two kinds of spaces are found between the spheres. The spaces at the centres of tetrahedra of four spheres, at sites marked ▼ in Figure 13-7, are tetrahedral in shape and are often described as *tetrahedral holes*. *Octahedral holes* are also found in cubic close-packing, and are most easily seen at the centre of the face-centred cubic lattice shown in Table 13-2. The sodium chloride structure can be described as a cubic close-packed structure of one type of ion, with the other ion situated in the octahedral holes.

In the cubic close-packed structure, and in the hexagonal close-packed structure, there is one octahedral hole and two tetrahedral holes for each atom. The zinc blende structure can be described as a cubic close-packed structure of one type of ion (either cation or anion) with the ions of opposite type occupying half of the tetrahedral holes. In the face-centred cubic unit cell, shown in Table 13-2, there are four lattice points, and the eight tetrahedral holes are to be found near the eight corners of the cell. In the zinc blende structure shown in Figure 13-12, every second one of these tetrahedral holes is occupied. Similarly

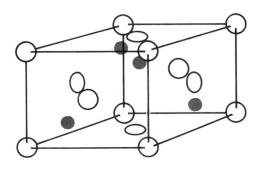

Figure 13-12 The zinc blende structure. The sulphide ions, which are designated by large spheres, form a cubic close-packed structure, and the zinc ions occupy half the tetrahedral holes, which in this diagram are to be found towards the corners of the cubic cell.

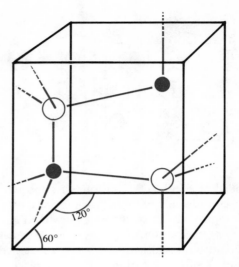

Figure 13-13 The unit cell of the hexagonal wurtzite structure. This drawing should be compared carefully with that in Figure 13-8. Each type of ion is arranged in a hexagonal close- packed structure, and the other ions are situated in the tetrahedral holes. Each ion is surrounded by a tetrahedron of the opposite ions. In this representation of the structure, none of the ions are at the lattice points at the corners of the unit cell.

the wurtzite structure, shown in Figure 13-13, can be described as a hexagonal close-packed structure of one type of ion, with the ions of opposite type occupying half the tetrahedral holes.

Table 13-4 lists some 1:1 compounds classified according to their crystal structures. As with the metals, many salts change their crystal structure at high temperature or pressure, and some salts are found in more than one crystal structure at ordinary conditions of temperature and pressure, a phenomenon called *polymorphism*.

TABLE 13-4   Some Compounds Forming Simple Ionic Crystal Structures

CsCl Structure	CsCl, CsBr, CsI. TlCl, TlBr, TlI. NH_4Cl, NH_4Br.
NaCl Structure	Group I halides except those mentioned above AgF, AgCl, AgBr. NH_4I Oxides and sulphides of Group II metals (except Be).

Zinc blende structure	ZnO, ZnS, ZnSe, ZnTe
	     CdS, CdSe, CdTe
	          HgS, HgSe, HgTe
	AlP, AlAs, AlSb
	GaP, GaAs, GaSb
	InP, InAs, InSb
	SiC

Wurtzite structure	ZnO, ZnS, ZnTe CdS, CdSe AlN, GaN, InN BeO

13-4   THE STRUCTURES OF MOLECULAR CRYSTALS

The structures of molecular crystals are more complicated than those of ionic crystals, and few generalizations are possible. Molecules are more complicated in shape than the spherical ions which were discussed in the last section, and the packing together of complex molecular shapes is hard to describe and to visualize. However, the mathematical techniques for describing the structures of molecular crystals are no different from those used for metals or ionic crystals. The lattice is specified, from amongst the Bravais lattices shown in Table 13-2. Then the positions of the atoms in the repeated figure (usually a molecule) are specified with respect to the lattice points. Many molecules do not have much symmetry, and do not form highly symmetrical crystals. Many of the lattices found in molecular crystals are of low symmetry compared with the cubic and hexagonal lattices which are common in ionic crystals.

As an example of a molecular crystal, consider iodine, with molecular formula I_2, which is a crystalline solid at room temperature. The unit cell is orthorhombic, and has unequal a, b and c axes at right angles to each other. The structure is based on the end-centred orthorhombic lattice, shown in Table 13-2. There are two lattice points per unit cell, and two molecules associated with each lattice point, making a total of four molecules per unit cell. The positions of the atoms relative to the lattice points are specified by the following vectors:

$$0.12\,b + 0.15\,c$$

$$-0.12\,b - 0.15\,c$$

$$0.50\,a + 0.62\,b - 0.15\,c$$

$$0.50\,a + 0.38\,b + 0.15\,c$$

The lengths of the edges of the unit cell are $a = 0.727$ nm, $b = 0.979$ nm and $c = 0.479$ nm. Figure 13-14 shows the crystal structure which is specified by these numbers. The iodine atoms are found to be placed geometrically in pairs. The atoms within a pair are much closer to each other than to any other atoms,

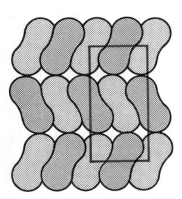

Figure 13-14 Two layers of iodine molecules in the crystal structure of solid iodine. The unit cell given in the text is shown. This view is along the a axis of the unit cell.

and these pairs of atoms of course constitute the diatomic molecules of iodine, which retain their identity in the crystal. This situation may be contrasted with that in the ionic crystal structures. For instance, in the sodium chloride structure, each sodium ion is surrounded by six equidistant chloride ions, and there are no molecules with the formula NaCl in the crystal.

The diatomic molecules are arranged in layers in the crystal, and two of those layers are shown in Figure 13-14. Within each layer the molecules are arranged in a zig-zag manner, a type of packing which is found in many molecular crystals.

The molecules in a molecular crystal are held together by forces caused by the interaction between the electrons in adjacent molecules. These forces are often called *Van der Waals forces* because they are also responsible for the term n^2a/V^2 in the Van der Waals equation of state. Since molecules are uncharged there is no Coulomb ($1/r^2$) electrostatic force between them. But molecules with electric dipole moments attract each other if their relative orientations are correct, like two bar magnets. Molecules without permanent electric dipole moments also attract each other by the following mechanism. Even though a molecule has zero dipole moment, its dipole moment at any instant can be different from zero, as long as this fluctuating dipole moment averages to zero over a period of time. The instantaneous dipole in one molecule induces an electric dipole moment in an adjacent molecule by distorting its electron distribution, and these two instantaneous dipoles attract each other. This explanation, though qualitative and crude, can be put into the form of an accurate quantum calculation. The result is that, whether or not they carry a dipole moment, two molecules are attracted weakly to each other with a force that varies with $1/r^6$, the inverse sixth power of the distance between them. The energies involved are of the order of 10-60 kJ/mol, much less than the energies of chemical bonds.

Molecules and ions containing hydrogen in a suitable chemical environment form hydrogen bonded crystals, in which the relative positions and orientations of the molecules are determined by intermolecular hydrogen bonds.

13-5   PLASTIC CRYSTALS AND LIQUID CRYSTALS

In ordinary crystals, the atoms are situated at well defined positions in relationship to each other, and remain at rest in those positions for long periods of time, except for oscillations of small amplitude. In ordinary molecular crystals, both the positions and orientations of the molecules remain fixed in the crystal. However, there are two classes of molecular crystals in which the molecules are not so severely constrained; these are called *plastic crystals* and *liquid crystals*. In crystals of these types, the molecules have more freedom of motion than in ordinary crystals, but less than in liquids. When heated, both these types of crystal form ordinary liquids, and when cooled they form ordinary crystals, and so they can be regarded as states of matter in between the ordinary crystalline state and the ordinary liquid state.

In crystals of molecules which are almost spherical in shape, the forces (or torques) restraining the molecules from rotating are small, and at temperatures which are not far below the melting point, the molecules begin to rotate. Crystals in shich the molecules are rotating rapidly are called *plastic crystals.* If the molecules are tetrahedral in shape, the rotational motion may persist down to very low temperatures. Such molecules are CH_4, which of course only exists as a solid at very low temperature, CCl_4, CBr_4 and $C(CH_3)_4$. However, many less symmetrical molecules also form plastic crystals, examples being CH_3CCl_3 and other substituted ethanes, and cyclic molecules such as cyclohexane.

When a molecule is rotating rapidly, it appears from the outside as a sphere, and is much less "lumpy" than the same molecule at rest. Hence the crystal structures of many plastic crystals are related to the simple structures which are familiar from the study of metals: body-centred cubic, cubic close-packed or hexagonal close-packed. When a plastic crystal is cooled, there is usually a well defined temperature at which the crystal structure changes from one of these highly symmetrical structures to a less symmetrical structure in which the molecules are not rotating. Energy is involved in this change of structure. When a plastic crystal is formed from an ordinary crystal, heat is absorbed at the phase transformation because of the onset of the rotational motion of the molecules. Ordinarily, this energy would have been absorbed at the melting point of the crystal as part of the latent heat of melting. Hence when a plastic crystal melts, the latent heat of melting is smaller than otherwise expected, for it reflects only the energy associated with the freeing of the translational motion of the molecules.

Liquid crystals are in a sense the opposite of plastic crystals. In a liquid crystal the orientations of the molecules remain fixed, but the molecules have some degree of translational freedom; the molecular orientations are ordered, but the positions of the molecules are disordered to some extent. Plastic crystals are found in compounds for which the molecules are almost spherical in shape, whereas liquid crystals are formed from molecules which are long and rod-like, and tend to lie parallel to each other.

Liquid crystals have some of the properties of liquids, and some of the properties of solids, and are often given the name *mesophase* to indicate their intermediate character. Some liquid crystals are formed upon heating a normal crystal, and upon further heating change to a normal liquid. This type of liquid crystal is called a *thermotropic* mesophase. The other general type of liquid crystal is described as *lyotropic*, and is formed as a result of the interaction between a solute and solvent.

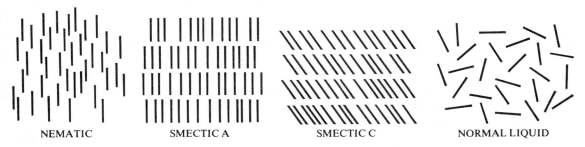

NEMATIC   SMECTIC A   SMECTIC C   NORMAL LIQUID

Figure 13-15 Representations of the molecular arrangements in liquid crystal mesophases and in a normal liquid.

There are three broad classes of thermotropic liquid crystal, which are described as the *nematic, cholesteric* and *smectic* mesophases, and the general characteristics of the structures of these are indicated in Figure 13-15. In a nematic mesophase the positions of the molecules are completely disordered, as in an ordinary liquid, but the rod-like molecules are all pointing in the same direction, or nearly so. Cholesteric mesophases are found in optically active substances; the structure of such mesophases is nematic in character, but the orientation of the molecules varies throughout the liquid in a spiral manner. In the smectic mesophases, the molecules are arranged in layers. There are three commonly recognized smectic mesophases, which are labelled A, B and C. In the smectic A mesophase, the positions of the molecules in each layer are disordered, but the molecules are all pointing perpendicular to the layer. The smectic C mesophase is similar, except that the molecules are tilted at an angle to the perpendicular. In the smectic B mesophase, the molecules are pointed perpendicular to the layers, and are arranged in a hexagonal array like that shown in Figure 13-6, making this type of liquid crystal very similar to an ordinary crystal.

Many compounds have been shown to form thermotropic liquid crystals. The structures of two examples are shown below. *p*-azoxyanisole forms a nematic mesophase between 118.2°C and 135.3°C, and ethyl *p*-azoxycinnamate forms a smectic A mesophase between 140°C and 250°C.

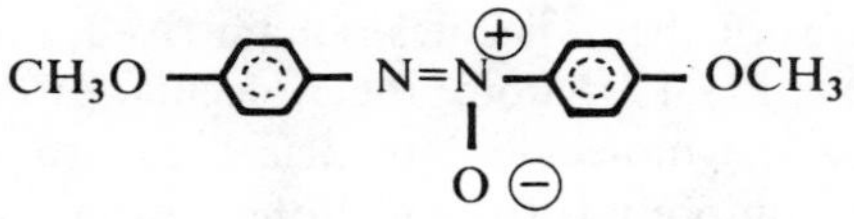

p-azoxyanisole

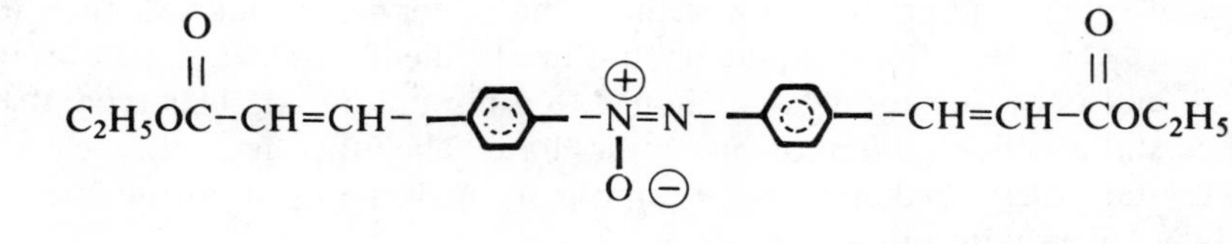

ethyl *p*-azoxycinnamate

Thermotropic liquid crystals have recently found a useful application in miniature display devices for microelectronics, particularly in wristwatches. A thin layer of a liquid crystal is sandwiched between glass plates which are electrically conducting. When an electrical potential difference is applied to the plates, the liquid crystal changes its optical properties because of the interaction between the electric field and the oriented molecules.

Lyotropic liquid crystals are solutions in which the solute is arranged in a pseudo-crystalline manner. A common example is a solution of a soap in water. A soap is an alkali metal salt of a long chain organic acid. Soaps are manufactured by alkaline hydrolysis of a fat, as shown in the following typical reaction:

$$
\begin{array}{ll}
\underset{\text{(fat)}}{\text{tristearin}} & \\
\end{array}
$$

```
        O
        ‖
CH₂−OC(CH₂)₁₆CH₃                      CH₂OH
│       O
│       ‖
CH −OC(CH₂)₁₆CH₃    + 3NaOH  →        CHOH    +3CH₃(CH₂)₁₆COO Na
│       O
│       ‖
CH₂−OC(CH₂)₁₆CH₃                      CH₂OH

     tristearin (fat)                glycerol    sodium stearate
```

In solution a salt such as sodium stearate is dissociated to Na^+ ions and stearate ions, $CH_3(CH_2)_{16}COO^-$. The stearate ion has a long hydrocarbon chain which is hydrophobic, or water-repelling, and the carboxyl group $-COO^-$ which is hydrophilic or water-attracting because the electronegative oxygen atoms can take part in hydrogen bonding to the solvent water molecules. The hydrocarbon chains can be protected from contact with the water by the formation of layers, cylinders or spheres with the hydrophilic carboxyl groups on the outside, as shown in Figure 13-16. The water solvent is then situated between these. If layers are formed, they lie parallel to each other. Cylinders are packed in hexagonal arrays, and spheres are packed in structures such as the body-centred cubic structure.

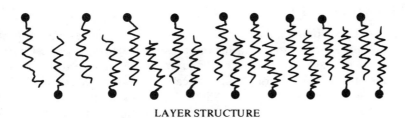

LAYER STRUCTURE

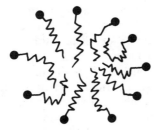

**CYLINDRICAL OR SPHERICAL STRUCTURE
IN CROSS-SECTION**

Figure 13-16 Structures which occur in lyotropic liquid crystals. The black dot represents the hydrophilic end groups, and the zig-zig represent hydrophobic hydrocarbon chains.

13-6   BONDING IN IONIC CRYSTALS

We turn now to a study of the bonding mechanism in crystals, starting with ionic crystals, such as the alkali metal halides. In such crystals, electrons are removed from the metal atoms, which have a low ionization energy, and transferred to the halogen atoms to form anions. The cations and anions are then attracted to each other electrostatically, and so form the crystal. In this process, the main contribution to the stability of the crystal is the electrostatic energy.

The process of formation of an alkali halide crystal from the elements in their standard states can be broken down into a number of steps for which individual enthalpy changes can be assigned. This analysis is called the Born-Haber cycle, after Max Born and Fritz Haber who first studied it. We will use as an example lithium fluoride, which crystallizes in the sodium chloride crystal structure. The process of formation of lithium fluoride from its elements in their standard states is very exothermic, ΔH being -618 kJ/mol. This process may be imagined to be carried out in the following steps.

		Enthalpy (kilojoule/mole)	Reference
(i)	$Li(c) \rightarrow Li(g)$	$+161$	Appendix I
(ii)	$\frac{1}{2}F_2(g) \rightarrow F(g)$	$+79$	Appendix I
(iii)	$Li(g) \rightarrow Li^+(g) + e$	$+520$	Table 10-2
(iv)	$e + F(g) \rightarrow F^-(g)$	-322	Table 10-3
(v)	$Li^+(g) + F^-(g) \rightarrow LiF(c)$	ΔH_L	

Net reaction:

	$Li(c) + \frac{1}{2}F_2(g) \rightarrow LiF(c)$	-618	Appendix I

In the first step, lithium metal is evaporated to form lithium atoms in the gas phase, and in the second step fluorine molecules are dissociated into fluorine atoms, also in the gas phase. In the third and fourth steps an electron is removed from the lithium atom to form a lithium cation, and the electron is added to the fluorine atom to form a fluoride anion. Both ions are in the gas phase at this stage. In the last step the gas phase cations and anions are assembled into the crystal, with each ion in its correct place relative to its neighbours.

The enthalpies of all but one of these steps have already been discussed. The enthalpy of the first step is the heat of vaporization of lithium metal, which can be determined from measurements of the vapour pressure of the metal at high temperatures. The enthalpy of the second step is half the bond energy of the fluorine molecule, and is determined from molecular spectroscopy. The enthalpy of the third step is the ionization energy of the lithium atom, which is measured from the series limit of the principal series of the atomic spectrum of lithium. The enthalpy of the fourth step is the negative of the electron affinity of the fluorine atom, which is measured from the spectrum of the fluoride ion in the gas phase. The enthalpy of the fifth step is not directly measurable, but the total enthalpy of the net reaction is the heat of formation of lithium fluoride, and is measured calorimetrically. The enthalpy of the fifth step can therefore be obtained by difference:

$$(+161) + (+79) + (+520) + (-322) + \Delta H_L = -618$$

and therefore $\Delta H_L = -1056 \text{ kJ mol}^{-1}$

The quantity ΔH_L is called the *lattice energy* of the crystal and is a measure of the energy required to take the crystal apart into its component ions in the gas phase separated from each other by large distances. The major contribution to the lattice energy is the electrostatic energy of the ions, which can be calculated theoretically, using the formula

$$E_{elec} = -\frac{q^2 A N_a}{4\pi\varepsilon_0 a} \qquad (2)$$

where q is the charge on the ions, N_a is the Avogadro constant, a is the length of the edge of the unit cell of the crystal, and ε_0 is the permittivity of free space. The quantity A is a constant, called the Madelung constant, which depends upon the crystal structure. For the sodium chloride structure, the Madelung constant is 3.4952 (which is the value we will use for lithium fluoride), and for the caesium chloride structure the Madelung constant is 2.0354. For lithium fluoride the length of the edge of the unit cell is 0.402 nm. Substituting values in the equation,

$$E_{elec} = -\frac{(1.60 \times 10^{-19})^2 \times 3.4952 \times 6.02 \times 10^{23}}{4 \times 3.142 \times 8.85 \times 10^{-12} \times 0.402 \times 10^{-9}}$$

$$= -1200 \text{ kJ mol}^{-1}$$

In addition to this electrostatic energy, the lattice energy includes a contribution from the repulsive energy of the ions, which makes a positive contribution of about 10% to the lattice energy in most ionic crystals. The repulsive energy is difficult to calculate precisely from the quantum theory of electrons.

In Figure 13-17, the energy changes in the five steps of the Born-Haber cycle are plotted on an energy scale. There are two important points to be made about this diagram. Firstly, the lattice energy is the largest negative contribution to ΔH_f, and in turn, the electrostatic energy is the largest contribution to the lattice energy. Hence the strongly exothermic value of ΔH_f is due primarily to the electrostatic interactions between the ions.

The second point is concerned with the octet rule of valence. It is sometimes thought that the transfer of an electron from the lithium atom to the fluorine atom is favoured because both atoms achieve a closed shell configuration as a result of the transfer. Examination of the diagram shows that the transfer process

$$Li(g) + F(g) \rightarrow Li^+(g) + F^-(g)$$

is in fact endothermic, and requires the input of 198 kJ/mol, as shown by the dotted line. This is not to say that the octet rule is irrelevant to ionic bonding. Indeed the valence of a metal taking part in ionic bonding is usually equal to the number of valence shell electrons, and the valence of a nonmetal is usually equal to the number of "holes" in the valence shell.

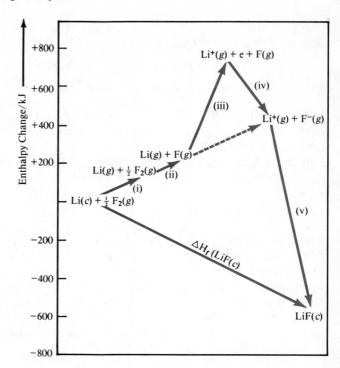

Figure 13-17 The enthalpy changes in the five steps of the Born-Haber cycle. The dotted line shows the transfer of an electron to form two ions in the gas phase.

Consider calcium oxide, CaO, for instance, which consists of Ca^{2+} ions and O^{2-} ions arranged in the sodium chloride structure. Since the electrostatic energy of the crystal is proportional to the square of the ionic charges, and the electrostatic energy is a dominant contribution to the overall energy, the crystal containing Ca^{2+} and O^{2-} ions is more stable than it would be if it consisted of singly charged ions. The electrostatic contribution to the total energy of the crystal favours the formation of ions of the largest possible charges.

Why then does LiF not contain doubly charged ions, Li^{2+} and F^{2-}? The answer is to be found in the effect of the exclusion principle on the consecutive ionization energies, which are shown in Table 10-2. The second ionization energy of lithium, 7300 kJ mol⁻¹, is an order of magnitude larger than the first ionization energy because there is one electron in the valence (2s) shell, and the second electron must come from an inner shell, which requires a very much larger energy. Hence the ionic valence of a metal is no larger than the number of electrons in the valence shell, as suggested by the octet rule.

13-7   METALS, INSULATORS AND SEMICONDUCTORS

In Chapter 10 the electronic structures of the atoms of the various elements were described. The electronic configurations described there are very useful in chemistry, but isolated atoms exist only under very special circumstances. Under standard state conditions, 298 K and 101 kPa, only eleven of the

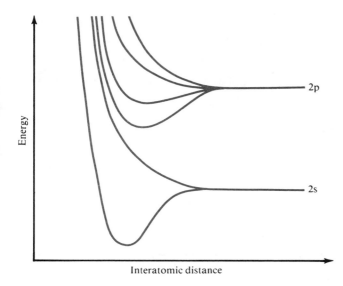

Figure 13-18 Sketch showing the variation of the energy levels of the Li_2 molecule with interatomic distance.

elements are gases, and of these only the noble gases are monatomic and have electronic structures which can be represented by atomic electronic configurations. For the remaining elements which are found in condensed states, the valence electrons of each atom are under the influence of neighbouring atoms. In this section we consider the electronic structures of crystals of various types, and the relationships between these structures and the properties of the atoms from which the crystals are formed.

Consider the pattern of energy levels formed when two lithium atoms, with electronic configurations $1s^2 2s^1$, are brought together. Figure 13-18 shows the way in which the atomic energy levels are split. The 1s levels are not significantly affected when the atoms are brought together, since the 1s electrons take no significant part in chemical bonding. The 2s atomic orbitals form σ and $\sigma*$ molecular orbitals, and the 2p atomic orbitals form σ, $\sigma*$, π and $\pi*$ molecular orbitals. In the Li_2 molecule the two valence electrons occupy the σ molecular orbital formed from the 2s atomic orbitals, and the bonding in this molecule is therefore very similar to that in H_2. The energy of the molecule is lower than that of the separated atoms, and so the molecule is stable with respect to dissociation into atoms.

The lithium molecule Li_2 is found in the vapour of this element at high temperature, but the normal form of lithium at ordinary temperatures is a metallic solid, in which a very large number of atoms are bonded together in a body-centred cubic structure. In this structure there are no identifiable diatomic molecules, and instead every atom is surrounded by eight other nearest-neighbour atoms. The properties of the metal are determined by the interactions of each atom with many neighbouring atoms, and our first approach to the electronic structure of metals is to consider an assembly of a large number of atoms.

When two lithium atoms are brought together, the two 2s atomic orbitals form two molecular orbitals. When a large number of atoms, say n atoms

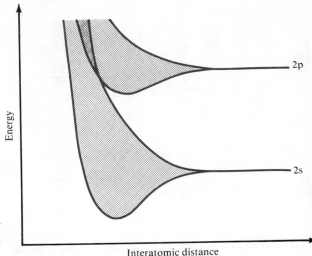

Figure 13-19 Sketch showing the variation of the bands of closely spaced energy levels in lithium metal with interatomic distance.

altogether, are brought together, there are n energy levels formed from the n 2s atomic orbitals, and these energy levels are characteristic of the geometry and internuclear distances of the n atoms in the structure. The general character of these levels is shown in Figure 13-19. The levels are distributed in a *band* between upper and lower limits, which are similar in shape to the σ and σ* levels of the Li_2 molecule. The shape of the band does not change greatly as the number of atoms in the cluster, n, increases. Hence for a very large value of n corresponding to a macroscopic sample of the metal, the energy levels are very closely spaced within the band.

The valence electrons in metallic lithium are contained in the energy levels of the 2s band, each level holding two electrons with opposite spin. Since there are n atoms in the sample and each atom has one valence electron, only half of the energy levels contain electrons when the electrons are placed in the lowest possible orbitals consistent with the Pauli exclusion principle. This is the situation at a temperature of zero kelvin; at higher temperatures the distribution of electrons is modified slightly in a way which will be discussed a little later.

The molecular orbitals in a diatomic molecule extend over the region of space containing both atoms, and in a metal the corresponding wavefunctions for the valence electrons extend over all the atoms in the metal. Electrons can move throughout the whole of the metal, and are not localized to particular atoms. To some extent, therefore, the atoms in the metal do not affect the properties of the valence electrons which give metals their characteristic properties. In a second approach to the electronic structure of metals, the atomic energy levels are ignored. It is assumed that the crystal consists of positive ions (i.e. atoms without their valence electrons) arranged in a regular structure, and the valence electrons are assumed to be common to all the ions in the metal. In the simplest form of the theory, the ions are ignored altogether, and the electrons are supposed to be free to move within the metal without suffering any forces at all. This theory was proposed first by the German physicist Arnold

Sommerfield. It is a theory based on wave mechanics, and is simple enough that the Schrödinger equation can be solved exactly.

The wavefunctions are essentially the same shape as the standing waves on a violin string shown in Figure 12-5, and are pure sine waves. The wavefunctions must be zero at the edge of the metal, since they are continuous functions and must be zero outside the metal where the electron density is zero. In applying the boundary conditions, it is convenient to assume that the piece of metal is in the shape of a cube with edges of length L; this is permissable since the properties of a piece of metal are the same no matter what its shape. If the length of the metal along the x-axis is L, the maximum allowed wavelength for the standing wave is 2L, and the shorter allowed wavelengths are 2L/2, 2L/3, 2L/4, ... or in general $2L/l$ where l is an integer which serves as a quantum number. Since the electrons are free to move in three dimensions, three quantum numbers l_x, l_y, and l_z must be specified in describing the wavefunction fully.

Since there are no forces on the electron in the metal the potential energy is a constant, and can be ignored. The energy of the electron is entirely kinetic energy and can be written

$$E = \tfrac{1}{2}m(v_x{}^2 + v_y{}^2 + v_z{}^2)$$

or in terms of the momentum of the electron,

$$E = \frac{1}{2m} (p_x{}^2 + p_y{}^2 + p_z{}^2) \tag{3}$$

Now by the de Broglie relation, the component of momentum p_x is related to the wavelength associated with the motion in the x-direction,

$$p_x = \frac{h}{\text{wavelength in x-direction}}$$

Since the wavelength is quantized, the momentum must be quantized too:

$$p_x = \frac{h}{2L/l_x}$$

$$= \frac{h\, l_x}{2L}$$

It is convenient in solid state work to write this equation

$$p_x = \hbar\, k_x \tag{4}$$

where $\hbar = h/2\pi$ and $k_x = \pi\, l_x/L$, with similar definitions for quantities k_y and k_z. Combining the equations (3) and (4), the energy of the electron can be written

$$E = \frac{\hbar^2}{2m} (k_x{}^2 + k_y{}^2 + k_z{}^2)$$

$$= \frac{\hbar^2 k^2}{2m} \tag{5}$$

where $k^2 = k_x{}^2 + k_y{}^2 + k_z{}^2$.

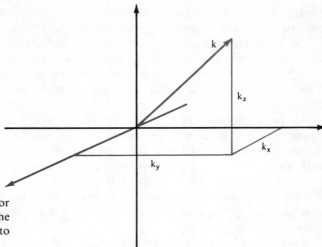

Figure 13-20 A representation of the *k* vector in k-space for an electron in a metal. The momentum of the electron is proportional to the *k* vector.

The three quantities (k_x, k_y, k_z) can be regarded as the components of a vector *k* in a space called *k-space*. The momentum of the electron is proportional to the length k or the vector *k*, the direction of motion is that of the vector *k*, and the energy of motion is related to the length of the vector *k* through equation (5). The quantization imposed through the integers l_x, l_y, and l_z means that only certain vectors *k* are permitted, namely those which point to one of a lattice of points in *k-space*.

Points in k-space which are equidistant from the origin correspond to states of motion which have equal energy, as shown in Figure 13-20. One can see intuitively that for states of high energy, the corresponding sphere in k-space is large, and has large surface area; hence the number of states having energies close to a given energy increases as the energy increases, because the area of the corresponding sphere in k-space increases. This relationship is expressed in terms of a quantity called the *density of states*, which measures the number of quantum states of the electrons in the metal having energies lying between a given energy E and a nearby energy E + dE. The density of states for the electrons described by the Sommerfeld model is shown in Figure 13-21. The form of the curve is a parabola lying on its side, for the density of states is proportional to the square root of the energy.

It might be asked why quantization of the energy levels of the electrons must be considered at all, since the electrons are free to move over the whole piece of metal, which is of macroscopic dimensions. It was stated in Section 12-6 that quantized energy levels are found only when electrons are confined in regions of atomic dimensions, which is not the case in the Sommerfeld model. The reason for considering quantized levels in metals is that electrons carry a spin of $\frac{1}{2}$, and are required to obey the Pauli exclusion principle, which limits the number of electrons per energy level to two. The density of electrons in a metal is high, and the exclusion principle is the major influence which determines the distribution of electrons amongst energy levels, and hence the properties of the electrons in the metal. Even though the energies of the electrons have been

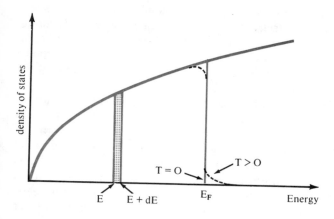

Figure 13-21 The density of states function in the Sommerfeld model. The shaded area indicates the number of quantum states with energies lying between E and E+dE. The Fermi energy is indicated by E_F. There is a sharp cut-off in the occupation of the energy levels at E_F at zero kelvin, but the cut-off becomes somewhat rounded at higher temperatures.

calculated from classical mechanics through equation (3), the existence of quantum states must be recognized in describing the properties of the entire collection of electrons.

Consider a monovalent metal such as lithium, and suppose that all the valence electrons have been removed from the atoms, leaving positive ions which are then assembled into the correct crystal structure. If the electrons are now fed into the energy levels which have been described, in a manner analogous to the aufbau process used in Chapter 10 to build up the electronic structures of the atoms of the elements, the lowest energy levels will be filled first. Each energy level can hold two electrons with opposite spin, according to the Pauli principle. Successive additions of electrons will fill progressively higher energy levels, until all of the valence electrons have been returned to the metal. The energy of the highest occupied energy level at zero kelvin is called the *Fermi energy*. The surface in k-space which connects all the states with energy equal to the Fermi energy is called the *Fermi surface*. In the Sommerfeld model of a metal the Fermi surface is a sphere. The shape of the Fermi surface can be measured experimentally for real metals, and is found to deviate somewhat from a spherical shape for most metals. The Fermi energy and the Fermi surface are characteristic properties of each metal, and are independent of the shape and size of the sample.

In a piece of metal of length L of macroscopic dimensions, the energy levels given by equation (5) are very close together. At zero kelvin, all the energy levels below the Fermi level are occupied, and all the levels above the Fermi energy are empty. However there are energy levels which are only slightly higher in energy than the Fermi energy, and at temperatures above zero kelvin some of the electrons are thermally excited into these slightly higher energy levels. The sharp cut-off in the occupation of the energy levels at the Fermi energy shown in Figure 13-21 becomes somewhat rounded or "blurred" at ordinary temperatures. Some energy levels above the Fermi energy become occupied, and some levels below the Fermi energy hold less than the two electrons allowed by the Pauli exclusion principle, as a result of thermal excitation.

Another result of the very close spacing of the quantized energy levels in a metal is that application of an electric field to a metal causes electrical conduction by exciting electrons preferentially to states with k-vectors in the direction of the field. Electrons in these states have linear momentum in the direction of the field, and so there is a net current carried by the electrons as a result of the application of the electric field.

In the Sommerfeld model, the electrons are assumed to move freely within the metal without interacting with the lattice of ions. In a real crystal, there is a potential energy associated with the interaction of the electrons with the positive ions. The ions are arranged in a regular array, and hence the potential energy of an electron is a periodic function of position. The existence of this periodic potential energy has important effects which can be understood as modifications to the Sommerfeld model. These effects occur for those electrons with de Broglie wavelengths which match the unit cell dimension. Major effects on the electron energies are found for electrons with de Broglie wavelengths equal to, or nearly equal to, $2a$, $2a/2$, $2a/3$, ... The corresponding values of k_x are π/a, $2\pi/a$, $3\pi/a$, ... The effects on the energy are demonstrated in Figure 13-22. The parabolic dependence of energy on k_x is altered for k_x values near the critical values π/a, $2\pi/a$, ... The energy is decreased for k_x just below each critical value, and increased for k_x just above each critical value, with the result that there are gaps in the allowed values of the electron energy at the critical values of k_x. The result of the existence of the periodic lattice then is to divide the k_x axis into a series of zones, called *Brillouin zones*, which are divided from each other by the critical values of k_x. The energy gaps between the *bands* occur at the critical values of k_x, which are often called *zone boundaries*.

In a three dimensional metal, the energy levels of the electrons are affected by the periodicity of the lattice in three different directions in space. In k-space, the Brillouin zone boundaries are planes which describe a polyhedron, the shape of which depends on the crystal structure of the material. The energy gap between different bands corresponding to different

Figure 13-22 A plot of energy versus k_x for motion in one dimension in a solid. The dotted line is a parabola, corresponding to the Sommerfeld model. The full lines show the formation of bands due to a periodic potential energy with a unit cell dimension a.

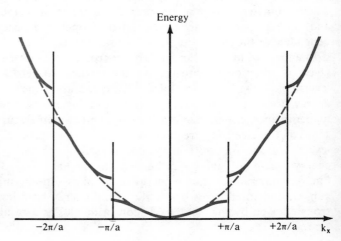

zones depends on the direction in k-space being considered. It is entirely possible that, although there is a gap between the first and second bands for all directions in k-space, there are energy levels in the second band which lie lower than the highest energy levels in the first band. In this case, when all directions are considered, there is no energy gap between the first and second bands. In other cases this is not so; all the energy levels of the second band lie above all the energy levels of the first band, and an energy gap appears between the bands. In such a case the properties of the system depend on the number of levels in the first zone, and the number of valence electrons to be accommodated. If the valence electrons of the atoms occupy all of the levels in the first zone and none in the second, then the system cannot be metallic, for the excitation of electrons to higher levels would require that they be raised in energy by an amount at least equal to the band gap, instead of the very small amount of energy required for excitation if there is no band gap.

It can be shown that the number of levels per atom in the first Brillouin zone for body-centred cubic lithium metal is one. Since lithium has only one valence electron, and each energy level can hold two electrons with opposite spin, only half of the levels in the first zone are occupied at zero kelvin. The Fermi surface in this metal is spherical, and the highest occupied level is well separated from the top of the band of energy levels for the first zone. Hence electrons can be excited to higher energy levels with very small energy input, and the properties of lithium are metallic in nature as a result.

Diamond, one of the polymorphs of carbon, has a face-centred cubic lattice. There are two atoms per lattice point; one atom is placed at the lattice point, and the other is displaced from it by the vector $\frac{1}{4}a + \frac{1}{4}b + \frac{1}{4}c$. The structure is shown in Chapter 8. The first Brillouin zone contains two energy levels per atom. Since carbon has four valence electrons per atom, all of the levels in the first zone are occupied at zero kelvin, provided that no energy overlap occurs between the first and second zones. In fact this condition is met, with an average energy gap of 533 kJ mol^{-1} between the bands. Very large energies relative to the thermal energy are required to excite an electron from the first band, or *valence band*, to the second band or *conduction band*. As a consequence the number of conduction electrons in diamond is exceedingly small even at very high temperatures.

Materials in which there is an energy gap E_g between the valence band and the conduction band sufficiently large to preclude occupancy of levels in the conduction band at moderate temperatures are known as *insulators*. Diamond is a very good insulator. Alkali halides and similar ionic crystals also have very large energy gaps, and can be regarded as lattices of ions in which all electrons are localized.

The values of the energy gap E_g for some diamond-structure elements and some binary AB compounds with the zinc blende structure are given in Table 13-5. The zinc blende structure is shown in Figure 13-12. The carbon atoms of the diamond structure are replaced alternately by A atoms and B atoms, so that each A atom is surrounded by a tetrahedron of B atoms and vice versa. It should be noted that since the elements in each compound come from either groups II and VI, or groups III and V, the total number of valence electrons for each AB pair is eight. Hence in these compounds, there are four electrons

TABLE 13-5 Band Gap Energies for Some Diamond-like Solids

Elements	Band gap E_g		Compounds	Band gap E_g	
	eV*	kJ mol^{-1}		eV*	kJ mol^{-1}
C (diamond)	5.33	514	GaP	2.25	217
Si	1.14	110	GaAs	1.4	130
Ge	0.67	65	ZnO	3.2	309
			ZnS	2.42	234
			InSb	0.23	22

*One electron volt per event (eV) is equivalent to 96.5 kJ mol^{-1}.

per atom, the same as in the Group IV solids, diamond, silicon, and germanium.

It may be seen from the table that as the atomic number of the elements involved increase, the energy gap E_g decreases. For InSb the gap is relatively small, and a significant number of electrons exist in the conduction band at ordinary temperatures. The number of electrons excited thermally to the conduction band is proportional to the quantity $\exp(-E_g/RT)$, and hence the conductivity of the material is strongly dependent on temperature, and can change by orders of magnitude over relatively small ranges of temperature. Such elements form a subclass of insulators called *semiconductors*. In the case of InSb the semiconducting properties are characteristic of the compound itself, rather than being due to impurities. Such semiconductors are called *intrinsic semiconductors*.

It is impossible to prepare elements or compounds which are absolutely pure. Impurity levels in the intrinsic semiconductors listed in Table 13-5 are seldom less than 1 ppm. In many instances the impurities form solid solutions, which will be discussed in Chapter 17, and the impurity atoms replace the *host* (or solvent) atoms on normal sites in the crystal structure. If the impurity atom has one more valence electron than the host, as is the case for an As impurity atom in Ge, then the extra electron for every impurity atom cannot be accommodated in the valence band, which is fully occupied. The impurity atom generates a special energy level, called an *impurity level* which lies just below the bottom of the conduction band. At relatively low temperatures this electron, normally localized on the impurity atom, can be excited to the conduction band, when it can then act to carry current through the material which would be an insulator if absolutely pure. Thus the presence of impurities can have significant effects on the conductivities of silicon and germanium. The impurity atoms may be present naturally, or may be added in a controlled way to otherwise very pure material, a process called *doping*. The resulting semiconductors are called *extrinsic semiconductors*.

Two classes of semiconductors can be produced, depending on whether the impurity atoms have larger or smaller numbers of valence electrons than the host material. In the example given above, the impurity atom, As, has 5 valence electrons, and the host, Ge, has 4. The excess electrons are contained in impurity levels, and upon excitation to the conduction band, the electrons can act as current carriers. Such a semiconductor is called an *n-type* semicon-

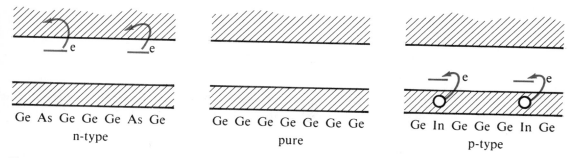

Ge As Ge Ge Ge As Ge   Ge Ge Ge Ge Ge Ge Ge   Ge In Ge Ge Ge In Ge
n-type   pure   p-type

Figure 13-23 A representation of impurity energy levels in germanium. In the centre the valence and conduction bands in pure germanium are shown. On the left, germanium doped with arsenic forms an n-type semiconductor, with impurity levels just below the conduction band. On the right, germanium doped with indium forms a p-type semiconductor, with impurity levels just above the valence band; excitation of electrons into these impurity levels leaves "holes" in the valence band.

ductor, because the current is carried by negatively charged particles. This process is shown in Figure 13-23.

If on the other hand In, with only three valence electrons, is used to dope Ge, impurity energy levels associated with these atoms appear in the band gap just above the valence band. These impurity levels are localized on the impurity atoms. The levels may be occupied by electrons from the valence band at ordinary temperatures, which results in the valence band being not quite full. It is said that there are *holes* in the valence band, and the presence of these holes allows mobility of charge. The transport of electric charge through the semiconductor can be described as the flow of positively charged holes rather than a flow of negatively charged electrons. The conductivity of the semiconductor depends on the number of holes present, and so it is really the holes which determine its properties. Such a semiconductor is called a *p-type* semiconductor.

The technology of semiconductor electronics depends on the production of extrinsic semiconductors of specified properties by the carefully controlled doping of exceedingly high purity silicon and germanium. This technology has now progressed to the stage where computing, control of equipment, and recording of data have been revolutionized. The nature of society itself is in the process of change as semiconductors are used in more and more industrial, commercial and scientific applications.

FURTHER READING

Structural Inorganic Chemistry, by A. F. Wells. 4th Edition (Oxford, 1975). A large textbook with a great deal of information on crystal structures.

Structure and Properties of Inorganic Solids, by F. S. Galasso (Pergamon, 1970). This book surveys the crystal structures and properties of the elements and many compounds and alloys.

Liquid Crystals, by S. Chandrasekhar (Cambridge University Press, 1977). A recent account of the subject with both theoretical and experimental discussions.

PROBLEMS

1. Tungsten has a density of 19 253 kg m^{-3}. Calculate the length of the edge of the unit cell, and the metallic radius of the tungsten atom.
[0.3165 nm, 0.137 nm]

2. Gold has a density of 19305 kg m^{-3}. Calculate the length of the edge of the unit cell, and the metallic radius of the gold atom.   [0.4077 nm, 0.144 nm]

3. When heated above 916°C, iron changes its crystal structure from body-centred cubic to cubic close-packed. Assuming that the metallic radius of the atoms does not change, calculate the ratio of the density of the BCC crystal to that of the CCP crystal.
[0.919]

4. Caesium chloride has a density of 3988 kg m^{-3}. Calculate the length of the edge of the unit cell.
[0.4123 nm]

5. Lithium hydride crystallizes in the NaCl structure, and the length of the edge of the unit cell is 0.409 nm. Calculate the molar volume of the crystal.
[10.3 mL]

6. Calculate the density of crystalline iodine from the data given in Section 13-4.
[4.95 × 10^3 kg m^{-3}]

7. Calculate the bond length in the I$_2$ molecule from the data given in Section 13-4
[0.27 nm]

8. Calculate the lattice energy of sodium bromide using the Born-Haber cycle.
[−751 kJ mol^{-1}]

9. Sodium bromide crystallizes in the NaCl structure, with a unit cell edge of length 0.597 nm. Calculate the electrostatic energy of the crystal and compare it with the lattice energy calculated in the last question.
[−811 kJ mol^{-1}]

10. Is there any combination of a metal (M) and a halogen (X) for which the transfer of an electron in the gas phase,

$$M(g) + X(g) \rightarrow M^+(g) + X^-(g)$$

is an exothermic reaction?

11. Given that the density of states in the Sommerfeld model is proportional to the square root of the energy (see Figure 13-21), show that the average energy of an electron in this model at zero kelvin is 3/5 of the Fermi energy E_F.

XIV POLYMERS AND SILICATES

Examination of Figure 8-13 shows that carbon and silicon lie among the elements with the least tendency to form ions. Both show an ability to form strong bonds with themselves, the carbon-carbon bond being particularly strong at 347 kJ mol^{-1}. The bond energy for a silicon-silicon bond is significantly less at 176 kJ mol^{-1} but what is evident from Table 11-2 is that silicon-oxygen bonds are very strong indeed at 369 kJ mol^{-1}. Both of these elements are capable of forming long strong chainlike structures, carbon by forming successive carbon-carbon bonds and silicon by a succession of alternating silicon and oxygen atoms.

Man has utilized the ability of carbon to form such giant molecules by learning to synthesize a variety of *polymers* which have properties suiting them to use as plastics, fibres and elastomers.

Whereas most, but not all, of the polymers of technical interest are man-made, the silicates are virtually all naturally occurring. Their diversity is extraordinary, a fact which is ultimately attributable to the strength of the silicon oxygen bond and to the structural potential of tetrahedral geometry.

14-1 POLYMER SYNTHESIS

A polymer is a chemical substance consisting of extremely long molecules. The bonding within each molecule is covalent, with the main chain almost always formed largely or entirely of carbon atoms. Polymers are formed by reacting *monomers* in a reaction known as polymerization. For example, ethylene will polymerize at high pressures, or in the presence of a suitable catalyst even at low pressures, to give polyethylene.

$$n C_2 H_4 \rightarrow \left[\begin{array}{c} H \quad H \\ | \quad\; | \\ -C-C- \\ | \quad\; | \\ H \quad H \end{array} \right]_n$$

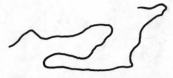

UNBRANCHED POLYMER MOLECULE

BRANCHED POLYMER MOLECULE

Polymers such as polyethylene may be either linear or branched, and they may have widely differing molar masses, and distributions of molar masses. Each of these factors affects the mechanical properties of the polymer, and thus provides a variable which the chemist and engineer seek to alter in order to achieve a product of specific qualities. The synthesis of polymer in this way, by simply adding monomers, is called **addition polymerization.**

Monomers with suitable functional groups may link with the resulting elimination of a small molecule, usually water. This process is called **condensation polymerization** or **step reaction polymerization.** A well known example is the linking of an amine to a carboxylic acid to yield a polyamide.

$$-R-\overset{\overset{\textstyle O}{\|}}{C}-OH \;+\; H_2N-R'- \;\rightarrow\; -R-\overset{\overset{\textstyle O}{\|}}{C}-\overset{\overset{\textstyle H}{|}}{N}-R'-\;+H_2O$$

Notice that polymers can be synthesized through this reaction in two different **ways,** one using a mixture of diamines and dicarboxylic acids and the other using an aminocarboxylic acid.

$$HO-\overset{\overset{\textstyle O}{\|}}{C}-R-\overset{\overset{\textstyle O}{\|}}{C}-OH \;+\; H_2N-R'-NH_2 \;\rightarrow\; HO\overset{\overset{\textstyle O}{\|}}{C}-R-\overset{\overset{\textstyle O}{\|}}{C}-\overset{\overset{\textstyle H}{|}}{N}-R'-NH_2 \;+\; H_2O$$

$$2 \quad HO-\overset{\overset{\textstyle O}{\|}}{C}-R''-NH_2 \;\rightarrow\; HO-\overset{\overset{\textstyle O}{\|}}{C}-R''-\overset{\overset{\textstyle H}{|}}{N}-\overset{\overset{\textstyle O}{\|}}{C}-R''-NH_2 \;+H_2O$$

or 2

$$\rightarrow \; -CH_2CH_2CH_2CH_2CH_2\overset{\overset{\textstyle O}{\|}}{C}\,\overset{\overset{\textstyle H}{|}}{N}-$$

Both methods leave an acid group at one end and an amine group at the other so that polymerization can continue indefinitely.

Polymer properties can be altered by introducing a *comonomer.* Copolymerization introduces several new parameters which may be used to vary and control polymer properties. One, obviously, is the ratio of the two monomers. A less obvious one is the regularity of insertion of the monomers. For some copolymerizations, catalysts are available which can produce a polymer in which the two monomers are alternate, random or in blocks.

$-M-M'-M-M'-M-M'-M-M'-M-M'-M-M'-$ alternating

$-M-M'-M'-M'-M-M-M'-M-M'-M'-M-M'-M-M'-$ random

$-M-M'-M'-M'-M'-M'-M'-M-M-M-M-M-M'-$ block

Even this very brief introduction makes it clear that there are many ways of varying the properties of a polymer. Correlation of physical properties with molecular structure involves subtleties which are still the subject of active research, but the main features are understood, and serve well to illustrate again the relationship of mechanical properties to bonding.

14-2 MOLECULAR STRUCTURE AND MACROSCOPIC PROPERTIES

While strong carbon-carbon bonds hold a polymer molecule together and can be said to account for the existence and importance of polymers, other factors must be examined in order to discover the reasons for differences among polymers. The most important of these is the nature of the bonding which binds a polymer molecule to its neighbours.

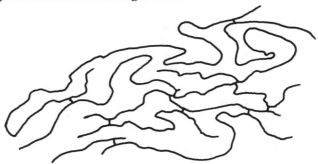

CROSSLINKING EFFECT OF VULCANIZATION

Sometimes these links are full covalent bonds. This very strong bonding is known as crosslinking and serves to turn the entire substance, in some degree, into a single giant molecule. Where the crosslinks are many, the polymer is rigid and hard, such as those used to make telephone casings and bowling balls. In some polymers, the degree of rigidity can be controlled by varying the degree of crosslinking. In elastomeric materials such as polyisoprene, the polymer backbone contains double bonds. The polymer is soft and rigid is the if sulphur is introduced, it reacts with some of the double bonds is known as adjacent molecules. The more sulphur that is introduced the resulting rubber. Such crosslinking of rubbers with vulcanizing.

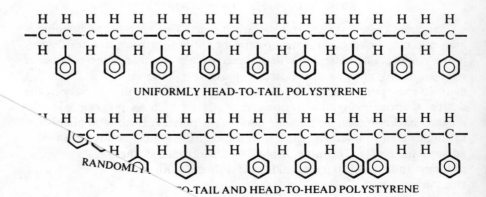

The next strongest intermolecular bonding is hydrogen bonding. It is notably important in polyamides, where the hydrogen on the nitrogen links strongly with the oxygen of an adjacent molecule. This makes the melting point of polyamides high, since melting requires the breaking of these intermolecular links.

The second factor important to determining mechanical properties is the conformation of the molecular chain, particularly the ease with which it bends and the ease with which it can be packed into crystalline sections. The flexibility, or conversely the stiffness since both at times are desirable, is much affected by the simple bulk of the side groups. Rotational motion is much restricted by a large, stiff group such as the C_6H_5 in styrene, and polystyrene is notably stiffer than is polyethylene.

UNIFORMLY HEAD-TO-TAIL POLYSTYRENE

RANDOMLY

TO-TAIL AND HEAD-TO-HEAD POLYSTYRENE

Several factors bear on crystallinity. One is the degree of branching. It is easy to pack long linear molecules into some sort of highly ordered lattice, but this becomes more difficult, and ultimately impossible, if the same substance is synthesized with branches which are randomly located and variable in length. Similarly, monomers can join regularly head-to-tail, or there can be random head-to-tail and head-to-head linkages.

Uniformly head-to-tail polymers have the regularity of structure required for crystallinity but a random mixture of the two does not. Finally, a head-to-tail polymer can still have varying orientations of the side group. All can be on the same side of the polymer chain (an *isotactic* polymer), or they can be alternatively above and below the chain (a *syndiotactic* polymer) or they can be randomly and unpredictably oriented (an *atactic* polymer). Again, the first two have the regularity suited to crystallinity while the third does not.

Crystallinity in polymers is never the total crystallinity observed in inorganic materials. Polymer molecules are so long that bends and folds are inevitably entrapped, and the solid of even linear polyethylene, with no side groups at all, still contains significant non-crystalline volumes known as amorphous regions.

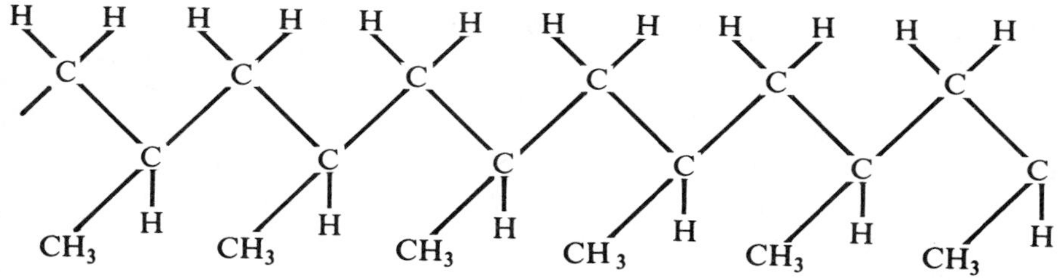

ISOTACTIC POLYPROPYLENE

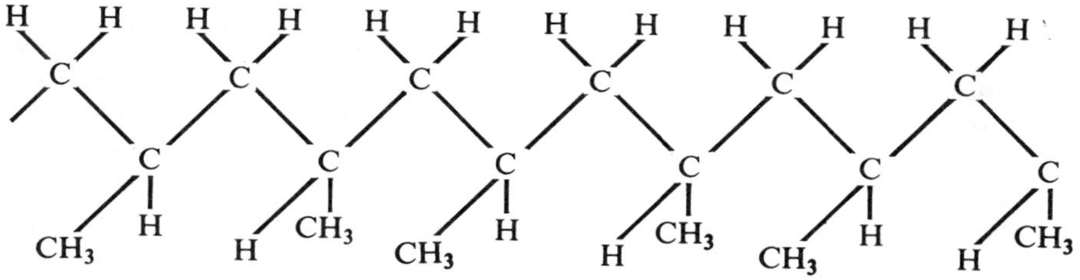

SYNDIOTACTIC POLYPROYLENE

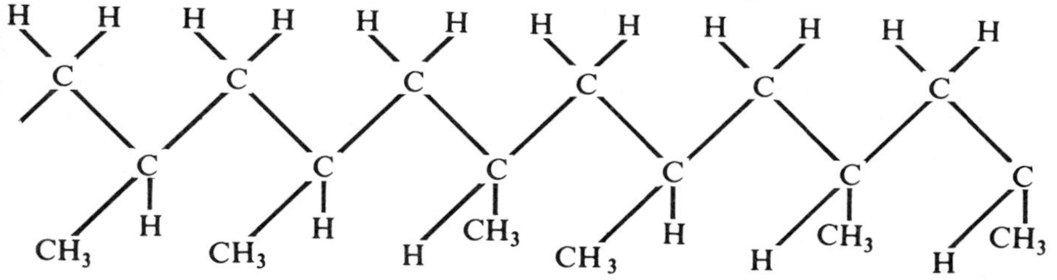

ATACTIC POLYPROPYLENE

CRYSTALLINE REGIONS AND AMORPHOUS REGION IN POLYMERS

A polymer which has large crystalline regions, when compared with an amorphous polymer of identical composition, average molar mass and molar mass distribution, will exhibit higher density, higher melting point and greater stiffness and tensile strength. These properties are not always desirable, of course, and both low density polyethylene and high density polyethylene enjoy large markets.

14-3 COMMERCIAL POLYMERS

There are three main divisions of polymers; plastics, fibres and elastromers. Plastics are usually considered to be those materials which can be molded or formed or extruded into useful shapes at high temperature. If the process can be repeated by reheating, the material is *thermoplastic*. If not, it is *thermosetting*. However, plastic is also used as a word to describe some paints and coatings, which is a somewhat different concept. Fibres are materials which have desirable properties when formed in shapes in which the length is at least two orders of magnitude greater than the other dimensions. With polymers, there is invariably a tendency for orientation of the polymer molecules to occur during the fibre forming process. The properties are much affected by what occurs during fibre forming, particularly in the orientation of crystalline regions. Some polymers can be used both as plastics and as fibres. Polyethylene is mainly used as a plastic but can be made into filaments. Polyamides are used chiefly as fibres but have some utility as plastics. Polypropylene is used extensively in both roles. Elastomers or rubbers are polymers which have a strong tendency to return to their original configuration when deformed. Until the Second World War, most rubber was obtained from Malaysia by tapping *hevea* trees which have a sap containing significant amounts of what can be regarded as polyisoprene. When this source was denied during the war to Canada, the United Kingdom and the United States, a 'synthetic rubber' industry was established which has since grown and diversified greatly.

An entire volume would be needed to provide a list of polymers and their properties which even approached being comprehensive. Table 14-1 merely lists a few of the more common ones.

Polymer	Monomer	Repeating unit	Properties and uses
1. Polyethylene, polyethene, Polythene, Sclair, Marlex, Lupolen H.	$CH_2{=}CH_2$	$-CH_2-CH_2-$	Often contains a small percentage of a comonomer, usually another alkene. Has good chemical resistance, impact strength and electrical resistance. Used mainly as a thermoplastic in sheet for bags and film, for pipe, wire insulation, containers and toys.
2. Polypropylene, polypropene, Propathene.	$CH_3-CH{=}CH_2$	$-CH(CH_3)-CH_2-$	Similar to polyethylene. Less impact strength but harder and superior in fibre usage. Much used as film, in rope and cord, and in small unstressed engineering parts.
3. Copolymers of ethylene and propylene, Royalene, Nordel, Keltan.	$CH_2{=}CH_2$ and $CH_3-CH{=}CH_2$	$-CH_2-CH_2-CH(CH_3)-CH_2-$	Elastomer when comparable amounts of ethylene and propylene are used. Good resistance to oxidation and chemical attack. Used in tires.

Monomer: $CH_2=CHCl$ Polymer: $-CH_2-CHCl-$	Monomer: $CH_2=CCl_2$ Polymer: $-CH_2-CCl_2-$	Monomer: $CH_2=C(CH_3)COOCH_3$ Polymer: $-CH_2-C(CH_3)(COOCH_3)-$	Monomer: $CF_2=CF_2$ Polymer: $-CF_2-CF_2-$
Rigid although can be made more flexible with additives. Good impact strength and electrical insulating value. Ranks with polyethylene as major industrial plastic. Does not burn readily. Used as wire and cable coating, in pipes and plumbing, and in film, packaging materials and floor coverings.	Normally includes significant quantity of vinyl chloride as comonomer. Good chemical resistance. Does not burn readily. Nearly impervious to water vapour. Used in moisture sealing films and in pipe linings.	Excellent transparency. Rigid, resistant to weathering, good impact strength. Used in sheets and in molded sections, often in applications where transparency is utilized.	Outstanding resistance to chemical attack. Somewhat soft. Extremely low coefficient of friction. Used in chemical resistant coatings, laboratory tubing, gaskets.
4. Poly(chloroethene) Poly(vinyl chloride), PVC, Vinoflex, Corvic, Tygon, Vinylite.	5. Poly(1.1 dichloroethene) poly(vinylidene chloride), Saran.	6. Poly(methyl methacrylate), Perspex, Plexiglas, Lucite.	7. poly(tetrafluoroethylene), PTFE, Teflon.

Name	Structure	Properties and uses
8. poly(chlorotrifluoro-ethylene), Kel-F.	$F_2C=CFCl$ monomer; chain $-CF_2-CFCl-$	Somewhat similar to polytetrafluoroethylene in properties and uses.
9. polyamides as a class, Nylon, Perlon.	$HO\,C(=O)-CH_2CH_2CH_2CH_2\,C(=O)\,OH$ $H_2NCH_2CH_2CH_2CH_2CH_2CH_2NH_2$ $-C(=O)-(CH_2)_4-C(=O)-N(H)-(CH_2)_6-N(H)-$ (Nylon 6,6)	Several variations depending on acid and amine chosen. Resistant to wear. Good tensile and impact strength. Does not burn readily. Most common as fibre in fabrics, tire cord and carpet yarn but also used in gears, rollers and moving parts where strength and resistance to wear are important.
10. polyesters as a class, Terylene, Fortrel, Dacron, Mylar.	ethylene glycol; terephthalic acid $HO(O=)C-C_6H_4-C(=O)OH$; polymer chain with $-CH_2-O-C(=O)-C_6H_4-C(=O)-O-CH_2-$	Some variations depending on choice of monomers but usually ethylene glycol and terephthalic acid. Excellent in fibre form and makes strong, tough film. Much used in fabrics. Less elastic than Nylon. Compounded with glass fibre gives exceptional tensile and flexural strength. Used in laminates in aircraft interiors, boat and furniture manufacture.

11. polyacrylonitrile, Orlon, Acrilan, Dralon.	Strong fibre much used in fabrics. Good resistance to sunlight, weathering, chemical attack.	monomer: $CH_2=CHCN$ → polymer chain with repeating $-CH_2-CH(CN)-$ units
12. polystyrene, Styrofoam.	Transparent, rigid, easily moulded. Readily made into rigid foam and as such much used as thermal insulation.	monomer: styrene $CH_2=CH(C_6H_5)$ → polymer chain with repeating $-CH_2-CH(C_6H_5)-$ units
13. polybutadiene, Budene.	Good resistance to wear, aging, heat. Used in tires.	monomer: $CH_2=CH\,CH=CH_2$ → 1,4 and 1,2 addition; mainly 1,4 addition but some 1,2 addition

	$CH_2=CHCH=CH$	An important general purpose rubber, much used in tire manufacture. Usually about 75% butadiene and 25% styrene. The butadiene is polymerized about 80% 1,4 and 20% 1,2.	14. copolymers of butadiene and styrene, GRS, SBR, Buna S, Ameripol.
	$CH_2 = CHC = CH_2$ with CH_3 poly (cis 1,4 isoprene) poly (trans 1,4 isoprene)	Cis-polyisoprene duplicates natural rubber and is used in a wide range of applications including tires. Trans polyisoprene is tough and hard, used in a limited range of applications such as golf ball covers.	15. polyisoprene, Natsyn, Shell IR.

	Structure	Properties and Uses
16. copolymers of isobutene and isoprene, butyl rubber, Polysar, Enjay Butyl.	$CH_2 = C(CH_3)CH_3$ $\quad$ $CH_2 = CH-C(CH_3) = CH_2$	Relatively impermeable to gases. Less elastic than most rubbers. Some use as inner tubes for tires and other specialized applications, liners, caulking.
17. copolymers of butadiene and acrylonitrile, Buna N, Hycar, Perbunan N, Krynac.	$CH_2 = CHC \equiv N$ $\quad$ $CH_2 = CHCH = CH_2$	A rubber with excellent resistance to grease and organic solvents. Used in gaskets, fuel hoses and similar applications.
18. poly (2-chloro-1,3-butadiene), Neoprene.	$CHCl = CHCCl = CH_2$	A specialty rubber noted for its excellent resistance to chemical attack.

14-4 SILICATES

In all silicates, silicon is tetravalent and lies at the centre of a tetrahedron of oxygen ions. The extraordinary variety of silicates arises in large part from the diversity of ways in which these tetrahedra can be put together. Both geologists and chemists classify silicates on the basis of how the tetrahedra are combined, as follows:

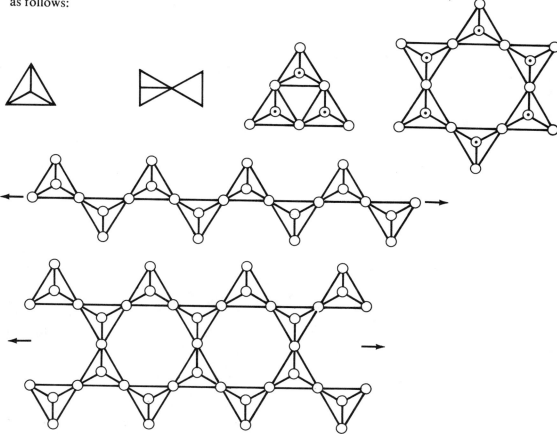

(1a) materials containing single SiO_4^{4-} ions, known as orthosilicates or nesosilicates

(1b) materials containing discrete ions made up of two to six tetrahedra attached linearly by common oxygen ions, known as sorosilicates

(1c) materials containing discrete ions made up of three or six tetrahedra in a ring, known as cyclosilicates

(2) materials in which the tetrahedra are linked through common oxygens in long strings of indefinite length, called inosilicates. There are many examples of both single chains called pyroxenes and double chains called amphiboles.

(3) materials in which three of the four oxygens in each tetrahedron are common to two tetrahedra, producing sheets. These substances are called phyllosilicates.

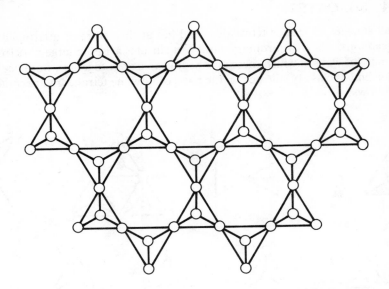

(4)   materials in which all oxygens are shared by two silicons producing a three dimensional framework structure which is uncharged unless some substitution occurs as discussed below. These materials are called tektosilicates.

Orthosilicates are not numerous. They are ionic materials no different in principle from any ionic substances with large anions, such as phosphates. Examples of orthosilicates are zircon, $ZrSiO_4$; olivine, $(Mg, Fe)_2SiO_4$ and willemite, Zn_2SiO_4. The bracketed group in the formula for olivine indicates that this material can exist with any proportion of Mg and Fe, from the mineral forsterite, Mg_2SiO_4 through to the mineral fayalite, Fe_2SiO_4. A geologist calls intermediate compositions isomorphous mixtures of forsterite and fayalite. A chemist calls such materials solid solutions of Mg_2SiO_4 and Fe_2SiO_4. The ability to substitute cations is a notable feature of phyllosilicates and tektosilicates, but is less common in orthosilicates.

Orthosilicates are hard and high melting. Zircon has a hardness of 7.5 on an empirical scale on which the hardness of diamond is 10. The hardness of glass is around 6, and copper is 3. Such hardness would be expected from a covalent network crystal, like diamond, and to a lesser extent from an ionic crystal. In fact, most evidence indicates that the orthosilicates lie somewhere between. Although the metal oxygen bonds are more polar than the silicon oxygen bonds, they have some covalent character, and the orthosilicates lie between being ionic and being giant molecules.

Also in this group are the garnets, which have the general formula $M_3N_2(SiO_4)_3$. M is a divalent cation, usually Ca^{2+}, Fe^{2+} or Mg^{2+} and N is a trivalent cation, usually Al^{3+}, Cr^{3+} or Fe^{3+}. An example is uvarovite, $Ca_3Cr_2(SiO_4)_3$.

Orthosilicates are important components of Portland cement. Cement is manufactured by mixing clays, which are silicates; limestone, $CaCO_3$; and some lesser components. These are fired at 1700 K to form a clinker of silicates.

$$CaCO_3(c) \rightarrow CaO\ (c) + CO_2\ (g)$$
$$2\ CaO(c) + SiO_2(c) \rightarrow Ca_2SiO_4(c)$$
$$CaO(c) + Ca_2SiO_4(c) \rightarrow Ca_3SiO_5(c)$$

Both Ca_2SiO_4 and Ca_3SiO_5 are important components of cement, as are aluminium analogues formed from the aluminium content of the clays.

$$CaO(c) + Al_2O_3(c) \rightarrow CaAl_2O_4(c)$$
$$2\ CaO(c) + CaAl_2O_4(c) \rightarrow Ca_3Al_2O_6(c)$$

The clinker, which consists of these orthosilicates, aluminates and other lesser but not unimportant constituents is powdered to give cement. On hydration with water, a sand and cement mixture forms a fluid which can be poured. Gravel or crushed rock is often added as reinforcement of the silicate matrix, the whole mixture setting to form what one calls concrete. The chemistry of these systems is complicated, and remains the subject of active research.

The sorosilicates involve anionic groups formed from two to six tetrahedra. The simplest of the anions is the pyrosilicate ion, $Si_2O_7^{6-}$, as found in the mineral hemimorphite, $Zn_4(OH)_2(Si_2O_7)$, which is an important zinc ore. Not fundamentally different are the cyclosilicates, in which the tetrahedra form a ring. Two such cyclic ions are known, one with three tetrahedra, $Si_3O_9^{6-}$, and one with six, $Si_6O_{18}^{12-}$. Examples are benitoite, $BaTiSi_3O_9$ and beryl, $Be_3Al_2Si_6O_{18}$. These materials, like the orthosilicates, show metal-oxygen bonding which is intermediate between being covalent and being ionic. This polar covalent bonding produces hard, high melting materials. Gems, as well as being beautiful, must be hard and durable and many are found among the orthosilicates, sorosilicates and cyclosilicates. These include beryl, where a trace replacement of Al^{3+} by Cr^{3+} yields emerald and of Al^{3+} by Fe^{3+} yields aquamarine; topaz, $Al_2(F,OH)SiO_4$; the garnets, notably the crimson almandine, $Fe_3Al_2(SiO_4)_3$, the red pyrope, $Mg_3Al_2(SiO_4)_3$ and the green andradite, $Ca_3Fe_2(SiO_4)_3$; olivene or peridot where the colour is determined by the proportion of magnesium and iron; and zircon itself, where again the replacement of a very small proportion of the zirconium by other metals gives rise to varying hues.

All of the previous classes have some common properties arising from each containing discrete ions. All of the following classes do not contain discrete silicate ions, but involve silicate anions of large and indefinite size.

The inosilicates contain long chains which are reminiscent of the polymers, but differ in a major way in that the silicate chains are negatively charged. These chains are held together by cations packed appropriately along the chain length. It will be evident that the precise nature of these cations is not important, since a variety of ion sizes can be accommodated by variations in the packing of the chains. Packing can also be varied to provide a variety of possible coordination numbers for the metal. As might be expected in these circumstances, the occurrence of isomorphism described earlier for olivine is not uncommon among inosilicates.

Single chain inosilicates are called pyroxenes, examples being jadeite, $NaAl(SiO_3)_2$; spudomene, $LiAl(SiO_3)_2$; diopside, $CaMg(SiO_3)_2$; and enstatite,

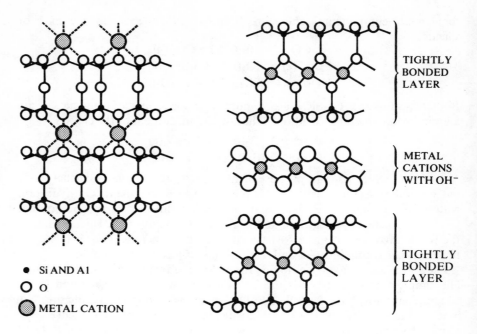

- ● Si AND Al
- ○ O
- ◉ METAL CATION

TIGHTLY BONDED LAYER

METAL CATIONS WITH OH⁻

TIGHTLY BONDED LAYER

$MgSiO_3$. Diopside is one which exhibits isomorphism, including in its structure any proportion of magnesium and iron in accordance with the formula $Ca(Mg,Fe)(SiO_3)_2$. The amphiboles differ from the pyroxenes in having double chains. All of the comments above on pyroxenes are substantially applicable to them as well. The chains in both classes of materials are very strong but the bonding of one chain to the next is variable. Where metal ions are closely packed, the bonding is strong and the resulting material is strong. Some of the pyroxenes are gems, including enstatite and spudomene. More often, especially with the amphiboles, the binding is weaker. The chains can be slipped over one another without bringing like charged ions into direct contact, which means that crystals can be cleaved easily in directions parallel to the chains. Indeed many are visibly fibrous in nature, with some amphiboles for example being among the minerals classed as asbestos.

The phyllosilicates are an even larger and more diverse class. The sheet-like structure with three shared oxygens and one unshared oxygen in each tetrahedron gives an overall formula of $Si_2O_5^{2-}$. These sheets, which may be formed of six member rings or of combinations of four and eight member rings, are bound together by cations. As with the inosilicates, many cations can serve this function. Variability in binding strength and examples of isomorphism are abundant. Many of the rare metals are found as trace substitutes in these materials. While the bonding is very strong within the plane, the weakness of interplane bonding leads to readily separated planes as is visually evident in the micas.

The phyllosilicates, as well as the tektosilicates described later, are notable for the examples of materials in which aluminium ions substitute for a fixed proportion of the silicon ions. This substitution is not random, as in isomorphous materials, but is a fixed stoichiometric substitution in which both aluminium and silicon have particular places in the unit cell. Since aluminium is trivalent and silicon tetravalent, substitution increases the negative charge on the silicate layers and increases the cationic charge required to balance it.

Phyllosilicates in which the tetrahedral sheet is double layered are common. If such a structure is a pure silicate without aluminium substitution, the double layer would be uncharged. However, if a fraction of the silicon atoms are replaced by aluminium atoms, the sheets will be negatively charged, and may be held together by cations. This is the usual case, an example being calcium aluminosilicate, $CaAl_2Si_2O_8$. In this compound, aluminium and silicon ions occur alternately in the sheets, and calcium ions bind the sheets together. Also common among the phyllosilicates are materials involving single layered sheets made up of hexagonal rings. These sheets are anionic even in the absence of aluminium substitution, and have the repeating unit $Si_2O_5^{2-}$. These sheets are bound together by metal cations with OH^- groups not infrequently occurring. In all silicates, the large units are the oxygen ions with radii of about 0.14 nm. These are clustered around relatively small silicon ions or aluminium ions which have radii of about 0.04 nm and 0.05 nm respectively. The large ions should be thought of as very nearly in contact, with the cations occupying tetrahedral holes. Many of the phyllosilicate structures are such that a repeating 'hole' would occur in the nearly close-packed oxygen ions, and it is in these 'holes' that OH^- groups fit so readily.

In some phyllosilicates, such as the clays, the forces holding the sheets together are weak. In dickite, $Al_2(OH)_4Si_2O_5$, much of the intersheet bonding is due to 'hydrogen bonding' between the OH^- of one layer and oxygen ions of the adjacent layer. While the forces are not negligible, they are small compared to those involved in covalent or ionic bonds. This weak bonding makes the clays soft and crumbly, and also provides for ready penetration by water, in which hydrogen bonding plays a major role. Clays swell in water as the water molecules penetrate the layers.

Natural clays usually consist of mixtures of tiny crystals of several different clay minerals. The amount of water which penetrates the layers of these crystals will vary with the moisture level of the soil. When much water has penetrated, ions from the soil can also penetrate, and can exchange with the cations binding the layers. These ions are therefore in active contact with the surrounding moisture, at least at times when that moisture level is high. The clays are important in storing moisture for plants and in storing and distributing nutrient ions.

In the tektosilicates, tetrahedral silicon-oxygen linkages extend indefinitely in all three directions. Since all oxygens are shared, the structure has no charge. Silica is the general name for this material, with formula SiO_2. It has two well defined crystal structures, quartz and cristobalite, and a number of variations in which microcrystalline, fine grained quartz is packed in various ways, often with some trace impurities included. Silica is a giant molecule or network solid and is very hard and durable. Many of its forms are valued as gems including cairngorm and amethyst, both quartz forms in which trace impurities account for the colour, and agate, jasper, onyx, chalcedony, carnelian and opal, all microcrystalline quartz variants. Opal differs somewhat from the rest in that it contains a variable water content and is less hard. Quartz has a much more abundant and less glamorous existence too, as the major component of most beach sand.

Substitution of some of the tetravalent silicon by trivalent aluminium generates a negatively charged framework and a profusion of possible structural variations. Many of these belong to the very abundant mineral grouping known as the felspars. Where one silicon in every four is replaced by an aluminium, a singly charged cation must be present as in orthoclase, $KAlSi_3O_8$ or albite, $NaAlSi_3O_8$. Where two silicons in every four are replaced, a divalent cation or two monovalent ones must be present as in celsian, $BaAl_2Si_2O_8$; anorthite, $CaAl_2Si_2O_8$; and nepheline, $KNa_3Al_4Si_4O_{16}$. Crystal structures vary, depending on the ordering of the silicon and aluminium ions and on the arrangement of the tetrahedra. Albite and anorthite are both triclinic, whereas orthoclase and celsian are both monoclinic. As is characteristic of many feldspars, a rather unusual isomorphism occurs. The isomorphic replacement of the *pair* of ions K^+ and Si^{4+} by Ba^{2+} and Al^{3+}, or its reverse, is possible over the entire range of composition. So too is the equivalent substitution in albite and anorthite. Many feldspars are, in chemical terms, solid solutions.

The feldspars are giant molecules and are hard, durable materials. The structures are more open than that of quartz, however, and the hardness less. Much more open structures still are found in the zeolites, the second most abundant group of tektosilicates. It is their open structure which distinguishes them from the feldspars. They readily absorb water into their porous structure. Replacement of cations of the zeolite by cations entering the pores in water is often accomplished easily. Replacement of calcium in water by sodium from a zeolite is a common way of 'softening' water, the sodium being restored by subsequently soaking the zeolite in brine. Zeolites absorb gases and liquids with differing degrees of preference. A zeolite with a particularly strong tendency to absorb water, say, may be used to remove traces of water from an organic solvent or from a stream of gases for which it has much less affinity. Zeolites sold for this purpose are known as molecular sieves.

ADVANCED READING

F. A. Bovey and F. H. Winslow, *Macromolecules*, Academic Press, New York, 1979
This book emphasizes the principles and experimental techniques of polymer science.

R. B. Seymour, *Introduction to Polymer Chemistry*, McGraw-Hill, New York, 1971
This is a general survey of most aspects of polymer chemistry and technology. Less quantitative or advanced than the book above, it does provide much useful information, especially on applications.

K. B. Krauskopf, *Introduction to Geochemistry*, McGraw-Hill, New York, 1967
Several sections of this textbook are devoted to silicate structures and properties.

XV CHEMICAL EQUILIBRIA IN THE GAS PHASE

It has long been known that many processes stop observably short of total conversion of reactants to products. When no further change is observable, such a process is said to have reached a state of equilibrium between reactants and products. The position of this equilibrium is altered by changes in conditions. For example, raising the temperature in a system at equilibrium will result in more products being formed if the process is endothermic, and in more reactants being formed if the process is exothermic. This observation is generalized in a rule due to Le Chatelier, who noted that a system in equilibrium will remain in equilibrium forever in the absence of any externally induced change, but that when the system is subjected to a change, the process will occur in whichever direction serves to reduce or oppose that change. This principle is quite general. For example, where the volume of the products is less than that of the reactants an increase in the pressure imposed on a system at equilibrium will produce more products, whereas a decrease will produce more reactants. Similarly, the addition of a small amount of any one reactant to a system of gases in equilibrium will produce more products whereas addition of a product will produce more reactants.

Le Chatelier's Principle is very important and contains a significant insight which every student of chemistry should understand. The task now is to construct machinery with which one can handle Le Chatelier's Principle quantitatively.

15-1 THE EQUILIBRIUM CONSTANT

The desire to predict the direction of a process in a mixture of reagents and products, and to predict the final or equilibrium state of the particular system has long been a matter of practical concern both to chemists and to industry. Some important relationships were discovered first empirically, before the development of thermodynamics permitted our grasping their relationship to other areas of chemistry. Such empirical tools remain useful, particularly the concept of the *equilibrium constant*.

This concept developed from experimentation with many systems in many laboratories. It became obvious that certain rules applied to the equilibrium positions of all processes, and that these rules could be applied with some confidence to systems or conditions which could not easily be investigated.

These rules may best be learned by examining the experimental data of a pair of early investigators. The reaction of SO_2 with O_2 to yield SO_3 is an important step in producing sulphuric acid and the equilibrium position of this process has long been of practical importance. One of the earliest accurate studies was done by Bodenstein and Pohl in 1905. They worked at several temperatures for various initial ratios of SO_2 to O_2, both in the presence of and absence of a non-participating gas, N_2. Some of their data at 1000 K are shown in Table 15-1.

TABLE 15-1   Experimental Determination of the Existence of an Equilibrium Constant

The data below are taken from a paper by Bodenstein and Pohl (Z. fur Elektrochemie, 11, 373-384 (1905)). The "experiment number" in the first column corresponds to their labelling. All experiments at 1000 K ± 1 K are included.

Experiment Number	Initial Ratios (mol/mol)		Equilibrium Partial Pressures (atm)			$\dfrac{(P_{SO_3}/P^o)^2}{(P_{SO_2}/P^o)^2(P_{O_2}/P^o)}$
	SO_2/O_2	x/O_2	SO_2	SO_3	O_2	
2	1.08	–	.279	.322	.399	3.34
3	1.24	–	.309	.338	.353	3.39
4	2.28	–	.456	.364	.180	3.54
5	2.40	–	.470	.365	.167	3.61
6	2.44	–	.481	.355	.164	3.32
7	3.36	–	.564	.334	.102	3.44
8	3.36	–	.566	.333	.101	3.43
9	7.94	–	.775	.203	.022	3.12
12	2.62	3.76 (N_2)	.248	.128	.080	3.33
13	3.10	3.76 (N_2)	.283	.136	.068	3.40
14	1.06	Large excess of SO_3	.273	.325	.402	3.53
						Average 3.40

It will be seen that the quantity formulated in the last column has the same value, within experimental error, for all cases. Thus, knowing the value of such a quantity, called the equilibrium constant, allows us to predict the direction and endpoint of this process at 1000 K.

These data demonstrate the most important principles of equilibrium constants.

(a) The equilibrium constant is independent of the initial ratios of reagents (compare 2, 4, 7 and 9) and of the absolute amounts of these reagents.

(b) The equilibrium constant is independent of the direction from which it is approached (compare 14 with all others).

(c) The equilibrium constant is independent of the presence of a species not participating in the equilibrium (consider 12 and 13).

The partial pressures *at equilibrium* were always such that the following expression had a value of approximately 3.4. $P°$ is chosen as 101.325 kPa, as it is throughout this textbook.

$$\frac{(P_{SO_3}/P°)^2}{(P_{SO_2}/P°)^2(P_{O_2}/P°)}$$

All studies of all gaseous equilibria at any temperature show the existence of an analogous equilibrium constant at each temperature.

For processes in which all of the reactants and all of the products are gases, the equilibrium expression places in the denominator the product of the ratio of partial pressure to reference pressure for each reactant, with each such expression taken to the power equal to the stoichiometric coefficient. The numerator is composed of equivalent terms for the products.

Thus in the SO_3 case

$$2\,SO_2(g)\; +\; O_2(g)\; \rightleftarrows\; 2\,SO_3(g)$$

$$K \;=\; \frac{(P_{SO_3}/P°)^2}{(P_{SO_2}/P°)^2(P_{O_2}/P°)}$$

where P_{SO_3}, P_{SO_2} and P_{O_2} are the partial pressures of the three substances *at equilibrium*.

It is essential that the meaning of the terms in this expression be understood. If P_{O_2}, P_{SO_2} and P_{SO_3} have values such that the equality is satisfied, the system is at equilibrium with respect to the process and P_{O_2}, P_{SO_2} and P_{SO_3} are equilibrium partial pressures. If the partial pressures do not satisfy this equation, the process can proceed in the direction of equilibrium and only as far as equilibrium, although for rate reasons it may proceed slowly, indeed so slowly that no reaction is observable at all, even over many years. Thus if a particular system at a particular temperature has values of P_{SO_2}, P_{O_2} and P_{SO_3} such that

$$\frac{(P_{SO_3}/P°)^2}{(P_{SO_2}/P°)^2(P_{O_2}/P°)} \;>K$$

then the reaction will proceed by the disappearance of SO_3 (reducing the numerator) and the appearance of SO_2 and O_2 (increasing the denominator) until new values of P_{O_2}, P_{SO_2} and P_{SO_3} are reached such that

$$\frac{(P_{SO_3}/P^\circ)^2}{(P_{SO_2}/P^\circ)^2(P_{O_2}/P^\circ)} = K$$

These new partial pressures of the three materials will be equilibrium pressures and the system is said to be at equilibrium with respect to the process.

It is common to define a quantity known as the reaction quotient, Q. For the particular case under discussion, Q is given by

$$Q = \frac{(P_{SO_3}/P^\circ)^2}{(P_{SO_2}/P^\circ)^2(P_{O_2}/P^\circ)}$$

The arguments of the preceding paragraph can then be phrased as follows. If $Q > K$ or $Q < K$ for a particular system, the process can proceed in whichever direction carries the value of Q towards K. The process will cease when $Q = K$.

The relationship between the form of the equilibrium expression and the stoichiometry of the process to which it refers should be noted carefully. In particular, the value of K for many processes is *specific to the particular statement of the process*. For example, consider the following.

$$2\,SO_2 + O_2 \rightleftarrows 2\,SO_3$$

$$K = \frac{(P_{SO_3}/P^\circ)^2}{(P_{SO_2}/P^\circ)^2(P_{O_2}/P^\circ)}$$

$$SO_2 + \tfrac{1}{2}O_2 \rightleftarrows SO_3$$

$$K' = \frac{(P_{SO_3}/P^\circ)}{(P_{SO_2}/P^\circ)(P_{O_2}/P^\circ)^{\frac{1}{2}}} = K^{\frac{1}{2}}$$

Therefore K and K' are *not* equal. It follows that in quoting an equilibrium constant for a particular process, the exact stoichiometric statement to which it relates must be included. To say that 3.4 is the equilibrium constant, K, for the process $2\,SO_2 + O_2 \rightleftarrows 2\,SO_3$ at 1000 K is an explicit and acceptable statement but it is ambiguous and therefore unacceptable to say that 3.4 is the equilibrium constant, K, at 1000 K, for the equilibrium among SO_2, SO_3 and O_2. Do keep in mind that these differences emerge from different ways of *describing* the process. There is only one reality, and any description will predict the same values for measurable quantities like partial pressures.

Example 15-1 Streams of SO_3, SO_2 and O_2 are fed into a previously evacuated vessel so that

$$P_{SO_3} = P_{SO_2} = P_{O_2} = 200 \text{ kPa}.$$

In what direction can the following process move at 1000 K if the equilibrium constant is 3.4?

$$2\,SO_2 + O_2 \rightleftharpoons 2\,SO_3$$

$$P_{SO_3}/P^\circ = P_{SO_2}/P^\circ = P_{O_2}/P^\circ$$

$$= 200 \times 10^3/101 \times 10^3 = 1.98$$

$$Q = \frac{(1.98)^2}{(1.98)^2(1.98)}$$

$$= 0.505$$

But K = 3.4 so that Q < K. Therefore Q can increase and the process can move to the right. SO_2 and O_2 react to give SO_3 until equilibrium is achieved.

Example 15-2   Carbon monoxide and chlorine are introduced into a vessel at 395 K, forming phosgene according to

$$CO(g) + Cl_2(g) \rightleftharpoons COCl_2(g)$$

At equilibrium, the partial pressures of the three gases are measured as 11.8 kPa, 13.0 kPa and 33.8 kPa respectively. Evaluate K and the total pressure P.

$$P_{CO}/P^\circ = 11.8 \times 10^3/101 \times 10^3 = 0.117$$
$$P_{Cl_2}/P^\circ = 13.0 \times 10^3/101 \times 10^3 = 0.129$$
$$P_{COCl_2}/P^\circ = 33.8 \times 10^3/101 \times 10^3 = 0.335$$

Hence the equilibrium constant is

$$K = \frac{0.335}{0.117 \times 0.129} = 22.2$$

By Dalton's law, the total pressure is

$$P = 11.8 + 13.0 + 33.8 = 58.6 \text{ kPa}$$

Example 15-3   CO, Cl_2 and $COCl_2$ are in equilibrium in a 1.0 L container at 395 K, with partial pressures as in the previous example. Would $COCl_2$ be formed, consumed or unchanged if argon were added (a) with the volume expanding so that total pressure remained at 58.6 kPa, (b) with the volume held constant?

(a) Suppose that the volume increases by a factor F, where F > 1. The immediate effect of this expansion is to decrease the partial pressure of each gas by a factor of $1/F$, and hence to change the reaction quotient from K to $(1/F)(1/F)^{-2}(K)=KF$.

Thus the reaction quotient is greater than K and the process will operate until Q decreases to K. This is done by loss of $COCl_2$ (decreasing the numerator in Q) and consequent formation of CO and Cl_2 (increasing the denominator in Q). Note that the equilibrium *constant* is unchanged, and indeed can be used to calculate the position of the new equilibrium.

(b) Since the partial pressures of the three materials are unchanged the process does not shift either way. Note carefully the distinction between adding an inert gas at constant P, which does cause the process to shift as in part (a), and adding an inert gas at constant V, which does not alter the position of equilibrium.

Example 15-4   A reaction vessel is charged with steam and ethene in a molar ratio of 10:1. Pressure is maintained at 1.0 MPa and temperature at 400 K. Assuming that the only process is

$$C_2H_4(g) + H_2O(g) \rightleftharpoons C_2H_5OH(g)$$

what fraction of ethene is converted to ethanol at equilibrium? K is 0.306.

For every original mole of ethene, suppose n mol of ethanol form. Therefore at equilibrium, for every n mole of C_2H_5OH, there is $1-n$ mol of C_2H_4 and $10-n$ mol of H_2O.

Hence

$$P_{C_2H_5OH} = \frac{n}{n+1-n+10-n}\,(1.0\times10^6) = \frac{n}{11-n}\,(1.0\times10^6)\text{ Pa}$$

$$P_{C_2H_4} = \frac{1-n}{11-n}\,(1.0\times10^6)\text{ Pa}$$

$$P_{H_2O} = \frac{10-n}{11-n}\,(1.0\times10^6)\text{ Pa}$$

Substituting in the equilibrium constant expression for this process,

$$0.306 = \frac{P_{C_2H_5OH}/P^\circ}{(P_{C_2H_4}/P^\circ)(P_{H_2O}/P^\circ)}$$

$$= \frac{\left(\frac{n}{11-n}\right)\left(\frac{P}{P^\circ}\right)}{\left(\frac{1-n}{11-n}\right)\left(\frac{P}{P^\circ}\right)\left(\frac{10-n}{11-n}\right)\left(\frac{P}{P^\circ}\right)}$$

where $P = 1.0\times10^6$ Pa and $P^\circ = 101325$ Pa.

Hence

$$\frac{n(11-n)}{(1-n)(10-n)} = 3.02$$

This is a quadratic equation and has two roots, of which one is greater than 1.0 (which cannot be the case); the other is n = 0.732.

Hence 73.2% of the ethene is converted to ethanol at this temperature and pressure and at this ratio of steam to ethene. Note that (i) increasing the pressure would increase the conversion and (ii) increasing the ratio of steam to ethene would increase the conversion. Work out an example if either of these statements is not clear to you.

Example 15-5 Chlorine dissociates increasingly as temperature increases. At 1800 K, K = 0.106 for the process

$$Cl_2(g) \rightleftharpoons 2Cl\,(g)$$

Calculate the fraction of Cl_2 which dissociates at this temperature for a total pressure of 134 kPa. What is the partial pressure of each species at equilibrium?

Let α be the fraction of Cl_2 to dissociate. If there were N mol of Cl_2 without dissociation, then at equilibrium there are N(1−α) mol of Cl_2 and 2Nα mol of Cl.

$$\frac{P_{Cl}}{P_{Cl_2}} = \frac{(2\alpha)N}{(1-\alpha)N} = \frac{2\alpha}{1-\alpha}$$

$$P_{Cl} = \frac{2\alpha}{1-\alpha}\,P_{Cl_2}$$

But

$$P_{Cl} + P_{Cl_2} = 1.34 \times 10^5 \text{ Pa}$$

Therefore

$$\frac{2\alpha}{1-\alpha}\,P_{Cl_2} + P_{Cl_2} = \frac{1+\alpha}{1-\alpha}\,P_{Cl_2} = 1.34 \times 10^5 \text{ Pa}$$

Also, the equilibrium condition gives

$$\frac{(P_{Cl}/P^\circ)^2}{(P_{Cl_2}/P^\circ)} = \frac{\left(\dfrac{2\alpha}{1-\alpha}\,P_{Cl_2}/1.01\times10^5\right)^2}{(P_{Cl_2}/1.01\times10^5)} = 0.106$$

From these two equations,

$$P_{Cl_2} = \frac{1.34\times10^5\,(1-\alpha)}{1+\alpha} = \frac{0.106\,(1-\alpha)^2(1.01\times10^5)}{(2\alpha)^2}$$

and hence

$$(1.34)(2\alpha)^2 = 0.106(1-\alpha)(1+\alpha)(1.01)$$

$$5.36\alpha^2 = \frac{0.107}{5.467} = 0.0196$$

$$\alpha = 0.140$$

The partial pressures are

$$P_{Cl_2} = \frac{(1-\alpha)}{(1+\alpha)} (1.34 \times 10^5) = 101 \text{ kPa}$$

$$P_{Cl} = \frac{2\alpha}{1-\alpha} P_{Cl_2} = \frac{0.280}{0.860} (101) = 33 \text{ kPa}$$

Example 15-6 At low pressure and high temperature, ethane dehydrogenates to make ethene (or ethylene as it is commonly known) and hydrogen according to the following,

$$C_2H_6(g) \rightleftarrows C_2H_4(g) + H_2(g).$$

If K is 0.0500 at 900 K, calculate the final composition if a mixture of 1000 mol of ethane and 4000 mol of inert nitrogen are passed over a catalyst which allows the above process to come to equilibrium. The pressure is maintained at 60.0 kPa. A catalyst affects the rate of a reaction but not the position of equilibrium.

Suppose n mol of C_2H_6 dehydrogenates.

Total amount of gas $= (1000-n) + (4000) + (n) + (n)$
$ = 5000 + n \text{ mol}$

At equilibrium,

$$P_{C_2H_6}/P^o = \left(\frac{1000-n}{5000+n} \right)\left(\frac{P}{P^o} \right)$$

$$P_{C_2H_4}/P^o = \left(\frac{n}{5000+n} \right)\left(\frac{P}{P^o} \right)$$

$$P_{H_2}/P^o = \left(\frac{n}{5000+n} \right)\left(\frac{P}{P^o} \right)$$

where P = 60 000 Pa and P° = 101 325 Pa.

Therefore

$$\frac{\frac{n^2}{(5000+n)^2} (0.592)^2}{\left(\frac{1000-n}{5000+n} \right) (0.592)} = 0.050$$

Simplifying,

$$11.8\,n^2 = (5000+n)\,(1000-n)$$

and so the following quadratic equation is reached:

$$12.8\,n^2 + 4\times10^3 n - 5\times10^6 = 0$$

This equation has one negative root, which is ignored, and the positive root

$$n = 488 \text{ mol.}$$

The final composition is 488 mol hydrogen, H_2; 488 mol ethylene, C_2H_4; 512 mol ethane, C_2H_6; and 4000 mol nitrogen, N_2 or in terms of mole fractions,

$$Y_{H_2} = Y_{C_2H_4} = 0.0889$$

$$Y_{C_2H_6} = 0.0933$$

$$Y_{N_2} = 0.729$$

15-2 EQUILIBRIUM CONSTANTS EXPRESSED IN TERMS OF CONCENTRATIONS

For some calculations, where data are available in concentrations, it may be convenient to use an equilibrium constant that permits direct calculation in these units.

The concentration of an ideal gas, its amount per unit volume, is proportional to its partial pressure. This can be seen by examining the ideal gas law,

$$PV = nRT$$

$$P = \left(\frac{n}{V}\right)RT = cRT$$

where c represents the concentration. In SI units, this concentration would normally be expressed in the units mol m^{-3}.

In the expression for the reaction quotient, one uses ratios of the partial pressure of each gas to the reference pressure, $P°$. These can be transformed readily into concentrations using the ideal gas law

$$P_A/P° = c_A RT/c°RT = c_A/c°$$

$c°$, the concentration of any ideal gas at $P°$, has a unique value for each temperature. For example at 25°C,

$$c°(25°C) = \frac{P°}{RT} = \frac{101325}{(8.314)(298.15)} = 40.88 \text{ mol m}^{-3}$$

and at 0°C

$$c^o(0°C) = \frac{101325}{(8.314)(273.15)} = 44.62 \text{ mol m}^{-3}$$

Note particularly that c^o is a function of temperature, since gases at any particular pressure become more rarified as the temperature increases.

This last value, at 0°C, is directly related to a number which many students remember, namely that one mole of an ideal gas occupies 22.4 L at P^o, although unfortunately, fewer remember that this applies only at 0°C. c^o is simply an expresssion of the reciprocal of this number. Using the more accurate value of 22.413 L mol^{-1}, one sees that

$$c^o(0°C) = \frac{1}{22.413} \text{ mol L}^{-1} = 0.04462 \text{ mol L}^{-1}$$

$$= 44.62 \text{ mol m}^{-3}$$

Since, at any temperature,

$$P_A/P^o = c_A/c^o$$

the reaction quotient can easily be written in concentration terms. For the general process

$$aA(g) + bB(g) \rightleftharpoons cC(g) + dD(g)$$

the reaction quotient is given by

$$Q = \frac{(P_C/P^o)^c(P_D/P^o)^d}{(P_A/P^o)^a(P_B/P^o)^b} = \frac{(c_C/c^o)^c(c_D/c^o)^d}{(c_A/c^o)^a(c_B/c^o)^b}$$

In the case of the particular example used earlier, this takes the following form.

$$2SO_2(g) + O_2(g) \rightleftharpoons 2SO_3(g)$$

$$Q = \frac{(P_{SO_3}/P^o)^2}{(P_{SO_2}/P^o)^2(P_{O_2}/P^o)} = \frac{(c_{SO_3}/c^o)^2}{(c_{SO_2}/c^o)^2(c_{O_2}/c^o)}$$

The use of this form of the reaction quotient is illustrated by the following example.

Example 15-7   For the process $N_2O_4(g) \rightleftharpoons 2NO_2(g)$, $K = 0.14$ at 298 K.

A vessel of volume 0.500 L contains 0.830 g of an equilibrium mixture of N_2O_4 and NO_2 at 298 K. What is the mass of NO_2 present?

Suppose that m gram of NO_2, and (0.830−m) g of N_2O_4, are present; then the amount of NO_2 is $(m/46.01)$ mol, and the amount of N_2O_4 is $((0.830-m)/92.01)$ mol.

Hence

$$c_{NO_2}/c^o = m/(46.01 \times 500 \times 10^{-6} \times 40.88) = 1.063\ m$$

$$c_{N_2O_4}/c^o = (0.830-m)/(92.01 \times 500 \times 10^{-6} \times 40.88)$$

$$= 0.532\,(0.830-m)$$

Substitution in the expression for the equilibrium constant gives

$$K = \frac{(1.063\ m)^2}{0.532(0.830-m)} = 0.14$$

This quadratic equation has one positive root, $m = 0.203$. Hence the equilibrium mixture contains 0.203 gram of NO_2, and $0.830 - 0.203 = 0.627$ gram of N_2O_4.

15-3   TEMPERATURE DEPENDENCE OF EQUILIBRIUM CONSTANTS

The values of equilibrium constants depend on temperature. Experimental work shows that, for all processes, the equilibrium constant increases with increasing temperature if the process is endothermic ($\Delta H > 0$) and decreases with increasing temperature if the process is exothermic ($\Delta H < 0$). This is, of course, completely in accordance with Le Chatelier's Principle. A compact and quantitative statement of this observation is due to van't Hoff and is of the form

$$\frac{d\ln K}{dT} = \frac{\Delta H}{RT^2}$$

If it can be assumed that ΔH is independent of temperature, an assumption which we saw earlier is fairly sound, then the expression can be integrated to give

$$\ln K'' - \ln K' = \ln \frac{K''}{K'} = \frac{\Delta H}{R}\left(\frac{1}{T'} - \frac{1}{T''}\right)$$

Notice again that this relationship gives quantitative form to one aspect of Le Chatelier's principle, namely that an exothermic reaction (ΔH negative) will be favoured at low temperature (equilibrium constant increased) and retarded at high temperature (equilibrium constant decreased).

Example 15-8   Calculate the equilibrium constant for the process $N_2O_4(g) \rightleftharpoons 2NO_2(g)$ at a temperature of 350 K, given that $K = 0.14$ at 298 K.

From data in Appendix I, the enthalpy change for the process is

$$\Delta H = 2(+33.2) - 9.16 = +57.24 \text{ kJ}$$

Hence

$$\ln \frac{K_{350}}{K_{298}} = \frac{+57240}{8.314} \left(\frac{1}{298} - \frac{1}{350} \right)$$

$$+3.43$$

and so

$$\frac{K_{350}}{K_{298}} = e^{+3.43} = 31.0$$

and therefore

$$K_{350} = 0.14 \times 31.0 = 4.3$$

Notice that ΔH must be converted from kilojoules to joules when it is substituted in this formula, if R is in J K^{-1} mol^{-1}.

The enthalpy change ΔH changes slightly with temperature, and in some cases, the integrated form of the equation will not lead to a sufficiently accurate value of the equilibrium constant if a large temperature change is being considered. This point is brought out in the next example.

Example 15-9   Calculate the equilibrium constant for the process
$2 SO_2 + O_2 \rightleftarrows 2 SO_3$ at 1100 K, assuming that K = 3.4 at 1000 K.

The enthalpy change at 298 K is

$$\Delta H_{298} = 2(-395.7) - 2(-296.83) = -197.74 \text{ kJ}.$$

However, the enthalpy change in the vicinity of 1000 K may be different from this value, and so ΔH at the mid point of 1050 K is calculated next using heat capacities.

$$\Delta H_{1050} = -197.74 + \frac{(1050-298)}{1000} (2 \times 50.7 - 2 \times 39.8 - 29.35)$$

$$= -203.4 \text{ kJ}$$

Using the van't Hoff equation with the corrected ΔH value gives

$$\ln \frac{K_{1100}}{K_{1000}} = \frac{(-203400)}{8.314} \left(\frac{1}{1000} - \frac{1}{1100} \right)$$

$$= -2.22$$

and so $K_{1100} = 3.4 \times e^{-2.22} = 0.37$

The result is not very much different from that obtained using ΔH_{298}, but the correction is sometimes worthwhile.

15-4 HETEROGENEOUS EQUILIBRIA: PROCESSES INVOLVING BOTH GASES AND CONDENSED PHASES

Consider the process below.

$$2\,CO(g) \rightleftharpoons CO_2(g) + C(c)$$

Suppose a container holds CO, CO_2 and graphite in equilibrium with respect to the above process of some high temperature. Addition of CO would result in a spontaneous formation of CO_2 and C, until equilibrium was again attained. Similarly, injection of CO_2 would result in the formation of CO, and the consumption of CO_2 and C, until equilibirium was re-established. However, the addition of solid carbon is found to cause no change in the equilibrium position. In fact, the equilibrium expression can be shown experimentally to be

$$K = \frac{(P_{CO_2}/P^\circ)}{(P_{CO}/P^\circ)^2}$$

In equilibria involving gases with pure solids and/or pure liquids, the equilibrium expression involves only the partial pressures (or concentrations where desired) of the gases. The quantity of either pure solid or pure liquid present does not affect the position of equilibrium although some of the solid or liquid material must be present.

Example 15-10 Write down the equilibrium constant expression for the calcining of limestone,

$$CaCO_3(c) \rightleftharpoons CaO\,(c) + CO_2(g).$$

Since limestone and quicklime are solids, they are ignored in writing down the equilibrium constant:

$$K = P_{CO_2}/P^\circ$$

Example 15-11 For the dehydration process

$$Na_2SO_4 \cdot 10\,H_2O(c) \rightleftharpoons Na_2SO_4(c) + 10\,H_2O(g)$$

the equilibrium pressure of water vapour is 2390 Pa at 298 K. What is K for the process?

The equilibrium constant is

$$K = (P_{H_2O}/P^o)^{10}$$
$$= (2390/101325)^{10}$$
$$= 5.33 \times 10^{-17} .$$

15-5 THE DISTINCTION BETWEEN EQUILIBRIUM CONSIDERATIONS AND RATE CONSIDERATIONS

It is extremely important to remember that equilibrium considerations tell us the direction in which a reaction can go or cannot go, but they tell us nothing about how rapidly it will go. In the process

$$C(c) + O_2(g) \rightleftarrows CO_2(g),$$

the formation of carbon dioxide is highly favoured and once started oxidation will proceed very rapidly and to such an extent that the reactants will appear to be transformed completely into products. The equilibrium constant is very large. Nevertheless, a diamond may be worn in the presence of oxygen for years without the slightest change. Despite the large K, the rate of oxidation under most conditions is so slow that the process, for all practical purposes, does not occur.

Where the equilibrium constant shows that a process *can* occur, reaction rates can often be increased by using a catalyst, a substance that permits the desired reaction to proceed towards equilibrium at a more rapid rate than in its absence. The importance of catalysts in industrial operations can scarcely be overstated. Catalysts permit reactions to go more rapidly than in their absence (thus producing a larger output from a given physical plant) and at more moderate conditions than in their absence (lower temperature and pressure implying less energy and smaller compressors), both of which are of great commercial importance. However, there is another benefit which is often even more important. In many systems, several reactions are possible and, if all possible reactions took place, the resulting mixture of products would waste reagents and would have to be treated in order to separate the required product from the by-products. A catalyst, however, can often be found which enhances the rate of only the desired reaction, and so the proportion of the desired product is increased. In most such circumstances, the process would be impractical without the catalyst.

Despite these formidable qualities of catalysts, however, the important point to be made here is one of limitation. A catalyst can only speed a reaction *toward* equilibrium. It *cannot* cause a process to proceed away from equilibrium, nor can it change the position of equilibrium.

15-6 OTHER FORMULATIONS OF EQUILIBRIUM CONSTANTS

As we have formulated the equilibrium constant in this chapter, the expression for K is dimensionless. This usage will be maintained throughout this text, and is recommended.

However, other treatments are common in the literature. Bodenstein and Pohl, for example, worked with the expression

$$K_p = \frac{P_{SO_3}{}^2}{P_{SO_2}{}^2 P_{O_2}}$$

for the process $2\,SO_2 + O_2 \rightleftharpoons 2\,SO_3$. The "equilibrium constant" in this approach is usually expressed as K_p, and has units related to pressure units. In this example, Bodenstein and Pohl used units of atm^{-1}. Because the reference pressure, $P°$ is unity in their units, the numerical value of their K_p is equal to the numerical value of K, although the latter is dimensionless. This would not be true for other pressure units, unless a different $P°$ is adopted. Whereas K = 3.40 no matter what units of pressure are used,

K_p = 3.40 (atm)$^{-1}$

    = 4.47×10^{-3} (torr)$^{-1}$

    = 0.231 (p.s.i.a.)$^{-1}$

    = 3.36×10^{-5} (Pa)$^{-1}$, depending upon the pressure units.

The use of K_p is to be discouraged, first because it necessitates remembering to express P in a particular set of units (a restraint frequently forgotten when the units are atmospheres and $P°$ is numerically unity) and secondly because it is so often incorrectly used in logarithmic expressions. It will be seen in the next chapter that the logarithm of the equilibrium constant is related to an important quantity in thermodynamics. It is undesirable to take the logarithm of any quantity which has dimensions. The use of K_p is common in the literature, but only the dimensionless K used in this book is properly, readily and rigorously usable in such logarithmic expressions.

Similarly a quantity called K_c is commonly introduced in the literature where K_p has been adopted. Just as K_p has units, so too does K_c. The two are numerically different, except for processes where the amount of gas (in mol) is unchanged when the process operates. For illustration, in the process

$$2\,SO_2(g) + O_2(g) \rightarrow 2\,SO_3(g)$$

$$K_p = 3.40\ \text{atm}^{-1} = \frac{P_{SO_3}{}^2}{P_{SO_2}{}^2 P_{O_2}}$$

By substituting from the ideal gas law for the partial pressures, one reaches

$$K_p = \frac{c_{SO_3}{}^2 R^2 T^2}{c_{SO_2}{}^2 R^2 T^2 c_{O_2} RT} = \frac{c_{SO_3}{}^2}{c_{SO_2}{}^2 c_{O_2}} \cdot \frac{1}{RT}$$

The quantity K_c is then defined as

$$K_c \equiv \frac{c_{SO_3}{}^2}{c_{SO_2}{}^2 c_{O_2}}$$

where c is in mol m^{-3} for S.I. units. Thus

$$K_p = K_c (RT)^{-1}$$

and in general,

$$K_p = K_c (RT)^{\Delta n}$$

where Δn is the change in amount of gaseous substances in the process of concern. Note that for a process such as

$$H_2(g) + Cl_2(g) \rightleftarrows 2\,HCl(g)$$

Δn is zero and $K_p = K_c$.

Where K_p is in units derived from atmospheres, it is usual to use R = 0.08205 atm L mol^{-1} K^{-1}, so that concentrations are in mol L^{-1}.

Mention of K_p and K_c is made only because they are so commonly met elsewhere. It must be emphasized that neither is necessary in order to make any calculation, and neither is used in further work in this book.

PROBLEMS

1. Sulphuryl chloride partially dissociates into sulphur dioxide and chlorine as shown.

$$SO_2Cl_2(g) \rightleftarrows SO_2(g) + Cl_2(g)$$

When the pressure is 98.0 kPa and the temperature 300 K, 12.1% of the sulphuryl chloride is decomposed at equilibrium. Evaluate K. Would the decomposition be less or more if the volume of the container were reduced in order to raise the pressure?

[0.0144; less]

2. The manufacture of hydrogen from coal, using steam, is a possible method of obtaining a readily transportable, non-polluting fuel from inac-

cessible coal reserves. Assume that the process is simply that shown below. Would the amount of hydrogen at equilibrium be increased at higher temperature? Would it be increased at higher pressure?

$$C(graphite) + 2 H_2O(g) \rightleftarrows CO_2(g) + 2 H_2(g)$$

[yes; no]

3. For the process

$$H_2(g) + I_2(g) \rightleftarrows 2 HI(g)$$

at 700 K, the equilibrium constant K is measured to be 55.3. What is the equilibrium constant at 700 K for the following process?

$$HI(g) \rightleftarrows \tfrac{1}{2} H_2(g) + \tfrac{1}{2} I_2(g)$$

[0.1345]

4. In a mixture of H_2, I_2 and HI at 700 K, $P_{HI} = 96$ kPa, $P_{H_2} = 2$ kPa and $P_{I_2} = 2$ kPa. Can a reaction occur? If so, will HI form or disappear?

[Yes, HI will disappear]

5. For the process

$$SO_2Cl_2(g) \rightleftarrows SO_2(g) + Cl_2(g)$$

at 375.0 K, K = 2.4. Suppose that 6.745 g of SO_2Cl_2 is placed in a previously evacuated one litre bulb and the temperature is raised to 375.0 K. What would be the pressure of SO_2Cl_2 if none of it dissociated? What is its partial pressure taking dissociation into account? What is the total pressure taking dissociation into account?

[155.8 kPa, 47.9 kPa, 263.6 kPa]

6. For the process

$$N_2O_4(g) \rightleftarrows 2 NO_2(g)$$

the equilibrium constant at 300 K is 0.14. What final pressure would result at equilibrium from placing 1.00 g of N_2O_4 into a previously evacuated one litre vessel at this temperature?

[35.4 kPa]

7. In Problem 6, the equilibrium involved 7.6×10^{-3} mol of N_2O_4 ($P_{N_2O_4} = 18.9$ kPa) and 6.6×10^{-3} mol of NO_2 ($P_{NO_2} = 16.5$ kPa). In what direction would the process go, if any, on adding 1.42×10^{-2} mol of argon (i) if the volume were simultaneously doubled to two litres, (ii) if the volume were increased so that the total pressure was held constant at

35.4 kPa, (iii) if the volume were held constant?

[(i) to form NO_2 (ii) to form NO_2 (iii) no change]

8. When a mixture containing initial mole fractions 0.75 of H_2 and 0.25 of N_2 was kept at 673 K and 1.0 MPa in the presence of a catalyst, the mole fraction of ammonia in the resulting equilibrium mixture was 0.0385. Calculate the pressure required to give a mole fraction of ammonia of 0.20 at equilibrium at the same temperature.

[7.50 MPa]

9. For the dissociation of iodine vapour

$$I_2(g) \rightleftarrows 2\,I(g)$$

the equilibrium constant is 0.0115 at 1073 K. If ΔH for this reaction is roughly constant at 149 kJ mol^{-1} in the range 1073 K to 1273 K, calculate K at 1273 K. What fraction of iodine is dissociated at 1273 K for a total pressure of 10.0 kPa?

[0.159, 0.536]

10. The equilibrium constants at 1000 K are as given for the two processes below.

$$N_2(g) + O_2(g) \rightarrow 2\,NO(g) \qquad K = 1.5 \times 10^{-4}$$
$$N_2(g) + 2\,O_2(g) \rightarrow 2\,NO_2(g) \qquad K = 1.0 \times 10^{-5}$$

Estimate the pressure at which an initial mixture of N_2 and O_2 in which the mole fraction of N_2 is 0.4 would produce equal amounts of NO and NO_2 at 1000 K. What are the mole fractions of all components under these conditions?

[2.56 MPa; $X_{NO} = X_{NO_2} = 6\times10^{-3}$, $X_{N_2} = 0.395$, $X_{O_2} = 0.593$]

11. The equilibrium constant for the process

$$FeO(c) + CO(g) \rightleftarrows Fe(c) + CO_2(g)$$

is K = 0.403 at a temperature of 1000 K. A stream of pure CO is passed over powdered FeO at 1000 K, so that equilibrium is reached. What is the mole fraction of CO in the gas stream after leaving the reaction zone?

[0.713]

XVI SPONTANEITY AND EQUILIBRIUM: THE SECOND LAW OF THERMODYNAMICS

In the previous chapter, the idea of an equilibrium constant was introduced as an empirical rationalization of experimental data for reacting systems. The equilibrium constant describes the position of equilibrium and, by implication, the possible direction of a chemical process, since a process can only go toward equilibrium, never away from it.

The value of the equilibrium constant can be related mathematically to measurements made in other areas of chemistry. This is done most conveniently through functions such as the Gibbs Energy, G, and the entropy, S. These are functions which were invented because the second law of thermodynamics makes it clear that functions so defined will be useful. It must be emphasized that the second law is not the only way to *prove* the existence of equilibrium constants. The fact that equilibrium constants have been shown experimentally to exist (within the limitations of the ideal gas law) wherever they have been measured is the basic reason for believing in them. Knowing that their existence is predicted by the second law is important evidence of the validity of that law. Nevertheless, the thermodynamic approach is extremely valuable. First, it shows that the experimental data on equilibria are consistent with the second law of thermodynamics. Secondly, the relationship permits the accurate calculation of equilibrium constants using thermochemical and other data acquired in quite different systems and experiments. Thirdly, it permits evaluation of the useful energy which can be extracted from a system in a non-equilibrium state as it proceeds to equilibrium. Finally, it indicates to us how equilibria can be handled mathematically in varied circumstances, such as at pressures that are too high for the ideal gas law to be accurate.

16-1 THERMODYNAMIC REVERSIBILITY

The first law of thermodynamics is a statement that energy cannot be created or destroyed. When energy is added to a system, it results in a change in the internal energy of the system equal to the energy added, be it as heat, as work, or as both. This was expressed by writing

$$\Delta U = q + w$$

Given the initial and final states of the system, the change in internal energy, ΔU, is the same no matter how the change came about; the change ΔU can come about through many different combinations of q and w.

In applying thermodynamics to equilibria and in making use of the second law, we must begin to take account of *how* a process is carried out. We must look in some detail at the *path* by which a system changes from one state to another. Of particular concern will be a kind of limiting case where the process is carried out *reversibly*, as distinct from processes that are *natural* or *spontaneous*.

When a process is carried out reversibly, it is possible to return both the system *and* its surroundings to their initial state. Reversibility in thermodynamics does not just mean that a process taking a system from A to B is such that the system can be returned to A. Most changes can be reversed in that sense, and the ability to carry out such reversal does not depend on the path taken originally. What is meant in thermodynamics by reversible is that if the state of the system changes from A to B via a reversible path, then it is always possible to return the system from B to A in such a way as to leave *both* the system and its surroundings unaltered.

Consider the explosive reaction of hydrogen gas with oxygen gas to form water. This reaction proceeds spontaneously, once initiated, and is therefore *natural.* The original hydrogen and oxygen could be recreated, by electrolysis of the water, but the electricity needed must be generated—by water flowing downhill, or by nuclear fission, or by combustion of some fossil fuel. Restoration of these systems, for instance returning the water to the top of the hill, in turn requires some change in some other system. The universe is permanently altered by the spontaneous combustion of hydrogen. Spontaneity implies irreversibility. *Natural* or irreversible processes are all those processes that do actually occur spontaneously. They proceed toward some final equilibrium condition and can normally do so by any one of many routes. *Unnatural* processes will be the term used to describe a process proceeding in a direction away from equilibrium. Such a process never occurs in an isolated system but may be induced by suitable input of energy, an example being the recharging of a battery by an electric current. *Reversible* processes are a limiting case between natural and unnatural processes, involving passage in either direction by such a route that no departure from equilibrium ever occurs. Reversible processes do not occur in nature but we can, by suitable choice of conditions, visualize and sometimes achieve experimentally a natural process differing from the reversible process by as small an amount as we choose. A mechanical example follows.

Figure 16-1 illustrates a cylinder containing a piston of mass *M*. The piston is attached to a tray on which extra mass can be placed. The entire apparatus is surrounded by a vacuum within a suitable enclosure as in Figure 5-1. The piston moves within the cylinder without friction, and forms at the same time a perfectly gas-tight seal. Although actual construction of a device with these

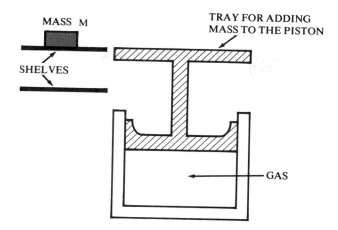

MASS M

TRAY FOR ADDING
MASS TO THE PISTON

SHELVES

GAS

Figure 16-1

properties is unlikely, it can be approached to whatever limit is set by the materials available and by the skill of the machinist.

The system under study is contained within the piston and cylinder. For simplicity, consider the system to be a gas. The piston and cylinder themselves are part of the surroundings.

If the cylinder has a cross sectional area A and the gravitational acceleration is g, then the pressure exerted on the system by the piston will be Mg/A. The total mass of the piston, and hence the pressure it exerts, can be altered by sliding extra mass from or to adjacent shelves. This operation is frictionless and work-free. In Figure 16-1, two shelves are shown. The height of the upper one is set to be equal to that of the tray when the gas is at equilibrium under the pressure of the piston alone.

If the mass, m, is slid from the upper shelf onto the tray of the piston, the downward force is increased and the piston falls. Such a spontaneous process is called a *natural* process. The falling piston compresses the gas and raises its pressure until a new equilibrium is reached with the gas pressure equal to $(M+m)g/A$.

Now, sliding the mass m aside onto the second of the shelves allows the piston to return to its initial position. The *system*, the gas within the cylinder, is now in its initial state exactly. This two-step process, the compression followed by the expansion, is called a *cycle*, a word used to describe any set of steps which leaves the system in the same state as it was initially. However, neither the compression nor the expansion were reversible processes.

Why not? Because a reversible process is such that the system can be restored to its initial state in such a way that the universe is unchanged. In our example, the universe has changed. The mass m, originally on a high shelf, is now on a low shelf. To restore it to its former position requires work, and the provision of that work would in turn leave something else changed. The universe has been permanently altered.

Could this compression of the gas have been carried out reversibly? The apparatus shown in Figure 16-2 allows compression of a gas in a way that can be made to approach reversibility. The piston and cylinder are the same, but the

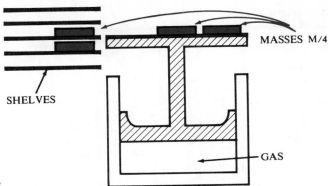

SHELVES

MASSES M/4

GAS

Figure 16-2

mass m has been divided into four equal parts and there are five shelves instead of two. The second shelf from the top is situated so that when mass $m/4$ is added to the tray, the tray lies opposite the second shelf. The third shelf is situated so that when mass $2m/2$ is added to the tray, the tray lies opposite the third shelf, and so on. The bottom shelf is in the same place as the bottom shelf of Figure 16-1. The compression is carried out by placing the four masses $m/4$ on the four upper shelves, and sliding them one by one on to the tray. When all four masses are on the tray, the total pressure in the gas is $(M+m)g/A$, exactly the same as it was after the first compression carried out with the apparatus of Figure 16-1.

Consider the reversal of this compression, which is carried out by sliding the masses one by one on to successively higher shelves. The shelves have been positioned so that this can be done without any friction. When all four masses are back on the shelves, the piston is back at its initial position, and the gas has been returned to its initial state. After the expansion, the four masses $m/4$ are situated on the four lower shelves; the net effect of the compression followed by the expansion has been to transfer mass $m/4$ from the top shelf to the bottom shelf. Clearly this is a smaller change in the surroundings than the transfer of the total mass m, which occurred in the apparatus of Figure 16-1. Hence the second method of compression is closer to being reversible than the first.

There is no theoretical limit to how finely the mass m can be divided, and hence the mass which is effectively transferred from the top shelf to the bottom shelf can be made as small as one pleases. In this case, the compression is a reversible process because the gas can be expanded by reversing the process to leave the system unchanged and the surroundings changed by only an infinitesimal amount.

In this argument using the piston and cylinder can be seen a second important aspect of reversibility. A process is reversible if it can be shown that the process changes direction at any point for small opposite changes in conditions such as temperature or pressure. In other words, the system is at all times at equilibrium with itself and with its surroundings during the process, except for infinitesimal departures. This concept applies equally to chemical and to mechanical equilibria, and it provides an experimental criteria for equilibrium.

In the example earlier, weights were removed in such infinitesimal steps during the reversible process that the system was at all times, except for infinitesimal departures, at equilibrium.

Yet another example would be the simple case of changing the temperature of a block of material, say 1.00 mol of copper at constant pressure. A heat bath is a device which can take in or give out heat without changing temperature, such as a mixture of ice and water. If the block of copper were at 100°C and one wished to change its temperature to 0°C, one could place it in a heat bath at 0°C until this was achieved. Since the heat capacity of copper is 24.4 J K^{-1} mol^{-1}, the system moves $(1)(24.4)(273-373) = -2440$ J to the heat bath. The system may be returned to 100°C by placing it in contact with a heat bath at 100°C, from which it draws 2440 J. From the viewpoint of the system, a cycle has been completed and the system is unchanged but the surroundings have been irreversibly altered. 2440 J has been lost by the heat bath at 100°C and gained by that at 0°C. This situation cannot be reversed except by changing something else.

In exact analogy with the mechanical system, a series of heat baths could be used to reduce the effect on the surroundings. The use of an additional bath at 50°C, which gains 1220 J in the cooling step and releases it again in the heating step, cuts the effect in half. The use of an infinite number of baths, each infinitesimally different in temperature from the next, would permit the processes to be carried out reversibly. What matters for reversibility to exist is not the amount of heat, which is in fact exactly the same in all the cooling steps and in all the heating steps, but that the system never differs in temperature by more than an infinitesimal amount from its surroundings.

Finally, it is essential to understand and to remember that when thinking about the terms *reversible* and *natural* both the system *and* the surroundings must be kept in mind. A process is reversible only if the entire universe, system and surroundings, can be brought back to its condition before the process took place.

16-2   THE SECOND LAW OF THERMODYNAMICS

The first law of thermodynamics is a statement that energy cannot be created or destroyed. Most statements of the first law are easy to understand and can be related to this simple idea easily. By contrast, the second law appears commonly in several different forms which appear at first to be quite unrelated to each other. The equivalence of the various forms is often not easy to prove, and the student must be prepared for difficulties in comparing the discussions in various books. The statement of the second law which will be used in this book is as follows.

> "It is impossible to take heat from a body of uniform temperature and convert it entirely into work without causing a change in the thermodynamic state of some other body."

One way to illustrate the commonsense basis for this statement of the second law is to consider a ship sailing in a sea of uniform temperature. It is consistent with the first law to imagine that the ship has an engine which extracts heat from seawater, converts the heat into the work necessary to drive the ship, and returns the cooled water to the sea, because all the work extracted from the seawater is dissipated in friction on the hull and propellers and is therefore converted back to heat within the sea. Thus, energy is not created or destroyed, the sea is unchanged, and yet the ship is moving steadily through the water. Experience tells us that such a ship is impossible even though the first law is not violated. The second law expresses this experience.

16-3   THE CARNOT MACHINE

The statement of the second law given in the last section is qualitative in nature, and it is difficult at the outset to imagine that it forms the basis for understanding an immense variety of phenomena in chemistry, physics and engineering on a quantitative, numerical basis. The building of this understanding is begun here by studying a theoretical machine devised by the engineer Carnot in his studies of thermodynamics.

The machine contains a frictionless, gas-tight cylinder and piston of the type described earlier. Such a device cannot be made in practice, but nevertheless one can derive accurate relationships by asking what would happen if operations were carried out in such a device. Doubters can approach the conditions of the ideal Carnot machine experimentally as closely as their skill, patience, and budget allow.

In addition to the piston and cylinder, the Carnot machine contains two heat baths and a block of insulation. The heat baths are at different temperatures, the cold bath at T_c and the hot bath at T_h. In the nature of heat baths, heat T_A and T_B. In the nature of heat baths, heat may be added or withdrawn

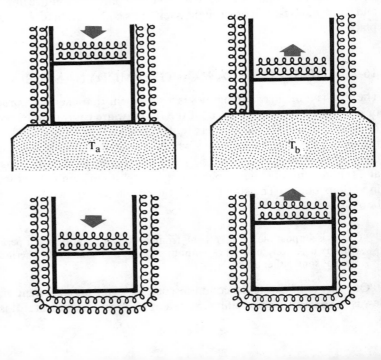

Figure 16-3

without changing the temperature of the bath, and such additions or withdrawals are always reversible with respect to the bath. The piston and cylinder fit perfectly and yet are frictionless. They are perfectly insulated from their surroundings but at some point, say the bottom of the cylinder, the insulation can be removed so that the cylinder can contact one or the other heat bath. The working substance, our system, is enclosed in the piston and cylinder.

Consider the following four-step cyclic process performed on any system in a Carnot apparatus. The heat and work terms associated with each step are defined, and then examined in the following sections.

Step One: While in contact with a heat bath at temperature T_A the system is compressed isothermally and reversibly. As a result, a quantity of heat q_A is transferred between the system and the heat bath. The sign of q_A will be discussed later. For step one, designate $q = q_A$ and $w = w_1$.

Step Two: The heat bath is replaced by insulation so that no heat can pass into or out of the system. Reversible adiabatic compression is carried out until the temperature has altered to T_B. For step two, $q = 0$ and w is designated as $w = w_2$.

Step Three: The insulation is replaced by a heat bath at temperature T_B. The pressure is reduced by a reversible, isothermal expansion; the extent of the expansion is chosen so that step four will return the system to its initial state. A quantity of heat q_B is transferred between the system and the heat bath. Again the sign of q_B will be considered later. $q = q_B$ and $w = w_3$.

Step Four: The heat bath at T_B is replaced by insulation, and the system is expanded reversibly and adiabatically until it reaches the initial state of temperature, pressure and volume. For step four $q = 0$ and w is designated as w_4.

If the total heat and total work for the complete cycle are designated respectively, q_t and w_t, then

$$q_t = q_A + 0 + q_B + 0 = q_A + q_B$$

$$w_t = w_1 + w_2 + w_3 + w_4$$

This set of operations is the basis for the arguments in the two following sections.

16-4   LIMITATIONS ON THE RELATIONSHIP OF HEAT AND WORK IN A CYCLE

In deriving the relationships of this section, it is assumed that the operations above are those of an engine, so that the total work over a cycle is negative ($w_t < 0$). The validity of the argument does not depend on this, however. Since every step in a Carnot cycle is reversible, the entire cycle can be carried out in reverse, beginning with a reversible, adiabatic compression, followed by a reversible, isothermal compression and so forth. Each heat and work quantity in this reverse cycle must be equal in magnitude but opposite in sign to its counterpart in the original cycle, or the processes would not be reversible.

Thus, if the original cycle had resulted in w_t being positive, the reversed cycle would produce a w_t that was negative and one could work from that.

The object of this section is to show that for a Carnot cycle in which w_t is negative, whichever q is associated with the colder temperature (call it q_c) must be negative, whichever q is associated with the hotter temperature (q_h) must be positive and $|q_h| > |q_c|$. Let us assume for now that

$$q_A = q_c$$

$$q_B = q_h$$

Notice that this assumption involves an implicit assumption about which method of operation (compression at T_c and expansion at T_h) leads to an output of work ($w_t < 0$). This assumption will be examined at the end of this section.

Because the system has completed a cycle, its internal energy is unchanged and therefore

$$\Delta U = 0 = q_t + w_t = q_c + q_h + w_t$$

$$\therefore w_t = -(q_c + q_h)$$

Since w_t is negative, the sum $(q_c + q_h)$ is positive. Hence

either   (i) q_c and q_h are positive
or   (ii) q_c is positive, q_h is negative $|q_c| > |q_h|$
or   (iii) q_c is negative, q_h is positive $|q_h| > |q_c|$

In words, this means that since the system has been restored to its initial state, the energy represented by the work came either from both baths, from the cold bath or from the hot bath. No other options are available.

Suppose that (i) is true. Since $T_h > T_c$, the two baths can be connected until an amount of heat q_c has flowed from the hot bath to the cold bath. The cold bath has now regained all it lost to the system. The hot bath has lost $q_c + q_h$ and work $= w_t = -(q_c + q_h)$ has been done by the system. But now heat has been transformed to work using heat from one bath only, which is contrary to the second law. Therefore the proposition (i) is impossible.

It can be shown by an analogous argument that proposition (ii) is wrong. Therefore q_c is negative, q_h is positive, and $|q_h| > |q_c|$.

It was noted in passing that if the above cycle were reversed, each of the terms, q_c, q_h and w would have the same absolute value but the opposite sign. Such a device would be a refrigerator, pumping heat from low temperature to high temperature. Notice that this application to refrigerators of an analogy to the Carnot cycle engine argument shows that, although a refrigerator can of course pump heat from hot to cold, it can pump heat *reversibly* only from cold to hot. Indeed it is obvious that pumping heat from hot to cold would be irreversible, since such a process is natural, and can occur even in the absence of a refrigerator system.

It is timely to examine the question of the sign of q for compression of the system. We have shown, quite generally for any system, that if w_t is negative (work comes from the system), q_h must be positive (heat is taken into the system from the high temperature bath) and q_c is negative (heat leaves the system to the low temperature bath). We further assumed, with a cautionary insert, that it was expansion of the system at T_h and compression at T_c that would bring this about. Nearly always, it will be so. For any system which expands when the temperature rises, this will be so, and that includes all gases as consideration of the ideal gas law will demonstrate. A very few systems, however, such as liquid water between 0°C and 4°C *contract* when the temperature rises. Water in this region will *cool* if compressed adiabatically and will draw heat in if compressed isothermally. All of the Carnot arguments would still apply but we should need to compress water at T_h and expand it at T_c in order to operate an engine.

In summary: For a reversible cycle operating on any system between two temperatures T_c and T_h, if $w < 0$, then $q_c < 0$ and $q_h > 0$.

16-5 THE DERIVATION OF AN ABSOLUTE SCALE OF TEMPERATURE

One can grasp the concept of temperature readily enough from daily experience. One body is "hotter" and one is "colder." Heat flows naturally from that which is hot to that which is cold. Until this point, however, we have been dependent for quantitative temperature scales on the properties of particular materials, such as the thermal expansion coefficient of mercury or, more general but less realizable, the volume of a quantity of ideal gas. In the argument below, one sees that the ratio of the amounts of heat transferred by the two baths to the system during each cycle of a Carnot engine is *independent of the system* and dependent only on the temperature of the two baths. A temperature scale defined in terms of the ratio of these two heat terms has an existence quite independent of the properties of any material or group of materials. Its derivation is as follows.

Consider N_A cycles of a Carnot engine containing the system A, where A can be any substance or substances. Designate the work produced by the N_A cycles as $N_A w_A$ and the heat terms associated with the two baths at T_c and T_h as $N_A q_{cA}$ and $N_A q_{hA}$ respectively.

Now we replace the system A with some other system B in the Carnot engine, and run the engine as a refrigerator, for a number of cycles, N_B, such that

$$N_A q_{cA} + N_B q_{cB} = 0.$$

This simply means that the cycle is operated as an engine with one system and as a refrigerator with the other, and N_A and N_B are chosen so that, with whatever accuracy we desire, the low temperature bath is left unchanged, having as much heat added to it in the engine cycles as is removed from it by the refrigerator cycles.

Because the operations performed on both A and B are cyclic, both systems are left unchanged and the value of ΔU for each must be zero. Hence by the first law

$$N_A(q_{cA} + q_{hA} + w_A) = 0$$

and

$$N_B(q_{cB} + q_{hB} + w_B) = 0$$

Summing these two gives

$$N_A q_{cA} + N_B q_{cB} + N_A q_{hA} + N_B q_{hB} + N_A w_A + N_B w_B = 0.$$

It is the essence of this hypothetical experiment that N_A and N_B are chosen such that, to any degree of accuracy desired,

$$N_A q_{cA} + N_B q_{cB} = 0$$

and therefore it follows that

$$N_A q_{hA} + N_B q_{hB} = -(N_A w_A + N_B w_B).$$

Now $-(N_A w_A + N_B w_B)$ is the total amount of work produced by the total process. This amount of work is produced entirely from heat from the hot bath and so cannot be positive, by the second law. This work cannot be negative either, for if it were, we could run the Carnot cycles on both A and B in reverse thereby changing the signs of all q's and w's, making the total work positive and in violation of the second law again. Hence the total work must be zero:

$$-(N_A w_A + N_B w_B) = 0$$

Hence also

$$N_A q_{hA} + N_B q_{hB} = 0$$

Therefore

$$\frac{q_{hA}}{q_{hB}} = -\frac{N_B}{N_A} = \frac{q_{cA}}{q_{cB}}$$

Therefore

$$\frac{q_{cA}}{q_{hA}} = \frac{q_{cB}}{q_{hB}}$$

The ratio q_c/q_h is thus shown to be the same no matter what system is used in the Carnot engine. It depends only on the temperatures of the two baths themselves.

Since the ratio q_c/q_h depends on the ratio of some function of temperature, and only on that, it is possible to choose this function as the *definition* of temperature itself.

$$\frac{T_c}{T_h} \equiv (\text{constant}) \frac{q_c}{q_h}$$

The student of thermodynamics should note that this statement is consistent with our earlier ideas about temperature. The most basic and qualitative statement is that heat always flows naturally from a hot system to a cold system. This definition takes as our *measure* of temperature *how much* heat flows under the precisely defined conditions of operating a Carnot Machine.

The choice of the constant is still open to definition. Since q_h and q_c must always have the opposite signs, a temperature scale which is always positive can be obtained by choosing a constant of -1. Thus

$$\frac{T_c}{T_h} = -\frac{q_c}{q_h}$$

Since the ratio of two temperatures, T_c/T_h, can be measured by the ratio of the heat terms of a Carnot Machine, q_c/q_h, using *any* substance including an ideal gas, this definition of temperature coincides exactly with that used earlier based on ideal gas properties. It assures us of the usefulness and importance of the ideal gas temperature scale while at the same time demonstrating that this scale is equally valid for any substance, and that such real substances may be used to calibrate the scale.

Two points should be made in summary.

(a) A reversible engine operating between a high temperature and a low temperature can only produce work by 'wasting' some of the heat which it receives from the high temperature side to the low temperature side.

(b) In the operation of a Carnot Machine, and indeed of every machine in which every step is carried out reversibly, the ratio q_h/q_c is independent of the size and composition of the system. That ratio depends only on the temperatures of the heat baths, and thus forms an excellent basis for the definition of temperature. Such a definition, when applied to any ideal machine in which all of the steps are reversible, leads to the important statement that

$$\frac{q_c}{T_c} + \frac{q_h}{T_h} = 0$$

16-6 ENTROPY

The concept of thermodynamically reversible processes leads to another concept, the function *entropy,* which is given the symbol S. Entropy is a state function, like P or H or U, but it is defined in an unusual way, as follows:

$$dS \equiv \frac{dq_{rev}}{T}$$

In this definition, dS is the infinitesimal change in the value of S as a system moves from one state (T, P, U, etc.) to another that is infinitesimally different (T + dT, P + dP, etc.). The change in entropy for a larger change in the system from state 1 to state 2 may be obtained by integration

$$S_2 - S_1 = \Delta S = \int_1^2 dS$$

The mechanics of such integration will be considered later using specific examples.

It may seem impossible, at first glance, to define a state function, S, in terms of a function, q, which is not *usually* uniquely determined by the initial and final state. However, it is not any dq, but a particular one, dq_{rev}, that is used.

The proof that S is a state function can be carried out using the Carnot cycle. It was proved in the last section that for a Carnot cycle, made up of reversible steps,

$$\frac{q_c}{T_c} + \frac{q_h}{T_h} = 0$$

Since the entropy changes are zero for each of the reversible adiabatic steps, q_{rev} being zero for each, this equation shows that ΔS for the entire Carnot cycle is zero. This is indeed true for any reversible cycle*, from which it follows that ΔS is a state function.

Where the chemical composition and the physical state are unchanged, entropy calculations are particularly simple. These are cases where the only process of interest is the 'heating' or 'cooling' of the substance. The heat required to achieve a given change in temperature is affected by whether the process is at constant pressure or constant volume, but as was pointed out in Section 16-1, it is not affected by whether or not the process is reversible. Hence the reversible heat term for a process at constant pressure can be stated to be

$$dq_{rev} = nC_p dT$$

from which it follows that

$$dS \equiv \frac{dq_{rev}}{T} = \frac{nC_p dT}{T}$$

and hence that

$$\Delta S = \int_{T_1}^{T_2} dS = \int_{T_1}^{T_2} \frac{nC_p dT}{T} = nC_p \ln \frac{T_2}{T_1}$$

The final integration above assumes that C_p does not change with temperature. As with enthalpy calculations, if C_p does change with temperature, the integration can be carried out conveniently using an algebraic expression for C_p as a function of temperature, usually of the form

$$C_p = a + bT + cT^2$$

Example 16-1 Calculate the entropy change when a 1.505 kg copper reaction vessel containing 1.004 kg of water is heated from 294.6 K to 300.0 K.

$$n_{Cu} = \frac{1.505 \text{ kg}}{0.063546 \text{ kg mol}^{-1}} = 23.68 \text{ mol}$$

$$n_{H_2O} = \frac{1.004 \text{ kg}}{0.018015 \text{ kg mol}^{-1}} = 55.73 \text{ mol}$$

It is usually sufficiently accurate to assume that C_p is independent of temperature. Appendix 1 tabulates values for C_p at 298.15 K, and these may be used for a reasonable temperature range on each side of this temperature. For

---

*For a proof, see The Principles of Chemical Equilibrium, K.G. Denbigh, Cambridge University Press, England, 1971.

the highest accuracy, C_p must be known as a function of T but here it is taken to be independent of T.

From Appendix 1

$$C_p(Cu) = 24.4 \text{ J K}^{-1} \text{ mol}^{-1}$$

$$C_p(H_2O(l)) = 75.29 \text{ J K}^{-1} \text{ mol}^{-1}$$

$$\Delta S = [(23.68)(24.4) + (55.73)(75.29)] \ln \left(\frac{300.0}{294.6} \right)$$

$$= 4773.7 \ln \frac{300.0}{294.6}$$

$$= 86.7 \text{ J K}^{-1}$$

It is worthwhile noting that for a process (other than an adiabatic process) to be reversible, it is necessary for the system undergoing that process to be at the same temperature as the surroundings, or differ at most by an infinitesimal amount. The q_{rev} terms for the surroundings must be equal in magnitude but opposite in sign from the same term for the system, since any heat passes from one to the other. Consequently, the entropy change for the surroundings due to a reversible process must be equal in magnitude but opposite in sign to that for the system. The entropy change for the universe, which is the sum of these two, is zero. A simple definition of reversibility therefore would be that a reversible process is one which does not alter the entropy of the universe.

16-7 ENTROPY CALCULATIONS FOR CHEMICAL REACTIONS

In order to permit calculations of entropy changes in chemical processes it is convenient to tabulate values of the *absolute entropy*, S°, for each substance. To define such a quantity requires making an assumption which may be stated, a little imprecisely, as that all substances which form crystalline solids would have zero entropy at 0 K. This is the so-called third law of thermodynamics. Its reasonableness should be considered after reading Section 16-11. Combined with a knowledge of the heat capacity of each substance over the range 0 K to 298.15 K, it can be used to define the entropy of a substance at $P = P^\circ$ and $T = 298.15$ K by

$$S^\circ = (S_{298.15} - S_0)_{P=P^\circ} = \int_0^{298.15} \frac{C_p(T)dT}{T}$$

Over this range, C_p always exhibits important temperature variations which must be known in order to evaluate S°. Appendix 1 includes values of S° for most substances listed. These can be used to calculate ΔS for any process at 101.325 kPa and 298.15 K, and, in combination with heat capacity data, to calculate ΔS for any process at 101.325 kPa and any temperature. It should be noted that the absolute entropies of the elements are not zero.

Example 16-2 Calculate ΔS for the following process at 298.15 K and 101.325 kPa

$$C(c) + 2\,Cl_2\,(g) \rightarrow CCl_4\,(l)$$

$$\Delta S = S°\,(CCl_4,\,l) - S°(C,\,c) - 2S°(Cl_2,\,g)$$

$$= 216.4 - 5.7 - 2(222.96)$$

$$= -235.3 \text{ J K}^{-1}$$

Example 16-3 Calculate ΔS for the following process at 373.15 K and 101.325 kPa

$$H_2O(l) \rightarrow H_2O(g)$$

After using tabulated data to calculate ΔS at 298.15 K, the value of ΔS at 373.15 K can be obtained by considering the following cyclic process.

$$H_2O(\,l\,,\,373.15\text{ K}) \xrightarrow{\Delta S} H_2O(g,\,373.15\text{ K})$$

$$\downarrow \Delta S_1 \qquad\qquad\qquad \uparrow \Delta S_3$$

$$H_2O(\,l\,,\,298.15\text{ K}) \xrightarrow{\Delta S_2} H_2O(g,\,298.15\text{ K})$$

$$\Delta S = \Delta S_1 + \Delta S_2 + \Delta S_3$$

$$= 75.29 \ \ln \frac{298.15}{373.15} + (188.72 - 69.91)$$

$$+ 33.58 \ \ln \frac{373.15}{298.15}$$

$$= 109.4 \text{ J K}^{-1}$$

16-8 ENTROPY AS A CRITERION FOR SPONTANEITY IN ADIABATIC PROCESSES

Suppose that a natural process carries a system from state 1 to state 2 within an insulated enclosure, so that the process is adiabatic.

$$dq_{1\rightarrow 2} = 0$$

$$dw_{1\rightarrow 2} = dw'$$

Now return the system to state 1 reversibly. Generally, this will not be adiabatic and there will be a transfer of heat to or from the surroundings.

$$dq_{2\rightarrow 1} = dq''$$

$$dw_{2\rightarrow 1} = dw''$$

Since the two step process completes a cycle for the system, application of the first law gives

$$dU = 0 = 0 + dw' + dq'' + dw''$$

and so

$$dq'' = -(dw' + dw'')$$

Since only one heat bath need be involved in the process, there can be no net output of work, by the second law. Therefore

$$(dw' + dw'') \geq 0$$

and hence

$$dq'' \leq 0$$

But

$$dq'' \equiv dq_{rev(2 \to 1)}$$

Therefore

$$dq_{rev(2 \to 1)} \leq 0$$

Since T is always positive, it follows that

$$\frac{dq_{rev(2 \to 1)}}{T} \leq 0$$

Therefore

$$dS_{2 \to 1} \leq 0$$

and hence

$$S_1 \leq S_2$$

No condition was put on the original process except that it was natural and adiabatic. Therefore such a process occurs only if it results in an increase in entropy. The limiting case in which $S_1 = S_2$ is the case where the original process which carried the system from state 1 to state 2 was itself reversible.

16-9 ENTROPY CHANGES IN ISOTHERMAL PROCESSES

Consider a system, Z, like that shown in Figure 16-4, contained in an adiabatic enclosure. It consists of two parts, a system X which may be anything and a system Y which is a heat bath at temperature T_r. A heat bath is a thermal reservoir capable of transferring any required amount of heat to or from another system without changing the temperature of the heat bath. It is part of the definition of a heat bath that such exchanges are reversible insofar as the heat bath is concerned but may or may not be so with regard to the system. Constant temperature heat baths are approached in reality by such devices as ice-water baths.

Consider some natural process taking place in X, involving a transfer of heat to or from the heat bath. This transfer may be in either direction and,

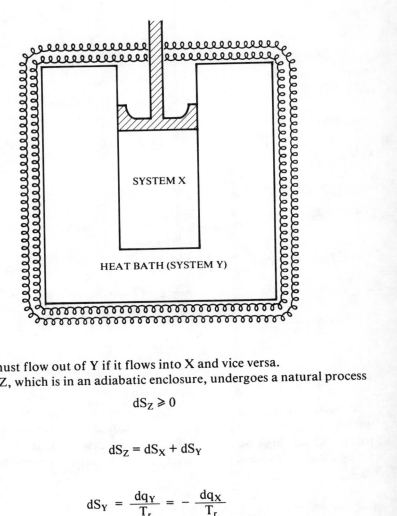

Figure 16-4

moreover, must flow out of Y if it flows into X and vice versa.

If system Z, which is in an adiabatic enclosure, undergoes a natural process

$$dS_Z \geqslant 0$$

But

$$dS_Z = dS_X + dS_Y$$

and

$$dS_Y = \frac{dq_Y}{T_r} = -\frac{dq_X}{T_r}$$

Hence

$$dS_X - \frac{dq_X}{T_r} \geqslant 0$$

and so

$$dS_X \geqslant \frac{dq_X}{T_r}$$

The equality sign applies, of course, to the limiting case where the process in X was reversible.

What has been shown here is that where a natural process occurs in any system at constant temperature, the heat term dq is such that

$$\frac{dq}{T} \leqslant dS$$

T is always positive, and this relationship remains true for the sum of differentials over macroscopic changes at constant temperature. Hence

$$\frac{q}{T} \leqslant \Delta S$$

or

$$q \leqslant T\Delta S$$

Since

$$T\Delta S \equiv q_{rev}$$

therefore

$$q \leqslant q_{rev}$$

This means that where q_{rev} is negative, implying that heat flows out of the system when the process is carried out reversibly, *more* heat will flow out of the system for any irreversible path than for the reversible path. If, for example, q_{rev} is -7.0 kJ, then the q for any natural path might be -7.1 kJ or -39.0 kJ or whatever, providing only that it is less than -7.0 kJ. Similarly where q_{rev} is positive, so that the reversible process involves heat flowing into the system, *less* heat will flow in for any natural path than for the reversible path. Again, illustrating by an example, if q_{rev} is 10.0 kJ, then q could be 8.4 kJ or 1.2 kJ or even -15.4 kJ or any value not greater than 10.0 kJ. Notice that this means that the natural path could be exothermic.

Recall that for reversible cycles operating between two temperatures T_h and T_c,

$$\frac{q_c}{T_c} + \frac{q_h}{T_h} = 0$$

Since q_c and q_h are associated with reversible processes, the definition of entropy allows this to be rewritten as

$$\Delta S_c + \Delta S_h = 0$$

It is now possible to state that for any real process

$$\frac{q_c}{T_c} \leqslant \Delta S_c$$

and

$$\frac{q_h}{T_h} \leqslant \Delta S_h$$

and hence that for the operation of any real engine between T_h and T_c

$$\frac{q_c}{T_c} + \frac{q_h}{T_h} \leqslant 0$$

Three important points are made in this section, and these may be summarized as follows.

(a) For any natural adiabatic process which carries a system from state A to state B, $S_B > S_A$.

(b) For any natural isothermal process, $q < T\Delta S$.

(c) For any engine operating between T_h and T_c,

$$\frac{q_h}{T_h} + \frac{q_c}{T_c} \leqslant 0$$

with the equality applying where all steps of the operation of the engine are reversible.

16-10   A DIGRESSION ON ENGINES, HEAT PUMPS AND GENERATING STATIONS

All means of converting work to heat or heat to work can be analyzed in terms of thermodynamic laws. In particular, the last relationship developed can be used to determine the limiting conversion factor for all such devices.

For refrigerators, which 'pump' heat and 'use' work, q_c is positive, q_h is negative and w is positive. By the second law

$$\frac{q_c}{T_c} + \frac{q_h}{T_h} \leqslant 0$$

By the first law

$$q_c + q_h + w = \Delta U = 0.$$

Substituting to eliminate q_h in the above equations leads to

$$\frac{q_c}{T_c} + \frac{-w - q_c}{T_h} \leqslant 0$$

which can be rearranged to give

$$\frac{w}{q_c} \geqslant \frac{T_h - T_c}{T_c}$$

The most efficient possible refrigerator will be that which requires the least input of work (w) to remove a given amount of heat from a cold object (q_c). In other words, the ratio w/q_c will be a minimum. The relationship which we have derived states that this ratio cannot be less than $(T_h - T_c)/T_c$, and will be greater than this for any other case. The limiting case is achieved for reversible processes. The important point is that the second law implies that there is a theoretical limit to the efficiency of a refrigerator beyond which no amount of mechanical ingenuity can take us.

The same is true for engines, where $q_h > 0$, $q_c < 0$ and w < 0. Engines are devices for converting heat to work. In an internal combustion engine, q_h is drawn from burning gasoline at high temperature, q_c is the heat leaving the engine to a radiator and w is the work used to move the car, charge the battery and so forth. Engines of any sort, turbines or piston, external or internal combustion, all are constrained by the second law. An analysis exactly analogous to that for refrigerators but choosing to eliminate q_c instead of q_h, leads to the following:

$$-\frac{w}{q_h} \leqslant \frac{T_h - T_c}{T_h.}$$

The most desirable engine is the one that converts the greatest fraction of the heat entering from a heat source (q_h) into work ($-w$). We wish to maximize the ratio $-w/q_h$. What we have shown is that this can never be greater than $(T_h - T_c)/T_h$, a situation achieved when all steps of the cycle are reversible. In all other cases, the ratio $-w/q_h$ will be less than $(T_h - T_c)/T_h$. No greater ratio of work to heat can be obtained for any engine operating between these two temperatures, however ingenious or well constructed it may be.

Electricity represents work in thermodynamic terms and thermal electric generating stations are subject to analysis by these laws. Here the hot side is the nuclear or fossil fueled boiler, and the cold side is a heat exchanger connected to a cooling tower or to the water from a nearby lake. Examination of the algebra shows that better conversion is possible if the difference between T_c and T_h can be very large. This difference is limited in practice by the structural strength of the vessels at T_h and by the atmospheric temperature at T_c. In nuclear stations, the additional requirement of resistance to radiation effects forces the use of materials with lower temperature limits than can be used in fossil fuel stations. As a result, nuclear stations are designed, at present, for lower T_h operation, and this is the major reason why they have a lower conversion factor than coal fired stations.

Typical of current design standards are three generating stations in Ontario. Pickering, with four 540 000 kW nuclear units, achieves 29.1% conversion from boiler temperatures of 520 K. Nanticoke, with four 500 000 kW coal fired units and Lennox, with two 575 000 kW oil fired units, achieve 40% conversion from boiler temperatures of 800 K.

Example 16-4 An electrically driven heat pump is used to heat a house. The house interior is at 20°C, the exterior at −3°C. The efficiency of the pump is such that four times as much electricity is required to pump a given amount of heat from outside as the theoretical best. Calculate the ratio of the heat entering the house to the electricity consumed. If the electricity was produced at a coal fired plant which converted 40% of its heat to electricity, and if 5% of the electricity is lost in transmission, what is the ratio of heat entering the house to heat generated at the electrical plant?

Suppose that for a quantity of heat q_s produced at the station, a quantity of heat q_h enters the house. The objective is to find the value of the ratio q_h/q_s.

Since the generating station achieves 40% conversion, the electrical energy produced equals $(0.40)q_s$.

Since 5% of the electricity is lost in transmission, the electrical energy reaching the heat pump is $(0.95)(0.40)q_s = (0.38)q_s$.

At the heat pump, we wish to know the ratio of heat entering the house to electricity used (q_h/w) but the information available is that the electrical energy required to pump a given quantity of heat from outside (w/q_c) is four times the ideal best.

The theoretical best is given by

$$\frac{w}{q_c} = \frac{T_h - T_c}{T_c}$$

Therefore for the heat pump in the question

$$\frac{w}{q_c} = (4)\,\frac{293 - 270}{270} = 0.341$$

But

$$q_h + q_c + w = 0$$

$$w = (0.38)(q_s)$$

Therefore

$$q_c = -q_h - w$$

$$= -q_h - 0.38\,q_s$$

Substitution to eliminate q_c and w yields

$$0.341 = \frac{w}{q_c} = \frac{(0.38)q_s}{-q_h - (0.38)q_s}$$

Therefore

$$\frac{q_h}{q_s} = 1.5$$

Notice that this means that heat pumps can deliver more heat to a building than would be available if the original fuel at the generating station had been burned directly in the house. Most domestic heat pumps are not this efficient but a target of four times theoretical best may well be realizable.

16-11   A MOLECULAR INTERPRETATION OF ENTROPY

Classical thermodynamics makes no references to molecules or atoms. On the other hand, chemists and those who apply chemistry know that thermodynamics, with its immense body of precise data in support of the three laws, provides a splendid test for any theory of atomic or molecular phenomena. Any molecular model which is inconsistent with the well established thermodynamic laws is almost surely defective.

A successful understanding of entropy, in atomic and molecular terms, stems from statistics. In Chapter 11, it was seen that energy flowing into a body could occupy various energy levels. These levels were associated with different motions of a molecule or atom; translational, vibrational or rotational. Molecules with many atoms have many more available motions than do molecules with few atoms, and require more energy for a given rise in temperature. Quantitatively, this means a higher heat capacity for the larger molecule. This relationship between complexity and the energy required to achieve a temperature rise is the basis of a statistical interpretation of entropy.

Suppose a substance is raised in temperature by placing it in contact with a heat bath at a higher temperature. Visualize the simplest possible situation in which no phase changes or chemical processes occur. The substance simply becomes 'hotter.' The measure of how much heat must flow into the system to achieve any particular increase in temperature is the heat capacity, and this is itself a function of temperature. Generally, at higher temperatures, more heat is required to achieve a given temperature rise for any substance. Expressed another way, the heat capacity of all substances increases with temperature.

It is now necessary to superimpose on this an understanding that not all molecules will have exactly the average molecular energy at any given moment. Molecules of oxygen in the gas phase, for example, will exhibit a wide range of velocities at any moment, corresponding to a wide range of kinetic energies. The translational energy calculated earlier is the average of this range. In all modes of motion, only certain states are allowed, so that this distribution of kinetic energies can be more accurately described in terms of what fraction of the molecules occupy a particular energy state. The separation of these energy states varies from mode to mode and depends, among other things, inversely on the masses of the atoms involved.

The total energy of a given molecule can be made up of numerous combinations of energy distributions among these modes. Two molecules with very similar total energy may differ in that one is travelling slowly but has much vibrational energy whereas the other is travelling more rapidly but has less vibrational energy.

Statistically, the more ways that a total molecular energy within a certain range can be achieved (by combining energies in the different modes), the more molecules in a given group will have that energy or, equally, the more probability there is that the total energy of any given molecule will be in that range.

The classic apparatus for demonstrating probability is a pair of dice. Each die has six faces and each face will 'come up' equally often. What *sum* will come up most often for two dice?

One sixth of the time, die A will produce a 1. One sixth of *these* times, die B will produce any one of the six numbers. One thirty-sixth of the time, therefore, we can expect a sum of 2=(1+1), and equally often of 3=(1+2), 4=(1+3), 5=(1+4), 6=(1+5) and 7=(1+6). Another sixth of the time, die A will produce a 2, and from these we get one thirty-sixth probability for 3, 4, 5, 6, 7, 8. Considering all the cases, we could prepare a table as on page 390.

It is thus seen that although the probability of A showing 1 and B showing 1 is the same as that of A showing 2 and B showing 5, the probability of A and B showing a total of 7 is greater than that of their showing any other sum because there are more individual distributions which add to give that sum than add to give any other.

Value of Die A	Probability of Total Value											
	2	3	4	5	6	7	8	9	10	11	12	2-12
1	$\frac{1}{36}$	$\frac{1}{36}$	$\frac{1}{36}$	$\frac{1}{36}$	$\frac{1}{36}$	$\frac{1}{36}$	0	0	0	0	0	$\frac{1}{6}$
2	0	$\frac{1}{36}$	$\frac{1}{36}$	$\frac{1}{36}$	$\frac{1}{36}$	$\frac{1}{36}$	$\frac{1}{36}$	0	0	0	0	$\frac{1}{6}$
3	0	0	$\frac{1}{36}$	$\frac{1}{36}$	$\frac{1}{36}$	$\frac{1}{36}$	$\frac{1}{36}$	$\frac{1}{36}$	0	0	0	$\frac{1}{6}$
4	0	0	0	$\frac{1}{36}$	$\frac{1}{36}$	$\frac{1}{36}$	$\frac{1}{36}$	$\frac{1}{36}$	$\frac{1}{36}$	0	0	$\frac{1}{6}$
5	0	0	0	0	$\frac{1}{36}$	$\frac{1}{36}$	$\frac{1}{36}$	$\frac{1}{36}$	$\frac{1}{36}$	$\frac{1}{36}$	0	$\frac{1}{6}$
6	0	0	0	0	0	$\frac{1}{36}$	$\frac{1}{36}$	$\frac{1}{36}$	$\frac{1}{36}$	$\frac{1}{36}$	$\frac{1}{36}$	$\frac{1}{6}$
1-6	$\frac{1}{36}$	$\frac{2}{36}$	$\frac{3}{36}$	$\frac{4}{36}$	$\frac{5}{36}$	$\frac{6}{36}$	$\frac{5}{36}$	$\frac{4}{36}$	$\frac{3}{36}$	$\frac{2}{36}$	$\frac{1}{36}$	1

In chemical systems, the more different ways there are to distribute a given total energy among the different modes in the molecules, the more probability there is of that state being achieved. Thus for two different states of a given system, equal in total energy but differing markedly in the number of ways in which that total can be achieved, the state involving the greater number of possible ways will be preferred. Transitions from the less likely to the more likely can be expected. Indeed a sufficient increase in entropy can allow a process to proceed in which enthalpy *increases*, a point central to the development below of the concept of Gibbs energy.

This very brief description leaves much unsaid—how the averaging process is carried out for the quantum states of macroscopic systems, for example. It serves nonetheless to make the point that spontaneous changes within adiabatic enclosures will occur if the system can go to a state of greater randomness. We have already seen that such changes involve an increase in entropy. Although an appeal to statistical thermodynamics is necessary in order to do it, these two can be linked quantitatively, entropy being related statistically to the number of available quantum states.

Appendix 1 shows that solids, and to a lesser extent liquids, have smaller values of $S°$ than for gases; one would expect this on the basis of the above interpretation, since gases have large translational movements. Chemical processes involving only solids and liquids have small entropy changes associated with them whereas those involving a change in the amount of gas, such as the boiling of a liquid to give its vapour, involve large entropy changes. Qualitative statements of this sort can often be made about other processes, such as the formation of complexes in solution where several molecules combine to give one with a resulting decrease in entropy.

16-12 GIBBS ENERGY

There is a function called *Gibbs energy*, G, which we define as follows

$$G \equiv H - TS$$

The function so defined has at least two useful properties. It predicts the maximum amount of useful work that can be obtained from any given process at constant temperature and pressure. The Gibbs energy also predicts the direction and the final equilibrium state for a given process at constant temperature and pressure. That there is a connection between these two properties is not immediately obvious but it is true and lies at the core of all arguments developed from the second law of thermodynamics. These properties of Gibbs energy may be demonstrated as follows. For any two states, 1 and 2, of a given system

$$\Delta G = G_2 - G_1 = H_2 - T_2 S_2 - H_1 + T_1 S_1$$

$$= U_2 - U_1 + P_2 V_2 - P_1 V_1 - (T_2 S_2 - T_1 S_1).$$

If the argument is confined to isothermal processes under constant external pressure

$$P_1 = P_2 = P$$

$$T_1 = T_2 = T$$

$$\Delta G = [U_2 - U_1] + [P(V_2 - V_1)] - [T(S_2 - S_1)]$$

$$= [q + w] + [-w] - [\geqslant q]$$

The substitutions in the three brackets reflect, respectively, the first law, the value of the work term in any process in which the only work is due to the expansion against (or contraction under) the atmosphere and the limitation on q in any isothermal process. Inspection shows that the sum of these three bracketed terms must always be less than or equal to zero, and so, for any natural process at constant T and P, in which the work term is as defined above,

$$\Delta G \leqslant 0$$

Thus the sign of ΔG provides a criterion for spontaneity under conditions of constant temperature and external pressure. If ΔG is negative, the reaction is a natural process and can proceed. If ΔG is positive, the reaction is unnatural and cannot proceed spontaneously. While these statements are strictly true, it will be seen shortly that this criterion must be applied with understanding and discretion.

The Gibbs energy has a second property of great importance. There are cases in which work is done beyond the work involved in moving the external pressure. Suppose one calls such extra work w′ so that

$$w = -P\Delta V + w'$$

This extra work term may arise in several ways. The process might be an electrochemical one within a cell, with the electrical output used to operate a motor which raises a weight. Alternatively, if an engine is arranged so that the piston expands against a pressure in addition to the atmospheric pressure, there is a work term beyond that due to expansion against the atmospheric pressure. Both of these extra work terms, and any others like them, are what is meant by w′. It follows that since

$$-w - P\Delta V \leqslant -\Delta G$$

Therefore $$P\Delta V - w' - P\Delta V \leqslant -\Delta G$$

$$-w' \leqslant -\Delta G$$

If the process is one that is natural, $\Delta G < 0$ and hence work may be obtained from the process. Moreover the maximum amount of work that can be so obtained is determined by the change in Gibbs energy associated with the process. This is, indeed, the origin of the historic term 'free energy' and is certainly one of the most useful properties of G.

16-13 $\Delta G°$: REACTION DIRECTION AND THE POSITION OF EQUILIBRIUM

The $\Delta G°$ of any process at 298.15 K and 101.325 kPa may be calculated from tabulated $\Delta G_f°$ values in a manner exactly analogous to obtaining $\Delta H°$. Later sections examine such calculation in detail.

The $\Delta G°$ so obtained, however, must be used with caution as a criterion for the spontaneity of the process.

For example

$$N_2(g) + 3\,H_2(g) \to 2\,NH_3(g) \qquad \Delta G° = -33.2\,kJ$$

This tells us that a mole of pure N_2 and three moles of pure H_2, all at 298.15 K and 101.325 kPa, have a greater Gibbs energy than two moles of NH_3 under the same conditions. We could rightly conclude that NH_3 could begin to form but it would be wrong to conclude that all of the N_2 and H_2 could be converted to NH_3. The equilibrium position lies between, with *partial* conversion of reagents to ammonia, albeit with a large excess of ammonia. Showing this quantitatively requires accounting for such factors as the natural mixing of nitrogen, hydrogen and ammonia.

A most useful expression for dealing with isothermal processes in any system is the following.

$$\Delta G = \Delta G° + RT\,\ln Q$$

Before undertaking a partial development of this relationship, it is important to understand the meaning of each term. Q is the reaction quotient for the process, as previously introduced in Section 15.1, but the meaning of the Gibbs energy term is less obvious than is sometimes implied. $\Delta G°$ is the Gibbs energy change associated with the process where all reagents and products are in a standard state. For example, the −33.2 kJ for the process above is the Gibbs energy change associated with the disappearance of one mole of nitrogen and three of hydrogen, and the formation of two moles of ammonia. Each of these is in a separate container, at 101.325 kPa and 298.15 K. The nitrogen container contains three moles less after the process than before and so on. Moreover, each of the products and reagents is at the same temperature and pressure before and after.

ΔG is the Gibbs energy change associated with the same chemical process (three moles of hydrogen disappear and so forth) but with the initial and final conditions being the temperature and pressure of interest rather than those of the standard state. The composition of any gaseous mixtures or the concentration of any participating solutions do not change. In any finite system the disappearance of reagents and the production of products would change these compositions but we can imagine approaching our hypothetical case by having huge systems. The nitrogen, hydrogen, ammonia system could be contained in a pressure tank holding thousands of moles of each. In such a large system, changes of one or two moles would not significantly change the overall composition of the gas, and the Gibbs energy change would be the ΔG for the conditions in question.

This expression provides a criterion for the direction of any process at constant temperature. The particular conditions of the state of the system are used to calculate Q. ΔG° can be evaluated using tabulated data. From these one can evaluate ΔG. If ΔG is negative, the system can 'move to the right,' with products forming and reactants disappearing. If ΔG is positive, the reverse can happen. If ΔG is zero, the reactants and products are in equilibrium. This criterion works because the treatment in terms of one mole in an infinite system is quite equivalent to considering an infinitesimal change in a finite system. Thus our criterion tells us the direction of initial change in a finite system and indeed could have been developed directly in those terms, using rather more calculus.

Example 16-5 A system contains N_2, H_2 and NH_3 with partial pressures of 14 kPa, 6 kPa and 9 kPa respectively. The temperature is 298 K. In which direction could the process below move?

$$N_2 + 3\,H_2 \rightarrow 2\,NH_3$$

Using data from Appendix 1.

$$\Delta G° = 2(-16.48) - 0 - 0 = -32.96 \text{ kJ}$$

Fitting the three partial pressures into the reaction quotient gives

$$Q = \frac{(P_{NH_3}/P°)^2}{(P_{N_2}/P°)(P_{H_2}/P°)^3} = \frac{(9000/101\,325)^2}{(14\,000/101\,325)(6000/101\,325)^3}$$

$$= 275$$

$$\Delta G = \Delta G° + RT \ln Q$$

$$= -32\,960 + 13\,920 = -19\,000 \text{ kJ}$$

ΔG is negative and ammonia could form. It is worth repeating that although ammonia can form, it will do so at an observable rate only in the presence of a catalyst. There are many processes for which this will be true. On the other hand, one can be absolutely certain that the reverse process, for which ΔG is positive, will never occur no matter what catalyst is used.

In order to develop a theoretical basis for this important relationship, it is necessary to digress briefly. For any process, the first law states that

$$dU = dq + dw$$

For a process which is reversible and isothermal

$$dq = TdS$$

and for a process in which the work is 'PV work' only,

$$dw = -PdV$$

For a process having both of these characteristics,

$$dU = TdS - PdV$$

But these variables are all state functions, having values which depend only on the initial and final state, and not at all on how the process was carried out. Therefore this last expression is true for any process, even those in which the work is not all 'PV work' or which are not reversible. Where these conditions are not met, of course,

$$dq \neq TdS$$

and

$$dw \neq -PdV$$

but the argument above shows nevertheless that under any circumstances, the sums are equal as below

$$dq + dw = TdS - PdV = dU$$

$$dU + PdV - TdS = 0$$

This relationship may now be put to use as follows.

$$G = U + PV - TS$$

$$dG = dU + PdV + VdP - TdS - SdT$$

$$= (dU + PdV - TdS) + VdP - SdT$$

$$= \qquad 0 \qquad + VdP - SdT$$

From this it may be seen that dG/dP equals V if temperature is held constant. In order to gain some insight into the significance of this, apply it to the case of an ideal gas. For an ideal gas

$$V = \frac{nRT}{P}$$

From the development above, it follows that

$$\frac{dG}{dP} = \frac{nRT}{P} \qquad \text{(constant T)}$$

Therefore

$$dG = \frac{nRT}{P}\,dP \qquad \text{(constant T)}$$

The difference between the Gibbs energy in the standard state and that in any state of interest can now be evaluated by integrating between these limits.

$$dG = \frac{nRT}{P}\,dP \qquad \text{(constant T)}$$

$$\int_{\substack{\text{reference}\\ \text{state}}}^{\substack{\text{actual}\\ \text{state}}} dG = G - G^\circ = \int_{\substack{\text{reference}\\ \text{state}}}^{\substack{\text{actual}\\ \text{state}}} \left(\frac{nRT}{P}\right)dP = nRT\,\ln\frac{P}{P^\circ}$$

On the basis of considering one mole, this can be expressed as

$$\overline{G} = \overline{G}^\circ + RT\,\ln\frac{P}{P^\circ}$$

where $\overline{G}$ and $\overline{G}^\circ$ represent the Gibbs energy *per mole* in the two states. This expression can be applied to reactions involving only gases in order to express ΔG for such processes in terms of ΔG°. Consider the particular example of forming ammonia from nitrogen and hydrogen.

$$N_2(g) + 3\,H_2(g) \rightarrow 2\,NH_3(g)$$

$$\Delta G = 2\overline{G}_{NH_3} - \overline{G}_{N_2} - 3\overline{G}_{H_2}$$

$$= 2\overline{G}^\circ_{NH_3} + 2RT\,\ln\frac{P_{NH_3}}{P^\circ} - \overline{G}^\circ_{N_2} - RT\,\ln\frac{P_{N_2}}{P^\circ} - 3\overline{G}^\circ_{H_2} - 3RT\,\ln\frac{P_{H_2}}{P^\circ}$$

$$= (2\overline{G}^\circ_{NH_3} - \overline{G}^\circ_{N_2} - 3\overline{G}^\circ_{H_2}) + RT\,\ln\frac{\left(\dfrac{P_{NH_3}}{P^\circ}\right)^2}{\left(\dfrac{P_{N_2}}{P^\circ}\right)\left(\dfrac{P_{H_2}}{P^\circ}\right)^3}$$

$$= \Delta G^\circ + RT\,\ln Q$$

Ways of applying this relationship to any process and any physical state are considered in the next section.

16-14   ACTIVITY

The observation that the *difference* of the Gibbs energies of two different states of an ideal gas depends on the *logarithm* of the *ratio* of the partial pressures in the two states can be used to provide a framework in which any material can be treated. The device used is the invention of a quantity called the absolute activity, λ, which is defined by the statement

$$\overline{G} = RT \ln \lambda$$

It should be noted in passing that this definition is usually expressed in terms of a quantity called the chemical potential, μ, which is equal to the Gibbs energy per mole under certain conditions but is an important and central quantity in thermodynamics which can be related equally to other variables. However, no rigour is lost by treating it here as $\overline{G}$.

If a material is considered in two different states designated 1 and 2, then for each state one can say

$$\overline{G}_1 = RT \ln \lambda_1$$

$$\overline{G}_2 = RT \ln \lambda_2$$

The difference in Gibbs energy between these two states is of course given by

$$\Delta G = \overline{G}_2 - \overline{G}_1 = RT \ln \frac{\lambda_2}{\lambda_1}$$

Calculation and tabulation is simplified by choosing a reference state or standard state designated by a superscript $^\circ$. Any other state can be expressed in terms of its departure from the reference state, as in

$$\overline{G} - \overline{G}^\circ = RT \ln \lambda/\lambda^\circ$$

So common is the expression λ/λ° that it is given a name, relative activity, and a symbol, a. Hence

$$\overline{G} = \overline{G}^\circ + RT \ln a$$

Although the form of the expression above arises in the relationship worked out explicitly for ideal gases, the fact that relative activity is an abstract concept means that one can assert that this applies rigorously to one mole of any compound, whether pure or in solution, and in any physical state. To make this relationship useful, one must find measurable quantities which change proportionally in the same way as activity.

For gases at pressures of 100 kPa or lower, relative activities can be accurately approximated by the ratio of pressure in the system of interest (the partial pressure of the species) to the pressure in its reference state (invariably 101.325 kPa). Hence for a process in which all reactants and products are gases, like our example, replacement of relative activities by this pressure ratio leads to the form which we introduced on empirical grounds in the previous chapter.

$$Q = \frac{(a_{SO_3})^2}{(a_{SO_2})^2(a_{O_2})} \approx \frac{(P_{SO_3}/P^\circ)^2}{(P_{SO_2}/P^\circ)^2(P_{O_2}/P^\circ)}$$

For pure solids or pure liquids, experience has shown that changes in pressure do not alter the activity greatly. Thus the activity in any state of interest, unless it is far removed from P°, is approximately the same as in the reference state and the relative activity is therefore 1. Thus the reaction quotient, Q, for the thermal decomposition of calcium carbonate

$$CaCO_3 (c) \rightleftarrows CaO (c) + O_2 (g)$$

can be approximated with reasonable accuracy by

$$Q = \frac{(a_{CaO})(a_{O_2})}{(a_{CaCO_3})} \approx \frac{(1)(P_{O_2}/P°)}{(1)} = P_{O_2}/P°$$

The reference state chosen for pure solids and liquids is the pure material at $P°$, and it is for this condition that the data in Appendix 1 are presented.

   Just as gases have activities which change proportionally to partial pressures (or, if one prefers, to concentrations) the relative activities of species in liquid solutions can be approximated by concentrations. This approximation is rarely accurate except for very dilute solutions, and errors arising from using this approximation can be very large. Methods of making calculations for these so-called *non-ideal* solutions is the subject of Chapter 21. Inaccurate as concentrations may sometimes be, however, they are often used in volumetric work with acids and bases, solubilities and so on. In such work, the usual units are mol L^{-1}, and the reference state of 1 mol kg^{-1} is, for *aqueous* solutions, close to being a one mol L^{-1} solution. That this too is not quite accurate will be discussed in Chapter 21.

   In order to have available a concise symbol for this ratio, the square bracket is used for concentrations and the square bracket with a subscript r is used for the ratio of this to the concentration in the reference state. Since the latter is almost unity for aqueous solutions, these two quantities, $[NO_3^-]$ and $[NO_3^-]_r$ may be considered to be numerically equal although the first has units mol L^{-1} and the second is dimensionless

$$a_{NO_3-} \approx [NO_3^-]_r = \frac{[NO_3^-](actual)}{[NO_3^-](reference)} \approx \frac{[NO_3^-]}{1}$$

   Thus, for example, an aqueous process like the attack on metallic zinc by aqueous hydrogen ion to yield hydrogen gas and aqueous zinc ion

$$Zn(c) + 2 H^+(aq) \rightarrow Zn^{2+}(aq) + H_2(g)$$

would have a reaction quotient as follows.

$$Q = \frac{[Zn^{2+}]_r (P_{H_2}/P°)}{(1)[H^+]_r^2}$$

Example 16-6   State the reaction quotients for the following processes in terms of relative activities and in terms of reasonable approximations by measureable quantities.

(a) $CuSO_4 \cdot 5 H_2O(c) \rightarrow CuSO_4 (c) + 5 H_2O(g)$

(b) $Hg(l) \rightarrow Hg(g)$

(c) $ZnO(c) + CO(g) \rightarrow Zn(c) + CO_2(g)$

(d) $CH_3COOH(aq) \rightarrow H^+(aq) + CH_3COO^-(aq)$

These are

(a) $Q = \dfrac{(a_{CuSO_4})(a_{H_2O})^5}{(a_{CuSO_4 \cdot 5H_2O})} \approx \dfrac{(1)(P_{H_2O}/P°)^5}{(1)} = (P_{H_2O}/P°)^5$

(b) $Q = \dfrac{a_{Hg(g)}}{a_{Hg(l)}} \approx \dfrac{P_{Hg}/P°}{(1)} \approx P_{Hg}/P°$

(c) $Q = \dfrac{(a_{Zn})(a_{CO_2})}{(a_{ZnO})(a_{CO})} \approx \dfrac{(1)(P_{CO_2}/P°)}{(1)(P_{CO}/P°)} = \dfrac{P_{CO_2}}{P_{CO}}$

(d) $Q = \dfrac{(a_{H^+})(a_{C_2H_3O_2^-})}{a_{HC_2H_3O_2}} \approx \dfrac{[H^+]_r[C_2H_3O_2^-]_r}{[HC_2H_3O_2]_r}$

Do keep in mind that in liquid solutions, particularly those involving ions, the approximation used in (d) may be very much in error.

16-15   THE RELATIONSHIP OF K TO $\Delta G°$

For a system in which the reactants and products are in equilibrium, ΔG in the particular sense defined in Section 16-13 must be zero. Similarly the reaction quotient, Q, has the value of the equilibrium constant, K. From this one obtains the very useful relationship

$$0 = \Delta G° + RT \ln K$$

or

$$K = e^{-\Delta G°/RT}$$

This provides a very useful way of calculating the equilibrium constant for any process from tabulated values of $\Delta G_f°$. Several examples follow.

Example 16-7   Use the thermochemical tables to evaluate $\Delta G°$ and K for the following process at 298 K. What is the equilibrium vapour pressure?

$$CuSO_4 \cdot 5 H_2O(c) \rightarrow CuSO_4(c) + 5 H_2O(g)$$

$$\Delta G° = (-662) + 5(-228.55) - (-1880.1) = 75.3 \text{ kJ}$$

$$K = e^{-75\,300/(8.314)(298)} = 6.4 \times 10^{-14}$$

$$K = \left(\frac{P_{H_2O}}{P°}\right)^5 = 6.4 \times 10^{-14} = \left(\frac{P_{H_2O}}{101\,325}\right)^5$$

$$P_{H_2O} = (6.4 \times 10^{-14})^{1/5}(101\,325) = 232 \text{ Pa}$$

Example 16-8   Calculate $\Delta G°$ and K for the following process at 298 K. It is the cell process in the Daniel Cell.

$$Zn(c) + Cu^{2+}(aq) \rightarrow Zn^{2+}(aq) + Cu(c)$$

$$\Delta G° = (-147.23) + 0 - 0 - (65.6) = -212.8 \, kJ$$

$$K = e^{-(-212\,800)/(8.314)(298)} = 1.9 \times 10^{37}$$

Example 16-9   Calculate ΔG for the following process at 298.15 K and a partial pressure of water of 5.0 kPa.

$$CuSO_4 \cdot 5\,H_2O(c) \rightarrow CuSO_4(c) + 5\,H_2O(g)$$

Can $CuSO_4 \cdot 5\,H_2O$ spontaneously give $CuSO_4$ and $H_2O(g)$ under these conditions? Can $CuSO_4$ take up water vapour to give $CuSO_4 \cdot 5\,H_2O$ under these conditions? What is the situation when P = 5.0 Pa?
From Example 16-7 $\Delta G° = 75.3$ kJ, therefore at 5 kPa

$$\Delta G = 75\,300 + (8.314)(298.15)\ln(5000/101\,325)^5$$

$$= 38\,000 \, J$$

Hence the process could only go to the left at 5.0 kPa. Now, evaluation of the value of ΔG when the pressure is 5 Pa gives

$$\Delta G = 75\,300 + (8.314)(298.15)\ln(5.0/101\,325)$$

$$= -47\,700 \, J$$

The process could only go to the right at 5.0 Pa. In this particularly simple case, both predictions could have been made on the basis of the equilibrium pressure calculated in Example 16-7. Pressures above it must come down and pressures below it must go up. In more complex cases, with several terms in Q, the calculation of ΔG is simpler and safer.

Example 16-10   Use the thermochemical tables to evaluate $\Delta G°$ and K for the condensation of one mole of mercury at 298.15 K. What is the vapour pressure of mercury at 298.15 K?

$$Hg(g) \rightarrow Hg(l)$$

$$\Delta G° = 0 - (31.88) = -31.88 \, kJ$$

$$K = e^{-\Delta G°/RT} = e^{\,31\,880/(8.314)(298.15)} = 3.85 \times 10^5$$

$$K = \frac{1}{P_{Hg}/P°} = 3.85 \times 10^5 = \frac{101\,325}{P_{Hg}}$$

$$P_{Hg} = 0.263 \, Pa$$

Example 16-11   Use the thermochemical tables to evaluate K at 298 K for the following process, and hence to calculate the equilibrium concentration of HI in a container at 298 K having equilibrium concentrations $C_{H_2} = 1.00$ mol m^{-3} and $C_{I_2} = 2.35$ mol m^{-3}.

The process is given by

$$2\,HI(g) \rightleftharpoons H_2(g) + I_2(g)$$

$$\Delta G° = 19.36 - 0 - 2(1.58) = 16.2\,kJ$$

$$K = e^{-\Delta G°/RT} = e^{-16\,200/(8.314)(298.15)} = 1.45 \times 10^{-3}$$

therefore

$$\frac{(C_{H_2}/C°)(C_{I_2}/C°)}{(C_{HI}/C°)^2} = 1.45 \times 10^{-3}$$

so

$$\frac{C_{H_2}C_{I_2}}{C_{HI}^2} = 1.45 \times 10^{-3}$$

Substituting

$$\frac{1.00 \times 2.35}{C_{HI}^2} = 1.45 \times 10^{-3}$$

$$C_{HI} = 40.2\,mol\,m^{-3}$$

Example 16-12   Use the thermochemical tables to calculate $\Delta G°$ and K for the following processes at 298 K. What is the ratio of the partial pressure of CO_2 to that of CO in the gas phase at equilibrium in the presence of zinc and zinc oxide? If total pressure is maintained at 50 kPa, what is P_{CO_2} at equilibrium?

$$ZnO(c) + CO(g) \rightleftharpoons Zn(c) + CO_2(g)$$

$$\Delta G° = 0 + (-394.37) - (-320.5) - (-137.15)$$

$$= 63.3\,kJ$$

$$K = e^{-63\,300/8.314 \times 298.15} = 8.2 \times 10^{-12}$$

$$\frac{P_{CO_2}/P°}{P_{CO}/P°} = \frac{P_{CO_2}}{P_{CO}} = K = 8.2 \times 10^{-12}$$

$$P = 5000 = P_{CO} + P_{CO_2}$$

$$P_{CO_2} = 4.1 \times 10^{-8}\,Pa$$

The gas is almost entirely CO and the process has not proceeded to any significant extent.

Example 16-13   Ammonium chloride crystals, NH_4Cl, evaporate to yield hydrogen chloride and ammonia. Use the thermochemical tables to predict the equilibrium vapour pressure if crystals of NH_4Cl are placed in a previously evacuated vessel at 298.2 K.

$$NH_4Cl(c) \rightleftharpoons NH_3(g) + HCl(g)$$

$$\Delta G° = -16.44 - 95.3 - (-202.9)$$

$$= +91.2 \text{ kJ}$$

$$K = e^{-91\,200/8.314 \times 298.2} = 1.07 \times 10^{-16}$$

$$(P_{NH_3}/P°)(P_{HCl}/P°) = 1.07 \times 10^{-16}$$

Since all material was originally NH_4Cl, there must be equimolar amounts of NH_3 and HCl in the gas phase. Therefore

$$P_{NH_3} = P_{HCl} = 101\,325 \times \sqrt{1.06 \times 10^{-16}}$$

$$= 1.05 \times 10^{-3} \text{ Pa}$$

$$\therefore \text{ equilibrium vapour pressure} = 1.05 \times 10^{-3} + 1.05 \times 10^{-3}$$

$$= 2.1 \times 10^{-3} \text{ Pa}$$

16-16   THE EXPERIMENTAL DETERMINATION OF ΔG°

There are three main methods of determining Gibbs energy changes experimentally. Where the process involves electron transfer, it is often possible to construct a cell in which the cell process is the process of interest. Electrochemical cells can be balanced by an equal and opposite potential so that measurements of a reversible or near reversible process are possible. Details of the evaluation of $\varepsilon°$, and hence of K and $\Delta G°$, are given in a later chapter. Less accurately but more generally, measurement of the actual equilibrium concentrations and conditions allows calculation of K and hence $\Delta G°$. This is the method used by Bodenstein and Pohl in the example given in Chapter 15 and is quite useful where the products and reagents all exist in accurately measurable quantities at equilibrium. This might be done by chemical analysis or by various spectrometric techniques. The third method of calculating $\Delta G°$ is by measuring S° and ΔH°. As mentioned in Section 16-7, S° is assumed to be zero for crystals at 0 K. Hence ΔS° will be zero for a process at 0 K, and hence $\Delta G° = \Delta H°$ at 0 K. A knowledge of the heat capacities of all reagents and products between 0 K and 298.15 K permits calculation of ΔH°, ΔS° and ΔG°.

16-17   THE TEMPERATURE DEPENDENCE OF K AND ΔG°

For any process

$$G = H - TS$$

$$\Delta G = \Delta H - \Delta(TS)$$

For a process at constant temperature

$$\Delta G = \Delta H - T\Delta S$$

It has already been noted that neither ΔH nor ΔS for a process vary strongly with temperature, but it is clear that ΔG must do so, depending directly on T. The equilibrium constant will therefore also vary with temperature and it is necessary to know how to calculate it at any temperature. Two levels of accuracy are of interest.

If the accuracy involved in assuming temperature independence for ΔH and ΔS is sufficient, a relatively simple calculation is possible, since

$$\Delta G_T^\circ = \Delta H^\circ - T\Delta S^\circ$$

$$\Delta G_{298}^\circ = \Delta H^\circ - 298\, \Delta S^\circ$$

$$\frac{\Delta G_T^\circ}{T} - \frac{\Delta G_{298}^\circ}{298} = \frac{\Delta H^\circ}{T} - \frac{\Delta H^\circ}{298} = \Delta H^\circ \left(\frac{1}{T} - \frac{1}{298} \right)$$

Since ΔG_{298}° and ΔH° can be evaluated from the tables, ΔG_T° can be calculated.

It is equally simple to calculate K at one temperature if K is known at another temperature.

Because $K = e^{-\Delta G^\circ / RT}$

therefore

$$\ln K_T = -\frac{\Delta G^\circ}{RT} = -\frac{\Delta H^\circ}{RT} + \frac{\Delta S^\circ}{R}$$

In the particular case of T being 298 K

$$\ln K_{298} = -\frac{\Delta H^\circ}{298\, R} + \frac{\Delta S^\circ}{R}$$

Subtraction gives

$$\ln K_T - \ln K_{298} = \frac{\Delta H^\circ}{R} \left(\frac{1}{298} - \frac{1}{T} \right)$$

$$\ln \frac{K_T}{K_{298}} = \frac{\Delta H^\circ}{R} \left(\frac{1}{298} - \frac{1}{T} \right)$$

Example 16-14 Using the thermochemical tables, calculate the equilibrium constant for the following process at 1000 K and compare it with the experimental value of Bodenstein and Pohl.

$$2\, SO_2(g) + O_2(g) \rightleftharpoons 2\, SO_3(g)$$

At 298 K

$$\Delta G^\circ = 2(-371.1) - 2(-300.10) = -142.0\, kJ$$

Therefore

$$K_{298} = e^{-\Delta G°/RT} = e^{142\,000/8.314 \times 298.15} = 7.56 \times 10^{24}$$

$$\Delta H° = 2(-395.7) - 2(-296.81) = -197.8\ kJ$$

Therefore

$$\ln \frac{K}{7.56 \times 10^{24}} = \frac{-197\,800}{8.314} \left(\frac{1}{298.15} - \frac{1}{1000} \right)$$

$$K = 3.6$$

Bodenstein and Pohl measured 3.4. The agreement is better than could be expected for a calculation over so large a temperature range using the assumption of constant $\Delta H°$.

Example 16-15   The equilibrium constant for the dehydration of $CuSO_4 \cdot 5\ H_2O$ was calculated in Example 16-7 to be 6.4×10^{-14} at 298.15 K. What would it be at 400 K, and what would be the equilibrium vapour pressure at this temperature?

$$K_{298} = 6.4 \times 10^{-14}$$

$$\Delta H° = -771 + 5(-241.81) - (-2279.7)$$

$$= 299.7\ kJ$$

$$\ln K_{400} = \ln(6.4 \times 10^{-14}) + \frac{299\,700}{8.314} \left(\frac{1}{298.15} - \frac{1}{400} \right)$$

$$K_{400} = 1.52$$

$$\left(\frac{P_{H_2O}}{P°} \right)^5 = 1.52$$

$$P_{H_2O} = 1.10 \times 10^5\ Pa = 110\ kPa$$

Example 16-16   Use the thermochemical tables to calculate K for the following process at 700 K.

$$C(c) + CO_2(g) \rightleftharpoons 2\ CO(g)$$

$$\Delta G° = 2(-137.15) - 0 - (-394.37) = 120.07\ kJ$$

$$\Delta H° = 2(-110.53) - 0 - (-393.51) = 172.45\ kJ$$

$$K_{298} = e^{-\Delta G°/RT} = e^{-120\,070/(8.314)(298.15)} = 9.2 \times 10^{-22}$$

$$\ln \frac{K}{K_{298}} = \frac{\Delta H°}{R} \left(\frac{1}{298.15} - \frac{1}{T} \right)$$

therefore

$$\ln K = \ln(9.2 \times 10^{-22}) + \frac{172\,450}{8.314}\left[\frac{1}{298.15} - \frac{1}{700}\right]$$

$$= -8.50$$

$$K = 2.0 \times 10^{-4}$$

Example 16-17 Use the data in the thermochemical tables to calculate the vapour pressure of n-octane, C_8H_{18}, at 25°C.

The process being considered is

$$C_8H_{18}(l) \rightleftharpoons C_8H_{18}(g)$$

for which

$$\Delta G° = 16.40 - 6.36 = 10.04\,\text{kJ}$$

$$K = P_{C_8H_{18}}/P° = e^{-10\,040/\,(8.314)(298.15)} = 0.0174$$

Therefore

$$P_{C_8H_{18}} = (0.0174)(101\,325) = 1765\,\text{Pa}$$

Example 16-18 Use the data in the thermochemical tables to calculate the boiling point (at 101 325 Pa) of normal hexane.

The process being considered is

$$C_6H_{14}(l) \rightleftharpoons C_6H_{14}(g)$$

$$\Delta G° = -0.29 - (-4.39) = 4.10\,\text{kJ}$$

$$\Delta H° = -167.1 - (-198.6) = 31.5\,\text{kJ at 298 K}$$

The 'boiling point' usually refers to the temperature at which a liquid has a vapour pressure of 101 325 Pa, and here that is explicitly stated. Therefore at T_b

$$P_{C_6H_{14}} = 101\,325\,\text{Pa}$$

Moreover, $P° = 101\,325$ Pa, and so at the boiling point,

$$K = (P_{C_6H_{14}}/P°) = 1$$

Therefore

$$\ln K = 0 = -\frac{\Delta G°}{RT_b}$$

therefore

$$\Delta G° \text{ at } T_b \text{ has the value zero.}$$

But

$$\frac{\Delta G'}{T'} - \frac{\Delta G''}{T''} = \Delta H\left(\frac{1}{T'} - \frac{1}{T''}\right)$$

Defining T'' as T_b and T' as 298.15 K,

$$\frac{4100}{298.15} - 0 = 31\,500 \left[\frac{1}{298.15} - \frac{1}{T_b} \right]$$

and therefore

$$T_b = 342.8 \text{ K}$$

Boiling points, incidentally, are usually measured directly and it would be rare to calculate one in this way.

More accurate calculation of $\Delta G°$ and K requires taking into account the temperature dependence of ΔH and ΔS. We have seen previously that this is not large, but for accurate work, the deviations cannot be neglected. Indeed for the highest accuracy, the temperature dependence of the heat capacity itself must also be considered. An example of each of these more detailed calculations follows.

Example 16-19   Calculate the equilibrium constant at 800 K for

$$N_2(g) + 3\,H_2(g) \rightleftarrows 2\,NH_3(g)$$

with three different degrees of accuracy; (a) assuming that $\Delta H°$ and $\Delta S°$ are independent of temperature; (b) assuming that $\Delta H°$ and $\Delta S°$ are dependent on temperature but that all heat capacities are independent of temperature; (c) using experimental values for the temperature dependence of the heat capacities expressed in the following analytical form:

for N_2 $C_p = 26.983 + 5.912 \times 10^{-3} T - 3.38 \times 10^{-7}\,T^2$

for H_2 $C_p = 29.066 - 8.368 \times 10^{-4} T + 2.01 \times 10^{-6}\,T^2$

for NH_3 $C_p = 25.985 + 3.300 \times 10^{-2} T - 3.05 \times 10^{-6}\,T^2$

(a) the solution assuming that $\Delta H°$ and $\Delta S°$ are independent of temperature

$$\Delta H° = 2(-45.94) - 0 - 3(0) = -91.88 \text{ kJ}$$

$$\Delta G°_{298} = 2(-16.44) - 0 - 3(0) = -32.88 \text{ kJ}$$

Since

$$K = e^{-\Delta G°/RT}$$

therefore

$$K_{298} = e^{+32\,880/(8.314)(298.15)}$$

$$= 5.763 \times 10^5$$

and hence

$$\ln K_{800} = \ln(5.763 \times 10^5) + \frac{(-91\,880)}{8.314} \left[\frac{1}{298.15} - \frac{1}{800} \right]$$

$$K_{800} = 4.6 \times 10^{-5}$$

(b) the solution assuming that C_p values are independent of temperature.

Consider carrying out the process in three steps as follows, for each of which $\Delta H°$ and $\Delta S°$ can be calculated from tabulated data.

$$N_2(800) + 3 H_2(800) \xrightarrow{\Delta H_1} N_2(298) + 3 H_2(298) \xrightarrow{\Delta H_2} 2 NH_3(298) \xrightarrow{\Delta H_3} 2 NH_3(800)$$

$$\Delta H°_{800} = \Delta H_1 + \Delta H_2 + \Delta H_3$$

$$= 29.12(298.15 - 800) + 3(28.824)(298.15 - 800)$$

$$+ (-91\,880) + 2(35.06)(800 - 298.15)$$

$$= -114\,700 \text{ J}$$

$$\Delta S°_{800} = \Delta S_1 + \Delta S_2 + \Delta S_3$$

$$= 29.12 \ln \frac{298.15}{800} + 3(28.824) \ln \frac{298.15}{800}$$

$$+ 2(192.67) - (191.50) - 3(130.57)$$

$$+ 2(35.06) \ln \frac{800}{298.15}$$

$$= -242.75 \text{ J K}^{-1}$$

Therefore

$$\Delta G°_{800} = \Delta H°_{800} - (800) \Delta S°_{800}$$

$$= (-114\,700) + (800)(-242.75)$$

$$= 79\,500 \text{ J}$$

and

$$K_{800} = e^{-79\,500/(8.314)(800)}$$

$$= 6.4 \times 10^{-6}$$

(c) the solution taking into account the temperature dependence of heat capacities.

Consider the same three step process described in (b). The terms for ΔH_2 and ΔS_2 are the same as in part (b) but the other terms, which all include heat capacities, are different. The calculations for ΔH_1 and ΔS_1 are shown.

$$\Delta H_1 = \int_{800}^{298.15} [26.983 + 5.912 \times 10^{-3}T - 3.38 \times 10^{-7}T^2$$

$$+ 3(29.066 - 8.368 \times 10^{-4}T + 2.01 \times 10^{-6}T^2)]dT$$

$$= -59\,160 \text{ J}$$

$$\Delta S_1 = \int_{800}^{298.15} \frac{1}{T} [C_p(N_2) + 3 C_p(H_2)]dT$$

$$= \int_{800}^{298.15} [\frac{26.983}{T} + 5.912 \times 10^{-3} - 3.38 \times 10^{-7}T$$

$$+ 3(\frac{29.066}{T} - 8.368 \times 10^{-4} + 2.01 \times 10^{-6}T)]dT$$

$$= -116.0 \text{ J K}^{-1}$$

Analogous calculations give ΔH_3 as 43 190 J and ΔS_3 as 84.60 J K^{-1}. Summing as before gives

$$\Delta H_{800}° = \Delta H_1 + \Delta H_2 + \Delta H_3$$

$$= -59\,160 - 91\,880 + 43\,190$$

$$= -107\,850 \text{ J}$$

$$\Delta S_{800}° = \Delta S_1 + \Delta S_2 + \Delta S_3$$

$$= -116.0 - 197.87 + 82.6$$

$$= -231.3 \text{ J K}^{-1}$$

Therefore

$$\Delta G_{800}° = -107\,850 - (800)(-231.3)$$

$$= 77\,200 \text{ J}$$

and

$$K_{800} = e^{-77\,200/(8.314)(800)}$$

$$= 9.1 \times 10^{-6}$$

This example also contains an important point of industrial economics. The equilibrium constant is very much smaller at 800 K than at 298 K. Indeed at 800 K and a total pressure of 1 MPa, less than one percent of the reagents are converted to ammonia at equilibrium. Nevertheless it is at 800 K and 1 MPa that industrial syntheses typically occur, testimony to the importance of kinetics in the economics of industrial production. The increased rates possible at 800 K more than offset the lower conversion. A catalyst which would provide high rates at low temperatures where the equilibrium is more favourable would be of great value. Indeed 'nitrogen fixation', the formation of nitrogen compounds directly from atmospheric nitrogen, is a large and active field of chemical and biological research.

SUMMARY

Beginning with only the first and second law, one can develop a number of important relationships. Chief among these for most chemists are those centred on the Gibbs energy which permit one to predict the direction and final equilibrium position of a process. The line of development from the two laws to these end points is clear and rigorous although the particular path followed in this chapter, via the so-called Carnot cycle, is not the only route which can be followed.

Important functions to the chemist which derive from consideration of the second law are the entropy, S, and the Gibbs energy, G. The first can be given physical meaning through the medium of statistical thermodynamics. It provides a measure of the number of ways in which a given amount of energy can be distributed within a system. Gibbs energy is less easily interpreted in physical terms, at least at this stage. Probably it is better to think of it purely as a mathematical function with a most useful property, namely that it must decrease in any natural process at constant temperature and pressure.

In the course of the chapter, several important relationships are developed. Chief among these are the following.

$$\text{(i)} \quad \frac{q_c}{T_c} + \frac{q_h}{T_h} = 0$$

This applies to the operation of a Carnot cycle or any other reversibly operated engine with *any* system therein. This relationship amounts to a definition of temperature and has the strength that such a definition is independent of the properties of any particular substance.

$$\text{(ii)} \quad \Delta S > 0$$

This must be true for any natural adiabatic process.

$$\text{(iii)} \quad q \leqslant T\Delta S$$

This must be true for any natural isothermal process.

$$\text{(iv)} \quad \frac{q_c}{T_c} + \frac{q_h}{T_h} \leqslant 0$$

This applies to the operation of any engine or heat pump. It provides a fundamental limit to the efficiency of such devices.

$$\text{(v)} \quad \Delta G \leqslant 0$$

This must be true for any natural process at constant temperature and pressure.

$$\text{(vi)} \quad \Delta G = \Delta G^\circ + RT \ln Q$$

This applies to any process at constant temperature. It is important to understand the precise process to which ΔG applies, as discussed in Section 16-13.

$$\text{(vii)} \quad K = e^{-\Delta G^\circ / RT}$$

This important relationship follows from the two above.

$$\text{(viii)} \quad \ln K_{T_2} = \ln K_{T_1} + \Delta H^\circ / R[1/T_1 - 1/T_2]$$

This relates equilibrium constants at different temperatures and is only as accurate as the assumption that ΔH° is unchanging over the temperature range in question.

FURTHER REFERENCES

Denbigh, Kenneth, The Principles of Chemical Equilibrium, Third Edition, Cambridge University Press, England, 1971.

This is a well written, well organized text which rarely if ever glosses over a difficulty. It is highly recommended to the chemist of somewhat-above-average ability.

Chemical Thermodynamics, Volume 1. Specialist Periodical Reports, The Chemical Society, London, England, 1973.

Chapter 1 (The Scope of Chemical Thermodynamics by M. L. McGlashan) and Chapter 2 (Thermodynamic Quantities, Thermodynamic Data and their Uses by E. F. G. Herington) provide an extremely concise but thorough survey of two important aspects of thermodynamics, standard states and data tabulations, written in impeccable S. I. language.

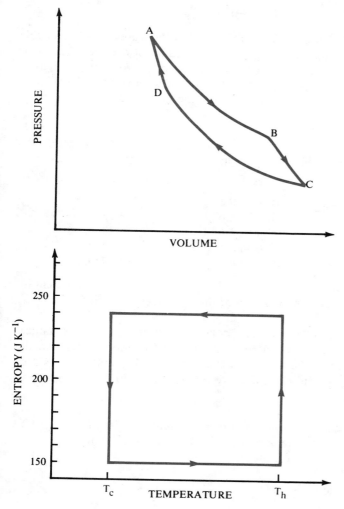

Figure 16-5

PROBLEMS

1. Figure 16-5 contains two diagrams depicting two aspects of a Carnot cycle.

   (a) Label the second diagram to show which 'side' of the initial diagram corresponds to each 'side' of the second diagram. Assume that the isothermal compression of the system results in heat flowing out of the system ($q < 0$).

   (b) If $T_c = 273$ K and the operation of this ideal heat engine between T_c and T_h produces 4000 J of work per cycle, calculate q_c and q_h for one cycle, as well as T_h. Notice that the entropy scale in the figure is calibrated.

   $$[q_c = -24\,600 \text{ J}; q_h = 28\,600 \text{ J}; T_h = 318 \text{ K}]$$

2. (a) Show that for the isothermal expansion of n mole of an ideal monatomic gas (for which you will doubtless remember, $U = 3/2\,nRT$), the value of ΔS is given by

   $$\Delta S = nR \ \ln \ \frac{V_2}{V_1}$$

   (b) ΔS as calculated above is related to q_{rev}, but there are many irreversible routes from 1 to 2 and an infinity of other values of q to go with them. Evaluate q for the case in which a stopcock is opened to permit the gas to expand from an initial volume of V_1 to a larger total volume V_2. What is the ΔS in this case? What is the ΔS for the universe? Was the process reversible? Why?

3. Compute the entropy change per mole for the vaporization of each of the following liquids at their boiling points.

Substance	ΔH_{vap}	Boiling Temperature
Cl_2	20.4 kJ mol^{-1}	238.5 K
C_6H_6	30.8 kJ mol^{-1}	353 K
$CHCl_3$	29.4 kJ mol^{-1}	334 K
$PbCl_2$	104.0 kJ mol^{-1}	1145 K
H_2O	40.7 kJ mol^{-1}	373 K

   An increased entropy is associated with a decrease in order. Comment on the sign and the relative magnitudes of the ΔS values calculated.

4. Suppose parts made of a particular polymer are found to lose mechanical strength when the parts are used at 400 K. Investigation shows that the polymer undergoes some process at that temperature. Study of this process reveals it to be endothermic. Are the products more or less ordered than the polymer?

5. (a) If n mole of gas in a bomb of constant volume is raised from T_c to T_h by dipping in an infinite number of baths, each dT hotter than the previous bath, show that for the gas

   $$\Delta S = nC_v \ \ln \ \frac{T_h}{T_c}$$

Assume that the value of C_v is independent of temperature.

(b) Calculate the entropy change from an identical initial state when the process is carried out by placing the bomb directly into a bath at T_h.

6. The following observations may be verified by consulting the thermochemical tables. Relate each observation to order/disorder considerations and entropy.

(a) For Cu_2O and CuO, ΔG_f^o is substantially more than ΔH_f^o, whereas they are roughly equal for both Cu_2S and CuS.

(b) In the series C_nH_{2n+2}, ΔH_f^o decreases as n increases but ΔG_f^o increases. Recall the bond energy concepts from Chapter 12.

7. A heat exchanger involves two sets of wound copper tubing in thermal contact, one carrying atmospheric air to do the cooling and the other carrying hot air that must be cooled. Suppose the atmospheric air is initially at 290 K and is raised to T_1. The hot air enters at 400 K and leaves at T_2. The flow rate of cool air can be increased to make T_2 lower. Assuming that air has heat capacity of 29 J K^{-1} mol^{-1}, calculate the entropy change per mole in both streams for $T_1 = 350$ K and $T_2 = 320$ K.

[5.5 J K^{-1} mol^{-1} and -6.5 J K^{-1} mol^{-1}]

8. A refrigerator operates at 50% of its theoretical maximum efficiency in a room at 298 K. If the heat of fusion of water is 335 J g^{-1}, calculate the work done in freezing 1 kg of water at 273 K and the heat discharged to the room in so doing.

[61 kJ; -396 kJ]

9. ΔG_f^o is -33.4 kJ mole^{-1} for $H_2S(g)$ and $+51.3$ kJ mole^{-1} for $NO_2(g)$. What can we conclude about the tendency of each of these two gases, at 298 K, to decompose into their constituent elements?

10. Use the data in the thermochemical tables to calculate $\Delta G°$ and K at 298 K for the following process

$$PCl_5(g) \rightleftharpoons PCl_3(g) + Cl_2(g)$$

Calculate $\Delta G°$ and K at 400 K, assuming that $\Delta H°$ does not vary significantly over this temperature range.

[37.2 kJ; 3.04×10^{-3}; 19.9 kJ; 2.54×10^{-3}]

11. Use the data in the thermochemical tables to calculate

(a) the vapour pressure of CCl_4 at 298 K and 330 K,

(b) the boiling point of methanol, CH_3OH, at 101 kPa. Neglect any temperature variation in $\Delta H°$.

[(a) 15.2 kPa; 54.4 kPa; (b) 337.8 K]

12. Suppose 10.0 g of phosgene, $COCl_2$, is injected into a previously evacuated 10.0 L container at 25.0°C. How many grams of CO will exist in the container at equilibrium due to the following process. Use the thermochemical tables to obtain K.

$$COCl_2(g) \rightleftarrows CO(g) + Cl_2(g)$$

[6.5×10^{-6} g]

13. Use the thermochemical tables to calculate $\Delta G°$ at 298 K for the following process.

$$N_2O_4(g) \rightleftarrows 2 NO_2(g)$$

If 1.01×10^5 Pa of N_2O_4 is introduced into a previously evacuated vessel, can any NO_2 form? Why?

[+4.78 kJ; Yes]

14. The equilibrium vapour pressure of water at 298 K over a mixture of $BaCl_2$ and its monohydrate is 333 Pa. Calculate $\Delta G°$ for the following process at 298 K.

$$BaCl_2 \cdot H_2O(c) \rightarrow BaCl_2(c) + H_2O(g)$$

[14.2 kJ]

15. Hydrazine, N_2H_4, was the subject of problem 6.13 because of its potential as a fuel. Calculate its vapour pressure at 298 K using thermochemical data.

[1.72 kPa]

16. Often the only tabulated data readily available on the liquid-vapour equilibrium of a compound are the boiling point (at P°) and the vapour pressure at one temperature (frequently 20°C). Use the vapour pressure of diethyl zinc at 11.7°C, 1330 Pa, and its boiling point, 118°C, to calculate its vapour pressure at 0°C.

[670 Pa]

17. The 'water gas shift reaction' has long been of interest to chemists.

$$CO(g) + H_2O(g) = CO_2(g) + H_2(g)$$

It is used to manufacture hydrogen for ammonia synthesis (where low grade fuels can be utilized to generate the CO) and in the removal of toxic CO from automobile exhaust gases (where the H_2 can sometimes be utilized to remove other unwanted components like nitrogen oxides). It offers hope of generating a useful fuel, hydrogen, by controlled in situ combustion of coal in remote fragmented coal seams which would be difficult to mine. Assuming that all C_p values are independent of temperature, calculate $\Delta G°$ and K for this process at 400 K. Is the process favoured by going to higher temperatures?

[−24.4 kJ; 1520; No]

18. In the hydroformylation process, aldehydes (RCHO) and alcohols (ROH)

are formed from carbon monoxide, hydrogen and the next lower alkene. Beginning with ethene, for example, this important industrial process operates as follows.

$$CH_2CH_2 + CO + 2\,H_2 \xrightarrow[\text{catalyst}]{i} CH_3CH_2\,CHO + H_2$$

$$\xrightarrow[\text{catalyst}]{ii} CH_3CH_2CH_2OH$$

A modification, which might be thought of as a combination of the water gas shift reaction and the hydroformylation reaction, is the Reppe process, which uses quite different catalysts, usually iron compounds.

$$CH_2CH_2 + 3\,CO + 2\,H_2O \xrightarrow{iii} CH_3CH_2\,CHO + H_2O + CO + CO_2$$

$$\downarrow iv$$

$$CH_3CH_2CH_2OH + 2\,CO_2$$

Taking all species as gases and $\Delta H°$ to be independent of temperature, calculate K for each of these overall processes, (i + ii) and (iii + iv) at 400 K.

$$[1 \times 10^8; 2 \times 10^{14}]$$

19. The above process could be continued, in order to synthesize progressively higher alcohols, if the following process could be carried out to form the next higher alkene.

$$CH_3CH_2CH_2OH(g) \rightarrow CH_3CHCH_2(g) + H_2O(g)$$

Assuming that $\Delta H°$ is independent of temperature, what is K for this process at 400 K?

$$[43]$$

20. Calculate ΔS for the system, the surroundings and the universe when 20.00 mol of $H_2O(l)$ at $P°$ is raised from 25.00°C to 35.00°C in each of the three following ways:

(i) by placing it in a heat bath at 35.00°C

(ii) by placing it in a succession of ten baths, each exactly 1 K hotter than the one before

(iii) by placing it in a succession of an infinite number of baths, each dT hotter than the one before

Consider the analogy between this and the mechanical system described in Section 16.1.

$$[\text{(i) } 49.68 \text{ JK}^{-1}; -48.87 \text{ JK}^{-1}; 0.81 \text{ JK}^{-1}$$
$$\text{(ii) } 49.68 \text{ JK}^{-1}; -49.60 \text{ JK}^{-1}; 0.08 \text{ JK}^{-1}$$
$$\text{(iii) } 49.68 \text{ JK}^{-1}; -49.68 \text{ JK}^{-1}; 0 \text{ JK}^{-1}]$$

21. The vapour pressure of crystals of o-dinitro-benzene has been found to

follow the relationship below at temperatures in the neighbourhood of 298 K.

$$\log_{10}\left(\frac{P}{P^\circ}\right) = 7.03 - \frac{4270}{T}$$

Calculate ΔH°, ΔS° and ΔG° for the sublimation of o-dinitro-benzene at 298.15 K.

$$[81.7 \text{ kJ mol}^{-1}; 135 \text{ J K}^{-1} \text{ mol}^{-1}; 41.6 \text{ kJ mol}^{-1}]$$

22. Crystals of rubidium iodide, RbI, sublime to give a gas containing both monomeric and dimeric rubidium iodide. In the range of temperature between 750 K and 920 K, the following experimental relationships have been reported.

$$\ln\left(\frac{P_{RbI}}{P^\circ}\right) = -21.84\times10^3\frac{1}{T} + 15.27$$

$$\ln\left(\frac{P_{Rb_2I_2}}{P^\circ}\right) = -25.81\times10^3\frac{1}{T} + 17.41$$

Calculate ΔG°_{900} and K_{900} for the following process.

$$Rb_2I_2(g) \rightarrow 2RbI(g)$$

$$[50.3 \text{ kJ}; 1.20\times10^{-3}]$$

23. The temperature dependence of the vapour pressure has been studied and reported for both solid and liquid thorium (IV) chloride as follows.

$$\text{solid: } \log_{10}\left(\frac{P_{ThCl_4}}{P^\circ}\right) = 10.098 - \frac{11\,612}{T}$$

$$\text{liquid: } \log_{10}\left(\frac{P_{ThCl_4}}{P^\circ}\right) = 6.648 - \frac{8013}{T}$$

Calculate the melting point of $ThCl_4(c)$ and explain briefly the basis of your calculation.

$$[1043 \text{ K}]$$

XVII PHASE EQUILIBRIA IN TWO COMPONENT SYSTEMS

Processes such as evaporating, boiling, precipitating, dissolving, subliming, melting and freezing are involved in every aspect of chemistry. In some cases, such as the refining of crude oil by distillation or the study of the properties of alloys, these processes, all of which involve 'phase changes', are central to understanding what occurs. Section 7-6 discusses phase changes for cases where a single substance is involved. Such systems, called one component systems, can exist in any of the three physical states of gas, liquid or solid. In addition, some one component systems can exist in more than one crystal structure in the solid state. The temperature and pressure regions in which each of these states is stable, and the temperatures and pressures at which one is transformed into the other, can be portrayed readily on a single diagram. In the most commonly met form of such a diagram, the vertical axis represents pressure and the horizontal axis, temperature. An example is shown in Figure 7-9.

With two component systems, these transformations are complicated by the existence of a new variable, composition. As with one component systems, it is convenient to display the experimental findings in diagram form. Before examining how this is done, however, it is important to define the terms employed.

17-1 THE MEANING OF PHASE AND COMPONENT

Within a given system, all of the matter having a particular set of properties constitutes one *phase*. If there is other matter in the system differing in any physical or chemical property, that matter belongs to another phase. Thus a mixture of sodium chloride crystals and ice crystals constitutes two phases, even although both are solids. Moreover it is *only* two phases, even although the particles of one or both materials may not be continuously connected. A mixture of ice and liquid water also constitutes two phases. Just as ice crystals have properties different from those of sodium chloride crystals, so too, do they have properties differing from those of liquid water.

However, while both of the systems above contain two phases, they differ in a fundamental way. Whereas the composition of the sodium chloride phase differs from that of the ice phase, the composition of the liquid water is identical to that of ice. Where it is possible to describe the composition of all phases in terms of a single material, the system is said to be a *one component system.* Where composition of the phases requires specification of the relative amounts of two materials, the system is said to be a two component system.

It is important to note in the above that components are defined in terms of the *minimum* number of materials needed to specify the composition. Composition can usually be described in many ways. All phases in the water system could be described in terms of the amounts of hydrogen and oxygen, but this does not make the water system a two component system. Because the hydrogen and oxygen are always present in the same proportion, a single specification suffices. Hydrogen and oxygen are *constituents* but the word components is reserved for the smallest set capable of describing the composition of any imaginable system.

In stating the above, certain limitations are implicit. These are described precisely by Denbigh in the text listed at the end of the chapter. Basically, however, in determining the number of components, the processes are restricted to 'physical' processes like melting, evaporating and dissolving. 'Chemical' processes like

$$H_2O(g) \rightarrow H_2(g) + \tfrac{1}{2} O_2(g)$$

are excluded from consideration.

17-2   THE PHASE RULE

It is found experimentally that there is an upper limit to the number of phases which can exist in equilibrium in any given system, and an upper limit to how many variables (temperature, pressure and the composition of the phases) which one can independently vary while still maintaining equilibrium among the phases. Both restrictions are expressed in a single, algebraically simple statement known as the phase rule,

$$P + F = C + 2$$

which was introduced in Section 7-6.

The phase rule can be developed on the basis of the second law of thermodynamics, by considering the number of independent relationships among the components in the various phases. It is equally convincing to note that no violation of this rule has been observed.

Chapter 7, in dealing with one component systems, recalled the everyday observation that water can exist as a liquid over a range of pressure, and that for *each* pressure it can exist over a range of temperature. For example, at $P°$, water is a liquid between 273.15 K and 373.15 K. Thus both pressure and temperature can be varied independently, albeit within a limited range, without causing a change in phase. The phase rule predicts these two degrees of freedom, since $C = 1$ and $P = 1$.

Similarly, at any given pressure, water exists in equilibrium with water vapour only at one temperature (the boiling point) or, conversely, only at one pressure (the vapour pressure) for any given temperature. As long as two phases are in equilibrium, there is only one degree of freedom. Again, the phase rule predicts this, since C = 1 and P = 2.

Finally, ice, water and water vapour can exist in equilibrium only at a unique temperature and pressure, the triple point. There is no freedom of choice in choosing either temperature or pressure. C = 1, P = 3 and consequently, F = 0.

The above discussion raises an interesting point. According to the argument, liquid water and water vapour cannot exist in equilibrium at 298 K and P°, and yet it is a matter of everyday experience that they do. There is, however, no inconsistency. Everyday experience is not with one component systems.

With a one component system, the vapour pressure must be the total pressure if a vapour phase exists. With multicomponent systems, other compounds can be in the gas phase contributing to the total pressure, and in these cases the total pressure is greater than the vapour pressure of a particular liquid.

Consider placing the two component system nitrogen and water in one of the piston and cylinder systems used in Chapter 16. One would find that at 298 K and P°, the system existed as two phases. One is a liquid consisting mostly of water but containing a trace of dissolved nitrogen. The other is a gas phase containing both water and nitrogen, the partial pressure of water being equal to the vapour pressure of water at 298 K. In the one component system, this vapour pressure is not large enough to lift the piston (except at or above 373 K) and hence there is no vapour phase. In the two component system, however, the nitrogen supports the remainder of the piston's mass, allowing two phases over a wide range of temperature and pressure. The nitrogen/water system is thus a more realistic model for this aspect of the natural environment.

17-3 PHASE DIAGRAMS

In the remainder of this chapter, data for a wider variety of real systems are presented. In studying them, you will gain both a sense of the types of situation which are encountered and a proficiency in reading phase diagrams. Both will help you in acquiring similar information about any system of interest to you in the future. The diagrams presented portray figures drawn from the chemical literature, and arise from experimental measurements carried out using a variety of techniques. They represent the work of many chemists and engineers over several decades. As such, they have varying degrees of accuracy. Exactly the same statement could be made of any body of data, such as the thermochemical data in Appendix 1. It is a point which the practicing scientist and engineer must always bear in mind.

A major difference between one component and two component systems is that in the latter one can form solutions. Solutions can be solid or liquid or gas. There is a modern preference for calling such phases mixtures when all components are thought of as equivalent (oxygen/nitrogen in air, gold/silver in jewellery alloys, ethanol/water in a mixed liquid solvent) and for reserving the word solution for cases where the components are regarded differently as *solvent* and *solute* (water/sodium chloride in sea water). Both types are called solutions in this text, partly because many people use the word mixture or mechanical mixture to refer to multiphase situations like the sodium chloride/ice crystals case which was used in Section 17-1. In this textbook, any phase containing two or more components, whatever its physical state, is a solution. Air is a solution. Sea water is a solution. Isomorphous mixtures of Fe_2SiO_4 and Mg_2SiO_4 in olivine are solutions.

Description of a solution requires specifying its composition. This poses an immediate complication in the portrayal of phase data diagrammatically for two component systems, since there are three variables of interest, temperature, pressure and composition. Thus not all of the data can be included in a single two-dimensional diagram. Usually one plots the relationship between composition and temperature at some fixed pressure, but composition/pressure diagrams at fixed temperature are not uncommon. Temperature/composition diagrams at fixed pressure are sometimes called reduced phase diagrams.

17-4 LIQUID-VAPOUR EQUILIBRIA IN TWO COMPONENT SYSTEMS

All gases are soluble in one another. One never finds two or more gas phases in equilibrium. At equilibrium there can be no gas phase or one gas phase but never more. This is not true for liquids, however, and the differences in liquid-vapour phase diagrams depend almost entirely on the differences in the way in which the liquids interact. Liquids can be totally soluble (miscible) in one another, partially soluble in one another or effectively insoluble in one another. These three situations give rise to three distinctively different phase diagrams.

Consider first the case of two liquids which are totally soluble in one another. Toluene, $C_6H_5CH_3$ and n-hexane, C_6H_{14} make such a system. A liquid phase containing these two can have any compostion from being 100% toluene to being 100% hexane. In such systems, there can never be more than one liquid phase at equilibrium. When these liquid solutions boil, the gas produced has a different composition from the liquid. Moreover, each different composition of liquid solution boils at a different temperature. By boil, one usually means 'has an equilibrium pressure equal to $P°$' but boiling points are frequently published for other pressures as well and it is important to check to see at what pressure any given set of measurements has been made.

It follows that a full description of the liquid/vapour equilibria in a system like toluene/n-hexane requires, for any given pressure, a knowledge of the boiling point of each composition of liquid, and a knowledge of the composition of the vapour which that boiling produces. Both can be measured in an apparatus like that shown in Figure 17-1. Liquids of known composition are placed in the flask and boiled. The gas rises, condenses on the cold walls of the condensor, and falls back. A thermometer measures the temperature and a

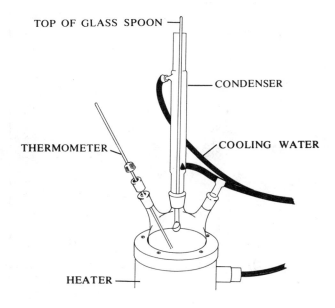

TOP OF GLASS SPOON

CONDENSER

THERMOMETER

COOLING WATER

HEATER

Figure 17-1

spoon permits collection for analysis of a small portion of the condensate. Sufficient time must be left for equilibrium to be established. Indeed, accurate work requires many precautions and calibrations.

When such an experiment has been carried out for several compositions, including the extreme cases of pure toluene and pure hexane, the data can be tabulated as shown in Table 17-1 and portrayed diagramatically as in Figure 17-2(a).

TABLE 17-1 Experimental Data for Boiling of System Toluene/n-Hexane at $P°$

Mole Fraction n-Hexane in Liquid Phase	Boiling Point/°C	Mole Fraction n-Hexane in Gas Phase
0.000	110.56	0.000
0.100	100.95	0.310
0.196	94.40	0.484
0.254	90.85	0.563
0.352	86.35	0.664
0.443	82.50	0.742
0.579	78.50	0.822
0.707	74.85	0.880
0.813	72.25	0.927
1.000	68.75	1.000

Source: L. Sieg, Chem. Ing. Techn. *22*(1950) 322

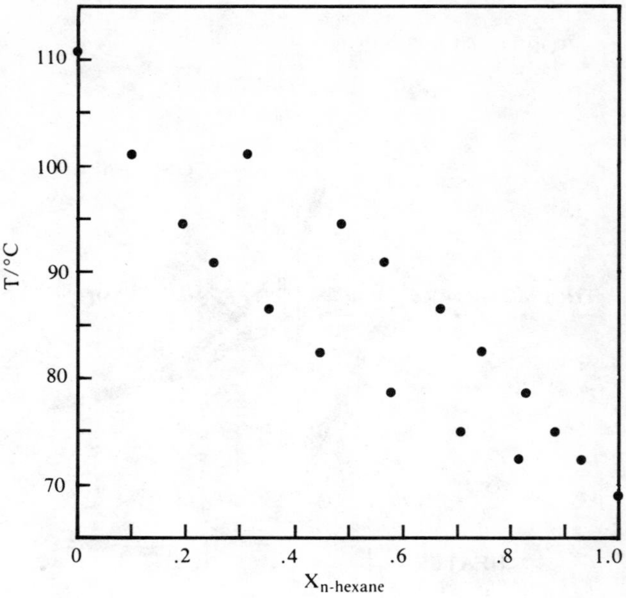

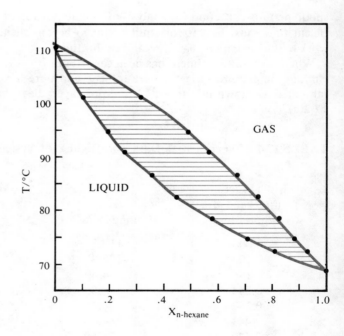

Figure 17-2a
The system Toluene/n-Hexane
$P = P°$: Temperature Range 65-105°C.
2b is identical to 2a except that the points
are replaced by two smooth curves, and
the area between these two curves is filled
with fine horizontal lines.

Figure 17-2b

Figure 17-2(b) results from drawing curves through the two sets of points.
The horizontal lines joining these two curves are *tie lines*. These join the compositions of phases which exist in equilibrium and so, of course, must be
horizontal since two phases at different temperatures cannot be in equilibrium.

It is instructive to consider how this diagram can be interpreted. Consider all possible relative amounts of toluene and hexane at some particular temperature, say 90°C. At this temperature, systems of less than 27% hexane exist, at equilibrium, as a single liquid phase. Systems of more than 57% hexane exist as a single gas phase. Systems with composition between 27% and 57% hexane cannot exist as a single liquid, since they have even more hexane than does the liquid which boils at this pressure. They cannot exist as a single gas phase either, since they have even less hexane than does the gas which condenses at this pressure. They exist as two phases, one a liquid which is 27% hexane and the other a gas which is 57% hexane. These are, of course, the compositions of the only gas and liquid which can exist at equilibrium in this system at this temperature. Varying the composition of the system in this range simply varies the relative amounts of the two phases, not the composition of either. Thus a system which is 54% hexane would contain mainly gas and little liquid whereas a system which is 29% hexane contains mainly the liquid phase. A method of calculating the exact proportions of the two phases is described in a subsequent section.

Notice that the phase rule shows that there is no freedom of choice in determining the composition of either the liquid or the gas.

$$F = C + 2 - P$$
$$= 2 + 2 - 2$$
$$= 2$$

Since the pressure and temperature have already been chosen, there is no freedom left to choose the compositions of the phases. Only one particular liquid (27% n-hexane) and one particular gas (57% n-hexane) can exist in equilibrium at 90°C and $P°$.

Extension of this argument to other temperatures shows that any toluene/n-hexane system having a temperature and composition represented by a point in the large clear field above the 'banana' will exist at equilibrium in a single gas phase. Any represented by a point below the banana will exist as a single liquid phase. Any represented by a point within the banana will exist in two phases, the compositions and physical states of which are indicated by the ends of the tie line on which the point lies.

Examination of a number of systems in which the two liquids are totally soluble in one another discloses that while the toluene/n-hexane pattern is common, there are also many systems in which there is either a maximum or a minimum at some intermediate composition. These maxima and minima are called azeotropic points. Examples are the systems hydrazine/water, Figure 17-3, which shows a maximum and pyridine/water, Figure 17-4, which shows a minimum.

The pyridine water system is such that $P°$ is reached at much lower temperatures at intermediate concentrations than it is for either of the pure components. This suggests that the energies of attraction between water molecules and pyridine molecules are less than those between water and water or pyridine and pyridine. If this unfavourable interaction were even greater, the two liquids could cease to be miscible in one another. New lines would have

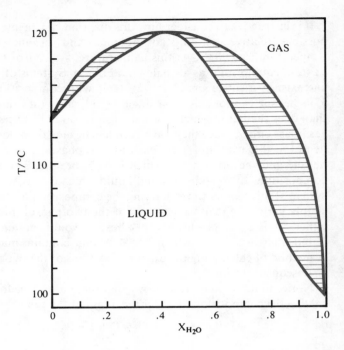

Figure 17-3 Hydrazine/Water
P=P°; Temperature Range 99-121°C

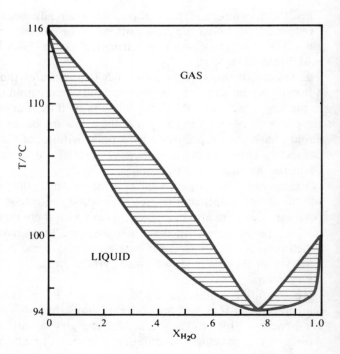

Figure 17-4 Pyridine/Water
P=P°; Temperature Range 94-116°C

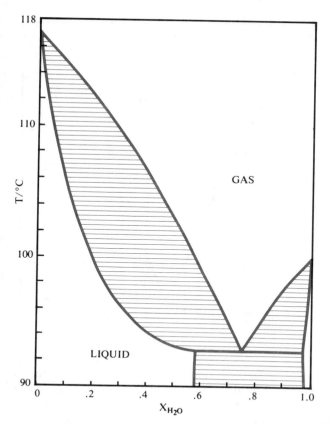

Figure 17-5   1–Butanol/Water
P = 102.3 kPa;
Temperature Range 90 – 118°C

to be added to the diagram to show the limits of solubility of each component in the other. Such a system is 1-butanol/water, the diagram of which appears in Figure 17-5. In the 'rabbit ears' region this figure is essentially the same as Figure 17-4 but in the liquid region at lower temperature there are three fields, two of which are one phase fields (below saturation by one or other component) and an intermediate field in which a system exists as two solutions in equilibrium. These two solutions may be thought of as a saturated solution of 1-butanol in water and a saturated solution of water in 1-butanol. They are in equilibrium with one another, as the tie lines indicate, and a small change in temperature results in a small change in the composition of each with a necessary transfer of material between the two phases to achieve this.

Finally, consider the case of a system in which the liquids are essentially insoluble in one another, such as n-heptane/water. The lines representing the solubility of the saturated solution would coincide with the axes, since essentially none of the other component is soluble. Such a diagram is shown in Figure 17-6.

The form of this diagram could have been predicted in another way. At P°, n-heptane boils at 98.4°C and water at 100°C. At temperatures below their boiling points each has, of course, a vapour pressure less than P°. There must

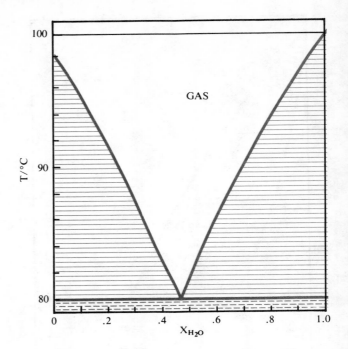

Figure 17-6   n-Heptane/Water
$P = P°$; Temperature Range $79° - 101°C$

be a temperature, in this system at 80.0°C, at which the sum of the two vapour pressures equals P°. At this temperature, both liquids may be simultaneously in equilibrium with a gas at P°. To achieve this in actual practice, one would need to shake the container or the like. Otherwise the less dense heptane would lie on top of the water and prevent the water from reaching the gas phase. Vigorous shaking would ensure that both liquid phases contacted the gas.

Below 80°C, the sum of the vapour pressures is less than P° and there will be no gas phase, just two liquid phases. The tie lines in this region are dotted on the diagram to indicate that although there are two phases, those phases are not in equilibrium. That is because no process between water and n-heptane is possible. They simply coexist. This is in contrast to the system 1-butanol/water where the two liquid *solutions are* in equilibrium, and temperature changes in either direction result in a change in the compositions of those solutions.

Returning to n-heptane/water, one sees that at temperatures above 80°C the sum of the vapour pressures is greater than P°. Thus at temperatures above 80°C if one component is present in liquid form so that its vapour is at the vapour pressure, the partial pressure of the other component must be at less than its vapour pressure. Thus only one liquid can be in equilibrium with the vapour above 80°C at P°. That there is only one temperature, for any given pressure, at which a vapour can be in equilibrium with both components is also evident from the phase rule, since for three phases present

$$F = C + 2 - P$$

$$= 2 + 2 - 3$$

$$= 1$$

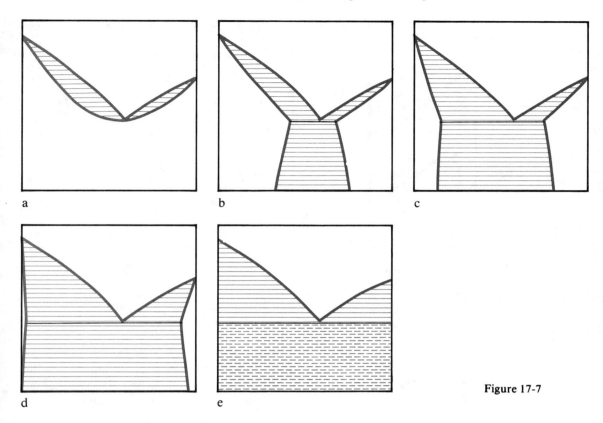

a

b

c

d

e

Figure 17-7

The pressure having been chosen, the temperature at which three phases can be in equilibrium is fixed.

These three diagrams can be seen as representing a continuum of possibilities from total solubility, as in Figure 17-7(a), to total insolubility as in Figure 17-7(e). Large solubilities imply saturation lines far from the axes as in Figure 17-7(b) whereas low solubilities imply lines close to the axes. Indeed the continuum concept fits the reality very well, because the systems which one usually regards as showing no solubility are usually really cases of extremely low solubility.

17-5 HEATING AND COOLING CURVES

Consider heating 7.0 mol toluene and 3.0 mol n-hexane at a uniform rate of addition of heat from 70°C to 100°C. Figure 17-8 shows that at 70°C, the system exists as a single liquid phase. Addition of heat raises the temperature, the rate of temperature rise depending on the rate of heat addition and on the heat capacity of the system. At about 75°C, a gas phase forms of composition 87% hexane by mol. As heat continues to flow in, the amount of gas increases at the expense of the liquid. The rate of temperature rise is less than that prior to gas forming because now the enthalpy of vaporization must be overcome.

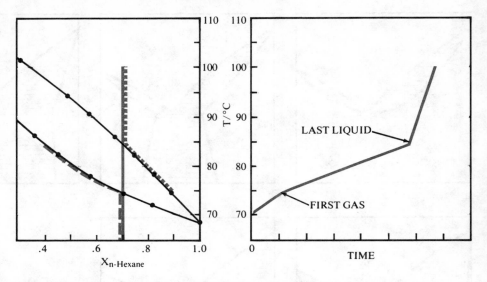

Figure 17-8   A portion of the toluene/n-hexane phase diagram (as in figure 17-2) and a hypothetical heating curve for a 70:30 solution between 70°C and 100°C

Notice that at each temperature the composition of both phases can be read from the curved lines. At 80°C for example, the liquid is 52% hexane and the gas is 79% hexane. At about 85°C, the gas composition is 70% hexane whereas the liquid is 38% hexane. Since the composition of the gas is the same as that of the system, it follows that there can be only a tiny drop of liquid left, since one cannot divide something which is 70%B and 30%A into two parts, one of which is 70%B and 30%A and the other of which is 38%B and 62%A unless the second is negligibly small in amount. In the system being considered, the liquid has evaporated continuously between 75°C and 85°C, and

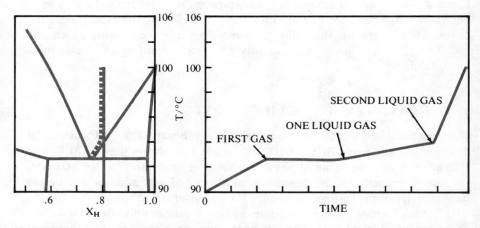

Figure 17-9   A portion of the 1-butanol/water phase diagram (as in figure 17-5) and a hypothetical heating curve for an 80:20 solution between 90°C and 100°C

is now all evaporated. Above 85°C the system exists as a single gas phase. The temperature rise will be steep relative to that in the 75°C to 85°C range since there is no longer an enthalpy of vaporization to overcome.

In the system 1-butanol/water, the heating of a liquid of less than 58% water or more than 98% water would follow a very similar course to that described above. Between these two compositions, however, one begins with two liquid phases, and there are, therefore, significant differences. Figure 17-9 illustrates the case of a system which is 8.0 mol of water and 2.0 mol of 1-butanol being heated from 90°C to 100°C. At 90°C there are two phases, both liquid, one 58% water and one 98% water. As heat enters, the temperature rises. The solubilities change slightly with temperature, so that the compositions of the two phases alter slightly with a necessary small transfer of material between the two phases to accomplish this. At about 92.7°C, a gas phase forms. Its composition is 76% water on a molar basis. Since three phases are now present, and since there can only be one temperature at any fixed pressure at which three phases can be in equilibrium in a two component system, further additions of heat will not merely convert liquid to gas, exactly as happens when two phases are present in a one component system. The temperature arrest will continue until one of the two liquids has disappeared. One way of seeing which liquid will evaporate first is to note that, just above this temperature, the system exists as a gas which is 76% water and a liquid which is 98% water. Therefore the phase which is exhausted first is the liquid which is 58% water. As soon as it is gone, the temperature resumes its rise. The rise will not be as steep as that below 92.7°C because liquid is still evaporating and the enthalpy of vaporization must be overcome. At about 94°C the last drop of liquid disappears and above that temperature the system exists as a single gas phase.

Figure 17-10 illustrates the case of a pair of insoluble liquids, a case which differs very little from that described above. The example chosen is a system containing equal parts of water and n-heptane on a molar basis. Between 79°C and 80°C there are two liquid phases, but in this case they are pure liquids rather than solutions. At 80°C a gas appears, of composition 47% water, and

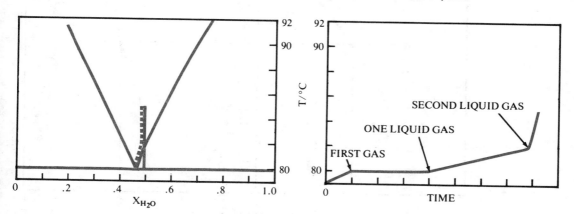

Figure 17-10 A portion of the n-heptane/water phase diagram (as in figure 17-6) and a hypothetical heating curve for 60:40 solution between 79°C and 85°C

since three phases are now present the temperature remains constant until one of them has disappeared. A glance at the diagram just above 80°C indicates that the system exists there as a gas plus liquid water, so the phase which evaporates first must be the heptane. Once it has gone, the temperature resumes its rise. Water continues to evaporate until, at about 82°C, it has all evaporated and the system exists as a single gas phase from that point on.

17-6   CALCULATION OF THE MASS OF EACH PHASE

If the mass, as well as the composition, of a system is known, and the composition of the phases which constitute the system can be obtained from a phase diagram, it is usually possible to calculate the mass of each phase. Consider Figure 17-11.

Suppose a system (in which the fraction of A is given by f) consists of two phases, labelled α and β. Phase α has a mass m_α and a composition f_α of A (and hence $1-f_\alpha$ of B). Phase β has a mass of m_β and a composition f_β of A. It follows that the mass of the system is $m_\alpha + m_\beta$, and that the mass of component A in the total system is $m_\alpha f_\alpha + m_\beta f_\beta$. f_α and f_β are the *mass* fractions, not the mole fractions of A in the two phases. Since the mass fraction of A in the total system, f, is the mass of A in the system divided by the total mass of the system, it follows that

$$f = \frac{m_\alpha f_\alpha + m_\beta f_\beta}{m_\alpha + m_\beta}$$

$$m_\alpha f + m_\beta f = m_\alpha f_\alpha + m_\beta f_\beta$$

$$\frac{m_\alpha}{m_\beta} = \frac{f_\beta - f}{f - f_\alpha}$$

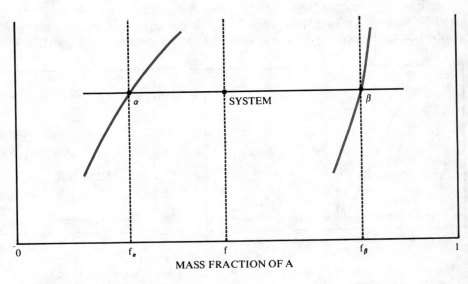

MASS FRACTION OF A

Figure 17-11

If actual masses, rather than ratios of masses, are required, these may be obtained in terms of the total mass of the system, M, as follows.

$$m_\alpha + m_\beta = M$$

Eliminating m_β from the last two equations above gives

$$m_\alpha = \frac{f_\beta - f}{f_\beta - f_\alpha} M$$

Similarly

$$m_\beta = \frac{f - f_\alpha}{f_\beta - f_\alpha} M$$

These relationships are often referred to as the lever rule, drawing attention to the fact that the greater mass stands on the shorter end.

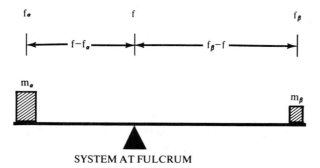

SYSTEM AT FULCRUM

This might be made more understandable by considering the reverse relationship for a trivial system. Suppose a store has two displays of fruit, one (α) with 100 apples and 300 oranges and the other (β) with 40 apples and 60 oranges. The total fruit in the store (our system) is $100 + 40 = 140$ apples and $300 + 60 = 360$ oranges. The composition of the total system is $\frac{140}{140 + 360} = 28\%$ apples and 72% oranges. The compositions of the two displays (phases) are $\frac{100}{100 + 300} = 25\%$ apples for α and $\frac{40}{40 + 60} = 40\%$ apples for β. Thus our system, which is 28% apples, exists as two separate units, one (α) of 25% apples and another (β) of 40% apples.

Now suppose we had been told the size and composition of the system (500 apples and oranges; 28% apples) and the composition of the two phases into which it was divided (25% apples in α and 40% apples in β) and had been asked to determine the amount of fruit in each display. If there are N_α fruits in α and N_β fruits in β, separate consideration of the distribution of apples and oranges gives

$$.25\, N_\alpha + .40\, N_\beta = .28(500)$$

$$(1 - .25)N_\alpha + (1 - .40)N_\beta = (1 - .28)(500)$$

Solving for N_α gives

$$N_\alpha = \frac{.40 - .28}{.40 - .25} \, (500)$$

Similarly,

$$N_\beta = \frac{.28 - .25}{.40 - .25} \, (500)$$

$$N_\alpha + N_\beta = \frac{.40 - .28}{.40 - .25} \, (500) + \frac{.28 - .25}{.40 - .25} \, (500) = 500$$

In terms of a diagram having a horizontal axis representing composition, length x is the composition difference between the system and α whereas length y is the composition difference between β and the system. The size of display having composition 25% apples is given by $\frac{y}{x+y}$ (500) and the size of display with composition 40% apples is given by $\frac{x}{x+y}$ (500).

Note that a system existing as two phases must always have a compostion intermediate between those of the phases. It is impossible for a system to divide itself into two portions, both of which are richer in one component than is the total system.

Example 17-1   From Figure 17-12, predict the mass of each phase present at equilibrium in a system consisting of 15.0 g of methanol and 35.0 g of water at 90°C and P°.

The system has a composition 30% alcohol and 70% water by mass. From the diagram, it can be seen that the system exists as two phases, one a liquid (about 12% alcohol) and the other a vapour (about 49% alcohol). The mass of liquid is therefore

$$\frac{49 - 30}{49 - 12} \, (50.0 \text{ g}) = 25.7 \text{ g}$$

and the mass of vapour is therefore

$$\frac{30 - 12}{49 - 12} \, (50.0 \text{ g}) = 24.3 \text{ g}$$

Obtaining the same information from a mole fraction diagram takes a few more steps. Example 17-2 illustrates what is necessary.

Example 17-2   Calculate the mass and composition of each phase present at equilibrium in a system containing 8.0 mol water and 2.0 mol hydrazine at P° and 113.0°C.

From Figure 17-3, it can be seen that this 80% water system exists as two phases, a liquid which is 70% water and a gas which is 88% water. These compositions are all molar percentages. Application of the lever rule gives

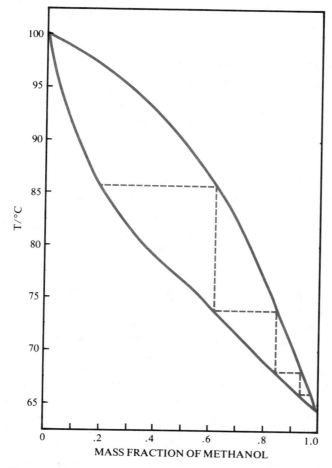

Figure 17-12   Methanol/Water
$P=P°$; Temperature Range 62.5°C to 102.5°C

$$\text{amount in liquid} = \frac{88 - 80}{88 - 70} \ (10.0) = 4.4 \ \text{mol}$$

$$\text{amount in gas} = \frac{80 - 70}{88 - 70} \ (10.0) = 5.6 \ \text{mol}$$

Notice that on a mass fraction diagram, the lever rule tells you what fraction of the mass is in each phase whereas on a mole fraction diagram, the lever rule tells you what fraction of the total moles is in each phase. In order to convert that information into mass, one must use the known compositions of the phases as follows.

In the liquid phase, 70% of the moles in that phase are water and 30% hydrazine. Hence

$$\text{amount of water in liquid} = (0.70)(4.4) = 3.1 \ \text{mol}$$

$$\text{amount of hydrazine in liquid} = (0.30)(4.4) = 1.3 \ \text{mol}$$

Using the molar mass of each component, one can then say

mass water in liquid = (3.1)(18.0) = 55.8 g

mass hydrazine in liquid = (1.3)(32.0) = 41.7 g

mass of liquid phase = 55.8 + 41.7 = 97 g

Since the mass of the total system is (2.0)(32.0) + (8.0)(18.0) which is 208 g, the mass of the gas phase must, by difference, be 208 − 97 = 101 g.

17-7 DISTILLATION

Even though they are soluble in one another, the components of a solution can often be totally separated from one another by a process known as distillation. The key to doing so lies in the fact that there is usually a difference in composition between a liquid solution and the gas which is in equilibrium with that solution.

Figure 17-12 contains a phase diagram of the system methanol/water. Suppose one wished to obtain pure methanol from a liquid solution containing 20 g of methanol and 80 g of water. For a pressure of $P°$, this solution boils at 85.6°C and yields a gas which is 62% methanol. This gas is much richer in methanol than the liquid, which is desirable in seeking to obtain pure methanol, but there is very little of the gas, which is undesirable. These two factors always work against one another. In order to obtain half of the system in the gas phase, the temperature would need to be raised to 94.0°C but at this temperature the gas would be only 34% methanol. Therefore in order to keep the gas rich in methanol, consider a temperature close to 85.6°C where, say, only 1% of the system exists as gas and that gas is approximately 62% methanol.

This gram of gas can be cooled and liquified entirely, producing a liquid which is 62% methanol. If this liquid is then heated, it will produce a gas which is 85% methanol at 73.8°C. As before, only a small fraction of gas can be produced and removed if that gas is to be this rich in methanol. Suppose that one again takes 1%.

This process can be repeated indefinitely. The next liquid boils at 68.0°C to give a gas which is 94% methanol. That, when liquified, boils at 65.9°C and gives a gas which is 98% methanol. Further steps would increase the percentage of methanol until any desired level of purity was reached. However, even the four steps described and illustrated in Figure 17-12 yield only $100(.01)^4 = 10^{-6}$ g. Such a method of separation is feasible but uselessly unproductive.

The separation can be carried out effectively and in reasonable time by the use of a distillation column or still, such as that illustrated in Figure 17-13. If a 20% methanol solution is boiled in the bottom of such a column, the vapour will rise, pass through the pipe above and condense on the underside of the bubble cap. Once the tray fills, further vapour must bubble from beneath the cap through the liquid. The heat produced by condensation heats the tray and vapour begins to rise to the next tray where the process repeats itself. The gas

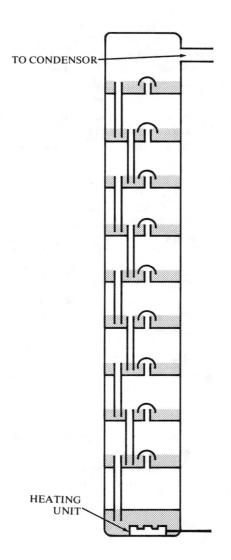

TO CONDENSOR

HEATING
UNIT

Figure 17-13

rising from each tray is at approximately the composition of the gas which is in equilibrium with the liquid in that tray. As each successive tray is filled, an overspill device carries excess liquid, depleted in methanol because the gas leaving it is rich in methanol, back to the tray below.

Eventually a steady state situation is established, with a temperature gradient toward progressively lower temperatures up the column, with solutions progressively richer in methanol boiling in each tray. Methanol rich gases rise from each tray and methanol poor liquids trickle back to the level below. In laboratory operations, it is usual to remove the gas at the top of the column and condense it. Industrial designs do this too, but there it is not uncommon to introduce new material continuously in a tray in the centre of the column. Water can then be removed continuously from the boiler and methanol removed by condensation of the gas.

The batch process described early in the section showed that, with the best imaginable enrichment at each stage, a still which produced 98% methanol from a solution which was 20% methanol required four stages to do so. In an ideal still, the first of these stages occurs in the boiler itself and three plates would be necessary to carry out the remaining stages. Thus a still which produced 98% methanol from a continuously fed solution of 20% methanol would be said to contain three *theoretical plates*. The performance of a column can be described quantitatively by comparing the separation it achieves with the minimum number of steps necessary to achieve that separation. This minimum number can be calculated from the phase diagram in exactly the same way as was done in Figure 17-12, by drawing the successive steps. Industrial columns are sometimes rated in terms of the physical column height equilvalent to a theoretical plate, or H.E.T.P. The smaller this quantity, the more effective the design, at least from this viewpoint. Industrial columns may be of the order of 100 m high. Laboratory columns are seldom more than a metre or two, and are usually less. There are many designs, and the best can achieve the equivalent of 200 theoretical plates in a height of a metre.

Systems with azeotropic points cannot be completely separated into the two components by distillation at that pressure. For example, a solution which is 70% water, 30% hydrazine, when distilled at $P°$ would yield a gas which was pure water, but the liquid left in the boiler would be 43% water, 57% hydrazine, the azeotropic solution. Similarly placing a solution in a still which was 30% water, 70% pyridine would result in the azeotropic mixture boiling off, but pure pyridine would eventually be left in the boiler.

Example 17-3   How much pyridine can be removed by distillation at $P°$ from a solution which contains 10 mol of each of water and pyridine?

The still could split a 50% water solution into two parts, the azeotropic solution (77% water) and pyridine (0% water!). Application of the lever rule gives

amount of pyridine $= \dfrac{77 - 50}{77 - 0}$ (20) = 7.0 mol

17-8   SOME SIMPLE SOLID-LIQUID EQUILIBRIA

There are many more kinds of solid/liquid phase diagrams than there are liquid/gas diagrams. Whereas gases are always totally soluble in one another, liquids may be soluble, partly soluble or insoluble. The solubilities of solids also vary but in addition some solids exhibit a variety of crystal structure as well as the formation of intermediate compounds.

Most of the patterns described for liquid/gas equilibria have analogues in solid/liquid equilibria. Figures 17-14 and 17-15 illustrate cases in which there is total solubility both as liquids and as solids. The similarity of these diagrams to those in Figures 17-2 and 17-4 is obvious. As a matter of interest, there are few if any systems known which exhibit a maximum in the melting point analogous to the boiling point maximum in Figure 17-3, although a few systems like the lead/thallium system discussed later come close to doing so.

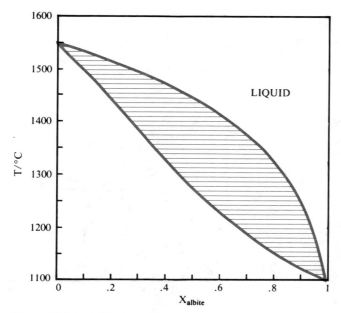

Figure 17-14 Albite/Anorthite
Temperature Range 1100-1600°C

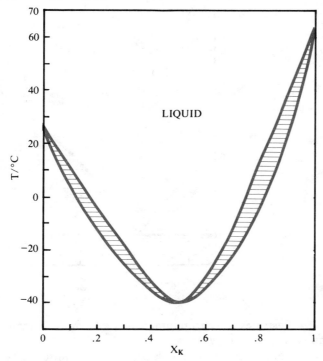

Figure 17-15 Potassium/Caesium
Temperature Range −50 to 70°C

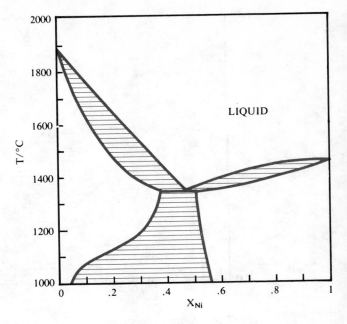

Figure 17-16 Chromium/Nickel

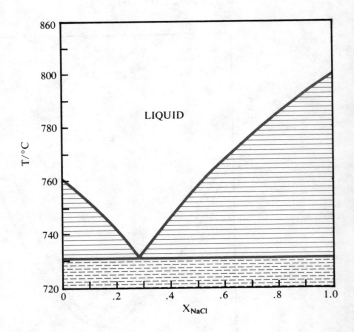

Figure 17-17 NaCl/NaBr
Temperature Range 720-820°C

Figure 17-16 illustrates the chromium/nickel system. The analogy between this figure and Figure 17-5 is again clear.

Finally, the diagram for NaCl and NaBr, which are miscible as liquids but insoluble as solids, is shown in Figure 17-17, a pattern with obvious similarities to Figure 17-6. There are numerous systems exhibiting a minimum melting point such as is shown by Cr/Ni and NaCl/NaBr. The minimum melting point is known as a *eutectic* point. The eutectic composition in NaCl/NaBr is 28% NaCl and the eutectic temperature is 731°C.

Cooling curves, or heating curves, for these solid/liquid equilibria will likewise follow the same patterns as their liquid/gas analogues.

Example 17-4 Describe what occurs, assuming equilibrium, as a system of (a) 40 kg of tin and 60 kg of lead is cooled from 340°C to 170°C (b) 15 kg of tin and 85 kg of lead is cooled through the same range.

(a) The system is 60% lead by mass. From the diagram in Figure 17-19, it can be seen that it exists as a single liquid phase at 340°C. On cooling, the first crystal of solid appears at about 240°C, having a composition of about 90% Pb by mass. Further cooling results in steadily increasing the mass of the solid and decreasing that of the liquid.

When the temperature reaches 183°C, the liquid has the composition and temperature (38.5% Pb, 183°C) that lies on both the line indicating saturation with respect to the lead rich solid solution (on which it has been since 240°C) and on the line indicating saturation with respect to the tin rich solution. This second solid solution now precipitates, giving three phases, two of them solid (3% Pb and 81% Pb respectively) and one of them liquid (38.5% Pb). The temperature will remain constant at 183°C until all of the liquid has precipitated as these two solids. Further removal of heat will then lower the temperature, with the composition of the two phases altering in accordance with the solubility limits indicated at each temperature. Although the figure does not extend far enough to show it, the solubility of lead in tin is extremely small below about 160°C and below this temperature one phase will be nearly pure tin.

(b) This system is 85% Pb by mass. At 340°C it is a single liquid phase. On cooling, a crystal of composition 95% Pb appears at about 296°C. As cooling continues the mass of liquid decreases and the mass of solid increases, the composition of each phase indicated at each temperature by the lines. At about 220°C, the last trace of liquid disappears and the system consists of a single solid phase, composition 85% Pb and mass 100 kg. It remains thus to about 176°C where the line of saturation is met. Further cooling will result, if equilibrium is achieved, in precipitation from this solid solution of a second solid solution (composition 8% Pb). As the temperature falls further more of this tin rich phase appears, with consequent changes in the amount and composition of the other phase.

In a technique known as thermal analysis, a small sample of a system of interest is compared with a comparably sized sample of some reference material. The comparison involves measuring the temperature difference between the two samples while at the same time a block which contacts both samples is slowly heated. The reference material is some stable substance having no phase changes in the temperature range of interest. The temperature of the block which both sample and reference contact can be altered either up or down at some programmed rate. As long as no change occurs in the sample, both it and the reference have the same temperature as the block except, perhaps, for a

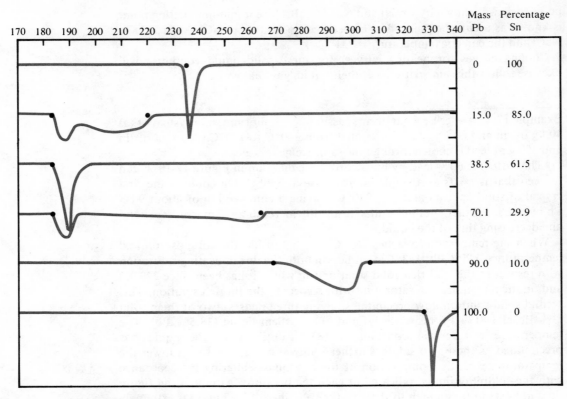

Figure 17-18   Thermal Analysis Curves
for Various Lead/Tin Systems

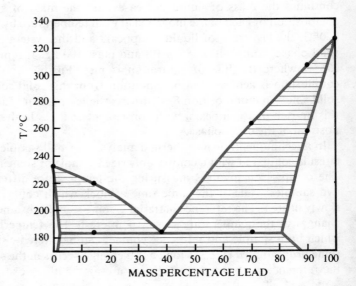

Figure 17-19   Phase Diagram for the
Lead/Tin System

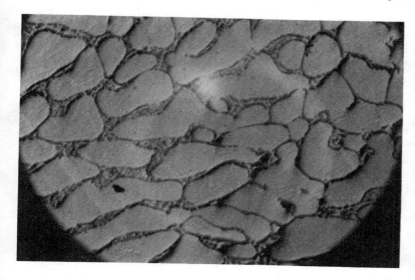

Figure 17-20

small lag. However if the sample undergoes some exothermic or endothermic process, such as melting or crystallization, its temperature will differ from that of the reference for a brief time. If the temperature difference between the sample and the reference is measured and recorded as a function of temperature, the temperature at which any exothermic or endothermic process occurs is indicated. Figure 17-18 shows such measurements for systems of tin and lead. The measurements were made for a temperature rise at the rate of 10 K (min)$^{-1}$. The eutectic temperature of 183°C is visible in three cases, those with 15.0, 38.5 and 70.1% lead. The 38.5% system is seen to be close to the eutectic composition since all or nearly all of the material melts close to the eutectic temperature. On the other hand, the 70.1% system shows a much smaller peak at the eutectic, with the rest of the melting taking place above 183°C, most rapidly between 250 and 265°C. Similarly each thermal analysis can be used to determine the temperature or temperature range of the melting of each mixture. The correlations between the points on the analysis plots and those on the phase diagram which would be generated are shown in Figures 17-18 and 17-19.

Figure 17-20 shows a photomicrograph of the sample produced by recooling the 15.0% lead system. Its microstructure consists of two kinds of material, one light coloured and apparently uniform and the other mottled as if consisting of two or more phases. The large light areas represent crystals of the tin rich material which precipitates first. The mottled material surrounding each of these crystals contains a mixture of tiny crystals of two different materials, the two solids which crystallize at the eutectic temperature.

One can visualize the initial precipitation and continuing growth of numerous crystals of the tin rich phase. These form a suspension within the liquid. Once the eutectic temperature is reached, the remaining liquid which occupies the volume among these crystals begins to solidify into crystals of two types, one the same tin rich material already present and the other the lead rich phase. This mixture of very fine crystals is characteristic of eutectics.

17-9   CORING

Consider a melt of 75 g of gold and 25 g of silver. The phase diagram for this system is shown in Figure 17-21. If the melt is cooled, a few tiny crystals will appear at about 1317 K and will have a composition near 86% gold by mass. Further cooling will produce crystals of lower gold concentration, and these will tend to isolate the first precipitated material from the liquid. What is observed is a layer of solid building up on the cooling element or vessel walls with a concentration gradient beginning with that of the first precipitate and ending with the composition of solid which, at the temperature in question, is in contact with, and in equilibrium with, the liquid. Given long enough, diffusion within the solid would eliminate this gradient and give a true equilibrium. In practice, this is not likely to be achieved in many cases.

The composition of the total solid will clearly lie between that of the first precipitate and that of the most recent. A reasonable path for total solid is therefore given by the dotted line in the detail.

For the particular case illustrated liquid disappears at 1296 K, 8 K lower than would be the case if equilibrium could be maintained. Moreover, it will be at this temperature that liquid first forms on heating the resulting solid.

This phenomenon, known as *coring,* is often a nuisance to metallurgists, producing non-uniform solids which melt or weaken at lower temperatures than would occur if equilibrium could be obtained. The difficulty is greatly reduced by slowing the rate of cooling and precipitation. *Annealing,* a process in which the solid is held for an extended period of time just below its melting point, is another answer. Diffusion processes in the solid are much more rapid at the higher temperature, and concentration gradients are thus reduced or eliminated.

17-10   PURIFICATION OF SOLIDS BY ZONE MELTING

In the refining of metals and other solid materials, it is sometimes necessary to achieve high degrees of purity (say 99.999%). This is usually done by *zone melting.*

Purification by melting, and subsequently cooling and separating the first solid precipitated, is well established in metallurgy and in preparative organic and inorganic chemistry. Where the impurity is soluble in the material of interest, a succession of such operations would gradually reduce the impurity in a manner exactly analogous to the batch process described for a liquid/vapour equilibrium involving methanol and water. Just as in that case, though, achievement of very high purity would produce very little material.

Consider a bar of 75% gold, 25% silver by mass, from which we wish to remove as much as possible of the silver. Suppose a tiny section at one end of the bar is melted. The resulting liquid, naturally, has a composition of 75% gold, 25% silver. Note that this liquid is *not* in equilibrium with the solid. A very long waiting period would be required before the slow process of solid state diffusion could operate to bring about equilibrium.

If we cool a portion of this liquid, the crystals which precipitate will, ac-

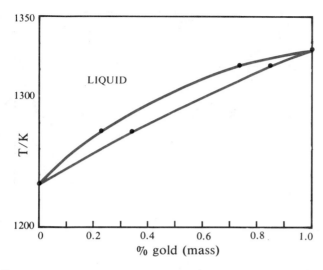

Figure 17-21 Silver/Gold

cording to Figure 17-21, have a composition of about 86% gold. If these crystals were then isolated and melted (giving a liquid that is 86% gold) and new crystals were precipitated from that melt, these crystals would have a composition of about 93% gold according to the diagram. Each successive repetition of the operation would remove more silver from the alloy.

Suppose, instead, that a long ingot in a tray were made of our alloy, and this was drawn very slowly through a device in which heating rings and cooling rings were alternatively arranged, as sketched in Figure 17-22. As each successive melt zone recrystallizes, it leaves a solid richer in gold than the melt from which it separates. The liquids, then, become progressively richer in silver as they move through the furnace. Each passing melt reduces the silver content, concentrating the silver in the back end of the bar, and leaving the forward end of the bar progressively richer in gold. This technique is, in many ways, analogous to the distillation technique used in liquid-vapour equilibria. Without zone refining, it is doubtful if semiconductors, which require materials such as germanium in extreme purity, would be in such widespread use.

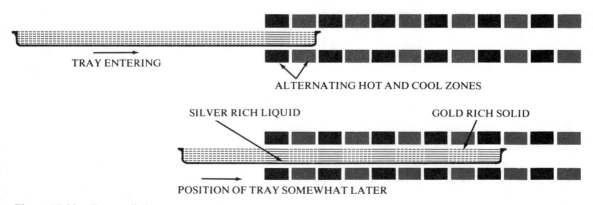

Figure 17-22 Zone refining

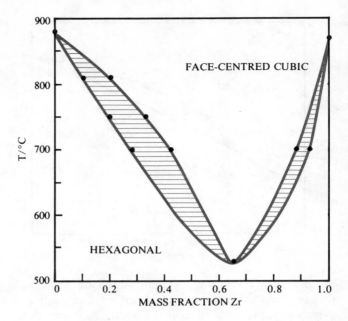

Figure 17-23   Titanium/Zirconium

17-11   SOLID/SOLID AND LIQUID/LIQUID EQUILIBRIA

Titanium has a hexagonal crystal structure below about 880°C and a body-centred cubic structure above that temperature. The closely related metal, zirconium, has almost exactly the same pattern, with the transition temperature slightly lower. These two metals are totally soluble in one another in both crystalline forms.

The phase diagram in Figure 17-23 portrays the region in which these structural changes occur while that in Figure 17-24 portrays a similar situation for

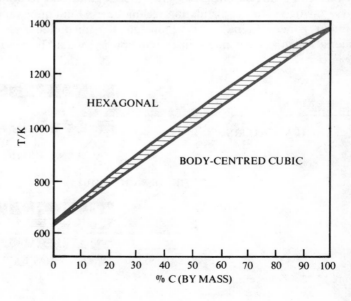

Figure 17-24   Nickel/Cobalt

the system nickel/cobalt. The similarity of these diagrams to those in Figures 17-2, 17-4, 17-14 and 17-15 suggests, and correctly so, that these transitions can be analyzed in exactly the same way as was done in the earlier cases.

Example 17-5 Describe what occurs under equilibrium conditions as 20.0 g of zirconium and 80.0 g of titanium are cooled from 900°C to 700°C.

At 900°C the system exists as a single phase. Every crystal has the body-centred cubic structure and a composition of 20% zirconium by mass.

On cooling, were equilibrium to exist, crystals of a different composition (10% zirconium) and structure (hexagonal) appear at about 810°C. Further cooling results in more hexagonal crystals forming, at the expense of the body-centred material, with the composition of both phases changing as indicated by the lines. At about 750°C, the last body-centred crystals (composition 32% zirconium) disappear. Below this temperature there is only one phase, all material being hexagonal in structure and 20% zirconium in composition. Note that in solids, equilibrium may be established very slowly, since changes in the composition of a solid require diffusion of atoms through the crystal, a slow process compared to the ease with which atoms can move in liquids or gases.

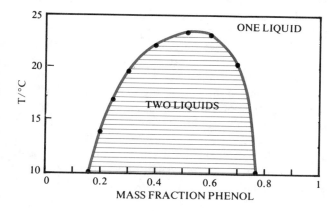

Figure 17-25 Heptane/phenol

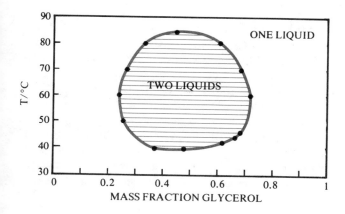

Figure 17-26 Glycerol/4-methoxyphenol
$C_3H_5(OH)_3/C_2H_4(OH)(OCH_3)$

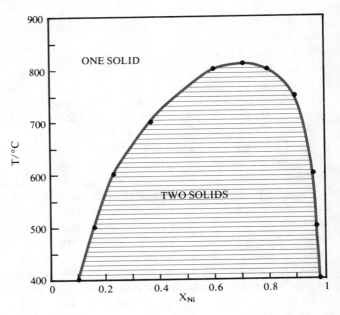

Figure 17-27   Gold/Nickel

Liquid/liquid equilibria are extremely simple. Where there is limited solubility between two liquids, the extent of that solubility will generally be a function of temperature. If solubility increases with temperature, there may be some temperature above which the two are miscible. If solubility decreases with temperature, there may be some temperature below which there is miscibility. There are even a few cases in which the effect of temperature on solubility is itself a function of temperature, resulting in miscibility at both high and low temperatures but a range of limited solubility in between. By far the most common case is that of miscibility at higher temperatures, resulting in a beehive shaped diagram as in Figure 17-25. Figure 17-26 illustrates one of the rare cases with miscibility at both higher and lower temperatures. Solids also show the beehive pattern as in the gold/nickel system of Figure 17-27. Both crystal types in the two phase region have the same crystal structure. Otherwise the miscibility at higher temperatures could not exist. The compositions of the two crystal types differ, of course, as will the lattice dimensions.

Example 17-6   Describe what happens under equilibrium conditions as 80.0 g of phenol is added slowly to 20.0 g of heptane at 20.0°C.

The hexane is, of course, a single liquid phase. As phenol is stirred in, it all dissolves until, when about 9.3 g has been added (giving a system composition of 3% phenol) a cloudiness appears in the liquid. If the source of this cloudiness is allowed to settle, it is found to be a separate liquid phase which is 71% phenol. As more phenol is stirred in, the compositions of these two liquids, one 32% phenol and the other 71% phenol, remain unchanged but the amount of the first increases and of the second decreases until, when 49 g of phenol has been added, all of the original phase has disappeared. Further additions of phenol simply change the composition of the one remaining phase until it is 80% phenol.

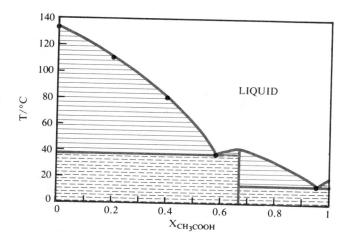

Figure 17-28   Urea/Acetic Acid
$CO(NH_2)_2/CH_3COOH$

17-12   INTERMEDIATE COMPOUNDS

The formation of one or more intermediate compounds introduces new and distinctive patterns to phase diagrams. Two main variants occur, depending on whether the compound melts *congruently* or *incongruently*.

Congruent melting compounds melt to give a liquid of the same composition as the solid. This is the situation with all elements (where no other possibility exists) and with most compounds. Where this occurs, the phase diagram is simply the combination of two of the forms already examined. Figure 17-28 illustrates the system acetic acid/urea. Since compounds are characterized by a unique composition which is independent of temperature, they will appear on the usual phase diagram as a vertical straight line. In this system the line at 66.7% acetic acid by mole corresponds to the compound $(CH_3COOH)_2 \cdot CO(NH_2)_2$. The formation of such a compound is not surprising in view of the possibility of bonding the acidic protons of the two monoprotic acid molecules to the basic $-NH_2$ groups of the urea. The portion of the diagram to the left of the compound line is a diagram for the system urea/compound and that to the right of the line is a diagram for the system compound/acetic acid. Both, as it happens, are simple eutectic diagrams but other forms such as that in Figure 17-16 are possible.

A compound which melts *incongruently* is one which gives a liquid of composition different from itself. Of necessity, some new solid of different composition must also form at the same time. On a phase diagram, the vertical line representing the compound will reach a horizontal line at the melting point which links the composition of the melting compound to those of the two phases into which it is transformed. Figure 17-29 illustrates the system sodium/potassium in which the compound Na_2K forms. This compound melts incongruently at 7°C to give a liquid which is 41% potassium and a solid which is pure sodium. Notice that this diagram *cannot* be separated into two independent diagrams at the composition of the incongruently melting compound since the phases into which that material turns lie one to the left and one to the

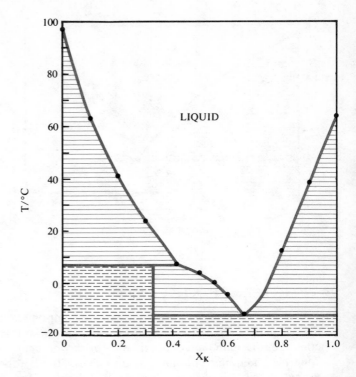

Figure 17-29 Sodium/Potassium

right. Both sodium and potassium react readily with water and both are used to dry high quality solvents in the laboratory. It is often advantageous to use a mixture of the two metals since it remains liquid and thus presents a fresh surface readily to the solvent being dried. Incidentally, this technique is limited to hydrocarbons and a few other solvents, since both metals can react explosively with chlorinated solvents such as CCl_4.

Example 17-7 Figure 17-30 contains the phase diagram for the system magnesium/nickel. What are the simplest formulas for the two intermediate compounds? Describe what happens, assuming equilibrium, as a system containing 35.0 g of nickel and 15.0 g of magnesium is cooled from 1500 K to 900 K.

This is a mass percentage diagram and so the formula of a compound is not so readily apparent as it is in a mole percentage diagram like Figure 17-29. Since the molar mass of nickel is 58.70 g mol^{-1} and that of magnesium is 24.305 g mol^{-1}, one can say of the compound which is 54.7% nickel by mass that

$$\frac{n_{Mg}}{n_{Ni}} = \frac{45.3/24.305}{54.7/58.70} = 2.00$$

Therefore the simplest formula is Mg_2Ni. By a similar calculation, the formula of the compound which is 82.9% by mass nickel can be shown to be $MgNi_2$.

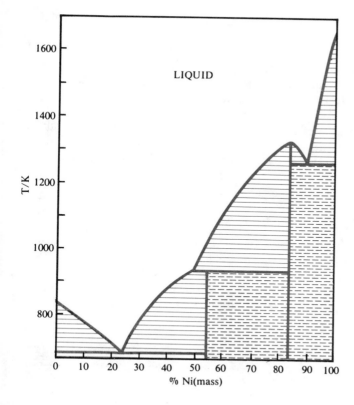

Figure 17-30   Magnesium/Nickel

A system which contains 35.0 g of nickel and 15.0 g of magnesium is 70% nickel by mass. The diagram shows this to be a single liquid phase at 1500 K. On cooling, a crystal of $MgNi_2$ appears at 1330 K. As cooling continues, the amount of $MgNi_2$ increases, while the composition of the liquid grows poorer in nickel accordingly until, at about 1020 K, crystals of Mg_2Ni appear as well. Since there are now three phases, crystals of Mg_2Ni, crystals of $MgNi_2$ and a liquid which is 49% nickel, the temperature remains constant until the liquid phase has gone. Below this temperature there are two phases, the two solid compounds.

Example 17-8   Describe what occurs if crystals of Mg_2Ni are heated from 900 K to 1400 K.

There is a single solid phase, crystals of Mg_2Ni, below 1020 K. At this temperature a liquid which is 49% nickel by mass appears, as do crystals of $MgNi_2$. The temperature remains constant until all of the Mg_2Ni solid has gone. Then the temperature rises with the amount of $MgNi_2$ solid decreasing steadily until, at about 1140 K, the last $MgNi_2$ crystals disappear. Above this temperature there is only a single liquid phase.

Example 17-9   Describe what happens as a system containing 53.0 g of Ni and 47.0 g of Mg is cooled from 1400 K to 700 K.

The system exists as a single liquid phase to about 1120 K at which point $MgNi_2$ begins to precipitate. The amount of $MgNi_2$ solid increases until, at 1020 K, solid Mg_2Ni also appears. The temperature remains constant until all of the solid $MgNi_2$ has gone. Notice that for a system having a composition to the left of the composition of Mg_2Ni, it is liquid which remains whereas for a system to the right like that in Example 17-7, liquid disappears and $MgNi_2$ remains.

Further cooling causes more Mg_2Ni to precipitate until, at 780 K, crystals of Mg appear. Again the temperature remains constant as long as there are three phases. When all of the liquid has gone, the temperature falls again. There are two solid phases, Mg and Mg_2 Ni.

17-13   SOLVENT/SOLUTE SYSTEMS

Where a substance which is a solid at ordinary conditions, like potassium iodide, dissolves in a substance which is a liquid at normal conditions, like water, one usually describes the first as a solute and the second as a solvent. Solutions of a non-volatile solute, like KI, will invariably have higher boiling points and lower melting points than will the pure solvent. Figure 17-31 con-

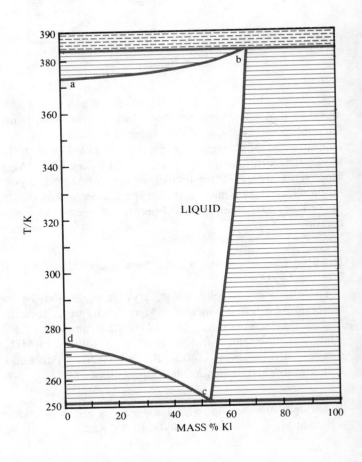

Figure 17-31   Water/Potassium Iodide

tains a phase diagram which illustrates these points. The area abcd represents the conditions of temperature and composition under which, at this pressure, the system exists as a single liquid phase. The system is in the form of an unsaturated solution under these conditions. The boiling points of the solutions are given by the line ab and the freezing points by the line dc. The line bc defines the solubility of KI in water at each temperature. Systems having a higher percentage of KI exist, at equilibrium, as two phases, crystals of KI and a saturated solution. Regarding bc as a solubility curve and dc as a freezing point curve is to some extent arbitrary, and arises from thinking of one component as a solute (which precipitates) and one as a solvent (which freezes). The lower part of the diagram could equally well be considered to be a eutectic diagram analogous to Figure 17-17.

Example 17-10 Describe what happens under equilibrium conditions as a system of 60.0 g of KI and 40.0 g of H_2O is heated from 240 K to 390 K at P°.

At 240 K the system exists as two phases, one pure KI and the other pure H_2O, both of which are solid. At about 251 K, a liquid appears which is 52% KI by mass. Since there are three phases, the temperature remains constant until all of the ice is gone. Then the temperature rises with more and more KI dissolving until, at about 310 K, the last solid KI disappears. From 310 K to about 379 K, the system point is in the clear field indicating that the system exists as a single liquid phase. At 379 K the solution boils and a gas which is 100% water appears. Further heating boils off more and more water, increasing the volume of steam at P°, and concentrating the solution in KI until, at about 383 K, the liquid is saturated with KI and solid KI begins to precipitate. Since there are three phases, the temperature remains constant until the liquid has gone. Above this temperature there are two phases, one a solid which is 100% KI and the other a gas which is 100% H_2O.

17-14 MORE COMPLICATED DIAGRAMS

Many systems have diagrams which appear to be complicated but which are merely combinations of the features observed in the simpler diagrams in the sections above. A few examples follow.

Figure 17-32 illustrates the system water/sodium sulphate. It differs from Figure 17-31 because of the existence, at temperatures below 305.53 K, of the compound $Na_2SO_4.10H_2O$ or Glauber's Salt. This compound melts incongruently.

Example 17-11 Describe what occurs under equilibrium conditions as a system of 10.0 g of Na_2SO_4 and 40.0 g of H_2O is raised in temperature from 250 K to 380 K at P°. Calculate the mass, physical state and composition of every phase present at 260 K and at 320 K.

The system is 20.0% sodium sulphate by mass. At 250 K it exists as two phases, both solid, one pure water and one pure Glauber's Salt. No change in

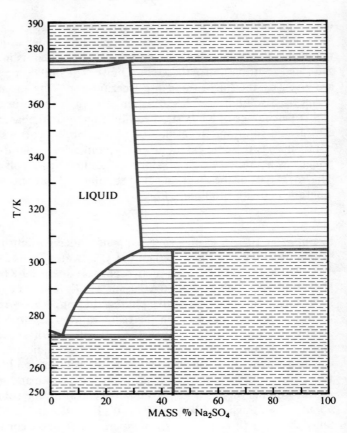

Figure 17-32 Water/Sodium Sulphate
P=P°

the mass or composition of these phases occurs up to 272.1 K so that, at 260 K, the system exists as follows.

phase 1; solid; 100% water; mass = $\dfrac{44.1 - 20.0}{44.1 - 0.0}$ (50.0) = 27.3 g

phase 2; solid; 44.1% Na_2SO_4; mass = $\dfrac{20.0 - 0.0}{44.1 - 0.0}$ (50.0) = 22.7 g

At 272.1 K, a liquid appears (3.9% Na_2SO_4) and, three phases now being present, the temperature remains constant until the ice has gone. Then the temperature rises and further Glauber's Salt dissolves until, at about 297 K, all solid has gone. From this temperature to about 374 K there is a single liquid so that, at 320 K, the one phase is liquid, 20.0% Na_2SO_4 and of mass 50.0 g.

At 374 K vapour appears which is 100% water. As the temperature rises the proportion of vapour increases and the liquid becomes steadily more concentrated in Na_2SO_4 up to 29.6% Na_2SO_4 at a temperature of 376.18 K. At this point solid Na_2SO_4 precipitates and the temperature remains constant until the liquid phase has gone. Above this temperature there is only solid Na_2SO_4 and steam.

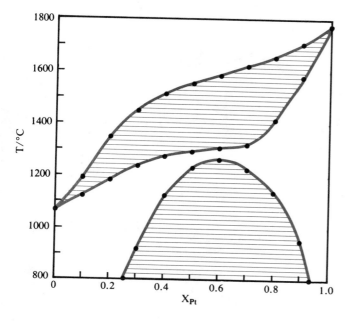

Figure 17-33 Gold/Platinum

The next example of a diagram which simply combines features met earlier is that of the gold/platinum system in Figure 17-33. It results from there being an overlap of the temperature range in which there is a solid/liquid transition like that in Figure 17-14 with that in which there is a solid solubility curve with a maximum like that in Figure 17-27. Analyzing this figure requires nothing more than combining the principles of the two earlier figures.

Example 17-12 Describe what occurs, under equilibrium conditions, as a system containing equimolar amounts of gold and platinum is cooled from 1600°C to 1100°C.

At 1600°C, the system exists as a single liquid phase. At 1550°C, a solid appears which is 89% Pt on a molar basis. Further cooling increases the amount of solid and decreases the amount of liquid, with the composition of both phases shifting in accordance with the curve until, at 1290°C, the last liquid disappears and only a solid which is 50% by mole exists. This situation continues until 1225°C at which temperature crystals of composition 70% Pt begin to form. Further cooling results in the formation of more of the platinum rich crystals, with the composition of both kinds of crystals changing steadily. At 1100°C the compositions of the two solid phases are 39% Pt and 82% Pt.

Figure 17-34 illustrates the thallium/lead system, one of the rare cases showing a maximum in the melting point curve. Thallium metal has two crystal structures, hexagonal below 232°C and body centred cubic above that temperature. Lead is face centred cubic throughout this temperature range. Much thallium can be dissolved in lead but comparatively little lead dissolves in either form of thallium.

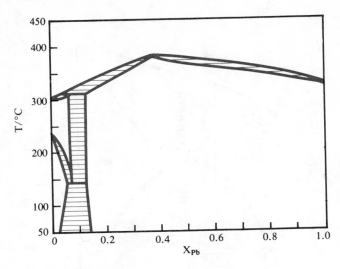

Figure 17-34 Thallium/Lead

Example 17-13 Describe what happens, at equilibrium, as a system containing 0.10 mol lead and 0.90 mol thallium is cooled from 400°C to 100°C.

The system begins as a single liquid phase. The first solid appears at 326°C and has a composition 18% lead by mole. Between 326°C and 310°C, the amount of solid increases and the amount of liquid decreases, the compositions of both changing. At 310°C, a new solid, 5% lead in composition, precipitates. The temperature remains constant until the liquid has disappeared. Then the temperature declines with only slight effects on the compositions of the two solids until, at 140°C, a third solid appears. The three solid phases now present are, respectively, 6% lead and hexagonal, 7% lead and body centred cubic and 12% lead and face centred cubic. The temperature remains constant until the disappearance of the phase which is 7% lead and body centred cubic. The temperature then resumes its decline, again with relatively small effect on the compositions of the two phases.

SUMMARY

Diagrams provide a concise method of portraying data for phase transitions of all kinds. This chapter deals with systems of two components, and it is for two component systems that diagrams are most useful and most used. However they also have a place in one component systems, as illustrated in Chapter 7, and in three component systems, where triangular diagrams are used.

The usual form of portrayal for two component systems, sometimes called a *reduced* phase diagram, is to plot the stable phase on a graph of temperature and composition at some fixed pressure. Examples of these have been given for a wide variety of systems and phase transitions.

FURTHER READING

The underlying thermodynamics of these processes may be found in "The Principles of Chemical Equilibria", by Kenneth Denbigh, the third edition of which was published by Cambridge University Press in 1971. The use of phase diagrams for both two and three component systems is described with brevity and precision in "Principles of Phase Equilibria", by F.E.W. Wetmore and D.J. LeRoy, published by Dover Publications, New York, in paperback in 1970.

A source of many diagrams is volume II (four books) of the data series published by Landolt-Bornstein.

PROBLEMS

1. Describe the physical state, composition and mass of every phase present at equilibrium in the following systems:

    (a) 4.0 mol water, 6.0 mol hydrazine at 118°C and P° (Figure 17-3)

    (b) 1.0 mol water, 1.0 mol n-heptane at 85°C and P° (Figure 17-6)

    (c) 60.0 g lead, 40.0 g tin at 200°C (Figure 17-19)

    (d) 3.5 g zirconium, 6.5 g titanium at 700°C (Figure 17-23)

    (e) 60.0 g glycerol, 40.0 g 4-methoxyphenol at 60°C (Figure 17-26)

    (f) 0.10 mol gold, 0.10 mol nickel at 500°C (Figure 17-27)

    (g) 0.20 mol potassium, 0.80 mol sodium at −10°C (Figure 17-29)

    (h) 0.30 mol platinum, 0.70 mol gold at 1150°C (Figure 17-33)

    [(a) one phase, liquid, 40% water by mole, 260 g
    (b) one phase, gas, 50% water by mole, 100 g
    (c) two phases (i) solid, 83% lead by mass, 41 g (ii) liquid, 44% lead by mass, 59 g
    (d) two phases (i) solid, b.c.c., 42% zirconium by mass, 5.0 g (ii) solid, hexagonal, 28% zirconium by mass,
    (e) two phases (i) liquid, 72% glycerol by mass, 75 g (ii) liquid, 24% glycerol by mass, 25 g
    (f) two phases (i) solid, 96% nickel by mole, 5.5 g (ii) solid, 16% nickel by mole, 20.1 g
    (g) two phases (i) solid, Na, 9.2 g (ii) solid, Na_2K, 17.0 g
    (h) one phase, solid, 30% platinum by mole, 196 g]

2. Describe what happens, assuming equilibrium, in the following cases.

    (a) The temperature is raised from 100°C to 120°C in a system consisting of 7.0 mol of water and 3.0 mol of hydrazine (Figure 17-3)

    (b) A melt consisting of equimolar amounts of sodium and potassium is cooled from 100°C to −20°C (Figure 17-29)

(c) Crystals of Glauber's Salt are heated from 260 K to 360 K. (Figure 17-32)

(d) A melt containing 0.030 mol of Pb and 0.970 mol of Tl is cooled from 400°C to 50°C. (Figure 17-34)

(e) A melt containing 0.970 mol of Pb and 0.030 mol of Tl is cooled from 400°C to 50°C.

3. Draw reasonable heating or cooling curves, as the case may be, for the processes of Question 2.

4. Lead and tin form a series of low melting alloys called solders. General purpose solder consists of 35 mol % lead, 65 mol % tin. Express this composition as a mass percentage. Use Figure 17-19 to determine at what temperature a melt of this solder would first solidify and at what temperature the last liquid would disappear. What are the compositions of the first solid and the last liquid?

[48% Pb; 210°C, 84% Pb; 183°C, 38% Pb]

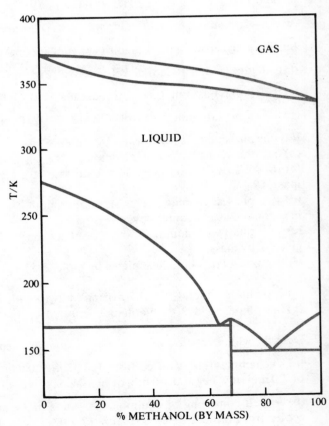

Figure 17-35 Water/Ethylene Glycol $H_2O/C_2H_6O_2$; $P=P°$

5. Figures 17-35 and 17-36 show phase diagrams for ethylene glycol/water and methanol/water. Consideration of the boiling point and freezing point of water should permit the interpretation of these diagrams.

(a) What is the minimum mass percentage of ethylene glycol in water necessary to prevent any freezing at 240 K? What is the boiling point of such a solution at P°? What is the composition of the vapour boiled off?

(b) What is the minimum mass percentage of methanol in water necessary to prevent any freezing at 240 K? What is the boiling point of such a solution at P°? What is the composition of the vapour boiled off?

(c) Since ethylene glycol costs more per unit mass than methanol, why is it the preferred antifreeze for automobile radiators?

[(a) 46% glycol, 382 K, 1% glycol;(b) 35% methanol, 353 K, 75% methanol]

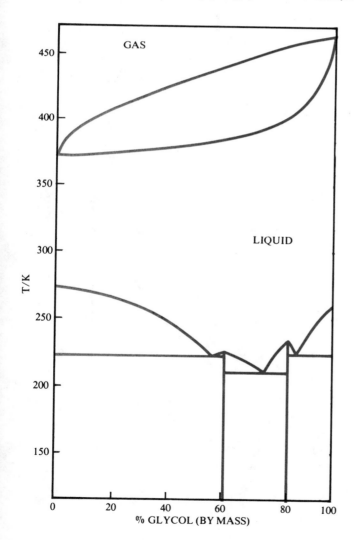

Figure 17-36 Water/Methanol
H_2O/CH_3OH; P=P°

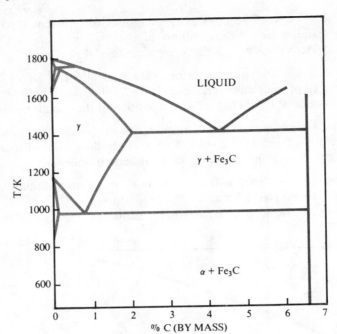

Figure 17-37 Iron/Carbon

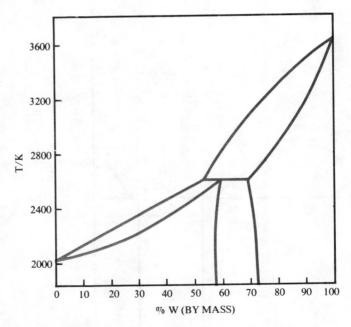

Figure 17-38 Platinum/Tungsten

6. The most widely used part of the iron/carbon diagram, the region of low carbon concentrations so important in steel making, is shown in Figure 17-37. Describe what happens, assuming equilibrium, as a melt of 1000 kg which is 1.0% carbon by mass is cooled from 1900 K to 800 K. What departures from equilibrium would be expected?

7. Figure 17-38 contains a phase diagram for the system Pt/W. The elements melt at 2046 K and 3643 K respectively. Describe what phases exist at equilibrium for a system represented by a point in each area of the diagram. Describe what happens, again assuming equilibrium, as 3.5 g of tungsten and 6.5 g of platinum are cooled from 3600 K to 2000 K. Repeat this for a melt containing 6.5 g of tungsten and 3.5 g of platinum.

8. Copper and aluminium do not dissolve in one another as solids, but are miscible as liquids. Measurement of the melting point of the two metals and of four mixtures of the two produced the following results.

% copper by mass	0	20	40	60	80	100
T/K	920	870	810	880	1200	1360

Draw a reasonable phase diagram for the copper/aluminium system and use it to estimate the mass, physical state and composition of every phase present at equilibrium in an equimolar mixture of these two metals having mass one kilogram and a temperature of 900 K.

[a liquid, mass 0.78 kg, composition 62% Cu by mass
a solid, mass 0.22 kg, which is pure copper]

XVIII THE PROPERTIES OF LIQUID SOLUTIONS

Liquid solutions are common and important both in industry and in the laboratory. In many cases there is a clearly defined *solvent*, in which are dissolved other substances, the *solutes*. These solutes may be gas, liquid or solid.

The most common solvent is water, but there are many organic solvents of importance. Since the solvent is usually present in a much greater proportion than the solutes in the solution, the properties of the solution are much more like those of the solvent than those of the solutes. However, the presence of the solutes makes the solution different from the pure solvent in many ways, and it is these differences in properties which are explored in this chapter. Perhaps the most important differences are found in the ways in which solutions vaporize or solidify when the temperature is changed, and much that is said in this chapter is related to phase equilibria.

From the many systems discussed in the last chapter, it should be clear that phase relationships are common to materials of all kinds. The same phenomena are found in organic chemicals and inorganic chemicals, in metals and in non-mentals. It is not surprising then that many formulas and rules have been developed for describing these phenomena.

These formulas and rules, like those governing chemical equilibria in the gas phase which are discussed in Chapter 15, are useful as empirical rules, and they are treated in that way in this chapter. However, like the gas phase relationships, they can be derived from the laws of thermodynamics. These derivations are to be found in more advanced discussions of physical chemistry, and are useful in two ways. First, the approximations and limitations of the empirical laws are made clear. For instance, many of the relationships are only accurate in dilute solutions. Secondly, the constants used in the empirical laws can usually be related to thermodynamic data obtained in other measurements.

18-1 RAOULT'S LAW

The simplest kind of liquid solution is found when two very similar substances are mixed together. Since the substances are very similar, the solution can be expected to be very similar in its properties to the substances forming the solution. The properties of the solution ought to be an average of the corresponding properties of the two components. Whenever this expectation is borne out, the solution is called an *ideal solution*. Most solutions deviate from ideal behaviour, just as most gases deviate from the behaviour described by the ideal gas law. But in solution theory, as in gas theory, ideal behaviour is a good place to begin study.

The vapour pressure of an ideal solution is described by Raoult's Law. If a solution obeys Raoult's Law, then the partial pressure of any component depends on how much of it is present, as measured by its mole fraction in the solution, and on how volatile it is, as measured by its vapour pressure when pure. Hence if P_A is the partial pressure of component A in equilibrium with the solution, P_A* is the vapour pressure of substance A when pure at the temperature of the solution, and x_A is the mole fraction of A in the solution, then,

$$P_A = x_A P_A* \tag{1}$$

with similar relationships applying to all the other components in the solution:

$$P_B = x_B P_B*$$
$$P_C = x_C P_C*, \text{ and so on.}$$

The total vapour pressure of the solution is equal to the sum of the partial pressures, according to Dalton's Law of partial pressures:

$$\begin{aligned} P &= P_A + P_B + P_C + \ldots \ldots \\ &= x_A P_A* + x_B P_B* + x_C P_C* + \ldots \ldots \end{aligned} \tag{2}$$

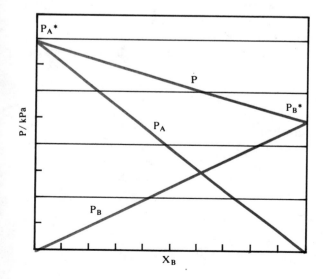

Figure 18-1 Raoult Law Prediction for Two Components A and B

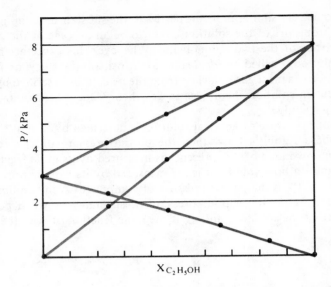

Figure 18-2   Example of a Nearly Ideal Solution: Ethanol and 1-Propanol at 298 K

This equation expresses mathematically the earlier statement that for a solution which obeys Raoult's Law, the total vapour pressure is an average of the vapour pressures of the substances which comprise the solution; the "weights" used in calculating the average are the mole fractions of the substances in the solution. The mathematical linearity of these equations is demonstrated graphically in Figure 18-1. Two substances which form almost ideal solutions are ethanol, CH_3CH_2OH, and 1-propanol, $CH_3CH_2CH_2OH$, and graphs of vapour pressure versus composition of the solution are shown in Figure 18-2. These two substances fit the requirement for substances to be chemically similar: they are both alcohols, since they contain the group −OH, and differ only in the length of the chain of carbon atoms. The data summarized in Figure 18-2 show that ethanol and 1-propanol form solutions which obey Raoult's Law, to a good approximation at least, and hence these solutions can be described as ideal.

Example 18-1   Benzene C_6H_6 and toluene (otherwise known as methylbenzene) $C_6H_5CH_3$ form solutions which are very close to ideal. The vapour pressure of pure benzene is 52.1 kPa and that of toluene is 18.7 kPa, both being at a temperature of 333 K. Calculate the vapour pressure of a solution containing 120 g of benzene and 450 g of toluene at 333 K.

$$\text{Amount of benzene (B)} = \frac{120\text{ g}}{78.1\text{ g/mol}} = 1.538\text{ mol}$$

$$\text{Amount of toluene (T)} = \frac{450\text{ g}}{92.1\text{ g/mol}} = 4.891\text{ mol}$$

Hence the mole fractions of the two components in the solution are

$$x_B = \frac{1.538}{1.538 + 4.891} = 0.239$$

$$x_T = 1 - 0.239 = 0.761$$

The partial pressures of the two components are

$$P_B = 0.239 \times 52.1 = 12.5 \text{ kPa}$$
$$P_T = 0.761 \times 18.7 = 14.2 \text{ kPa}$$

and the total pressure is

$$P = 12.5 + 14.2 = 26.7 \text{ kPa.}$$

Do not confuse Raoult's Law, which *predicts* partial pressures on the basis of the composition of the *liquid*, with the *definition* of partial pressure, which defines the partial pressure of component A, P_A, as

$$P_A = y_A P \qquad\qquad (3)$$

where y_A is the mole fraction of A in the *gas* phase, and P is the total pressure. Contrast this with Raoult's Law which states that

$$P_A = x_A P_A{}^* \qquad\qquad (1)$$

where x_A is the mole fraction of A in the *liquid* phase, and $P_A{}^*$ is the vapour pressure of pure A at the temperature in question. Study these two equations until the difference between them is understood thoroughly.

Consideration of the system in Example 18-1 shows that composition of the vapour phase is quite different from the composition of the liquid phase. This could have been seen from a comparison of equations (1) and (3) and arises from the generally different volatilities of the two components. Example 18-2 illustrates the point.

Example 18-2   Calculate the mole fraction of benzene in the vapour in equilibrium with the solution specified in Example 18-1.

The mole fraction of benzene in the vapour phase is equal to the ratio of the partial pressure of benzene to the total pressure:

$$y_B = 12.5 \text{ kPa}/26.7 \text{ kPa} = 0.468$$

The mole fraction of toluene is

$$y_T = 1 - 0.468 = 0.532$$

In this case the benzene is more volatile than the toluene, and the mole fraction of benzene in the vapour is much larger than the mole fraction of benzene in the liquid solution.

The fact that compounds similar enough to form ideal solutions often have widely different vapour pressures means that such compounds can be separated by distillation. When a vapour is formed from such a solution, its composition is different from the composition of the liquid. If the vapour is condensed to a new liquid solution, the new solution is richer in the more volatile component. If this process of evaporation and condensation is repeated, the process of enrichment of the more volatile component will be continued. By this process of fractional distillation, a separation of the two components can be achieved even though they may be very similar in their chemical properties. This process is of central importance in the such diverse industries as the refining of petroleum and the production of whiskey, and was discussed in the context of phase diagrams in the previous chapter.

In an ideal solution of two chemically similar compounds, such as benzene and toluene, the energy of attraction between a benzene molecule and a toluene molecule is approximately the same as the energy of attraction between two benzene molecules or between two toluene molecules. The behaviour of a molecule is then the same whether it is surrounded mostly by benzene molecules or mostly by toluene molecules, and so molecular behaviour is independent of composition. Each component exerts a vapour pressure which is proportional to the number of molecules of each in the liquid solution, as stated by Raoult's Law.

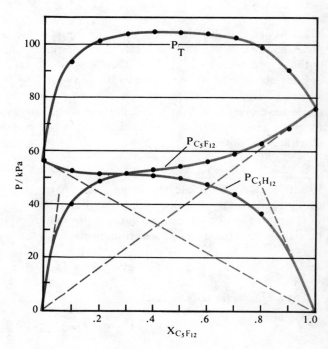

Figure 18-3 C_5H_{12}/C_5F_{12} at 293.0 K

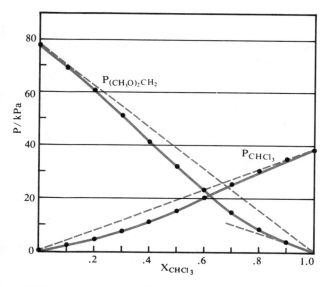

Figure 18-4 $(CH_3O)_2CH_2/CHCl_3$ at 308.2 K

When two compounds form a complete range of liquid solutions, but are not so similar that the solutions are ideal, two situations are met. In the case of *positive* deviations from Raoult's Law, both components have greater partial pressures than they would have if the solution were ideal. Such a case is shown in Figure 18-3. In this case the deviations are large enough that the total vapour pressure of the solution shows a maximum, and the boiling point shows a minimum, at a characteristic composition. Positive deviations occur when the cohesive energies between the two different molecules are less than the cohesive energies between like molecules. Cases of minimum boiling azeotropes were met in the last chapter.

In the opposite case, of *negative* deviations from Raoult's Law, both components have smaller partial pressures than they would if the solution were ideal. Figure 18-4 shows a case where there are small negative deviations. If the deviations are large enough, there is a minimum in the total vapour pressure of the solution and a corresponding maximum in the boiling point. Negative deviations occur when the cohesive energy between unlike molecules is larger than that between like molecules.

It should be noted that in both Figures 18-3 and 18-4 the partial pressure of a component is close to the value given by Raoult's Law in solutions where that component has a mole fraction near unity. To take a specific example, the partial pressure of pentane in a mixture of pentane and fluoropentane (Figure 18-3) is close to the value given by Raoult's Law as long as the mole fraction of pentane is larger than about 0.9. In the figure, this corresponds to the left hand edge of the graph, where the mole fraction of fluoropentane is less than 0.1. This result is always true, because in a dilute solution, most *solvent* molecules are surrounded and influenced by other solvent molecules and their behaviour is similar to their behaviour in the pure solvent whatever the nature of the solute. Hence Raoult's Law can be applied with a good deal of confidence when considering the *solvent* in a dilute solution, without regard to whether the solution is ideal or not.

18-2   HENRY'S LAW

There is more to be learned from examination of the graphs in Figures 18-3 and 18-4 at the opposite end of the concentration scale. In solutions which are dilute, the partial pressure of the solute (i.e. that component which has the small mole fraction) may be very different from the Raoult's Law value, but nevertheless be proportional to the mole fraction of the solute. For example, the graph of partial pressure of fluoropentane against mole fraction of pentane is linear as long as the mole fraction of fluoropentane is less than about 0.04. This linearity is found in a great variety of solutions, and is summarized in Henry's Law for the vapour pressure of a solute in a dilute solution:

$$P_B = x_B K(B, A)$$

where P_B is the partial pressure of the solute B in a dilute solution in a solvent A, x_B is the mole fraction of B in the solution, and K(A, B) is the Henry's Law constant for this particular combination of solute and solvent.

Example 18-3   For the mixture of pentane and fluoropentane represented in Figure 18-3, the partial vapour pressure of pentane is 12 kPa when the mole fraction of fluoropentane is 0.95. What is the Henry's Law constant for pentane dissolved in fluoropentane?

The mole fraction of pentane is 0.05, and so

$$K(C_5H_{12}, C_5F_{12}) = 12 \text{ kPa}/0.05$$
$$= 240 \text{ kPa}$$

The Henry's Law constant determined in this way can be used to calculate the partial vapour pressure of pentane in equilibrium with dilute solutions of pentane in fluoropentane. It should be noted that the Henry's Law constant is given by the intersection of the extrapolation of the linear part of the partial vapour pressure curve with the vertical axis at the opposite side of the graph. For positive deviations from Raoult's Law, the Henry's Law constant is larger than the vapour pressure of the pure solute, P*, and for negative deviations it is less.

Henry's Law is commonly applied to describe dilute solutions of gases in liquid solvents, and some useful values are given in Table 18.1. The gases nitrogen, hydrogen and oxygen are only slightly soluble in water and their Henry's Law constants are correspondingly very large.

Example 18-4   It is found that at a temperature of 293 K, carbon dioxide dissolves in water to the extent of 0.1688 g in 100 g of water when the partial pressure of carbon dioxide is 101 kPa. Calculate the Henry's Law constant, and the solubility at a partial pressure of 500 kPa, for this temperature.

For the solution described, the mole fraction of CO_2 is

TABLE 18.1   Henry's Law Constants

The units in this table are MPa.

Solute	Solvent		
	Water (298 K)	Water (333 K)	Benzene (298 K)
H_2	7100	7700	370
N_2	8700	12000	240
O_2	4400	6500	
CO_2	170	340	11

$$x_{CO_2} = \frac{0.1688/44.0}{0.1688/44.0 + 100/18.0} = 6.90 \times 10^{-4}$$

The Henry's Law constant is therefore

$$K(CO_2, H_2O) = 101 \times 10^3 \text{ Pa}/6.90 \times 10^{-4}$$
$$= 146 \text{ MPa}$$

At a partial pressure of 500 kPa, then the mole fraction of CO_2 in the solution is

$$x_{CO_2} = 500 \times 10^3 \text{ Pa}/146 \times 10^6 \text{ Pa}$$
$$= 3.42 \times 10^{-3}$$

which corresponds to a solubility of 0.836 g of CO_2 per 100 g H_2O.

Removing oxygen from water used in industrial equipment is a common method of reducing corrosion. Dissolved oxygen can be removed by heating, since the Henry's Law constant increases at high temperatures corresponding to a reduction of the solubility. Another method is to reduce the partial pressure of oxygen in contact with the water by pumping the air away with a vacuum pump. Perhaps the easiest method is to bubble an oxygen-free gas such as nitrogen or argon through the water in a confined container with a small outlet for the gas. This removes the oxygen from the gas in contact with the water, and hence the partial pressure of oxygen is greatly reduced from its normal value of about 20 kPa in the atmosphere. According to Henry's Law the amount of oxygen dissolved in the water is also greatly reduced. This process is known as *sparging*.

Example 18-5   Water for a closed cycle heat exchanger is to be de-oxygenated by sparging with nitrogen at a temperature of 298 K. The amount of water required is 27.5 t. After four hours of bubbling gas through the water, the oxygen content of the gas leaving the water is 0.0046% by volume. Calculate the total amount of oxygen dissolved in the water.

For ideal gases, the volume fraction in a mixture is equal to the mole fraction. Hence assuming that the total pressure of the gas bubbling out of the water is 100 kPa, the partial pressure of oxygen in contact with the water is

$$P_{O_2} = 4.6 \times 10^{-5} \times 100 \times 10^3 \text{ Pa}$$
$$= 4.6 \text{ Pa}$$

Using the Henry's Law constant from Table 18.1, the mole fraction of oxygen in the water is

$$x_{O_2} = 4.6 \text{ Pa}/4.4 \times 10^9 \text{ Pa}$$
$$= 1.0 \times 10^{-9}$$

This is a very dilute solution, containing 1.0×10^{-9} mole of oxygen per 18 g of water. The total amount of oxygen dissolved is

$$n = \frac{1.0 \times 10^{-9} \text{ mol} \times 27.5 \times 10^6 \text{ g}}{18 \text{ g}}$$
$$= 1.5 \times 10^{-3} \text{ mol}$$

Finally, do keep in mind both the similarity and the difference between Raoult's Law and Henry's Law. Both contain the same essential relationship, predicting the partial pressures in the vapour phase on the basis of compositions in the liquid phase, but they do so at opposite extremes of composition. For any dilute solution, Raoult's Law applies to the *solvent* and Henry's Law applies to the *solute*. For ideal solutions, of course, Raoult's Law applies to all components over the entire range of composition.

18-3   DILUTE SOLUTIONS OF NON-VOLATILE SOLUTES

When the solute in a dilute solution has a very low vapour pressure, P^*_{solute}, as pure material, it will contribute a negligible amount to the vapour pressure of the solution and the vapour pressure of the solution will be equal to the partial pressure of the solvent. As was seen in the last section, the partial pressure of the solvent in a dilute solution can be calculated to a good approximation using Raoult's Law, no matter what the nature of the solute. This is expressed mathematically by the equation

$$P = P_{solvent} = x_{solvent}P^*_{solvent}$$

Since $x_{solvent}$ is less than unity, the vapour pressure of the solution is less than that of the pure solvent. This effect is known as *vapour pressure lower-*

ing. The amount of the lowering is proportional to the mole fraction of all the solutes present in the solution:

$$\Delta P = P^*_{solvent} - P_{solution}$$

$$= P^*_{solvent} (1 - x_{solvent})$$

$$= P^*_{solvent} \, x_{solutes}$$

since

$$x_{solvent} + x_{solutes} = 1.$$

In these equations, the quantity $x_{solutes}$ refers to the total mole fraction of all the solutes dissolved in the solution. This has particular significance in the case of solutions of strong electrolytes dissolved in water, for when an electrolyte dissociates and forms ions, each ionic species acts as a separate solute in lowering the vapour pressure.

Example 18-6   Calculate the vapour pressure lowering for a solution of 8.0 g sucrose $C_{12}H_{22}O_{11}$ in 100 g water, at a temperature at which the vapour pressure of water is 3.7 kPa.

The mole fraction of sucrose in the solution is 0.0042, and this is the total mole fraction of all solutes in the solution. Hence the vapour pressure lowering is

$$\Delta P = 0.0042 \times 3.7 \, kPa = 1.6 \, Pa.$$

Example 18-7   Calculate the vapour pressure lowering for a solution containing 8.0 g sodium chloride in 100 g of water at the same temperature as in the last example.

The mole fraction of NaCl in the solution is 0.024, but since the solute is an electrolyte which forms two ions in aqueous solution, the total mole fraction of solutes is 0.048. Hence the vapour pressure lowering is

$$\Delta P = 0.048 \times 3.7 \, kPa = 178 \, Pa.$$

One of the earliest pieces of evidence for the existence of ions as separate entities in aqueous solutions was the fact that electrolytes are more effective in reducing the vapour pressure of water than non-electrolytes, by a factor which was found in measurements to be approximately an integer. Accurate measurements show that ionic solutions show marked deviations from ideal behaviour, except in very dilute solutions, and these deviations are reflected in the measured vapour pressure lowering. The properties of non-ideal ionic solutions will be discussed later, and for the moment it is sufficient to note that the individual ions act independently in reducing the vapour pressure of solutions.

Measurements of the vapour pressure of solutions are occasionally used to determine the molar mass of solutes in solution. While not particularly accurate as a way of determining molar mass, it is accurate enough to determine the molecular formula of a solute in solution when the empirical formula is known. The principle of the calculation is illustrated in the following example.

Example 18-8   1.042 g of a substance of unknown formula is dissolved in 49.537 g of benzene. The solute is not volatile and does not dissociate into ions in this solvent. At the temperature of the measurements, the vapour pressure of pure benzene is 13.33 kPa, and that of the solution is 147.2 Pa lower than this. What is the molar mass of the solute?

From the basic formula for vapour pressure lowering, the mole fraction of the solute in the solution is

$$x = 147.2 \text{ Pa}/13.33{\times}10^3 \text{ Pa}$$
$$= 1.104{\times}10^{-2}$$

In such a dilute solution, the mole fraction of solute is approximately equal to $n_{solute}/n_{solvent}$, and since

$$n_{solvent} = 49.537 \text{ g}/78.0 \text{ g mol}^{-1}$$
$$= 0.635 \text{ mol}$$

the amount of solute present in the solution is

$$n_{solute} = 1.104{\times}10^{-2} \times 0.635 \text{ mol}$$
$$= 7.01{\times}10^{-3} \text{ mol}$$

Hence the molar mass of the solute is

$$M = 1.042 \text{ g}/7.01{\times}10^{-3} \text{ mol}$$
$$= 148 \text{ g/mol}$$

The "boiling point" of a liquid is the temperature at which the vapour pressure is equal to the pressure of the atmosphere. It has been seen that the addition of a non-volatile solute to a solvent causes a lowering of the vapour pressure relative to that of the pure solvent. In Figure 18-5, the vapour pressures of a solvent and of a solution of a non-volatile solute in that solvent are plotted against temperature, and it can be seen that the effect of the solute is to increase the temperature of the boiling point. For dilute solutions, the increase in the boiling point temperature is proportional to the displacement of the two curves, that is, the reduction in the vapour pressure. Hence the increase in the boiling point temperature is proportional to the mole fraction of the solute (or solutes if there is more than one):

$$\Delta T_b \; \alpha \; x_{solutes}$$

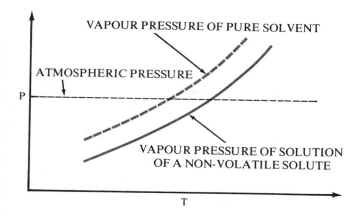

Figure 18-5 Vapour pressure of a pure solvent, and of a solution of a non-volatile solute, plotted as a function of temperature. Boiling occurs when the vapour pressure is equal to the atmospheric pressure, indicated by a horizontal dotted line. Reduction of the vapour pressure due to the presence of the solute results in an increase of the boiling point temperature.

When describing the composition of dilute solutions, it is easier and more usual to measure composition in terms of molality rather than mole fraction. To a good approximation, the molality of a solution is proportional to the mole fraction of the solute, as long as the solution is dilute, and so the boiling point elevation is proportional to the molality:

$$\Delta T_b = k_b\, m$$

where k_b is the "molal boiling point constant" or "ebullioscopic constant" and m is the total molality of all the solutes in the solution. In calculating the molality of solutions of electrolytes, the separate ions are to be regarded as separate solutes. The solutes must be non-volatile and the solutions must be dilute for this formula to give accurate results. The value of the boiling point constant k_b is specific to the solvent, and does not depend on the nature of the solute, and this makes the measurement of boiling point elevations useful as a method of determining the molar mass of solutes. The method is easier and more accurate than the vapour pressure method. Table 18.2 lists the values of the boiling point constant for a number of possible solvents for carrying out these measurements. It is important to note that the boiling point of a liquid is very sensitive to changes in the atmospheric pressure, so the change in the boiling point must be measured by direct comparison with that of the pure solvent at the same pressure.

Example 18-9 A solution containing 36.0 g of a non-volatile compound in 125 g of water boils at 373.21 K at a pressure at which pure water boils at 372.95 K. What is the molar mass of the compound in the solution, assuming that it does not ionize?

The change in the boiling point is 373.21 − 372.95 = 0.26 K. From Table 18.2, the molal boiling point constant for water is 0.52 K/(mol kg⁻¹), and so the basic equation for the boiling point elevation is

$$0.26\ \text{K} = 0.52\ \text{K/(mol kg}^{-1})\, m$$

and so the molality is

$$m = (0.26/0.52) \text{ mol kg}^{-1}$$
$$= 0.50 \text{ mol kg}^{-1}$$

Since the solution contained 0.125 kg of solvent, the amount of solute in the solution is

$$n = (0.50 \text{ mol kg}^{-1})(0.125 \text{ kg})$$
$$= 0.0625 \text{ mol}$$

Hence the molar mass of the solute is

$$M = 36.0 \text{ g}/0.0625 \text{ mol}$$
$$= 576 \text{ g mol}^{-1}$$

The boiling point constant may be related to other properties of the solvent as follows. Suppose that a solution of a non-volatile solute boils at T''. Let x_A be the mole fraction of the solvent and T' the boiling point of the pure solvent.

For the process

$$A(l) \rightarrow A(g)$$

the equilibrium expressions at T' and T'' are

$$K_{T'} = \frac{P_A^{*'}}{P^\circ} = \frac{P^\circ}{P^\circ} = 1$$

$$K_{T''} = \frac{P_A^{*''}}{P^\circ}$$

But the solution boils at T'' so that its vapour pressure at that temperature is P° and by Raoult's Law it follows that

$$P^\circ = x_A P_A^{*''}$$

Therefore

$$K_{T''} = \frac{P_A^{*''}}{P^\circ} = \frac{P_A^{*''}}{x_A P_A^{*''}} = \frac{1}{x_A}$$

But the relationship between two equilibrium constants at different temperatures is

$$\ln K_{T''} - \ln K_{T'} = \frac{\Delta H_b}{R} \left[\frac{1}{T'} - \frac{1}{T''} \right]$$

$$\ln (1/x_A) - 0 = \frac{\Delta H_b}{R} \left[\frac{T'' - T'}{T'T''} \right] = \frac{\Delta H_b}{R} \frac{\Delta T}{T'T''}$$

where ΔH_b is the enthalpy of vaporization at the boiling point and ΔT is the difference between the boiling points of the solvent and solution. Two points remain. One is to make a series of approximations which all depend on the solution being dilute.

$$\ln (1/x_A) = -\ln x_A$$
$$= -\ln (1 - x_B)$$
$$\approx x_B$$
$$= n_B/(n_A + n_B)$$
$$\approx n_B/n_A$$
$$= n_B M_A/n_A M_A$$
$$= n_B M_A/(\text{mass of A})$$
$$= M_A m_B$$

where m_B is the molality of B. The approximation of $\ln (1 - x_B)$ by $-x_B$ arises from applying Taylor's series and is very accurate for small values of x_B. The other approximation to be made also depends on the solution being dilute, since then

$$T'T'' \approx (T')^2 = (T_b)^2$$

Substitution of these two approximations in the earlier equation yields

$$M_A \, m_B = \frac{\Delta H_b}{R} \cdot \frac{\Delta T}{T_b^2}$$

$$\Delta T = \frac{R T_b^2 M_A}{\Delta H_b} \, m_B$$

Therefore

$$k_b = \frac{R T_b^2 M_A}{\Delta H_b}$$

Thus k_b can be evaluated for any solvent from the boiling point, the molar mass and the molar enthalpy of vaporization. In the case of water, for example, T_b is 373.15 K, M is 0.01802 kg mol^{-1} and ΔH_b is 40 600 J mol^{-1}. Substitution of these values into the formula gives

$$k_b = \frac{(8.314 \text{ J K}^{-1} \text{ mol}^{-1})(373.15 \text{ K})^2 (0.01802 \text{ kg mol}^{-1})}{40 \, 600 \text{ J mol}^{-1}}$$

$$= 0.51 \text{ K}/(\text{mol kg}^{-1})$$

This result is in satisfactory agreement with the experimental value of k_b which is quoted in Table 18.2. Measurement of the molal boiling point constant for a solvent is a method of determining the heat of vaporization of the solvent.

TABLE 18-2   Boiling Point Elevation Constants

Solvent	k_b $K(mol\ kg^{-1})^{-1}$	T_b K
Water, H_2O	0.52	373.15
Methanol, CH_3OH	0.83	338.1
Ethanol, C_2H_5OH	1.2	351.7
2-Propanone, $(CH_3)_2CO$ (acetone)	1.7	329.4
Diethyl ether, $(C_2H_5)_2O$	2.2	307.7
Acetic Acid, CH_3COOH	3.1	391.1
Trichloromethane, $CHCl_3$ (chloroform)	3.8	334.9
Tetrachloromethane, CCl_4 (carbon tetrachloride)	5.0	349.7
Benzene, C_6H_6	2.6	353.3
Nitrobenzene, $C_6H_5NO_2$	5.2	484.0
Hydroxybenzene, C_6H_5OH (phenol)	3.6	454.9
Naphthalene, $C_{10}H_8$	5.7	491

18-4   THE FREEZING POINT OF SOLUTIONS

When a solution is cooled, solid begins to separate from the liquid when the temperature is made low enough. For solutions which are not too concentrated, and in which the solvent is either water or one of the more common organic solvents, the solid is usually pure solvent, and only rarely a solid solution.

In the phase diagrams for water and potassium iodide, and for benzene and chloroform in the previous chapter it is clear that the solid which first separates from the solution when cooled is the pure solvent. Furthermore the temperature at which the solid first appears is *lower* than the freezing point of the pure solvent. The initial part of the freezing point curve on the phase diagram is approximately a straight line, and so the lowering of the freezing point, ΔT_f, is proportional to the amount of solute in the solution. Just as for the vapour pressure and the boiling point elevation, each solute acts independently in lowering the freezing point, and in the case of electrolytes each ionic species acts as a separate solute. Thus the freezing point lowering can be written

$$\Delta T_f = k_f\ m$$

where m is the total molality of all the solutes in the solution, and k_f is the "molal freezing point depression constant." The value of k_f depends only on the nature of the solvent, and is independent of the solute. Table 18.3 contains some values of k_f for a number of solvents. The formula for ΔT_f can be applied to solutions which are fairly dilute, and there is no restriction on the volatility of the solute.

Freezing point measurements can be used to determine the molar mass of a solute, in the same way as boiling point elevations or vapour pressure lowering. Generally the freezing point method is to be preferred. Freezing points are not affected appreciably by changes in atmospheric pressure, and some solutes may decompose at the boiling point of the solvent. Generally k_f values are larger than k_b values, so temperature changes can be more accurately measured and more dilute solutions can be used.

Just as for the boiling point constant, the freezing point constant can be related to other properties of the solvent:

$$k_f = \frac{RT_m{}^2 M}{\Delta H_m}$$

where T_m is the melting (or freezing) point temperature of the pure solvent, and ΔH_m is the molar heat of melting. Some solvents have unusually large values of k_f, an example being CCl_4. In these cases the molar heat of melting is unusually small, and the effect of this on k_f is readily seen from the form of the above equation.

TABLE 18-3   Freezing Point Depression Constants

Solvent	k_f K $(mol\ kg^{-1})^{-1}$	T_m K
Water, H_2O	1.9	273.15
Ethanol, C_2H_5OH	2.0	155.9
Acetic Acid, CH_3COOH	3.8	289.75
Sulphuric Acid, H_2SO_4	6.1	283.4
Benzene, C_6H_6	5.1	278.7
Nitrobenzene, $C_6H_5NO_2$	8.1	278.9
Hydroxybenzene, C_6H_5OH	7.3	316
Naphthalene, $C_{10}H_8$	6.9	353.70
Tetrachloromethane, CCl_4	32.	250.16

Example 18-10   Calculate the freezing point lowering of a solution of 8.0 g of sucrose in 100 g of water.

The molality of the solution is 0.23 mol kg^{-1}, and from Table 18.3, k_f is 1.9 K/(mol kg^{-1}), so the freezing point is lowered by an amount

$$\Delta T_f = 1.9\ K\ (mol\ kg^{-1})^{-1} \times 0.23\ mol\ kg^{-1}$$
$$= 0.44\ K$$

Such a change in temperature is readily measured, whereas the vapour pressure lowering calculated in Example 18-6 would be very difficult to measure with accuracy.

The freezing point depression formula can be applied to the problem of melting ice off sidewalks in winter. Enough solute must be added to convert the ice into an aqueous solution with a freezing point at or below the ambient temperature. The lower the temperature, the more solute has to be added.

Example 18-11   Estimate the amount of $CaCl_2$ required to melt completely 5.0 kg of ice from a sidewalk at a temperature of $-3°C$.

Since the freezing point of the solution must be 3 K lower than that of water, the molality of the solution formed by melting the ice must be

$$m = 3 \, K/(1.9 \, K/(mol \, kg^{-1}))$$
$$= 1.6 \, mol \, kg^{-1}$$

However, $CaCl_2$ is an electrolyte which dissociates into 3 moles of ions per mole of the electrolyte

$$CaCl_2(c) \xrightarrow{H_2O} Ca^{2+}(aq) + 2 \, Cl^-(aq)$$

and so 1.6/3 mole of $CaCl_2$ is required per kilogram of water. Hence the amount of $CaCl_2$ is $(1.6/3) \times 5$ mole, and the mass is

$$(1.6/3) \times 5 \, mol \times 111 \, g \, mol^{-1} = 300 \, g.$$

This calculation is approximate because the solution is concentrated and far from being ideal.

18-5   OSMOTIC PRESSURE

It is well known that a solution placed in contact with an amount of pure solvent becomes more dilute through diffusion. Solvent molecules diffuse into the solution, and solute molecules diffuse into the pure solvent, until the whole system is uniform in concentration. This process occurs spontaneously at constant temperature and pressure, and so must involve a decrease in the Gibbs energy of the system.

It is possible to make a membrane which is porous to solvent molecules, but not to solute molecules, as long as the latter are sufficiently large. Many natural biological membranes have this property, but similar artificial membranes can also be made. If a solution is placed on one side of such a membrane, and pure solvent is placed on the other side, then solvent molecules will pass through the membrane into the solution spontaneously, since this process will lead to the mixing of the solvent and solution, and so to a lower Gibbs energy for the system as a whole. This process is called osmosis.

The tendency for solvent to pass through the membrane into the solution can be reversed if pressure is applied to the solution. Assuming that the membrane is mechanically strong enough to hold the pressure without breaking,

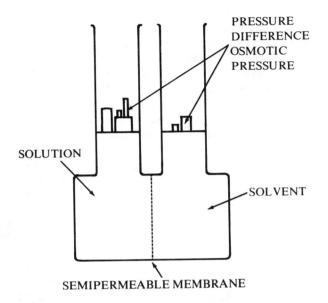

PRESSURE
DIFFERENCE
OSMOTIC
PRESSURE

SOLUTION

SOLVENT

SEMIPERMEABLE MEMBRANE

Figure 18-6 Apparatus for investigating osmosis. The pressure on the solution is higher than that on the pure solvent. The pressure difference is adjusted until the two liquids are in thermodynamic equilibrium, and there is no tendency for solvent to pass through the membrane in either direction.

solvent molecules can be made to travel from the solution side into the pure solvent, if the pressure is high enough. It is possible to adjust the pressure on the solution so that the two tendencies for motion of solvent molecules are in balance, and the solution is then in thermodynamic equilibrium with the pure solvent. This special pressure is called the *osmotic pressure* of the solution, and can be investigated using the apparatus shown in Figure 18-6. The osmotic pressure of a solution, denoted by the capital Greek letter π, is a function of the concentration of the solution and the temperature. For dilute solutions it is found that the osmotic pressure obeys an equation exactly the same in form as the ideal gas equation:

$$\pi V = n_{solutes}RT$$

where $n_{solutes}$ is the total number of moles of all solutes in volume V of the solution, R is the gas constant, and T is the temperature.

Example 18-12 Calculate the osmotic pressure of a solution of 0.80 g of sucrose $C_{12}H_{22}O_{11}$, in 100 g of water at 27°C.

The amount of solute is 0.0023 mole, and the volume of the solution is approximately 100 mL. Hence the osmotic pressure is

$$\pi = \frac{0.0023 \text{ mol} \times 8.314 \text{ J K}^{-1} \text{mol}^{-1} \times 300 \text{ K}}{100 \times 10^{-6} \text{ m}^3}$$

$$= 57 \text{ kPa}.$$

It should be noted that osmotic pressures can be large. Osmotic pressure effects are of great importance in biological systems, in which solutions of different concentrations are separated by semi-permeable membranes.

The "ideal" equation for osmotic pressure is accurate only for very dilute solutions in which the osmotic pressure is small. Corrections for non-ideal behaviour can be made, however, and measurements of osmotic pressure are of importance as a method of measuring molar mass of solutes, especially biological molecules and polymers.

Semi-permeable membranes can be used for desalination of seawater on an industrial scale. If seawater is placed in a vessel with a semipermeable membrane and compressed to a pressure higher than the osmotic pressure, then pure water passes through the membrane, leaving the salts and other solutes in a concentrated solution.

ADVANCED REFERENCES

Denbigh, K., The Principles of Chemical Equilibrium, Third Edition, Cambridge University Press (1971). As in most matters of chemical thermodynamics, this book by Denbigh is a useful standard reference on the work of this chapter.

Moyes, R.B., Atomic and Molecular Weight Determinations. Methuen, 1971. This book includes a brief summary of the use of several of these methods for determination of molar mass of solutes.

PROBLEMS

1. Calculate the vapour pressure of a solution containing 50.0 g of 1,4-dimethylbenzene (often called para xylene, $C_6H_4(CH_3)_2$) and 150.0 g of benzene (C_6H_6) at 327.6 K. The vapour pressures of pure p-xylene and benzene at this temperature are, respectively, 5330 Pa and 42 640 Pa.

   [35.3 kPa] ✓

2. A 2.00% (by mass) toluene solution of an unknown non-dissociating and non-volatile solute has a vapour pressure of 100.5 kPa at 383.79 K (the boiling point of pure toluene) and boils at 384.04 K. Calculate the molar mass of the solute and the molar heat of vaporization of toluene. Toluene is methylbenzene.

   [0.229 kg mol^{-1}; 40.2 kJ mol^{-1}]

3. Use the data in Appendix 1 to calculate the vapour pressures of tetrachloromethane and trichloromethane at 279 K. Assume that $\Delta H°$ for the process of vaporization does not vary significantly with temperature. Then use the values so calculated to estimate the vapour pressure of a liquid solution consisting of 350 g of each.

   [6.16 kPa; 11.7 kPa; 9.28 kPa]

4. Estimate the freezing point of a solution containing 40% ethylene glycol (by mass) in water. How does your estimate compare with the experimental value in Figure 17-35? The molar mass of ethylene glycol, $C_2H_6O_2$, is 0.0621 kg mol^{-1}. Would you expect good agreement? Why?

    [253 K]

5. A polymer of low average molar mass is dissolved in naphthalene, 1.64 g of polymer to 95.31 g of naphthalene. The freezing point of the solution is 353.02 K whereas pure naphthalene freezes at 353.37 K. Using the datum in Table 18-3, estimate the average molar mass of the polymer.

    [0.339 kg mol^{-1}]

6. Estimate the osmotic pressure of the following solutions. Take water to have a density of 1.00 g cm^{-3} and CH_2Cl_2 to have a density of 1.34 g cm^{-3} at 298 K.
    (a) 0.0050 g of sucrose, $C_{12}H_{22}O_{11}$ in 100 g of water;
    (b) 0.010 g of $CaCl_2$ in 100 g of water;
    (c) 0.10 g of low molar mass polymer (average M = 0.240 kg mol^{-1}) in 100 g of dichloromethane, CH_2Cl_2. The density of CH_2Cl_2 is 1.34 g mL^{-1}.

    [360 Pa; 6700 Pa; 13.8 kPa]

7. Estimate the solubility of oxygen in water at 298 K under a partial pressure of oxygen of 20 kPa, using Henry's Law. Express your answer in mol kg^{-1} and in p.p.m.

    [2.5×10^{-4} mol kg^{-1}; 8 p.p.m.]

8. Chlorobenzene, C_6H_5Cl, has a vapour pressure of 115.1 kPa at 410 K and bromobenzene, C_6H_5Br, has a vapour pressure of 60.4 kPa at the same temperature. Mixtures of the two behave ideally. Calculate the composition of a mixture of these two liquids which would have a vapour pressure of 100 kPa at 410 K. What is the composition of the vapour?

    [in liquid, $x_{C_6H_5Cl} = 0.724$ in vapour, $x_{C_6H_5Cl} = 0.833$]

XIX SLIGHTLY SOLUBLE ELECTROLYTES

Electrolytes are substances which, when dissolved in water, form ions. They are discussed at somewhat greater length in Section 20.1. This chapter is concerned with those electrolytes, and there are many of them, which have such a small solubility in water that they are usually described as being insoluble. However, while one normally and quite properly describes a substance like silver chloride as being insoluble in water because it is difficult to see any change in solid silver chloride when it is added to water, the fact is that a very slight amount of it does dissolve. Electrolytes having very small solubilities in water are of some importance, and form the subject of this chapter.

19-1 THE SOLUBILITY PRODUCT

For saturated solutions of relatively insoluble electrolytes like silver chloride, it has long been known that the product of the concentrations of the electrolyte's ions was approximately constant at any temperature for any solution in equilibrium with the solid electrolyte. This took the following algebraic form.

$$AgCl: \qquad (c_{Ag^+})(c_{Cl^-}) \approx \text{constant}$$
$$Ag_2SO_4: \qquad (c_{Ag^+})^2(c_{SO_4^{2-}}) \approx \text{constant}$$

These relationships hold true independently of the presence in the same solution of non-participating ions such as sodium ion. The constant involved is called the solubility product of the electrolyte and is given the symbol K_{sp}.

These relationships can be understood in a more general context if one applies the analyses of Chapter 16. The dissolving process is the following.

$$AgCl(c) \rightleftarrows Ag^+(aq) + Cl^-(aq)$$

The equilibrium constant for such a process is

$$K = \frac{a_{Ag^+(aq)} a_{Cl^-(aq)}}{a_{AgCl(c)}} \; ;$$
$$a_{Ag^+(aq)} a_{Cl^-(aq)} = K(a_{AgCl})$$

As in earlier cases of heterogeneous equilibria in Chapter 15, the relative activity of the crystalline solid can be taken to be unity. For the species in solution, the relative activity is approximately equal to the ratio of the molality (or molarity) to that in some chosen reference state. In electrochemistry and thermochemistry the composition is usually described in terms of molality and the reference state, with one important qualification discussed in Section 21.1, is a one molal solution of the species concerned.

In solubility studies, acid/base studies and other areas where volumetric measurements are made, composition is usally described in terms of molarity, and relative activities are approximated by the ratio of the concentration (in mol L^{-1}) to that in the reference state. For *aqueous* solutions, the reference state of 1 mol kg^{-1} is nearly equal to 1 mol L^{-1}, so that the term in the denominator remains close to unity. Thus

$$a_{Ag^+} \approx \frac{[Ag^+]}{1} = [Ag^+]_r$$

$$a_{Cl^-} \approx \frac{[Cl^-]}{1} = [Cl^-]_r$$

The square bracket provides a convenient symbol to represent concentration. It is an accepted S.I. symbol and is synonymous with a subscripted c.

$$c_{Ag^+} \equiv [Ag^+]$$

The subscript r on a square bracket is used throughout this book to indicate the ratio of the concentration to that of the standard state. Since this text (like most texts) uses mol L^{-1} exclusively in dealing with the concentrations of aqueous solutions and since the concentration of the standard state is approximately 1 mol L^{-1}, the denominator in the approximation of relative activity is invariably close to unity. Thus the numerical value of [A] is always nearly the same as that of $[A]_r$. However, the former has units mol L^{-1} and the latter is dimensionless. In most books, this distinction is ignored or forgotten, and since the two are numerically equal, the loss is not great. It ought to be remembered, however, that all equilibrium constants are properly dimensionless so that

$$K_{sp} = [Ag^+]_r[Cl^-]_r$$

The same form of analysis applies, of course, to more complicated electrolytes. For silver sulfate, the equations are

$$Ag_2SO_4(c) \rightleftarrows 2Ag^+(aq) + SO_4^{2-}(aq)$$

$$K_{sp} \approx [Ag^+]_r^2[SO_4^{2-}]_r$$

while for barium fluoride, they are

$$BaF_2(c) \rightleftarrows Ba^{2+}(aq) + 2F^-(aq)$$

$$K_{sp} \approx [Ba^{2+}]_r[F^-]_r^2$$

Table 19-1 lists the solubility products for a number of insoluble electrolytes, and can be used to calculate the solubilities of these electrolytes.

TABLE 19-1

Solubility Products at 25°C

AgCl	2×10^{-10}	$Fe(OH)_2$	8×10^{-16}
AgBr	5×10^{-13}	$Fe(OH)_3$	4×10^{-40}
AgI	8×10^{-17}	FeS	5×10^{-18}
Ag_2CO_3	8×10^{-12}	Hg_2Cl_2	1×10^{-18}
Ag_2CrO_4	3×10^{-12}	$Hg_2(OH)_2$	2×10^{-24}
Ag_2S	6×10^{-50}	$Hg(OH)_2$	4×10^{-26}
Ag_2SO_4	2×10^{-5}	HgS (red)	4×10^{-53}
$Al(OH)_3$	1×10^{-33}	HgS (black)	1×10^{-52}
$BaCO_3$	5×10^{-9}	$MgCO_3$	1×10^{-5}
$BaCrO_4$	1×10^{-10}	$Mg(OH)_2$	1×10^{-11}
$Ba(OH)_2$	5×10^{-3}	$Mn(OH)_2$	2×10^{-13}
$BaSO_4$	1×10^{-10}	MnS (green)	3×10^{-13}
$Be(OH)_2$	1×10^{-21}	$Ni(OH)_2$	6×10^{-18}
Bi_2S_3	1×10^{-97}	NiS	2×10^{-26}
$CaCO_3$	5×10^{-9}	$PbCl_2$	2×10^{-5}
CaC_2O_4	2×10^{-9}	$PbBr_2$	9×10^{-6}
CaF_2	3×10^{-11}	$PbCO_3$	6×10^{-14}
$Ca(OH)_2$	4×10^{-6}	$PbCrO_4$	3×10^{-13}
$CaSO_4$	9×10^{-6}	$Pb(OH)_2$	6×10^{-16}
$Cd(OH)_2$	4×10^{-15}	PbS	1×10^{-28}
CdS	2×10^{-28}	$PbSO_4$	2×10^{-8}
$Co(OH)_2$	6×10^{-15}	$Sn(OH)_2$	8×10^{-29}
$Co(OH)_3$	3×10^{-41}	SnS	1×10^{-25}
CoS	2×10^{-25}	$SrCO_3$	1×10^{-10}
$Cr(OH)_2$	1×10^{-17}	$SrCrO_4$	2×10^{-5}
$Cr(OH)_3$	1×10^{-30}	$Sr(OH)_2$	3×10^{-4}
CuCl	4×10^{-7}	$SrSO_4$	3×10^{-7}
CuBr	8×10^{-9}	$Zn(OH)_2$	3×10^{-17}
CuI	2×10^{-12}	ZnS (zincblende)	2×10^{-24}
$Cu(OH)_2$	1×10^{-20}	ZnS (wurtzite)	3×10^{-22}
CuS	6×10^{-36}		

Example 19-1   Estimate the solubility of AgCl in pure water.

Let s be the solubility in mole AgCl/litre. Now if s mole of AgCl dissolves in a litre of water then, since AgCl is a strong electrolyte and completely dissociated into ions, the concentration of Ag^+ is s mol L^{-1} and the concentration of Cl^- is also s. Hence

$$[Ag^+]_r = s,$$

$$[Cl^-]_r = s$$

Hence

$$[Ag^+]_r[Cl^-]_r = s^2 \approx 2 \times 10^{-10} = K_{sp}$$

so

$$s = (2 \times 10^{-10})^{1/2} = 1.4 \times 10^{-5}$$

The solubility is 1.4×10^{-5} mol L^{-1}.

Example 19-2 Estimate the solubility of Ag_2SO_4 in pure water.

In this case one must be careful of the stoichiometry. Let s be the solubility in mole Ag_2SO_4/litre. The dissociation equilibrium is

$$Ag_2SO_4(c) \rightleftarrows 2Ag^+(aq) + SO_4{}^{2-}(aq)$$

and so the concentration of Ag^+ is 2s and the concentration of $SO_4{}^{2-}$ is s. Hence

$$[Ag^+]_r^2[SO_4{}^{2-}]_r = (2s)^2.s = 4s^3 \approx 2 \times 10^{-5} = K_{sp}$$

so

$$s = (2 \times 10^{-5}/4)^{1/3} = 0.018$$

The solubility is 0.018 mol L^{-1}.

The solubility of an electrolyte is very strongly affected by the presence of a second solute containing the same ion. If a solution contains even a small concentration of chloride ion derived from a soluble salt (such as sodium chloride), the solubility of silver chloride *in that solution* is directly affected through the solubility product. This effect is called the common ion effect. It is of course, simply another example of Le Chatelier's Principle.

Example 19-3 What is the solubility of AgCl in a 0.005F NaCl solution?

Let s be the solubility of AgCl. The concentration of Ag^+ is then s, while the concentration of Cl^- is (0.005 + s) since chloride ion is derived from both the NaCl and the AgCl. Hence

$$[Ag^+]_r[Cl^-]_r = s(0.005 + s) \approx 2 \times 10^{-10} = K_{sp}$$

We have to solve the quadratic equation

$$s^2 + 0.005s - 2 \times 10^{-10} = 0$$

The positive root of this equation is

$$s = \frac{-0.005 + \sqrt{25 \times 10^{-6} + 8 \times 10^{-10}}}{2} = 4 \times 10^{-8}$$

Therefore the solubility of AgCl in 0.005F NaCl is about 4×10^{-8} mol L^{-1}. Notice that the solubility is about a thousand times smaller than when the solvent is pure water (Example 19-1).

19-2   APPROXIMATE METHODS OF SOLVING EQUATIONS

The student who skimmed very quickly over the conventional solution to the quadratic equation which had to be solved in Example 19.3 should now take calculator in hand and follow through the arithmetic.

It is necessary to take the square root of 25.008×10^{-6}, which is 0.00500008, and then to subtract 0.005 from this number, leaving a very small difference of 8×10^{-8}. The accuracy with which this difference can be calculated is not very high, and some calculators may not be able to calculate it at all. Furthermore, this is not an extreme case, for if the solubility of AgI in 0.1F NaI were to be calculated the following solution to the quadratic equation would be found:

$$s = \frac{-0.1 + \sqrt{0.01 + 3.2 \times 10^{-16}}}{2}$$

It is beyond the capacity of most hand calculators to evaluate this expression directly, and yet this is a perfectly reasonable question in chemistry.

Another type of difficulty is discovered if one tries to calculate the solubility of Ag_2SO_4 in a solution of $AgNO_3$. It is found that the solubility can only be obtained by solving a cubic equation. The general solution to a cubic equation is difficult to write down, very difficult to remember, and awkward to evaluate numerically. However, this equation is a perfectly reasonable one and some kind of approach to the problem must be found.

Both of these problems of arithmetic can be solved by using approximate methods of solving the quadratic and cubic equations. It will be found that the same numerical methods will be of great use in dealing with acid-base equilibria, and so it is worth studying the methods carefully at this stage, where the chemistry is simpler.

Consider again the solution to Example 19-3. Looking at the expression for K_{sp}

$$K_{sp} \approx [Ag^+]_r [Cl^-]_r$$

consider a solution in equilibrium with AgCl(c). If the Cl^- concentration is increased, the Ag^+ concentration must be decreased, and so the solubility of AgCl must be decreased. The common ion effect always reduces solubility, unless some other reaction takes place. Now K_{sp} for AgCl is very small, and so the solubility of AgCl in pure water is very small and the presence of NaCl must make the solubility even smaller. Hence in solving the equation

$$s(0.005 + s) \approx 2 \times 10^{-10}$$

first assume that $s \ll 0.005$, solve the resulting simplified equation, and then check the assumption. If the assumption turns out to be wrong, the first calculation is corrected.

If $s \ll 0.005$, the equation is reduced to

$$s(0.005) \approx 2 \times 10^{-10}$$

which is a linear equation with the solution

$$s = \frac{2 \times 10^{-10}}{0.005} = 4 \times 10^{-8}$$

This solution is indeed much less than 0.005, and so no further work is required. The result agrees exactly with the full solution to the quadratic equation. In the following example, a second iteration of the procedure is needed.

Example 19-4   What is the solubility of AgCl in 3×10^{-5} F NaCl solution?
As before, $[Ag^+]_r = s$, $[Cl^-]_r = 3 \times 10^{-5} + s$, so

$$s(3 \times 10^{-5} + s) \approx 2 \times 10^{-10} = K_{sp}$$

Assuming that $s \ll 3 \times 10^{-5}$, set $[Cl^-]_r = 3 \times 10^{-5}$ as a first approximation, and solve the linear equation

$$s = 2 \times 10^{-10}/3 \times 10^{-5} = 0.7 \times 10^{-5}$$

It is clear the 0.7 is not "much less than" 3, and so this result is not correct. However, one can now make a better estimate of the chloride ion concentration,

$$[Cl^-]_r \approx (3 + 0.7) \times 10^{-5} = 3.7 \times 10^{-5}$$

Assuming this new value, one finds

$$s = 2 \times 10^{-10}/3.7 \times 10^{-5} = 0.5 \times 10^{-5}$$

The new value for s is not changed much from the first estimate. One further iteration gives

$$[Cl^-]_r \approx (3 + 0.5) \times 10^{-5} = 3.5 \times 10^{-5}$$

$$s = 2 \times 10^{-10}/3.5 \times 10^{-5} = 0.6 \times 10^{-5}$$

Hence the solubility is 0.6×10^{-5} mol L^{-1}.

The exact solution to this problem is $s = 0.56 \times 10^{-5}$. After a little practice, the iterative method for such equations can be executed more quickly and more accurately than the exact solution, even when several iterations are required.

This approximate method for solving the algebraic equations may not work when the concentration of the electrolyte with the common ion is very small. If the successive results of the iterative steps are getting further apart instead of closer together, the approximations are said to be "diverging," and another method of approximate solution must be found.

Example 19-5   Calculate the mass of Ag_2SO_4 which will dissolve in 500 mL of 0.10F $AgNO_3$.
Let s mol Ag_2SO_4/litre be the solubility. Then

$$[Ag^+]_r = 0.10 + 2s$$

$$[SO_4{}^{2-}]_r = s$$

Hence

$$(0.10 + 2s)^2 s \approx 2 \times 10^{-5} = K_{sp}$$

This is a cubic equation, requiring an iterative solution. Assuming that $s \ll 0.10$,

$$s = 2 \times 10^{-5}/(0.10)^2 = 0.002$$

Carrying out a second iteration,

$$[Ag^+]_r = 0.10 + 2(0.002) = 0.104$$

Hence

$$s = 2 \times 10^{-5}/(0.104)^2 = 0.0018$$

This is a sufficiently small change in s that no further iterations are necessary. The solubility is 0.0018 mol L^{-1} and so the mass which dissolves

$$= 0.0018 \text{ mol } L^{-1} \times 0.500 \text{ L} \times 311.7 \text{ g mol}^{-1}$$
$$= 0.28 \text{ g.}$$

Most solubility products are not known very accurately, and vary with temperature and other conditions, and it is seldom justified to give more than two significant figures in calculations such as these.

19-3   SEPARATION BY PRECIPITATION

Differences in solubilities of salts are very commonly used to separate ions in solution. For instance, the ions in a solution containing both silver ions and sodium ions can be readily separated by addition of dilute hydrochloric acid: silver chloride precipitates and can be filtered off, leaving a solution of sodium chloride. This is an extreme case, where one salt is very soluble, and the other is insoluble.

Separation can also be carried out when two ions form salts which are both fairly insoluble, but which have very different solubilities nevertheless. Table 19-1 shows many pairs of salts with a common ion, having solubilities which differ by a large factor. The principles behind the separation are illustrated in the next example.

Example 19-6   A solution contains Ba^{2+} at a concentration of 0.010 mol L^{-1} and Sr^{2+} at 0.015 mol L^{-1}. A solution of sodium sulphate is added slowly in order to precipitate the two metals separately as the insoluble sulphates. Which metal precipitates first? What fraction of the first metal remains when the second metal begins to precipitate?

The solubility products are 1×10^{-10} for $BaSO_4$, and 3×10^{-7} for $SrSO_4$. Hence $BaSO_4$ begins to precipitate when $[SO_4^{2-}]$ reaches the value $1 \times 10^{-10}/0.010 = 10^{-8}$ mol L^{-1} and $SrSO_4$ begins to precipitate when $[SO_4^{2-}]$ reaches the value $3 \times 10^{-7}/0.015 = 2 \times 10^{-5}$ mol L^{-1}. Beginning at zero, $[SO_4^{2-}]$ increases as the sodium sulphate solution is added, and so $[SO_4^{2-}]$ reaches 10^{-8} mol L^{-1} before it reaches the larger value 2×10^{-5}. Hence $BaSO_4$ precipitates first.

When $SrSO_4$ begins to precipitate, $[SO_4^{2-}]_r = 2 \times 10^{-5}$. Hence the Ba^{2+} concentration is

$$[Ba^{2+}]_r = 1 \times 10^{-10}/2 \times 10^{-5} = 5 \times 10^{-6}$$

Hence the barium ion concentration is very low, and essentially all the barium has been removed by precipitation as the sodium sulphate solution is added. The fraction remaining in solution is $5 \times 10^{-6}/0.010$, or 5×10^{-4} or 0.05%, so that 99.95% of the barium is precipitated before any strontium is precipitated.

In practice such separations must be carried out very carefully. If the sulphate solution is added too quickly, or without proper stirring, the sulphate ion concentration may exceed 2×10^{-5} mol L^{-1} in some parts of the solution, and then some strontium sulphate would precipitate before the above calculation says that it ought to. Hence, some contamination of the $BaSO_4$ precipitate can be expected under normal conditions. On the other hand, it is certain that the subsequent $SrSO_4$ precipitate will be contaminated with 0.05% of the $BaSO_4$.

Separations of this type are commonly carried out for metals which form insoluble sulphides. The concentration of sulphide ion in solution is controlled by using the acid/base properties of the sulphide ion, and so will be discussed in more detail in the next chapter.

19-4   INFLUENCE OF OTHER PROCESSES

The solubility of silver sulphate was calculated in Example 19-2 as 0.018 mol L^{-1} at 298 K, but the published experimental value is somewhat greater, 0.027 mol L^{-1}. This inaccuracy in predicting the solubility by using solubility product is common. Indeed, systems showing exact agreement are rarities. The cause of this disagreement is not, however, that the concept of solubility product is incorrect, but that the process to which it refers is rarely the only one operating.

For example, the sulphate ion hydrolyses to some extent in aqueous solution:

$$H_2O + SO_4^{2-}(aq) \rightleftharpoons HSO_4^{-}(aq) + H_3O^{+}(aq)$$

This process will be examined more fully in Chapter 20. The effect is to reduce the concentration of sulphate ions, thus permitting more silver sulphate to dissolve.

An analogous reaction occurs with fluorides

$$H_2O + F^{-}(aq) \rightleftharpoons HF(aq) + H_3O^{+}(aq)$$

but can be ignored for chlorides, bromides and iodides. All of this may be understood in terms of HF being a weak acid, whereas HCl, HBr and HI are strong acids.

Reactions with water, hydrogen ions or hydroxide ions are the most common processes to require consideration, but other equilibria sometimes occur involving only the species produced by dissolution. For example silver cyanide, the usual material for solutions in silver plating, gives an important soluble complex as follows:

$$Ag^+(aq) + 2\,CN^-(aq) \rightleftarrows Ag(CN)_2^-(aq)$$

This process is so important in this case that AgCN is actually more soluble in CN^- solutions than in water, the inverse of the common ion effect.

Similarly lead ions and iodide ions form a complex according to

$$Pb^{2+}(aq) + 4\,I^-(aq) \rightleftarrows PbI_4^{2-}(aq)$$

and this would require a correction (not large as it happens) in calculating the solubility of lead iodide. Inorganic materials in aqueous solutions are well understood in most instances, and the equilibrium constants are usually available for accurate calculation. Those working with these systems must be aware of the variety of processes that occur.

Further errors occur in more concentrated solutions which are not "ideal" in a thermodynamic sense where the relative activities are not equal to the relative concentrations. The corrections necessary are called activity coefficients, and are the subject of Chapter 21.

19-5 THERMODYNAMICS OF SOLUBILITY PRODUCT

The equilibrium between a solid insoluble electrolyte in contact with a solution can be analyzed thermodynamically, like any other chemical or phase equilibrium. For instance, for

$$BaSO_4(c) \rightleftarrows Ba^{2+}(aq) + SO_4^{2-}(aq)$$

the standard state free energy change ΔG° can be written

$$\Delta G^\circ = \Delta G_f^\circ(Ba^{2+}(aq)) + \Delta G_f^\circ(SO_4^{2-}(aq)) - \Delta G_f^\circ(BaSO_4(c))$$

and then, as usual,

$$K_{sp} = e^{-\Delta G^\circ/RT}$$

Moreover, the temperature dependence of K_{sp} is governed by ΔH° for the above process, and hence K_{sp} can be evaluated at any temperature as outlined previously.

There is a difficulty in assigning ΔH_f° and ΔG_f° values for aqueous ions. It is not possible to make and study a solution containing *only* one kind of ion. Always at least one type of ion of opposite charge must be present to achieve electrical neutrality. The thermodynamics of such ions are handled by adopting a convention that ΔH_f° and ΔG_f° are zero for $H^+(aq)$ at all temperatures.

$$\tfrac{1}{2}\,H_2(g) \xrightarrow{H_2O} H^+(aq) + e$$
$$\Delta H^\circ \equiv 0; \ \Delta G^\circ \equiv 0$$

ΔG_f° and ΔH_f° of other ions can then be assigned by experimental measurements on real processes such as the following:

$$Zn(c) + 2\,H^+(aq) \rightarrow Zn^{2+}(aq) + H_2(g)$$

If $\Delta H°$ for the above process is determined experimentally to be, say, X, then one can state that

$$X = \Delta H_f^\circ(Zn^{2+}(aq)) + \Delta H_f^\circ(H_2(g)) - \Delta H_f^\circ(Zn(c)) - 2\,\Delta H_f^\circ(H^+(aq))$$

$$= \Delta H_f^\circ(Zn^{2+}(aq)) + 0 - 0 - 0$$

$$= \Delta H_f^\circ(Zn^{2+}(aq))$$

This, and a similar calculation for $\Delta G°$, determine the values of ΔH_f° and ΔG_f° for $Zn^{2+}(aq)$ in accordance with out convention.

Appendix 1 contains thermodynamic data for single ions in aqueous solutions at 298.15 K. It should be noted that the standard state implied by the superscript ° is, for these species, a one molal solution. Note should also be taken of a point to be dealt with more extensively in Chapter 21, namely that the solution chosen as the standard state is not the real one molal solution but a hypothetical one in which the activity coefficient is zero. This point, difficult in itself, causes no difficulties whatsoever in using these data, as the following example shows.

Example 19-7 Calculate K_{sp} for $BaSO_4$ at 25°C and at 50°C using thermochemical data.

The process is

$$BaSO_4(c) \rightleftarrows Ba^{2+}(aq) + SO_4{}^{2-}(aq)$$

From Appendix 1,

$$\Delta G_{298}^\circ = (-560.7) + (-744.63) - (-1362)$$

$$= 57\ kJ$$

Hence, in agreement with the value in Table 19-1, K_{sp} at 25°C is

$$K_{sp} = e^{-(57000)/(8.314)(298.15)} = 1 \times 10^{-10}$$

Also,

$$\Delta H° = (-537.6) + (-909.27) - (-1473)$$

$$= 26\ kJ$$

and hence

$$\ln K_{323} = \ln(1 \times 10^{-10}) + \frac{-26\,000}{8.314}\left[\frac{1}{298.15} - \frac{1}{323.15}\right]$$

$$= 2 \times 10^{-10}$$

The solubility product of barium sulphate, and hence the solubility, increase with increasing temperature, in accordance with Le Chatelier's Principle for an endothermic reaction.

SUMMARY

The concept of solubility product is a most useful one for quantitative treatments of the solubilities of ionic species. It is particularly valuable for calculating solubilities in solutions containing common ions. The fact that the solubility product is an equilibrium constant related to $\Delta G°$ for the dissolution process adds a further element of calculating power, permitting solubilities to be determined at any temperature.

It must be remembered, however, that this approach is accurate only for very slightly soluble materials. Deviations from ideality make this approach meaningless for soluble materials like sodium chloride. Methods for dealing with these deviations are dicussed in Chapter 21.

FURTHER READING

J.N. Butler, Solubility and pH Calculations, Addison-Wesley (1964); This is a fine introduction to solubility product. The methodology is clear and the problems extensive but the book is perhaps most memorable for the exceptionally relevant allegory threaded through the book.

PROBLEMS

1. Calculate the solubility of $BaSO_4$ in (a) pure water (b) 0.1F Na_2SO_4 (c) 5×10^{-5}F $BaCl_2$, all at 25°C.
    $$[1 \times 10^{-5}\, mol\, L^{-1}, 1 \times 10^{-9}\, mol\, L^{-1}, 1.9 \times 10^{-6}\, mol\, L^{-1}]$$

2. Calculate the solubility of $PbBr_2$ in (a) pure water   (b) 0.1F KBr   (c) 0.05F KBr, all at 25°C.
    $$[1.3 \times 10^{-2}\, mol\, L^{-1}, 9 \times 10^{-4}\, mol\, L^{-1}, 2.9 \times 10^{-3}\, mol\, L^{-1}]$$

3. What mass of lead sulphate $PbSO_4$ would be dissolved per cubic metre of otherwise pure water in contact with solid $PbSO_4$ at 25°C?
    $$[42\, g]$$

4. A solution contains 0.05 mole L^{-1} Ba^{2+} ions, and 0.002 mol L^{-1} Ag^+ ions. The metals are to be precipitated in turn by addition of chromate ion, $CrO_4{}^{2-}$. Which ion precipitates first? What percentage of this ion remains in solution when the second ion begins to precipitate?
    $$[Ba^{2+}, 0.26\%]$$

5. Calculate the solubility product of lead iodide PbI_2 at 25°C and at 50°C using thermochemical data.
    $$[1.1 \times 10^{-8}, 7.8 \times 10^{-8}]$$

6. What is the ratio of the solubility of $PbCl_2$ at 40°C to that at 25°C?

   [1.18]

7. Use the solubility product of $Ca(OH)_2$ and the thermochemical data for $Ca^{2+}(aq)$ and $Ca(OH)_2(c)$ to calculate ΔG_f° for $OH^-(aq)$. Repeat using the magnesium analogues.

   [−158 kJ; −158 kJ]

8. The solubility of AgBr at 20°C is listed as being 8.4×10^{-6} g of AgBr per 100 g water. What is the solubility in mol L^{-1} and the solubility product for AgBr at this temperature?

   [4.5×10^{-7} mol L^{-1}, 2×10^{-13}]

XX PROTON TRANSFER: ACIDS AND BASES

"Acid" is a very old word. Its meaning has evolved over many years, acquiring different connotations at different times. Very early, for example, a sour taste was one property associated with acids although it is a criterion few would wish to use in these safety-conscious times. Indeed, the word acid is derived from the Latin word for sour and the property is amply illustrated by acetic acid, the basis of vinegar, and by citric acid, the constituent of lemon juice responsible for its sharp taste. Some of the other early properties attributed to acids, such as "high solvent power," still have relevance whereas others, such as "an ability to precipitate sulphur from liver of sulphur," would not even be intelligible to most modern chemists.

Early in the nineteenth century, as ideas of composition developed generally, the composition of acids began to be debated. From 1838, it was recognized not only that acids contained hydrogen but also that the hydrogen was in such a form that it could be replaced by metals. There are materials now recognized as acids to which this definition does not apply, but it is an important idea which is relevant still.

Growing understanding of ions in solution led to proposals by Ostwald and Arrhenius, late in the nineteenth century, that acids gave rise to H^+ in aqueous solution. Bases, which had little definition up to now other than an ability to neutralize acids, were seen to be compounds which gave rise to OH^- in aqueous solution. These ideas, while limited to water as a solvent and less powerful than either of those to follow, nevertheless represent an important insight and they permitted rational and quantitative treatment of many systems.

This approach has two deficiencies, however. It cannot deal with bases reacting in the absence of water nor can it deal with solvents other than water. Brønsted and Lowry saw that acid/base behaviour was involved in a reaction such as the simple gas phase reaction of hydrochloric acid with ammonia

$$HCl(g) + NH_3(g) \rightarrow NH_4Cl(c)$$

and that a full definition must incorporate such cases. They proposed that an acid be defined as a substance which donates a proton, and a base as a substance which accepts a proton. A particularly common case of interest is that in which the base (or acid) is the solvent, and it is this case that allows us to compare the Brønsted/Lowry view with that of Arrhenius. Many solvents, and most notably water, can act either as a base or as an acid. Thus Brønsted acids and bases will exhibit reactions of the following form in such solvents.

$$HA(aq) + H_2O \rightarrow H_3O^+ + A^-(aq)$$

$$A^-(aq) + H_2O \rightarrow HA(aq) + OH^-(aq)$$

The symbols $H^+(aq)$ and H_3O^+ are both used in chemical literature to indicate a proton in water. They are interchangeable and mean exactly the same thing. Neither should be taken as being a literal interpretation of the actual form of the proton. Certainly free protons are unlikely to exist, but it is probable that the number of water molecules associated with any one proton will vary with time. Such detailed molecular considerations are not, however, part of this chapter. Both $H^+(aq)$ and H_3O^+ should be taken to mean a proton in water, whatever the actual nature of such a species may be. The nature of a proton in water is discussed in Section 23-4.

Although the Brønsted approach is of great importance, and will be the basis of the treatment in this chapter, a still more general definition is of value to chemists. This definition, due to Lewis, defines acids as electron acceptors rather than as proton donors, and bases as electron donors rather than as proton acceptors. Moreover, it is extended to the important cases of coordination complex formation where the electrons are not fully "donated" but rather change from being associated with the base only to being associated with both species. Examples are the following:

$$Cu^{2+} + 4\,H_2O \rightarrow Cu(H_2O)_4^{2+}$$
$$\text{acid} \qquad \text{base}$$

$$BF_3 + F^- \rightarrow BF_4^-$$
$$\text{acid \ base}$$

$$Cd^{2+} + 4\,NH_3 \rightarrow Cd(NH_3)_4^{2+}$$
$$\text{acid} \qquad \text{base}$$

In an earlier chapter, the importance of the non-bonding pair in NH_3 was noted in connection with the structure. The non-bonding pair in this or any ion or molecule is an important factor in determining its reactivity, always rendering the species a potential "Lewis base." Note that NH_3 can also accept H^+ itself, forming NH_4^+, and thus acting as a base in the *Brønsted* definition. The Lewis concept is much broader, and extends to areas of chemistry where there is *not* proton transfer, as well as encompassing all those that do. In this chapter, as the title states, we are concerned only with proton transfer reactions and hence with acids and bases within the narrower Brønsted definition.

20-1   ELECTROLYTES AND ION FORMATION IN SOLUTION

Electrolytes are compounds, which, when dissolved in a suitable solvent (often water), form ions which impart electrical conductivity to the solution. Other solutes which remain electrically neutral in solution and do not enhance the electrical conductivity of the solution are termed *non-electrolytes*. Pure water itself is a poor conductor of electricity owing to the small fraction of water molecules which are dissociated into the aqueous ions, $H^+(aq)$ and $OH^-(aq)$. If an electrolyte such as sodium chloride, NaCl, is added to the water and dissolved, the electrical conductivity of the liquid may be increased many thousand fold owing to the presence of the ions, Na^+ and Cl^-. A non-electrolyte such as sucrose in the water does practically nothing to enhance the conductivity. No formation of ions takes place.

The formation of ions occurs in two ways. In some solid electrolytes the ions are already present as such in the solid lattice. The dissolving process breaks up the crystal lattice and separates the ions. Such a process is termed *dissociation*. NaCl and KOH are electrolytes which dissolve to form ions in solution in this way. Ions may also form in solution, however, from species in which no ions exist prior to dissolving. Hydrogen chloride is a gas of covalently bonded molecules but when it dissolves in water, these are found almost exclusively as $H^+(aq)$ and $Cl^-(aq)$. This process is called *ionization* and is an example of *hydration*. Notice that in both cases the resulting ions are surrounded in water by oriented water molecules. This *solvation* of the ions is a major factor in determining both ΔH and ΔS for the dissolving process.

Electrolytes for which the dissociation or ionization to form ions is virtually complete are called *strong* electrolytes. *Weak* electrolytes are those for which dissociation or ionization is significantly incomplete. The distinction is not a sharp one, and the electrolyte is usually regarded as being weak in doubtful cases.

Acids and bases are also designated as being strong or weak. A strong acid is one which gives virtually one mole of $H^+(aq)$ per mole of dissolved acid (or even more in the case of sulphuric acid). A strong base is one which gives one mole of $OH^-(aq)$ per mole of dissolved base. There are in fact few strong acids and bases and these should be memorized.

Strong Acids

three of the hydrogen halides;
   HCl, HBr and HI (but *not* HF)
sulphuric acid; H_2SO_4 (the first
   hydrogen only)
perchloric acid; $HClO_4$
nitric acid; HNO_3
the sulphonic acids,
   such as phenylsulphonic acid

Strong Bases

alkali metal hydroxides;
   LiOH, NaOH, KOH, RbOH, CsOH
thallous hydroxide; TlOH
alkaline earth hydroxides;
   $Mg(OH)_2$, $Ca(OH)_2$, $Sr(OH)_2$, $Ba(OH)_2$
tetraalkyl ammonium hydroxides, such as
   tetramethyl ammonium hydroxide,
   $(CH_3)_4NOH$

While a strong acid or strong base is necessarily a strong electrolyte, there are many strong electrolytes which are not strongly acidic or basic. These are the materials frequently referred to as salts. The word salt is one most easily understood within the context of the Arrhenius approach, where an acid reacts with a base to give a salt. Three examples follow.

$$HCl + KOH \rightarrow KCl + H_2O$$

$$CH_3COOH + KOH \rightarrow CH_3COOK + H_2O$$

$$HCl + NH_3 \rightarrow NH_4Cl$$

KCl, CH_3COOK and NH_4Cl are all salts and salts, with few exceptions, are strong electrolytes. Exceptions are the cadmium halides; $CdCl_2$, $CdBr_2$ and CdI_2, and the mercury (II) halides; $HgCl_2$, $HgBr_2$ and HgI_2, all of which are weak electrolytes.

20-2 BRØNSTED/LOWRY CONCEPTS APPLIED TO AQUEOUS SOLUTIONS

The basis of the Brønsted/Lowry concept is that an acid is a substance which donates a proton and a base is a substance which accepts a proton. Water is by far the most important medium in which acid/base reactions are studied and so it is important to see how the Brønsted/Lowry approach applies to aqueous solutions.

Water is itself capable both of donating and of accepting a proton. Thus it may act as an acid or as a base. In the presence of an acid stronger than itself, it will act as a base and accept a proton from that acid.

$$HCl(aq) + H_2O \rightarrow H_3O^+ + Cl^-(aq)$$

$$CH_3COOH(aq) + H_2O \rightleftharpoons H_3O^+ + CH_3COO^-(aq)$$

For a strong acid, like HCl, the reaction proceeds almost completely to the right and the equilibrium constant is very large. For a weak acid like CH_3COOH, most of the acid stays in the undissociated form, CH_3COOH, and only a little exists as H_3O^+ and CH_3COO^-. The equilibrium constant for the reaction is small.

Similarly, water acts as an acid in the presence of a base stronger than itself.

$$NH_3(aq) + H_2O \rightleftharpoons NH_4^+(aq) + OH^-(aq)$$

$$F^-(aq) + H_2O \rightleftharpoons HF(aq) + OH^-(aq)$$

These weak bases conform directly to the Brønsted view of bases. They are *weak* bases because the equilibrium constants for the processes above are small and hence the amount of OH^- produced is small. Strong bases, in analogy with strong acids, have large equilibrium constants.

Even in the absence of a solute, of course, water retains the ability to donate and accept protons, and so the following process occurs in water.

$$2 H_2O \rightleftharpoons H_3O^+ + OH^-(aq)$$

Even the purest water is slightly conducting due to this small amount of ionization. At 25°C, the equilibrium concentration of H_3O^+ (and of OH^-) is about 1×10^{-7} mol L^{-1} in pure water. Water is by far the most common solvent in acid/base chemistry but it should be noted in passing that there are other solvents capable of both donating and accepting protons, and they too exhibit self-ionization, as with methanol below.

$$2 \, CH_3OH \rightarrow CH_3OH_2^+ + CH_3O^-$$

20-3   THE ACID IONIZATION CONSTANT K_a

The ionization of any acid is an equilibrium. For strong acids the ionization is almost complete, corresponding to a very large equilibrium constant, and for weak acids there is very little ionization, corresponding to a very small equilibrium constant. It is convenient in our discussion to talk about a fictitious acid having the formula HA, which ionizes as shown:

$$HA + H_2O \rightleftharpoons H_3O^+ + A^-$$

HA may represent such species as acetic acid CH_3COOH in which case A^- represents the acetate ion CH_3COO^-, or hydrochloric acid HCl with A^- being the chloride ion, or ammonium ion NH_4^+ with A^- being the ammonia molecule NH_3.

The equilibrium constant for the above equilibrium can be written in terms of relative activities of the four species present:

$$K_a = \frac{a_{H_3O^+} \, a_{A^-}}{a_{HA} \, a_{H_2O}}$$

This expression is simplified for practical use by making approximations similar to those made for the solubility product. First, in dilute solutions, water is by far the most abundant species, and its relative activity is almost the same as in pure water, namely unity. Notice that this assigns a different standard state to the solvent (pure material) than is assigned to each of the solutes (one molal solution). Hence one gets

$$a_{H_2O} = 1$$

and can ignore the solvent water in all that follows. Secondly, the relative activities of the solute species are assumed to be equal to the ratio of concentration to a standard state concentration:

$$a_{HA} \approx c_{HA}/c^\circ = [HA]_r$$

$$a_{H_3O^+} \approx c_{H_3O^+}/c^\circ = [H_3O^+]_r$$

$$a_{A^-} \approx c_{A^-}/c^\circ = [A^-]_r$$

Hence

$$K_a = \frac{[H_3O^+]_r [A^-]_r}{[HA]_r}$$

Numerical values of K_a are often very small numbers, and it is convenient to take the logarithm of K_a (to base 10) with sign changed as a measure of K_a. This quantity is denoted pK_a and is definitely

$$pK_a \equiv - \log K_a$$

Notice that relative activities, and K_a, are dimensionless.

TABLE 20-1 Ionization Constants for Weak Acids and Bases

Acid	K_a	pK_a	Base	K_b	pK_b
oxalic $(COOH)_2$	5.4×10^{-2}	1.3	binoxalate ion $COOHCOO^-$	1.9×10^{-13}	12.7
sulphurous H_2SO_3	1.7×10^{-2}	1.8	bisulphite ion HSO_3^-	5.9×10^{-13}	12.2
phosphoric H_3PO_4	7.1×10^{-3}	2.1	dihydrogen phosphate $H_2PO_4^-$	1.4×10^{-12}	11.9
hydrofluoric HF	6.7×10^{-4}	3.2	fluoride ion F^-	1.5×10^{-11}	11.8
nitrous HNO_2	5.1×10^{-4}	3.3	nitrite ion NO_2^-	2.0×10^{-11}	10.7
formic HCOOH	2.1×10^{-4}	3.7	formate ion $HCOO^-$	4.8×10^{-11}	10.3
binoxalate ion $COOHCOO^-$	5.4×10^{-5}	4.3	oxalate ion $(COO^-)_2$	1.9×10^{-10}	9.7
$C_6H_5NH_3^+$	2.5×10^{-5}	4.6	aniline $C_6H_5NH_2$	4.0×10^{-10}	9.4
acetic CH_3COOH	1.8×10^{-5}	4.7	acetate ion CH_3COO^-	5.6×10^{-10}	9.3
carbonic H_2CO_3	4.4×10^{-7}	6.4	bicarbonate ion HCO_3^-	2.3×10^{-8}	7.6
hydrosulphuric H_2S	1.1×10^{-7}	7.0	bisulphide ion HS^-	9.1×10^{-8}	7.0
dihydrogen phosphate $H_2PO_4^-$	6.3×10^{-8}	7.2	monohydrogen phosphate HPO_4^{2-}	1.6×10^{-7}	6.8
bisulphite ion HSO_3^-	6.2×10^{-8}	7.2	sulphite ion SO_3^{2-}	1.6×10^{-7}	6.8
ammonium ion NH_4^+	5.6×10^{-10}	9.3	ammonia NH_3	1.8×10^{-5}	4.7
hydrocyanic HCN	4.0×10^{-10}	9.4	cyanide ion CN^-	2.5×10^{-5}	4.6
bicarbonate ion HCO_3^-	4.7×10^{-11}	10.3	carbonate ion CO_3^{2-}	2.1×10^{-4}	3.7
monohydrogen phosphate HPO_4^{2-}	4.4×10^{-13}	12.4	phosphate ion PO_4^{3-}	2.2×10^{-2}	1.7
bisulphide ion HS^-	1.0×10^{-14}	14.0	sulphide ion S^{2-}	1.0	0.0

Table 20-1 lists K_a values for some common acids. The ionization of water itself is a special case. For the equilibrium

$$2\,H_2O \rightleftarrows H_3O^+ + OH^-$$

the equilibrium constant is given the special symbol K_w. Using the above approximations, this reduces to

$$K_w \approx [H_3O^+]_r[OH^-]_r$$

Although K_w varies somewhat with temperature, it is close to 10^{-14} at temperatures at which solutions are ordinarily handled, and it is usual to assume

$$K_w = 10^{-14} \text{ or } pK_w = 14.$$

Note however, that the value is temperature dependent.

20-4 THE pH OF SOLUTIONS

In pure water, the only source of ions is the water itself, and from the stoichiometry of the ionization, the concentrations of the hydrogen ions and hydroxide ions are equal:

$$[H_3O^+]_r = [OH^-]_r$$

Hence

$$K_w = [H_3O^+]_r{}^2 = 10^{-14},$$

so

$$[H_3O^+]_r = 10^{-7}.$$

The hydrogen ion and hydroxide ion concentrations in pure water are therefore 10^{-7} mol L^{-1}. If some acid is added to the water, the hydrogen ion concentration is increased; if some base is added, the hydroxide ion concentration is increased. In either case, the product of the two concentrations must remain constant, since the ions must remain in equilibrium with the water:

$$[H_3O^+]_r[OH^-]_r = K_w = 10^{-14}$$

The state of a solution with respect to acidity or basicity is commonly judged by measuring the hydrogen ion concentration. This is usually expressed as the negative logarithm of $[H_3O^+]_r$ denoted as pH and defined by

$$pH \equiv -\log a_{H^+} \approx -\log [H^+]_r$$

Sometimes the quantity pOH is used as well:

$$pOH \equiv -\log a_{OH^-} \approx -\log [OH^-]_r$$

From these definitions, it follows that

$$pH + pOH = pK_w = 14$$

In a neutral solution pH = pOH = 7. In an acidic solution the pH is less than 7, and in a basic solution the pH is greater than 7. Table 20-2 summarizes these relationships.

TABLE 20-2 [H⁺], pH and [OH⁻], pOH for Aqueous Solutions at Room Temperature

[H⁺]	pH	[OH⁻]	pOH	
10^{+1}	-1	10^{-15}	15	↑
10^{-1}	1	10^{-13}	13	
10^{-3}	3	10^{-11}	11	acidic
10^{-5}	5	10^{-9}	9	↓
10^{-7}	7	10^{-7}	7	neutral
10^{-9}	9	10^{-5}	5	↑
10^{-11}	11	10^{-3}	3	alkaline
10^{-13}	13	10^{-1}	1	
10^{-15}	15	10^{+1}	-1	↓

The pH scale is a very useful one, for it can be measured by a direct-reading instrument called a pH meter; a suitable pair of electrodes is immersed in the solution to be measured, and the voltage developed electrochemically is measured with a voltmeter. Indicators can also be used to judge the pH of a solution through their colour; indicators are particularly useful for judging the endpoints of titrations.

It should be noted that the pH does not measure the total concentration of acid or base in the solution, but rather the concentration of hydrogen ions, resulting from proton transfer to or from the solvent water molecules. At equal *formal* concentrations a strong acid produces a solution of lower pH than a weak acid, because more hydrogen ions are produced by the stronger acid. The total concentration of acid in a solution can be measured by titration with a suitable base, and vice-versa.

20-5 THE BASE IONIZATION CONSTANT K_b

The ionization reaction for a weak base, B, such as ammonia, NH_3, can be represented by the reaction

$$B(aq) + H_2O \rightleftarrows BH^+(aq) + OH^-(aq)$$

This reaction shows that the hydroxide ion concentration in the solution is increased due to the transfer of protons from the water to the base. The equilibrium constant for this reaction is written, within our approximations,

$$K_b = \frac{[BH^+]_r[OH^-]_r}{[B]_r}$$

For instance, for ammonia,

$$NH_3 + H_2O \rightleftarrows NH_4^+ + OH^-$$

$$K_b = \frac{[NH_4^+]_r[OH^-]_r}{[NH_3]_r}$$

20-6   CONJUGATE ACIDS AND BASES

It is inherent in the Brønsted/Lowry approach that an acid reacts with water to give a basic species which can accept a proton to reform the original acid.

$$NH_4^+ + H_2O \rightleftarrows H_3O^+ + NH_3$$
acid   base   acid   *base*

$$NH_3 + H_2O \rightleftarrows NH_4^+ + OH^-$$
base   acid   *acid*   base

NH_4^+ and NH_3 are a *conjugate acid/base pair*, each immediately producing the other when placed in water. Similarly, the fluoride ion F^- is the *conjugate base* to the acid HF and HF is the *conjugate acid* to the base F^-.

Returning to ammonia, we see that

$$K_a = \frac{[NH_3]_r[H_3O^+]_r}{[NH_4^+]_r}$$

$$K_b = \frac{[NH_4^+]_r[OH^-]_r}{[NH_3]_r}$$

$$K_aK_b = [H_3O^+]_r[OH^-]_r = K_w$$

This is not just a useful arithmetic relationship. It contains a most useful and important point. One cannot have an acid or a base in water without producing its conjugate. Both will always be present. Hence K_a and K_b contain the same piece of information, the *ratio* of the concentrations of the two conjugates at equilibrium. Thus the values of K_a and K_b are not independent.

From the relation $K_aK_b = K_w$, it may be seen that the stronger an acid is, the weaker is its conjugate base, and vice-versa. Thus hydrochloric acid is a very strong acid, so the chloride ion is a very weak base.

Because of the close relationship between K_a and K_b for conjugate acids and bases, only one of the two need be quoted in a tabulation of data, and some workers prefer to use only one of the constants (usually K_a) in working out acid-base problems for any given system.

20-7   CALCULATIONS: THE INTUITIVE APPROACH

The usual problem in acid/base chemistry is calculation of the concentration of some species from a knowledge of the amounts of material originally mixed. These amounts are most readily expressed as formal concentrations. Thus when we say that we have one litre of .027 *F* HCl in water, we mean that we have a litre of a solution which could be reproduced by mixing .027 mole of HCl with the appropriate amount of water to make one litre. What we usually want to know is the *actual* concentrations of HCl, H_3O^+, Cl^- and OH^- at equilibrium.

While such a calculation is trivial in this example, it can be very complex in others. The principles are simple but the arithmetic is not. While the modern chemist increasingly uses computers for the more complex cases, one nevertheless has to calculate many by hand. The essential feature of all solution methods is simplification of the arithmetic by making a reasonable approximation. There is a range of approaches to doing this, which might be represented best by the two extremes, which we shall call throughout this chapter the *intuitive* approach and the *systematic* approach.

The intuitive approach is used by most chemists in all but complex problems because it is shorter and simpler than the systematic approach. On the other hand, the systematic approach has the advantage that all assumptions and approximations are explicit and thus are subject to checking. Users of the intuitive approach must keep in mind the kinds of conditions under which their intuition will possibly fail them.

In this chapter, the intuitive approach is used in all but a few examples. Those who wish to see the systematic approach applied to the entire range of problems are referred to the excellent book "Solubility and pH Calculations" listed at the end of the chapter.

20-8 CALCULATIONS FOR STRONG ACIDS AND BASES

Example 20-1 (Solution of a Strong Acid)
Calculate the pH of a 0.027 F solution of HCl at 25°C.

Intuitive Approach

$$HCl + H_2O \rightarrow H_3O^+ + Cl^-$$

Since ionization is complete, $[H_3O^+]_r = 0.027$, and

$$pH = (-\log 0.027) = 1.6$$

Notice that the concentration of OH^- is very small, about 10^{-12} mol L^{-1}. The addition of a strong acid to water reduces the self-ionization of the water to a negligible amount.

Notice that the quantities $[H_3O^+]_r$, $[OH^-]_r$, $[Cl^-]_r$ and the like are approximations for *relative* activities, and are dimensionless. Since the reference state in the denominator is 1.00 mol L^{-1}, these quantities are numerically equal to the concentrations of the species. Throughout this chapter, this numerical identity of two closely related but distinguishable quantities will be used so often that the reader may come to think of quantities in square brackets as being concentrations. There is no great harm in this but the distinction should be remembered when it is needed.

Example 20-2 (Solution of a Strong Base)
Calculate the pH of a 0.042 F solution of NaOH at 25°C.

Intuitive Approach

$$NaOH \rightarrow Na^+ + OH^-$$

Since ionization is complete, $[OH^-]_r = 0.042$, and so

$$pOH = -\log 0.042 = 1.4$$

and

$$pH = 14 - 1.4 = 12.6$$

Notice that in the presence of a strong base, it is implicitly assumed that the contribution to OH^- from self-ionization of water is negligible. Techniques of calculation applicable where this is not valid are described in Section 20-14.

20-9   CALCULATIONS FOR WEAK ACIDS

Weak acids are those for which ionization is incomplete and some significant amount of undissociated acid remains at equilibrium. The concentrations of reactants and products at equilibrium can be calculated using the equilibrium constant just as was done with gas phase equilibria in Chapter 15 and solubility equilibria in Chapter 19.

Consider the general equation

$$HA + H_2O \rightleftharpoons H_3O^+ + A^-$$

and let f be the formal concentration of acid in the solution and x be the equilibrium concentration of H_3O^+. Assuming as in the previous section that no significant part of the H_3O^+ arises from the self-ionization of water, the concentration of the three solute species at equilibrium can be written in terms of a single variable as follows.

$$\underset{f-x}{HA} + H_2O \rightleftharpoons \underset{x}{H_3O^+} + \underset{x}{A^-}$$

The notation of writing the symbol for the concentration of a species below the corresponding symbol in the equation will be used throughout this chapter.

For this process, the equilibrium expression can now be written as

$$K_a = \frac{x^2}{f-x}$$

which is a quadratic equation which can be solved for x either by the usual formula or by the iterative method demonstrated in the last chapter. For if $f \gg x$, then

$$x^2 \approx K_a f,$$

$$x \approx \sqrt{K_a f}$$

Example 20-3   (Solution of a Weak Acid)
Calculate the pH of a 0.078 F solution of acetic acid, CH_3COOH at 25°C.

Intuitive Approach

$$\underset{0.078-x}{CH_3COOH} + H_2O \rightleftharpoons \underset{x}{H_3O^+} + \underset{x}{CH_3COO^-}$$

$$K_a = \frac{x^2}{0.078-x} = 1.8 \times 10^{-5}$$

$$x^2 + (1.8 \times 10^{-5})x - 1.40 \times 10^{-6} = 0$$

Solving the quadratic equation gives

$$x = \frac{-1.8\times10^{-5} \pm [(1.8\times10^{-5})^2 - 4(-1.40\times10^{-6})]^{\frac{1}{2}}}{2}$$

Only the positive answer has physical meaning, so

$$x = 1.2\times10^{-3}$$

$$pH = -\log 1.2\times10^{-3} = 2.9$$

Example 20-4 (Solution of a Weak Acid which is a Salt)
Calculate the pH of a 0.050 F solution of ammonium chloride at 25°C.

Intuitive Approach
Salts are materials which can be formed by reacting an acid with a base. NH_3 and HCl react to give NH_4Cl. The ammonium ion is the conjugate acid to a weak base, ammonia, and so is acidic in character, with a $K_a = 5.6\times10^{-10}$ (Table 20-1). However, Cl^- is an *extremely* weak base since the conjugate is HCl, and no appreciable amount of Cl^- will accept protons. Thus ammonium chloride is acidic.

$$NH_4^+ + H_2O \rightleftharpoons H_3O^+ + NH_3$$
$$0.050-x \qquad\qquad x \qquad x$$

$$K_a = \frac{x^2}{0.050-x} = 5.6 \times 10^{-10}$$

$$x^2 + (5.6 \times 10^{-10})x - (2.8 \times 10^{-11}) = 0$$

$$x = \frac{-5.6 \times 10^{-10} \pm [(5.6 \times 10^{-10})^2 - 4(-2.8 \times 10^{-11})]^{1/2}}{2}$$

$$= 5.3 \times 10^{-6}$$

$$pH = 5.3$$

In this as in many other such problems, the alert chemist may spot ways of shortening the calculation. Here, for example, the small K_a suggests that only a small part of the NH_4^+ goes to H_3O^+. Thus

$$x \ll 0.050$$

and the equilibrium expression reduces to

$$x^2 \approx (5.6 \times 10^{-10})(0.050)$$

$$x \approx 5.3 \times 10^{-6}$$

Whenever an approximation is made always check to see that the final answer, as here, is consistent with the assumption.

Example 20-5 Calculate the pH and the concentration of HNO_2 in a 1.5×10^{-4} F solution of HNO_2 at 25°C.

Intuitive Approach

$$HNO_2 + H_2O \rightleftharpoons H_3O^+ + NO_2^-$$

$$1.5\times10^{-4}-x \qquad\qquad x \qquad x$$

$$K_a = \frac{x^2}{1.5\times10^{-4} - x} = 5.1 \times 10^{-4}$$

$$x^2 + 5.1\times10^{-4}\,x - 7.6\times10^{-8} = 0$$

The positive root is

$$x = 1.21\times10^{-4}$$

$$pH = -\log(1.21\times10^{-4}) = 3.9$$

Finally, the concentration of acid not ionized is

$$[HNO_2]_r = 1.5\times10^{-4} - 1.21\times10^{-4} = 2.9\times10^{-5}$$

$$[HNO_2] = 2.9\times10^{-5}\ mol\ L^{-1}$$

Calculations in this section follow almost exactly the procedures for weak acids and can be followed best by examples.

Example 20-6   (Solution of a Weak Base)

Calculate the pH and $[NH_3]$ for a $0.200\ F\ NH_3$ solution at 25°C.

Intuitive Approach

$$NH_3 + H_2O \rightleftharpoons NH_4^+ + OH^-$$

$$0.200-y \qquad\qquad y \qquad y$$

$$K_b = \frac{y^2}{0.200-y} = 1.8\times10^{-5}$$

$$y^2 + 1.8\times10^{-5}\,y - 3.6\times10^{-6} = 0$$

$$y = 1.9 \times 10^{-3}$$

$$pOH = -\log(1.9\times10^{-3}) = 2.7$$

and

$$pH = 14.0 - 2.7 = 11.3$$

The ammonia concentration is

$$[NH_3]_r = 0.200 - 1.9\times10^{-3} = 0.198$$

$$[NH_3] = 0.198\ mol\ L^{-1}$$

Hence almost none of the ammonia in solution is ionized. Such an ammonia solution is a common laboratory reagent, and is often stored in bottles labelled

"NH$_4$OH." The calculation in this example shows that such labelling is misleading. Aside from the small concentrations of NH$_4^+$ and OH$^-$ ions in such a solution, the material exists as NH$_3$.

Example 20-7 (Solution of a Weak Base which is a Salt)
Calculate the pH of a 0.17 F solution of sodium acetate at 25°C.

Intuitive Approach

Sodium acetate is a salt, but the acetate ion is the conjugate base of a weak acid, acetic acid, and so a solution of sodium acetate is expected to be basic, with a pH greater than 7. The hydrolysis of the acetate ion is described by the equation

$$CH_3COO^- + H_2O \rightleftarrows CH_3COOH + OH^-$$
$$0.17{-}y \qquad\qquad\qquad y \qquad\quad y$$

$$K_b = \frac{y^2}{0.17-y} = 5.6\times10^{-10}$$

$$y^2 + (5.6 \times 10^{-10})y - (9.5 \times 10^{-11}) = 0$$

$$y = 9.7 \times 10^{-6}$$

$$pOH = 5.0$$

$$pH = 14.0 - 5.0 = 9.0$$

20-11 BUFFER SOLUTIONS

A solution containing both an acid and its conjugate base has the interesting property that the pH is almost unaffected by the addition of another acid, or a base, or solvent. Such a solution is called a *buffer solution*. Buffer solutions are important in biological systems, and in some industries, where processes would be interrupted by large changes in pH.

A buffer solution contains roughly equal formal concentrations of a weak acid and its conjugate base. Let f_a and f_b be the *formal* concentrations of the acid and of the base respectively. At equilibrium the concentration of non-ionized acid, [HA], is almost exactly equal to f_a, and the concentration of unhydrolyzed anion from the salt, [A$^-$], is numerically almost exactly equal to f_b. This may be seen by the following argument. Consider the ionization process for the acid.

$$HA + H_2O \rightleftarrows H_3O^+ + A^-$$

Recalling that the acid is weak, the extent of dissociation of the acid in water solution is small, and the presence of the anion A$^-$ from the base will make the extent of dissociation smaller still by the "common ion effect."

Similarly the anion A$^-$ is a weak base, and the slight extent of hydrolysis of this weak base is reduced by addition of the HA. Writing the expression for the equilibrium constant,

$$K_a = \frac{[H_3O^+]_r[A^-]_r}{[HA]_r} \approx \frac{[H_3O^+]f_b}{f_a}$$

Hence

$$[H_3O^+]_r \approx K_a \cdot \frac{f_a}{f_b}$$

Notice that larger values of K_a and of f_a increase $[H_3O^+]$ while a larger value of f_b decreases it, all of which is as one would expect. Another form of the above expression is

$$pH \approx pK_a - \log(f_a/f_b)$$

Example 20-8   Calculate the pH of a buffer solution containing 0.20 F acetic acid and 0.25 F sodium acetate at 25°C. K_a is 1.8×10^{-5}.

$$f_a = 0.20 \text{ mol L}^{-1}$$
$$f_b = 0.25 \text{ mol L}^{-1}$$
$$[H_3O^+]_r = (1.8 \times 10^{-5})(0.20/0.25)$$
$$= 1.4 \times 10^{-5}$$
$$pH = 4.8$$

Example 20-9   Calculate the pH of a buffer containing 0.42 F NH_3 and 0.17 F NH_4Cl.
   Since $f_b = 0.42$ mol L^{-1} and $f_a = 0.17$ mol L^{-1}

$$[OH^-] = 1.8 \times 10^{-5} \times (0.42/0.17)$$
$$= 4.4 \times 10^{-5} \text{ mol L}^{-1}$$
$$pOH = 4.4, \text{ so } pH = 14 - 4.4 = 9.6$$

The remarkable property of *buffering* the pH of a solution against additions of solvent, acid or base is shown by considering two solutions, each having a pH of 4.8:
   Solution A: 1.4×10^{-5} F HCl solution
   Solution B: the buffer solution of Example 20-8.
   Suppose 200 mL of water is added to 100 mL of each solution. The concentration of H_3O^+ in Solution A is reduced to a third of its original value, and so the pH increases by log 3 = 0.5 units, from 4.8 to 5.3. The pH of the buffer Solution B is entirely *unaffected* since both acid and salt are diluted equally and so the ratio f_a/f_b is not changed.

Suppose that 10.0 mL of 0.1 F HCl were added to 100 mL of each solution. The concentration of H_3O^+ in Solution A would then be

$$[H_3O^+] = (0.001 + 1.4 \times 10^{-6}) \text{ mol}/0.110 \text{ L}$$

$$\approx 0.009 \text{ mol L}^{-1}$$

and the pH is 2.0. The total pH change is 2.8 units. For Solution B, the addition of HCl converts some of the acetate ion into acetic acid, by the reaction

$$HCl + CH_3COO^- \rightarrow CH_3COOH + Cl^-$$

and so the concentration of acid in the buffer is increased and the concentration of base is decreased. After the addition,

$$[H_3O^+]_r = 1.8 \times 10^{-5} \times (0.020 + 0.001)/(0.025 - 0.001)$$

$$= 1.6 \times 10^{-5}$$

$$pH = 4.8$$

To two-figure accuracy, the pH of the buffer solution is unchanged. Notice that the calculation need only use the amounts (number of moles) of acid and base in the solution, and does not depend directly on the final volume of the solution.

Suppose now that 10.0 mL of 0.1 F NaOH is added to 100.0 mL of each solution. In Solution A this is an excess of base, which reacts with all of the HCl in solution, and so after the addition,

$$[OH^-] = (0.001 - 1.4 \times 10^{-6}) \text{ mol}/0.110 \text{ L}$$

$$= 0.009 \text{ mol L}^{-1}$$

$$pOH = 2.0 \text{ and pH} = 12.0$$

The total pH change is 7.2 units.

For Solution B, addition of NaOH converts some of the acetic acid into acetate ion, by the reaction

$$CH_3COOH + NaOH \rightarrow Na^+ + CH_3COO^- + H_2O$$

and so the concentration of acid in the buffer is decreased and the concentration of salt is increased:

$$[H_3O^+] = 1.8 \times 10^{-5} \times (0.020 - 0.001)/(0.025 + 0.001)$$

$$= 1.3 \times 10^{-5} \text{ mol L}^{-1}$$

$$pH = 4.9$$

Again, the pH of the buffer solution is virtually unchanged.

Buffer solutions are effective when the ratio f_a/f_b is roughly between 1/10 and 10, and so the pH lies between $pK_a + 1$ and $pK_a - 1$. The selection of the appropriate acid/conjugate base to be used depends upon the pH which is required in the buffer solution. Chemical supply companies sell certified buffer solutions covering the range 1.0 to 11.0 as standard items for analytical or biological work. For less precise work, buffer solutions are readily made from a suitable acid and salt (or base).

20-12   A MIXTURE OF AN ACID AND A BASE

There are many situations in which one wishes to calculate the pH of a system in which an acid has been mixed with a base. Four possibilities exist; strong acid plus strong base, strong acid plus weak base, weak acid plus strong base and weak acid plus weak base. In each of these one may have either component in excess or one may have equal amounts of the two.

The case of weak acid plus weak base will not be dealt with in this book, except for the very special case of the buffer solution already discussed. All of the other possibilities listed above can, however, be handled simply using the techniques already learned. In doing so it is usually useful to adopt a method which might be called the technique of equivalent systems.

In this technique, one treats the system as if the component present in smaller amount had been totally neutralized by the other component. This state is not the equilibrium state, but it is one from which the equilibrium state is invariably easier to calculate. Consider the following examples.

Example 20-10   Calculate the pH of a solution made from 35.0 mL of 0.15 F NaOH and 25.0 mL of 0.15 F HCl.

Formally, one has 5.25×10^{-3} mol of NaOH and 3.75×10^{-3} mol of HCl. Applying the technique, total neutralization would produce 3.75×10^{-3} mol of NaCl, 1.50×10^{-3} mol of excess NaOH and 3.75×10^{-3} mol of H_2O, the last negligible with respect to the water already present. It is important to realize that the system being considered is identical to one in which we start with 3.75×10^{-3} mol of NaCl and 1.50×10^{-3} mol of NaOH in 60.0 mL of water. Both will go to the same state of equilibrium, but in this latter case it is rather easier to see where that equilibrium lies. The NaCl will remain as $Na^+(aq)$ and $Cl^-(aq)$ and will not affect the acidity. Therefore the pH is determined solely by the concentration of NaOH.

$$[OH^-]_r = 1.50 \times 10^{-3}/0.060 = 2.50 \times 10^{-2}$$

$$[H^+]_r = 10^{-14}/2.50 \times 10^{-2} = 4.0 \times 10^{-13}$$

$$pH = 12.4$$

Example 20-11   Calculate the pH of a solution made from 5.0 mL of 0.15 F NaOH and 25.0 mL of 0.15 F CH_3COOH.

Formally, there is 7.5×10^{-4} mol NaOH and 3.75×10^{-3} mol of CH_3COOH in 0.030 L of solution. Consider instead the system obtained by total neutralization of the base, namely 7.5×10^{-4} mol CH_3COONa, 3.00×10^{-3} mol of excess CH_3COOH and 7.5×10^{-4} mol H_2O, the last negligible with respect to the 30 g or approximately 1.6 mol H_2O already present. Now one replaces the question "What is the pH of a solution of 7.5×10^{-4} mol NaOH and 3.75×10^{-3} mol CH_3COOH in 30 mL of water?" with the question "What is the pH of a solution of 7.5×10^{-4} mol CH_3COONa and 3.0×10^{-3} mol of CH_3COOH in 30 mL of water?" It can be seen at once that this is a buffer solution for which

$$[H^+]_r \approx \frac{f_a}{f_b}(K_a) = \frac{3.0 \times 10^{-3}/0.030}{7.5 \times 10^{-4}/0.030} \ (1.8 \times 10^{-5}) = 7.2 \times 10^{-5}$$

$$pH = 4.14$$

Notice that titration of a weak base with a strong acid or of a weak acid with a strong base leads to a buffer solution over a very significant part of the titration, during which the pH will change very little.

Example 20-12 Calculate the pH of a solution made from 30.0 mL of 0.15 F NaOH and 25.0 mL of 0.15 F CH_3COOH.

Rather than considering the 4.50×10^{-3} mol of NaOH and 3.75×10^{-3} mol CH_3COOH in .055 L, consider 3.75×10^{-3} mol of CH_3COONa and 0.75×10^{-3} mol of NaOH in 0.055 L. Sodium acetate will ionize completely to give Na^+ and CH_3COO^-. The Na^+ will remain unchanged in solution, but the acetate ion is a weak base and might be expected to produce a small amount of OH^- according to

$$CH_3COO^- + H_2O \rightarrow OH^- + CH_3COOH$$

However the contribution of the weak base to $[OH^-]$ would be small compared to that from the strong base NaOH even if they were in separate solutions, and since they are in the same solution, the presence of a large OH^- concentration from the NaOH will suppress the process above even further. Thus in such cases the pH is determined entirely by the strong base.

$$[OH^-]_r = 0.75 \times 10^{-3}/0.055 = 1.36 \times 10^{-2}$$

$$[H^+]_r = 7.3 \times 10^{-13}$$

$$pH = 12.1$$

The nine situations of interest are illustrated in Table 20-3 by particular examples. It will be seen that the technique of equivalent systems reduces each of them to one of the relatively simple cases examined earlier in the chapter.

20-13 ACID-BASE TITRATIONS AND INDICATORS

Acid-base titrations are among the most important basic chemical measurements. The essence of a titration is that the concentration of a solution of acid (or base) is measured by allowing it to react with a solution of base (or acid) of *known* concentration; the volume of one of the solutions is fixed, usually at 10.0 or 25.0 mL using a pipette, and the other solution is added using a burette which allows the volume to be measured accurately. The titration is stopped at an *endpoint* which is determined using an *indicator*. The endpoint is reached

TABLE 20-3

(a) Strong Acid plus Strong Base

Case	Example	Equivalent System	Analysis
acid in excess	7.0×10^{-3} mol HCl 3.0×10^{-3} mol NaOH 50 mL	3.0×10^{-3} mol NaCl 3.0×10^{-3} mol H_2O 4.0×10^{-3} mol HCl 50 mL	essentially just a strong acid $[H^+]_r = \dfrac{4.0 \times 10^{-3}}{.050}$
equal amounts	7.0×10^{-3} mol HCl 7.0×10^{-3} mol NaOH 50 mL	7.0×10^{-3} mol NaCl 7.0×10^{-3} mol H_2O 50 mL	neutral pH = 7
base in excess	3.0×10^{-3} mol HCl 7.0×10^{-3} mol NaOH 50 mL	3.0×10^{-3} mol NaCl 3.0×10^{-3} mol H_2O 4.0×10^{-3} mol NaOH 50 mL	essentially just a strong base $[OH^-]_r = \dfrac{4.0 \times 10^{-3}}{.050}$

(b) Strong Acid plus Weak Base

Case	Example	Equivalent System	Analysis
acid in excess	7.0×10^{-3} mol HCl 3.0×10^{-3} mol NaAc 50 mL	3.0×10^{-3} mol NaCl 3.0×10^{-3} mol HAc 4.0×10^{-3} mol HCl 50 mL	weak acid negligible compared to strong $[H^+]_r = \dfrac{4.0 \times 10^{-3}}{.050}$
equal amounts	7.0×10^{-3} mol HCl 7.0×10^{-3} mol NaAc 50 mL	7.0×10^{-3} mol NaCl 7.0×10^{-3} mol HAc 50 mL	essentially just a weak acid $K_a = \dfrac{(x)(x)}{\dfrac{7.0 \times 10^{-3}}{.050} - x}$
base in excess	3.0×10^{-3} mol HCl 7.0×10^{-3} mol NaAc 50 mL	3.0×10^{-3} mol HAc 3.0×10^{-3} mol NaCl 4.0×10^{-3} mol NaAc 50 mL	buffer solution $[H^+]_r = \dfrac{3.0 \times 10^{-3}/.050}{4.0 \times 10^{-3}/.050} K_a$

(c) Strong Base plus Weak Acid

Case	Example	Equivalent System	Analysis
acid in excess	7.0×10^{-3} mol HAc 3.0×10^{-3} mol NaOH 50 mL	3.0×10^{-3} mol NaAc 3.0×10^{-3} mol H_2O 4.0×10^{-3} mol HAc 50 mL	buffer solution $[H^+]_r = \dfrac{4.0 \times 10^{-3}/.050}{3.0 \times 10^{-3}/.050} K_a$
equal amounts	7.0×10^{-3} mol HAc 7.0×10^{-3} mol NaOH 50 mL	7.0×10^{-3} mol NaAc 7.0×10^{-3} mol H_2O 50 mL	essentially just a weak base $K_b = \dfrac{(x)(x)}{\dfrac{7.0 \times 10^{-3}}{.050} - x}$
base in excess	3.0×10^{-3} mol HAc 7.0×10^{-3} mol NaOH 50 mL	3.0×10^{-3} mol NaAc 3.0×10^{-3} mol H_2O 4.0×10^{-3} mol NaOH 50 mL	weak base negligible compared to strong $[OH^-]_r = \dfrac{4.0 \times 10^{-3}}{.050}$

when a donatable proton is present for every proton acceptor. Notice that at the endpoint, the mixture of solutions is not necessarily neutral, i.e. the pH is not necessarily 7.

The progress of a titration can be followed by calculating the pH of the mixture of the two solutions at various stages. Two separate types of problem will be treated, one where a strong acid is titrated with a strong base and the other where a weak acid is titrated with a strong base.

Taking the strong acid/strong base first, consider taking 25.0 mL of 0.15 F solution of HCl, and adding 0.15 F NaOH from a burette. There are four clearly defined stages in the titration:

(a) Before any NaOH is added, the solution contains only HCl.

(b) If less than 25.0 mL of NaOH is added, the solution contains NaCl and the excess HCl which remains unreacted.

(c) If exactly 25.0 mL of NaOH is added, the resulting solution is a solution of NaCl.

(d) If more than 25.0 mL of NaOH solution is added, the resulting solution contains NaCl and an excess of NaOH.

It can be seen that the pH can be calculated for any amount of added NaOH using the techniques described in the previous section, and particularly those summarized in Table 20-3(a). The results of a number of calculations are plotted in graphical form in Figure 20-1.

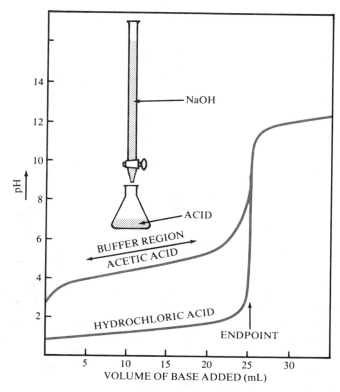

Figure 20-1   Titration of 25.0 ml of 0.15F acids with 0.15F NaOH.

The titration of a weak acid by a strong base can also be analyzed by dividing the titration into four stages and applying the techniques of the previous section. The stages are as follows.

(a) Before any base is added, the case is simply that of a weak acid.

(b) At the intermediate stages of the titration, the case is that of a buffer solution, as may be seen by considering Table 20-3(b). At the exact midpoint of the titration, the pH is equal to pK_a for the acid.

(c) At the endpoint, only the salt is present and the calculation is essentially that of a weak base.

(d) Beyond the endpoint, the excess strong base determines the pH, almost as if no other reagent were present.

These data too are portrayed in Figure 20-1. Notice that beyond the endpoint, the pH curve is essentially the same for the titration of both strong and weak acids by a strong base. A selection of calculated data for these two titrations is presented in Table 20-4 and Table 20-5. Students are urged to be certain that they could calculate any of these pH values.

TABLE 20-4   Titration of 25.0 mL 0.15 F HCl with 0.15 F NaOH

Volume of base added	$[H_3O^+]_r$	$[OH^-]_r$	pH
0.0 mL	0.15	—	0.82
5.0 mL	0.10	—	1.00
20.0 mL	0.0167	—	1.78
24.9 mL	0.000301	—	3.52
25.0 mL	10^{-7}	10^{-7}	7.00
25.1 mL	—	0.000299	10.48
35.0 mL	—	0.025	12.39

TABLE 20-5   Titration of 25.0 mL 0.15 F CH_3COOH with 0.15 F NaOH

Volume of base added	$[H_3O^+]_r$	$[OH^-]_r$	pH
0.0 mL	1.6×10^{-3}	—	2.79
5.0 mL	7.2×10^{-5}	—	4.14
12.5 mL	1.8×10^{-5}	—	4.74
20.0 mL	4.5×10^{-6}	—	5.35
25.0 mL	—	6.4×10^{-6}	8.81

Comparing the two curves in Figure 20-1, one sees that the curve for a weak acid lies everywhere at higher pH than the strong acid curve. The buffer region on the weak acid curve is easily recognized as the central region in which pH changes little as base is added. The extent of the change of pH in the vicinity of the endpoint is smaller for weak acids than for strong, and the pH at the endpoint itself is basic for the case of a weak acid with a strong base.

In practice the endpoint is usually detected with an *indicator*, which is a weak acid or base having a markedly different colour from its conjugate. For example methyl orange is an indicator which is red in an acid solution with pH < 3.2 but is yellow in a solution with pH > 4.4. The equilibrium for an indicator can be represented by the following.

$$HIn + H_2O \rightleftarrows H_3O^+ + In^-$$

$$K_{in} = \frac{[H_3O^+]_r[In^-]_r}{[HIn]_r}$$

basic

acidic

Only a very small amount of an indicator is added so that it itself does not affect the pH significantly. The ratio of concentrations of In^- and HIn is therefore determined by the pH of the solution, as shown below.

$$\frac{[In^-]_r}{[HIn]_r} = \frac{K_{in}}{[H_3O^+]_r}$$

or

$$\log([In^-]_r/[HIn]_r) = pH - pK_{in}$$

In a solution in which pH is larger than ($pK_{in} + 1$), the ratio $[In^-]/[HIn]$ will be larger than 10, and the colour of the solution will be that of In^-. If the pH is smaller than ($pK_{in} - 1$), the ratio $[In^-]/[HIn]$ will be smaller than 0.1 and the colour of the solution will be that of the acidic form HIn. Thus the colour of a solution containing an indicator changes over roughly two pH units, centred at pH equal to pK_{in}.

Table 20-6 lists some common indicators, together with the pH range in which the colour change occurs. This list can be used to select an indicator appropriate to the titration. For the titration of a strong acid with a strong base,

TABLE 20-6 Indicators for Acids and Bases

Indicator	Acid Colour	Base Colour	pH Range for Colour Change	K_{in}	pK_{in}
thymol blue	red	yellow	1.2 to 2.8	1.0×10^{-2}	2.0
methyl orange	red	yellow	3.2 to 4.4	1.6×10^{-4}	3.8
bromcresol green	yellow	blue	3.9 to 5.5	2.0×10^{-5}	4.7
methyl red	red	yellow	4.7 to 6.0	4.5×10^{-6}	5.3
litmus	red	blue	5.0 to 8.0	3.2×10^{-7}	6.5
bromthymol blue	yellow	blue	6.1 to 7.6	1.4×10^{-7}	6.9
thymol blue	yellow	blue	8.0 to 9.6	1.6×10^{-9}	8.8
phenolphthalein	colourless	red	8.3 to 10.0	7.1×10^{-10}	9.1
alazarin yellow	yellow	red	10.1 to 12.0	8.9×10^{-12}	11.1

any indicator changing colour between pH values of 4 and 10 would give a sharp endpoint at the correct addition of base. However for the weak acid/strong base titration described, a sharp endpoint at the correct amount of base will be obtained only by using an indicator with a pH range of 8 to 10. Phenolphthalein is a logical choice. When a weak base is being titrated with a strong acid, the pH at the endpoint is in the acidic range, and an indicator such as methyl orange would be suitable.

20-14   CALCULATIONS: THE SYSTEMATIC APPROACH

In introducing the intuitive approach in Section 20-7, mention was made of the systematic approach as an alternative. The systematic approach has two advantages and one major disadvantage. The advantages are that it works in cases where the intuitive approach fails and that because its assumptions are made explicitly rather than implicitly, it is always possible to test their validity. The disadvantage is that it usually involves many more variables and relationships than the intuitive approach, which tends to confuse the chemist. The solution of these is, however, always straightforward however arduous. Since computers are undaunted by arduous straightforward calculations, and since the systematic approach will work in a number of cases where the intuitive approach will not, the systematic approach is the one to use as a basis for creating computer programs to solve acid/base problems.

In the systematic approach, a set of independent equations is created sufficient to solve for all of the unknown concentrations. These equations are usually the charge balance equation (the sum of all of the concentrations of positive charges must equal the sum of all of the concentrations of negative charges), equilibrium expression for all operative equilibria including the self-ionization of water, and as many mass balance statements as are available. This is best seen by example.

Example 20-13   Calculate the pH of a $5.0 \times 10^{-7} F$ solution of HNO_3, using first the intuitive and then the systematic approach.

Intuitive Approach

The unwary might might think that since this is a strong acid, the answer would be that $[H_3O^+]_r$ is 5.0×10^{-7}. This is so close to what one gets for pure water, however, that one must ask if the water makes a significant contribution through

$$2 H_2O \rightleftarrows H_3O^+ + OH^-$$

Let y be the value of $[OH^-]_r$. Because of the stoichiometry of this reaction,

$$[H_3O^+]_r = y + (5 \times 10^{-7})$$

Therefore

$$K_w = 10^{-14} = (y + 5 \times 10^{-7})(y)$$

This gives a quadratic equation $y^2 + 5 \times 10^{-7} y - 10^{-14} = 0$, which has only one positive root, $y = 1.9 \times 10^{-8}$. Hence

$$[OH^-]_r = 1.9 \times 10^{-8}$$

$$pOH = 7.7$$

$$pH = 6.3$$

Notice that had the ionization of the water been ignored in setting up the equation, one would have effectively assumed $y \ll 5 \times 10^{-7}$, so that the solution would have been

$$y = 10^{-14}/5 \times 10^{-7} = 2 \times 10^{-8}$$

which would not have been a very serious error.

This conclusion can be made general: *when the pH is less than 6 or greater than 8, the ionization of the water can be ignored.* The exact limit depends on the accuracy sought and where doubt exists, the systematic approach is worthwhile.

Systematic Approach

The systematic approach involves stating sufficient mathematical relationships to allow solutions to be obtained for all of the variables. In this case, there are three variables and three relationships.

(a) Since nitric acid is a strong acid and ionizes essentially completely, and since there is no other source of nitrate, we can write down a "mass balance" in nitrate ion.

$$[NO_3^-] = 5.0 \times 10^{-7} \text{ mol L}^{-1}$$

(b) Since the solution is uncharged, the sum of all of the positive charges in a litre equals the sum of all of the negative charges.

$$[H_3O^+] = [OH^-] + [NO_3^-]$$

(c) In any aqueous solution at 298 K

$$[H_3O^+]_r[OH^-]_r = 10^{-14}$$

Substituting from (a) and (c) to eliminate $[OH^-]$ and $[NO_3^-]$ from (b) gives

$$[H_3O^+]_r = \frac{10^{-14}}{[H_3O^+]_r} + 5.0 \times 10^{-7}$$

$$[H_3O^+]_r^2 - 5.0 \times 10^{-7} [H_3O^+]_r - 10^{-14} = 0$$

$$[H_3O^+]_r = 5.2 \times 10^{-7}$$

$$pH = 6.3$$

Example 20-14   Use the systematic approach to produce a general expression for pH in a buffer solution in which the formal concentration of acid is f_a and the formal concentration of its conjugate base is f_b. Let the acid be HA and the base MA.

(a) mass balance in A

$$[HA] + [A^-] = f_a + f_b$$

(b) mass balance in metal ion

$$[M^+] = f_b$$

(c) charge balance

$$[M^+] + [H_3O^+] = [A^-] + [OH^-]$$

(d) equilibrium condition giving the ratio of the concentrations of the conjugates

$$\frac{[H_3O^+]_r[A^-]_r}{[HA]_r} = K_a$$

(e) water equilibrium

$$[H_3O^+]_r[OH^-]_r = 10^{-14}$$

Substituting from (b) into (c)

$$f_b + [H_3O^+] = [A^-] + [OH^-]$$

Adding (a) to the above gives

$$[H_3O^+] - f_a = [OH^-] - [HA]$$

$$[HA] = f_a + [OH^-] - [H_3O^+]$$

Substituting in (a)

$$[A^-] = f_a + f_b - [HA]$$

$$= f_b - [OH^-] + [H_3O^+]$$

Substituting in (d)

$$[H_3O^+]_r = K_a \frac{[HA]}{[A^-]} = K_a \frac{f_a + [OH^-] - [H_3O^+]}{f_b - [OH^-] + [H_3O^+]}$$

It can be seen that this simplifies to

$$[H_3O^+] \approx K_a \frac{f_a}{f_b}$$

providing that the formal concentrations of both conjugates are much larger than the concentrations of both H_3O^+ and OH^-. It will therefore fail if either or both formal concentrations are very small, or if one is much larger than the other. The simple buffer formula is enormously useful but its limitations must be kept in mind.

20-15   POLYPROTIC ACIDS

Some acids have more than one acidic hydrogen atom per molecule. Some examples are sulphuric acid, oxalic acid and carbonic acid

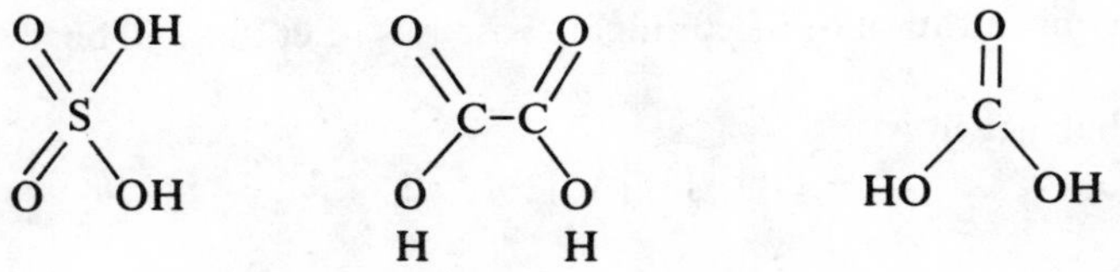

These three examples are all diprotic acids, which could be represented as H_2A. Such acids donate their protons in two stages as follows.

$$(1)\ H_2A + H_2O \rightarrow H_3O^+ + HA^-$$

$$(2)\ HA^- + H_2O \rightarrow H_3O^+ + A^{2-}$$

The equilibrium expressions for these two processes are

$$K_{a1} = \frac{[H_3O^+]_r[HA^-]_r}{[H_2A]_r}$$

$$K_{a2} = \frac{[H_3O^+]_r[A^{2-}]_r}{[HA^-]_r}$$

For triprotic acids, three ionization steps are available and three values of K_a are required. Such values are included in Table 20-1 for four polyprotic acids. In almost all polyprotic acids, $K_{a1} \gg K_{a2}$ and, for triprotic acids, $K_{a2} \gg K_{a3}$. For sulphurous acid for example, K_{a1} is 1.7×10^{-2} and K_{a2} is 6.2×10^{-8}. These figures show that the bisulphite ion, HSO_3^-, is a much weaker acid than sulphurous acid, H_2SO_3.

The properties of such acids can be better understood by considering the titration curve when one of them is titrated with a strong base. An approximate curve is shown in Figure 20-2, and it can be seen that it consists of two curves for monoprotic acids joined together, with two endpoints and two buffer regions. In either of the buffer regions, the other process can be ignored. The pH equals pK_{a1} at the centre of the first buffer region and pK_{a2} at the centre of the second. The initial pH is simply that of a solution of H_2SO_3 with the first ionization process the only significant one in determining pH. At the

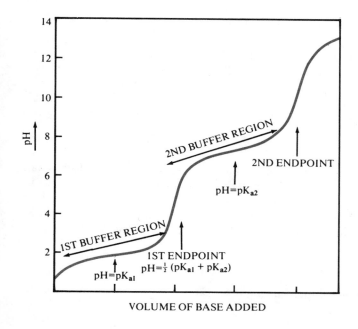

Figure 20-2 Titration of a diprotic acid (H_2SO_3) with NaOH

second endpoint, the pH is determined by the weak base SO_3^{2-}. The only interesting point not discussed so far is the first endpoint.

At the first endpoint, one has essentially a solution of $NaHSO_3$. It will ionize completely to give Na^+ and HSO_3^-. The Na^+ remains unchanged in solution but the HSO_3^- can act both as a base and as an acid.

$$HSO_3^-(aq) + H_2O \rightarrow H_2SO_3(aq) + OH^-(aq) \qquad K_b'$$

$$HSO_3^-(aq) + H_2O \rightarrow SO_3^{2-}(aq) + H_3O^+ \qquad K_a''$$

Notice that K_b' is expressable in terms of the conjugate acid, H_2SO_3, since

$$K_b' = K_w/K_a'$$

so that K_a' and K_a'' are, in fact, the first and second acid constants for H_2SO_3.

Application of the systematic approach to this system produces the following result, taking the $NaHSO_3$ formality as F.

(i) the equilibrium expression for the first process

$$\frac{[H_2SO_3]_r[OH^-]_r}{[HSO_3^-]_r} = \frac{K_w}{K_a'}$$

(ii) the equilibrium expression for the second process

$$\frac{[H^+]_r[SO_3^{2-}]_r}{[HSO_3^-]_r} = K_a''$$

(iii) mass balance statements for Na^+ and sulphite ion

$$[Na^+] = F$$

$$[HSO_3^-] + [H_2SO_3] + [SO_3^{2-}] = F$$

(iv) charge balance

$$[Na^+] + [H^+] = [OH^-] + [HSO_3^-] + 2[SO_3^{2-}]$$

Begin by considering the last two statements. Each contains a term, F in the first and its equivalent $[Na^+]$ in the second, which is larger than any other term present. In order to focus on the smaller terms, it is convenient to eliminate this large term by adding the two equations, which gives, after cancelling like terms on both sides of the summed equation,

$$[H^+] + [H_2SO_3] = [OH^-] + [SO_3^{2-}]$$

Another reasonable assumption is that $[H^+]$ and $[OH^-]$ are both small relative to $[H_2SO_3]$ and $[SO_3^{2-}]$. Although it is an assumption which needs to be tested for self consistency when the calculation is complete, it is a reasonable one since an H^+ is formed for every SO_3^{2-} and an OH^- is formed for every H_2SO_3 but the H^+ and OH^- will then be largely removed through the operation of

$$H^+ + OH^- \rightarrow H_2O$$

while the other species remain unchanged. Applying this assumption to the previous equation gives

$$[H_2SO_3] \approx [SO_3^{2-}]$$

Let this quantity be designated y.

$$[H_2SO_3] = [SO_3^{2-}] = y$$

Substitution of these terms in the charge balance equation, and continuing our assumption that H^+ and OH^- are small gives

$$F = [HSO_3^-] + 2y$$

$$[HSO_3^-] = F - 2y$$

The concentrations of all three sulphite species are now expressable in terms of F and y. Making those substitutions in the two equilibrium expressions gives

$$\frac{[H^+]_r(y)}{(F-2y)} = K_a''$$

$$\frac{(y)[OH^-]_r}{(F-2y)} = \frac{K_w}{K_a'}$$

These two expressions can be rearranged as follows.

$$\frac{y}{F-2y} = \frac{K_a''}{[H^+]_r}$$

$$\frac{y}{F-2y} = \frac{K_w}{K_a'[OH^-]_r} = \frac{K_w[H^+]_r}{K_a'K_w} = \frac{[H^+]_r}{K_a'}$$

Finally, since the left hand sides of the above equations are the same, the right hand sides must be so too.

$$\frac{K_a''}{[H^+]_r} = \frac{[H^+]_r}{K_a'}$$

$$[H^+]_r^2 = K_a'K_a''$$

$$pH = \tfrac{1}{2}(pK_a' + pK_a'')$$

This expression is extremely useful for calculating the pH of solutions of materials which can act either as acids or as bases. Notice that there was an assumption, namely that

$$[H^+], [OH^-] \ll [H_2SO_3], [SO_3^{2-}]$$

This cannot be tested except by considering some specific value of F but it will be found always to be true except in very dilute solutions. Wherever doubt exists, all four quantities should be calculated and the assumption verified.

Example 20-15 What is the pH of a solution which is 0.30 F in $NaHCO_3$?

The pH will be independent of the concentration except in extremely dilute solutions, in accordance with the calculation above. Thus using the values of

K_{a1} and K_{a2} for carbonic acid from Table 20-1, the pH is given by

$$pH = \tfrac{1}{2}(pK_{a1} + pK_{a2})$$
$$= \tfrac{1}{2}(-\log(4.4 \times 10^{-7}) - \log(4.7 \times 10^{-11}))$$
$$= 8.34$$

Although machinery has been described now by which all manner of polyprotic acid calculations can be made, there is one case so common and important that an example must be included. This is the case of a solution of a polyprotic acid alone.

Example 20-16   Calculate the pH of the solution and the concentrations of all species in a solution which is 0.25 F in oxalic acid. In solutions of pure polyprotic acids, the first K_a is invariably very much larger than the second. Therefore the H$^+$ contributed by the second and subsequent steps is negligible with respect to that contributed from the first and the pH is determined almost entirely by the first step.

$$H_2C_2O_4 + H_2O \rightleftarrows H_3O^+ + HC_2O_4^-$$

$$\begin{array}{ccc} 0.25-x & x & x \end{array}$$

$$K_{a1} = 5.4 \times 10^{-2} = \frac{x^2}{0.25-x}$$

The solution is $x = 0.092$, so

$$[H_3O^+]_r = 0.092, \ pH = 1.03$$
$$[H_2C_2O_4]_r = 0.25 - 0.092 = 0.158$$
$$[HC_2O_4^-]_r = 0.092$$

$[C_2O_4^{2-}]$ is calculated from the second ionization equilibrium

$$HC_2O_4^{2-} + H_2O \rightleftarrows H_3O^+ + C_2O_4^{2-}$$

From the definition of K_{a2},

$$[C_2O_4^{2-}]_r = \frac{K_{a2}[HC_2O_4^-]_r}{[H_3O^+]_r}$$

But from the first equilibrium, the two concentrations on the right hand side are equal, and so

$$[C_2O_4^{2-}]_r = K_{a2} = 5.4 \times 10^{-5}$$

This result is much less than $[H_3O^+]$ and so, as assumed throughout this calculation, the second ionization does not have any significant effect on the first ionization, and the pH is determined by the first ionization step alone.

20-16 A NOTE ON CARBON DIOXIDE

Carbon dioxide is always present in the air, being particularly abundant in areas where combustion processes are common. All natural waters thus contain some dissolved carbon dioxide, the Henry's Law constant being 1.7×10^8 Pa. An ability to make calculations related to dissolved CO_2 is thus important to the chemistry of all natural waters, as well as in many other circumstances such as the manufacture of carbonated beverages and studies of body respiration.

The equilibrium constant for the formation of carbonic acid from dissolved CO_2 is not very high, about 2×10^{-3} at 298 K. Both species will exist in solution in significant amounts, with carbonic acid much the less abundant. Calculation of the concentrations of each species requires the following equations.

$$CO_2(aq) + H_2O \rightleftarrows H_2CO_3(aq) \qquad\qquad K = \frac{[H_2CO_3]_r}{[CO_2]_r} = 2 \times 10^{-3}$$

$$H_2CO_3(aq) + H_2O \rightleftarrows H_3O^+(aq) + HCO_3^-(aq)$$

$$K_{a1} = \frac{[H_3O^+]_r[HCO_3^-]_r}{[H_2CO_3]_r} = 2 \times 10^{-4}$$

$$HCO_3^-(aq) + H_2O \rightleftarrows H_3O^+(aq) + CO_3^{2-}(aq)$$

$$K_{a2} = \frac{[H_3O^+]_r[CO_3^{2-}]_r}{[HCO_3^-]_r} = 6 \times 10^{-11}$$

Use of the above equations is recommended. Caution must be exercised when using tabulated data however, since it is not uncommon to apply a simplified treatment and to quote data on that basis. In particular, it is common to treat all non-ionized, dissolved carbon dioxide as if it were all H_2CO_3, which is far from the truth but can lead to correct pH calculations if K_a is taken as 4×10^{-7}, the product of K and K_{a1} in the treatment above. This approach is treacherous and should be avoided.

Example 20-17 Calculate the concentrations of all species present at equilibrium if 0.20 g of CO_2 is dissolved in 1.00 L of water.

Total amount of CO_2 per litre, all forms, $= 0.20/44.0$

$$= 4.55 \times 10^{-3} \text{ mol}$$

Let $p = [H_2CO_3]_r$, $q = [HCO_3^-]_r$, and $r = [CO_3^{2-}]_r$

$$\frac{p}{4.55 \times 10^{-3} - p - q - r} = 2 \times 10^{-3}$$

But most of the CO_2 remains as $CO_2(aq)$ and so one may assume that $p, q, r \ll 4.55 \times 10^{-3}$

$$p = 9.1 \times 10^{-6}$$

Also assume that most H_3O^+ arises from the first ionization, and relatively little from the second ionization or from the self ionization of water, since the

first ionization constant is much greater than the second.
Therefore

$$[H_3O^+]_r = [HCO_3^-]_r = q$$

Substitution in the first equilibrium expression gives

$$K_{a1} = 2 \times 10^{-4} = \frac{q^2}{9.1 \times 10^{-6}}$$

and therefore

$$q = 4.3 \times 10^{-5}$$

Finally, substitution of these values in the second equilibrium expression gives

$$\frac{(4.3 \times 10^{-5})(r)}{4.3 \times 10^{-5}} = K_{a2} = 6 \times 10^{-11}$$

$$r = 6 \times 10^{-11}$$

Thus the concentrations of H_2CO_3, HCO_3^- and CO_3^{2-} are respectively 9.1×10^{-6} mol L^{-1}, 4.3×10^{-5} mol L^{-1} and 6×10^{-11} mol L^{-1}, all of which are much less than 4.5×10^{-3} so that the assumption is consistent with the result.

20-17 SILLEN DIAGRAMS

In previous sections, the distinction between a systematic approach and an intuitive approach has been made and exemplified. The systematic approach is in theory capable of solving any acid base problem. One finds a set of independent equations equal in number to the number of variables and uses these to obtain solutions for each variable.

Even in some of the cases examined so far, however, the algebra becomes complicated and solutions are possible only with the aid of simplifying assumptions or of a computer. Where such assumptions cannot be made or where the situation is even more complicated, it is nearly impossible to solve the equations without a computer. This is the preferred route if repeated calculations are being made with a particular system but where few calculations are required, a non-computer route is desirable.

Such a technique, applicable to many systems, was developed in Scandinavia long before the computer came to prominence and owes its greatest advance to Lars Gunnar Sillén. It involves a graphical presentation of data in what we choose to call Sillén diagrams.

The Sillén diagram plots the logarithm of the concentration of each species as a function of some "master variable," frequently pH in acid/base systems. Although a full presentation of this valuable technique would require a chapter in itself, an illustration is worthwhile. The example chosen for this purpose is a simple system which does not in fact require the technique, being easy to analyze by the methods presented earlier in the chapter. It serves however to show how a Sillén diagram is constructed, and how one subsequently recovers needed information from one.

The systems chosen are those containing a weak acid, HA, and its conjugate

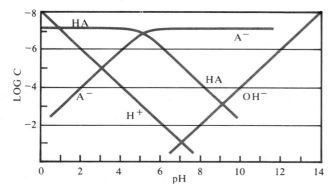

Figure 20-3 Sillén diagram for the general acid/base system HA/A^-; $K_a = 10^{-5}$; $f = 0.10$.

base, A^-, at 25°C. The *total* formality of the acid and base is f and the acid dissociation constant is K_a. For purposes of constructing the initial diagram in Figure 20-3, f is taken as 0.10 mol L^{-1} and K_a as 1.0×10^{-5}.

In the diagram, plots are made of log $[H^+]_r$, log $[OH^-]_r$, log $[HA]_r$, and log $[A^-]_r$ as functions of pH. The simplest to obtain, of course, is log $[H^+]_r$ since

$$\log [H^+]_r \approx -pH$$

This is a straight line of slope -1 and intercept 0. Almost as simple is the line for log $[OH^-]_r$. Since at 25°C

$$[H^+]_r[OH^-]_r = 10^{-14}$$

$$\log [H^+]_r + \log [OH^-]_r = -14$$

$$\log [OH^-]_r = pH - 14$$

This too is easily plotted, a straight line of slope 1 with log $[OH^-]_r$ being 0 at a pH value of 14.

Obtaining equations for the remaining two functions requires consideration of the mass balance condition and the equilibrium expression.

$$[HA] + [A^-] = f$$

$$\frac{[H^+]_r[A^-]_r}{[HA]_r} = K_a$$

Eliminating first [HA] and then $[A^-]$ from these equations leads to the following relationships in which the distinction between [x] and $[x]_r$ is ignored.

$$[A^-] = \frac{(K_a)(f)}{[H^+] + K_a}$$

$$[HA] = \frac{(f)[H^+]}{[H^+] + K_a}$$

If the solution is acidic, and the pH small, so that

$$[H^+] \gg K_a$$

then the above relationships simplify to

$$[A^-] = \frac{(K_a)(f)}{[H^+]}$$

$$\log [A^-] = \log K_a + \log f + pH$$

$$[HA] = f$$

$$\log [HA] = \log f$$

Thus at low pH values, the plot of $\log [A^-]$ is a straight line of slope 1, with an intercept equal to $\log K_a + \log f$ at pH equal to 0, and the plot of $\log [HA]$ is a horizontal straight line at $\log f$.

Conversely, where the solution is more basic so that

$$[H^+] \ll K_a$$

the same two relationships for $[A^-]$ and $[HA]$ simplify instead to

$$[A^-] = f$$

$$\log [A^-] = \log f$$

and

$$[HA] = \frac{f[H^+]}{K_a}$$

$$\log [HA] = \log f - \log K - pH$$

These are again straight lines, one horizontal and one of slope -1, as shown in the figure.

While this analysis has been successful in describing the behaviour of all species at high and at low pH, it remains necessary to describe the behaviour of $[HA]$ and $[A^-]$ in the vicinity of the region where

$$[H^+] = K_a$$

It is easily seen from the equilibrium condition that $[HA] = [A^-]$ at this point, since

$$\frac{[H^+][A^-]}{[HA]} = K_a$$

$$\frac{[A^-]}{[HA]} = \frac{K_a}{[H^+]} = 1$$

Therefore at the point where $pH = -\log K_a$,

$$\log [HA] = \log [A^-] = \log(f/2) = \log f - \log 2$$

With these points known as well as the lines at high and low pH, reasonably accurate plots can be made even in the difficult region where $[H^+]$ is close in value to K_a. Such a diagram can now be used to provide answers quickly in a variety of situations, examples of which are below.

Example 20-18   Evaluate the concentrations of all species in a solution which is 0.10 F in HA.

One can see that in this case, where no A^- has been added directly,

$$[H^+]_r = [A^-]_r$$

The diagram shows that this occurs at a pH of 3.0 where

$$\log [H^+]_r = \log [A^-]_r = -3.0$$

$$[H^+]_r = [A^-]_r = 10^{-3}$$

The other entities may also be read directly.

$$\log [HA]_r = -1.0$$

$$\log [OH^-]_r = -11.0$$

Example 20-19   If a buffer is made up which is 0.05 F in each of HA and NaA, what are the concentrations of all species at equilibrium?
   From the diagram, these are equal at pH equal to 5 so that

$$\log [H^+]_r = -5.0$$

$$\log [OH^-]_r = -9.0$$

$$\log [HA]_r = \log [A^-]_r = -1.3$$

Example 20-20   A buffer is to be made up using HA and NaA to have a pH of 4.0 and a total formality in HA and NaA of 0.10. What proportions of HA and NaA are required?
   From the diagram, at pH equal to 4,

$$\log [HA]_r = -1.0$$

$$\log [A^-]_r = -2.0$$

Therefore

$$\frac{[HA]_r}{[A^-]_r} = \frac{10^{-1}}{10^{-2}} = 10$$

Example 20-21   A system is made up to a total formality of HA and NaA of 0.10 and is found to have a pH of 7. What are the concentrations of all species?
   From the diagram, at pH equal to 7,

$$\log [H^+]_r = \log [OH^-]_r = -7.0$$

$$\log [A^-]_r = -1.0$$

$$\log [HA]_r = -3.0$$

Example 20-22   What is the concentration of each species present in a solution which is 0.10 F in NaA?

Since the process of importance is

$$A^- + H_2O \rightarrow HA + OH^-$$

it follows that, to a very good approximation,

$$[HA]_r = [OH^-]_r$$

The diagram shows that this occurs at pH equal to 9.0 at which point

$$\log [HA]_r = \log [OH^-]_r = -5.0$$

$$\log [A^-]_r = -1.0$$

$$\log [H^+]_r = -9.0$$

The diagram in Figure 20-3 suffers from one major handicap. It applies only to systems having a total formality in HA and A^- of 0.10. This can be overcome, and the diagram made applicable to any concentrations of these species, by preparing two graphs as in Figure 20-4. The H^+ and OH^- plots do not depend on the formality of the two species and are drawn on a base diagram as in Figure 20-4(a). The HA and A^- plots are drawn on a transparent sheet as in Figure 20-4(b). By placing the horizontal sections of the transparency at log F

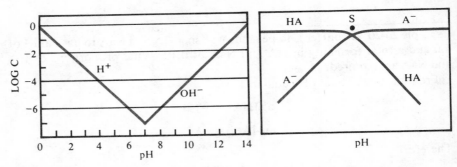

Figure 20-4   Two master plots for superposition to form Sillén Diagrams

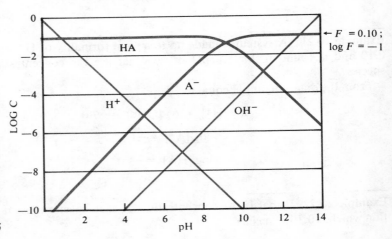

Figure 20-5

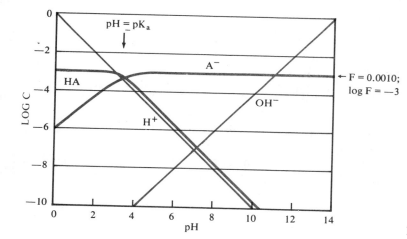

Figure 20-6

on the base diagram, and the crossover point of the transparency plot at a pH value of pK_a for the acid in question, the plot can be made to apply to any concentration of any acid and its conjugate base. Figures 20-5 and 20-6 illustrate this for, respectively, NH_4^+ and NH_3 of total formality 0.10 (K_a being 5.6×10^{-10}) and HF and F^- of total formality 0.0010 (K_a being 6.7×10^{-4}).

The Sillén diagram permits one to visualize the whole range of values, showing which species are important and which not under various conditions. The advantages in using them are very great in dealing with complicated systems like polyprotic acids or the mixtures one finds in sea water.

SUMMARY

Acid/base reactions are extremely common and important, even within the restricted definition of proton donation due to Brønsted and Lowry. Moreover, the level of H^+ concentration is extremely important to the rate of many reactions, including enzyme reactions in biochemistry and corrosion of metals in aqueous environments. For those reasons an understanding of acid/base reactions and an ability to handle them quantitatively is an essential part of a chemist's background.

The most common need quantitatively is a knowledge of the concentration of all species in solution, especially H^+. For this purpose, many systems fit the common classifications organized and described in Sections 20-8, 20-9, 20-10, 20-11 and 20-12, namely a strong acid or base in solution, a weak acid or base in solution, or various combinations of these. For such common and relatively simple situations, an intuitive approach is simple and effective.

More difficult cases do arise, though, such as the period in the titration of a weak acid by a strong base between the beginning and the buffer region and between the buffer region and the endpoint. Polyprotic acids or additional equilibria such as solubility equilibria are other common complications. For these cases, a systematic or a diagram approach is necessary. It has always been a difficult area for the beginner to master, but it should yield to those who work numerous problems of a variety of types.

ADVANCED READING

R.P. Bell, *The Proton in Chemistry* (Second Edition), Cornell University Press, Ithaca, N.Y., 1973
This book is a classic. It emphasizes principles and understanding, not techniques of calculation.

J.N. Butler, *Solubility and pH Calculations*, Addison-Wesley, Reading, Massachusetts, 1964
This is a compact systematic treatment of acid/base and solubility equilibria. In level it extends slightly beyond the material of this chapter.

J.N. Butler, *Ionic Equilibria*, Addison-Wesley, Reading, Massachusetts, 1964. The treatment in this text extends far beyond that in the book above.

I.M. Kolthoff and P.J. Elving (Editors) *Treatise on Analytical Chemistry*, Volume 1, Part 1 Chapter 8 "Graphic Presentation of Equilibrium Data" by L.G. Sillén
In addition to this chapter on Sillén diagrams, this book contains chapters on other aspects of acid/base chemistry.

PROBLEMS

1. The following data are taken from the labels on bottles of concentrated reagents. The precentage refers to the mass fraction, and the specific gravity is equal to the density in $g \, mL^{-1}$.

	Formula Mass /$g \, mol^{-1}$	Relative Density
Hydrochloric acid, 36% HCl	36.47	1.19
Nitric acid, 69% HNO_3	63.02	1.41
Acetic acid, 99% CH_3COOH	60.05	1.05
Sulphuric acid, 95% H_2SO_4	98.08	1.84
Phosphoric acid, 85% H_3PO_4	98.00	1.74

Calculate the formality of each reagent.

[11.7, 15.4, 17.3, 17.8, 15.1, mol L^{-1}]

2. It is desired to make 105 L of sulphuric acid, S.G. 1.20, 27.3% H_2SO_4. What volume of the concentrated acid must be used?

[19.7 L]

3. A sample of potassium hydrogen phthalate ($KHC_8H_4O_4$) required 48.37 mL of NaOH solution to reach an endpoint with phenolphthalein. If the

mass of sample was 4.000 g what was the formality of the base?

$$[0.405 \text{ mol L}^{-1}]$$

4. A sample of anhydrous sodium carbonate of mass 0.2118 g is dissolved in water. This solution is titrated against a solution of hydrochloric acid using methyl orange as indicator and 44.55 mL of the acid is required to neutralize it. Calculate the formality of the acid.

$$[0.0897 \text{ mol L}^{-1}]$$

5. Calculate the pH of the following aqueous solutions: (a) 0.10 F HCl; (b) 0.20 F CH_3COOH; (c) 0.010 F HCN; (d) 0.30 F NH_3; (e) 0.30 F KOH; (f) 1.0×10^{-4} F HCOOH.

$$[(a) 1.0, (b) 2.7, (c) 5.7, (d) 11.4, (e) 13.5, (f) 4.1]$$

6. The fractional ionization of a monoprotic acid in 0.050 F solution is 0.058. What fraction is ionized in 0.20 F solution?

$$[0.029]$$

7. A solution is made up 1.00×10^{-8} F with respect to HCl. Estimate the pH.

$$[6.98]$$

8. What formal concentration of acetic acid would have a pH of 3.00?

$$[0.056]$$

9. Calculate the pH of the following solutions: (a) 0.20 F NH_4Cl; (b) 0.20 F NaCN; (c) 0.30 F Na_2CO_3; (d) 0.40 F $NaHCO_3$; (e) 0.15 F K_2SO_3.

$$[(a) 5.0, (b) 11.3, (c) 11.9, (d) 8.3, (e) 10.2]$$

10. Calculate the pH of the solution made by mixing the following. The technique of equivalent systems will simplify the calculations.

(a) 20. mL 0.50 F HCl and 30. mL 0.10 F CH_3COONa

(b) 30. mL 0.10 F HCl and 20. mL 0.50 F CH_3COONa

(c) 20. mL 0.050 F NH_4Cl and 30. mL 0.20 F NH_3

(d) 20. mL 0.10 F $NaHCO_3$ and 40. mL 0.10 F H_2CO_3

(e) 20. mL 0.10 F $NaHCO_3$ and 40. mL 0.10 F Na_2CO_3

$$[0.9, 5.1, 10.0, 6.1, 10.6]$$

11. Calculate the pH *change* which results when 50.0 mL of 0.100 F nitric acid is added at 25°C to each of the following:

(a) 1.00 L of pure water

(b) 1.00 L of a solution containing acetic acid and sodium acetate, each at a formal concentration of 1.0 mol L^{-1}.

$$[-4.68, -0.04]$$

12. Calculate the *change* in pH which results when the following are separately

added to 1.00 L of a solution containing NH_3 and NH_4Cl, each at a formal concentration of 1.00 mol L^{-1} at 25°C.

(a) 0.100 L water

(b) 0.200 mL 0.200 F KOH

[0.00, +0.04]

13. A certain monoprotic weak acid serves as an indicator. Assuming that the colour change is seen when 1/3 of the indicator has been converted to ions and that at that point the pH of the solution is 6.00, what is the value of pK_{in}?

[6.3]

14. Estimate a pH range within which ZnS would precipitate but MnS would not from a solution originally 0.1 F with respect to these ions and saturated with H_2S.

[−0.3 to 5.2]

15. A solution is titrated by adding 100.1 mL of 0.01000 F NaOH to 100.0 mL of 0.01000 F HCl. If a few drops of phenolphthalein are added, what fraction of the indicator is converted to the red (basic) form?

[0.26]

16. Sketch the titration curve showing how the pH varies as a concentrated solution of HCl is added to a 0.20 F solution of sodium carbonate. On the curve mark the pH values, buffer regions, equivalence points and the places where the indicators methyl orange and phenolphthalein change colour.

17. The value of K_{a1} for H_2SO_4 is very large, this being a strong acid. However, the HSO_4^- ion is not a very strong acid and K_{a2} is 1.2×10^{-2}. Estimate the pH, $[HSO_4^-]$ and $[SO_4^{2-}]$ in a 0.50 F H_2SO_4 solution.

[0.3, 0.49 mol L^{-1}, 0.012 mol L^{-1}]

18. An unknown acid is shown to be monoprotic by an initial rough titration in NaOH. In a second, careful titration, the pH of the solution is measured to be 4.7 after 13.7 mL of base is added; the endpoint is determined by the rapid increase in pH which occurs in the neighbourhood of 35.2 mL. Calculate the K_a for the acid.

[1.3×10^{-5}]

19. Estimate the pH of "milk of lime" a precipitate of $Ca(OH)_2$ in equilibrium with water.

[12]

20. Using Figure 20.5, evaluate the pH of a solution which is 0.050 F in each of NH_4^+ and NH_3. If a buffer solution is arbitrarily defined as being one in which the formalities of HA and A^- differ by not more than a factor of 10,

over what pH range could an NH_4^+/NH_3 system be used as a buffer at total formality of 0.10? Does altering the total formality alter this range?

[9.2; 8.1 to 10.2; no]

21. Draw or describe structures, using the ideas on molecular structures developed in earlier chapters, for the acids H_3PO_4, H_2SO_4 and $HClO_4$, which might better be written as $PO(OH)_3$. $SO_2(OH)_2$ and $ClO_3(OH)$.

22. $Mn(OH)_2$ is relatively insoluble but it is a strong electrolyte. Calculate the pH of a saturated solution in water at 25°C.

[9.9]

23. What is the minimum concentration of $[H_3O^+]$ required to ensure that Mg^{2+} at a concentration of 2.5 mol L^{-1} does not precipitate from water at 25°C as $Mg(OH)_2$?

[5×10^{-9} mol L^{-1}]

24. Calculate K_{ind} for the indicator α-naphthyl red which is effective for endpoints in the pH range 3.7 to 5.0 and for phenol red, which is effective in the range 6.4 to 8.0.

[4×10^{-5}, 6×10^{-8}]

25. In a solution in which the formality of a strong acid, HA, is y, it has been shown that ignoring the contribution to H^+ from the self ionization of water leads to

$$[H^+]_r = y$$

whereas taking the water contribution into account leads to

$$[H^+]_r = y + \frac{10^{-14}}{[H^+]_r}$$

Establish the error involved in making the first approximation for HNO_3 solutions which are 1.00×10^{-6} F, 1.00×10^{-7} F and 1.00×10^{-8} F.

[approximate: 1.00×10^{-6}, 1.00×10^{-7}, 1.00×10^{-8}

accurate: 1.00×10^{-6}, 1.62×10^{-7}, 1.05×10^{-7}]

XXI CHEMICAL EQUILIBRIUM IN NON-IDEAL SOLUTIONS

In Chapter 15, gas phase reaction quotients and equilibrium expressions were introduced empirically in terms of ratios of partial pressures to $P°$. Thus for the formation of ammonia from hydrogen and nitrogen, one writes

$$N_2(g) + 3 H_2(g) \rightarrow 2 NH_3(g)$$

$$Q = \frac{(P_{NH_3}/P°)^2}{(P_{N_2}/P°)(P_{H_2}/P°)^3}$$

At the same time, it was observed that pure liquids and pure solids may be ignored in the reaction quotient.

In Chapter 16, these observed dependencies of Q and K on the amounts of each reactant and product were generalized in terms of relative activity, a. Thus the dependencies discussed in Chapter 15 could be expressed as follows, using as an example the thermal decomposition of calcium carbonate.

$$CaCO_3(c) \rightarrow CaO(c) + CO_2(g)$$

$$Q = \frac{a_{CaO} a_{CO_2}}{a_{CaCO_3}}$$

$$a_{CaO} \approx 1$$

$$a_{CO_2} \approx P_{CO_2}/P°$$

$$a_{CaCO_3} \approx 1$$

and hence

$$Q \approx P_{CO_2}/P°$$

This treatment was also extended to reactions involving solutions, as in the following example of the attack of aqueous acid on metallic zinc.

$$Zn(c) + 2 H^+(aq) \rightarrow Zn^{2+}(aq) + H_2(g)$$

$$Q = \frac{a_{Zn^{2+}(aq)}\, a_{H_2(g)}}{a_{Zn(c)}\, (a_{H^+(aq)})^2}$$

$$a_{Zn^{2+}(aq)} \approx [Zn^{2+}]_r$$

$$a_{H_2(g)} \approx P_{H_2}/P°$$

$$a_{Zn(c)} \approx 1$$

$$a_{H^+(aq)} \approx [H^+]_r$$

and hence

$$Q \approx [Zn^{2+}]_r\, (P_{H_2}/P°)/[H^+]_r^2$$

Systems in which these approximations for gases and liquid solutions are valid are said to be ideal. What they have in common is that most of the solute particles are so far apart that interactions among them may be neglected. Hence they work well for gases at low pressures, or for solutes in dilute solutions. The approximation of the relative activity of a gas by $P/P°$ is usually a very good one at pressures of 100 kPa or below, and thus applies to most systems of interest, but the approximation of the relative activity of a solute by the ratio of concentrations is usually accurate only for very dilute solutions, especially where the solute forms ions. That is why these approximations are used for 'insoluble' electrolytes as in Chapter 19 but are never applied to solubility calculations with more soluble electrolytes.

In all cases of non-ideality, calculations may be handled by the introduction of an *activity coefficient*. In this chapter, this technique is illustrated for the common and important case of ions in aqueous solution but the same principles can be applied to any non-ideal system.

21-1   THE MATTER OF UNITS

Consider the specific case of Ag_2SO_4. The equilibrium between the solid salt and its ions in aqueous solution is

$$Ag_2SO_4(c) \rightleftharpoons 2\, Ag^+(aq) + SO_4^{2-}(aq)$$

At equilibrium, the relative activities of the ions must satisfy the equation

$$K = (a_{Ag^+})^2(a_{SO_2^{2-}})$$

with the relative activity of the crystalline material being taken as unity. For such an insoluble salt, a reasonable further approximation is to take

$$a_{Ag^+} \approx [Ag^+]_r$$

$$a_{SO_4^{2-}} \approx [SO_4^{2-}]_r$$

The quantity $[Ag^+]_r$ represents the ratio of c_{Ag^+} to a reference state of $1\ mol\ L^{-1}$. It is dimensionless, but is numerically equal to the concentration.

The decision on which units to choose is a vexing one. Experimentalists in the field choose molality, not molarity, with a reference state of $1\ mol\ kg^{-1}$

(subject to the qualification in the next paragraph). Tabulated thermochemical data for aqueous ions refer to this 1 mol kg^{-1} reference state, and accurate experimental works on solubility products and related quantities are usually published in molalities. On the other hand solubility products are usually used in order to calculate concentrations in work involving volumes, and it is convenient to work in mol L^{-1}. For aqueous solutions, and especially for dilute aqueous solutions, molarity and molality are very nearly the same and the distinction is often of no practical importance. Chemists often use tabulated data (based on molalities) to calculate K, and use that K to obtain concentrations (in mol L^{-1}) without correction or comment. In some places in this text, the same course is followed. For precise work, however, the units must be noted carefully and used consistently. Molarity, molality and mole fraction are all used in published work and activity coefficients are defined in terms of each.

The choice of units could also affect the choice of reference state but in fact virtually all tabulated data are for a hypothetical reference state of 1 mol kg^{-1}. Just as calculations with gases are based on reference to a hypothetical *ideal* gas at P°, calculations for species in aqueous solution are based on reference to a hypothetical *ideal* solution of unit molality. A difference in practice is that whereas real gases at P° are very close to being ideal, real one molal solutions are far from being ideal. Thus the thermodynamic properties listed in Appendix 1 for ions in their standard state differ considerably from those of the same ions in real one molal solutions. This choice of an ideal reference state, however exotic it may appear to be on first acquaintance, yields significant simplification of the tabulation and use of data.

In summary then, molality is the unit of choice in precise work, and all thermochemical data are based on a hypothetical ideal solution of unit molality. In much work with aqueous solutions, however, molarities are used out of convenience, and the distinction between molarity and molality even ignored. That the two are indeed numerically similar for dilute aqueous solutions is illustrated by the following example.

Example 21-1   The density of a 10.00% by mass aqueous solution of KOH is 1.0918 kg L^{-1}. What are the molarity and molality of the KOH? What are they for a 1.00% solution of density 1.0083 kg L^{-1}?

$$1 \text{ L has a mass of } 1.0918 \text{ kg and hence contains}$$

$$(0.1000)(1.0918)/(0.056106) = 1.9460 \text{ mol KOH}$$

$$\text{and } (0.9000)(1.0918) = 0.9826 \text{ kg of water}$$

Therefore

$$\text{molarity} = (1.9640 \text{ mol})/(1 \text{ L}) = 1.9640 \text{ mol L}^{-1}$$

$$\text{molality} = (1.9640 \text{ mol})/(0.9826 \text{ kg}) = 1.9804 \text{ mol kg}^{-1}$$

It is readily seen that the two are similar even in this very concentrated solution. The difference grows less with dilution. Analogous calculations for the

1% solution give

$$\text{molarity} = (0.01)(1.0083)/(0.056106)(1) = 0.1797 \text{ mol L}^{-1}$$

$$\text{molality} = (0.1797)/(0.9900)(1.0083) = 0.1800 \text{ mol kg}^{-1}$$

21-2   THE ACTIVITY COEFFICIENT

Returning to the example of the previous section, how can one express the reaction quotient in terms which relate to measurable quantities but which nevertheless are capable of providing a precisely correct answer? The first step is the introduction of an activity coefficient, γ, such that

$$a_{Ag^+} = \gamma_{Ag^+}(m_{Ag^+}/m^\circ) = \gamma_{Ag^+}(m_{Ag^+}/1)$$

Notice that $m_{Ag^+}/1$ is a ratio of two molalities, and that γ_{Ag^+} would have a slightly different value if $m_{Ag^+}/1$ were replaced by the ratio of the molarity of the solution to that of a one molar reference solution. The activity coefficients in this book apply precisely only for a molality ratio. In accordance with the remarks in Section 21-1, that distinction will often be ignored and the two sets of units will be used almost interchangeably. The error introduced in so doing is negligible compared to the one being eliminated by the introduction of γ itself. Once again it must be stressed, however, that this easy sliding back and forth between molarity and molality, so common in textbooks often without it even being mentioned, is possible only for aqueous solutions, is inaccurate for concentrated solutions, and is to be avoided wherever high precision is required.

The activity coefficient is simply the multiplier of $m_{Ag^+}/1$ required to give correct predictions of the properties of a solution. Such a definition may seem to be unmitigated 'fudging.' In a sense it is, but the 'fudge factor,' the activity coefficient γ, is of such universal applicability that it is more appropriate to think of it as being a thermodynamic property of the solution in its own right. The activity coefficient which one determines for Ag_2SO_4 from solubility product measurements is exactly the correct activity coefficient to use in calculations of osmotic pressures for Ag_2SO_4 solutions or for calculations of potentials in cells in which Ag_2SO_4 solutions are involved.

Notice that it is impossible to produce a solution containing Ag^+ ions only. Solutions are uncharged and always there must be a balancing quantity of some negative ion present. Hence γ_{Ag^+} cannot be evaluated independently, at least not without making some assumptions. What can be measured directly is the mean ionic activity coefficient, $\gamma_\pm$. For the particular example of Ag_2SO_4, this is defined as follows in molalities, the unit of choice in precise work.

$$K = (a_{Ag^+})^2(a_{SO_4^{2-}})$$

$$= (\gamma_{Ag^+})^2(m_{Ag^+}/1)^2(\gamma_{SO_4^{2-}})(m_{SO_4^{2-}}/1)$$

$$= (\gamma_{Ag^+})^2(\gamma_{SO_4^{2-}})(m_{Ag^+}/1)^2(m_{SO_4^{2-}}/1)$$

$$= (\gamma_\pm)^3(m_{Ag^+}/1)^2(m_{SO_4^{2-}}/1)$$

The mean ionic activity coefficient is the geometric mean of the individual activity coefficients, so that in general for a cation activity a_c and an anion activity a_a where

$$K = (a_c)^m(a_a)^n$$

then the mean ionic activity coefficient will be defined by the equation

$$(\gamma_\pm)^{m+n} = (\gamma_c)^m(\gamma_a)^n$$

The mean ionic activity coefficient has a value for a particular solution of a particular electrolyte. It is directly measurable and is a function of concentration.

Example 21-2   Write down expressions for the mean ionic activity coefficients of KOH, $CaSO_4$ and $AlCl_3$ in terms of the activity coefficients of the individual ions.

$$KOH: \; (\gamma_\pm)^2 = (\gamma_{K^+})(\gamma_{OH^-})$$

$$CaSO_4: \; (\gamma_\pm)^2 = (\gamma_{Ca^{2+}})(\gamma_{SO_4^{2-}})$$

$$AlCl_3: \; (\gamma_\pm)^4 = (\gamma_{Al^{3+}})(\gamma_{Cl^-})^3$$

For ionic materials in aqueous solution, the mean ionic activity coefficient approaches unity as the concentration of ions approaches zero. It is these cases of very dilute solutions in which the approximations introduced earlier are valid, with the activity coefficient at or close to unity. That is why solubility product calculations are done as they are for very insoluble salts from which few ions are produced, but are never applied to more soluble salts.

TABLE 21-1:   Mean Ionic Activity Coefficients at 25°C in water
(a) five 1:1 electrolytes over a large molality range

mol kg^{-1}	HCl	HBr	NaCl	KCl	KNO$_3$
0. 000 1	0.989	—	—	—	—
0.001	0.966	0.966	0.965	0.965	0.965
0.002	0.952	0.952	0.952	0.952	—
0.005	0.929	0.930	0.927	0.927	0.926
0.01	0.905	0.906	0.902	0.902	0.898
0.02	0.876	0.879	0.871	0.869	—
0.05	0.840	0.838	0.819	0.816	0.799
0.1	0.796	0.805	0.778	0.769	0.738
0.2	0.767	0.782	0.734	0.719	0.659
0.5	0.757	0.789	0.682	0.651	0.546
1.	0.809	0.871	0.658	0.606	0.443
2.	1.009	1.168	0.671	0.576	0.327
5.	2.38	—	0.885	—	—
10.	10.44	—	—	—	—

(b) various electrolytes over the molality range 0.1 to 3.

Electrolyte	molality					
	0.1	0.2	0.5	1.	2.	3.
1:1						
HBr	0.805	0.782	0.789	0.871	1.168	1.674
HCl	0.796	0.767	0.757	0.809	1.009	1.316
HClO$_4$	0.803	0.778	0.769	0.823	1.055	1.448
HI	0.818	0.807	0.839	0.963	1.356	2.015
HNO$_3$	0.791	0.754	0.720	0.724	0.793	0.909
KCl	0.770	0.718	0.649	0.604	0.573	0.569
KNO$_3$	0.738	0.659	0.546	0.443	0.327	0.266
KOH	0.776	0.739	0.712	0.735	0.863	1.051
LiCl	0.790	0.757	0.739	0.774	0.921	1.156
LiClO$_4$	0.812	0.794	0.808	0.887	1.158	1.582
LiOH	0.718	0.663	0.583	0.523	0.485	0.467
NaCl	0.778	0.735	0.681	0.657	0.668	0.714
NaClO$_4$	0.775	0.729	0.668	0.629	0.609	0.611
NaOH	0.764	0.725	0.688	0.677	0.707	0.782
1:2, 2:1						
CaBr$_2$	0.532	0.491	0.490	0.596	1.119	2.53
CaCl$_2$	0.518	0.472	0.448	0.500	0.792	1.483
Cu(NO$_3$)$_2$	0.512	0.461	0.427	0.456	0.610	0.905
K$_2$CrO$_4$	0.466	0.390	0.298	0.240	0.200	0.194
Li$_2$SO$_4$	0.478	0.406	0.326	0.283	0.269	0.294
MgBr$_2$	0.542	0.512	0.538	0.714	1.593	4.20
MgCl$_2$	0.528	0.488	0.480	0.569	1.051	2.32
Na$_2$SO$_4$	0.452	0.371	0.270	0.204	0.154	0.139
Na$_2$S$_2$O$_3$	0.466	0.390	0.298	0.239	0.202	0.203
ZnCl$_2$	0.518	0.465	0.396	0.341	0.291	0.289
2:2, 3:1, 4:1						
AlCl$_3$	0.337	0.305	0.331	0.539	—	—
CrCl$_3$	0.331	0.298	0.314	0.481	—	—
CuSO$_4$	0.150	0.104	0.0620	0.0423	—	—
MgSO$_4$	0.150	0.107	0.0675	0.0485	0.0417	0.0492
ThCl$_4$	0.292	0.257	0.275	0.643	—	—
ZnSO$_4$	0.150	0.104	0.0630	0.0435	0.0357	0.0408

Even at concentrations as low as 10^{-2} or 10^{-3} mol kg^{-1}, departures from unity are significant. Experimental values for a few salts are listed in Table 21-1. Examine the trends with concentration, and the effects of high charges on one or more of the ions. Note too that species having the same charge distribution (especially those having both the anion and the cation singly charged) tend to have roughly similar activity coefficients at lower concentrations.

The factor responsible for departures from ideality is interaction among the particles. That is why gases approach ideality at low pressures and solutes at low concentrations. The reason why such departures are so large with ions in solution is that the interactions are coulombic attractions and repulsions among the ions, and coulombic forces are much greater, and operate significantly at much greater range, than do the forces among gas molecules or among uncharged species in solution.

It follows from this that *any* ion in a solution will affect the mean ionic activity coefficients of all ionic species present. For example, Table 21-1 shows an experimentally determined $\gamma_\pm$ of 0.778 for 0.1 mol kg^{-1} NaCl in water at 298 K. This differs from unity because of the interactions among 0.1 mol of Na$^+$ ions and 0.1 mol of Cl$^-$ ions distributed through one kilogram of water. The interactions among charged particles, however, are not dependent on the source of the charge. Thus, the introduction of 0.01 mol of KCl decreases $\gamma_\pm$ for NaCl, much the same as the addition of 0.01 mol of NaCl would do.

The properties of aqueous solutions of ionic materials may be thought of in terms of three ranges. The boundaries suggested below for these ranges are quite arbitrary.

(a) Below 10^{-5} mol kg^{-1} where all ions are singly charged and below 10^{-7} mol kg^{-1} where some are multiply charged, departures from ideality are extremely small ($<1\%$) and need to be taken into account only where accuracy greater than this is sought. For compounds having such low solubilities that their saturated solutions have concentrations in this range, solubility product calculations work very well without considering activity coefficients.

(b) In the range 10^{-5} mol kg^{-1} to 10^{-3} mol kg^{-1} for singly charged ions and 10^{-7} mol kg^{-1} to 10^{-4} mol kg^{-1} for multiply charged ions, the activity coefficient becomes significant but is determined almost entirely by the charge on the species. It may be accurately predicted using the concept of ionic strength as shown below. Such calculations were originally devised by Debye and Hückel.

(c) Above these concentrations, individual characteristics of the ions become more and more important, and the predictions of the Debye Hückel law less and less dependable. Experimental data are the only sure route to obtaining accurate values. Remember, however, that $\gamma_\pm$ may be measured in one experiment and then used with confidence for the same solution in another circumstance. It can, for example, be measured using an electrochemical cell and then applied to predict solubility or osmotic pressure.

21-3 IONIC STRENGTH

In order to show how the activity coefficient depended primarily on the charge and concentration of all ions, especially where two or more electrolytes are present, Lewis and Randall introduced the concept of ionic strength, I. It may be defined either in terms of mol kg^{-1} (I_m) or mol L^{-1} (I_c). As often noted, the difference is small for dilute aqueous solutions but cannot be ignored in accurate work.

$$I_m = 1/2\Sigma m_i Z_i^2$$

$$I_c = 1/2\Sigma c_i Z_i^2$$

m_i is the amount of each ion per kg of solvent. c_i is the amount of each ion per litre of solution. Z_i is the charge number of each ion. It is positive for cations and negative for anions.

Example 21-3   Calculate I_m (a) for 0.10 mol kg^{-1} NaCl, (b) for a mixed electrolyte that is 0.10 mol kg^{-1} in NaCl and 0.050 mol kg^{-1} in KCl, and (c) for a solution that is 0.10 mol kg^{-1} in Na$_2$SO$_4$.
  (a) For the NaCl solution

$$m_{Na+} = m_{Cl-} = 0.10 \, \text{mol kg}^{-1}$$

$$I_m = 1/2[0.10(1)^2 + 0.10(-1)^2] = 0.10 \, \text{mol kg}^{-1}$$

  (b) For the NaCl and KCl solution

$$m_{Na+} = 0.10 \, \text{mol kg}^{-1}$$

$$m_{K+} = 0.05 \, \text{mol kg}^{-1}$$

$$m_{Cl-} = 0.15 \, \text{mol kg}^{-1}$$

$$I_m = 1/2[(0.1)(1)^2 + (0.05)(1)^2 + (0.15)(-1)^2] = 0.15 \, \text{mol kg}^{-1}$$

  (c) For the Na$_2$SO$_4$ solution

$$m_{Na+} = 0.20 \, \text{mol kg}^{-1}$$

$$m_{SO_4{}^{2-}} = 0.10 \, \text{mol kg}^{-1}$$

$$I_m = 1/2[(0.20)(1)^2 + (0.10)(-2)^2] = 0.30 \, \text{mol kg}^{-1}$$

Working from a model in which point charge ions are moving freely through an inert solvent of known dielectric constant, Debye and Hückel developed a limiting law relating $\gamma_\pm$ to I_m. They and others have modified this limiting law to permit its use to higher concentrations, but it should be noted that it assumes fundamentally that differences among the species bearing the charge do not affect the result, so that it cannot predict $\gamma_\pm$ accurately above about 10^{-3} mol kg^{-1} where these differences often become significant. The Debye-Hückel law would predict the same $\gamma_\pm$ for all electrolytes of a given charge and concentration (say equimolal solutions of Na$_2$SO$_4$, K$_2$SO$_4$, Ca(NO$_3$)$_2$, Li$_2$CO$_3$ and so on) but it is only below 10^{-4} mol L^{-1} that they would, in fact, have nearly similar values.
  For aqueous solutions at 298 K, the Debye-Hückel "limiting" law is

$$\log \gamma_\pm = -.51 \left| Z_+ Z_- \right| \sqrt{I_m}$$

where $\gamma_\pm$ is the mean ionic activity coefficient of an ionic species, Z_+ is the charge number of the cation, Z^- is the charge number of the anion and I_m is the ionic strength of the solution, including contributions both from the ions of the species and from those of other electrolytes that may be present. The .51 term, incidentally, carries units so that the entire right hand side (and left hand side!) is dimensionless.

Example 21-4 Calculate $\gamma_\pm$ for $AlCl_3$ in a 2.5×10^{-6} mol kg^{-1} aqueous solution of $AlCl_3$ at 298 K.

$$I_m = 1/2[(2.5 \times 10^{-6})(+3)^2 + (7.5 \times 10^{-6})(-1)^2] = 1.5 \times 10^{-5} \text{ mol kg}^{-1}$$

$$\log \gamma_\pm = (0.51)(+3)(-1)\sqrt{1.5 \times 10^{-5}} = -0.006$$

$$\gamma_\pm = 0.986$$

Example 21-5 Calculate $\gamma_\pm$ for NaCl in an aqueous solution containing 1.4×10^{-4} mol kg^{-1} of NaCl and 1.6×10^{-5} mol kg^{-1} of $CaCl_2$.

$$m_{Na+} = 1.4 \times 10^{-4} \text{ and } m_{Ca2+} = 1.6 \times 10^{-5}$$

$$m_{Cl-} = 1.4 \times 10^{-4} + 2(1.6 \times 10^{-5}) = 1.72 \times 10^{-4}$$

$$I_m = 1/2[(1.4 \times 10^{-4})(1)^2 + (1.6 \times 10^{-5})(2)^2 + (1.72 \times 10^{-4})(-1)^2] = 1.88 \times 10^{-4}$$

$$\log \gamma_\pm (\text{for NaCl}) = (0.509)(1)(-1)\sqrt{1.88 \times 10^{-4}} = -0.007$$

$$\gamma_\pm = 0.984$$

Many refinements of Debye-Hückel exist, but for the range in which it is truly valid, none are needed. Above this range, however, especially with mixed electrolytes, it is often better to have a means of obtaining an approximate value of $\gamma_\pm$ than to have no means at all. A useful form for our purposes, often called the Davies equation, is

$$\log \gamma_\pm = -(0.5)\left| Z_+ Z_- \right| \left[\frac{I_m^{\frac{1}{2}}}{1 + I_m^{\frac{1}{2}}} - 0.30 I_m \right]$$

At very low values of I_m, $I_m \ll \sqrt{I_m}$ and $\sqrt{I_m} \ll 1$, so that this form collapses to that of the limiting law. This form may be used to make approximate calculations up to 1 mol kg^{-1}. At that level, it will usually be accurate to $\pm 5\%$ for electrolytes with only singly charged ions, but deviations could go to 100% or more.

21-4 APPLICATION OF ACTIVITY COEFFICIENTS TO SOLUBILITY PRODUCTS

It is worth exploring one of the simplest applications of activity coefficients in order to demonstrate their use. Later, they will be needed again in the study of electrochemical cells.

Solubility products can be used to calculate solubilities exactly, even in mixed electrolytes, using activity coefficients. Conversely, solubilities provide a simple means of measuring many activity coefficients experimentally. Some examples follow.

Example 21-6   The solubility of AgCl in water at 25°C is measured to be 1.31×10^{-5} mol kg^{-1}. Calculate the mean ionic activity coefficient of AgCl in a saturated solution, using the Davies equation, and hence calculate K_{sp} for AgCl at 25°C.

$$I_m = \tfrac{1}{2}[(1.31 \times 10^{-5})(1)^2 + (1.31 \times 10^{-5})(-1)^2]$$

$$= 1.31 \times 10^{-5} \text{ mol kg}^{-1}$$

$$\log \gamma_\pm = -(0.5)(1)\left[\frac{(1.31 \times 10^{-5})^{\frac{1}{2}}}{1 + (1.31 \times 10^{-5})^{\frac{1}{2}}} - 0.30\,(1.31 \times 10^{-5})\right]$$

$$\gamma_\pm = 0.996$$

Therefore

$$K_{sp} = (a_{Ag^+})(a_{Cl^-})$$

$$= (\gamma_{Ag^+})(m_{Ag^+}/1)(\gamma_{Cl^-})(m_{Cl^-}/1)$$

$$= (\gamma_\pm)^2(1.31 \times 10^{-5})^2$$

$$= 1.70 \times 10^{-10}$$

Example 21-7   If K_{sp} for BaF$_2$ is 1.73×10^{-6} at 25°C, calculate the solubility of BaF$_2$ in water at this temperature. Use the Davies equation to evaluate the activity coefficient for BaF$_2$ in the saturated solution.

An iterative solution is necessary since an estimate of molality is required by the Davies equation. Obtain this by ignoring activity coefficients in the first stage so that

$$K_{sp} = 1.73 \times 10^{-6}$$

$$\approx (s)(2s)^2$$

This provides an estimated solubility of 7.6×10^{-3} mol kg^{-1}. When activity coefficients are ignored, this is the final answer but in this example a more accurate evaluation is sought. Substitution of this value into the Davies equation gives

$$I_m = \tfrac{1}{2}[(7.6 \times 10^{-3})(2)^2 + (15.2 \times 10^{-3})(-1)^2]$$

$$= 0.0228$$

$$\log \gamma_\pm = -0.5(2)\left[\frac{(0.0228)^{\frac{1}{2}}}{1 + (0.0228)^{\frac{1}{2}}} - 0.30(0.0228)\right]$$

$$\gamma_\pm = 0.75$$

Using this value predicts a solubility m such that

$$1.73 \times 10^{-6} = (0.75)^3 (m/1)(2m/1)^2$$

$$m = 1.01 \times 10^{-2} \, mol \, kg^{-1}$$

This value can then be used to obtain a more accurate value for $\gamma_\pm$ with which the whole process can be repeated. Such repetition leads finally to a solubility of $1.04 \times 10^{-2} \, mol \, kg^{-1}$.

Example 21-8 Using the solubility product calculated in Example 21-6, calculate the solubility of AgCl at 25°C in a solution which is 1.4×10^{-2} molal in NaF.

Since the concentration of NaF is much higher than the AgCl is likely to be, judging from Example 6, the ionic strength will be determined almost entirely by the concentration of the NaF.

$$I_m = \tfrac{1}{2}[(1.4 \times 10^{-2})(1)^2 + (1.4 \times 10^{-2})(-1)^2]$$

$$= 1.4 \times 10^{-2}$$

This value is used in the Davies equation to evaluate $\gamma_\pm$ for AgCl.

$$\log \gamma_\pm = -0.5(1) \left[\frac{(1.4 \times 10^{-2})^{\frac{1}{2}}}{1 + (1.4 \times 10^{-2})^{\frac{1}{2}}} - 0.30(1.4 \times 10^{-2}) \right]$$

$$\gamma_\pm = 0.89$$

The solubility, m, can now be calculated as follows.

$$K_{sp} = 1.70 \times 10^{-10}$$

$$= (0.89)^2 (m/1)(m/1)$$

$$m = 1.5 \times 10^{-5} \, mol \, kg^{-1}$$

Notice that the solubility is increased slightly by the presence of another electrolyte.

SUMMARY

Deviations from ideality can be ignored when dealing with very dilute solutions, but they become too large to ignore in concentrated solutions, especially in solutions of ions where deviations may be significant for even modest accuracy at a molality of $10^{-7} \, mol \, kg^{-1}$.

The treatment of non-ideal solutions is complicated by the variety of conventions and units used in the literature. Care is needed in reading papers or textbooks. One must note the units used (molality or molarity or, rarely, mole fraction), and the convention used for the standard state (pure material or ideal one molal solution).

This chapter develops briefly the most common approach to accurate work with aqueous solutions of ionic materials (molality).

FURTHER READING

J.N. Butler; *Ionic Equilibria;* Addison-Wesley, Massachusetts, 1964
Always well written, this text provides an account of various ways of measuring mean ionic activity coefficients in chapter 2, and a fair treatment of theory in chapter 12. The emphasis is on *using* activity coefficients.

J.O.M. Bockris and A.K.N. Reddy; *Modern Electrochemistry;* Plenum Press, New York, 1970
Chapter 3 of this advanced but highly readable textbook treats most aspects of mean ionic activity coefficients.

PROBLEMS

1. Calculate mole fraction, molality and molarity for an aqueous solution of NaOH which is 5.0000 % NaOH by mass at both 20°C, where the solution has a density of 1.0538 kg L^{-1}, and at 60°C, where it has a density of 1.0359 kg L^{-1}.

    [.02316, 1.3159, 1.3173; .02316, 1.3159, 1.2950]

2. Calculate I_m for each of the following aqueous solutions:

    (a) 0.100 molal KCl

    (b) 0.00500 molal CaBr$_2$

    (c) 0.100 molal in KCl and 0.00500 molal in CaBr$_2$

    [.100 mol kg^{-1}, .0150 mol kg^{-1}, .115 mol kg^{-1}]

3. Calculate the mean ionic activity coefficient, $\gamma_\pm$, for the following solutes at the molalities given and at a temperature of 25°C. Use the Davies equation. Compare the results with the experimental values in Table 21-1.

    (a) 0.10 molal HBr

    (b) 0.10 molal CaCl$_2$

    (c) 0.10 molal Li$_2$SO$_4$

    (d) 0.10 molal MgSO$_4$

    (e) 0.10 molal CrCl$_3$

4. Calculate the solubility of $SrSO_4$ at 25°C in (a) pure water, (b) 0.10 molal NaCl and (c) 0.10 molal Na_2SO_4. The solubility product is 2.82×10^{-7}. Use the Davies equation to evaluate $\gamma_{\pm}$.

$$[6.6 \times 10^{-4} \text{ mol kg}^{-1}, 1.4 \times 10^{-3} \text{ mol kg}^{-1}, 3.1 \times 10^{-5} \text{ mol kg}^{-1}]$$

5. Calculate the solubility product of silver chromate at 298.15 K using thermochemical data from Appendix 1. Using the Davies equation to evaluate $\gamma_{\pm}$, calculate the solubility of silver chromate in water at this temperature.

$$[1.2 \times 10^{-12}, 6.7 \times 10^{-5} \text{ mol kg}^{-1}]$$

XXII ELECTROCHEMISTRY

Processes involving transfer of electrons are extremely important both in science and in technology. These processes and their associated thermodynamic functions are the subject of this chapter.

Such processes are often referred to as oxidation/reduction processes or redox processes, arising from an early view that oxidation implied combination of a substance with oxygen. Later, the definition of oxidation was broadened to include any case in which the 'oxidation state' of a species is increased. In this general view, oxidation corresponds to a loss of electrons and its inverse, reduction, to a gain of electrons.

22-1 THE NATURE OF OXIDATION AND REDUCTION REACTIONS

Whether sodium metal reacts with O_2 to form the oxide (Na_2O), or with Cl_2 to form the chloride (NaCl), we say that the Na has been oxidized to Na^+, with an increase in oxidation state from 0 to +1.

$$2\,Na + \tfrac{1}{2}\,O_2 \rightarrow (2\,Na^+ + O^{2-}) \qquad \begin{cases} 2\,Na \rightarrow 2\,Na^+ + 2e \\ \tfrac{1}{2}O_2 + 2e \rightarrow O^{2-} \end{cases}$$

$$Na + \tfrac{1}{2}\,Cl_2 \rightarrow (Na^+ + Cl^-) \qquad \begin{cases} Na \rightarrow Na^+ + e \\ \tfrac{1}{2}\,Cl_2 + e \rightarrow Cl^- \end{cases}$$

In the formation of both Na_2O and NaCl, whether in solution or in the solid, sodium ions (Na^+) are formed according to what is termed an oxidation *half-reaction*, $Na \rightarrow Na^+ + e$. There is, of course, a matching or coupled reduction half-reaction involving, respectively, the reduction of O_2 to O^{2-}, or Cl_2 to Cl^-. But to concentrate on the oxidation half-reaction for the moment, the oxidation of 1 mol of Na to 1 mol of Na^+, as well as involving an increase in oxidation state from 0 to +1, is seen to involve a loss of 1 mol of electrons. As well as involving oxidation of metals to cations, oxidation processes may involve anions and neutral molecules, but all have in common the loss of electrons, as given in Table 22-1.

TABLE 22-1 Some Oxidation Half-reactions

$Al \rightarrow Al^{3+} + 3e$	metal to cation
$2\,Cl^- \rightarrow Cl_2 + 2e$	anion to non-metal
$NO_2^- + H_2O \rightarrow NO_3^- + 2\,H^+ + 2e$	anion to another anion
$H_2C_2O_4 \rightarrow 2\,CO_2 + 2\,H^+ + 2e$	molecule to another molecule
$CH_4 + 2\,H_2O \rightarrow CO_2 + 8\,H^+ + 8e$	molecule to another molecule

The reverse processes to the oxidation half-reactions shown in the table are reduction half-reactions. When various oxidation and reduction half-reactions are considered together it becomes apparent that the electrons required or consumed in a particular reduction must be supplied by some oxidation. In other words, a pair of oxidation and reduction half-reactions *couple* to produce a complete *redox reaction*. For example, the oxidation half-reaction, $Na \rightarrow Na^+ + e$, may supply the electrons required for the reduction half-reaction, $\frac{1}{2}\,Cl_2 + e \rightarrow Cl^-$, to give the overall results shown below.

$Na \rightarrow Na^+ + e$	oxidation half-reaction
$\frac{1}{2}\,Cl_2 + e \rightarrow Cl^-$	reduction half-reaction
$Na + \frac{1}{2}\,Cl_2 \rightarrow Na^+ + Cl^-$	complete redox reaction

Redox reactions are electron transfer processes. By comparison, the acid/base reactions of Chapter 20 are proton transfer processes.

Most materials can be involved in oxidation and reduction processes but there are some laboratory reagents used very often to oxidize other species. A list of some of these materials, known as oxidizing agents, and of their reducing counterparts, known as reducing agents, is found in Table 22-2.

TABLE 22-2 Some Common Reducing and Oxidizing Agents

(a) **Reducing Agents**
lithium aluminium hydride, $LiAlH_4 \rightarrow H_2$

$$\qquad\qquad\qquad\quad \overset{\displaystyle O}{\overset{\displaystyle \|}{}}$$

e.g. $LiAlH_4 + RCOH + H_2O \rightarrow RCH_2OH + LiAlO_2 + 2\,H_2$

carbon $C \rightarrow CO$
and carbon monoxide $CO \rightarrow CO_2$
e.g. $FeO + CO \rightarrow Fe + CO_2$

hydrazine dihydrochloride, $N_2H_4 \cdot 2\,HCl \rightarrow$ nitrogen, N_2
e.g. $N_2H_4 \cdot 2\,HCl + 2\,Cl_2 \rightarrow N_2 + 6\,HCl$

arsenious oxide, $As_2O_3 \rightarrow$ arsenic oxide As_2O_5
e.g. $As_2O_3 + 2\,Cl_2 + 5\,H_2O \rightarrow 2\,H_3AsO_4 + 4\,HCl$

hydrogen, $H_2 \rightarrow H^+$
e.g. $2\,H_2 + GeO_2 \rightarrow Ge(c) + 2\,H_2O$

(b) Oxidizing Agents

chromic acid CrO_4^{2-} → chromic ion, Cr^{3+}

$$\text{e.g. } 3 \, R_2C\overset{H}{-}OH + 2 \, H_2CrO_4 \rightarrow 3 \, R_2C = O + 2 \, Cr(OH)_3 + 2 \, H_2O$$

---

hydrogen peroxide H_2O_2 → water, H_2O

$$\text{e.g. } R\overset{O}{\overset{\|}{C}}H + HOOH \rightarrow R\overset{O}{\overset{\|}{C}}OH + H_2O$$

---

permanganate ion, MnO_4^- $\overset{H^+}{\rightarrow}$ manganous ion, Mn^{2+}

e.g. $2 \, KMnO_4 + 10 \, KI + 8 \, H_2SO_4 \rightarrow 6 \, K_2SO_4 + 2 \, MnSO_4 + 5 \, I_2 + 8 \, H_2O$

---

permanganate ion, MnO_4^- $\overset{OH^-}{\rightarrow}$ manganese dioxide, MnO_2

e.g. $2 \, KMnO_4 + KI + H_2O \overset{OH^-}{\rightarrow} 2 \, MnO_2 + 2 \, KOH + KIO_3$

---

oxygen, O_2 → oxide, O^{2-}

e.g. $2 \, Na + \frac{1}{2} O_2 \rightarrow Na_2O$

---

iodine, I_2 → iodide, I^-

e.g. $(CH_3)_2S + I_2 \rightarrow (CH_3)_2SI_2$

---

chlorine, Cl_2 → chloride, Cl^-

e.g. $SnCl_2 + Cl_2 \rightarrow SnCl_4$

---

palladium dichloride, $PdCl_2$ → palladium, Pd

$$\text{e.g. } C_2H_4 + PdCl_2 + H_2O \rightarrow CH_3\overset{O}{\overset{\|}{C}}H + Pd + 2 \, HCl$$

---

cupric ion, Cu^{2+} → cuprous ion, Cu^+

$$\text{e.g. } R\overset{O}{\overset{\|}{C}}H + 2 \, Cu(OH)_2 + NaOH \rightarrow R\overset{O}{\overset{\|}{C}}ONa + Cu_2O + 3 \, H_2O$$

Cupric ion complexed with tartrate ion is known as Fehling's reagent. The precipitation of the red Cu_2O makes it useful as a test for the presence of aldehydes.

22-2   OXIDATION NUMBER

The concept of oxidation number has its origin in inorganic chemistry. If a neutral atom acquires an electron the resulting ion is said to have an oxidation number of -1. Chlorine has an oxidation number of -1 in the chloride ion,

Cl^-. Similarly, iron is said to have an oxidation number of +2 in Fe^{2+} and of +3 in Fe^{3+}.

The concept of oxidation number or oxidation state as it is also called can be extended to include species where the electron transfer is far from complete. This is somewhat artificial but can be achieved using the following set of rules.

(a) All elements have an oxidation number of zero in their normal uncharged form, e.g. $Cu(c)$, $Cl_2(g)$, $Hg(l)$.

(b) The element in any monatomic ion has an oxidation number equal to the charge on the ion, e.g. sodium has an oxidation number of +1 in Na^+.

(c) Oxygen has an oxidation number of -2 in any compound except a peroxide (a compound having oxygens bonded $-O-O-$) in which case it has an oxidation state of -1.

  e.g. in MgO, oxygen has an oxidation number of -2,
  in CO_2 oxygen has an oxidation number of -2,
  but in H_2O_2 oxygen has an oxidation number of -1.

(d) Hydrogen has an oxidation number of +1 in any compound except metal hydrides, where the oxidation number is -1.

  e.g. in H_2O, hydrogen has an oxidation number of +1,
  in C_2H_6, hydrogen has an oxidation number of +1,
  but in LiH, hydrogen has an oxidation number of -1.

(e) Halogens have an oxidation number of -1 in any compound except oxides and interhalogen compounds

  e.g. In HCl, chlorine has an oxidation number of -1,
  in CCl_4, chlorine has an oxidation number of -1,
  but in ClO_2, chlorine has an oxidation number of +4,
  and in ClF_3, chlorine has an oxidation number of +3.

(f) In a polyatomic molecule, the sum of the oxidation numbers of the atoms is zero. In a polyatomic ion, the sum of the oxidation numbers of the atoms is equal to the charge on the ion.

It must be emphasized that oxidation states should not be interpreted too literally. While chemists do associate an increase in oxidation state with a decrease in electron density around the atom, it is far from complete. CCl_4, with carbon in an oxidation state of +4, certainly has less electron density associated with the carbon than is found in CH_4, where the carbon has an oxidation state of -4 but the difference is nowhere near the equivalent of complete transfer of 8 electrons. In inorganic chemistry too, difficulties may arise if these states are interpreted as predicting actual charge distributions in metal complexes. Basically, oxidation states should be thought of as a useful tool in interpreting and balancing oxidation/reduction processes, and as a rough but not infallible guide to the direction in which electron densities shift in such processes.

22-3   BALANCING REDOX EQUATIONS

While most chemical equations can be balanced easily, redox equations often provide a challenge and require a systematic approach. More than one technique exists for doing this. The particular one described below has the advantage that one need only be able to discern which species are reduced and oxidized.

Consider the redox process in which permanganate ion, MnO_4^-, in aqueous acid solution oxidizes ferrous ion, Fe^{2+}, to ferric ion, Fe^{3+}. The manganese is reduced to Mn^{2+}.

The *unbalanced* overall equation

$$MnO_4^- + Fe^{2+} \rightarrow Mn^{2+} + Fe^{3+}$$

can be split into two half-processes as follows

$$Fe^{2+} \rightarrow Fe^{3+}$$

$$MnO_4^- \rightarrow Mn^{2+}$$

However in this latter case we see that the Mn content is the same on both sides but the right side requires more O. How can this be supplied with some respect for reality? In aqueous solution the entities H_2O, H^+ and OH^- are always present to some extent. It is apparent that we could add the required oxygen in the form of H_2O or OH^-. Let us avoid the latter since the reaction is specified as going on in acid solution, and write,

$$MnO_4^- \rightarrow Mn^{2+} + 4\,H_2O.$$

But now 8H is required on the left. Supply this by adding $8H^+$,

$$MnO_4^- + 8\,H^+ \rightarrow Mn^{2+} + 4\,H_2O.$$

The half-reaction equations are now balanced for chemical elements as inspection will show. All that is required is to balance the charges, which can be done by adding electrons. The two half-reactions are now:

Oxidation	Reduction
$(Fe^{2+} \rightarrow Fe^{3+} + e) \times 5$	$MnO_4^- + 8\,H^+ + 5e \rightarrow Mn^{2+} + 4\,H_2O$

The oxidation half-reaction has been multiplied by 5 to make the electrons available the same as the number required by the reduction half-reaction. The complete cell reaction is, by summation,

$$5\,Fe^{2+} + MnO_4^- + 8\,H^+ \rightarrow 5\,Fe^{3+} + Mn^{2+} + 4\,H_2O$$

This is sometimes termed a *net* reaction as it leaves out all the unnecessary items which do not change in the reaction, such as the anion for Fe^{2+} and the cation for MnO_4^-.

The basis for handling the reaction as two half-reactions is a real one and not just an artifice. The electric cell which performs the above reaction can be set up as two physical half-cells and the transfer of electrons indicated on an instrument.

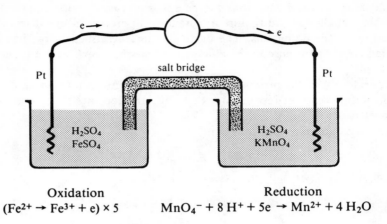

Oxidation

$(Fe^{2+} \rightarrow Fe^{3+} + e) \times 5$

Reduction

$MnO_4^- + 8\,H^+ + 5e \rightarrow Mn^{2+} + 4\,H_2O$

Figure 22-1

Any redox equation can be balanced by applying the following formal procedure. Students should learn this procedure by studying Examples 22-1 to 22-5.

1. Identify the reductant and oxidant by inspection of their respective oxidation states. Write skeleton half-reactions showing the reductant going to its oxidized state (oxidation) and the oxidant going to its reduced state (reduction). In each of these reactions balance the chemicals except for oxygen and hydrogen.

2. Balance the oxygen in each half-cell reaction by adding an appropriate amount of H_2O to the proper side. If oxygen is absent this step is not necessary.

3. Balance the hydrogen in each half-reaction by adding an appropriate amount of H^+ to the proper side. If hydrogen is absent this step is not necessary.

4. Balance the charges in each half-reaction by adding an appropriate number of electrons to the proper side.

5. Multiply the respective half-reactions by coefficients such that the oxidation supplies the same number of electrons that the reduction requires and add them to give the complete reaction.

6. If the reaction given is in basic solution eliminate any H^+ in the final result by adding the appropriate amount of OH^- to both sides of the equation. Combine H^+ and OH^- as H_2O and cancel H_2O from both sides if necessary.

Example 22-1   Balance $Pb(c) + PbO_2(c) + SO_4^{2-} \rightarrow PbSO_4(c)$ in acid solution

(1) Pb is the reductant (going to $PbSO_4$) and PbO_2 is the oxidant (also going to $PbSO_4$)

<table>
<tr><td colspan="2" align="center">Oxidation</td><td align="center">Reduction</td></tr>
<tr><td colspan="2" align="center">$Pb(c) + SO_4^{2-} \rightarrow PbSO_4(c)$</td><td align="center">$PbO_2(c) + SO_4^{2-} \rightarrow PbSO_4(c)$</td></tr>
<tr><td>(2)</td><td>(unnecessary)</td><td>$PbO_2(c) + SO_4^{2-} \rightarrow PbSO_4(c)\ 2\,H_2O$</td></tr>
<tr><td>(3)</td><td>(unnecessary)</td><td>$PbO_2(c) + SO_4^{2-} + 4\,H^+ \rightarrow PbSO_4(c) + 2\,H_2O$</td></tr>
<tr><td>(4)</td><td>$Pb(c) + SO_4^{2-} \rightarrow PbSO_4(c) + 2e$</td><td>$PbO_2(c) + SO_4^{2-} + 4\,H^+ + 2e \rightarrow PbSO_4(c) + 2\,H_2O$</td></tr>
</table>

(5)

$$Pb(c) + PbO_2(c) + 2\,SO_4^{2-} + 4\,H^+ \rightarrow 2\,PbSO_4(c) + 2\,H_2O$$

$$or\ Pb(c) + PbO_2(c) + 2\,H_2SO_4 \rightarrow 2\,PbSO_4(c) + 2\,H_2O$$

The above is the discharging reaction of the common lead storage battery with electrodes of Pb and PbO_2, both going to $PbSO_4(c)$ (white crystals) on discharge. If left in this condition the crystals will damage the cell. Since H_2SO_4 is used up to form H_2O in the discharge process, the specific gravity can be used to indicate the progress of discharge and recharge.

Example 22-2   Balance $H_2O_2 + SCN^- \rightarrow NH_4^+ + H_2O + HCO_3^- + HSO_4^-$
(in basic solution)

Oxidation	Reduction
(1) SCN^- is the reductant being oxidized to NH_4^+, HCO_3^-, HSO_4^-	H_2O_2 is the oxidant being reduced to H_2O
$SCN^- \rightarrow NH_4^+ + HCO_3^- + HSO_4^-$	$H_2O_2 \rightarrow H_2O$
(2) $SCN^- + 7\,H_2O \rightarrow NH_4^+ + HCO_3^- + HSO_4^-$	$H_2O_2 \rightarrow 2\,H_2O$
(3) $SCN^- + 7\,H_2O \rightarrow NH_4^+ + HCO_3^- + HSO_4^- + 8\,H^+$	$H_2O_2 + 2\,H^+ \rightarrow 2\,H_2O$
(4) $SCN^- + 7\,H_2O \rightarrow NH_4^+ + HCO_3^- + HSO_4^- + 8\,H^+ + 8e$	$(H_2O_2 + 2\,H^+ + 2e \rightarrow 2H_2O) \times 4$

(5)

$$SCN^- + 4H_2O_2 \rightarrow NH_4^+ + HCO_3^- + HSO_4^- + H_2O$$

(6)   (unnecessary)

Example 22-3   Balance $Cu(NH_3)_4^{2+} + CN^- \rightarrow CNO^- + Cu(CN)_3^{2-} + NH_3$ (in basic solution)

Oxidation	Reduction
(1) CN_- is the reductant being oxidized to CNO^-	$Cu(NH_3)_4^{2+}$ is the oxidant being reduced to $Cu(CN)_3^{2-}$
$CN^- \rightarrow CNO^-$	$Cu(NH_3)_4^{2+} + 3\,CN^- \rightarrow Cu(CN)_3^{2-} + 4\,NH_3$

Example 3 *continued*

(2) $CN^- + H_2O \rightarrow CNO^-$ (unnecessary)

(3) $CN^- + H_2O \rightarrow CNO^- + 2 H^+$ (unnecessary)

(4) $CN^- + H_2O \rightarrow CNO^- + 2 H^+ + 2e$ $(Cu(NH_3)_4{}^{2+} + 3 CN^- + 1e \rightarrow Cu(CN)_3{}^{2-} + 4 NH_3) \times 2$

(5) $2 Cu(NH_3)_4{}^{2+} + 7 CN^- + H_2O \rightarrow CNO^- + 2 Cu(CN)_3{}^{2-} + 8 NH_3 + 2 H^+$

(6) $2 OH^- \rightarrow 2 OH^-$

$2 Cu(NH_3)_4{}^{2+} + 7 CN^- + 2 OH^- \rightarrow CNO^- + 2 Cu(CN)_3{}^{2-} + 8 NH_3 + H_2O$

Example 22-4 Balance $Pb_3O_4(c) + Cl^- \rightarrow PbCl_2(c) + Cl_2$ (in acid solution)

Oxidation	Reduction
(1) Cl^- is the reductant being oxidized to Cl_2	Pb_3O_4 is the oxidant being reduced to $PbCl_2$

$$2 Cl^- \rightarrow Cl_2$$

$$Pb_3O_4(c) + 6 Cl^- \rightarrow 3 PbCl_2(c)$$

(2) (unnecessary)

$$Pb_3O_4(c) + 6 Cl^- \rightarrow 3 PbCl_2(c) + 4 H_2O$$

(3) (unnecessary)

$$Pb_3O_4(c) + 6 Cl^- + 8 H^+ \rightarrow 3 PbCl_2(c) + 4 H_2O$$

(4) $2 Cl^- \rightarrow Cl_2 + 2e$

$$Pb_3O_4(c) + 6 Cl^- + 8 H^+ + 2e \rightarrow 3 PbCl_2(c) + 4 H_2O$$

(5) $Pb_3O_4(c) + 8 H^+ + 8 Cl^- \rightarrow 3 PbCl_2(c) + Cl_2 + 4 H_2O$

(6) (unnecessary)

Example 22-5 Balance $ClO_3{}^- + As_2S_3(c) \rightarrow Cl^- + H_2AsO_4{}^- + S(c)$ (in acid solution)

Oxidation	Reduction
(1) As_2S_3 is the reductant being oxidized to $H_2AsO_4{}^-$ and S	$ClO_3{}^-$ is the oxidant being reduced to Cl^-

$$As_2S_3(c) \rightarrow 2 H_2AsO_4{}^- + 3 S(c)$$

$$ClO_3{}^- \rightarrow Cl^-$$

(2) $As_2S_3(c) + 8 H_2O \rightarrow 2 H_2AsO_4{}^- + 3 S(c)$

$$ClO_3{}^- \rightarrow Cl^- + 3 H_2O$$

(3) $As_2S_3(c) + 8 H_2O \rightarrow 2 H_2AsO_4{}^- + 3 S(c) + 12 H^+$

$$ClO_3{}^- + 6 H^+ \rightarrow Cl^- + 3 H_2O$$

(4) $As_2S_3(c) + 8 H_2O \rightarrow 2 H_2AsO_4{}^- + 3 S(c) + 12 H^+ + 10e$ $ClO_3{}^- + 6 H^+ + 6e \rightarrow Cl^- + 3 H_2O$

$\times 3$	$\times 5$

(5) $5 ClO_3{}^- + 3 As_2S_3(c) + 9 H_2O \rightarrow 5 Cl^- + 6 H_2AsO_4{}^- + 9 S(c) + 6 H^+$

(6) (unnecessary)

In the preceding examples it can be seen that a certain chemical sense or knowledge is required to write the original skeleton equations of Step 1. On the other hand the remaining steps require only care in manipulation. They follow logically from Step 1. Unfortunately, the success of the whole operation depends on Step 1. It is important that the student realize just what is required in the matter of memorization. Otherwise he or she might get the false impression that the study of chemistry requires an infinite memory.

At this stage the student should have a working knowledge of the behaviour of some common oxidants and reductants, lists of which have been given already. With further experience the list should grow. The student should also be acquainted with the common oxidation states of the most common elements and so be able to predict without too much strain on the memory just what will happen to a certain element undergoing oxidation or reduction.

22-4   THE ELECTROCHEMICAL CELL

Water is a poor conductor of electricity. So are most ionic crystals such as $CaCl_2$ or NaF. If, however, the ionic material is dissolved in water, an excellent conductor is produced. Any ionic material which produces a highly conducting aqueous solution is called an electrolyte. Whereas in a metal, electricity is conducted by electrons moving, in a solution of an electrolyte it is ions which move.

To make a cell, two conducting *electrodes* must be inserted into the solution, one to bring electrons in and one to conduct them away. In the solution, the current is carried between the electrodes by the ions. At one electrode, incoming electrons are transferred *to* some species, which is a reduction process. The electrode at which this occurs is the *cathode*. At the other electrode, some species give up electrons which the electrode then carries away. This is oxidation, and the electrode at which it occurs is called the *anode*.

When energy is supplied to the cell, the cell is called an electrolytic cell. When the cell is a source of energy, it is called a galvanic or voltaic cell. In both of these, oxidation occurs at the anode and reduction at the cathode.

Conventions exist for stating the construction of a galvanic cell in a condensed way. The various phases are shown in the order in which they contact one another, beginning with the anode on the left. Separate phases are shown separated by a vertical line. The cell components to which external connections are made are on the extreme left and right. If the cell includes two solutions joined by a salt bridge (of which more later), the salt bridge is represented by two vertical lines. It is usually assumed that the salt bridge does not affect the cell potential.

Example 22-6   A galvanic cell consists of a solution that is 0.10 mol kg^{-1} in Cu^{2+} into which is placed a copper bar, and a solution that is 0.050 mol kg^{-1} in Ag^+, into which is inserted a silver bar. The solutions are joined by a salt bridge. The silver is the cathode. (Note that we ignore the ions which do not participate. The Cu^{2+}, for example, may be there as $CuSO_4$ but the SO_4^{2-} is not part of the cell process and is omitted.) Draw the cell diagram.

$$Cu \mid Cu^{2+} \, (aq. \, 0.10m) \parallel Ag^+ \, (aq. \, 0.050m) \mid Ag$$

Example 22-7 Consider a cell in which the Cu | Cu²⁺ portion of the above is replaced with a platinum conductor contained in a glass tube into which is passed hydrogen gas at 110 kPa. The platinum wire dips into a 0.15 mol kg⁻¹ HCl solution into which the hydrogen is bubbled. The silver is the cathode. Draw the cell diagram

$$Pt \mid H_2(g, 110 \text{ kPa}) \mid H^+(aq. 0.15m) \mid\mid Ag^+(aq. 0.050m) \mid Ag$$

22-5 THE THERMODYNAMICS OF GALVANIC CELLS

The cell process of the cell in Example 22-6 is as follows:

$$Cu(c) + 2 Ag^+(aq) \rightarrow Cu^{2+}(aq) + 2 Ag(c)$$

For this, as for any process at constant T and P we may write

$$\Delta G = \Delta G^\circ + RT \ln Q$$

where

$$Q = \frac{a_{Cu^{2+}} \, a_{Ag}^{\,2}}{a_{Cu} \, (a_{Ag^+})^2}$$

As before, the activity of a pure solid metal is equal to unity, and the expression simplifies to

$$\Delta G = \Delta G^\circ + RT \ln \frac{a_{Cu^{2+}}}{(a_{Ag^+})^2}$$

The potential of a cell, measured under conditions of zero current, is called the electromotive force or emf, and has the symbol E. A galvanic cell is capable of doing work, such as running a motor which lifts a weight. We saw earlier that the maximum work which a process can do, when run reversibly, is ΔG. With a galvanic cell, it is possible to run it reversibly in practice, as well as in theory. The cell in our example produces some particular emf, E. The work that is available externally is the equal to qE where q is the charge that passes through the potential difference E in the external circuit.

To determine q, consider the cell process as comprised of two *half-cell processes*, as follows:

$$Cu \rightarrow Cu^{2+} + 2e$$

$$Ag^+ + 2e \rightarrow 2 Ag$$

From this one sees that the consumption of one mole of Cu and two of Ag⁺, and the formation of one mole of Cu²⁺ and two of Ag, results in the passage of two mole of electrons, bearing a charge of 2 faraday. Since this is the process to which ΔG refers, one can now complete the relationship as follows

$$\Delta G = -qE = -2FE$$

The minus sign arises because a cell voltage is defined as being positive for a real cell with a natural cell process, for which ΔG is negative. The symbol F is used to denote the Faraday constant, 96 485 coulomb mol⁻¹.

One problem remains. If one mole of copper really did dissolve, the concentration of Cu^{2+} would be increasing throughout. Simultaneously, the concentration of Ag^+ would be in decline and E would be changing. What one really wishes to know is the dG associated with the passage of an infinitesimal charge dq but we can reach the correct conclusion, without an appeal to the calculus, by considering a very large cell - swimming pool size at least. In such a huge cell, a mole of copper could dissolve without significantly changing Q. For such a cell, ΔG and E could be related as above. For a smaller cell, of the usual size, the relationship is equally valid as an expression of the Gibbs energy change **per mole** of Cu. The real passage of current and change in concentration in our cell, finite in size and balanced as it is by an external potential to ensure reversibility, is infinitesimal, but the change in G, per mole, and the charge passed, per mole, is as we have calculated. All of this is exactly in agreement with the analogous comments on gas phase reactions in Section 16-13.

Finally, note that if all the materials involved in the cell process are in their standard states, and one defines $E°$ as the cell emf produced by such a cell, then Q = 1 when all materials are in their standard states, so that

$$-2FE° = \Delta G° + 0$$

$$2FE = 2FE° + RT \ln Q$$

$$E = E° - \frac{RT}{2F} \ln Q$$

Put more generally, for a cell process involving n mole of electrons passing through an external circuit,

$$E = E° - \frac{RT}{nF} \ln Q = E° - \frac{0.0592}{n} \log Q \text{ at } 25°C$$

This equation, known as the Nernst equation, permits calculation of the emf of any cell from the activities of its constituents and a knowledge of $E°$. There are, in fact, some difficulties with this but it does form the basis for a reasonable approximation in most cases. How, then, does one establish a value for $E°$? This question is answered in the next section.

22-6   SINGLE ELECTRODE POTENTIALS

The necessary data for calculating $E°$ for any cell can be tabulated much more compactly if a value $\varepsilon°$ can be assigned to each *half*-cell. Although one can regard a voltaic cell as consisting of two half-cells, one with an oxidation process and one with a reduction process, it is impossible to measure an $\varepsilon°$ for such a half-cell absolutely. The ΔG associated with the process

$$Cu^{2+} (aq,m) + 2e \rightarrow Cu(c)$$

depends on the ease with which the electrons are supplied. This problem can be overcome by arbitrarily choosing a reference potential and measuring all other potentials relative to it. The universal choice is the potential which accepts (or provides) electrons reversibly for the following process.

$$\tfrac{1}{2} H_2(g, P^\circ, \textit{ideal}) \rightleftharpoons H^+(aq, m=unity, \textit{ideal}) + e$$

ΔG° for this process is defined as being zero at all temperatures. Note that since both the H_2 and the H^+ are in their standard states, the ΔG and ε associated with this process are the ΔG° and ε° for the process. Note too, that they are zero for both directions of the process. The standard state for ions in solution was introduced in Section 21-1. Just as the standard state for gases is a hypothetical one involving $P = P^\circ$ but ideal gas properties, so for solutions it involves $m = $ unity but ideal solution properties. Although ε is zero for this ideal half-cell, the half-cell potential for a real hydrogen half-cell with $P_{H_2} = P^\circ$ and molality of H^+ equal to unity will *not* be zero, because both the real gas and the real solution, especially the latter, differ from their hypothetical ideal counterparts on which the standard state half-cell potential, ε°, is based.

If one then constructs a cell involving a hydrogen electrode and another electrode, measurement of the E° of the cell allows calculation of the electrode potential, ε°, of the second electrode. Experimental methods of making such measurements are described in Section 22-16. Either of these electrodes could then be used in combination with other electrodes to establish ε° values for them. These are expressed as standard *reduction* potentials as in Table 22-3.

A few texts and tables express them as oxidation potentials, which have the same numerical value but the opposite sign. Care must therefore be taken in using tables of ε°. Tabulated ε° values represent exceedingly compact data storage. A table of 100 such values can be coupled two at a time to give the E° for nearly 5000 cells and their corresponding processes. Note that a large positive ε° corresponds to a strong tendency for the electrode to be reduced and a large negative ε° corresponds to a strong tendency for the electrode to be oxidized.

Example 22-8   Calculate E° for the two cells in Examples 6 and 7.

In Example 6

$Cu \rightarrow Cu^{2+} + 2e$	$\varepsilon^\circ = -0.34$ V
$2\,Ag^+ + 2e \rightarrow 2\,Ag$	$\varepsilon^\circ = 0.80$ V
$Cu + 2\,Ag^+ \rightarrow Cu^{2+} + 2Ag$	$E^\circ = 0.46$ V

In Example 7

$\tfrac{1}{2} H_2 \rightarrow H^+ + e$	$\varepsilon^\circ = 0.00$ V
$Ag^+ + e \rightarrow Ag$	$\varepsilon^\circ = 0.80$ V
$\tfrac{1}{2} H_2 + Ag^+ \rightarrow H^+ + Ag$	$E^\circ = 0.80$ V

TABLE 22-3 Standard Reduction Potentials at 298.15 K

Reduction Process	$\varepsilon°/V$
$\frac{1}{2}F_2 + H^+ + e \rightarrow HF$	3.06
$\frac{1}{2}F_2 + e \rightarrow F^-$	2.92
$O_3 + 2H^+ + 2e \rightarrow O_2 + H_2O$	2.07
$\frac{1}{2}S_2O_8^{2-} + e \rightarrow SO_4^{2-}$	2.01
$Co^{3+} + e \rightarrow Co^{2+}$	1.82
$\frac{1}{2}H_2O_2 + H^+ + e \rightarrow H_2O$	1.77
$MnO_4^- + 4H^+ + 3e \rightarrow MnO_2 + 2H_2O$	1.70
$PbO_2 + 4H^+ + SO_4^{2-} + 2e \rightarrow PbSO_4 + 2H_2O$	1.68
$Ce^{4+} + e \rightarrow Ce^{3+}\ (1F\,HNO_3)$	1.61
$BrO_3^- + 6H^+ + 5e \rightarrow \frac{1}{2}Br_2 + 3H_2O$	1.52
$MnO_4^- + 8H^+ + 5e \rightarrow Mn^{2+} + 4H_2O$	1.51
$ClO_3^- + 6H^+ + 5e \rightarrow \frac{1}{2}Cl_2 + 3H_2O$	1.47
$\frac{1}{2}Cl_2 + e \rightarrow Cl^-$	1.361
$Cr_2O_7^{2-} + 14H^+ + 6e \rightarrow 2Cr^{3+} + 7H_2O$	1.33
$O_2 + 4H^+ + 4e \rightarrow 2H_2O$	1.229
$IO_3^- + 6H^+ + 5e \rightarrow \frac{1}{2}I_2 + 3H_2O$	1.119
$\frac{1}{2}Br_2 + e \rightarrow Br^-$	1.08
$NO_3^- + 4H^+ + 3e \rightarrow NO + 2H_2O$	0.96
$Hg^{2+} + e \rightarrow \frac{1}{2}Hg_2^{2+}$	0.90
$Hg^{2+} + 2e \rightarrow Hg$	0.852
$Ag^+ + e \rightarrow Ag$	0.7990
$\frac{1}{2}Hg_2^{2+} + e \rightarrow Hg$	0.792
$Fe^{3+} + e \rightarrow Fe^{2+}$	0.771
$O_2 + 2H^+ + 2e \rightarrow H_2O_2$	0.68
$\frac{1}{2}I_2 + e \rightarrow I^-$	0.538
$Cu^+ + e \rightarrow Cu$	0.518
$VO^{2+} + 2H^+ + e \rightarrow V^{3+} + H_2O$	0.36
$Fe(CN)_6^{3-} + e \rightarrow Fe(CN)_6^{4-}$	0.356
$Cu^{2+} + 2e \rightarrow Cu$	0.340
$\frac{1}{2}Hg_2Cl_2 + e \rightarrow Hg + Cl^-$	0.2680
$AgCl + e \rightarrow Ag + Cl^-$	0.2224
$Cu^{2+} + e \rightarrow Cu^+$	0.153
$Sn^{4+} + 2e \rightarrow Sn^{2+}$	0.15
$S + 2H^+ + 2e \rightarrow H_2S$	0.14
$AgBr + e \rightarrow Ag + Br^-$	0.071
$\frac{1}{2}S_4O_6^{2-} + e \rightarrow S_2O_3^{2-}$	0.08
$H^+ + e \rightarrow \frac{1}{2}H_2$	0.00
$Pb^{2+} + 2e \rightarrow Pb$	-0.13
$Sn^{2+} + 2e \rightarrow Sn$	-0.14
$AgI + e \rightarrow Ag + I^-$	-0.152
$Ni^{2+} + 2e \rightarrow Ni$	-0.24
$V^{3+} + e \rightarrow V^{2+}$	-0.26
$Co^{2+} + 2e \rightarrow Co$	-0.28
$PbSO_4 + 2e \rightarrow Pb + SO_4^{2-}$	-0.361
$Ti^{3+} + e \rightarrow Ti^{2+}$	-0.37
$Cd^{2+} + 2e \rightarrow Cd$	-0.403
$Cr^{3+} + e \rightarrow Cr^{2+}$	-0.41
$Fe^{2+} + 2e \rightarrow Fe$	-0.440
$2CO_2 + 2H^+ + 2e \rightarrow H_2C_2O_4$	-0.44
$Cr^{3+} + 3e \rightarrow Cr$	-0.74
$Zn^{2+} + 2e \rightarrow Zn$	-0.7630
$Cr^{2+} + 2e \rightarrow Cr$	-0.91
$V^{2+} + 2e \rightarrow V$	-1.18
$Mn^{2+} + 2e \rightarrow Mn$	-1.18
$Al^{3+} + 3e \rightarrow Al$	-1.69
$Mg^{2+} + 2e \rightarrow Mg$	-2.36
$Na^+ + e \rightarrow Na$	-2.71
$Ca^{2+} + 2e \rightarrow Ca$	-2.865
$K^+ + e \rightarrow K$	-2.928
$Li^+ + e \rightarrow Li$	-3.033

Note that writing the process of silver ion giving silver in a different way, double in 6 what it is in 7, does not alter $E°$ for that half cell process. A given cell has a given voltage no matter how large you make it or how you express the processes. What is larger is $\Delta G°$, as will be clear from the next example.

Example 22-9 Calculate $\Delta G°$ for the cell in Example 6.

For Example 6, the cell process is

$$Cu \rightarrow Cu^{2+} + 2e$$

$$\underline{2\,Ag^+ + 2e \rightarrow 2\,Ag}$$

$$Cu + 2\,Ag^+ \rightarrow Cu^{2+} + 2\,Ag$$

Hence, $\Delta G° = -nFE°$

$$= -(2)(96\,485)(0.46) = -88.8\,kJ$$

Notice that if we had written the process as

$$\tfrac{1}{2}\,Cu + Ag^+ \rightarrow \tfrac{1}{2}\,Cu^{2+} + Ag$$

$$E° = 0.46\,V \text{ (unchanged)}$$

$$n = 1 \text{ (down proportionately)}$$

$$\Delta G° = -(1)(96\,485)(0.46) = -44.4\,kJ$$

Example 22-10 Use $E°$ data to calculate $\Delta G_f°$ for H^+, F^- and Mg^{2+} ions in aqueous solution.

For H^+, the formation process is

$$\tfrac{1}{2}\,H_2(g,\,P°,\,ideal) \rightarrow H^+(aq,\,m{=}1,\,ideal) + e$$

$$\varepsilon° = 0$$

$$\Delta G° = 0$$

For F^-, the formation process is

$$\tfrac{1}{2}\,F_2(g,\,P°,\,ideal) + e \rightarrow F^-(aq,\,m{=}1,\,ideal)$$

$$\varepsilon° = 2.87\,V$$

$$n = 1$$

$$\Delta G° = -277\,kJ$$

For Mg^{2+}, the formation process is

$$Mg(c) \rightarrow Mg^{2+}(aq, m = 1, ideal) + 2e$$

$$\varepsilon^\circ = +2.37 \text{ V}$$

$$n = 2$$

$$\Delta G^\circ = -457 \text{ kJ}$$

The tabulated value is -456 kJ.

Example 22-11   Assuming that activity coefficients can be ignored, so that $a_{Cu2} \approx [Cu^{2+}]_r$ and so forth, calculate E for the cells in Examples 6 and 7 at 298.15 K.

In Example 6

$$a_{Cu^{2+}} \approx [Cu^{2+}]_r = 0.10$$

$$a_{Ag^+} \approx [Ag^+]_r = 0.050$$

The cell process is

$$Cu(c) + 2 Ag^+(0.050 \text{ m}, aq.) \rightarrow Cu^{2+}(0.10 \text{ m}, aq) + 2 Ag(c)$$

The value of E° (see Example 8) is 0.46 V

$$E = E^\circ - \frac{RT}{n F} \ln \frac{[Cu^{2+}]_r}{[Ag^+]_r^2}$$

$$= 0.46 - \frac{(8.314)(298.15)}{(2)(96\ 485)} \ln \frac{0.10}{0.050}$$

$$= 0.45 \text{ V}.$$

In Example 7

$$a_{H_2} \approx \frac{P_{H_2}}{P^\circ} = \frac{110}{101.325} = 1.09$$

$$a_{Ag^+} \approx [Ag^+]_r = 0.050$$

$$a_{H^+} \approx [H^+]_r = 0.15$$

The cell process is

$$H_2(g, 110 \text{ kPa}) + 2 Ag^+(aq, 0.050\text{m}) \rightarrow 2 H^+ (aq, 0.15\text{m}) + 2 Ag(c)$$

The value of E° (see Example 8) is 0.80 V

$$E = E^\circ - \frac{RT}{n F} \ln \frac{[H^+]_r^2}{(P_{H_2}/P^\circ)[Ag^+]_r^2}$$

$$= 0.80 - \frac{(8.314)(298.15)}{(2)(96\ 485)} \ln \frac{(0.15)^2}{(1.09)(0.050)^2}$$

$$= 0.77 \text{ V}.$$

Example 22-12 Calculate ε° for $Cu^{2+} + e \rightarrow Cu^+$ from ε° values for $Cu^{2+} + 2e \rightarrow Cu(c)$ and $Cu^+ + e \rightarrow Cu(c)$.

Consider the following half cells:

$$Cu^{2+} + 2e \rightarrow Cu(c) \qquad\qquad \Delta G_A^\circ = -2\,F\,\varepsilon_A^\circ$$

$$Cu^+ + e \rightarrow Cu(c) \qquad\qquad \Delta G_B^\circ = -1\,F\,\varepsilon_B^\circ$$

Subtracting one equation from the other

$$Cu^{2+} + e \rightarrow Cu^+ \qquad\qquad \Delta G_c^\circ = \Delta G_A^\circ - \Delta G_B^\circ$$

$$-1\,F\varepsilon_c^\circ = -2\,F\,\varepsilon_A^\circ + 1\,F\,\varepsilon_B^\circ$$

$$\varepsilon_c^\circ = 2\,\varepsilon_A^\circ - \varepsilon_B^\circ$$

$$= 2(+0.34) - (+0.52)$$

$$= +0.16\ \text{V}$$

The conservation of Gibbs energy is illustrated in the following diagram summarizing the n and ε° values.

$$Cu^{2+} \xrightarrow{\ 1 \times 0.16\ } Cu^+ \xrightarrow{\ 1 \times 0.52\ } Cu(c)$$
$$\underset{2 \times 0.34}{\underline{\qquad\qquad\qquad\qquad\qquad}}$$

Similar diagrams for other metals may be constucted to show the relationships between different oxidation states in solution in the standard state:

$$Fe^{3+} \xrightarrow{\ 1 \times 0.77\ } Fe^{2+} \xrightarrow{\ 2 \times (-0.44)\ } Fe(c)$$
$$\underset{3 \times (-0.04)}{\underline{\qquad\qquad\qquad\qquad\qquad}}$$

$$Hg^{2+} \xrightarrow{\ 1 \times 0.92\ } \tfrac{1}{2}\,Hg_2^{2+} \xrightarrow{\ 1 \times 0.79\ } Hg(l)$$
$$\underset{2 \times 0.86}{\underline{\qquad\qquad\qquad\qquad\qquad}}$$

22-7 GALVANIC CELLS IN PRACTICE

All galvanic cells involve reactants being oxidized at the anode and reduced at the cathode with consequent production of an electric current. Cells which are discarded when spent and are not recharged either chemically or electrically are called *primary cells*. An example is the ordinary dry cell used in a flashlight. Galvanic cells in which new reactants are fed in continuously are called *fuel cells*. Galvanic cells which are reversible in the sense that they can be recharged after use by application of a reverse electric current are called *storage cells* or *secondary cells*. The best known example is the lead/acid battery used in most automobiles.

Primary cells and fuel cells are sometimes grouped as *convertors,* in reference to the fact that both serve to effect a one-way conversion of chemical energy to electrical energy. Secondary cells by definition work both ways. In general language, all of these types of cells are often called *batteries* although the word battery should properly be used to describe two or more cells in series in a package.

22-8   PRIMARY CELLS

These are cells in which chemical substances are consumed in the electrode reactions which provide electrical energy. The substances are not replaced nor is the cell recharged. At the end of its life the cell is discarded as an electrical source but the materials may be recovered for re-use. Often these cells are called dry cells, meaning that the electrolyte is used as a paste or impregnated in a matrix rather than as a liquid. Most dry cells work best in intermittent use, recuperating somewhat in between. They deteriorate even on the shelf. Testing with a voltmeter is almost useless, unless under load, since even a badly discharged cell will still test at the nominal voltage on open circuit. Tests should be at the maximum rated current.

The three most commonly used primary cells are described below.

(a) Zn/MnO_2 or Leclanché Cells

$$\text{Anode: } Zn \rightarrow Zn^{2+} + 2e \text{ (negative)}$$

$$\underline{\text{Cathode: } 2\,MnO_2 + 2\,NH_4^+ + 2e \rightarrow Mn_2O_3 + 2\,NH_3 + H_2O}$$

$$\text{Cell: } Zn + 2\,MnO_2 + 2\,NH_4^+ \rightarrow Zn(NH_3)_2^{2+} + Mn_2O_3 + H_2O$$

This cell has a solid Zn anode and a complex cathode which consists of a central rod of carbon contacting a paste containing MnO_2, aqueous NH_4Cl and $ZnCl_2$, and graphite. The Zn anode is a can which serves as the container. The MnO_2 is obviously the oxidant which consumes electrons, but it is technically termed a depolarizer. This is the cell which is normally sold as a "flashlight battery," having a nominal voltage of 1.5 V.

(b) Alkaline Zn/MnO_2

$$\text{Anode: } Zn + 2\,OH^- \rightarrow Zn(OH)_2 + 2e \text{ (negative)}$$

$$\underline{\text{Cathode: } 2\,MnO_2 + 2\,H_2O \rightarrow 2MnOOH + 2\,OH^-}$$

$$\text{Cell: } Zn + 2\,MnO_2 + 2\,H_2O \rightarrow Zn(OH)_2 + 2\,MnOOH$$

An outgrowth of the above is what is called the alkaline Zn/MnO_2 cell or simply the "alkaline cell." KOH is used as the electrolyte and the container is made of steel, with the anode spongy Zn. The emf is 1.55 V but the cells are nominally sold as 1.5 V. They have improved shelf-life, the capacity is doubled and does not fall off under load, the current is higher, and the cell operates down to $-40°C$. For a more reliable source under load or in the cold this cell is recommended, but the price is roughly quadrupled. They are used to power instruments, cameras, toys and other small appliances.

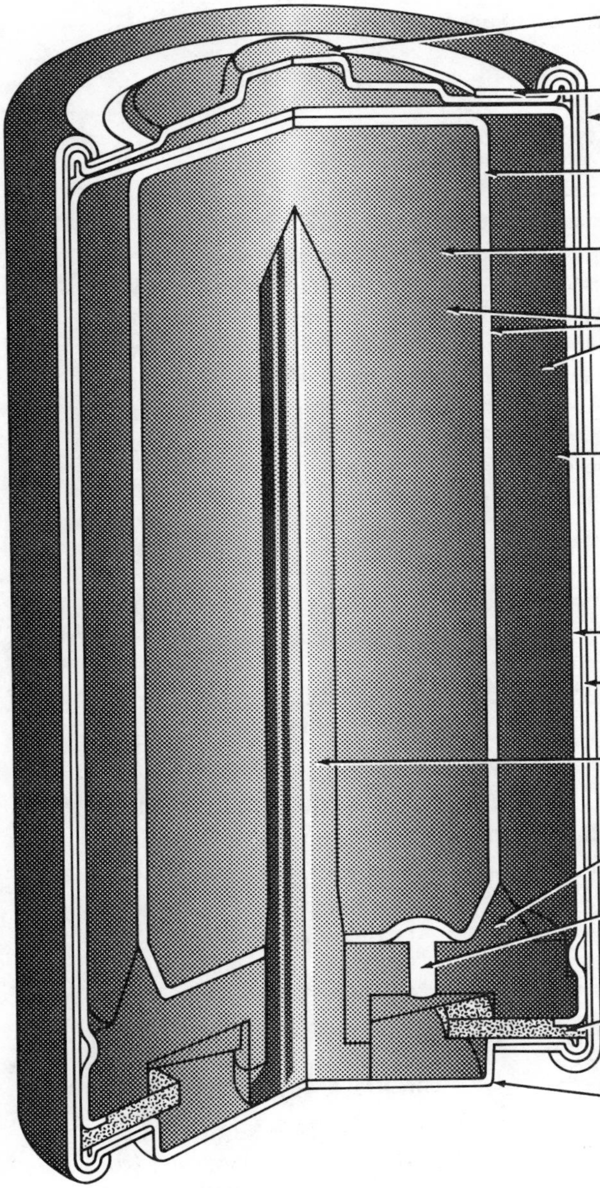

Cathode Cap (Positive Terminal)
Protrusion in contact with steel
cell case.

Insulating Washer

Outer Steel Jacket
Lithographed in copper and black.

Separator
A sleeve of porous, synthetic fiber
impregnated with electrolyte.

Anode
Powdered zinc, highly amalgamated
and compacted.

Electrolyte
Potassium hydroxide (KOH)
solution absorbed into separator,
anode material and cathode
material.

Cathode
Compressed mix of electrolytic
manganese dioxide MnO_2 and
graphite, introduced either by
extrusion or by insertion in the
form of pre-formed, tight-fitting
cylindrical rings.

Cathode Collector
Steel cell case.

Plastic Sleeve
Separates steel case from outer steel
jacket.

Anode Collector
Metal "nail."

Plastic Grommet
Forms a structural, insulating seal
for cell.

Vent
Wax-sealed hole in plastic grommet
(releases gases if they build up and
prevents cell rupture).

Insulator
Separates (and insulates) steel cell
case (positive) from the end cap
(negative).

Anode Cap (Negative Terminal)
Protrusion in contract with collector
"nail."

Figure 22-2   Alkaline Manganese Cell

(c) Zn/HgO

$$\text{(negative)} \quad \text{Anode: } Zn + O^{2-} \rightarrow ZnO + 2e$$

$$\text{Cathode: } HgO + 2e \rightarrow Hg + O^{2-}$$

$$\text{Cell: } Zn + HgO \rightarrow Hg + ZnO$$

These primary cells are referred to as mercury or Ruben-Mallory Cells. They have a steel case connecting to the HgO cathode and a cap contacting the Zn (amalgam) anode. Insulating gaskets prevent the case and cap from shorting. The electrolyte of KOH is contained in a disc of porous material. In potential this cell is unusually constant over the discharge period and also holds up well on the shelf. The emf of 1.35 V is remarkably constant from cell to cell. These cells were developed during World War II out of a need for maximum energy per volume in portable equipment. They have greater capacity than the alkaline Zn/MnO_2, but suffer more under load. They are about five times as expensive as alkaline cells. Their prime use is for a reliably constant voltage source as required often in medical and scientific equipment. A similar cell, which is often in the form of a flat small button, has a Ag_2O cathode.

22-9 FUEL CELLS

Such cells have an anode at which reductant is supplied for the duration of the operation. The reductant or fuel is consumed by oxidation, usually by O_2 in air supplied at the cathode, but other oxidants are used such as Cl_2. Fuels which have been seriously considered have been both liquid and gaseous H_2, hydrazine, N_2H_4, methanol, and hydro-carbons. H_2 is not much more dangerous to handle than is gasoline, but it is more easily handled. It has much less energy per volume than the liquid fuels. Hydrazine is probably too toxic for general commercial use.

Intense interest in fuel cells arises in part from their ability to achieve an efficiency in conversion of the order of 60% or better. Furthermore, most of the important fuel cells have non-polluting products such as H_2O, N_2 and CO_2. If in the future our energy economy becomes based on hydrogen from the electrolysis of water, then H_2/O_2 fuel cells will have important advantages.

A schematic representation of a H_2/O_2 fuel cell is given in Figure 22-3.

One of the major challenges in the design of fuel cells has been the development of suitable catalysts, particularly at the O_2 cathode. Platinum metals have been used successfully but are too expensive. Cheaper transition metals such as nickel are also common, while new developments favour the use of nickel and cobalt superlattices, spinel and perovskite.

Fuel cells have been produced for automobile and truck use, for tractors, as power plants for apartment houses, and for aerospace units such as the U.S. Gemini and Apollo spacecraft. This last fuel cell had 1 kW output with 63% efficiency. Mass is also an important consideration. The fuel cells in the General Motors "Electrovan" weigh about 1500 kg, almost half the total mass of the vehicle.

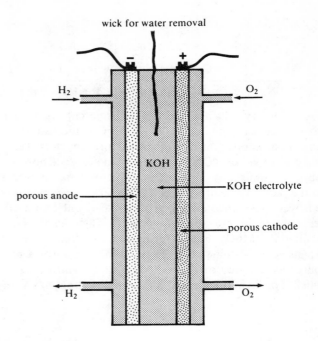

Figure 22-3 H_2/O_2 Fuel Cell (Schematic).

22-10   SECONDARY OR STORAGE CELLS

Perusal of a thermodynamic table of electrode reactions with their corresponding potentials might lead one to the impression that most of these reactions are reversible in practice as well as in theory. Otherwise why should they be treated thermodynamically at all?

There are two definite occasions when thermodynamics apply rigorously to cell reactions. One is when the cell is on open circuit with no appreciable reaction and no appreciable current. Then the full cell emf is obtained. The other is when the cell has been fully discharged so that all substances in it have reached equilibrium and the emf is zero.

But when a cell is under load it does not deliver the full cell emf because of losses owing to the resistance drop within the cell, and a kinetic effect termed overvoltage. Furthermore most electrode reactions are not easily reversed, particularly those which involve solid substances, where chemical changes cannot occur quickly enough to keep pace with the electrical flow required. These factors effectively eliminate the possibility of recharging most cells. There are successful secondary cells, however, of which the most common is the lead/acid cell.

(a) Lead/acid

Anode: $Pb + SO_4^{2-} \rightarrow PbSO_4 + 2e$

Cathode: $PbO_2 + 4\,H^+ + SO_4^{2-} + 2e \rightarrow PbSO_4 + 2\,H_2O$

$$\text{Cell: } Pb + PbO_2 + 2\,H_2SO_4 \underset{\text{charge}}{\overset{\text{discharge}}{\rightleftharpoons}} 2\,PbSO_4 + 2\,H_2O$$

A battery consists of a number of such cells contained in a hard rubber or plastic case. Each cell has an anode which when charged consists of spongy Pb. This is the negative plate which on discharge is converted to solid $PbSO_4$. The cathode of each cell consists of solid PbO_2. This is the positive plate which on discharge is reduced to solid $PbSO_4$. Solid $PbSO_4$, the product of both electrode reactions, is a white crystalline solid which has two harmful effects. The first is that although all the other substances including the electrolyte of H_2SO_4 are good electrical conductors, $PbSO_4$ is not. The second is that if there is a significant build-up of $PbSO_4$ crystals, as there would be at a low state of charge, the growth of crystals is bound to distort the plates and spacers and sometimes even split the case. Notice that on discharge H_2SO_4 is consumed and H_2O is formed. Both of these processes dilute the electrolyte resulting in lower density. On charging the reverse occurs. Thus the state of charge can be monitored by measurement of the relative density of the solution. Table 22-4 shows the relationship among relative density, open circuit potential, and percentage charge. The battery (12 V) mass for a car is about 20 kg of which roughly one third can be assigned to each of: the redox materials; the H_2SO_4 electrolyte; and the grids and case. The lead/acid battery is well suited to the operation of the gasoline driven automobile because the battery is alternately being charged and discharged, almost like respiration. Also the lead/acid battery is capable of furnishing the sudden high current required for a short time to start the engine. For an electric car, however, the periods of charge and discharge must be more extended. A severe drawback of the lead/acid battery is its propensity for damage at a low state of charge. Also these batteries are quite heavy for their energy or power output, so that it would not be unusual for an electric car to have seven 12 V batteries with a total mass of about 130 kg.

TABLE 22-4   Characteristics of Lead/Acid Batteries

Percent of Full Charge	Relative Density	Potential (volt)
100	1.26	2.11
75	1.22	2.07
50	1.18	2.03
25	1.14	1.99
0*	1.10	1.95

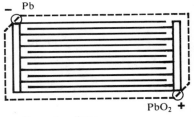

7 negative plates
6 positive plates
12 separators
Dimensions 19 × 4 × 11 cm
Mass 6 kg
Electrolyte .85 L H_2SO_4 solution
(S.G. 1.28)

*Zero charge corresponds not to complete usage of reactants but to internal conductivity becoming too low for the cell to deliver current.

Recent improvements in the design of the lead/acid cell include increasing area of electrode and decreasing spacing between them to lower resistance; lighter construction with greater porosity; improved electrode support on nickel grids (called clad type); stirring of electrolyte by thermal design; and addition of H_3PO_4 to improve cycling life and prohibit evolution of hydrogen on charging.

(b) Cd/Ni

$$\text{Anode: } Cd + 2\,OH^- \rightarrow Cd(OH)_2 + 2e$$

$$\text{Cathode: } 2\,NiOOH + 2\,H_2O + 2e \rightarrow Ni(OH)_2 + 2\,OH^-$$

$$\text{Cell: } Cd + 2\,NiOOH + 2\,H_2O \underset{\text{charge}}{\overset{\text{discharge}}{\rightleftarrows}} Cd(OH)_2 + 2\,Ni(OH)_2$$

This cell has the advantage that no significant changes occur in the electrolyte composition on discharge so that output voltage is independent of the electrolyte. Highly porous plaques formed by sintering Ni powder to a Ni screen have been used as support in cells where highest quality and light weight are required. The plaques are separately immersed in solutions of cadmium or nickel nitrate to which alkali is added to form the hydroxide. The hydroxides $Cd(OH)_2$ and $Ni(OH)_2$ are electrolyzed to produce respectively negative plates impregnated with Cd and positive plates impregnated with NiOOH. Separators of polypropylene are used to keep the reactants apart. The electrolyte used for the cell is 30 percent KOH and the cell emf is 1.29 V.

The advantages of the Cd/Ni cell are sturdy construction, long life, rapid charging, and the fact that it can be left uncharged without damage. Disadvantages are its low potential per cell and the high cost of its materials.

(c) Zn/Ag

$$\text{Anode: } Zn + O^{2-} \rightarrow ZnO + 2e$$

$$\text{Cathode: } AgO + 2e \rightarrow Ag + O^{2-}$$

$$\text{Cell: } Zn + AgO \underset{\text{charge}}{\overset{\text{discharge}}{\rightleftarrows}} ZnO + Ag$$

In this cell the anode of Zn and cathode of AgO are separated by a semipermeable membrane of cellophane. Both electrodes are of porous construction and the electrolyte is of 40-45% KOH. The cathodic reaction actually takes place in two steps ($2\,AgO \rightarrow Ag_2O \rightarrow 2\,Ag$) so that in practice two discharge potentials are obtained: an upper level at about 1.7 V and lower level at 1.5 V. This cell has the highest energy density per unit mass of the common commercial storage cells. Disadvantages are interactions among the materials and the high cost of the silver.

22-11   NEW DEVELOPMENTS IN STORAGE CELLS

If storage cells are to have a more significant role in future energy technology such as providing the motive power for cars, trucks and buses rather than just for starting heat engines, their performance relative to their mass and cost must be greatly improved. There is a number of ways of attempting this:

(i) using less expensive materials
(ii) using lighter electrode and cell construction materials
(iii) increasing electrode area and decreasing spacing to reduce electrical resistance
(iv) selecting electrode materials with greater emf per cell
(v) improving electrode kinetics to achieve higher current
(vi) improving insulation between electrodes to minimize losses
(vii) operating cells at higher temperature to increase electrode rates and create liquid electrodes which have important kinetic advantages.

The achievement of all the above improvements in one cell has not taken place, but a number of cells have reached the research and pilot stage which incorporate some of these points. Since successful design requires years of testing, none of these is commercially available but it is clear that greater energy density from commonly available materials is now at hand. Because of their low densities and large negative electrode potentials the alkali metals and alkaline earth metals make highly desirable anodes at low cost. But these metals are too reactive with water so they must be used with either a molten or solid electrolyte, or possibly an organic (aprotic) liquid. Common and light cathode materials are O_2 (air); the halogens Cl_2 and Br_2; and MnO_2. The properties of five of these developmental ambient temperature cells are summarized below.

(a) Zn/Ni

$$\text{Anode: } Zn + 2\,OH^- \rightarrow Zn(OH)_2 + 2e$$

$$\text{Cathode: } 2\,NiOOH + 2\,H_2O + 2e \rightarrow 2\,Ni(OH)_2 + 2\,OH^-$$

$$\text{Cell: } Zn + 2\,NiOOH + 2\,H_2O \rightleftarrows 2\,Ni(OH)_2 + Zn(OH)_2$$

The electolyte is $30 - 40\%$ KOH and emf 1.72 V. This cell has high energy density but has had problems with reactions between the electrode materials and the separators. The high cost of nickel prevents large-scale manufacture.

(b) Zn/MnO₂

$$\text{Anode: } Zn + O^{2-} \rightarrow ZnO + 2e$$

$$\text{Cathode: } MnO_2 + H_2O + 2e \rightarrow Mn(OH)_2 + O^{2-}$$

$$\text{Cell: } Zn + MnO_2 + H_2O \rightleftarrows ZnO + Mn(OH)_2$$

Here the cathode reaction is actually in two stages via trivalent Mn. The cell emf is 1.55 V and the electrolyte is KOH. This cell was an adaptation of the primary alkaline cell when it was found possible under certain conditions to recharge it. It has the advantages of available materials of reasonable cost, a good shelf life and a high rate of discharge, but operates irreversibly.

(c) Zn/Air

$$\text{Anode: } Zn + O^{2-} \rightarrow ZnO + 2e$$

$$\text{Cathode: } \tfrac{1}{2} O_2 + 2e \rightarrow O^{2-}$$

$$\text{Cell: } Zn + \tfrac{1}{2} O_2 \rightleftarrows ZnO$$

The electrolyte would normally be KOH with emf of 1.61 V. Although capable of high energy density, difficulties with the development of this cell include: excessive hydrogen evolution on charge; poor charge retention; and poor performance at a high rate of discharge.

(d) Li/Br$_2$ with organic electrolyte

$$\text{Anode: } Li \rightarrow Li^+ + e$$

$$\text{Cathode: } \tfrac{1}{2} Br_2 + e \rightarrow Br^-$$

$$\text{Cell: } Li + \tfrac{1}{2} Br_2 \rightleftarrows LiBr$$

This cell has a Li anode and a Br$_2$ (on carbon) cathode, with porous polyethylene separators. An organic electrolyte which is aprotic must be used such as propylene carbonate, nitromethane, tetrahydrofuran, acetonitrile or dimethylformamide. Such cells are capable of achieving high energy both by mass and volume. However power output tends to be low because of the high resistance of the electrolyte.

(e) Seawater cells

These cells use seawater as the electrolyte usually with an anode of an aluminium alloy and the cathode some oxidant such as MnO$_2$, CuC$_2$O$_4$, HgCl$_2$ or AgCl.

An even more exciting possibility for some uses is the development of high temperature cells. These cells usually employ molten salts as electrolytes, with much higher electrical conductivity than for aqueous conditions. Also electrode reactions occur rapidly and active metals such as Ni, Na, Mg and Be can be used as liquids. For cathodes F$_2$ and O$_2$ would be optimum for purposes of high cell emf but so far suitable electrodes have not been developed. The next best are Cl$_2$ and S, which are workable but limiting. While high energy densities are possible, disadvantages of high temperature cells are that some form of heating control must be applied in order to hold the temperature at the required level of operation. Moreover hot molten electrolyte is damaging to almost all known containers and cell component parts.

(a) Li/Cl$_2$

$$\text{Anode: } Li \rightarrow Li^+ + e$$

$$\text{Cathode: } \tfrac{1}{2} Cl_2 + e \rightarrow Cl^-$$

$$\text{Cell: } Li + \tfrac{1}{2} Cl_2 \rightleftarrows LiCl$$

The electrolyte is LiCl which melts at 614°C and has exceptionally high electrical conductivity at the operating temperature of 650°C, Liquid Li, being light, floats on top of the electrolyte and is fed in by means of a porous wick.

The Cl_2 gas is fed in through porous carbon. The anode does not become polarized at high current density but the cathode does, even at low values. Neither Li nor Cl_2 are appreciably soluble in the electrolyte so no separators are necessary to prevent direct reaction. The advantages of this cell are the high energy density and the fact that the cell emf is constant at 3.5 V. Disadvantages are the high temperature requirement, storage and flow of chlorine and, most difficult of all, the lack of cheap and suitable construction materials to withstand such powerful and active substances at high temperature.

(b) $Zn/Cl_2 \cdot 8 H_2O$

$$Anode: Zn \rightarrow Zn^{2+} + 2e$$
$$Cathode: Cl_2 \cdot 8 H_2O + 2e \rightarrow 2 Cl^- + 8 H_2O$$

$$Cell: Zn + Cl_2 \cdot 8 H_2O \rightleftarrows Zn^{2+} + 2 Cl^- + 8 H_2O$$

This cell has an emf of 2.12 V. The anode is the usual Zn metal on plates, but the cathode is innovative in that it avoids the difficulties in controlling Cl_2 gas both as to feed and toxicity, by storing the gas as the hydrate, which is crystalline.

A complement of these batteries (five 40 V units in series) was used to operate an automobile, which achieved speeds up to about 100 km h^{-1} on a 240 km trip.

(c) Li/S

$$Anode: 2 Li \rightarrow 2 Li^+ + 2e$$

$$Cathode: S + 2e \rightarrow S^{2-}$$

$$Cell: 2 Li + S \rightleftarrows Li_2S$$

This cell is operated at about 400°C with an emf of 2.3 V. The above expression of the cell reaction is an over simplification and in fact non-stoichiometric compounds may be formed as represented by Li_2S_x. Here again the anode reaction is rapid and non-polarized but the cathode reaction is difficult. The liquid Li is contained in a porous metal frame and is fed in capillarily. The liquid S is contained in a porous matrix of metal or carbon. The operation of the cathode process is not well understood. One difficulty is that S is a non-conductor so diffusion of products must play a part in allowing the electrode to function. The cell is capable of producing high energy density and has the advantage that both electrode-active materials are liquid, capable of being stored within the electrode and reacting quickly. Also the operating temperature is not too high.

Sulphur is in plentiful supply and inexpensive. However, this cell has the usual disadvantage that lithium, sulphur and lithium sulphide are all very reactive at high temperature and damage the materials used to construct the cell.

(d) Li/FeS_2

$$Anode: 4 Li + 2 S^{2-} \rightarrow 2 Li_2S + 4e$$

$$Cathode: FeS_2 + 4e \rightarrow Fe + 2 S^{2-}$$

$$Cell: 4 Li + FeS_2 \rightleftarrows Fe + 2 Li_2S$$

The operating temperature range is 400-500°C and various eutectic electrolytes have been used. The operating potential is 1.4 V and energy density is fairly high at about 200 kJ kg^{-1}. The cell life is estimated at about 1000 cycles. Fe_2S is inexpensive. There are difficulties however with this cathode.

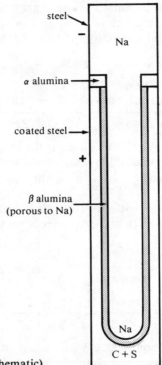

Figure 22-4   Na/S Cell (Schematic).

(e) Na/S

$$\text{Anode: } 2\,Na + S^{2-} \rightarrow Na_2S + 2e$$

$$\text{Cathode: } S + 2e \rightarrow S^{2-}$$

$$\overline{\text{Cell: } 2\,Na + S \rightleftharpoons Na_2S}$$

The above equations are simplified. Complex sulphides are formed. The cell emf is about 2.1 V and operating temperatures 300-350°C. The design of this important cell is complicated. It has an unusual solid electrolyte of β alumina, $Na_2O \cdot 11\,Al_2O_3$, which acts as a semi-permeable separator by allowing Na^+ to pass through directional spaces in its lattice. On the other hand α alumina is not porous and serves as a separator and insulator. The anode is of liquid Na which is stored in the centre of the cylindrical cell, Figure 22-4. The cathode is a mixture of carbon, S and Na_2S which is held on graphite felt.

Table 22-5 affords a comparison of the Na/S cell with the Pb/acid cell. The Na/S cell has generated much interest both for motor vehicles and for municipal utility load levelling, and roughly half of the total of all recent cell research in the U.S.A. has been devoted to it. In the U.K. design work has been done on a flywheel combination with Na/S cells. The battery provides the main source of energy but the flywheel is used to attain peaks. The combination is also suited to regenerative discharge braking, by which much energy is saved when a vehicle is slowed.

TABLE 22-5   Comparison of Pb/acid Cell with Na/S Cell*

	Pb/acid	Na/S
Discharge time / hour	2 − 4	2 − 4
Charge time / hour	6 − 8	1 − 6
Energy density (mass) / kJ kg^{-1}	100	600
Power density (mass) / W kg^{-1}	30	70
Energy density (volume) / kJ L^{-1}	110	720
Average life / year	5	10
Average life / cycles	300	800
Conversion efficiency / percent	65	50

*J.R. Birk, F. Klunder and J.C. Smith I.E.E.F. Spectrum (1979) **16** 49-55

Both existing commercial cells and new designs like the Na/S cell are likely to be very important in future energy technology, since they can store and transport electricity which can itself be generated from a wide variety of sources, including renewable hydroelectricity. Table 22-6 compares the energy density, lifetime and relative cost of commercial batteries, while Table 22-7 indicates the impressive energy densities sought in new designs.

TABLE 22-6

Comparison of Energy Density, Life and Cost of Commercial Storage Cells

Cell	Energy Density kJ kg^{-1}	Life cycles	Relative Cost
Zn/Ag	400	100 − 300	18
Cd/Ni	140	300 − 2000	12
Fe/Ni	120	3000	8
Pb/acid			
in motor car	80	1500 − 2000	1
in submarine	100	400	1.5
in electric vehicle	125	500 − 800	2

TABLE 22-7

Energy Densities of Developmental and Commercial Storage Cells/kJ kg^{-1}

(a) Developmental High Temperature Cells

Li/Cl$_2$	1080 − 1440
Li/S	560 − 1510
Na/S	650 − 1180

(b) Developmental Ambient Temperature Cells

Zn/Ni	90 − 220
Zn/MnO$_2$	70 − 200
Zn/O$_2$	400 − 650

(c) Commercial Cells

Pb/acid	25 − 125
Cd/Ni	70 − 200
Zn/Ag	200 − 400

22-12 GENERAL COMMENT ON STORAGE AND RETRIEVAL OF ELECTRICAL ENERGY

The most obvious way of storing electrical energy is by charging a suitable battery of storage cells. One hopes that these batteries will have low mass and volume per unit of energy stored, low self-discharge, long life both in and out of service, and high turnaround efficiency, as well as being rugged, safe and affordable. Since no one cell offers all of these properties, one must seek the cell to fit particular priorities. Huge batteries used to store the intermittently generated energy from solar, wind or wave sources must be inexpensive. Cells in pacemakers must be safe, reliable and light. Low cost and high storage per unit mass are among the important characteristics of vehicle batteries. All of these matches of source to use are but a part of the larger task of deploying our energy sources in the most effective way.

22-13 ELECTROLYTIC CELLS

As the case of secondary cells demonstrates, there are many redox processes which exhibit true reversibility. By applying a potential to the electrodes equal in magnitude but opposite in sign to the cell potential, the cell process can be held in balance. Decrease the applied potential by an infinitesimal amount and the cell process will occur. Increase the applied potential by an infinitesimal amount and the cell process will be reversed.

In the previous sections, galvanic cells were described in which a process occurs naturally and the energy produced is withdrawn. As indicated in Chapter 3, however, there are also many important applications of electrolytic cells where the normal process is driven backward by putting energy into the cell.

One obvious application is in the refining of metals. Most metals are oxidized in the natural environment. Over the long periods of geologic history, most have reached relatively stable forms as oxides, sulphides, silicates and halides. Obtaining metal for human use requires driving these natural oxida-

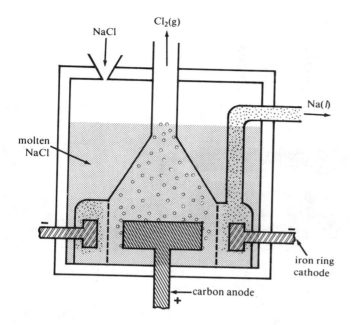

NaCl

Cl$_2$(g)

Na(l)

molten
NaCl

$-$

iron ring
cathode

carbon anode
$+$

Figure 22-5 The Downs cell for electrolysis of molten sodium chloride.

tion processes backward, and this is often done electrochemically. For example sodium is often produced by the electrolysis of molten sodium chloride in the Downs cell. The cell processes are as follows.

$$Na^+ + e \rightarrow Na(l) \qquad \text{(cathode process)}$$

$$Cl^- \rightarrow \tfrac{1}{2} Cl_2 (g) + e \qquad \text{(anode process)}$$

$$Na^+ + Cl^- \rightarrow Na(l) + \tfrac{1}{2} Cl_2(g) \qquad \text{(overall process)}$$

Another important metallurgical application is the production of aluminium. The extremely large electrical requirements of large scale aluminium production result in most smelters being located near large but relatively remote hydroelectric sources such as Arvida in Quebec and Kitimat in British Columbia. Similar considerations have placed large smelters in Ghana, Norway and other locations. Energy costs dominate the cost of aluminium, and have made it difficult for Japan, competitive in so many fields, to compete in this industry.

After removing impurities from bauxite, Al_2O_3, it is dissolved in molten cryolite, Na_3AlF_6. Cryolite melts at 1012°C, whereas alumina melts at about 2000°C, a temperature too high for commercial electrolysis. The melting point of cryolite is lowered by the addition of alumina, and there is a eutectic point at about 960°C and 10% alumina by mass. The solution in the electrolytic cells is generally near the eutectic composition but has other components including CaF_2 (5-10%) which further lowers the melting point. The cathode of the cell is molten aluminium metal, which is in electrical contact with a carbon lining of the cell. The carbon anode is made from a paste mixture of pitch and ground petroleum coke called Soderberg paste; as this paste comes in contact with the

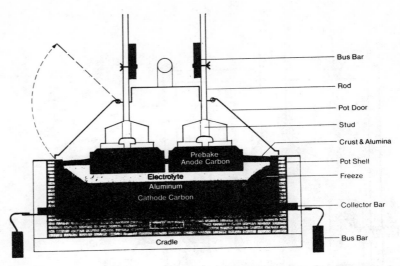

Figure 22-6 Electrolytic cell for the production of aluminium metal. The drawing represents the so-called prebake design of Alcan Aluminium Limited.

hot cell, it softens, flows together, and then bakes to form a rigid carbon anode. The anode is eroded by the electrolytic oxidation:

$$3\,C + 6\,O^{2-} \rightarrow 3\,CO_2(g) + 6e$$

The reduced aluminium metal is simply added to the cathode:

$$Al^{3+} + 3e \rightarrow Al(l).$$

The temperature of the cell is maintained just above the eutectic temperature by passage of the current through the electrical resistance of the electrolyte in the cell. Typically, the current is about 150 000 A. The potential across the cell is 4 to 5 V, and about 120 cells are connected in series.

The production of each kg of aluminium requires 0.6 kg of carbon and 7.9×10^7 J of energy (22 kwh). The energy to be saved is the most compelling reason for saving and recycling metallic aluminium articles when they are scrapped.

Some metals can be produced electrolytically from aqueous solution. In the electrolytic production of zinc, for example, aqueous solutions which have ex-

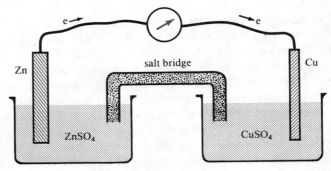

Figure 22-7

tracted zinc from its ore are passed continuously through tanks. Cathodes suspended in these tanks accumulate zinc metal and can be removed and replaced by new cathodes whenever required. Typically 50 to 100 kg of zinc might be accumulated per cathode, operating at current densities of 400 to 700 A m^{-2}. In a large plant this means several thousand crane lifts a day to replace cathodes.

Electrolysis cells are also used for electroplating. A metal article for plating is the cathode in a solution containing the ion of the plate material, such as Ag$^+$. Passage of current plates out the material.

Example 22-13   How long must a current of 0.0120 A be passed through a solution of Ag(CN)$_2$$^-$ in order to plate a spoon of area 20.0 cm^2 to a depth of 0.10 mm? The density of silver is 10 500 kg m^{-3}.

The cathode process is

$$Ag(CN)_2^-(aq) + e \rightarrow Ag(c) + 2\ CN^-(aq)$$

One faraday will plate out one mole of Ag.

$$\text{The plating requires } (20.0)(0.010) = 0.200 \text{ cm}^3 \text{ of silver}$$

$$= (0.200)(10.5) = 2.10 \text{ g of silver}$$

$$= \frac{2.10}{106} = 1.94 \times 10^{-2} \text{ mol of silver}$$

and therefore 1.94×10^{-2} faraday is required

Therefore   charge $= (1.94 \times 10^{-2})(96\ 485) = 1870$ C

$$\text{time} = \frac{1870 \text{ C}}{0.0120 \text{ C s}^{-1}} = 156\ 000 \text{ s}$$

$$= 433 \text{ h.}$$

22-14   USE OF ELECTROCHEMICAL DATA TO EVALUATE AN EQUILIBRIUM CONSTANT.

Since, for any cell process,

$$\Delta G° = -\ nFE°$$

it follows that the equilibrium constant for that process is given by

$$K = e^{-\Delta G°/RT} = e^{nFE°/RT}$$

The practical importance of this is that the equilibrium constant can be evaluated indirectly, from easily and accurately measurable electrochemical data, for many processes in which the equilibrium constant could not be measured directly with nearly the same accuracy. A prime example is the case of solubility products. Direct measurement of the solubility product of so-called insoluble electrolytes is error prone because of the very small amounts of substance which dissolve. Consider silver iodide.

$$AgI(c) \rightleftarrows Ag^+(aq) + I^-(aq)$$

The equilibrium constant for this process is, of course, the solubility product of silver iodide. The process is not itself a redox process, since silver maintains an oxidation state of +1 and iodide of −1 throughout. However the process can be split into two parts which are redox processes.

$$AgI(c) + e \rightleftarrows Ag(c) + I^-(aq) \qquad \varepsilon° = -0.1518 \text{ V}$$

$$\underline{Ag(c) \rightleftarrows Ag^+(aq) + e \qquad\qquad\quad \varepsilon° = -0.7991 \text{ V}}$$

$$AgI(c) \rightleftarrows Ag^+(aq) + I^-(aq) \qquad E° = -0.9509 \text{ V}$$

$$K = e^{(1)(96\ 485)(-.9509)/(8.314)(298.15)}$$

$$= 8.42 \times 10^{-17}$$

Notice that the two $\varepsilon°$ values could have been measured, and almost certainly were measured, using cells with quite different cell processes. The method by which E° values, and hence $\varepsilon°$ values, are measured is described in Section 22-17.

Because E° data are intrinsically related to equilibrium constants, a table of $\varepsilon°$ values can be used conveniently to determine the direction in which a redox process can move. The following examples illustrate the point.

Example 22-14 Will zinc dissolve to any significant extent in an aqueous solution of $CuSO_4$?

The possible process is

$$Cu^{2+}(aq) + Zn(c) \rightarrow Cu(c) + Zn^{2+}(aq)$$

In this case, one can use either the data in Appendix 1 to calculate $\Delta G°$ or the data in Table 22-3 to calculate E° and hence K. Using Appendix 1,

$$\Delta G° = -212.5 \text{ kJ}$$

and

$$K = 1.7 \times 10^{37}$$

The process will proceed very far to the right. Zinc metal can dissolve in a solution containing Cu^{2+}, resulting in the precipitation of copper metal.

Example 22-15 Will chlorine displace F^- from an aqueous solution of fluoride? Br^- from a bromide solution?

The chemical reaction being considered is

$$\tfrac{1}{2} Cl_2(g) + F^-(aq) \rightarrow Cl^-(aq) + \tfrac{1}{2} F_2(g)$$

Using Appendix 1, one sees that

$$\Delta G° = -131.26 - (-278.8) = +147.54 \text{ kJ}$$

$$K = 1.4 \times 10^{-26}$$

Displacement would be insignificant.

To illustrate the alternative means of calculation, the second part will be worked out using reduction potentials. The reduction and oxidation processes are:

$$\tfrac{1}{2}\,Cl_2 + e \rightarrow Cl^- \qquad \varepsilon° = +1.36 \text{ V}$$

$$Br^- \rightarrow \tfrac{1}{2}\,Br_2 + e \qquad \varepsilon° = -1.07 \text{ V}$$

Hence
$$E° = +0.29 \text{ V}$$

$$K = e^{+\,1 \times 96\,485 \times 0.29/8.314 \times 298.15}$$

$$= 8.0 \times 10^4$$

The large value of K indicates that there would be almost complete displacement of the bromide ion due to oxidation by chlorine.

The ability of Cl_2 to displace Br^- and I^- from aqueous solutions, and the distinctive colours of Cl_2, Br_2 and I_2 combine to provide a useful qualitative test for the presence of Br^- or I^- in an unknown material.

22-15   THE SALT BRIDGE

Electrochemical cells provide many cases in which redox processes can be carried out reversibly. A small decrease in the balancing voltage allows the process to proceed, while a small increase drives the process backwards from its natural direction. Such cells are called reversible cells. In a reversible cell, both the half-cells must be reversible.

In some cells, both electrodes dip into the same solution of electrolyte. An example is as follows:

$$Pt \mid H_2(g,\ 100 \text{ kPa}) \mid HCl\ (aq,\ 0.1 \text{ m}) \mid AgCl(c) \mid Ag$$

in which the half-cells are

$$\tfrac{1}{2}\,H_2 \rightarrow H^+ + e$$

$$AgCl + e \rightarrow Ag + Cl^-.$$

Such cells are called cells without transference.

In other cases, the two electrodes dip in separate solutions, such as those in Examples 22-6 and 22-7. These are called cells with transference. The necessity for separate cells can be understood by reference to Example 22-6.

$$Cu \mid Cu^{2+}(aq) \mid\mid Ag^+(aq) \mid Ag$$

If the copper electrode is dipped into a solution containing silver ion, the silver ions would form silver metal plated on the copper, and the copper bar would dissolve:

$$2\,Ag^+ + Cu \rightarrow 2\,Ag + Cu^{2+} \qquad E° = +0.46 \text{V}$$

The electron transfer would take place directly at the copper electrode. The presence of the silver electrode and the copper ions in solution would be irrelevant to a great extent, and no potential would be developed between the electrodes. In order to develop a potential, the two solutions and their associated electrodes must be separated in this case.

This then raises the problem of making an electrical connection between the solutions in the two half-cells. If the two solutions are placed in contact, in a capillary tube for instance, the different ions mix at the junction due to diffusion. Since the different ions have different masses and sizes and different interactions with the solvent molecules, they diffuse at different rates, and a difference in electric potential between the two solutions is developed. This potential difference is called the *liquid junction potential* and cannot be measured. It has no relationship to the reversible redox potentials due to processes occurring at the electrodes, and so is not of interest in the present context. It has been found that the liquid junction potential is minimized if the electrical connection between the solutions is made through a *salt bridge.* The salt bridge is often a U-tube containing a semi-rigid gel containing a concentrated solution of KCl. This bridge prevents mixing of the solutions by diffusion, and equalizes the potentials of the solutions by transport of K^+ and Cl^- ions which can move through the gel. The theory of the salt bridge is difficult, but in practice it allows consideration of the redox potentials developed at the electrodes without the interference of the liquid junction potential.

22-16   ACTIVITY COEFFICIENTS

So far in this chapter relative activities have been approximated by ratios of molalities or concentrations or pressures. Such approximations are not always accurate for electrolytes, especially at the high concentrations customarily found in operating galvanic cells.

Applying activity coefficients to cells involving salt bridges is possible but difficult, but there is no difficulty in doing so for cells with a single solution, as the following examples show.

Example 22-16   Calculate the emf of the following cell, using tabulated data to evaluate $\gamma_{\pm}$.

$$\text{Zn}(c) \mid \text{ZnCl}_2(aq, m=0.10) \mid \text{AgCl}(c) \mid \text{Ag}(c)$$

The cell process is

$$\text{Zn}(c) + 2\,\text{AgCl}(c) \rightarrow \text{Zn}^{2+}(aq) + 2\,\text{Cl}^-(aq) + 2\,\text{Ag}(c)$$

$$E = E^\circ - \frac{RT}{2F}\ \ln\ (a_{\text{Zn}^{2+}})(a_{\text{Cl}^-})^2 = E^\circ - \frac{RT}{2F}\ \ln\ (\gamma_{\pm})^3 m_{\text{Zn}^{2+}}(m_{\text{Cl}^-})^2$$

From Table 22-3 the standard potential for the process is

$$E^\circ = 0.763 + 0.222 = 0.985 \text{ V}$$

From Table 21-1, $\gamma_{\pm} = 0.518$ for ZnCl_2 at m = 0.10.

$$m_{\text{Zn}}{}^{2+} = 0.10$$

$$m_{\text{Cl}}{}^- = 0.20$$

$$E = 0.985 - \frac{(8.314)(298.15)}{2(96\ 485)}\ \ln\ (0.518)^3(0.10)(0.20)^2$$

$$= 1.08 \text{ V}.$$

Example 22-17   Calculate E for the following cell at 298K, using tabulated data to evaluate $\gamma_\pm$.

$$Zn(c) \left| ZnSO_4(aq, m=1.0) \right| PbSO_4(c) \left| Pb(c) \right.$$

The cell process is

$$Zn(c) + PbSO_4(c) \rightarrow Zn^{2+}(aq) + SO_4^{2-}(aq) + Pb(c)$$

$$E° = 0.76 + (-0.36) = 0.40 \text{ V}$$

$$E = 0.40 - \frac{RT}{2F} \ln (a_{Zn^{2+}})(a_{SO_4^{2-}})$$

$$= 0.40 - \frac{(8.314)(298.15)}{2(96\ 485)} \ln (0.0435)^2(1)^2$$

$$= 0.48 \text{ V}.$$

22-17   MEASUREMENT OF ACTIVITY COEFFICIENTS AND E°

Consider the following cell at 25°C.

$$Pt \left| H_2(g, P°) \right| HCl(aq, m) \left| AgCl(c) \right| Ag(c)$$

The value of E of this cell can be measured for many values of m.
The cell process is

$$\tfrac{1}{2} H_2(g) + AgCl(c) \rightarrow H^+(aq) + Cl^-(aq) + Ag(c)$$

Hence, E is given by

$$E = E° - \frac{RT}{F} \ln \frac{a_{H^+}a_{Cl^-}}{(a_{H_2})^{\frac{1}{2}}}$$

Since the pressure of the gas is maintained at P°, $a_{H_2} = 1$ (almost!), and hence

$$E = E° - \frac{(8.314)(298.15)}{(96\ 485)} \ln (\gamma_\pm)^2 m^2$$

$$E + 0.02569 \ln(m)^2 = E° - 0.02569 \ln(\gamma_\pm)^2$$

$$E + 0.05138 \ln m = E° - 0.05138 \ln \gamma_\pm$$

$$\text{or } E + 0.1183 \log m = E° - 0.1183 \log \gamma_\pm$$

Since all terms on the left are known, the left hand side can be plotted as a function of m. This, of course, is the same as plotting the right hand side as a function of m. Since as $m \rightarrow 0$, $\gamma_\pm \rightarrow 1$, the intercept of the vertical axis will be E°.

This experiment has been carried out by Harned and Ehlers. In presenting the results, the left hand side of the equation is plotted against $\sqrt{m}$ instead of m, since consideration of Debye-Hückel theory shows that such a plot will be more nearly linear at low concentrations and hence can be extrapolated more

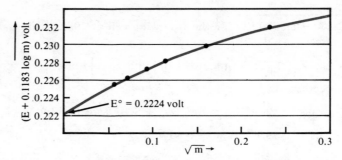

Figure 22-8   Evaluation of E° for the cell Pt │ H₂ (g,P°) │ HCl(aq, m) │ AgCl(c) │ Ag.

accurately. The extrapolation of E + 0.1183 log m to zero molality is shown in Figure 22-8, from which the value E° = 0.2224 V is obtained.

Once the value of E° has been established, the activity coefficient, $\gamma_\pm$, can be evaluated for any molality, m, from the equation.

$$0.1183 \log \gamma_\pm = 0.2224 - 0.1183 \log m - E$$

The dependence of log $\gamma_\pm$ on molality is illustrated in Figure 22-9. It can be seen that log $\gamma_\pm$ is negative for low and intermediate concentrations of HCl, so that $\gamma_\pm$ is less than one in this range. At high concentrations, $\gamma_\pm$ is greater than one. This behaviour can be seen for many of the electrolytes included in Table 21-1. As noted above, the linearity of the plot of log $\gamma_\pm$ against $\sqrt{m}$ at low concentrations is consistent with the applicability of the Debye-Hückel law at low concentrations, since

$$\log \gamma_\pm = -0.50 \, \big| (z_+)(z_-) \big| \sqrt{I_m}$$
$$= -0.50 \, \big| (z_+)(z_-) \big| \, [\tfrac{1}{2}[m(z_+)^2 + m(z_-)^2]]^{\frac{1}{2}}$$
$$= -0.50(1)(\tfrac{1}{2})^{\frac{1}{2}} \, \sqrt{m}$$
$$= -0.36\sqrt{m}$$

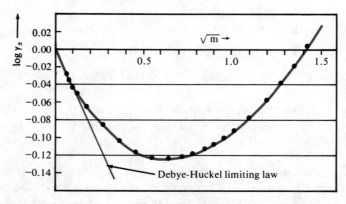

Figure 22-9   Plot of log $\gamma_\pm$ against $m^{1/2}$ for HCl.

22-18   THE ELECTROMETRIC MEASUREMENT OF pH

A common, accurate and extremely convenient way of measuring pH is by using a pH meter. Such a device is simply a galvanic cell in which the potential is dependent on the relative activity of H^+. Consider the following cell at 25°C.

$$\text{Pt, } H_2(g, P°) \mid HCl(aq) \mid AgCl(c) \mid Ag(c)$$

The cell process is

$$H_2(g) + AgCl(c) \rightarrow H^+(aq) + Cl^-(aq) + Ag(c)$$

and the Nernst equation for this particular cell with the hydrogen gas at unit relative activity is

$$E = E° - \frac{RT}{F} \ln a_{H^+} a_{Cl^-}$$

$$= 0.2224 - .0592 \log a_{H^+} - .0592 \log a_{Cl^-}$$

$$= 0.2224 + .0592(pH) - .0592 \log a_{Cl^-}$$

Notice that pH is now regarded as being $-\log a_{H^+}$, rather than as being based on the concentration of H^+ as was done in the less rigorous treatment in Chapter 18 and, indeed, as is usually done in work with acids and bases. Evaluation of the equation above to obtain pH from a measured value of E would be possible if a_{Cl^-} could be evaluated. The S.I. system circumvents the problems associated with this by adopting a purely empirical definition of pH, based on a set of arbitrary standards. pH values are assigned to a group of standard substances in aqueous solution as shown in Table 22-8. The pH of any unknown solution can then be obtained by comparing the potential of a cell containing it with the potential of the same cell altered by substituting one of the standard solutions for the unknown. Thus in the S.I. system, the pH of any solution, pH_x, is *defined* in terms of the pH of a reference solution, pH_s, by the equation

$$pH_x = pH_s + \frac{E_x - E_s}{(RT/F)\ln 10}$$

$$= pH_s + \frac{E_x - E_s}{(1.984 \times 10^{-4})T}$$

TABLE 22-8   Some Assigned pH_S Values for Standard Aqueous Solutions

		20°C	25°C	30°C
A.	KH tartrate (sat'd at 25°C)	—	3.557	3.552
B.	KH tartrate (0.05 m)	4.002	4.008	4.015
C.	KH_2PO_4 (0.025 m) Na_2HPO_4 (0.025 m)	6.881	6.865	6.853
D.	KH_2PO_4 (0.008695 m) Na_2HPO_4 (0.03043 m)	7.429	7.413	7.400
E.	$Na_2B_4O_7$ (0.01 m)	9.225	9.180	9.139

where E_x is the cell emf with the unknown in place and E_s is the cell emf with the reference standard in place. The S.I. treatment describes exactly the cells to be used and the variations necessary in different circumstances.

In common laboratory measurements, a pH meter is usually calibrated by checking the pH registered for a buffer solution of known pH. This is, in principle, analogous to the S.I. procedure. However if an absolute value of pH is required, and the S.I. procedures are not to be used, great care must be taken to ensure that the standardizing procedure is as closely matched as possible in symmetry, liquid junctions and temperature with the measurement of the unknown. On the other hand for most titrations, absolute values are not important and the main requirement is a means of observing the sudden change of pH near equivalence. In such cases, less precise calibration is completely satisfactory.

22-19   THE USE OF DIAGRAMS TO COMBINE REDOX AND ACID/BASE PROCESSES

The interaction of redox processes with acid/base processes is of great practical importance and some complexity. For most systems, however, it is possible to portray all of the necessary information on a single diagram.

Suppose that some general oxidized species, Ox, acquires electrons to produce a reduced species, Rd. Suppose too that the process is affected by the presence of H^+, so that the overall equation of this generalized half-cell process may be written as

$$x\,Ox + m\,H^+ + n\,e \rightarrow y\,Rd + z\,H_2O$$

The Nernst equation for this half-cell process would be

$$\varepsilon = \varepsilon^\circ - \frac{RT}{nF}\ln Q$$

$$= \varepsilon^\circ - \frac{RT}{nF}\ln \frac{(a_{Rd})^y\,(a_{H_2O})^z}{(a_{Ox})^x\,(a_{H^+})^m}$$

Accepting unity as an approximation for a_{H_2O} and changing to logarithms of base 10 gives

$$\varepsilon = \varepsilon^\circ - \frac{2.303RT}{F}\frac{m}{n}\,(pH) + \frac{2.303RT}{nF}\log \frac{a_{Ox}{}^x}{a_{Rd}{}^y}$$

Multiplication of this equation by $F/2.303RT$ yields

$$\frac{F}{2.303RT}\,\varepsilon = \frac{F}{2.303RT}\,\varepsilon^\circ - \frac{m}{n}\,(pH) + \frac{1}{n}\log \frac{a_{Ox}{}^x}{a_{Rd}{}^y}$$

which, for a temperature of 298.15 K is

$$\frac{\varepsilon}{.0592} = \frac{\varepsilon^\circ}{.0592} - \frac{m}{n}\,(pH) + \frac{1}{n}\log \frac{a_{Ox}{}^x}{a_{Rd}{}^y}$$

Not infrequently, the terms $\varepsilon/.0592$ and $\varepsilon°/.0592$ (or their equivalent at other temperatures) are called $p\varepsilon$ and $p\varepsilon°$ respectively.

Rather than continuing with a general case, the use of such a relationship will be illustrated by applying it to the important case of iron. The equation will be applied to each of the possible processes in order to generate a '$p\varepsilon/pH$ diagram.' In such a diagram, for 25°C, the vertical scale is $p\varepsilon$ and the horizontal scale is pH. On such a diagram, the conditions of ε and pH at which one species turns to another are indicated by lines. The areas bounded by these lines represent the conditions under which one species is stable. Consider now each important process in the iron system.

Line (1), $Fe^{3+} + e \rightarrow Fe^{2+}$

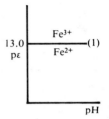

$$p\varepsilon° = \frac{0.77}{0.059} = 13.0$$

$$p\varepsilon = 13.0 + \log a_{Fe^{3+}}/a_{Fe^{2+}}$$

Taking $a_{Fe^{3+}}/a_{Fe^{2+}} = 1/1$, $p\varepsilon = 13.0$

This plot is independent of pH, being a simple horizontal line at $p\varepsilon = 13.0$. When $a_{Fe^{3+}} > a_{Fe^{2+}}$, $p\varepsilon > 13.0$, so the domain above the line at $p\varepsilon = 13.0$ represents the dominance of Fe^{3+}. Below the line at $p\varepsilon = 13.0$ represents the dominance of Fe^{2+}.

Line (2), $Fe^{3+} + 3\ OH^- \rightarrow Fe(OH)_3(c)$

$$a_{Fe^{3+}}\ a_{OH^-}^{3} = K_{sp}$$

or since $a_{OH^-} = K_w/a_{H^+}$

$$a_{Fe^{3+}} = \frac{K_{sp}}{K_w^3} \cdot a_{H^+}^3$$

Taking logarithms and inserting values of K_w and K_{sp}, $\log a_{Fe^{3+}} = 4.62 - 3pH$ and when $a_{Fe^{3+}}$ is taken as 1, pH $= 1.5$. This is the plot of a vertical straight line with $a_{Fe^{3+}}$ dominating to the left and $a_{Fe(OH)_3}$ to the right.

Line (3), $Fe(OH)_3(c) + 3\ H^+ + e \rightarrow Fe^{2+} + 3\ H_2O$

$$p\varepsilon° = \frac{1.04}{0.059} = 17.6$$

$$p\varepsilon = 17.6 - 3pH - \log a_{Fe^{2+}}$$

and when $a_{Fe^{2+}}$ is taken as 1, $p\varepsilon = 17.6 - 3pH$, a straight line with intercept 17.6 and slope -3.

Line (4), $Fe^{2+} + 2e \rightarrow Fe(c)$

$$p\varepsilon° = \frac{-0.44}{0.059} = -7.4$$

$p\varepsilon = -7.4 + \frac{1}{2} \log a_{Fe^{2+}}$ and when $a_{Fe^{2+}} = 1$

$p\varepsilon = -7.4$, a horizontal line independent of pH. Fe^{2+} dominates above the line, $Fe(c)$ below.

Line (5), $Fe^{2+} + 2\,OH^- \rightarrow Fe(OH)_2(c)$

$a_{Fe^{2+}}\, a_{OH}^{-2} = K_{sp}$

$$a_{Fe^{2+}} = \frac{K_{sp}}{K_w^2} \cdot a_H^{+2}$$

$\log a_{Fe^{2+}} = 13.2 - 2pH$, and when $a_{Fe^{2+}} = 1$, $pH = 6.6$.

Line (6), $Fe(OH)_2(c) + 2\,H^+ + 2e \rightarrow Fe(c) + 2\,H_2O$

$$p\varepsilon^\circ = \frac{-0.49}{0.059} = -0.8$$

$p\varepsilon = -0.8 - pH$

This is a straight line of intercept -0.8 and slope -1.

Line (7), $Fe(OH)_3(c) + H^+ + e \rightarrow Fe(OH)_2(c) + H_2O$

$$p\varepsilon^\circ = \frac{0.262}{0.059} = 4.4$$

$p\varepsilon = 4.4 - pH$

This is a straight line of intercept 4.4 and slope -1.

For species in aqueous solution it is valuable to include on the diagram lines for the aqueous system H^+/H_2 and O_2/H_2O. Especially for the latter system there is some doubt whether such an equilibrium is really attained, but at least it can be regarded as a limiting condition.

Line (A), $H^+ + e \rightarrow \frac{1}{2}\,H_2$

$p\varepsilon^\circ = 0$

$p\varepsilon = -pH - \frac{1}{2}(P_{H_2}/P^\circ)$

When P_{H_2} becomes greater than P°, $p\varepsilon$ becomes more negative so the domain below the line (A) is dominated by H_2, above by $H^+(aq)$
When $P_{H_2} = P^\circ$, $p\varepsilon = -pH$

This simple relation results from the fact that the H^+ system is used as a basis for both proton transfer and electron transfer processes.
Line (A) slopes down from 0.0 at -1.

Line (B), $\frac{1}{2}\,O_2 + 2\,H^+ + 2e \rightarrow H_2O$

$$p\varepsilon^\circ = \frac{1.23}{0.059} = 20.8$$

$p\varepsilon = 20.8 - pH + \frac{1}{2}(P_{O_2}/P^\circ)$

By testing it is found that the region above line (B) is dominated by O_2 and below by H_2O. When $P_{O_2} = P^\circ$, $p\varepsilon = 20.8 - pH$.

Thus line (B) has intercept 20.8 and slope -1. Between lines (A) and (B) is a region of stability for the aqueous species H_2O, $H^+(aq)$ and $OH^-(aq)$.

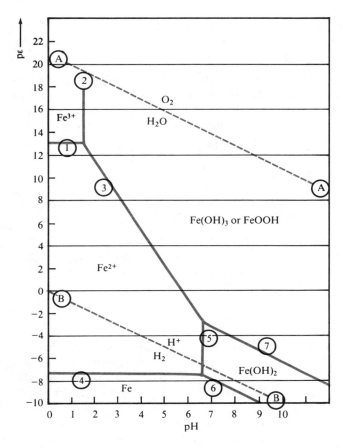

Figure 22-10 $p\varepsilon/pH$ Diagram for Fe.

The inclusion of lines (A) and (B) on any $p\varepsilon/pH$ diagram for a particular element adds considerable information with regard to stability under environmental conditions and in reactions with the species H_2O, $H^+(aq)$ and $OH^-(aq)$.

Figure 22-10 shows the final $p\varepsilon/pH$ diagram for iron with all of these lines included. Some short examples of its use are given below. In using this or any other such diagram, it is important to remember that the construction is based on equilibrium being obtained. In the real world, metastable states often exist, remaining so unchanged that an observer could not know that they are not the stable form. Nevertheless these diagrams serve as a most useful source of chemical knowledge. For example, the following facts, among many others, can be gleaned from the diagram for the iron system.

(i)   The position of line (4) relative to line (A) shows that Fe(c) as a reductant can evolve H_2 from H_2O in acid solution. That is, Fe(c) reduces H^+ to H_2, while Fe(c) is oxidized to Fe^{2+}.

$$Fe(c) + 2\,H^+ \rightarrow Fe^{2+} + H_2$$

A vertical line drawn at such a position represents a redox or cell reaction.

(ii) The species Fe^{3+} is found only in very acidic solutions, pH<1.5, whereas Fe^{2+} may be found in solutions of pH<6.6. Thus $Fe(OH)_3$ is much less soluble than $Fe(OH)_2$ in aqueous solutions.

(iii) The position of line (7) relative to line (B) shows that freshly precipitated $Fe(OH)_2$ above pH 6 will be oxidized by O_2 up to $Fe(OH)_3$ according to the reaction

$$\tfrac{1}{2} O_2 + H_2O + 2\,Fe(OH)_2(c) \rightarrow 2\,Fe(OH)_3(c)$$

(iv) An iron nail added to a solution of Fe^{2+} or $Fe(OH)_2$ will prevent it being oxidized up to the ferric state as shown by the position of line (4) relative to line (3) or line (6) relative to line (7).

(v) Under the usual environmental conditions, between lines (A) and (B), say at pε 8, pH 8, the stable form of iron is as $Fe(OH)_3$, or common rust.

These few examples give an indication of the vast storage potential of these diagrams, and the many practical situations to which they can be applied. The textbooks by Pourbaix and by Garrels and Christ will be particularly useful to those wishing to develop a facility in this area.

SUMMARY

Oxidation/reduction reactions, which are also called redox reactions, involve the coupling of a reduction (with gain of electrons) to an oxidation (with loss of electrons). The same redox reaction which occurs when a reductant and oxidant are reacted directly can also be arranged to occur electro-chemically by having the reduction half-reaction (at the cathode) and the oxidation half-reaction (at the anode) occur in separate compartments. For a given amount of chemical reaction in such a cell the current must be the same throughout, and the number of electrons gained at the cathode in one compartment must be the same as the number of electrons lost at the anode in the other compartment.

An electrochemical cell develops a potential difference between the two electrode terminals which has a maximum value when no current is passed, called the electromotive force (emf). If an equal and opposing external potential difference were applied to the cell, the whole system would be in balance and no net reaction would occur. If the externally applied potential difference were less than that of the cell or non-existent, the cell reaction on discharge would occur and chemical energy would be converted to electrical energy; such an arrangement is termed a *galvanic* or *voltaic* cell. On the other hand if the external, opposing potential difference were greater than that of the cell, the cell reaction would be driven in the opposite direction and the cell would be electrolyzed or charged, and called an *electrolytic cell*. Thus galvanic cells use chemical changes to produce electrical energy; electrolytic cells use external electrical energy in order to bring about desired chemical changes.

Electrolytic cells have definite advantages over direct chemical processes in the operation of redox reactions to yield required products. For example, in oxidation by a direct chemical process, the strongest oxidant we have is F_2, with a single reduction potential (on the hydrogen scale) of about +3 V. The strongest chemical reductant would be one of the alkali metals, such as Li, with a single reduction potential of about -3 V. But in an electrolytic cell the externally applied potential has no such limitation and so much more drastic oxidizing and reducing conditions can be imposed as, for example, in the electroreduction to win an alkali metal such as Na, or a highly oxidized product such as F_2. Another advantage is in the matter of control. A controlled potential at the cathode allows the selective plating out of metals from a mixture of ions in solution. In the reduction of nitrobenzene, $C_6H_5NO_2$, to aniline, $C_6H_5NH_2$, there is a variety of possible intermediate products from which the desired one can be got by control of potential. In the future, electrolysis should play a more important role in preparative organic and inorganic chemistry, as well as in the more conventional refinement of metals, in the chlorine-alkali process, and particularly in the electrolysis of water to afford hydrogen as a mobile and storable source of energy.

Galvanic cells are important in both theory and practice. As practical sources of electrical power there are primary cells which are discarded when the chemical ingredients are spent; secondary or storage cells which can be recharged electrically; and fuel cells which are kept fed with supplies of fuel (reductant) and oxidant. Modern technology has led to improvements in such classical cells as the lead/acid and nickel/cadmium storage cells, and the Leclanché type primary cell, as well as to the development of new cells for municipal power levelling and as power supplies for motor vehicles. Fuel cells have the possibility of delivering 100% of the ΔG of a process as work whereas allowing that energy to degrade to heat (as by burning hydrogen in oxygen) and then recovering work by applying the heat to an engine is inevitably less efficient.

Galvanic cells are splendid sources of thermodynamic data. The standard emf of a cell, $E°$, is directly related to the value of $\Delta G°$ by $\Delta G° = -nFE°$. If the change of $E°$ with temperature is known for the cell the standard entropy change can be found from the relation $\Delta S° = nF(\partial E/\partial T)$. Also $\Delta H°$ can now be found from the equation $\Delta G° = \Delta H° - T\Delta S°$. The equilibrium constant, K, can be found from the relation $\Delta G° = -RT\ln K$. It should be understood that all of the above thermodynamic quantities pertain to the cell reaction in question.

Single electrode potentials are not measurable; however by arbitrarily giving the standard hydrogen electrode potential a value of zero at all temperatures, single electrode potentials for other electrodes can be determined from cell emf's on this relative basis. These are conventionally listed in tables under standard conditions as reduction potentials, $\varepsilon°$, constituting a remarkably efficient means of storing these data.

Lastly, the measurement of the emf of a cell as a function of concentration permits the evaluation of $E°$, of activities of species, and of activity coefficients using the appropriate detailed form of the Nernst equation

$$E = E° - \frac{RT}{nF}\ln Q$$

where Q is the reaction quotient for the cell reaction.

ADVANCED REFERENCES

J. O'M. Bockris and A.K.N. Reddy, "*Modern Electrochemistry*" Plenum Press, New York, 1970
This highly readable, two volume text covers almost all important areas of electrochemistry.

D.A. MacInnes, "*The Principles of Electrochemistry*" Dover, New York, 1961
The experimental details are particularly well described in this rigorous text by one of the leading developers of the subject.

R.M. Garrels and C.L. Christ, "*Solutions, Minerals and Equilibria*" Harper and Row, New York, 1965
For the geologist and geochemist, this excellent text describes equilibrium concepts and the application of pε/pH diagrams.

M. Pourbaix, "*Atlas of Electrochemical Equilibria*" Pergamon Press, Toronto, 1966
This monumental treatment of pε/pH diagrams is a goldmine of thermodynamic data.

J. O'M. Bockris, "*Electrochemistry of Cleaner Environments*" Plenum Press, New York, 1972
This book discusses the role of electrochemistry within an economy responding to changing environmental criteria and energy costs.

Many articles of interest, particularly on galvanic cells, will be found in the "Journal of the Electrochemical Society" and in a continuing series entitled "Modern Aspects of Electrochemistry", the latter published by Plenum Press, New York.

PROBLEMS

1. State the oxidation number of Pb in $PbCl_6{}^{2-}$; Sn in $Sn_2F_5{}^-$; Re in $ReO_4{}^-$; Xe in $HXeO_4{}^-$; Bi in BiO^+; N in NH_3OH^+.

2. Balance the following equations. All reactions are in acid solution. Supply H_2O and H^+ as needed.

$$PbS(c) + H_2O_2 \rightarrow PbSO_4(c) + H_2O$$

$$Mn^{2+} + BiO_3{}^- \rightarrow MnO_4{}^- + Bi^{3+}$$

$$NO + NO_3{}^- \rightarrow N_2O_4$$

$$CS(NH_2)_2 + BrO_3^- \rightarrow CO(NH_2)_2 + SO_4^{2-} + Br^-$$

$$KMnO_4 + KCNS + H_2SO_4 \rightarrow MnSO_4 + K_2SO_4 + CO_2 + N_2 + H_2O$$

3. Balance the following equations. All reactions are in alkaline solution. Supply H_2O, and OH^- as needed.

$$Al(c) + NO_3^- \rightarrow Al(OH)_4^- + NH_3$$

$$Bi(OH)_3 + Sn(OH)_4^{2-} \rightarrow Bi + Sn(OH)_6^{2-}$$

$$MnO_4^- + CN^- \rightarrow MnO_2(c) + CNO^-$$

$$S(c) + HO_2^- \rightarrow SO_4^{2-} + OH^-$$

4. Designate in conventional form voltaic cells which have the following cell reactions:

$$Ni(c) + 2 Ag^+ \rightarrow Ni^{2+} + 2 Ag(c)$$

$$6 Fe^{2+} + Cr_2O_7^{2-} + 14 H^+ \rightarrow 2 Cr^{3+} + 6 Fe^{3+} + 7 H_2O$$

$$Ag^+ + Br^- \rightarrow AgBr(c)$$

$$Cu^{2+} \rightarrow Cu^{2+}$$
$$0.1m \qquad 0.01m$$

5. For the cell at 298 K:

$$Cd(c) \left| Cd^{2+}(aq,m') \right|\left| I^-(aq, m'') \right| I_2(c) \left| Pt \right.$$

write the electrode and cell reactions. Calculate for this reaction $E°$, K, and $\Delta G°$ per mole of cadmium. Mark the polarity of the electrodes. What is the effect on $E°$ and K of doubling the cell reaction? What is the effect on $E°$ and K of reversing the cell reaction?

$$[0.94, 5.6 \times 10^{31}, -181 \text{ kJ}]$$

6. Hills and Ives measured the emf of the following cell at 298 K and $P°$ at a series of molalities. Data at low molalities are below:

m of HCl	E in volt for $H_2(g,P°) \left\| HCl(aq,m) \right\| Hg_2Cl_2(c) \left\| Hg(l) \right.$
0.013 968	0.493 39
0.010 947 4	0.505 32
0.007 693 8	0.522 675
0.005 040 3	0.543 665
0.003 076 9	0.568 25
0.001 607 7	0.600 80

By extrapolation to infinite dilution on a plot of E versus $m^{\frac{1}{2}}$ determine $E°$. Also calculate $\gamma_\pm$ for HCl at 0.005 m and compare it with the values predicted by various forms of the Debye-Hückel equation from Chapter 21.

$$[0.2679 \text{ V}, 0.926]$$

7. A study of the following cell at 298.15 K measured $E°$ to be 0.984 28 V.

$$ZnHg(amalgam)\,\big|\,ZnCl_2(aq)\,\big|\,AgCl(c)\,\big|\,Ag(c)$$

At the most dilute concentration of $ZnCl_2$ studied, 4.3035×10^{-4} mol kg^{-1}, E was measured as 1.268 05 V. What is the mean ionic activity coefficient of $ZnCl_2$ in aqueous solution at this concentration and temperature?

[0.928]

8. From the values of $\varepsilon°$ for the $Ag^+\,|\,Ag$ and $AgBr\,|\,Ag$, Br^- electrodes calculate the value of the solubility product constant for $AgBr(c)$.

[4.9×10^{-13}]

9. A 0.3130 g sample of an oxidant with formula mass about 250 g mol^{-1} liberates from an excess of KI solution enough I_2 to require in titration 2000. mL of 0.1250 F $Na_2S_2O_3$ solution. Calculate the accurate formula mass of the oxidant and write the equation for the titration.

[250.4 g mol^{-1}]

10. Calculate the pressure of hydrogen necessary to maintain equilibrium with respect to the following process at 298 K if the concentration of lead (II) ion is 0.01 mol kg^{-1} and the solution is buffered at pH 1. Use standard electrode potentials rather than thermochemical data to evaluate K. Ignore activity coefficients.

$$Pb(c) + 2\,H^+(aq) \rightarrow Pb^{2+}(aq) + H_2(g)$$

[1800 MPa]

11. You wish to reduce an I_2 solution and decide to use a solution of sodium thiosulphate, $Na_2S_2O_3$. From the $\varepsilon°$ values in the table predict the equilibrium constant for this reaction (for 1 mol I_2). Is the reaction spontaneous? Is the reaction quantitative by some reasonable criterion? Sketch the progress of the titration.

[3.5×10^{15}]

12. Using Figures 22-10 and 22-11 answer the following questions

(a) In an excavation you find samples of both hematite (Fe_2O_3) and pyrite (FeS_2) at pH 7. Estimate the pε of the formation.

[−4]

(b) At pH 6 what potential should be applied to a piece of iron to prevent it from corroding?

[−0.44 V]

13. The pε/pH diagram shows two redox processes, one of which is pH dependent and one of which is not. Write the equations for the two processes. If one wanted to oxidize Cr^{3+} to CrO_4^{2-}, would it make sense to do it in acidic or in alkaline solution?

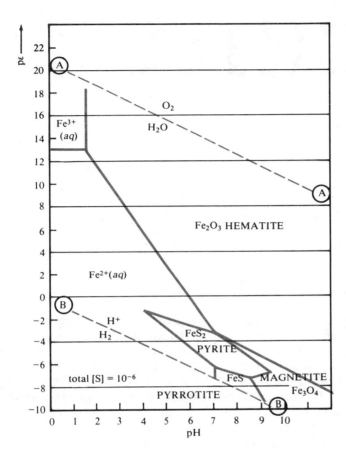

Figure 22-11 pε/pH Diagram for Iron modified for Geological Use.

XXIII WATER

23-1 PLANETARY SIGNIFICANCE

For the purpose of support of life one of the most important chemical compounds is water. For one thing, water constitutes a suitable body fluid, a medium in which the various required biochemicals are assembled within the organism and allowed to react. Some organisms such as jellyfish are about 98% water, while trees may be only about 50% water. Human blood and the body fluids of other animals bear remarkable similarities to sea water, which is not surprising if one accepts the premise that life emerged from the sea. All forms of life, even in the desert, require a reliable intake of water and most of the nutritional and excretory functions are water based. Water even acts as a source of oxygen.

For plants, oxygen is required along with carbon dioxide in photosynthesis, which can be approximately represented in an overall way by the equation:

$$CO_2 + 2\,H_2O^* \xrightarrow{h\nu} \frac{1}{n}\,(CH_2O)_n + H_2O + O_2^*$$

The above equation has been written in this particular way to stress the known fact that the two oxygen atoms (in O_2) come from the water and not from the carbon dioxide. In natural water bodies the water acts not only as an essential ingredient in its own right, but also as a vehicle for the CO_2 in the form of bicarbonate ion (HCO_3^-). The reverse process to photosynthesis is called respiration and is required by both plants and animals, demanding a reliable supply of oxygen in the air or water inhabited by the organism. Here the water can be regarded as a reliable source of O_2, whether by the photosynthetic process indicated above, or by the photodecomposition of water in the atmosphere under the influence of ultraviolet radiation from the sun, according to

$$2\,H_2O \xrightarrow{h\nu} 2\,H_2 + 2\,O \rightarrow 2\,H_2 + O_2$$

Most of the water on the earth resides in the outer skin of the planet whether as oceans, fresh water lakes and streams, ground water, snow and ice, or in the atmosphere. This water is termed collectively the hydrosphere. 98% of it is sea water which covers about 71% of the surface of the earth. Not surprisingly, this vast surface of water drives our climate patterns. Water born aloft by evaporation and as fine particles forms clouds with high electrical charges as well as regions of high and low atmospheric pressure creating the potential for winds and storms with attendant precipitation in the forms of rain, snow, sleet and hail. This precipitated water reaches the water bodies on land and sea directly or by drainage routes. In certain places the energy of flowing water is converted to electrical energy which in Canada is commonly termed ''hydro'' power. Also, water bodies have a steadying effect on the climate of nearby land by absorbing large quantities of heat, or the reverse, with small change in temperature owing to the high heat capacity and high latent heats of fusion and vaporization. The high heat capacity is partly owing to the vast amount of matter in water bodies such as the seas and the Great Lakes, and partly because, per unit amount of substance, water has the highest heat capacity of all liquids and solids, except liquid NH_3. Water also has the highest latent heats of vaporization and fusion, again with the exception of NH_3.

The value of seas, lakes and rivers in the provision of a medium for economical transport of people and materials needs no explanation here, nor does their use for recreational purposes.

23-2 STRUCTURE AND BONDING

The structure of the *individual* H_2O molecule has already been discussed as a bent triatomic molecule with the $H\diagdown{}_O{}\diagup H$ angle of 104.5°; and the two interatomic O−H distances the same, 0.096 nm. The bond energy for these covalent O−H bonds can be determined as one half the enthalpy of the reaction,

$$H_2O(g) \rightarrow 2\,H(g) + O(g)$$

$$\text{bond energy} = \frac{2(218.00) + 1(249.17) - (-241.81)}{2}$$

$$= 463.5 \text{ kJ}$$

This is one of the strongest single bonds, being stronger than those for H−H, H−Cl, O−O, C−H, C−C, and N−H, although it is not as strong as for H−F, as might be predicted from the relative electronegativities. For each molecule in the gas phase, the arrangement of valence shell electron pairs is almost tetrahedral, but with the repulsion between lone pairs of electrons squeezing the pure tetrahedral angle of 109° down to 104.5°. Also the molecule has its centre of positive charge displaced from the centre of negative charge, resulting in an important dipole moment.

Occasionally in the gas phase a dimer will be formed by 'hydrogen bonding' as indicated below. Notice that when this occurs each H_2O molecule retains its

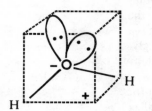
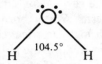
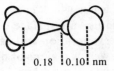

identity. Hydrogen bonding is significant only when an H bridge is formed electrostatically between small, electronegative atoms such as F, O, and N, or combinations of these.

In the solid state as ice there are several possible structures. In the usual form at atmospheric pressure, termed ice I, the H_2O molecules are arranged in a completely ordered lattice wherein each O atom has attached to it at tetrahedral angles, four H atoms, two of which are close (0.099 nm) and two of which, being H—bonded, are farther away (0.177 nm), so that here again each water molecule retains its identity, yet all water molecules are bonded alike in an array which has the appearance of layers of puckered hexagonal rings as illustrated. This microscopic arrangement is commonly manifested macroscopically in the hexagon patterns of snowflakes. Different experimental methods give different values for the energy of the H—bond, with a range of 10—30 kJ per mole of H—bonds, averaging an order of magnitude higher than values for Van der Waals attractions, and an order lower than the usual covalent bond energies. Hence one might say that H—bonds are intermediate in importance.

When ice melts, some of the H—bonds are broken. Judging from the low value of the heat of fusion (6.02 kJ mol^{-1}) breaking is not extensive but it is enough that long-range order is destroyed and fluidity established. The temperature remains equal to 0°C until all the ice is melted, after which more H—bonds are broken as the temperature of the water is raised, and the water becomes progressively more fluid. When the boiling point is reached, still more H—bonds are broken as the water is vaporized and when all is in the vapour state we may assume that all of these bonds have gone. Judged by the magnitude of the heat of vaporization (40.63 kJ mol^{-1}) the boiling process overcomes much more H−bonding than does fusion, implying that much such bonding remains in the liquid state. An approach to assessing the energy of H−bonding considers the heat of sublimation of a mole of ice to a mole of water vapour at 0°C, namely 51.00 kJ mol^{-1}. If we regard ice as completely H−bonded with two H−bonds per molecule, and water vapour to have no H−bonds, then the energy of a mole of H−bonds comes out to be roughly 25 kJ at 0°C. In liquid water the extent of H−bonding is intermediate between the extremes of ice and water vapour, and dependent on temperature.

The intermolecular structure of liquid water has not been fully established, although many theories exist. These will not be developed here except to say that all such theories require two kinds of molecular structure, the relative proportions of which govern the measured physical properties which must be explained by theory. For our purpose in this chapter we may visualize that as the temperature of cold water is raised, H-bonds are progressively overcome and long-range order destroyed. The destruction of cross-linking may allow chains of H-bonded water molecules, as well as single molecules, to slip past one another and exhibit the fluidity which we know is a property of liquid water with such temperature dependence. As the temperature is further increased it is to be expected that the average chain length will decrease and the proportion of monomeric water will increase. However, the relatively high latent heat of vaporization at 100°C indicates that even at the boiling point the extent of structure in the water is considerable.

A last important point should be appreciated in connection with bonding and structure. One usually thinks of a structure as holding the composite entities together; in the case of water it is valuable to realize also that the intermolecular H-bonded structure serves to hold the entities *apart*. This concept and the contribution of H-bonding generally is the key to understanding the unusual properties of water which follow.

23-3   THE PHYSICAL PROPERTIES OF WATER

Judged by its physical properties water is an extraordinary liquid, as the following list emphasizes.

Property	Value	Comment
Specific heat capacity (20°C)	4.18 J K^{-1} g^{-1}	highest (expect NH$_3$)
Heat of fusion (0°C)	0.333 kJ g^{-1}	highest (except NH$_3$)
Heat of vaporization (100°C)	2.257 kJ g^{-1}	highest
Density (4°C)	1.000 kg L^{-1}	anomalous
Surface tension (20°C)	72.8×10^{-3} J m^{-2}	highest
Dipole moment (20°C)	6.14×10^{-30} C m	highest (except HCN)
Dielectric constant (20°C)	80	highest (except H$_2$SO$_4$)
Heat conductivity (20°C)	59.8 J s^{-1} m^{-2}	highest of all liquids
Transparency	relatively good	but absorbs strongly in IR and UV
Colour	none	when pure
Odour	none	when pure
Taste	none	when pure

The reason for the extraordinary behaviour of water as a liquid as shown in the above properties is to be found in the relatively strong intermolecular forces inherent in H-bonding. In most liquids the intermolecular forces are of the Van der Waals type, and are approximately an order of magnitude lower than those found in H-bonded liquids such as H_2O, NH_3 and HF. A comparison of the melting and boiling points for water and its closely related hydrides (H_2S, H_2Se, H_2Te) is useful, as shown in Figure 23-1. It is clear that H_2O has a relatively higher resistance to phase change on heating as a consequence of its strong H-bonding. If H_2O had the same trends shown by its fellow hydrides, it should melt at about $-100°C$ and boil at about $-70°C$, with disastrous environmental consequences. The thermal behaviour of water in the various phases is best visualized in the heating curve of Figure 23-2 and the one-component phase diagram of Figure 23-3. The heating curve is generated by starting with solid ice and taking temperatures with time as heat is supplied at a constant rate. Thus, on the abscissa, time is proportional to heat supplied. At $0°C$ the ice begins to melt to liquid, and so long as both of these phases are present in equilibrium, the temperature remains at $0°C$. When all of the ice has disappeared, the temperature rises again. The horizontal length of the thermal arrest is a measure of the heat supplied to cause fusion, called the "latent" heat of fusion because the effect of the heat is hidden in that it is not manifest in temperature rise. Between $0°C$ and $100°C$ the heat supplied is used in raising the temperature. When $100°C$ is reached a new (vapour) phase forms and the

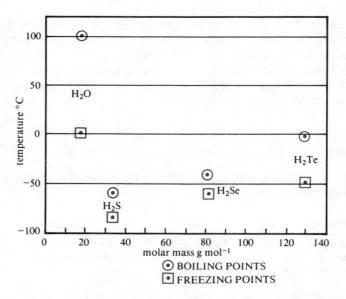

Figure 23-1   Freezing and Boiling Points of Water and Related Hydrides.

temperature is arrested until all the water disappears. This second thermal arrest, coresponding to the latent heat of vaporization, has a larger horizontal span than the latent heat of fusion, in keeping with the knowledge that the heat of vaporization is considerably larger than the heat of fusion.

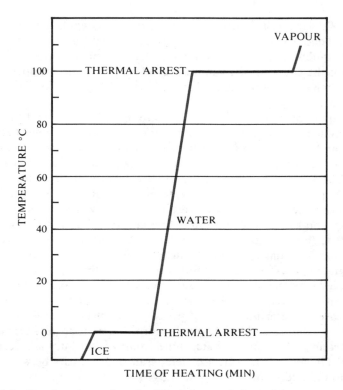

Figure   23-2   Heating Curve for the Water System (schematic).

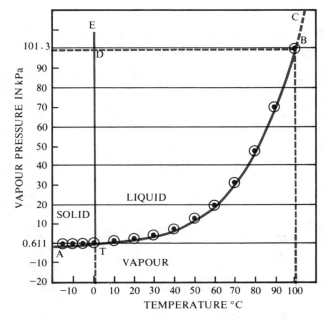

Figure   23-3   Phase Diagram for the Water System.

The phase diagram of Figure 23-3 for the water system is derived from the experimental data for three separate curves: one is that for the vapour pressure of water in equilibrium with its vapour at a series of temperatures (Table 23.1); the second is the curve for the vapour pressure of ice against temperature; the third is the line showing the dependence of the melting point of ice on the external pressure.

At the triple point, T, all three phases are in equilibrium and this point is invariant in temperature and pressure. It occurs at a vapour pressure of 0.611 kPa and temperature 0.0098°C and makes an excellent reference point for temperature calibration. The normal melting point, D, occurs at a pressure of 101.325 kPa (P°) and temperature exactly 0°C (by definition). In general the melting point depends on the external pressure. Increase in external pressure lowers the melting point, a result which every skater enjoys. The normal boiling point occurs at a vapour pressure of P° and a temperature of exactly 100°C (by definition). The boiling point decreases with decreased external pressure, so that on a mountain top water may boil without being at high enough temperature to cook food in the normal time.

The effect of increased pressure on water structure is to cause breaking of H-bonds, with a decrease in specific and molar volume, or an increase in density. In the case of water the effect of pressure on density, as measured by the coefficient of compressibility, is much more drastic than in normal liquids (such as mercury). Not only is water more compressible but the effect is quite non-linear. The anomalous effect of temperature on density begs an explanation which might contribute to a qualitative picture of liquid water structure.

TABLE 23-1   Vapour Pressures of Water and Ice with Temperature
(vapour pressure in kPa)

T (°C)	Ice	Water
−15	0.165	
−10	0.260	
− 5	0.402	
0	0.611	0.611
10		1.227
20		2.337
25		3.166
30		4.242
40		7.377
50		12.34
60		19.94
70		31.17
80		47.36
90		70.10
100		101.3

Ice, with a density at 0°C of 0.9168 kg L⁻¹ is considerably lighter than liquid water at the same temperature with a density of 0.9998 kg L⁻¹. As the temperature is raised above 0°C, water becomes anomalously more dense until it reaches a maximum density of 1.000 kg L⁻¹ at 3.98°C. Above this temperature the density decreases with increased temperature as would normally be expected. The effect of temperature on density at low temperatures is illustrated in Figure 23-4. It is apparently the case that the complete H-bonding in ice keeps the molecules well apart (i.e. about 0.276 nm between O centres). As the temperature is raised and ice melts, a considerable number of H-bonds will be broken, allowing the remnants to come closer together with a marked increase in density. Some estimate of the percent of bonding broken per mole of water at various stages might be made from the following data, allowing for the fact that there are two H-bonds per molecule.

	$\Delta H(\text{kJ mol}^{-1})$
Heat of sublimation at 0°C	51.0
Heat of fusion at 0°C	6.0
Heat of vaporization at 100°C	40.6
Bond energy overcome by heating (0° − 100°C)	
by difference = 51.0 − 46.6 = 4.4 kJ mol⁻¹.	

This leads to the estimate that about 12% of the H-bonds are broken on fusion, no more than 8% on heating from 0° to 100°C, and 80% on vaporization.

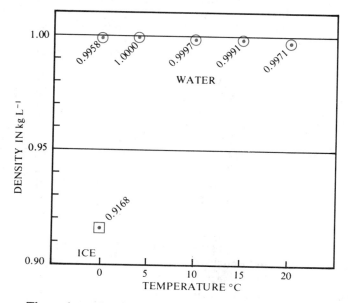

Figure 23-4   Densities of Ice and Water.

The awkward range of temperature is between 0°C and 3.98°C when the liquid increases in density slightly on heating. Two effects have opposing tendencies: the breaking of H-bonds tends to increase the density slightly as molecules come closer together; and opposing this is the thermal expansion effect whereby increased kinetic energy at higher temperature causes them to occupy more space (as is the case with most substances). Below 3.98°C the first effect predominates; at 3.98°C the effects are balanced; above 3.98°C the thermal expansion effect is overriding. The consequences of the above density relations are important in the environment. At the onset of cold weather water is cooled to maximum density at 3.98°C when it sinks through less dense layers causing an autumn overturn. On further cooling below 3.98°C the density decreases slightly until 0°C is reached when the liquid freezes with a marked decrease in density (or increase in volume which can rupture containers). This marked decrease in density causes the ice formed to float on top of the water and insulate it from the cold air above. In this way the body of water, if deep enough, is prevented from freezing solid with much benefit to aquatic life. Furthermore in fresh water harbours such as at Kingston, Canada, bubbling systems are used in winter to drive the bottom water (at 3.98°C) up to the top to prevent the harbour routes from freezing up.

The natural abundance of deuterium, the hydrogen isotope with one neutron, is 0.015% by mole in natural hydrogen. Water with only deuterium present is called heavy water. Usually in chemistry, the effects of isotopic differences are slight. An atom of ^{13}C is, after all, only 8% heavier than one of ^{12}C and one of ^{37}Cl is only 6% heavier than one of ^{35}Cl. These differences can be easily detected spectroscopically but they have small effects on the chemical and physical properties of compounds containing them. In the case of hydrogen, however, the deuterium isotope is 100% heavier and this does have a more significant impact on the properties of water and other compounds containing such hydrogen. The importance of this isotope is great enough that it is often given its own symbol, D, as if it were a separate element. Some of the differences in physical properties between H_2O and D_2O are exemplified below.

		H_2O	D_2O
Molar mass	(g mol^{-1})	18.015	20.028
Density at 25°C	(kg L^{-1})	0.9970	1.1044
Temperature of maximum density	(°C)	3.98	11.23
Heat capacity C_p at 25°C	(J K^{-1}mol^{-1})	75.29	84.35
Vapour pressure at 25°C	(Pa)	3166	2734
ΔH of vapour at 25°C	(kJ mol^{-1})	44.0	45.4
Boiling point at P°	(°C)	100.0	101.42
Freezing point at P°	(°C)	0.00	3.81
ΔH of fusion at F.P.	(kJ mol^{-1})	6.01	6.34
Bond energy	(kJ mol^{-1})	463.5	470.9

Heavy water is now produced on a large scale, since it is used as a moderator in the natural uranium fuelled Candu nuclear power reactors. Heavy water is also a simple starting point for the synthesis of a wide range of organic compounds with partial or total deuteration. Such compounds are used as 'labels' to study the mechanism of reactions by finding out where in the structure of a product molecule one locates a given kind of reactant molecule. Nuclear magnetic resonance (n.m.r.) spectroscopy in particular has made this a powerful technique.

23-4   THE CHEMICAL PROPERTIES OF WATER

The excellence of water as a versatile solvent can be attributed to five properties:

1. the capability of reacting with certain substances to give soluble products.
2. the capability of H-bonding with certain substances.
3. the small size of the water molecule.
4. the fact that water has a dipole moment.
5. the fact that water has a high dielectric constant.

Before elaborating on these properties some general comments on the dissolution of substances should be made. In order for a substance to dissolve, the solute-solute forces and solvent-solvent forces must be overcome. These are called "cohesive" forces. On the other hand, there will be compensation in the energy released when new forces come into play between solute-solvent, called "adhesive" forces. Likewise entropy considerations involve a balance between the gain associated with breaking up the solid lattice and the decrease associated with solvating dissolved molecules and ions. When we consider the chemical nature of water and the substances which it dissolves we are led to the realization that the most important factor is electrostatic in nature and leads to producing aqueous ions. Water is a particularly good solvent for ionic inorganic compounds and small, polar organic compounds, whereas it is not a good solvent for large, non-polar organic compounds. Now let us look at the five properties listed above:

Water can dissolve such substances as HCl(g), CH$_3$COOH(l) and Na(s) by reacting with them to produce hydrated ions in solution with bonding of an ion-dipole type. Hence water has been termed an ionizing solvent.

$$HCl(g) + H_2O(l) \rightarrow H^+(aq) + Cl^-(aq)$$

$$CH_3COOH(l) + H_2O(l) \rightarrow H^+(aq) + CH_3COO^-(aq)$$

$$Na(s) + H_2O(l) \rightarrow Na^+(aq) + 2 OH^-(aq) + H_2(g)$$

The ions above have an indefinite number of solvent molecules attached, and are said to be *solvated*, or in this particular case, *hydrated*. It is not certain just how many water molecules (termed the hydration number), are associated with a particular proton or sodium ion at any particular temperature, pressure, composition or ionic strength. A variety of experimental techniques have been tried, with lack of agreement in the results. Various techniques show hydration numbers from 3 to 13 for Na$^+$, from 2 to 7 for K$^+$, from 8 to 36 for Mg^{2+}, from 8 to 29 for Ca^{2+} and from 2 to 5 for Br$^-$.

A vital question is the nature of the hydrogen ion in dilute aqueous solution. The intense charge/size ratio for a proton precludes any reasonable chance of finding bare unattached protons in aqueous solution. On the other hand, the chemical bonding of the proton to *one* H$_2$O diminishes greatly this intensity of charge/size, affording the interesting entity, H$_3$O$^+$, which has been predicted and detected by infrared and x-ray diffraction studies. Here the O−H bonds formed are even shorter and stronger than in H$_2$O and enclose an angle near 110°, which is closer to tetrahedral than that in H$_2$O. Its VSEPR picture is thus quite regular with three bonding pairs and one lone pair arranged almost symmetrically in space at close to tetrahedral angles. The entity H_3O^+ is capable of forming H-bonds to other H_2O molecules (often 3, but fewer if in concentrated acid solution), but this bonding is much weaker than the chemical bond to the first H_2O. The component parts of this hydrated structure largely retain their own character so that most of the positive charge resides on the H_3O part, which has an electrostatic attraction for a further water dipole. The problem is how to represent the hydrated structure. To distinguish the strength of bonds and location of charge the formula $H_3O^+ \cdot 3\ H_2O$ is best. When these are not required, $H_3O^+(aq)$ and $H^+(aq)$ are used in this book. By comparison, the hydroxide ion in aqueous solution also H-bonds to form $OH^- \cdot 3\ H_2O$, which can be simplified to $OH^-(aq)$, as is done for other ions such as $Na^+(aq)$ and $Cl^-(aq)$.

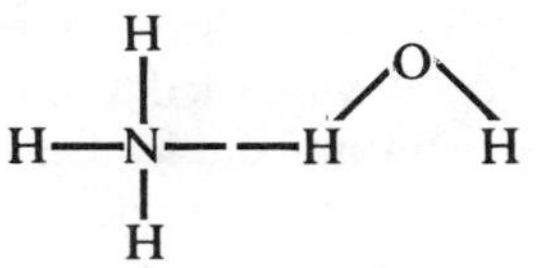

AMMONIA

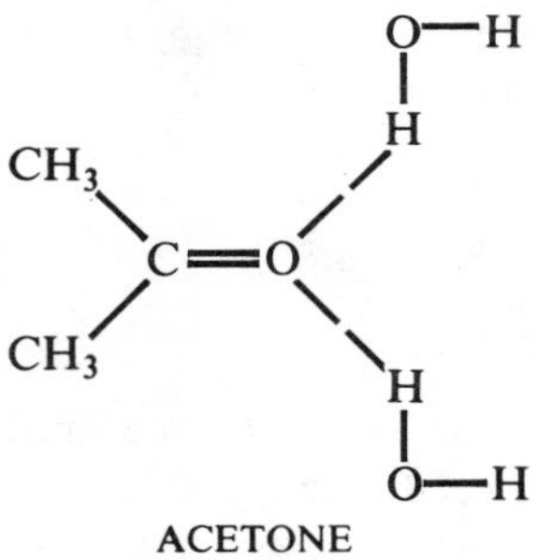

ACETONE

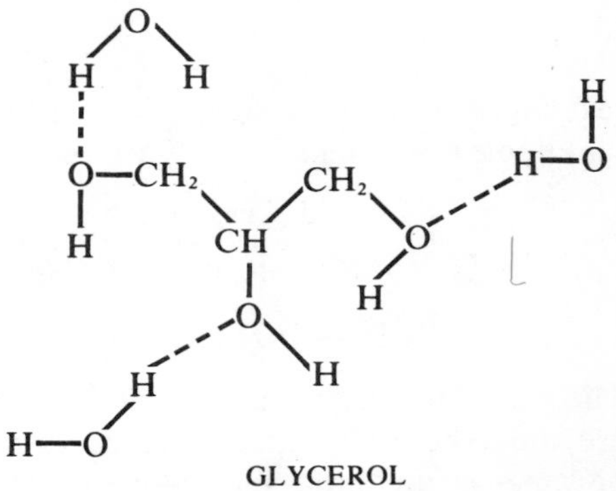

GLYCEROL

In spite of the above mentioned variation in experimental hydration numbers, some trends are evident.

(a) Smaller ions in the same periodic group tend to have higher hydration numbers than the larger ions, i.e. $Li^+ > Na^+ > K^+$; $Mg^{2+} > Ca^{2+} > Sr^{2+}$.

(b) Ions with higher charges have higher hydration numbers, e.g. $Mg^{2+} > Na^+$.

(c) Cations are generally smaller than anions with the same charge and approximate mass and being more intensely charged relative to size, hold more water molecules of hydration, e.g. $Na^+ > F^-$; $K^+ > Cl^-$. It appears that large ions such as Cs^+ and I^- are scarcely hydrated at all.

Water can dissolve organic molecules of small size with polar groups, and especially those with many OH groups such as the carbohydrates (e.g. sucrose) and polyalcohols (e.g. glycerol) by H-bonding. H-bonds can be formed with small polar molecules such as ammonia, NH_3; ether, CH_3OCH_3; and acetone, CH_3COCH_3.

The small size of the water molecule, with a diameter about 0.2 nm, allows it to penetrate into crystalline lattices between ions and in solution between molecules once they have been loosened by the forces of adhesion. The forces of adhesion need to be strong to produce dissolution if the cohesive forces are strong, but can be weaker if the cohesion is weaker.

The fact that the water molecule has a dipole moment allows it to orient itself to advantage in overcoming the cohesive forces and release and disperse the ion or polar solute molecule, with or without hydration. The point is that water molecules constitute an oriented medium which isolates the solute entities from one another.

We have noted that water has an exceptionally high dielectric constant of 80. Writing Coulomb's law with force F in newton, charge q in coulomb, and the permittivity in vacuum $\varepsilon_o = 8.85 \times 10^{-12}\ J^{-1}\ C^2\ m^{-1}$,

$$F = \frac{^-q \cdot q_2}{K(4\pi\varepsilon_o r^2)}$$

with K=1 for a vacuum and for water as the dielectric medium, K=80 so that

$$F = \frac{^-q \cdot q_2}{80(4\pi\varepsilon_o r^2)}$$

This signifies that the force between charges has been reduced to 1/80 of the force between ions in the crystal. In other words, water is a good medium for keeping the ions apart.

An attempt is made in Figure 23-5 to illustrate the process of dissolution of an ionic crystal lattice in favour of dispersed and hydrated ions. The release of

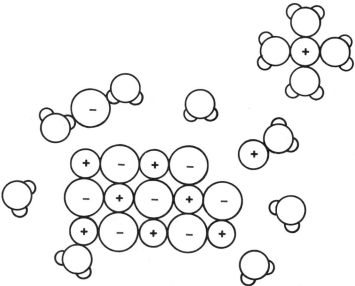

Figure 23-5   Aqueous dissolution of an ionic lattice.

energy on hydration must be sufficient to overcome the lattice energy of the crystal and that of the intermolecular structure of the solvent. The disruption of these cohesive forces is always endothermic. The hydration of the ion may be exothermic or endothermic; if endothermic then the whole dissolution process must be endothermic and increased solubility favoured with increased temperature. If the whole process is exothermic then the solubility will decrease with increased temperature. The most common situation is that the hydration process is exothermic, the overcoming of the cohesion endothermic and the overall dissolution is net endothermic and solubilities most commonly increase with higher temperature. Some salts have water of hydration even in the crystalline state and the lattices for $CuSO_4 \cdot 5 H_2O$ and $CuSO_4 \cdot H_2O$ are different, as are their colours. Four of the water molecules of hydration in $CuSO_4 \cdot 5 H_2O$ are complexed with the Cu^{2+} ion, while the fifth occupies a separate site in a bridging function. In other words the cations in the lattice are $Cu(H_2O)_4^{2+}$ ions and these are connected to SO_4^{2-} ions in a three dimensional array through the fifth molecule, and so the formula would be more informative if written $Cu(H_2O)_4SO_4 \cdot H_2O$. On heating these crystals, four molecules are lost at 110°C and the fifth at 150°C. Both types of water in such a crystal, that which is coordinated to a particular ion and that which is not, are usually called *water of hydration*. Salts which contain either kind of water are called *salt hydrates*, whereas the same salt with all of the water of hydration removed is said to be *anhydrous*.

The dissociation of water according to,

$$H_2O \rightleftharpoons H^+(aq) + OH^-(aq)$$

$$K_W = 1.0 \times 10^{-14} \text{ at } 25°C$$

has been discussed in Chapter 20. According to the above equation H_2O is acting as a Brønsted/Lowry acid by furnishing a proton to the base, $OH^-(aq)$. But one might also consider water as a Brønsted/Lowry base according to the equation,

$$H_3O^+ \rightleftharpoons H^+ + H_2O$$

wherein H_2O is acting as a base in accepting the proton. Classically, water would be said to be amphoteric; but in Brønsted/Lowry terms water is said to be amphiprotic, meaning that it has the potential to donate or accept a proton. Evidence for the weak dissociation of water can be found in the fact that pure water conducts electricity by movement of the ions formed. Values for K_W at a series of temperatures along with the electrical conductivity x (in $\mu S \ m^{-1}$) are given below in Table 23-2. It can be seen that the conductivity of water in-

TABLE 23-2 Temperature Dependence of Dissociation and Conductivity of Water

T(°C)	0	10	20	25	30	40	50
$10^{14} \cdot K_W$	0.114	0.292	0.688	1.008	1.47	2.92	5.5
$x \ (\mu S \ m^{-1})$	1.2	2.3	4.2	5.5	7.1	11.3	17.1

Data taken in part from Aylward and Findlay: SI Chemical Data courtesy John Wiley and Sons, Australia Pty Ltd.

creases with temperature as does the dissociation constant. However, the temperature dependence of conductivity reflects the speed of the ions as well as degree of dissociation and an abnormal transport mechanism. Furthermore there are two different ions involved, with attendant hydration, so the relationships are not simple. While the conductivity of the water itself is relatively low, the conductivity of a solution of electrolyte is relatively high. For example, x for a 0.1 F aqueous solution of KCl at 25°C is 1.16 S m^{-1}, or almost a million times that for pure water, demonstrating why water has been called an ionizing solvent. The conductivity of strong acids and bases is even higher than for salts. For 0.1 F solutions of HCl and NaOH values of x at 25°C are respectively 3.32 and 2.18 S m^{-1}. This has been attributed to the fact that H_3O^+ and OH^- bear a special relation to the solvent structure, which adds to the normal ferrying of charge as a result of rapid transfer of protonic charge within the H-bonded water chains. For H_3O^+ and OH^- the mechanisms can be pictured as in Figure 23-6.

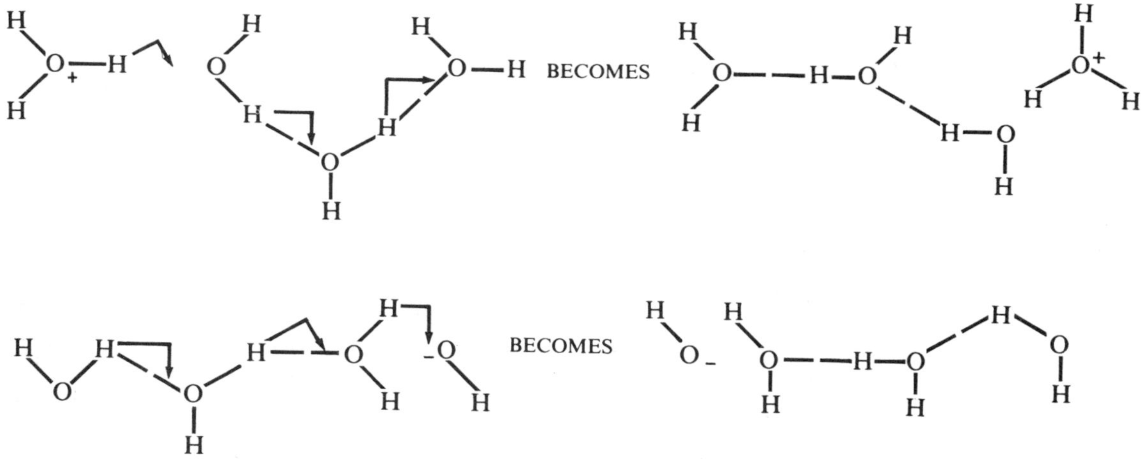

Figure 23-6 Tranfer of Charge through Water Chains.

As a redox reagent H_2O can be regarded as an oxidant or reductant; it is the reduced product from O_2, or the oxidized product from H_2. The appropriate standard reactions are:

$$\tfrac{1}{2} O_2(g) + 2 H^+(aq) + 2e \rightarrow H_2O(l) \qquad\qquad \varepsilon° = 1.23 \text{ V}$$

$$H_2(g) \rightarrow 2 H^+(aq) + 2e \qquad\qquad \varepsilon° = 0.00 \text{ V}$$

$$H_2(g) + \tfrac{1}{2} O_2(g) \rightarrow H_2O(l) \qquad\qquad E° = 1.23 \text{ V}$$

The above is a valuable energetic relation from a thermodynamic standpoint since the cell emf of 1.23 volt corresponds to an equilibrium constant at 25°C,

$$E° = 1.23 = \frac{0.0592}{2} \log K$$

$$K = 4.4 \times 10^{41}$$

$$\Delta G° = \Delta G_f° \text{ of } H_2O(l) = -237.13 \text{ kJ mol}^{-1}$$

However, in spite of the thermodynamic favourability implied by any of the above criteria, when $H_2(g)$ and $O_2(g)$ are put together in a container, nothing happens unless certain catalytic conditions are met. With hot platinized asbestos, for example, the reaction is explosive. To control the energy release of the reaction from a voltaic cell the oxidant (O_2) and reductant or fuel (H_2) must be kept separate so that they cannot react directly, and separate catalysts are used. The reaction is carried out in what is termed a *fuel cell*, because energy is derived from the oxidation of reduced material by the use of a cheap and available oxidant, namely O_2 in the air. For the oxidation of $H_2(g)$ the platinum-group metals are satisfactory catalysts when deposited on pure carbon electrodes. Nickel also is satisfactory. But the reduction of $O_2(g)$ all the way to H_2O is a more complicated matter kinetically. For one thing, per mole of $O_2(g)$, a four-electron change is involved, which is mechanistically unlikely to occur in one step. Rather the overall reduction can be viewed as two sequential steps:

$$O_2(g) + 2 H^+(aq) + 2e \rightarrow H_2O_2$$

$$H_2O_2(aq) + 2 H^+(aq) + 2e \rightarrow 2 H_2O(l)$$

The first of these is not so kinetically difficult as the second, and can be catalyzed by any of the catalysts for chemisorption of $O_2(g)$. But the second step is the difficult one since it involves breaking the strong oxygen to oxygen bond in H_2O_2 with the use of an appropriate dissociation catalyst. Used as catalysts have been black platinum, silver, and oxides of the noble metals (Cu, Ag, Au). Other fuels can be considered such as hydrazine (N_2H_4), or methane (CH_4) from natural gas or from cracked hydrocarbons, with $O_2(g)$ in air again as the oxidant.

$$N_2H_4(g) + O_2(g) \rightarrow N_2(g) + 2 H_2O(l)$$

$$CH_4(g) + 2 O_2(g) \rightarrow CO_2(g) + 2 H_2O(l)$$

In all of these cases the products of the fuel cell reactions are relatively innocuous (H_2O, N_2, CO_2). Other advantages of the fuel cell are that it has not the same thermodynamic limit on efficiency which constrains heat-converted mechanical devices (engines). Also the H_2/O_2 fuel cell particularly suits a hydrogen-based energy economy (whereby $H_2(g)$ from electrolysis of water, and any other sources, is circulated country-wide rather than electricity). The use of fuel cells is not apt to become dominant, however, so long as petroleum and other fossil fuel reserves remain competitive. Nevertheless, the present use of fuel cells in commercial tractors, and as energy sources in space vehicles is worth noting, as well as their function as back-up power supplies at generating stations.

23-5   WATER MANAGEMENT: SUPPLY, TREATMENT AND DISPOSAL

We have already stressed the unique abundance of water on our planet and the dependence on it which all life has developed. Man in particular uses water for drinking, cooking, bathing, laundry, recreation, irrigation, cooling, movement of sewage, transportation and special industrial purposes. Yet two major problems have not been overcome. In spite of the overall abundance of water, some areas are desperately short and its cost is high in money or labour. Secondly, even where water is plentiful, the quality is sometimes so bad as to be detrimental to health. Good water management is sorely needed for world nutrition and health.

Water sources vary with locale. Most municipalities rely on surface water from lakes and rivers but farms and rural communities often rely on ground water from wells which tap the water table or underground streams. The island of Barbados has a vast supply of such water underground; Bermuda has not and relies on water caught on tiled roofs and drained into cisterns in which fish are kept to control the algal growth. In polar regions ice and snow can be melted while in a dry region such as Baja California, desalination of sea water is current. Also, within any one community different waters may be used for different purposes. In Canada, the water from a certain lake may be used for all purposes while in Southern California untreated surface water may be used for irrigation, ion-exchanged water for industrial purposes, distilled water for institutions, while the householder may buy his sparkling water in a jug at the supermarket. Water sources are not thoroughly homogeneous. The chemical properties of the water in the Colorado River near its origin in the Rocky Mountains are a far cry from those in the miserable trickle which survives to enter Mexico. And the water in Saginaw Bay, Michigan, is much different from that in the main body of Lake Huron.

As to treatment, water for agricultural use is normally not treated chemically although at times this ought to be done wherever there is a threat that toxic substances in the water may be taken up by plants. By contrast, the uses of water in industry are highly specific, ranging from water used for cooling, which may need little treatment, to water used for food processing and analytical chemical purposes, which will require high purity. These will not be discussed here since the individual treatments for some industrial purpose will often be a combination of those in use in municipal water purification, which follow. A municipality will use some sequence of the following processes, depending on the quality of the raw water:

(a) removal of solids by sedimentation
(b) chemical coagulation of suspended solids and colloids
(c) filtration to remove coagulated solids
(d) aeration to oxidize undesirable compounds and, by raising $p\epsilon$ and pH, improving taste and odour
(e) chlorination to control harmful bacteria and algae, improving taste and odour
(f) softening and corrosion prevention
(g) removal of ions by distillation or ion-exchange
(h) polishing with activated carbon to remove organic compounds objectionable for reasons of taste, odour, or toxicity.

The suspension of particles in water is stabilized by the mutual repulsion of like charges on the particles, often negative. Neutralization of the charges is achieved most effectively by an ion of high valence such as aluminium ion, usually in the form of the compound aluminium sulphate (misnamed alum). Ferric ion has also been used and both of the above cations have the added advantage that they form insoluble phosphates, thus helping to clarify eutrophic waters. The $Al_2(SO_4)_3$ dissociates to form $Al^{3+}(aq)$ which combines with $OH^-(aq)$ to form a gelatinous precipitate of $Al(OH)_3$. This precipitate in bulk is positively charged and gathers the negatively charged suspended particles causing discharge and coagulation into a gelatinous mass with settling and clarification of the water on filtration through sand beds.

$$Al_2(SO_4)_3(c) \rightarrow 2\, Al^{3+}(aq) + 3\, SO_4{}^{2-}(aq)$$

$$Al^{3+}(aq) + 3\, OH^-(aq) \rightarrow Al(OH)_3(c)$$

Aeration of water supplies is used primarily as an economic means of oxidizing undesirable substances present. In the case of iron and manganese, which are usually common in ground water in reduced condition (as Fe (II) and Mn (II)), these elements are oxidized to the higher valent insoluble compounds, MnO_2 and $Fe(OH)_3$. An alternative is to precipitate the carbonates $FeCO_3$ and $MnCO_3$ with sodium carbonate. Aeration will also cause the oxidation of some organic compounds to CO_2 and sulphides to SO_2, sulphite, or sulphate, thus eliminating some causes of bad taste and odour.

The most common disinfectant for controlling bacteria in water is chlorine, Cl_2. It can be added in gaseous form, in which case most of it forms the weak acid, hypochlorous acid.

$$Cl_2(g) + H_2O(l) \rightarrow H^+(aq) + Cl^-(aq) + HOCl(aq); \qquad K = 4.5 \times 10^{-4}$$

$$HOCl \rightarrow H^+(aq) + OCl^-(aq); \qquad K_a = 2.7 \times 10^{-8}$$

For some purposes (e.g. swimming pools) it is more convenient to add calcium hypochlorite.

$$Ca(OCl)_2 \rightarrow Ca^{2+}(aq) + 2\, OCl^-(aq)$$

In the usual pH range, OCl^- will be protonated to produce $HOCl$. Both OCl^- and $HOCl$ are effective bacteriocides. Also effective are the chloramines: NH_2Cl, $NHCl_2$ and NCl_3, formed by the addition of ammonia,

$$HOCl + NH_3(g) \rightarrow H_2O + NH_2Cl(aq)$$

$$2\, HOCl + NH_3(g) \rightarrow 2\, H_2O + NHCl_2(aq)$$

$$3\, HOCl + NH_3(g) \rightarrow 3\, H_2O + NCl_3(aq)$$

In practice the mass ratio of Cl/NH_3 is kept high enough so that there is always an excess of $HOCl$, ensuring removal of NH_3 from the product. Another disinfectant used is ozone, O_3, produced by strong electrical discharge (20 000 V) through clean, dry, compressed air and passage of the $O_3(g)$ through the water for ten to fifteen minutes. Oxidizing agents such as chlorine, hypochlorite ion, and ozone are beneficial beyond disinfection in that they are capable of oxidizing undesirable organic and inorganic compounds and removing offensive taste and odour as well as potential toxicity.

Water is said to be "hard" when objectionable salts come out of solution when the water is heated or used for washing or industrial purposes. In general hard waters contain dissolved substances, of which the divalent ions calcium and magnesium are the real culprits because they are plentiful, have insoluble compounds, and, in particular, form objectionable curds or sludges with soaps. With these abundant cations, Ca^{2+} and Mg^{2+}, in hard waters the commonest anion is bicarbonate, but others such as sulphate and chloride may occur in water supplies. When the common anion is bicarbonate the hardness is said to be "temporary" since it can be removed by simply boiling the water to cause the removal of the cation by precipitation.

$$Ca(HCO_3)_2(aq) \xrightarrow{\text{heat}} CaCO_3(c) + CO_2(g) + H_2O.$$

However, with anions such as sulphate or chloride no such removal is effected and so the hardness is termed "permanent." The reaction above whereby $CaCO_3$ is deposited on heating temporary hard water explains why scale occurs in kettles, hot water heaters, industrial boilers and pipes. At higher temperature, $CaSO_4$, owing to an inverted solubility effect of temperature, can also constitute a threat to boiling by forming scale.

Hardness is commonly determined by a complexing titration using a chelate called EDTA. The divalent cations found are *assumed* to be all calcium with carbonate as anion. Thus, results for hardness of water are expressed as $CaCO_3$, usually in parts per million (ppm) by mass. Water with hardness over 100 ppm would be regarded as quite hard. Soft waters, on the other hand, are more corrosive than hard waters, having lower pH. An optimum hardness for swimming pools and indoor plumbing would be about 70 ppm $CaCO_3$. Reduction of hardness in water by treatment is termed softening. Of course one way to avoid excess hardness in water is by use of a softer water source. One automated scientific operation used a ground water supply with an almost unbelievably high hardness of 1500 ppm which caused the plumbing to seize up within a few months. After trying to soften this terribly hard water, it was found that bringing softer water from a nearby river was a better solution to the problem. For washing purposes, considerable hardness can be tolerated if synthetic detergents are used but not soaps. The reason for this is that the detergents, often organic compounds with a sulphonate functional group ($-SO_3H$) attached, form soluble calcium and magnesium complexes, while soaps form insoluble sludges. For household washing the divalent cations can be precipitated by adding washing soda, $Na_2CO_3 \cdot 10H_2O$.

$$Ca^{2+}(aq) + 2\,Na^+(aq) + CO_3{}^{2-}(aq) \rightarrow CaCO_3(c) + 2\,Na^+(aq)$$

Larger scale treatments such as for municipal water supply use lime water, $Ca(OH)_2$, for softening, with the capability of removing both calcium and magnesium ions at relatively high pH.

$$Ca(HCO_3)_2 + Ca(OH)_2 \rightarrow 2\,CaCO_3(c) + 2\,H_2O$$

$$Mg(HCO_3)_2 + 2\,Ca(OH)_2 \rightarrow Mg(OH)_2(c) + 2\,CaCO_3(c) + 2\,H_2O$$

Natural or synthetic ion-exchange resins may be used on the household or industrial scale to soften water. For a cation-exchange resin with R_x representing the large anionic portion of the polymeric resin, the action may be represented by

$$Na_2R_x + Ca^{2+} \rightarrow CaR_x + 2\,Na^+$$

The sodium ion released does not form undesirable curds or scales as do the corresponding calcium and magnesium compounds. The resin can be regenerated when required by adding concentrated NaCl solution, according to the reverse reaction of that above. Common natural clays such as montmorillonite are excellent ion-exchangers. Zeolites are also natural silicates which have been used commercially. Within these porous materials, sodium cations are relatively mobile and replaceable by calcium and other cations. The operation and regeneration of zeolites as ion exchange resins can be represented respectively by the above equation and its reverse.

That soft water has been found to be more aggressive in corrosion than hard water is mostly a matter of acidity. Waters made more acidic than pH 7 become depleted in bicarbonate and evolve carbon dioxide. Thus acidifying hard water softens the water but lowers the pH and renders the water more corrosive. This latter tendency can be overcome by adding base economically in the form of lime, $Ca(OH)_2$. Certain anions such as the halides favour conditions for corrosion; they can be removed by distillation, or by anion-exchange using resins of type R_xOH, according to

$$R_xOH + Cl^- \rightarrow R_xCl + OH^-$$

For certain special applications such as protection of car radiators, corrosion inhibitors (e.g. potassium dichromate solution) are used to encourage the formation of a protective oxide coat (passivation). The removal of air or oxygen from the water discourages corrosion by eliminating one of the potential cathodic systems.

The use of activated carbon for the final polishing of water is not yet extensive but is likely to increase in the future. The carbon used is derived as a by-product from such carbonaceous materials as wood, peat, lignite, coconut shell and pulp-mill char. These materials are charred in the absence of air below 600°C and activated by partial oxidation. The success of the activated carbon technique depends on affording an enormous surface area for chemical adsorption and the fact that after it is spent the carbon can be reactivated at high temperature.

Waste water may contain human, animal and industrial organic matter, inorganic salts, living organisms such as algae, bacteria and viruses, plus sediments, scums, trace metal compounds, and a host of discarded articles and materials. Before disposal into any natural water body, waste water should have these substances reduced to reasonable levels by a waste water treatment, which normally is considered to consist of three distinct stages.

Primary treatment involves removal of insoluble matter such as large objects, grease, grit and scum as well as a sedimentation process to clarify the water by removal as a sludge. This sludge is concentrated and treated biologically before disposal. Much waste water entering our waterways receives only this simple and mainly physical treatment.

Secondary treatment consists mainly of the removal of organic matter by oxidation and consumption, aided by the action of a host of micro-organisms which are kept cultured in ready supply. These micro-organisms incorporate some of the organic substance into cell material, while most of it is oxidized to CO_2, which is emitted. In addition, organic nitrogen and phosphate compounds are converted to their inorganic forms respectively: ammonium ion, nitrite and nitrate, and orthophosphate ion. For the above oxidation, molecular O_2 is required and is supplied by aeration or by exposure to air in a trickling process over rocks or other supports.

The oxygen consumed in the microbially mediated oxidation of organic content is termed the Biochemical Oxygen Demand (BOD) and is measured over an arbitrary five day period. A more definite and quicker test is the Chemical Oxygen Demand (COD) found by titration of the organic matter in the water by excess standard dichromate solution in 50% H_2SO_4, and back titration with a standard reducing agent. Total Organic Carbon (TOC) is assessed by catalytically oxidizing the carbon and detecting the carbon dioxide evolved.

The treatment system most commonly used by large municipalities is the "activated sludge" process. Effluent from primary treatment enters a large, aerated tank wherein micro-organisms from previous sludge convert organic matter to biomass and CO_2, which is evolved. After a certain time the biomass material is readily flocculated and sedimented in a settler. Some of this sludge is recycled to provide fresh micro-organisms; the rest may be processed for fertilizer. The success of the activated sludge process depends on having a large population of fresh and hungry organisms meeting a rich food supply in the sewage.

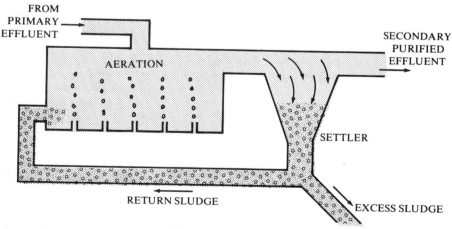

Figure 23-7 The Activated Sludge Process.

The secondary purified effluent will contain as little as 5.1% of the original solids. The excess sludge may contain desirable substances for fertilizers such as 5% N, 3% P, 0.5% K by dry mass, as well as humic substances for soil conditioning. However, the sludge is still mostly water so much of this must be removed, often by vacuum filtration, centrifuging, or drying. Proving a serious threat to its use on market gardens or near habitations is its content of pathogenic biota (such as salmonella, fecal coliforms and viruses), toxic metals and dangerous organic compounds. The first of these may be controlled by chlorination but the last two categories require careful monitoring where food crops are involved. If tighter control were established for industrial loading of toxic metals and organic compounds on the sewage, it is possible that all the excess sludge could be used for its fertile content.

Tertiary treatment refers to any process beyond the secondary, such as removal of suspended solids, dissolved organic compounds, or dissolved inorganic compounds. The first of these is undesirable in water because of oxygen demand, the second because of toxicity, and the last because of eutrophication caused by the nitrate and phosphate content. Tertiary waste water treatment is all too rare in practice. The processes required are similar to those used in treatment of water supplies. Suspended solids are most effectively removed by a combination of coagulation and filtration using an agent such as aluminium sulphate. Dissolved organic compounds are usually adsorbed on activated charcoal, packed as granules in columns. Adsorbent organic polymers have also been found effective, particularly for such potentially dangerous substances as pesticides. Removal of dissolved inorganic compounds can be effected by a number of relatively expensive processes such as distillation, freezing, ion-exchange, electrodialysis, and reverse osmosis. These are discussed in the section on natural waters.

23-6   NATURAL WATERS

The sum total of all natural waters on earth is called the hydrosphere. The study of fresh waters in lakes and streams is termed limnology and that of the salt water in the seas, oceanography. Over 70% of the surface of the planet is covered by water, about 98% of which is salty. But the small 2% in lakes and streams is vital to all living systems and essential to civilization. Marine organisms are by adaptation sustained by salt water in the seas, but fresh water organisms, including man, are not. However, at considerable cost fresh water can be obtained from salt water by a number of processes including distillation, flash evaporation, freezing, reverse osmosis, and ion-exchange. Stagnant fresh water bodies can constitute a health hazard by harboring organisms capable of transmitting serious diseases. A country with a reliably steady supply of fresh, running water for drinking, irrigation, recreation, transportation and industrial purposes has a tremendous economic advantage.

Compositions of surface and ground waters are highly variable, ranging from that of almost pure H_2O from freshly fallen rain in streams to that of the salt water in estuaries and salt lakes. Sea water in general has a much higher concentration of solutes, mostly inorganic ions and complexes, the total of which is usually expressed in grams per kilogram ($g\ kg^{-1}$) of sea water as are the individual solute concentrations. Table 23-3 contains a comparison of typical compositions of a variety of natural waters for the major constituents only. Apart from the generally greater abundance of ions in sea water it should be noted that calcium and bicarbonate ions have *relatively* greater importance in fresh waters, and magnesium and sodium ions relatively more importance in sea water. The ratio of [Mg]/[Ca] has been used to differentiate marine from terrestrial conditions.

TABLE 23-3 Some Compositions of Major Ions in Sea and Fresh Waters

Major Ions	Average Sea Water		Average River Water		Eutrophic Lake Water	
	g kg^{-1}	mol L^{-1}	g kg^{-1}	mol L^{-1}	g kg^{-1}	mol L^{-1}
Cl$^-$	19.35	0.55	0.008	$<10^{-4}$	0.026	0.00075
Na$^+$	10.76	0.47	0.006	,,	0.012	0.00053
SO$_4^{2-}$	2.71	0.03	0.011	,,	0.027	0.00028
Mg^{2+}	1.29	0.05	0.004	,,	0.006	0.00026
Ca^{2+}	0.41	0.01	0.015	,,	0.043	0.00107
K$^+$	0.39	0.01	0.002	,,	0.0015	0.00004
HCO$_3^-$	0.14	0.002	0.059	,,	0.155	0.00189
Br$^-$	0.07	$<10^{-3}$	—	,,	—	—
Sr^{2+}	0.008	$<10^{-3}$	—	,,	—	—

The total ionic content of sea water, the salinity, is designated by the symbol, S ^{o}/oo, with units of g per kg (of sea water), or sometimes termed parts per thousand or per mille. The salinity of the world ocean changes with locale, in general being low where precipitation is high relative to evaporation and vice versa. But a remarkable uniform feature of the world ocean is found in the fact that although the salinity varies with time and place, the relative proportions of the major ionic species, one to another, remain very nearly the same. This enables the overall salinity to be characterized by the determination of only one major species such as chloride ion, according to the following relation,

$$S\ ^o/oo = 0.03 + 1.80\,(Cl\ ^o/oo)$$

where Cl ^{o}/oo signifies the chloride (or bromide, iodide) content in g per kg of sea water, originally determined by titrating a weighed sample of the sea water with standard silver nitrate solution using a suitable analytical procedure (such as those of Fajan, Mohr or Volhard). In modern practice, however, the salinity has been found to be proportional to the electrical conductivity, measured on an instrument called a salinometer which has been calibrated against standard sea water of known salinity. Of course the salinity of fresh waters can also be determined by the same technique, but the values so obtained are less than unity. Fresh waters therefore are more apt to be categorized by analysis of individual species, alkalinity, pH, redox potential, and dissolved oxygen content.

Trace elements, present in a few parts per million, and ultra-trace elements, in parts per billion, are also found in sea water and fresh waters. For these elements both the absolute and relative amounts vary considerably from place to place and seasonally, as well as with depth, so representative figures are difficult to tabulate without being misleading. Furthermore, as a result of more careful sampling and of analysis by improved techniques, it has been found that many concentrations of trace elements in natural waters previously reported were too high owing to contamination during sampling, storage and analysis. It should be made plain that the analysis of trace and ultra-trace elements in natural waters cannot be carried out directly in ordinary chemical laboratories. Preconcentration steps and "clean-lab" conditions are required to keep the analyte to contaminant ratio high enough to obtain reliable results.

Important extensive properties measured in natural waters are the alkalinity and the dissolved oxygen content. The former is a measure of the capacity of the water for absorbing protons, obtained by titrating a sample of the water with standard HCl solution using a methyl orange indicator. In most natural waters the major contributors to alkalinity are bicarbonate and carbonate, but silicate, phosphate and borate species also play a significant part, taking up hydrated protons as follows:

$$CO_3^{2-} (aq) + H^+(aq) \rightleftharpoons HCO_3^- (aq)$$

$$HCO_3^- (aq) + H^+(aq) \rightleftharpoons H_2O + CO_2(aq)$$

$$Si(OH)_3O^- (aq) + H^+(aq) \rightleftharpoons Si(OH)_4(aq)$$

$$PO_4^{3-} (aq) + H^+(aq) \rightleftharpoons HPO_4^{2-} (aq)$$

$$HPO_4^{2-} (aq) + H^+(aq) \rightleftharpoons H_2PO_4^- (aq)$$

$$H_2BO_3^- (aq) + H^+(aq) \rightleftharpoons H_3BO_3(aq)$$

Since all the above systems can be regarded as conjugate pairs of Brønsted/Lowry acids and bases they can also be considered as buffer systems which regulate the pH of the water by gaining or losing $H^+(aq)$ as required. In sea water, as well as in much fresh water and in natural blood systems, bicarbonate/carbonate is the most important buffer pair. In the sea this is followed by the silicate, borate and phosphate buffers. Owing to the great predominance of silicates in the earth's crust, many consider them to provide the ultimate buffering reservoir with the carbonate system as the immediately available buffer.

The amount of oxygen dissolved in the water was formerly determined by a Winkler titration, which uses freshly precipitated $Mn(OH)_2$ to absorb the oxygen from the water sample and to form the trivalent $Mn_2O_3(H_2O)_n$. This in turn is reacted with a solution of iodide (in excess) to produce an equivalent amount of I_2, to be titrated against a standard reducing agent such as sodium thiosulphate solution. Nowadays most scientists use a 'dissolved oxygen meter,' one form of which applies a negative potential of about 0.8 V to reduce oxygen at a polarographic cathode. This produces an electric current which is proportional to the concentration of dissolved oxygen, usually expressed in parts per million of water, but sometimes as mL of oxygen per L of water. The meter is usually calibrated against the reliable oxygen content of the air, or any solution of known O_2 content. Most natural waters contain some oxygen derived from the air and from photosynthesis, and are said to be oxic. In the ground or soil, or in water bodies which contain organic matter and are prevented from mixing, or within the sediments, the oxygen may become depleted and reducing conditions prevail with sulphide ion and hydrogen sulphide being the stable and controlling redox species. The dissolved oxygen content of the water is a quantitative measure of the capacity of the water to absorb the effects of reducing agents to which the water might be exposed, whether of chemical or biological origin.

23-7   pε/pH DIAGRAMS

As opposed to the extensive properties above, the intensive properties, pH and pε can be used to define the acid-base and redox conditions of a natural water. There are no serious problems with measuring the pH of a water sample, even in situ, providing care and common sense prevail. But it should be appreciated that, as a logarithmic function of a buffered activity, the pH is a relatively insensitive parameter so that in the world ocean, the pH never differs much from a value of 8.0. There is considerable difficulty, however, in establishing the pε of natural waters. Involved experimentally is the measurement of Eh, the redox potential of the water on the hydrogen scale, based on $\varepsilon^{\circ}_{H^+/H_2}$ being taken as zero at all T, even though the measurement may actually be taken using a standard reference electrode such as a saturated calomel or silver chloride electrode. It is sad to relate that no satisfactory indicator electrode has been established for monitoring natural redox conditions. Electrochemists have long been aware that a platinum electrode absorbs a layer of oxygen atoms on its surface which affords what is termed a "mixed potential," signifying that the electrode does not behave reversibly, having different potentials when operating anodically and cathodically. It can be stated, therefore, that the measurements of Eh using platinum electrodes have no absolute significance, but may have considerable merit for comparative purposes. The pε which has been defined as $p\varepsilon = -\log a_{e^-}$ by analogy with $pH = -\log a_{H^+}$ can be related to the Eh at 25°C by a simple factor,

$$p\varepsilon = Eh/0.0592$$

Normally most ocean, lake and river waters are oxic, but in localities where mixing is restricted, the decomposition of plant and animal organic detritus can deplete the oxygen supply. Oxic waters contain about 8 ppm oxygen or more. Cold waters have a higher solubility for oxygen and constitute a healthy environment for marine life. When the oxygen content of the water falls below 5 ppm it becomes difficult for fish to survive.

The pH and pε parameters in nature should not be thought of as operating separately, although that is possible. Many natural redox reactions also involve acid-base changes, for example:

$$O_2(g) + 4\,H^+(aq) + 4e \rightarrow 2\,H_2O(l)$$

$$2\,H^+(aq) + 2e \rightarrow H_2(g)$$

$$Fe(OH)_3(c) + H^+(aq) + e \rightarrow Fe(OH)_2(c) + H_2O(l)$$

The respective Nernst equations for the above reactions follow for 25°C:

$$\varepsilon = 1.23 - \frac{0.0592}{4} \cdot \log \frac{1}{(P_{O_2}/P°)a_{H^+}{}^4}$$

$$\varepsilon = 0 - \frac{0.0592}{2} \cdot \log \frac{P_{H_2}/P°}{a_{H^+}{}^2}$$

$$\varepsilon = 0.262 - \frac{0.0592}{1} \cdot \log \frac{1}{a_{H^+}}$$

In the above equations relative activities of $H_2O(l)$, $Fe(OH)_3(c)$ and $Fe(OH)_2(c)$ are all taken as unity. In terms of pε and pH the above equations become respectively:

$$p\varepsilon = \frac{1.23}{0.0592} + \tfrac{1}{4} \log (P_{O_2}/P°) - pH = 20.8 + \tfrac{1}{4} \log (P_{O_2}/P°) - pH$$

$$p\varepsilon = \frac{0}{0.0592} - \tfrac{1}{2} \log (P_{H_2}/P°) - pH = 0 - \tfrac{1}{2} \log (P_{H_2}/P°) - pH$$

$$p\varepsilon = \frac{0.262}{0.0592} - pH = 4.43 - pH$$

These equations are plotted on what is known as a pε/pH diagram, Figure 23-8, for partial pressures of O_2 and H_2 of 0.1, 1.0 and 10.0 bar, showing that the positions of the lines are not sensitive to the values of the respective gas pressures. Figure 23-8 gives the locations on the pε/pH diagram of various natural waters in relation to the O_2/H_2O and H_2O/H_2 lines. When oxic water is reduced by decay of organic matter both pε and pH are affected; oxygen is used up, reducing the pε, and CO_2 is produced, lowering the pH.

$$O_2(g) + 4\,H^+(aq) + 4e \rightarrow 2\,H_2O$$

$$\tfrac{1}{n}\,(CH_2O)_n + 2\,H_2O \rightarrow 5\,H^+(aq) + HCO_3^-\,(aq)$$

overall $$O_2(g) + \tfrac{1}{n}\,(CH_2O)_n \rightarrow H^+(aq) + HCO_3^-\,(aq)$$

Within the pore waters of sediments the lowering of pε and pH mobilizes most of the transition elements, particularly manganese and iron, by reducing them to the divalent state and rendering them more soluble and more subject to diffusion. At the surface of the sediment, on contacting oxic water, they are reconverted to the more insoluble higher valent oxides which deposit on suitable substrates, such as sand grains, clay pellets, shells, sharks' teeth and other objects. The above explanation is one proposed to account for the formation of manganese nodules with rich transition metal content.

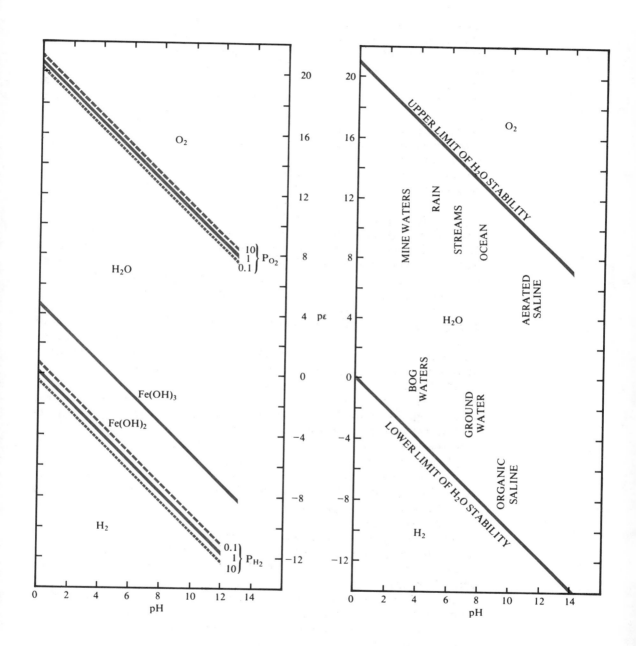

Figure 23-8 (a) O_2, H_2, H_2O and $Fe(OH)_3/Fe(OH)_2$ (b) Natural waters.

23-8   DESALINATION

The total amount of fresh water on earth is reasonably constant and it has been noted that the distribution of reliable renewed supplies is restricted. Limitations on fresh water for the growing of food are likely to become critical. On the other hand, sea water is generally in plentiful supply, even in the tropics. The challenge is to produce fresh water from sea water (termed desalination) by some economically viable process. Of course the natural evaporation of sea water and subsequent condensation constitute nature's own desalination. Processes for desalination will be outlined here in principle but not in respect to technical details which are apt to change with time.

Sea water on the average has a salinity of about 35 ^{o}/oo, or 35 g kg^{-1} and is unsuitable for drinking, irrigation and most industrial uses. Even for industrial cooling purposes, its high tendency to corrode metal makes it unsuitable. For human consumption the salt content should be reduced to no more than 1 g kg^{-1}. For agricultural purposes the maximum could be up to 2 g kg^{-1}. Except for cooling, similar limits are required by most industries in order to avoid damage from scaling and corrosion. In principle there are two kinds of desalination: the water may be removed as the product from the sea water; or the salts may be sufficiently removed to leave essentially water as the product. Processes involving removal of water as product are distillation, freezing, and reverse osmosis; those involving removal of salts are ion-exchange and electrodialysis. All of the above methods require expenditure of energy, itself a precious commodity. The economics involved in the form of energy available at the site, or transported to it, as well as the scale of the operation, should govern the method of desalination. Where the climate is cool, such as in the United Kingdom, freezing may be favoured, whereas in a Middle Eastern state, with oil aplenty, and warm temperatures, some form of distillation process will have merit. Another energy consideration is that desalination processes afford a good outlet for utilization of low-grade energy such as that available from electrical generating stations.

Simple distillation of sea water to afford pure water as condensate is expensive but has been carried out on shipboard and in laboratories for a long time. Solar stills, invented for use in lifeboats during World War II have been adapted for desert conditions, particularly in Israel, but simple distillation is not yet economic for large scale operation.

In the simple still the salt solution must be heated to its boiling point at a temperature slightly above the boiling point of pure water. The heat required to raise the temperature of the water to the boiling point and the latent heat of vaporization required to convert liquid to vapour are in theory recoverable when the product water condenses and cools, but in practice the recovery is not complete. The above reasoning leads to the practice of using the heat released on condensation and cooling to preheat the incoming solution of a succeeding still and so on in what is called multiple-effect distillation. Another practical consideration for large-scale operation is that the heat to the still is usually conveniently supplied by piped steam at 100°C which is below the boiling point of the sea water. This difficulty is overcome by lowering the boiling point of the sea water by reducing the pressure in the still, as illustrated in Figure 23-9 where the boiling point T_b' of the solution (at reduced pressure P') is below that of pure water T_b^o at atmospheric pressure, P^o. A different and popular process which follows the same principle of lowering the boiling point of the sea water by reduction in pressure is called multiple-stage flash evaporation, whereby preheated sea water is injected into an evaporator with pressure well below that corresponding to the boiling point. Some of the sea water suddenly flashes (evaporates) while the rest passes on to a subsequent stage at even lower pressure. The pipes bringing sea water preheated by contact with subsequent evaporation stages serve as condensor coils. A third multiple distillation process evaporates the sea water by contact with heat derived from compression of water vapour in later stages of the process.

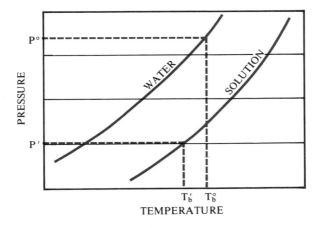

Figure 23-9   Lowering of Boiling Point at Reduced Pressure.

Two types of freezing process have been used. In the first sea water is frozen directly at its solute-lowered freezing point. If the process is carried out slowly (close to equilibrium) pure water freezes out without entrapping much brine. Since the first salt to come out of solution on lowering the temperature sufficiently is $Na_2SO_4 \cdot 10\,H_2O$, the freezing of sea water close to equilibrium can be studied in accord with the Na_2SO_4/H_2O binary phase diagram. The freezing out of pure water as ice and the subsequent melting is analogous to the distillation/condensation process but opposite, and the heat given out when water is frozen to ice should be conserved for remelting ice to yield pure water from a previous effect, confirming the economy of a multi-effect process. The second method of freezing sea water employs a volatile and immiscible liquid such as butane as a refrigerant, in that its rapid evaporation extracts enough heat from sea water to freeze ice which can be separated from the immiscible butane on remelting.

The phenomenon of osmosis has been described in Chapter 18 as a process in which pure solvent, separated from solution by a suitable semi-permeable membrane, tends to flow through the membrane as in Figure 23-10(a) and dilute the solution until a head of solution is established, the extra pressure (π) of which just prevents any further net flow, as in Figure 23-10(b). On the other hand, the process can be reversed as in Figure 23-10(c) by the application of a pressure, P, greater than the osmotic pressure, π, to force pure water from the solution side through the membrane, but detaining the solute. One crucial matter is the development of a suitably strong and porous membrane with the right surface properties. The usual material used is cellulose acetate. Reverse osmosis has been successfully adapted for water of low salinity (brackish) as well as to waste water (tertiary) effluent, but not to ordinary sea water.

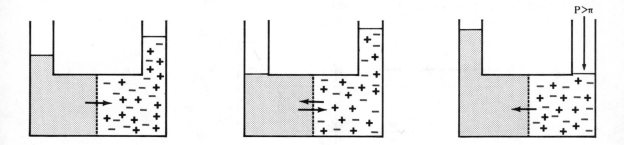

Figure 23-10   Conditions of Osmosis, Equilibrium, and Reverse Osmosis.

Several methods have been tried in the alternative approach, the removal of salts. One is the use of ion-exchange resin beds, natural and synthetic, which have been discussed in principle earlier. Another solute removing process is termed electrodialysis, which is an electrolysis procedure to deplete the water of positive and negative ions by attracting them respectively according to their polarity through selective cation-permeable and anion-permeable membranes, which are thin beds of cation- and anion-exchange resins. This process can be compared with reverse osmosis, but with the hydrostatic pressure of osmosis replaced by a driving force of electric potential. However, it should be noted that in osmosis it is the solvent which is forced to move, while in electrodialysis it is the solute ions which are transported. Successful use has only been effected with waters of low salinity.

In the present state of world economy all of the above processes are expensive. With fossil fuels still available in reasonable supply, about 95% of desalination is done by distillation. This cost is considerably more than that required for treatment of waste fresh waters, but as the desalination processes are scaled up and low-grade energy is available from many generating stations, the price will become more competitive, especially where fresh water is scarce. In theory, freezing has some advantages in that the latent heat of fusion is much less than the latent heat of vaporization, and at low temperatures the corrosion and scaling problems are minimal. On the other hand, much difficulty has been encountered with the physical separation of pure water from the refrigerated slush. Reverse osmosis, ion-exchange and electrodialysis appear to be competitive only when the salinity is low and membrane technology well developed.

Although pure water as a product is probably the greatest benefit available to man from the sea, there are many other water assets in the inventory of Table 23-4.

TABLE 23-4   Man's Use of the Sea

Assets:
   Ports, transport, trading, warfare and defense
   Communications
   Cooling water
   Power: tidal, wave, thermal, chemical, electrolytic
   Waste elimination capacity
   Materials

Renewable Materials	Non-Renewable Materials
Pure water	Metals: Fe, Al, Cr, Mn, Ti,
Food from marine	Mg, Cu, Pb, Zn, Sn,
organisms	W, U, Au, Ag, Pt, Hg.
	manganese nodules,
	sulphide muds.
	Non-metals: NaCl, PO_4^{3-}, NO_3^-,
	S, Br
	seaweed products,
	fertilizer
	building materials:
	cement, sand, gravel,
	gypsum
	petroleum

23-9   WATER POLLUTION

Water pollution may be defined as the introduction into natural waters of an effect or substance which is deleterious to the use of the water as a natural habitat for its indigenous aquatic life or for purposes such as drinking, washing, recreation, irrigation or industrial consumption. Pollutants are classified in Table 23-5. That certain qualifications are assumed in compiling such a simplified list of pollutants can be seen by a couple of examples. That too much input of heat in the wrong place is harmful does not imply that absence of heat is necessarily a beneficial state of affairs for life as we know it. Also, while a certain level of the essential bionutrients of nitrogen and phosphorus is mandatory for life, an overabundance of these produces the growth and decay imbalance which is termed eutrophication. Finally, many of the metals such as V, Mn, Fe, Cd, Ni, Cu, Zn, Sn and Pb, while essential to life at extremely low levels (say ppb) may become toxic at concentrations of ppm or higher.

TABLE 23-5   Classification of Pollutants

Thermal discard:
  from industry and generating stations

Inorganic compounds:
  metal ions of Hg, Cd, Pb, Cu, Zn, V, etc.
  non-metals such as As, S, Se, F
  acid rain, mainly H_2SO_4
  radioactive elements

Organic compounds:
  petroleum spills
  fungicides, herbicides, pesticides
  decay products

Bionutrients:
  compounds of nitrogen and phosphorus from sewage and land run-off,
  mainly nitrates and phosphates

Micro-organisms:
  blue-green algae
  bacteria
  viruses

Enough knowledge has not yet been acquired on the effects of thermal pollution on natural water systems. The problem is not small and not simple. It has been estimated, for example, that when all the generating stations now planned for the Great Lakes region of North America are in operation, about one third of the total water flowing in the St. Lawrence River will have been used as coolant. The most obvious effects of thermal pollution are the production of a plume of warm surface water containing an overabundance of plant life and the asphyxiation of fish accustomed to lower temperature and higher oxygen levels. On occasion the argument is advanced that the changes in climate, which are beyond our control, are apt to produce higher temperatures in the effluent plume than does its use as coolant, which is often of the order of one to ten kelvin. Such arguments ignore the reality that the intake water may be taken from a deep supply of the order of 10 or 20 kelvin below the temperature at the surface. Rarely considered is the potentially large effect of pumping cooling water from a region which, being deep and below the thermocline, is *cold, energy poor* and *nutrient rich,* through the plant and out on the surface which is *warm, energy rich* and *nutrient poor,* not to mention the introduction of important catalytic trace elements. Such a transposition constitutes "man- made upwelling" and begs for a biological explosion far exceeding that to be expected on the mere basis of the small elevation in the temperature of the surface layer. Some of the possible benefits mentioned are that the warm effluent might be used to grow marketable crops, and that the heat supplied to a waterway might keep it from freezing over during the winter.

Some criteria of acceptable levels of inorganic and organic substances in water are compiled below for various purposes as prepared by the Ministry of the Environment for Ontario, Canada.* It is assumed that readers from other regions and countries will realize that the data are exemplary and that similar or other criteria may be available to them which are more pertinent to the particular locale. Table 23-6 gives a partial list of levels which are desirable for surface waters used for recreation and for the protection of the native aquatic life. Changes in our knowledge of toxicity of materials and in our ability to detect materials lead to constant revision of such standards.

For some substances the permissible limits are set at zero because even when these substances are at ultra trace levels they are bioaccumulated and biomagnified at higher trophic levels to concentrations which are potentially dangerous. It would be well if these could be eliminated from the natural environment; the least that can be done is not to discharge any of these substances. It is recognized that some of these substances (e.g. Hg) may have natural sources.

TABLE 23-6   Water Quality Objectives (for aquatic life and recreation)

(a)   pH 6.5−8.5   alkalinity not less than 25% of natural value

(b)   Non-metals (mg L^{-1})

NH_3	<0.02
Cl_2	<0.002
CN	<0.005
As	<0.1
Se	<0.1
H_2S	<0.002
total P	0.01−0.03
phenols	<0.001

(c) O_2 (mg L^{-1}) Minimum oxygen levels recommended depend on temperature and locale.

T(°C)	Cold water biota	Warm water biota
0	8	7
10	6	5
20	5	4
25	5	4

* "Water Management," Ministry of the Environment of Ontario, November, 1978.

(d) Trace metals (μg L^{-1})

Be	<11
Cd	<0.2
Cr	<100
Cu	<5
Fe	<300
Pb	<5−25 (depends on alkalinity)
Hg	<0.2 (<0.5 μg g^{-1} in whole fish)
Ni	<25
Ag	<0.1
Zn	<30

(e) Pesticides (μg L^{-1})

Chlordane	<0.06
Malathion	<0.1
Methoxychlor	<0.04
Pyrethrum	<0.01

(f) Herbicides (μg L^{-1})

2,4-D	<4.0
Diuron	<1.6
Dalapon	<110

(g) Industrial organics (μg L^{-1})

dibutylphthalate	<4.0
dichlorane (Mirex)	<0.001
PCB	<0.001

(h) Radionuclides (pCi L^{-1}) *

gross beta emitters	<1000
Ra^{226}	<3

(i) Pathogens

fecal coliforms	<100 per 100 mL
total coliforms	<1000 per 100 mL

TABLE 23-7   Substances with Zero Tolerance Limits

Hg	mercury
DDT, DDD, DDE,	dichlorodiphenyltrichloroethane and metabolites
PCB's	polychlorinated biphenyls
PBB's	polybrominated biphenyls
Mirex	Dichlorane, $C_{10}Cl_{12}$

* 1 becquerel (1 Bq) represents 1 disintegration per second and equals 27.03 picocurie. The becquerel is the SI unit.

TABLE 23-8   Substances with Undefined Limits (but recognized danger)

Metals:
Al, Sb, Ba, B, Cs, Co, Mn, Mo, Sr, Tl, Sn, V

Organics: (partially)
acrylonitrile, alkyl amines, aryl amines, acyl chlorides, aryl sulphonic acids, azo- and diazo- compounds, benzene and aliphatic derivatives, carbon tetrachloride, chlorinated ethylenes, chlorophenols, furfural, haloforms, mercaptans, nitrosoamines, nitroaromatics, phenols and derivatives, cresols, polycyclic aromatics, hydrocarbons (esp. naphthalene and benzopyrene), quinoline, styrene, sulphonates

Herbicides	Insecticides	Fungicides
Alachlor	Altosid	Captan
Amitrole	Carbofuran	Dacanil
Paraquat	Dimilin	Pentachlorophenol
2,4,5-T	Temephos	

Substances entered in Table 23-8 may present some danger but they have not been investigated well enough to set proper limits. Table 23-9 follows with criteria for drinking water.

TABLE 23-9   Drinking Water Criteria

Chemical Limits* (mg L^{-1})		Radioactivity (pCi L^{-1}) **	
As	0.01	Gross beta	
Cl	250	activity	1000
Cu	1.0	Ra^{226}	3
CN	0.01	Sr^{90}	10
F	1.2		
Fe	0.3		
Mn	0.05		
NO$_3^-$	10.0		
SO$_4^{2-}$	250		
Zn	5.0		
CHCl$_3$ extract	0.2		
phenols	0.001		
total diss. solids	500		
total org. C	5.0		
organic N	0.15		

* The chemical substances shown should not be present in a water supply in excess of the listed concentrations where more suitable supplies can be made available.

** See footnote to Table 23-6.

Tolerance limits which are somewhat less stringent than for drinking water are also available for water for irrigation and for watering livestock. In general, the sources, means of transport and mechanisms of toxicity of inorganic and organic pollutants cannot be said to be known. With a substance as dangerous as mercury, intensive studies have led to a knowledge of how such a dense and relatively noble metal can be mobilized by biota to yield organometallic species such as CH_3Hg^+ and $(CH_3)_2Hg$. CH_3Hg^+ is an ionic species capable of diffusing through membranes of fish, while $(CH_3)_2Hg$ is quite volatile. Furthermore, the physiological effects of mercury compounds in man have been much studied, but the analysis of organic compounds in natural waters is in its infancy. For example, in the sea it is estimated that only about one tenth of the organic content has even been categorized. Among organic substances the polychlorinated hydrocarbons (particularly PCB's and PBB's) as a class include some of the most persistent and noxious chemicals. Some of these are definitely contributed by industrial activity, such as the PCB's used in transformers and heat exchangers, but scientists are also wondering if Cl_2 used to purify water is chlorinating hydrocarbons from various polluting sources. Other pollutants are particularly associated with riches of our technological culture. Mercury contamination has been derived mainly from chlorine-alkali plants, pulp and paper manufacture and seed treatment, as well as many minor contributors including the natural component. Large amounts of lead have been added to the verges of roads, atmosphere and eventually water systems by the combustion of leaded gasoline. Fierce debate is current as to whether or not the addition of more fluoride to the environment is too high a price to pay for the benefit children may gain from the prophylactic use of fluoride against dental caries, when other means are at hand. Identification of sources of pollution has led to appreciable reduction in some cases, such as the reduced use of DDT, and of tetraethyl lead in motor gasoline.

Another form of pollution called "acid rain," is rapidly growing and is believed by some to be the most serious pollution problem in North America. Roasting of sulphide and arsenide ores, the generation of power in thermal generating stations and, in fact, any industrial use of fossil fuels as an energy source are all bound to produce airborne gases of non-metals such as SO_2, SO_3, HCl and oxides of nitrogen. When these dissolve in water, as found in rain, clouds, mist, or water bodies, they produce acids which may lower the pH significantly and in some cases release ions which might normally be tied up as hydroxides or carbonates.

$$Al(OH)_3(c) + 3\,H^+(aq) \rightarrow Al^{3+}(aq) + 3\,H_2O(l)$$

$$CuCO_3(c) + 2\,H^+(aq) \rightarrow Cu^{2+}(aq) + H_2O(l) + CO_2(g)$$

Lakes or streams in basins which are largely composed of carbonate rock may be well buffered against the influx of acid but waters in basins of granitic or other acidic rocks will be vulnerable to considerable pH change, release of cations, and death of plant and animal species. In Sweden, the liming of lakes has been under way for a number of years with beneficial results, but the prospect of treating the vast array of lakes in Canada is staggering, and the change of energy emphasis from oil to coal gives no cause for optimism. It has been estimated that 48 000 Canadian lakes will be affected.

Radioactive pollutants must be viewed in the context of natural levels. A few of the natural radionuclides in the world ocean are shown below in Table 23-10.*

TABLE 23-10　A Few Radionuclides in the Sea
(before nuclear tests 1953)

Nuclide	Half-life (year)	Concentration (g L^{-1})	Isotopic Abundance (%)	Emits
K^{40}	1.3×10^9	4.5×10^{-5}	1.2×10^{-2}	$\beta + \alpha$
Rb^{87}	5×10^{10}	3.4×10^{-5}	27.8	β
U^{238}	4.5×10^9	2×10^{-6}	99.3	α
U^{235}	7.1×10^8	1.4×10^{-11}	0.7	α
Ra^{226}	1.6×10^3	8×10^{-14}	≈ 100	α
C^{14}	5.5×10^3	3×10^{-14}	1.3×10^{-10}	β

In general radioactive concentrations in the sea are lower than in the crust of the earth and not in the same relative proportions. K^{40} accounts for about 90% of the natural radioactivity in the seas with Rb^{87} less than 1%. The common radioactive contaminants from nuclear testing and man's activities are the fission products of U^{235} and Pu^{239}, which in the long run abound in Sr^{90} and Cs^{137}, important sentinels and themselves troublesome because they persist for long periods (half lives about 28 years). Sr^{90} has the dangerous property of replacing Ca in bone structure. The storage or dispersal of radioactive wastes has not yet been satisfactorily solved and poses a serious potential problem if the sea is chosen as a dumping place. Burial in dumps has been disastrous and encapsulation in such materials as concrete has been found ineffective over a period of time. Depositing wastes in deep plutons* within the earth or in subduction zones in the sea has been considered. Subduction zones are deep trenches where the ocean crust leads down to the mantle.*

Progress has been made in dealing with large oil spills by containment with booms and recovery by special boats. Some spills have been ignited but this can be difficult and unsatisfactory from the viewpoint of either recovery or disposal. Detergents and dispersants have in some cases caused more damage than they prevented. Some progress has been made on the highly desirable biodegradation of the petroleum by developing suitable bacterial populations, aided by the addition of some crucial nutrients of nitrogen and phosphorus. On the negative side, however, the sinking of tankers has become common, often with disastrous effects on European or American nature and shorelines. Even larger spills arise from "blowouts" of undersea wells such as the Mexican well in the Bay of Campeche.

---

* Taken in part from R.A. Horne, Marine Chemistry, Wiley 1969.

* See Glossary

Questionable political judgement also prevails with regard to the bionutrient compounds of nitrogen and phosphorus. The sparseness of their concentrations limit growth of algae and other organisms on a worldwide basis. We persist in using these assets as pollutants in some of our valuable fresh water systems. The influx of nitrates, ammonia, and phosphates from municipal sewage and run-off from fertile land causes two problems. One is a predisposition for the algal population to favour the undesirable colonies of blue-green species which choke off sunlight from more desirable algae. The other is the bloom produced by the overabundance of nutrients, a condition leading to eutrophication. Although it is accompanied by the production of oxygen, abundant growth gives the water a cloudy green turbidity, and macrophytes foul the shallow nearshore waters. Even greater damage is done in the decay or respiration phase when the large and microscopic biomass consumes oxygen rapidly to produce rotten foul-smelling mats. When the level of oxygen falls below about 5 ppm, even for a short time, fish and other aquatic life which must respire constantly are in danger. When oxygen is still further depleted the formation of reduced species such as H_2S and S^{2-} make life impossible for all organisms except anerobic bacteria.

Knowledge of the population of bacteria and viruses in natural waters is sparse indeed. In the absence of any better method of assessing the potential damage to the water quality from these sources, the count of fecal coliforms (such as E. Coli) is usually taken as an indication of the presence of human and animal wastes, which are definitely to be avoided for health reasons.

Scientists and engineers have an important role in the stewardship of our resources. By insisting that economic criteria are not enough, and by conscientiously considering their technical decisions in the widest possible environmental and social context, they can do much to improve the quality of life. Outstanding achievements such as the improvement of the Thames River in England, and the conserving technical attitudes that permeate almost all decisions in Sweden, give hope that such attitudes and results will spread.

SUMMARY

It is difficult to overstate the importance of water on this planet. It is by far the most abundant chemical substance in the thin skin of the earth which supports all life, and it is involved in the numerous means, including climate, of supporting that life: as a body fluid, as a vehicle for nutritional intake and excretory output, and as a source of oxygen by photosynthesis and photodecomposition. Man has developed numerous additional uses, such as transportation, cooling, and recreation.

Moreover, the chemical and physical properties of water are unusual, and in some instances unique, as exemplified by its abnormally high melting and boiling points, high surface tension, high latent heats of fusion and vaporization, and its special function as a universal solvent for ionic and polar substances. These properties arise, by and large, by the characteristic scope for hydrogen bonding in water, with two protons and two non-bonding electron pairs per oxygen atom. This structure also leads to water being amphiprotic and having prominence in acid/base chemistry, and to its being highly polar, and thus an ionizing solvent of importance in dissolving electrolytes. In redox reactions water is sometimes oxidized to O_2, at other times reduced to H_2, depending on the chemical system with which it is coupled. In electrolysis water is oxidized to O_2 at the anode, and reduced to H_2 at the cathode simultaneously. Also, water is a non-polluting product of H_2/O_2 fuel cells.

Natural waters differ considerably in their properties, including composition, ranging from almost pure water in rain to the strongly ionic solution of sea water. About 98% of the total hydrosphere is sea water, with a saline content averaging 35 g kg^{-1}. But while the salinity of sea water may vary considerably, the proportions of the major solute species remain nearly constant. The oceans support adapted marine life, but this salt water is unfit for terrestrial consumption by people and animals, and for irrigation. The roughly 2% of fresh water is relatively constant in amount and continuously cycling through the atmosphere, but is not evenly distributed nor properly conserved. At considerable cost at present, fresh water can be obtained from sea water by a number of processes including: distillation, flash evaporation, freezing, reverse osmosis, and ion-exchange, each of which enjoys particular advantages in given situations.

The dissolved and suspended content of water can alter its quality and utility drastically. Water management includes control of supply, beneficial treatment, and responsible disposal or recycling. Man has rendered many waters unusable by introducing pollutants. The treatment of wastes to prevent pollution reaching harmful levels and the recovery of pure water from substandard stock are important concerns of chemistry and engineering, from both economic and ethical points of view. The inescapable conclusion is that the water on the planet should be recycled by man, as it is by nature.

REFERENCES

Speakman, J.C., *The Hydrogen Bond,* The Chemical Society, London, 1975.
This is a brief, inexpensive and effective introduction to its subject, with a section devoted to ice and water and with ample references for more extensive reading.

Horne, R.A., *Marine Chemistry,* Wiley Interscience, 1969.
This book specializes in the chemical aspects of oceanography and is especially strong on the physical chemistry of the oceans and the structure of water.

James, G.V., *Water Treatment,* The Technical Press, London, 1966.
A technical book with many of the practical details of water treatment.

Turk, A., Turk, J., and Wittes, J.T., *Ecology, Pollution, Environment,* W.B. Saunders, Philadelphia, 1972.
A small book which includes details of water treatment, pollutants and agricultural problems.

Gymer, Roger G., *Chemistry, an Ecological Approach?*, Harper and Row.

An introductory chemistry text with emphasis on ecology and the environment, particularly for those who wish to relate chemistry to other disciplines and vice-versa. There is a thorough chapter on water, as well as on the atmosphere and there is an excellent connection between chemistry and biology throughout the book.

PROBLEMS

1. Sketch the structures of the following entities: H_2O, the dimer $(H_2O)_2$, H_3O^+, $H_3O^+ \cdot 3\,H_2O$, $OH^- \cdot 3\,H_2O$.

2. Estimate the ratio of the strength of the $O-H$ bond to that of a hydrogen bond.

   [18/1]

3. What is the effect of raising the external pressure on:

   (a) the boiling point of water?

   (b) the freezing point of water?

   Which of the above effects is unusual for liquids in general?

   [raise; lower; (b)]

4. Estimate the freezing point of a solution of 100 g of ethylene glycol, $HOCH_2-CH_2OH$, in a litre of water.

   [$-3.0°C$]

5. Using the data from Table 23-3 calculate for sea water and lake water the following ratios:

   $[Mg^{2+}]/[Ca^{2+}]$ $[SO_4^{2-}]/[HCO_3^-]$ $[Cl^-]/[Na^+]$

   [sea 5, 15, 1.2; lake 0.24, 0.15, 1.4]

6. If sea water has a concentration of chloride ion of 0.55 mol L^{-1}, estimate the maximum concentration of silver ion permitted by the solubility product, in ppm. Analysis of sea water for total silver gives a concentration of 4×10^{-5} ppm. How can you explain these results? Does the sea appear to be saturated with silver chloride?

   [3.3×10^{-5}; some silver as AgCl, $AgCl_2^-$; yes]

7. Calculate the highest concentration of $Fe^{3+}(aq)$ in mol L^{-1} allowable in Lake Ontario water of pH 7.8.

   [1.6×10^{-21}]

8. If Lake Ontario water has concentrations of Ca^{2+} and Mg^{2+} respectively 0.00107 and 0.00026 mol L^{-1}, what is the hardness of the water expressed in ppm? If the concentration of bicarbonate ion in the lake is 0.115 g kg^{-1}, what fraction of the total water hardness is temporary?

   [133; 115/133]

9. Cl_2 gas can be used to sanitize swimming pool water. A 100 mL sample of chlorinated pool water was treated with excess KI solution, generating I_2 which was then titrated with 0.0100 F sodium thiosulphate solution, requiring 10.0 mL, according to the reactions:

$$Cl_2 + 2\,I^- \rightarrow I_2 + 2\,Cl^-$$

$$I_2 + 2\,S_2O_3{}^{2-} \rightarrow 2\,I^- + S_4O_6{}^{2-}$$

Calculate the Cl_2 added to the water in ppm assuming no loss to the air.

[35.46]

10. Sketch the $p\varepsilon$/pH lines for the half-reactions:

$$1/2\,O_2 + 2\,H^+ + 2e \rightarrow H_2O$$

$$2\,H^+ + 2e \rightarrow H_2$$

taking the pressures of gases to be $P°$ and temperature 298 K.

(a) Also draw the line for the first half-reaction but now taking P_{O_2} to be 0.2 bar.

(b) Represent on the diagram the condition for an H_2/O_2 fuel cell which operates at pH 10. What is the emf? Do the same at pH 12.

Figure 23-11   Ontario's heavy water installation at the Bruce Plant on the shore of Lake Huron.

XXIV KINETICS

One of the most interesting and important aspects of chemistry is understanding the reactions among materials. Thermodynamics tells us what *can* happen but it tells us nothing about *how* it happens or how rapidly it happens. How a reaction takes place is called the *mechanism* of the reaction. The mechanism determines how rapidly a reaction will occur and what factors will affect that rate. The study of reaction rates and of the factors affecting them is called kinetics. By interpretation of kinetic data, a chemist seeks to understand mechanisms.

Kinetics is a broad topic because of the diversity of reactions which occur. The gas phase decomposition of nitrogen oxides, the liquid phase substitution of coordinated ammonia for coordinated water around a metal cation and the solid phase explosive decomposition of a crystal of silver azide are just three random examples of this diversity. The factors which influence the rates of these processes are correspondingly diverse. Nevertheless, considerable classification is possible.

First, there are distinguishing features of gas phase reactions, liquid phase reactions and solid phase reactions although the first two have much in common. Secondly, there is a major distinction to be made between homogeneous reactions, which involve only a single phase, and heterogeneous reactions, which involve two or more phases. Some reactions are inherently heterogeneous, like the reaction between zinc metal and an aqueous solution of an acid. In others, the second phase is introduced because of its effect on the rate of a process. The reaction of nitrogen with hydrogen to form ammonia takes place much more rapidly on a surface of iron or iron oxide mixed with alumina than it does in the absence of such a surface, although the iron and other solid phase materials do not occur in the equation describing the process. A material which increases the rate of a process but is left unchanged itself is called a *catalyst*. If the catalyst is a separate phase to that containing the reactants and products as in the ammonia example, it is called a heterogeneous catalyst. If it is part of the same phase, it is a homogeneous catalyst.

It is well to establish early in the chapter that our knowledge of how a reaction proceeds is rarely as certain as the text may imply. One is trying to determine what happens at the molecular level using information gathered for systems consisting of huge numbers of molecules in which there is a large range of energies and orientations to name but two factors. A mechanism is postulated and tests are made of the consistency of this mechanism with the known evidence. One is encouraged if there is consistency but there are usually two or three plausible proposals which could equally well be consistent. From that point one defends one's choice by pointing to analogous situations or, more often, by arguments based on the structure and energy levels of the reactants. Real progress is made this way, but there are some well known cases where mechanisms were believed for decades to be the only likely choice, only to be disproven by some new experimental test. Then a new mechanism, hitherto believed to be unlikely, becomes the choice. It is a lesson always to be borne in mind.

24-1 THE IDEA OF A MECHANISM

Ideally, one might like to observe reacting molecules directly in order to see what characteristics differentiate those molecules which do react from those which collide but do not react. One can visualize strolling around in space observing colliding molecules everywhere, and making field notes on what velocities, what relative orientations, and so forth combine to lead to reaction. One could also observe what subsequent steps led to the final products. Of course such observations are impossible, and indeed it is rarely possible to devise an experiment which tells us much about the particular characterisitics of a particular pair of reacting molecules. So-called crossed molecular beam experiments have given information on energies for a few systems amenable to this approach, but most information on mechanisms must be deduced from data representing countless successful and unsuccessful collisions. The nature of these data and the approaches used in analyzing them form the subject of the following sections.

There are several levels of understanding which a chemist seeks. First, what sequence of elementary reactions and events goes into producing the observed process? Secondly, what structural and electronic characteristics of the reacting molecules are important to the operation of these elementary steps? If a step requires close contact between a particular atom in one molecule and a particular atom in another molecule, the size and position of other atoms and groups of atoms in the two molecules affect the ease with which such contact comes about. Such factors are known as *steric* factors. Strong electron donating or withdrawing groups in either or both molecules can alter the electron density at the site either favourably or unfavourably insofar as the process is concerned. These factors are referred to as *electronic* factors. In many cases the steric and electronic effects of a particular group are difficult to separate and the interpretation of the mechanism is then open to dispute. Such disputes, and the ensuing experimental efforts to resolve them, are valuable in that they add to our understanding of electron distribution within molecules and the way in which those distributions respond to the approach of another molecule. The quantum mechanics required in the pursuit of these arguments puts them beyond the scope of this book, but that is not true of the first step in describing a mechanism, the identification of a set of elementary processes which are consistent with the observed experimental facts.

24-2 DEFINITIONS OF RATE AND ORDER

If concentrations are measured and plotted as a function of time after introducing some N_2O_5 into a vessel, a plot such as that in Figure 24-1(a) would result from the operation of the process

$$2\,N_2O_5(g) \rightarrow 4\,NO_2(g) + O_2(g)$$

At any time the amount of NO_2 formed is twice that of the N_2O_5 lost while the amount of O_2 formed is half that of the N_2O_5 lost. This is a direct consequence of the stoichiometry.

The plot shows that the rate at which the process is happening decreases with time. Notice that the stoichiometry imposes an interrelationship on the rates too. The rate of formation of NO_2 at time, t_1, as indicated by the tangent drawn in Figure 24-1(b), is double the rate at which N_2O_5 is decomposing at that time. At a later time, t_2, both of these rates have declined but the stoichiometry requires that the ratio of the two remains unchanged.

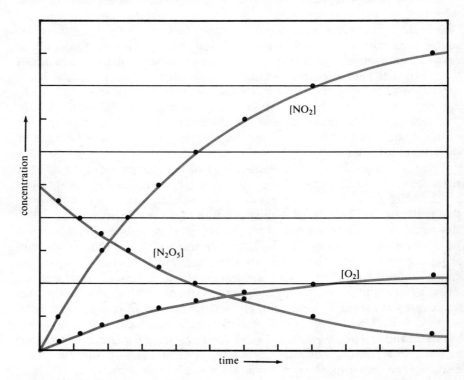

Figure 24-1(a) Sketch of Changes in Concentration for Process
$2\,N_2O_5(g) \rightarrow 4\,NO_2(g) + O_2(g)$

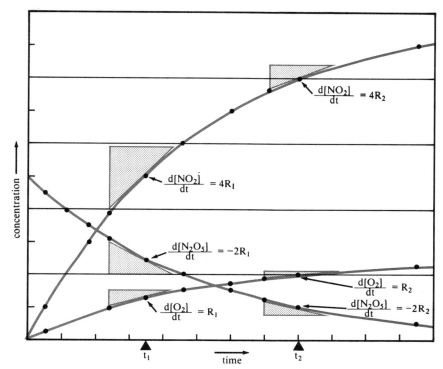

Figure 24-1(b)

In view of the different rates at which the concentrations of different species are changing at any point in a reaction, it is important to specify exactly what is meant by the *rate* of a reaction. The rate can be defined equally well in terms of the rate of decrease of the concentration of a reactant or of the rate of increase of the concentration of a product, since, as we have seen, the two are precisely related. In S.I. terminology, a rate defined in concentration terms is called the *rate of reaction per unit volume*, for which the symbol is r. The shorter and more familiar term *rate of reaction* is reserved for the rate of change in total amount with respect to time, and has the symbol J. Thus

$$J \equiv \frac{dn_A}{dt}$$

$$r \equiv \frac{d[A]}{dt}$$

In this text, only the rate of change in concentrations is required and it is defined, in terms of the N_2O_5 example, as follows.

$$r \equiv -\frac{1}{2}\frac{d[N_2O_5]}{dt} = \frac{1}{4}\frac{d[NO_2]}{dt} = \frac{d[O_2]}{dt}$$

If the entire set of equations is not obvious to the reader, they may be seen clearly if taken two at a time. For example, NO_2 is produced at four times the rate at which O_2 is produced and hence

$$\frac{d[NO_2]}{dt} = 4 \frac{d[O_2]}{dt}$$

$$\tfrac{1}{4} \frac{d[NO_2]}{dt} = \frac{d[O_2]}{dt}$$

Experimentally, rates are found to depend on the concentrations of one or more reactants and, sometimes, on the concentration of a product as well. Indeed there are many cases where the rate depends on the concentration of some species not contained in the equation describing the overall process.

For the process

$$aA + bB \rightarrow cC + dD$$

the rate might be found experimentally to depend on the concentrations of A, B and D but to be independent of the concentration of C in accordance with the following expression:

$$r = -\frac{1}{a} \frac{d[A]}{dt} = k[A]^m[B]^n[D]^p$$

Such an expression is called the *rate law* for the process and the process is said to be m^{th} order in A, n^{th} order in B, p^{th} order in D and of order $m+n+p$ overall. Notice that m, n and p are determined experimentally and usually do *not* bear any relationship to the stoichiometric coefficients a, b, c and d.

k is called the rate constant and is sometimes called k_{obs}, the observed rate constant, to differentiate it from the rate constants postulated for the elementary processes described in the next section. k is a function of temperature and, to a very much lesser extent, of pressure. In almost all published work, the unit of concentration is mol L^{-1} and k takes its units accordingly. In the example above, the units of k are $(mol\ L^{-1})^{-(m+n+p-1)}(s)^{-1}$. The following examples serve to illustrate these points.

(a) The gas phase decomposition of N_2O_5

$$2\ N_2O_5(g) \rightarrow 4\ NO_2(g) + O_2(g)$$

is found experimentally to obey the following rate law.

$$r = -\tfrac{1}{2}\frac{d[N_2O_5]}{dt} = k[N_2O_5]$$

This process is said to be first order in N_2O_5 and first order overall. The units of k are s^{-1}.

(b) The gas phase decomposition of acetaldehyde,

$$CH_3CHO(g) \rightarrow CH_4(g) + CO(g)$$

is found to obey the rate law

$$r = k[CH_3CHO]^{3/2}$$

This process is three halves order in acetaldehyde and three halves order overall. The units of k are $L^{1/2}$ $mol^{-1/2}$ s^{-1}.

(c) In the presence of a tungsten catalyst, ammonia decomposes to N_2 and H_2 at a rate which is independent of concentration.

$$2\ NH_3 \rightarrow N_2 + 3\ H_2$$

$$r = -\tfrac{1}{2}\frac{d[NH_3]}{dt} = k = k[NH_3]^0$$

This process is zeroth order, both in ammonia and overall. It is appropriate to note, in view of the extensive discussion in earlier chapters of equilibrium in this process, that this statement deals with the decomposition process only.

(d) The reaction

$$Hg_2^{2+}(aq) + Tl^{3+}(aq) \rightarrow 2\ Hg^{2+}(aq) + Tl^+(aq)$$

obeys the rate law

$$r = k[Hg_2^{2+}][Tl^{3+}][Hg^{2+}]^{-1}$$

This process is first order in Hg_2^{2+}, first order in Tl^{3+}, negative first order in Hg^{2+} and first order overall. The units of k are s^{-1}.

(e) Some processes follow rate laws much more complex than any of those above. The classic example, de rigueur in introductory textbooks on chemistry, is the reaction of hydrogen with bromine to give HBr.

$$H_2(g) + Br_2(g) \rightarrow 2\ HBr(g)$$

For this process the rate law has been found to be

$$r = -\frac{d[H_2]}{dt} = \frac{k'[H_2][Br_2]^{\frac{1}{2}}}{1 + k''[HBr][Br_2]^{-1}}$$

The concept of order is inapplicable to processes with complicated rate laws of this sort.

Example 24-1   The thermal decomposition of N_2O_5 is first order in N_2O_5. If the rate constant at 25°C is 1.7×10^{-5} s^{-1}, at what rate does N_2O_5 decompose at this temperature if its partial pressure is 50.0 kPa? The rate constant quoted is for the process stated as

$$2\ N_2O_5(g) \rightarrow 4\ NO_2(g) + O_2(g)$$

The concentration of N_2O_5 is given by

$$\frac{n}{V} = \frac{P}{RT} = \frac{50000}{(8.314)(298.15)} = 20.2\ \text{mol m}^{-3}$$

$$= 0.0202\ \text{mol L}^{-1}$$

$$-\tfrac{1}{2}\,\frac{d[N_2O_5]}{dt} = (1.7 \times 10^{-5})(.0202)$$

$$\frac{d[N_2O_5]}{dt} = -6.9 \times 10^{-7}\ \text{mol L}^{-1}\,\text{s}^{-1}$$

Keep in mind that a rate constant, like an equilibrium constant, has a value dependent on the way in which the equation for the process is written. Actual physical quantities, such as the rate of change of concentration of N_2O_5, are of course independent of how the process is described. Thus if the above process were described as

$$N_2O_5(g) \rightarrow 2\,NO_2(g) + \tfrac{1}{2}\,O_2(g)$$

the rate constant would be $3.4 \times 10^{-5}\ \text{s}^{-1}$ but the calculated rate of disappearance of N_2O_5 would be the same at $-6.9 \times 10^{-7}\ \text{mol L}^{-1}\,\text{s}^{-1}$.

24-3 ELEMENTARY REACTIONS

Typically a process takes place in a number of steps. Each such step is called an *elementary reaction*. The formulation of a set of elementary equations which is both plausible and consistent with the rate law is a major step in understanding the mechanism of a process. Elementary reactions are conceived as being the reactions which actually occur at the molecular level, and one refers to their *molecularity*. An elementary reaction involving a single reactant is said to be *unimolecular* while one which involves the collision of two molecules is said to be *bimolecular*. Since three molecules colliding simultaneously is a rare event, these will be the only two situations commonly met. The terms unimolecular and bimolecular are reserved for elementary processes.

If an elementary reaction is unimolecular

$$A \rightarrow \text{products}$$

it is first order in A

$$-\frac{d[A]}{dt} = k[A]$$

whereas if an elementary reaction is bimolecular, it is second order overall according to one or the other of the following cases.

$$A + A \rightarrow \text{products}$$

$$-\tfrac{1}{2}\,\frac{d[A]}{dt} = k[A]^2$$

$$A + B \rightarrow \text{products}$$

$$-\frac{d[A]}{dt} = k[A][B]$$

It must be emphasized that this automatic relationship between order and stoichiometry is valid *for elementary reactions only*. Where overall reactions are concerned, any such connection must *not* be assumed, as the many examples in the previous section indicate. Only experiment can determine the order of overall processes.

In formulating elementary processes, one usually assumes the existence of one or more intermediate species which are not among the reactants or products. Sometimes, physical evidence of these unstable species is available and sometimes their existence is pure supposition based on one's experience and chemical intuition. The development of increasingly sensitive instruments, such as electron spin resonance spectrometers to detect free radicals, has helped to detect evidence of many species which were previously just conjecture. Whatever the status of the supporting evidence, unstable intermediates are species which exist at all times in very small concentrations. Since the concentrations are always small, the changes in concentration as a function of time must be smaller still. To a good approximation these rates of change can be set equal to zero, thus providing the necessary relationships with which one can solve for the concentrations of these species and hence develop an expression for the rate law. This is sometimes called the steady state approximation. The following examples illustrate this technique.

The decomposition of N_2O_5, which is known to be first order in N_2O_5, is believed to proceed in three steps as follows.

$$N_2O_5(g) \underset{k_{-1}}{\overset{k_1}{\rightleftharpoons}} NO_2(g) + NO_3(g)$$

$$NO_2(g) + NO_3(g) \overset{k_2}{\rightarrow} NO(g) + O_2(g) + NO_2(g)$$

$$NO(g) + NO_3(g) \overset{k_3}{\rightarrow} 2\,NO_2(g)$$

Now for the process stated as

$$N_2O_5(g) \rightarrow 2\,NO_2(g) + \tfrac{1}{2}\,O_2(g)$$

the rate, r, and its experimentally determined first order dependence on N_2O_5 is given by

$$r = -\frac{d[N_2O_5]}{dt} = k_{obs}[N_2O_5]$$

If the postulated elementary reactions are correct, this can be related to the rate constants for those elementary reactions.

$$r = -\frac{d[N_2O_5]}{dt} = k_1[N_2O_5] - k_{-1}[NO_2][NO_3]$$

In order to evaluate the concentration of the unstable intermediate, NO_3, in terms of measurable quantities, it is necessary to utilize the so-called steady state approximation discussed above. Notice that NO is a relatively stable compound but since it is observed to exist only in trace amounts in this process, it is perfectly legitimate to apply to it the steady state approximation.

$$\frac{d[NO]}{dt} = 0 = k_2[NO_2][NO_3] - k_3[NO][NO_3]$$

Therefore

$$[NO] = \frac{k_2[NO_2]}{k_3}$$

$$\frac{d[NO_3]}{dt} = 0 = k_1[N_2O_5] - k_{-1}[NO_2][NO_3] - k_2[NO_2][NO_3] - k_3[NO][NO_3]$$

and therefore

$$[NO_3] = \frac{k_1[N_2O_5]}{(k_{-1} + k_2)[NO_2] + k_3[NO]} = \frac{k_1[N_2O_5]}{(k_{-1} + k_2)[NO_2] + k_2[NO_2]} = \frac{k_1}{k_{-1} + 2\,k_2}\frac{[N_2O_5]}{[NO_2]}$$

Finally, it is possible to use this value to eliminate the only unmeasurable quantity in the derived rate law.

$$r = -\frac{d[N_2O_5]}{dt} = k_1[N_2O_5] - k_{-1}[NO_2][NO_3]$$

$$= k_1[N_2O_5] - k_{-1}[NO_2]\frac{k_1[N_2O_5]}{(k_{-1} + 2\,k_2)[NO_2]}$$

$$= \left(\frac{2\,k_1k_2}{k_{-1} + 2\,k_2}\right)[N_2O_5]$$

Thus the postulated mechanism does lead to the correct conclusion, namely that the rate is first order in N_2O_5 and first order overall. It carries us a step forward too in showing us that k_{obs} is made up of the rate constants for three elementary processes. Caution is necessary, however. The proposal was reasonable and any chemist would be heartened that it was consistent with the experimental results and could proceed to use it or, better still, to devise further tests of it. Nevertheless one must always remember that other postulates will almost certainly exist which would also lead to first order kinetics. There is always the possibility that it is one of these other mechanisms which actually occurs.

A second example serves to introduce the concept of a *rate determining step*. Consider the decomposition of ozone to oxygen.

$$2\,O_3(g) \rightarrow 3\,O_2(g)$$

The experimentally determined rate law for this process is

$$r = -\tfrac{1}{2}\frac{d[O_3]}{dt} = k_{obs}[O_3]^2[O_2]^{-1}$$

A mechanism which is consistent with this observed rate law is the following.

$$O_3(g) \underset{k_{-1}}{\overset{k_1}{\rightleftharpoons}} O_2(g) + O(g)$$

$$O_3(g) + O(g) \xrightarrow{k_2} 2\,O_2(g)$$

Applying the steady state approximation to O gives

$$\frac{d[O]}{dt} = 0 = k_1[O_3] - k_{-1}[O_2][O] - k_2[O][O_3]$$

$$[O] = \frac{k_1[O_3]}{k_{-1}[O_2] + k_2[O_3]}$$

Therefore the rate, r, is given by

$$r = -\tfrac{1}{2}\frac{d[O_3]}{dt} = -\tfrac{1}{2}\left(-k_1[O_3] + k_{-1}[O_2][O] - k_2[O][O_3]\right)$$

$$= \tfrac{1}{2}\left(k_1[O_3] + (k_2[O_3] - k_{-1}[O_2])[O]\right)$$

$$= \tfrac{1}{2}\left(k_1[O_3] + (k_2[O_3] - k_{-1}[O_2])\left(\frac{k_1[O_3]}{k_{-1}[O_2] + k_2[O_3]}\right)\right)$$

$$= \frac{k_1 k_2[O_3]^2}{k_{-1}[O_2] + k_2[O_3]}$$

The mechanism is consistent with the known rate law only if one further postulate is made, namely that

$$k_{-1}[O_2] \gg k_2[O_3]$$

in which case

$$r \approx \frac{k_1 k_2[O_3]^2}{k_{-1}[O_2]} = \frac{k_1 k_2}{k_{-1}}\,[O_3]^2[O_2]^{-1}$$

Such postulates about the relative magnitudes of rate constants are often required and, if the whole proposal is correct, they provide additional insight. In this case, for example, it can be seen that the back reaction for which k_{-1} is the rate constant is much more rapid than the reaction for which k_2 is the rate constant. Thus the proposed mechanism involves a very rapid process in which O_3 will be in equilibrium with, or nearly in equilibrium with, O_2 molecules and O atoms. Oxygen atoms will sometimes react with O_3 molecules to give $2\,O_2$ but they will very much more often react with O_2 to give O_3. The important point is that the rate of the overall process is ultimately controlled by the rate of one particular step and its rate constant, k_2. An even more rapid exchange in the first process would require that k_1 and k_{-1} both increase. If they changed by different factors, the equilibrium concentration of O would change and the overall rate would change accordingly. If, however, they changed by the same proportion, even if it were an increase of several orders of magnitude, the overall rate would not change. That is because an equilibrium concentration of O is established rapidly, and the overall rate is determined by the rate at which the O_3 can react with this small pool of O atoms. This can all be seen in the algebra, where the rate depends on the ratio k_1/k_{-1} so that changing each by a constant factor has no effect. On the other hand a change in k_2, the rate constant for the slow step, affects the rate directly. The slow step in a reaction, the one responsible for determining the overall rate, is called the *rate determining step.*

Finally, a third example serves to illustrate the possible role of a species not included in the equation of the process itself. The following reaction occurs much more rapidly in the presence of bromide ion than in its absence, although bromide is not found in the equation of the overall process.

$$HNO_2(aq) + C_6H_5NH_2(aq) + H^+(aq) \rightarrow C_6H_5N_2^+(aq) + 2\,H_2O$$

The experimentally observed rate law for this process in the presence of bromide ion is

$$r = k[H^+][HNO_2][Br^-]$$

Such a rate law is consistent with the following mechanism.

$$H^+ + HNO_2 \underset{k_{-1}}{\overset{k_1}{\rightleftharpoons}} H_2NO_2^+$$

$$H_2NO_2^+ + Br^- \overset{k_2}{\rightarrow} NOBr + H_2O$$

$$NOBr + C_6H_5NH_2 \overset{k_3}{\rightarrow} C_6H_5N_2^+ + H_2O + Br^-$$

Notice that this scheme leaves the bromide ion unchanged in the end so that bromide in this process is a homogeneous catalyst. Application of the steady state approximation to the unstable intermediate $H_2NO_2^+$ results in the following rationalization of this mechanism.

$$\frac{d[H_2NO_2^+]}{dt} = 0 = k_1[H^+][HNO_2] - k_{-1}[H_2NO_2^+] - k_2[H_2NO_2^+][Br^-]$$

$$[H_2NO_2^+] = \frac{k_1[H^+][HNO_2]}{k_{-1} + k_2[Br^-]}$$

$$r = -\frac{d[HNO_2]}{dt} = k_1[H^+][HNO_2] - k_{-1}[H_2NO_2^+]$$

$$= k_1[H^+][HNO_2] - \left(\frac{k_1 k_{-1}[H^+][HNO_2]}{k_{-1} + k_2[Br^-]} \right)$$

$$= \frac{k_1 k_2[H^+][HNO_2][Br^-]}{k_{-1} + k_2[Br^-]}$$

As in the previous example, it is necessary to make a postulate about the relative size of two rate constants.

$$k_{-1} \gg k_2[Br^-]$$

Hence

$$r = \frac{k_1 k_2}{k_{-1}}[H^+][HNO_2][Br^-]$$

The above is an example of catalysis, where the addition of a substance speeds the reaction without the substance itself being changed. One can equally well find examples of inhibitors which slow the rate of a reaction but do not appear in the overall process. An example would be OH^- in the process

$$ClO^-(aq) + I^-(aq) \rightarrow IO^-(aq) + Cl^-(aq)$$

for which the rate law is found to be

$$r = - \frac{d[ClO^-]}{dt} = k[ClO^-][I^-][OH^-]^{-1}$$

24-4 INTEGRATED RATE LAWS

Integrated rate laws often provide the most convenient way of testing the order of a reaction and the most accurate way of extracting a value for the rate constant from experimental data. The integrated rate laws for some simple and commonly met cases are developed below.

(a) a reaction which is first order in reactant A only:

$$aA + other\ reactants \rightarrow products$$

$$r = -\frac{1}{a}\frac{d[A]}{dt} = k[A]$$

$$\frac{d[A]}{[A]} = -ak\ dt$$

Integration gives

$$\ln [A] = -akt + constant$$

To solve for the constant in terms of measurable quantities, designate the concentration of A at t=0 as $[A]_0$. Therefore

$$\ln [A]_0 = 0 + constant$$

$$\ln [A] = -akt + \ln[A]_0$$

$$\ln\frac{[A]}{[A]_0} = -akt$$

Thus, if [A] is measured as a function of time and $\ln[A]/[A]_0$ is plotted as a function of time, a first order process will yield a straight line passing through the origin. The linearity of such a plot is therefore a test of whether or not a process is first order in A. If it is, the slope of such a line is $-ak$ and provides an accurate route to evaluating k since all the data points are used and since the best straight line, in a statistical sense, can be fitted easily. Indeed many hand calculators are capable of performing the necessary calculations.

A plot as described above would not yield a straight line of course, if in addition to being first order in A, the process was such that the rate law contained other concentration terms and those concentrations were changing. The example is for a reaction which is first order in A only. It is worth noting, however, that straight lines are often obtained where there is a second concentration dependence but that concentration is essentially constant. In particular, this occurs where the solvent is a participant in the process. Such a process is said to be *pseudo first order*.

$$r = k[A][S] = k'[A]$$

A common example of reactions that follow first order kinetics is the case of nuclear disintegrations. Indeed in this case the analysis can be extended to the solid state since the rate is really proportional to the number of nuclei. Thus in the gas phase or in the liquid,

$$-\frac{d[A]}{dt} = k[A]$$

while in the solid

$$-\frac{dN_A}{dt} = kN_a$$

These two statements differ only in that the first is per unit volume and the second is not. It is common to quote the disintegration rate of unstable nuclei in terms of *half-life*, the time required for half of the nuclei present at t=0 to disintegrate. For example, ^{14}C is an unstable nucleus much used for tracer work in organic chemistry and as a means of dating archeological materials. The half-life of ^{14}C is 5570 years. Since this is the time required for

$$[A] = \tfrac{1}{2}[A]_0$$

it follows that

$$\ln [A]/[A]_0 = \ln \tfrac{1}{2} = - k(5570)$$

$$k = 1.24 \times 10^{-4} \text{ year}^{-1}$$

Thus for any first order reaction, an alternative way of measuring or expressing k is to measure or record the half-life. Notice that 5570 years is the time taken for half of any amount of ^{14}C to disintegrate. Thus a mole would become a half mole in 5570 years, a quarter mole in 11 140 years and an eighth mole in 16 710 years.

(b) a reaction which is second order in reactant A only:

$$aA + \text{other reactants} \rightarrow \text{products}$$

$$r = -\frac{1}{a} \frac{d[A]}{dt} = k[A]^2$$

$$\frac{d[A]}{[A]^2} = - ak\, dt$$

$$-\frac{1}{[A]} = - akt + \text{constant}$$

Again solving for the constant in terms of $[A]_0$ gives

$$-\frac{1}{[A]_0} = 0 + \text{constant}$$

$$\frac{1}{[A]} - \frac{1}{[A]_0} = akt$$

From this it can be seen that a test of this rate law would be a plot of $1/[A]$ as a function of t. If the rate law is second order in A only, such a plot will be a straight line from the slope of which one can calculate k.

(c) a reaction which is first order in A, and first order in B. In such cases, A and B are usually both reactants, but there are cases where one is a product. In such cases, the rate increases during the initial buildup of that particular product. Such processes are said to be autocatalytic. For purposes of this example, it is assumed that both A and B are reactants, and that the equation and rate law are as follows.

$$aA + bB + \text{other reactants} \rightarrow \text{products}$$

$$r = -\frac{1}{a}\frac{d[A]}{dt} = k[A][B]$$

The changes in the concentrations of A and B are not independent. If, at time t, α mol of A and β mol of B have reacted per litre, then,

$$\frac{\beta}{\alpha} = \frac{b}{a}$$

Therefore

$$[A] = [A]_0 - \alpha$$

$$[B] = [B]_0 - \beta = [B]_0 - (b/a)(\alpha)$$

$$= [B]_0 - (b/a)([A]_0 - [A])$$

This expression allows one to express the rate law in a form in which [A] is the only concentration variable.

$$-\frac{1}{a}\frac{d[A]}{dt} = k[A][B]$$

$$= k[A]([B]_0 - (b/a)([A]_0 - [A]))$$

A table of integrals shows that, for $p \neq 0$, the integral of the expression

$$\frac{dx}{x(p+qx)}$$

is given by

$$-\frac{1}{p}\ln\frac{p+qx}{x} + \text{constant}$$

Rearrangement of the rate law into concentration terms on the left and $-ak\,dt$ on the right, as in previous cases, produces on the left hand side an expression which is essentially of this form, so that integration yields

$$\frac{1}{a[B]_0 - b[A]_0} \ln \frac{[B]}{[B]_0} - \ln \frac{[A]}{[A]_0} = kt$$

This solution does not apply, as was noted above, where $p \neq 0$. The case of $p=0$ corresponds to

$$\frac{[B]_0}{[A]_0} = \frac{b}{a}$$

in which case B and A are present in stoichiometric proportions throughout. A solution for this special case gives

$$\frac{1}{[A]} - \frac{1}{[A]_0} = bkt$$

This case illustrates the complexity of integrated rate laws for higher order rate laws. The same is true for other complexities of interest, such as cases where there is a significant back reaction leading to equilibrium. The mathematics in these cases can be untidy, but the principles are no different from those in the cases examined.

24-5   TEMPERATURE DEPENDENCE OF RATE CONSTANTS

Rate constants invariably increase with increasing temperature. The temperature dependence is often of the form

$$\ln k = \ln A - (B/T)$$

where A and B are positive numbers. This pattern is reminiscent of the temperature dependence of an equilibrium constant

$$\ln K = \Delta S^\circ/R - (\Delta H^\circ/RT)$$

The analogy is a dangerous one and will not be pursued here except to note that it is useful to identify the coefficient B with an energy divided by R. This energy is called the activation energy, E_a. Thus one forms the Arrhenius expression which is

$$\ln k = \ln A - (E_a/RT)$$

or

$$k = Ae^{-E_a/RT}$$

A large value of E_a leads to a small value of k and thus to a slow reaction. A small E_a leads to a fast reaction. E_a is interpreted as being an energy barrier which reactants must cross in order to react. The higher that barrier, the less frequently colliding molecules will have enough energy to cross it. Experimentally, E_a may be measured for a particular reaction by determining k at different temperatures. A plot of $\ln k$ against $1/T$ gives a straight line of slope $-E_a/R$.

Theory associates the pre-exponential factor, A, with a number of effects, notably the rate of collisions and restrictions on the relative orientations which two colliding molecules must have if they are to react. In this approach both A and E_a are independent of temperature but some modern theoretical treatments lead to similar expressions in which both are functions of temperature. In fact, any temperature dependence is usually too small to measure, not least because kinetic data are notoriously imprecise. In this chapter, both A and E_a are treated as being constants but it is worth noting that there is a definition of each which applies whether or not they are temperature independent.

$$E_a \equiv RT^2 \ \frac{d(\ln k)}{dT}$$

$$A \equiv k e^{E_a/RT}$$

Example 24-2 The rate of a process is found to be twice as fast at 300 K as at 290 K. What is the activation energy of the process?

$$k' = Ae^{-E_a/R(290)}$$

$$k'' = 2k' = Ae^{-E_a/R(300)}$$

Dividing gives

$$2 = e^{-E_a/R(300)}e^{E_a/R(290)} = e^{\,0.000115E_a/8.314}$$

$$E_a = 50000 \text{ J mol}^{-1} = 50 \text{ kJ mol}^{-1}$$

24-6 GAS PHASE REACTIONS AND LIQUID PHASE REACTIONS

In much of what appears in this chapter so far, the distinction between gas phase reactions and liquid phase reactions is largely ignored. It is certainly true that gas phase reactions and liquid phase reactions are very much more similar to one another than either is to solid phase reactions, and in some cases the solvent plays little role. As an example, consider again the process

$$2 N_2O_5 \rightarrow 4 NO_2 + O_2$$

It is found to follow the same rate law in gas and in liquid solution. Moreover the similarity of the values of k and E_a in Table 24-1 suggests that the role of the solvent is minor.

Interpretation of liquid phase reactions is more difficult than the interpretation of gas phase reactions, but it is clear that in the liquid there are much greater interactions with neighbouring molecules. Where this interaction is minimal, the case will be most like a gas. Even where the interaction is small, however, some differences between gas and liquid phase reactions remain. In the liquid, a reactant molecule tends to bounce around among its immediate neighbours for some time before enough rearrangement occurs to give it one or two new neighbours. Thus if a neighbouring molecule is one with which it

TABLE 24-1 Some Experimental Values of k and E_a at 25°C for the Process $2 N_2O_5 \rightarrow 4 NO_2 + O_2$

Medium	k/s^{-1}	$E_a/kJ\ mol^{-1}$
gas	1.7×10^{-5}	103
$CCl_4(l)$	4.7×10^{-5}	101
$Br_2(l)$	4.3×10^{-5}	100
$CH_3NO_2(l)$	3.1×10^{-5}	103
$CHCl_2CCl_3(l)$	4.3×10^{-5}	105

can react, it has several opportunities to do so whereas if its neighbours are all solvent molecules, there can be no reaction until some rearrangement occurs. This effect is sometimes described as the *cage effect*. The rate at which reactant molecules can work towards one another, the diffusion rate, can be much slower than the rate of the subsequent reaction steps. In such cases diffusion becomes the rate determining step and the reaction is said to be diffusion controlled. Note that a reaction may be diffusion controlled if the reactants are very dilute but follow a different law for more concentrated solutions.

Solvent effects are much more important, of course, where the reactants and solvent interact strongly. If solvent molecules coordinate with molecules of one of the reactants, the frequency of collisions may be reduced and both steric and electronic factors may be altered.

24-7 NUCLEOPHILIC SUBSTITUTION AND OTHER CLASSIFICATIONS OF REACTIONS

Some mechanisms are so common that they have acquired their own particular terminology. Such is the case with *nucleophilic substitution reactions*, which are of particular importance to organic chemists.

The synthesis of many organic compounds is achieved by substituting one functional group for another. A particularly common route is to prepare an alkyl halide from a hydrocarbon, which is a relatively easy process to carry out in many cases, and then to substitute another functional group for the halogen. The carbon to which the halogen is attached will be somewhat positively charged because of the electronegativity of the halogen atom. Mechanisms frequently involve 'attack' by a *nucleophile* on this positive carbon atom.

A nucleophile is an atom or ion which readily coordinates to a positive centre through a non-bonding pair of electrons in its valence shell. In the terms used in Chapter 20, a nucleophile is a base. A base has electrons which can accept a proton, as in Brønsted acid/base chemistry, but which can accept other positively charged centres as well.

Two important substitution reaction classes are labelled S_N2 (for substitution nucleophilic bimolecular) and S_N1 (for substitution nucleophilic unimolecular). In the S_N2 reaction, a nucleophile attacks the positive centre and, in the process, displaces a group already bonded to that centre. The displaced

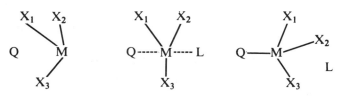

(a) reactants   (b) intermediate stage   (c) products

Figure 24-2 Visualization of S_N2 Mechanism by Back-side Attack.

group is called the *leaving group*. In the S_N2 process, the formation of a bond with the attacking group and the breakage of the bond with the leaving group are simultaneous, and the reaction is said to be a *concerted process*.

Since a nucleophile is a base, it is not surprising that OH^- is an effective nucleophile. In terms of the kind of process mentioned above, for example, it attacks CH_3Br to produce CH_3OH. Species which have a strong tendency to displace others in this way are often referred to as 'good' nucleophiles while those with a strong tendency to be displaced, like the halogens, are called 'good' leaving groups. By and large, good nucleophiles are poor leaving groups and vice versa.

So far in discussing mechanisms, no mention has been made of the role of configuration in analyzing a mechanism and, conversely, of the importance of mechanism in determining the configuration of the product. In many cases the configuration of the product is a most important piece of evidence in discovering the mechanism. S_N2 reactions afford such a case. Suppose that a nucleophile, designated as Q in Figure 24-2, approaches a positive centre, M, from the side remote from the leaving group, L. The figure is drawn in terms of tetrahedral symmetry around M because the case of M being carbon is of such great importance, and the following comments on configuration are framed in the context of tetrahedral symmetry. As shown in Figure 24-2, the back-side approach leads to *inversion* of the molecule whereas the front-side approach, illustrated in Figure 24-3, leads to retention of the same configuration. Note that the elementary reactions so visualized are bimolecular, in accordance with the 2 in S_N2. Assuming that this is the rate determining step, the rate of such a process is first order in the species being attacked, first order in the nucleophile and second order overall.

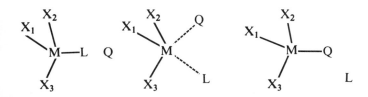

(a) reactants   (b) intermediate stage   (c) products

Figure 24-3 Visualization of S_N2 Mechanism by Front-side Attack.

The fact that the hydrolysis of an alkyl halide results exclusively in inversion is evidence that only back-side approach is successful in bringing about substitution. This is, indeed, the usual case, an example being the attack of hydroxide ion on 2-chlorobutane to give exclusively 2-butanol with the inverted configuration.

Now whereas S_N2 reactions usually result in the continuation of optical activity but with inversion of configuration, S_N1 reactions result in the loss of optical activity. The S_N1 reaction is not a concerted reaction. It is a two step process with dissociation into an anion and a triangular planar cation as the first step and reaction of the nucleophile with the cation as the second step. If the nucleophile can attack either side of the planar cation equally, then both configurations would result equally and the product would not be optically active. The nature of the cation is obviously of great importance in determining this outcome. Cations in which the positive charge resides on the carbon have been called *carbonium ions* and they are an important example of *reactive intermediates*, the kind of highly reactive species existing in low concentration, the existence of which we postulated in developing the steady state approximation. In S_N1 reactions, the slow rate-determining step is the initial dissociation into ions. Providing there are no complications and this step is indeed rate-determining, the rate will be first order in the species on which substitution occurs, first order overall and independent of the concentration of the attacking species.

In inorganic and organometallic chemistry, the same S_N1 and S_N2 terminology is still used, although decreasingly so. The symmetry at a metal centre is not, of course, always tetrahedral. The various groups attached to the metal are called ligands and S_N1 and S_N2 are examples of *ligand replacement reactions*. However, so many subtle intermediate or complicated cases have been discovered, particularly in organometallic chemistry, that the S_N1 and S_N2 terminology is less useful there than in organic chemistry. In inorganic chemistry, the tendency is to classify reactions in terms of dissociative mechanisms (D mechanisms) in which a relatively long-lived reactive intermediate is produced as in S_N1; dissociative interchange mechanisms (I_d mechanisms) in which the dissociation is influenced weakly by the approach of the attacking group; associative interchange mechanisms (I_a mechanisms) in which the effect of the attacking group on the bond breaking is much more important; and associative mechanisms (A mechanisms) in which both the attacking and leaving groups are simultaneously bonded to the metal centre in the intermediate complex. These four classifications cover a continuous range of possibilities. It should also be noted that a first order rate law in such reactions usually but *not* always indicates a dissociative mechanism and that a second order rate law usually but *not* always indicates an associative mechanism.

Example 24-3   Suppose a complex ML_4 goes to ML_3Q by a two-step mechanism involving first a rapid dissociative equilibrium into ML_3 and L followed by a one-way formation of ML_3Q. Show how even this simple mechanism which appears to have all of the characteristics of an S_N1 reaction, can have a rate which is either first order or second order overall.

$$ML_4 \underset{k_{-1}}{\overset{k_1}{\rightleftharpoons}} ML_3 + L$$

$$ML_3 + Q \overset{k_2}{\to} ML_3Q$$

$$r = \frac{d[ML_3Q]}{dt} = k_2[ML_3][Q]$$

The steady state approximation gives

$$\frac{d[ML_3]}{dt} = 0 = k_1[ML_4] - k_{-1}[ML_3][L] - k_2[ML_3][Q]$$

Notice that [L] may be quite large and that L is not infrequently the solvent. Thus it is inappropriate to apply the steady state approximation to it in any general case.

Therefore

$$[ML_3] = \frac{k_1[ML_4]}{k_{-1}[L] + k_2[Q]}$$

$$r = k_2[Q]\left(\frac{k_1[ML_4]}{k_{-1}[L] + k_2[Q]} \right)$$

Thus if $k_{-1}[L] \gg k_2[Q]$

$$r = k_2[Q] \; \frac{k_1[ML_4]}{k_{-1}[L]}$$

Here, if L were the solvent, the denominator would be effectively constant and a pseudo second order rate law would be observed.

If, on the other hand, $k_2[Q] \gg k_{-1}[L]$

$$r = k_2[Q] \; \frac{k_1[ML_4]}{k_2[Q]} = k_1[ML_4]$$

This process is first order.

There is a wide range of other terms used to classify reactions, especially by organic chemists. Just as there are nucleophilic attacks, there are *electrophilic* attacks. One of the best known examples is the addition of a halogen, X_2, or a hydrogen halide, HX, to the double bond of an alkene, as for example

$$CH_3CH = CH_2 + Br_2 \to CH_3CHBrCH_2 Br$$

Bromine is believed to produce a small concentration of Br^+ which attacks the high electron density of the double bond.

$$Br_2 \rightleftharpoons Br^+ + Br^-$$

$$CH_3CH = CH_2 + Br^+ \to CH_3 \overset{\overset{\displaystyle H}{|}}{C} - \overset{\overset{\displaystyle Br^+}{|}}{CH_2}$$

$$\begin{array}{ccc} H & Br^+ \\ | & | \\ CH_3 - C - CH_2 & \to CH_3CHBrCH_2Br \\ \overset{\displaystyle Br^-}{\diagup} \end{array}$$

Of importance to both organic and organometallic chemists are *elimination reactions*. Examples are the following.

$$CH_3CHBrCH_3 \to CH_3CH = CH_2 + HBr$$

$$(C_6H_5)_3P\,Au(CH_3)_3 \to (C_6H_5)_3P\,AuCH_3 + C_2H_6$$

Elimination reactions, like substitution reactions, include a wide variety of different mechanisms, and have their own specialized terminology in both organic and inorganic chemistry. Almost any introductory text in each of these two subdisciplines can serve as an introduction to these important classes of reaction, and to the mechanisms associated with them.

24-8 REACTIONS IN THE SOLID STATE

Molecules in the liquid or gas state are free to move and reaction rates are much influenced by the frequency of collisions, by the relative orientations of colliding molecules, and by the kinetic energies of the reactants. In solids, most material is fixed in position, and rates are often controlled by the relatively slow speed at which material can migrate through a crystal. Solid state reactions are few compared to those in gas or liquid state, especially those which involve the reaction of one crystalline material with another. However, there are some significant groups of reactions such as detonations, thermal decompositions and the heterogeneous reaction of a solid with a gas or liquid. This latter group includes corrosion.

The two factors most frequently encountered as limiting the rate of solid state processes are transfer of material through a crystal and transfer of charge through a crystal. An elegant demonstration of the reality of diffusion was published by Wagner* near the beginning of a long career in which he made many contributions to our understanding of corrosion processes. The black tarnish which forms on silver arises from formation of silver sulphide. In the atmosphere this is usually due to minute traces of sulphur compounds but silver sulphide is also formed by direct contact of silver with molten sulphur.

In this experiment two crystals of Ag_2S are tightly clamped between a piece of silver and a vessel containing molten sulphur. The silver and the two pieces of silver sulphide were weighed before the device was constructed and again after the molten sulphur had been present for an hour. The silver had become lighter and the silver sulphide had become heavier by the expected amount, but the interesting point in Table 24-2 is that the additional mass was entirely in the upper silver sulphide slice. This strongly supports a mechanism in which silver

---

* C. Wagner Z. Phys. Chem. *B21* (1933) 25-41

TABLE 24-2 Wagner's Experimental Results. Five determinations were done. For each the temperature was 220°C and the time was one hour.

Experiment Number	Mass Change/mg		
	Ag	$Ag_2S(I)$	$Ag_2S(II)$
1	−108	+3	+117
2	−137	+1	+135
3	− 84	+1	+ 96
4	−108	+2	+126
5	−121	+5	+131

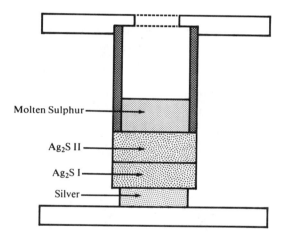

Molten Sulphur

Ag_2S II

Ag_2S I

Silver

Figure 24-4 Wagner's Apparatus for Study of the Diffusion of Ag through Ag_2S.

diffuses through the silver sulphide to the sulphur/silver sulphide interface where it reacts. Diffusion of metal cations is illustrated diagrammatically in Figure 24-5. Notice that it could be regarded equally well as the migration of a vacancy in the other direction. In the oxidation of aluminium by oxygen, metal atoms again diffuse through the oxide layer to react at the oxygen/aluminium oxide interface, but this case serves to show that diffusion is not necessarily the rate determining step. Studies show that although the diffusion of the metal is slow, the rate determining step appears to be the transfer of aluminium ion across the aluminium oxide/aluminium boundary. The ease of this jump is determined by the potential of the oxide layer adjacent to the metal. This is made more negative, and the jump consequently easier, by oxygen adsorption on the film of aluminium oxide at the oxygen/aluminium oxide interface. As the film becomes thicker, the adsorbed oxygen has less and less effect on the potential at the oxide/metal boundary and the jump process effectively ceases.

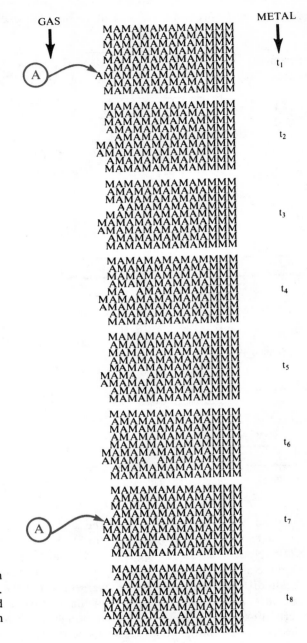

Figure 24-5 Diffusion of metal through a surface film. A represents the anion. The important question of charge, and the transfer of charge when a new anion forms from a gas molecule, is ignored.

A third process by which product films grow at a solid/liquid or solid/gas interface is represented by the rusting of iron. Neither of the mechanisms above apply because rust cracks, peels and washes away so readily that the fresh iron surface is constantly being exposed at one point or another. Iron therefore corrodes readily unless protected by a coating or unless alloyed with carbon and certain transition metals in the form of stainless steel.

These three examples, which are by no means all-inclusive, serve to illustrate the relationship between mechanism and rate law for reactions of a solid with a gas or liquid. In the case of silver sulphide, the diffusion process is associated with a gradient in silver concentration or conversely a gradient in cation vacancies, across the film. This gradient is inversely proportional to the thickness of the film, y. Since diffusion is the rate determining step in this process, the rate is inversely proportional to y, and the rate law can be written

$$\frac{dy}{dt} = k \, \frac{1}{y}$$

which in its integrated form can be written

$$y^2 = 2kt$$

if the film is taken to have zero thickness at t=0. This equation is the equation of a parabola and such processes are sometimes referred to as exhibiting parabolic growth.

In the case of an oxide film forming on aluminium, the relationship between the film thickness and the influence on potential which the adsorbed oxygen exerts through that thickness of oxide film is complex. The rate law takes the form

$$\frac{dy}{dt} = Ae^{(B + C/y)/T}$$

where the constants A, B and C have been related successfully to some more fundamental properties of the metal. For such a rate law, the rate is very large when y is very small, but the rate decreases rapidly as y increases. For aluminium at 20°C, it is effectively zero when y is only 2 nm.

In the case of the rusting of iron, the rate of oxidation is usually constant with time until the iron has gone. There is some irregularity because of the irregularity in the timing of the splitting and peeling of the rust, but over a long period of time the rate is constant. This is referred to as linear growth.

Thermal decomposition processes constitute a second important class of reactions in solids. Except for a few exotic cases like Ag_2C_2, these processes lead to at least one gaseous product and their progress is often followed experimentally by monitoring the pressure, and if necessary the composition, of the gas produced. Typical examples of such processes are the following.

$$AgN_3(c) \rightarrow Ag(c) + 1\tfrac{1}{2} \, N_2(g)$$

$$Na_2SO_4 \cdot 10 \, H_2O(c) \rightarrow Na_2SO_4(c) + 10 \, H_2O(g)$$

$$CaCO_3(c) \rightarrow CaO(c) + CO_2(g)$$

The decompositions of these solids usually occur in two stages, the first involving formation of nuclei of the solid decomposition product and the second involving diffusion or surface migration of material to those nuclei. Either of these processes can be rate controlling.

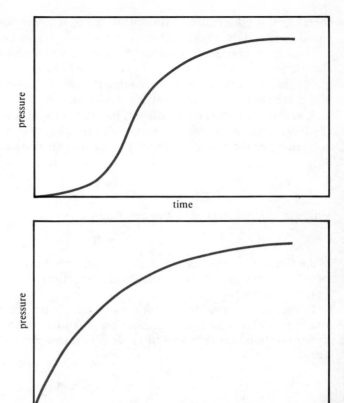

Figure 24-6 Sigmoidal Growth of Gas Pressure for Process: Solid → Solid + Gas.

Figure 24-7 Decomposition without Induction Period for Process: Solid → Solid + Gas.

Nuclei usually form at surface discontinuities where the energy is higher due to strain and the amount of extra energy required from local fluctuations in order to satisfy the activation energy is less. The surface location permits the product gas to escape, creating lattice vacancies, usually anionic, around the nucleus. If the growth of these product crystals is much faster than the rate at which nuclei form, the decomposition will be slow in the early stages but will accelerate later as nuclei begin to grow. The pressure of product gas would alter with time in the way shown in Figure 24-6. The period of slow growth is called the *induction period*. Eventually the rate declines, of course, when most of the material has decomposed, as growing nuclei begin to touch and thus to decrease the area of interface between reactant and product. This pattern of decomposition is called sigmoidal.

If, on the other hand, nuclei form readily, the rate is determined throughout by the diffusion rate. A curve of the form shown in Figure 24-7 is then obtained. There are many cases known in which the two processes, nuclei formation and product growth, have comparable rates and neither is exclusively rate determining.

This brief section illustrates the fact that solid state reactions are controlled by factors quite different from those that control reactions in liquids or gases. Much experimental and theoretical work has been done on them and is available to those with an interest in this specialized but important area.

FURTHER READING

There are many useful introductory texts on chemical kinetics. One which begins with fundametals, is well organized and is notably careful in its explanations is "Chemical Kinetics and Reaction Mechanisms," F. Wilkinson, Van Nostrand Reinhold, New York (1980).

PROBLEMS

1. Methyl acetate reacts with water to give acetic acid and methanol. Experiments in the laboratory showed that the disappearance of methyl acetate in a dilute aqueous solution was governed by the following rate law at 25°C.

$$\frac{d[CH_3COOCH_3]}{dt} = 3.6 \times 10^{-5}[CH_3COOCH_3]$$

A solution is prepared having a concentration of methyl acetate of 0.105 mol L^{-1} at t=0. What is the concentration after twenty minutes at 25°C? What is it after 24 hours?

[0.101 mol L^{-1}; 0.005 mol L^{-1}]

2. Plots such as that in Figure 24-1 were prepared for five experimental studies of the reaction

$$A(aq) + B(aq) \rightarrow C(aq)$$

A value of the initial rate of disappearance of A was determined for each experiment by drawing a tangent to the experimental curve at t=0. Results were as follows.

$[A]_0$/mol L^{-1}	$[B]_0$/mol L^{-1}	$\left(\frac{d[A]}{dt}\right)_0$ /mol L^{-1} s^{-1}
1.0	2.0	-1.5×10^{-2}
0.50	1.0	-1.9×10^{-3}
0.50	0.50	-9.3×10^{-4}
0.20	0.20	-5.9×10^{-5}
1.0	0.20	-1.5×10^{-3}

If the rate law is of the form

$$-\frac{d[A]}{dt} = k[A]^m[B]^n$$

what are the values of k, m and n? What is the overall order?

[7.5×10^{-4}; 2; 1; third]

3. Use the data in Table 24-1 to calculate the rate constant at 100°C for the process

$$2 N_2O_5(g) \rightarrow 4 NO_2(g) + O_2(g)$$

[.072 s^{-1}]

4. Why is the concept of half-life useful for first order processes but not for second order processes?

5. The reaction between hydrogen and iodine to form hydrogen iodide,

$$H_2(g) + I_2(g) \rightarrow 2\,HI(g)$$

is found experimentally to follow the rate law

$$r = k[H_2][I_2]$$

Assuming that the rate law is of this form, is this reaction necessarily second order overall? Is it necessarily bimolecular? What is the distinction?

[yes; no]

6. An undergraduate is measuring the catalytic effect of iodide ion on the following reaction.

$$2\,H_2O_2(aq) \rightarrow 2\,H_2O(l) + O_2(g)$$

The reaction was followed by collecting the oxygen and measuring its volume as a function of time. One particular run, for one particular concentration of potassium iodide, produced the following results. The temperature was 23.8°C and the pressure was 98.5 kPa

t/s	V_{gas}/mL
0	0
300	7.7
600	15.2
900	21.3
1200	27.1
1500	32.6
1800	37.8
2100	40.8
2400	45.5

The initial concentration of H_2O_2 was 0.300 mol L^{-1} and the volume of the solution was 21.1 mL. What is the order of the reaction, n, in H_2O_2 as expressed in the following rate law?

$$-\frac{d[H_2O_2]}{dt} = \tfrac{1}{2}(k_{obs})[H_2O_2]^n$$

What is the value of k_{obs} at this temperature? Remember that since the oxygen is collected above the aqueous solution, it will be saturated with water vapour. Estimate the contribution which this water makes to the volume figures before attempting to answer the question. Simplify the process by treating the solution as pure water, for which the vapour pressure can be found from the following data.

$T/°C$	P/Pa
22.0	2643
23.0	2809
24.0	2983

Why is it wise to emphasize the obs in k_{obs} in this example?

[first; $1.7 \times 10^{-4}\,s^{-1}$]

7. In the gas phase reaction of hydrogen with photolytically produced iodine atoms,

$$H_2(g) + 2\,I(g) \rightarrow 2\,HI(g)$$

the rate law is found to be

$$r = k[H_2][I]^2$$

Such a rate law would be consistent with a single termolecular step. Devise an alternative mechanism which involves only unimolecular and/or bimolecular steps and which is equally consistent with the rate law.

8. The gas phase reaction of H_2 with I_2 follows the rate law indicated in Problem 5. k has the value $2.5 \times 10^{-3}\,L\;mol^{-1}\;s^{-1}$ at $356\,°C$ and $1.4 \times 10^{-2}\,L\;mol^{-1}\;s^{-1}$ at $393\,°C$. If, at t=0, the concentration of H_2 is $1.05 \times 10^{-2}\,mol\;L^{-1}$ and that of I_2 is $4.60 \times 10^{-4}\,mol\;L^{-1}$, what would be the concentration of I_2 after one hour at each of these temperatures? What is the activation energy of the process?

[$4.58 \times 10^{-4}\,mol\;L^{-1}$; $4.50 \times 10^{-4}\,mol\;L^{-1}$; $162\,kJ$]

9. The reaction

$$2\,NO_2(g) + F_2(g) \rightarrow 2\,NO_2F(g)$$

has the rate law

$$r = k[NO_2][F_2]$$

Develop a set of reasonable elementary equations which are consistent with this rate law.

10. The reactant A decomposes in aqueous solution to give P and Q.

$$A(aq) \rightarrow P(aq) + Q(aq)$$

In an experiment in which $[A]_0$ was $0.420\,mol\;L^{-1}$, [Q] was measured as a function of time, producing the following experimental data.

t/s	[Q]/mol L^{-1}
0	0.0
100	0.101
200	0.165
300	0.206
400	0.239
500	0.263
600	0.281
700	0.294
800	0.306

By plotting ln [A] and 1/[A] as functions of t, determine if this process is first order in A only, second order in A only or neither of these. If a suitable fit is found, evaluate k.

11. Some reactions are zeroth order, such that

$$A \rightarrow P$$

$$r = k$$

Develop an integrated form of this rate law. Can this integrated rate law be valid at all times, as for example at $t=2[A]_0/k$? Could the rate law itself be valid at such times? Speculate on the physical interpretation of your answers.

12. The isomerization of cyclopropane to propene is typical of many isomerizations in that it appears to follow the mechanism below.

$$CH_2CH_2CH_2(g) + M \underset{k_{-1}}{\overset{k_1}{\rightleftharpoons}} CH_2CH_2CH_2^*(g) + M$$

$$CH_2CH_2CH_2^*(g) \overset{k_2}{\rightarrow} CH_3CHCH_2(g)$$

M represents a molecule, perhaps cyclopropane and perhaps not, from which the cyclopropane molecule acquires energy on collision and is thus more likely to react. Energized cyclopropane is indicated by an asterisk. Collisions can lead equally well to loss of energy, as represented by k_{-1}. Such processes can have rate laws including the concentration of other species present, and even such chemically inert species as argon can serve to provide the energy needed. Develop the rate law for the isomerization of cyclopropane. What form would it take if [M] were very small? What form would it have if [M] were very large?

13. Walsh and his coworkers studied the gas phase reaction of iodine with trimethylsilane in the temperature range from 565 K to 599 K.

$$(CH_3)_3SiH(g) + I_2(g) \rightarrow (CH_3)_3SiI(g) + HI(g)$$

The reaction is found to obey the rate law

$$r = \frac{k[I_2]^{1/2}[(CH_3)_3SiH]}{1 + k'[HI][I_2]^{-1}}$$

Does this reaction have an order and, if so, what is it? At the moment t=0, when [HI] and [(CH_3)_3SiI] are both zero, what form would the rate law take? Does the process have an order at that moment and, if so, what is it? Show that the following mechanism is consistent with the observed rate law.

$$I_2(g) \underset{k_{-1}}{\overset{k_1}{\rightleftharpoons}} 2 I(g)$$

$$I(g) + (CH_3)_3SiH(g) \underset{k_{-2}}{\overset{k_2}{\rightleftharpoons}} (CH_3)_3Si \cdot (g) + HI(g)$$

$$(CH_3)_3Si \cdot (g) + I_2(g) \xrightarrow{k_3} (CH_3)_3SiI(g) + I(g)$$

Relate k and k′ in the experimental rate law to k_1, k_{-1}, k_2, k_{-2} and k_3. This question is long.

14. In the question above, $(CH_3)_3Si\cdot$ is a free radical, a species with an unpaired electron. Indeed so are I atoms although one does not always think of them in this way. Free radicals may be produced by ultraviolet radiation or other means and are highly reactive once generated. Study of their reaction has both fundamental and commercial objectives. Free radical reactions often involve regeneration of the radical so that the process carries on until some terminating process destroys the radical. Such processes are examples of *chain reactions*.

Tedder and his associates produced $(CF_3)_3C\cdot$ radicals by photolysis of $(CF_3)_3CI$

$$(CF_3)_3CI(g) \xrightarrow{hv} (CF_3)_3C \cdot (g) + I \cdot (g)$$

and studied the reaction of these radicals with ethene and substituted ethenes. It was found that the only steps in the mechanism appeared to be the following.

$$(CF_3)_3C \cdot (g) + CH_2CHR(g) \xrightarrow{k_1} (CF_3)_3CCH_2CHR \cdot (g)$$

$$(CF_3)_3CCH_2CHR \cdot (g) + (CF_3)_3CI(g) \xrightarrow{k_2} (CF_3)_3CCH_2CHRI(g) + (CF_3)_3C \cdot (g)$$

The radical can add to either end of the alkene and the following data have been reported for the case of CH_2CHF. Chromotography was used to measure the ratio of the final amounts of the two possible products at several temperatures.

T/°C	Product Ratio
72	.0018
94	.0027
107	.0031
123	.0036
140	.0041
163	.0054

What is the difference between the activation energies of the two competing processes shown below?

$$(CF_3)_3C \cdot (g) + CH_2CHF(g) \rightarrow (CF_3)_3CCH_2CHF \cdot (g)$$

$$(CF_3)_3C \cdot (g) + CH_2CHF(g) \rightarrow (CF_3)_3CCHFCH_2 \cdot (g)$$

[15 kJ]

15. Recombinations are an important aspect of free radical chemistry. For example, in studies of methyl radicals, one must take account of the terminating reaction

$$CH_3 \cdot (g) + CH_3 \cdot (g) \rightarrow C_2H_6(g)$$

for which the rate law is

$$r = k[CH_3 \cdot]^2$$

Experimental values of k have been published as follows.

T/K	k/L mol^{-1} s^{-1}
293	2.5×10^{10} ($\pm 0.3 \times 10^{10}$)
295	2.4×10^{10} ($\pm 0.2 \times 10^{10}$)
298	2.7×10^{10} ($\pm 0.4 \times 10^{10}$)
313	2.5×10^{10} ($\pm 0.1 \times 10^{10}$)

What value would you consider to be reasonable for the activation energy of this process? What is the practical meaning of such a value?

16. A metal forms an oxide layer with a rate which follows a parabolic rate law. If the first 10.0 nm of oxide grows in 100 s after the production of a fresh metal surface, how long does it take for the second 10.0 nm to form?

[a further 300 s]

17. A well known phenomenon in upper atmosphere chemistry is the generation of a small concentration of ozone by sunlight. This is believed to be due to the following slightly simplified mechanism.

$$NO_2 \overset{h\nu}{\underset{k_1}{\rightarrow}} NO + O$$

$$O + O_2 \overset{k_2}{\rightarrow} O_3$$

$$NO + O_3 \overset{k_3}{\rightarrow} NO_2 + O_2$$

Show that in the presence of steady illumination by sunlight, the steady state concentration of ozone is given by

$$[O_3] = \frac{k_1[NO_2]}{k_3[NO]}$$

18. The cyclic dimerization of chlorotrifluoroethene

$$2C_2F_3Cl(g) \rightarrow C_4F_6Cl_2(g)$$

has been studied by Atkinson and Tsiamis. The rate law is found to be

$$-\tfrac{1}{2} \frac{d[C_2F_3Cl]}{dt} = k[C_2F_3Cl]^2$$

k was evaluated at several temperatures, only some of which evaluations are listed below. Use these data to calculate the activation energy for the process.

T/K	P/Pa	$-\log(k/\mathrm{m^3\,mol^{-1}\,s^{-1}})$
523.5	39.790	6.665
523.5	39.790	6.690
523.5	25.434	6.654
523.5	25.434	6.688
523.5	25.434	6.678
498.2	40.041	7.198
498.2	40.041	7.205
498.2	40.041	7.189
498.2	25.198	7.203
498.2	25.198	7.197
473.0	42.434	7.770
473.0	42.434	7.783
473.0	42.434	7.769
473.0	30.144	7.774
473.0	30.144	7.768

XXV CORROSION OF METALS

Corrosion may be defined as an undesirable and harmful reaction of a metal product with its environment. That such unwanted reactions are worthy of the attention of scientists and engineers may be judged from the fact that annual losses due to corrosion are in the multi-billion dollar range. For steel it has been estimated that 25% of production is lost through corrosion, although our economy admittedly still countenances obsolescence and replacement.

Corrosion is a natural and spontaneous process at constant temperature and pressure and must therefore involve a decrease of Gibbs energy. Most metals occur in the natural state after eons of time as compounds of oxygen, sulphur, or silicon. The pure metal is obtained metallurgically by a reduction process. For example, iron is produced by reduction of oxides with carbon monoxide in the blast furnace, while aluminium is won from its oxide by electrolysis. It is only natural that the metal so won will tend to return to its original stable compounds if allowed to react with an environment which allows the required oxidation. In the case of iron, when exposed to a climate of air and moisture, it will return to an oxide form as first found in the ground. One might intone, "ashes to ashes, dust to dust, and rust to rust."

25-1 CORROSION IN DRY AIR

TABLE 25-1 gives the standard Gibbs energies of formation of a number of metal oxides. In each case the value is given per mole of combined oxide ions,

TABLE 25-1 Values of ΔG_f° for Some Metal Oxides
(in kJ per mole of O^{2-} combined at 298 K)

Ag_2O	-11.2	ZnO	-318
Cu_2O	-146	$\frac{1}{3}Cr_2O_3$	-353
PbO	-188	$\frac{1}{3}Al_2O_3$	-527
NiO	-212	MgO	-569
FeO	-228		
$\frac{1}{3}Fe_2O_3$	-247		
$\frac{1}{4}Fe_3O_4$	-254		

or per two faraday change of charge, so the values are intensive and line up in the same order as metals in the usual electrochemical series with the most noble metal (Ag) at the top left and the most active metal (Mg) at the bottom right. All values of ΔG_f° in the table are negative, signifying that the reaction of each metal with oxygen to form the appropriate oxide is spontaneous. However, one must be careful not to oversimplify. At higher temperatures the values of ΔG_f° are less negative, signifying lower stability as the oxide. In fact above about 200°C the oxide of the noblest metal in the table, Ag_2O, decomposes into the metal and oxygen. In the case of the other oxides, their *rates* of formation from the metal are enhanced at the higher temperature, in spite of the fact that the decreases in Gibbs energy on forming the oxides are less. The importance of kinetics as a complement to thermodynamics is evident.

The oxides first form as a thin transparent layer. On further oxidation the film thickens and interference colours may appear. When the oxide coat becomes thick enough it may flake off, especially on cooling. For polyvalent metals such as iron or copper, a series of oxidized layers may form, becoming more oxidized the farther from the pure metal surface. At high temperature the arrangement of iron oxide layers may be different from that at low temperature, where the FeO layer is missing. On a really corroded piece of iron the various layers can be recognized by colour or analysis, and in the case of Fe_3O_4 by its magnetic property.

The growth of metal oxide films has been studied kinetically by observing the increase in mass per unit area of surface with time. The three rate laws of most importance in the corrosion of metals by gases are those already described in Section 24-8. A parabolic growth rate results when the rate depends upon the rate of diffusion of metal through the oxide layer. A logarithmic rate law arises where the rate determining step is the jump of metal ions from metal to metal oxide. A linear growth rate is the case where after a short period of film formation, the film cracks or peels to expose fresh metal. The process is then repeated, yielding a series of parabolas which combine to give a pseudo-linear effect. Parabolic rates are more common at high temperature, examples being iron, nickel and copper. Logarithmic rates are more common at lower temperatures.

Most metal oxides exhibit lattice deficiencies. Cu_2O, NiO and FeO are examples of oxides found to be cation deficient. These oxide films grow by diffusion of cations from one vacancy to another to reach the surface and react with oxygen. On the other hand, where ionic and electronic conductance are poor, a thin protective oxide coat may be formed as in the case of aluminium and chromium.

25-2 AQUEOUS CORROSION: THERMODYNAMICS AND PASSIVATION

A metal in contact with an aqueous solution functions as an electrode. The potential of this electrode is a measure of the tendency of the metal to act as an anode and become oxidized when coupled with some other material, or with localized portions of the same metal which can act as cathodes. The anodic or

O_2
Fe_2O_3
Fe_3O_4
$Fe°$

low temperature

O_2
Fe_2O_3
Fe_3O_4
FeO
$Fe°$

high temperature

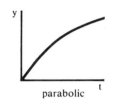

parabolic

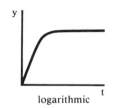

logarithmic

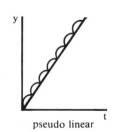

pseudo linear

Zn^{2+}	Zn^{2+}	Zn^{2+}
	Zn^{2+} + 2e	
Zn^{2+}	Zn^{2+}	Zn^{2+}
Zn^{2+}	Zn^{2+}	Zn^{2+}

cation excess

Cu^+	Cu^+	Cu^+
Cu^+	Cu^+	Cu^+
Cu^+		Cu^+

cation deficient

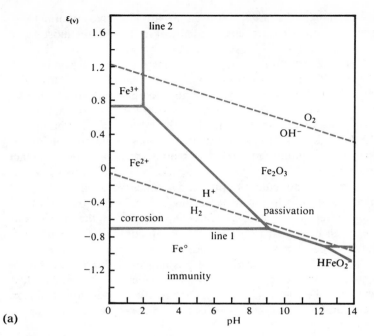

(a)

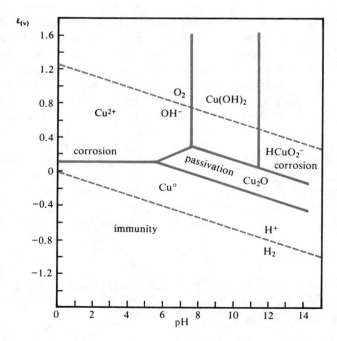

(b)

Figure 25-1   Pourbaix Diagrams.

corrosive half-reaction can be represented,

$$M_1 \rightarrow M_1{}^{z+} + ze$$

where M_1 is the metal corroded; the emf of the galvanic corrosion cell formed,

$$E_{cell} = -\varepsilon_{anode} + \varepsilon_{cathode}$$

gives the driving force behind the process under equilibrium conditions. The values of ε in the above expression for both anode and cathode are considered as reduction potentials which explains the negative sign for the anode. The pH of the solution is also highly important, with corrosion usually more severe under acid conditions, or sometimes under strongly alkaline conditions. All of these effects can be represented on an ε/pH or Pourbaix diagram wherein the selection of the relative activity of an ion in solution is arbitrarily but conveniently taken as 10^{-6} at temperature 25°C. Figure 25-1 displays Pourbaix diagrams for four important metals (Fe, Cu, Zn, Al) with different corrosive tendencies under aqueous conditions. The ε/pH lines for the aqueous redox systems O_2/OH^- and H^+/H_2 are included for reference. Pourbaix's "Atlas of Electrochemical Equilibria" contains such plots for all the elements, as well as accompanying diagrams specifically adapted for corrosion studies. It is a scientific treasury of combined redox and pH information. However, it is important to realize that these diagrams are all developed from thermodynamic data and so serve to show the equilibrium position to which a system *can* possibly go. For a complete comprehension of corrosion, kinetic studies are also essential.

On the iron diagram of Figure 25-1(a), points on line (1) represent the potential of iron metal, Fe°, acting in electrical contact with an aqueous solution of Fe^{2+} of relative activity 10^{-6}. It can be seen that this potential is not pH dependent. Below this line is the *immunity* domain wherein the metal is stable and immune to corrosion at these potentials. If to the Fe is applied a potential more negative than the value on line (1) (for example by contact with zinc metal) the iron system will act cathodically and the zinc anodically,

$$Zn° \rightarrow Zn^{2+} + 2e; \qquad Fe^{2+} + 2e \rightarrow Fe°$$

so that the iron is protected at the expense of the zinc. Of course the relative tendencies of various metals to act as cathodes (under standard conditions) are given in a table of standard reduction potentials. Conversely, if a more positive potential is applied, such as by the presence of an oxidant like O_2 or Cu°, then the iron system will act anodically, the Fe° being corroded, with the O_2 or Cu° acting cathodically. The vertical lines on the ε/pH diagram, such as line (2) on Figure 25-1(a), represent insolubility equilibria involving hydroxides or insoluble oxides of the metals with the metal ions at relative activity 10^{-6}. The formation of these hydroxides (or hydrous oxides) as coatings on the metal must impede the corrosion process by denying access to the metal surface by the electrolyte solution. The domains where these hydroxides prevail are designated as regions of *passivation*. Obviously the effectiveness of passivation will depend on the integrity of the hydroxide coating. Domains where the free ions Fe^{2+}, Fe^{3+}, and $HFeO_2^-$ prevail are regions where the effects of corrosion are worst, as these areas represent the solubilization of the

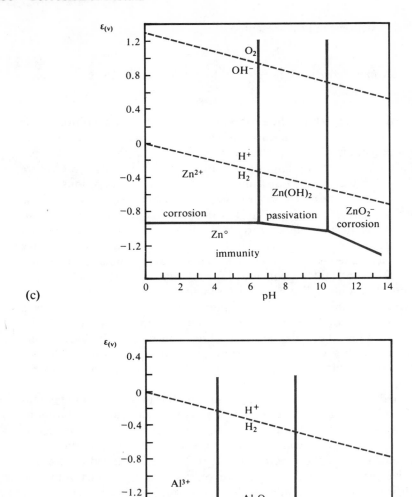

Figure 25-1 Pourbaix Diagrams.

metal, usually at low pH and high ε; but iron is also prone to corrode at high pH (>12) by formation of the bihypoferrite ion, $HFeO_2^-$.

In Figure 25-1(b) it will be observed that Cu° has a much higher domain of immunity than Fe°, in keeping with its recognized nobility and high value of ε°. Here too is a region of passivation in the pH range where the $Cu(OH)_2$ is formed, but again corrosion can occur at high pH (>12) owing to the formation of $HCuO_2^-$, as well as at low pH. The ε/pH diagrams for zinc and aluminium are similar in that the immunity domains are lower than for iron and copper, both have regions of passivation owing to hydrous oxide formation, and both have soluble anionic corrosion products at high pH. The domains are summarized below.

Domain	Action	Comment
Immunity	Metal cannot dissolve	Thermodynamics forbids
Corrosion	Metal does dissolve	Corrosion occurs
Passivation	Metal dissolution is hindered	Thermodynamics permits but kinetics retards

To form a complete corrosion cell, possible cathodic reactions which may accompany the anodic corrosion of a given metal are listed below. In air, with both O_2 and H_2O present, the first of these processes is the most likely. In the fourth possibility listed, M_2 represents a metal which is more noble than the anodic metal, M_1. The corrosion of the metal M_1 can be formulated in each case as follows (for a 2 electron change):

Anode Reaction	Cathode Reaction	Cell Reaction
$M_1{}^\circ \rightarrow M_1{}^{2+} + 2e$	$\frac{1}{2} O_2 + H_2O + 2e \rightarrow 2\,OH^-$	$M_1{}^\circ + \frac{1}{2} O_2 + H_2O \rightarrow M_1{}^{2+} + 2\,OH^-$
$M_1{}^\circ \rightarrow M_1{}^{2+} + 2e$	$2\,H_2O + 2e \rightarrow H_2 + 2\,OH^-$	$M_1{}^\circ + 2\,H_2O \rightarrow M_1{}^{2+} + 2\,OH^- + H_2$
$M_1{}^\circ \rightarrow M_1{}^{2+} + 2e$	$2\,H^+ + 2e \rightarrow H_2$	$M_1{}^\circ + 2\,H^+ \rightarrow M_1{}^{2+} + H_2$
$M_1{}^\circ \rightarrow M_1{}^{2+} + 2e$	$M_2{}^{2+} + 2e \rightarrow M_2{}^\circ$	$M_1{}^\circ + M_2{}^{2+} \rightarrow M_1{}^{2+} + M_2{}^\circ$

The potential of the important O_2/OH^- electrode at 25°C is theoretically given by,

$$\varepsilon_{O_2/OH^-} = \varepsilon^\circ_{O_2/OH^-} + \frac{0.0592}{2} \log \frac{(P_{O_2}/P^\circ)^{\frac{1}{2}}}{a^2_{OH^-}} \; ; \text{where } \varepsilon^\circ_{O_2/OH^-} = 0.403 \text{ V}$$

The above equation signifies that the potential is a function of P_{O_2}, being more cathodic the higher the value. Furthermore, if there are different values of P_{O_2} at different points on the same metal, a cell emf can arise owing to this *differential oxygenation or aeration*. One arrangement leading to differential aeration will arise when the surface of the metal is partially restricted from

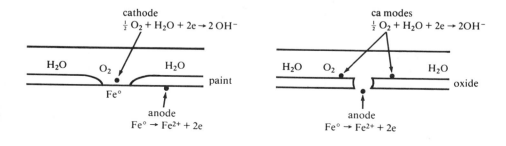

contact with air by virtue of an incomplete protective coating, such as a coat of paint. On the other hand, the oxide coat on a piece of metal may act as the cathode with the anode being located at a crack in the oxide film. It is assumed in the latter case that the oxide can act as an electrode and conduct electrons. The ultimate corrosion product in the case of iron will be rust by reason of the incompletely balanced reactions below.

$$Fe^{2+}(aq) \xrightarrow{O_2} Fe^{3+}(aq) + 3\,OH^-(aq) \rightarrow \underset{rust}{Fe_2O_3} \cdot xH_2O(c)$$

If the oxygen content of the electrolyte is high, the rust forms as a porous coating near the anode; if low, precipitation of rust occurs farther away and passivation is not possible. Also the presence of dissolved ions in the solution will enhance the conductance and increase the rate and extent of corrosion.

Where the oxide layer serves to protect the metal, as with aluminium, a somewhat thicker layer of controlled porosity may be intentionally developed as a protective coat. *Anodizing* is an electrochemical process by which metals such as aluminium, titanium and tantalum are purposely made the anode and, under controlled potential and acidity, oxidized to form an oxide layer of particular thickness and porosity. In the case of aluminium a typical bath might consist of 5-10% H_2SO_4, 3-10% CrO_3, 2-5% $H_2C_2O_4$ to give a suitably porous structure of alumina, with an impervious base layer next to the metal. The pores can be impregnated with dyes to produce a desired colour and the whole layer sealed by expansion on exposure to steam. Inhibitors can also be sealed in the pores.

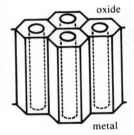

oxide

metal

25-3 EFFECT OF POLARIZATION ON RATE OF CORROSION IN AQUEOUS SOLUTION

We have seen that in aqueous solution a galvanic corrosion cell can develop in which one part of the system acts as an anode and becomes corroded, while another part of the system functions as a cathode. For such a cell the emf or maximum potential is established only on open circuit or when negligible current is allowed to flow in the cell circuit. The rate of corrosion is proportional to the current density and this, in turn, is proportional to the cell potential. The cell potential is in part determined by a purely thermodynamic quantity, the cell emf, but if any current actually flows, a number of purely kinetic factors come into play. These factors, which reduce the cell potential and alter the rate, are listed below.

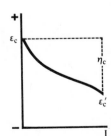

1. Both the anode and cathode reactions may have an energy of activation which decreases the potential difference by an amount known as activation polarization or overvoltage.

2. Concentration gradients may develop in solution which limit the supply or removal of ions and hence limit the flow of current from the cell reaction. This effect is termed concentration polarization.

3. Internally and externally the electric cell must have some resistance to current flow and this will reduce the potential difference obtained from the cell by an amount known as the IR drop.

All of the above factors may be involved in a given corrosion process. In a case where a gas is involved in the electrode process, energy of activation has to be 'localized' for the gaseous process to occur and the slow nature of the electrode reaction is apt to cause activation polarization unless a good catalyst is present. When metallic oxidation or reduction is involved as the electrode process, concentration polarization rather than activation polarization is likely to dominate, especially if access to the electrode is poor and stirring is absent. Under marine conditions where ions are plentiful the limiting slow process is unlikely to be conduction in the cell; but in a terrestrial environment, particularly where dry as in a desert, the galvanic cell reaction may be prevented or slowed drastically by high cell resistance. Motor cars last considerably longer where salt is not used on the roads in winter.

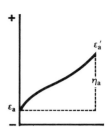

Whatever the cause or combination of factors causing polarization in a galvanic cell, as the current is increased the effect at the cathode will be for the potential to become less cathodic (less positive) by an amount known as the cathodic polarization, η_c, and the effect at the anode will be for the potential to become less anodic (less negative) by an amount known as the anodic polarization, η_a. Both cathodic and anodic polarization can occur in the same cell and the contribution of the IR drop can be included as well. The emf of the cell, $E_{cell} = -\varepsilon_a + \varepsilon_c$, is the potential difference measured on open circuit (I = 0). The potential difference of the cell obtained when an actual current, I', flows is less than the emf and is given by,

$$\varepsilon_c' - \varepsilon_a' = \varepsilon_c - \varepsilon_a - \eta_c + \eta_a$$

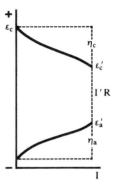

The drop in potential, $I'R$, will depend on the total resistance in the corrosion cell circuit, both internal and external. Had the cathodic and anodic polarization terms been less severe, η_c and η_a would have been smaller, $\varepsilon_c' - \varepsilon_a'$ would have been larger, and the current passed would have been larger. Of course if ε_c' and ε_a' pertain to the same cell, the current I' must be the same throughout the cell and apply to both anode and cathode. Severe polarization thus restricts the current flow, the rate of the cell reaction, and rate of corrosion.

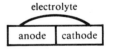

A particular corrosion situation can be depicted in which a more noble metal and less noble metal are touching, or these could be even more cathodic and less cathodic parts of the same metal. Since the metals touch and are connected by electrolyte, the resistance must be minimal and the current maximal; in fact the cell is short-circuited. The total potential drop is equal to the cathodic and anodic polarization terms, and the current, which again must be the same for both cathode and anode, is given by the intersection of the polarization curves and termed I_{max}. It is also called the corrosion current, I_{corr}. The potential measured on these connected metals, ε_{corr}, termed the corrosion potential, will be a mixed potential, having a value somewhere between the reversible electrode potentials for the cathode, ε_c, and anode, ε_a.

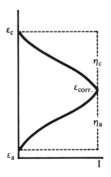

The curves depicting the polarization have been merely sketched. It would be important to know the actual shape of these curves and to be able to write equations for them. Progress has been made for the two cases of activation polarization and concentration polarization. That for the latter is a form of the Nernst equation which is not included here. It is sigmoidal. However, in an experimental study of the activation polarization involved in gas evolution on a number of metals of different known catalytic ability, Tafel found a linear relationship between polarization, η, and current density, i, expressed by the commonly used "Tafel equation,"

$$\eta = a - b \log i$$

where i, the current density, is the current per unit area, I/A, and a and b are constants characteristic of the metal surface. Furthermore a theoretical kinetic treatment according to the concepts of activation energy has reproduced the above equation and evaluated the constants. While the Tafel equation in many cases is valid over a large range of current densities, activation polarization is not the whole story and the curves can be complex. Thus the limiting process at low values of η may well not be the same one at high values of η. Particularly at low values of η the Tafel equation breaks down and η is often found to be directly proportional to i. Further, at high values of η, i is often found to become concentration limited owing to the restricted supply of one of the reactants such as oxygen. For the above reasons the curves in the diagrams have been represented as having complex shapes.

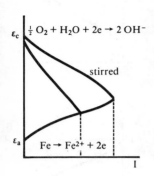

Oxygen reduction will often constitute the reaction at the cathode of a corrosion cell. In neutral or alkaline solution the supply of oxygen to the cathode becomes rate controlling and the polarization at the cathode is large when the supply of oxygen becomes low, as with no stirring or mixing. Stirring moves more oxygen to the cathode, reduces the polarization, and permits higher current and rate of corrosion. In strongly acid solution the cathodic reaction of importance is

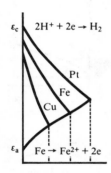

$$2\,H^+ + 2e \rightarrow H_2$$

This process can be controlled by the surface properties of a number of metals such as platinum, iron and copper.

Anodic control by polarization is also possible whereby in aerated solution oxide layers coat the anode, passivating the corrosion by limiting access of the electrolyte to the metal. Oxides of the various metals have different efficiencies in passivation, with aluminium and stainless steel oxide layers being most effective in that they have higher potentials than do the corresponding pure metals, as well as steeper polarization curves. Nevertheless certain ions such as the halides attack the oxide film in places which permit local corrosion. Empirical tests have shown some stainless steels to be better than others for salt water use, although titanium has the best resistance to sea water of all metals.

Corrosion rates have been studied by means of electrical measurements. One method controls the potential applied to a metallic specimen by means of a potentiostat and measures the current density which develops at the metal surface to maintain that potential. Plots of $\varepsilon_{applied}$ and log i produce curves of the type shown. Anodic dissolution begins at A and log i rises linearly with $\varepsilon_{applied}$ along what is called the Tafel line at B until passivation due to oxide formation sets in at C with a sharp halt in current density and sudden reduction to a minimum at D, at a potential, ε_F, called the Flade potential, after which increase in potential is not at once accompanied by increased current density. At high enough potential, that for oxygen evolution is reached, with attendant increase in current at E. Metals easily passivated like chromium and aluminium

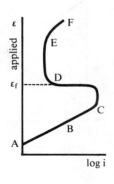

have low Flade potentials while that for iron is higher. Especially at the anode current density is important. A small anode coupled to a large cathode effects extensive damage with severe pitting. Milder damage would result from the use of a small cathode with large anode. The above might be termed an electrical picture of anodic corrosion.

25-4 ABATEMENT OF CORROSION

Under most common environmental conditions the total elimination of corrosion is not likely except in particular situations which warrant large investment in expensive metals, alloys, and controlled environment. The challenge will usually be to minimize the losses owing to the corrosion of less expensive materials. Below are listed some of the main principles employed in corrosion control:

1. Contact between dissimilar metals should be avoided, particularly contact with a more noble metal such as copper in the case of iron. If dissimilar metals are mandatory they should be insulated by spacers. When only one metal is involved, inhomogeneities arrising from mechanical treatment and protective coatings should be kept to a minimum.

2. Choice of metals and alloys should be made to best suit the particular corrosive environment. For example, under oxidizing conditions, stainless steels and titanium are resistant to acid conditions because of oxide layer formation; but these oxide coats may be damaged under less oxidizing conditions, where Monel metal (an alloy of Cu and Ni) would be a better choice. Under strongly alkaline conditions iron, aluminium and zinc are all badly attacked, but magnesium and nickel are fairly resistant to attack.

3. Removal of oxygen and air from solution eliminates the most likely natural cathodic reaction as well as the tendency for differential aeration.

4. Contact with aggressive electrolytes should be avoided or minimized.

5. Under atmospheric conditions corrosion is very dependent on the relative humidity. At high humidity a layer of water is adsorbed on the metal surface. If the air can be dried the corrosion can be greatly reduced. Air contaminants such as sulphur dioxide, sulphur trioxide, chlorine, and oxides of nitrogen enhance the corrosion effects.

6. Anodic inhibitors may be used to stifle the anodic process. These include sodium hydroxide, carbonate, silicate, borate, and phosphates. All produce alkaline solutions, with OH^- present to contact Fe^{2+} at the point of attack by the anodic process in order to repair the film by formation of hydrous oxides. In acid solution chromate compounds are used to oxidize metal ions to form insoluble oxide films.

7. Cathodic inhibitors include magnesium and zinc sulphates. The cations react with OH^- produced by the reduction of oxygen at the cathode to form insoluble $Mg(OH)_2$ and $Zn(OH)_2$, both of which are capable of smothering the cathode process and are non-conductors. Also effective is $Ca(HCO_3)_2$ which with OH^- forms $CaCO_3$ to stifle the cathode process.

8. Restrainers impede but do not stop the anodic process. They are organic substances including amines, pyridine, and substituted thioureas which coat the anode surface by adsorption.

9. Protective metallic coatings can be applied by cladding, dipping, spraying, plating, and cementing. Coatings of more noble metals must be complete, otherwise the noble metal will act as a cathode and promote the anodic attack of the partly covered metal. Coatings of baser but kinetically less corrodable metals, like chromium and zinc, will act as anodes even if a hole in the coating is present. This technique overlaps that termed cathodic polarization.

10. Non-metallic coatings include oxide films produced by deliberately anodizing the surface of metals like aluminium and titanium, as well as other inorganic substances which form glassy coats or enamels. Organic coatings include oils and greases, tar, bitumen, and a variety of modern plastics. Ordinary paints inhibit corrosion because they act as non-conductors and slow down access to the metal by oxygen, water, and electrolyte. The surface cleaning and preparation prior to painting is most crucial. Some paints contain anodic inhibitors such as zinc chromate or red lead. The technology of protective coatings is vast. Specific treatises should be consulted for details.

11. The principle behind cathodic protection is to force the protected metal to become cathodic by purposely providing a more active metal to act as the anode, and to locate this sacrificial anode where it can be inspected and replaced when required. Cathodic protection has been extensively

Figure 25-2

employed in the case of ships, piers, buried piping and cables, underground tanks, and household hot water tanks. A more direct method of making the protected metal the cathode is to apply a direct-current supply which has the negative terminal attached to the protected structure and the positive to a replaceable anode which is immersed or buried nearby.

12. Mechanical abuse of a metal product in its formation or subsequently may cause corrosion. Examples are stresses applied to the metal from within or without, fatigue by persistent flexing, fretting, rivetting, as well as scratching. In all cases a protective coat may be injured and the underlying metal act anodically to extend the injury into a bad crack. Anodic regions can be detected on ordinary nails made from steel wire, at the point and head where the metal has been deformed, as well as on the threads and heads of steel screws and bolts. Stresses can be relieved at some cost by annealling, but all the art, skill and science of the metallurgist are required, for even the different orientation of crystal faces at grain boundaries cause these regions to be more anodic than metal in the body of the crystal.

13. Design of structure is important in avoiding corrosion at crevices and restricted places which act anodically, and in planning access to proper welds and bolted connections, well spaced for painting and insulated where required. A drainage design which does not allow water and dust to accumulate is important, for example in automobiles. Choice of materials and how they are arranged, protected and joined should be well planned in advance.

25-5 SOME EXEMPLARY STUDIES

1. Panels designed for the absorption of solar energy were constructed of copper to avoid corrosion. The panels contained a heat conducting fluid, propylene glycol. After some months of operation the liquid was analyzed by atomic absorption spectrophotometry to detect traces of metals dissolved by corrosive action. Significant amounts of tin and lead were found but not copper. It was realized that the source of the tin and lead was the soft Sn/Pb solder by which the inlet and outlet tubes had been attached. Silver solder was used instead and proved more satisfactory but expensive. Aluminium panels were substituted both for economy and ease of fabrication without joints. The panels are sealed and the air is removed to avoid possible oxygen cathodes. However, hydrogen has been detected as a cathode product and some pitting has been observed on the aluminium as anode. Choice of the particular aluminium alloy, both for corrosion and erosion (wear due to flow), is under investigation.

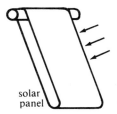

solar panel

2. An East Coast city board of works became discouraged with replacing the sheet steel eavestroughing on its public buildings, necessitated by the aggressive maritime climate, and went to the expense of installing copper troughs. Unfortunately steel fasteners were used for strength and con-

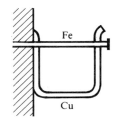

Fe

Cu

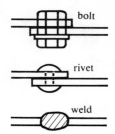

venience. The relatively small fasteners became intensely anodic and lasted only a short time.

The solution lies in assuring that the fastening is somewhat cathodic or in properly insulating the dissimilar metals. Metals are joined by bolting, rivetting, soldering, and welding. In all these cases the material at the joint is smaller than the adjacent parts and being crucial to the security of the joint should not be allowed to become anodic. Crevices and inaccessible spaces should be avoided.

3. The cause of pitting of such corrosion resistant materials as stainless steel and aluminium alloys is not well understood but it must bear some relation to inhomogeneities or gaps in the protective oxide film on the metal. Once formed, the action of the propagation of the attack can be pictured. The oxide layer on the metal acts as the cathode with the reaction

$$\tfrac{1}{2} O_2 + H_2O + 2e \rightarrow 2\,OH^-$$

occurring there. At some break in the oxide layer the anodic process occurs, for example,

$$Fe^\circ \rightarrow Fe^{2+} + 2e$$

whereby metal goes into solution, forming a hole or pit. As the metal ion, for example Fe^{2+}, diffuses out it meets the OH^- ions from the cathode process and forms a precipitate,

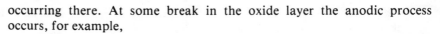

$$Fe^{2+} + 2\,OH^- \rightarrow Fe(OH)_2 \xrightarrow{O_2} Fe(OH)_3$$

at a place where the anodic attack is not passivated, and in fact eats deeper into the metal. The presence of the oxide film as cathode prevents lateral spreading of the pit. Chloride ions are particularly apt to promote pitting, probably by damage of the oxide film.

4. Particularly in Canada many thousands of kilometres of pipelines have been laid in inaccessible places under severe climatic conditions. Pipelines may be in some cases buried or partially buried with different sections in such diverse terrain as sand, clay, gravel, and marshland, as well as under roads. Where the pipe is hardest to get at is where it is likely to be most anodic and corroded. The solution is to use a pattern of well placed sacrificial anodes buried alongside to enforce cathodic protection of the pipe. The pipes are normally covered with a protective coating so that only the gaps in the protective coat need protection. This keeps the current low and saves on the sacrificial anode. The anodes must be inspected periodically and replaced as necessary.

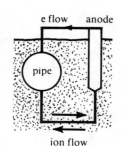

5. In a marine environment experiments have shown that, on combining separate couples of metals and alloys, the normal electrochemical series is sometimes not followed. Rather the following practical "sea water" galvanic series has been adapted from "Principles of Metallic Corrosion" by J.P. Chilton, with decreasing nobility from the top down:

Titanium	Lead
Monel	Stainless steel, active
Stainless steel, passivated	Cast iron
Silver	Mild steel
Nickel	Aluminium
Copper	Zinc
Brass	Magnesium
Tin	

The difference in galvanic activity between passivated and active stainless steels is noteworthy. This implies that in a passivated specimen, if the oxide layer becomes damaged, the injury will be anodic and a galvanic corrosion cell will be constituted. Sea water is an especially aggressive environment both because of high conductivity owing to the ionic content, and the presence of a high concentration of chloride ion, which is particularly destructive to otherwise passive oxide films.

SUMMARY

Corrosion of a metal is a harmful reaction by which the metal becomes oxidized. It is a spontaneous process which occurs naturally with the metal going back to an original oxide form. The stability of metal oxides can be studied by comparing their standard Gibbs' energies of formation, yielding an order analogous to the usual electrochemical series. Kinetic experiments on the rate of growth of different oxide films in air under different conditions have given rate laws which are parabolic, logarithmic, and linear, as well as more complicated functions. Conduction of matter and charge through the oxide film is necessary for growth.

Metal in contact with an aqueous solution can constitute a galvanic corrosion cell with metal being attacked or oxidized at the anode. Coupled to this is a cathodic reaction which most often is the aqueous reduction of oxygen from air. The higher the partial pressure or concentration of oxygen the greater the tendency for this last reaction to occur at a cathode. The differential exposure of metal to air or oxygen is capable of producing a potential difference and causing galvanic attack of metal at the anode.

The reduction potential, ε, for a particular metal is a measure of its tendency to act cathodically and go to the reduced form and so is a measure of the nobility of the metal. Plots of ε versus pH are called Pourbaix diagrams. These map out the regions of stability of the various species of the metal. The condition under which the pure metal is stable is called a region of immunity; that where the aqueous metal ion is dominant is a region of corrosion; and that where an oxide film impedes corrosion is termed a region of passivation. Valuable as the above are in corrosion studies, they are strictly applicable only under equilibrium conditions, when electric current flow is negligible.

Under real, dynamic conditions in a galvanic corrosion cell, current does flow and is taken as a measure of the rate of corrosion. With appreciable current flow the cell becomes polarized, the potential difference is less than the emf, and the cell process becomes limited in one of two ways:

(1) The electrode reaction is slow in the absence of catalysis, requiring activation. This is termed activation polarization.

(2) The diffusion of electrode-active ions to and from the electrode is slow in the absence of stirring. This is concentration polarization.

The curves for the electrode potential, ε, at a polarized electrode as a function of current or current density have been studied for both activation and concentration polarization and the utilization of these polarization curves allows some kinetic control of corrosion rate to be exercised. Also on passage of current the cell develops an IR drop both internally and in the external circuit which also diminishes the cell potential difference. Thus high resistance retards corrosion.

For control or at least minimization of corrosion the following should be avoided:

Contact between dissimilar metals   Strong acid or base
Inhomogeneities in the same metal   Uneven coatings
Differential aeration   Mechanical abuse
Aggressive electrolytes   High conductivity
High humidity   Poor drainage design

Both metallic and organic coatings have been applied to protect metal surfaces and specific substances are available for inhibiting and restraining cathodic and anodic reactions. Cathodic protection is achieved by purposely arranging a more active metal to serve as a sacrificial anode.

FURTHER READING

Principles of Metallic Corrosion, J.P. Chilton, Royal Institute of Chemistry (London, 1961)
An excellent book for both principles and practical details, and very readable as an introduction to the subject.

The Fundamentals of Corrosion, J.C. Scully, Pergamon Press (Oxford, 1975)
This book is intermediate in difficulty and is more extensive.

An Introduction to Metallic Corrosion, Ulick R. Evans, Edward Arnold (London, 1965)
A classic treatise, written by a leading authority.

APPENDIX 1

THERMOCHEMICAL TABLES

All values refer to the standard state. Excellent descriptions of the standard states may be found in all of the four sources listed below. These four provided almost all of the data in these tables. Wherever a datum was available in more than one source, that from the higher listed source is used.

1. CODATA Recommended Key Values for Thermodynamics, CODATA Bulletin Number 28, Paris, France 1978. This is a list of internationally accepted values for a small number of substances. It is being extended continually. Both ΔH_f° and S° are listed.

2. Sussex — N.P.L. Computer Analyzed Thermochemical Data for Organic and Organometallic Compounds. J.B. Pedley and J. Rylance, University of Sussex, England, 1977. This table provides an extensive list of ΔH_f° values.

3. National Bureau of Standards, Washington, D.C., U.S.A.
(a) Selected Thermochemical Data Compatible with CODATA Recommendations, 1976
(b) Chemical Thermodynamic Properties of Compounds of Sodium, Potassium and Rubidium, 1976
(c) Technical Notes 270-3, 1968; 270-4, 1969; 270-5, 1971; 270-6, 1971, and 270-7, 1973
This is an extensive and important collection concerned mainly with inorganic compounds. ΔH_f°, ΔG_f°, S° and C_p are all listed. Unfortunately, data are in calories.

4. Selected Values of Properties of Hydrocarbons and Related Compounds, Thermodynamics Research Center, API 44 Hydrocarbon Project, Texas A & M University, College Station, Texas, U.S.A. This work provides a continually updated source for the important set of compounds described in the title. Again, values are in calories.

Problems arise in the selection of data, even when the sources are confined to such authoritative and critically evaluated tables as those above. CODATA, while up-to-date and meticulously prepared, omits many numbers of interest to chemists. Adding these from the other sources introduces a problem of internal inconsistency. Typically the calculation of a new entry in the thermochemical tables involves combining one or more new measurements on the material of interest with accepted data for other compounds. For example, all entries for organic compounds depend on the accepted values for $H_2O(l)$ and $CO_2(g)$. When an entry in a table is changed, all of those entries which depended on it in their calculation must be changed too. These in turn generate other changes. N.P.L. and others are developing computer methods of accomplishing these changes automatically. The relevance of this to selecting data from multiple sources is that those data drawn from older tables may be based on older values of certain entries than those shown. While each of the four sources is internally consistent, they are not necessarily completely consistent with one another, and these minor inconsistencies will be found in the table below.

In the matter of significant figures, some sources give tolerances on each entry and some do not. In the table below, most entries are quoted in such a way that the last figure is in doubt. For example, CODATA gives ΔH_f° for $SnO_2(c)$ as $-580.78 \pm .40$ kJ mol^{-1}. We quote this as -580.8 kJ. Departures from this policy occur only when the author's attention lapses.

Finally a word must be added about the order of presentation. All large tabulations follow a well established order which is well suited to large tabulations but which is hard to remember for casual users and new students. In the table below we have adopted an arbitrary order which is not completely logical but which has proven to be simple for student use. The rules are the following. Elements are listed in alphabetical order. Compounds containing a metal are listed under the metal, e.g. NaCl under sodium. Compounds with two or more metals are under that which occurs first alphabetically, e.g. KMnO$_4$ under manganese. Compounds of carbon, except metal carbonates and organometallics, are under carbon e.g. CS$_2$ under carbon. As to other non-metals, compounds with oxygen and/or hydrogen are listed under the non-metal while those few cases of compounds with other non-metals are usually listed under the more electropositive of the two, e.g. SiCl$_4$ under silicon and XeF$_4$ under xenon. All oxides are listed under the elements with which it is combined, as are all compounds of hydrogen except water, e.g. Cl$_2$O under chlorine and HCl under chlorine.

All entries are for standard states at 25°C and P°.

Formula	ΔH_f° kJ mol^{-1}	ΔG_f° kJ mol^{-1}	S° J K^{-1} mol^{-1}	C_p° J K^{-1} mol^{-1}
Aluminium				
Al (c)	0.0	0.0	28.35	24.4
(g)	330	286	164.44	21.4
Al^{3+} (aq)	-538	-491	—	—
Al$_2$O$_3$ (c,α)	-1676	-1582	50.9	79.0
AlF$_3$ (c)	-1510	-1431	66.5	75.1
AlCl$_3$ (c)	-704.2	-628.9	110.7	91.8
AlI$_3$ (c)	-313.8	-300.8	159	98.7
Al$_2$(SO$_4$)$_3$ (c)	-3440.8	-3100.1	239.2	259.4
AlPO$_4$ (c, berlinite)	-1733.9	-1601.2	90.79	93.2
(CH$_3$)$_3$Al (l)	-151	-10.0	209	155.6
Al(BH$_4$)$_3$ (l)	-16.3	144.8	289	194.6
Al$_2$SiO$_5$ (c, andalusite)	-2744.3	-2597.4	93.22	122.7
(c, kyanite)	-2746.4	-2596.2	83.81	121.7
(c, sillimanite)	-2772.3	-2625.9	96.19	122.6
Antimony				
Sb (c)	0.0	0.0	45.69	25.1
Sb$_4$O$_6$ (c, cubic)	-1440	-1268	221	—
(c, orthorhombic)	-1417	-1253	246	202.7
Sb$_2$O$_5$ (c)	-971.9	-829.3	125.1	—
SbH$_3$ (g)	145.11	147.7	232.7	41.0
SbCl$_3$ (g)	-314	-301	337.7	76.7
(c)	-382.0	-323.7	184.1	107.9
Argon				
Ar (g)	0.0	0.0	154.732	20.786
Arsenic				
As (c, gray)	0.0	0.0	35.1	24.7
(g)	288	261.1	174.1	20.9
As$_4$ (g)	144	92.5	314	—
As$_4$O$_6$ (c, octahedral)	-1313.9	-1152.5	214	191.3
(c, monoclinic)	-1309.6	-1154.0	234	—
As$_2$O$_5$ (c)	-924.9	-782.4	105.4	116.5
AsH$_3$ (g)	66.4	68.9	222.7	38.1
AsF$_3$ (g)	-920.647	-905.669	288.99	65.6
(l)	-956.253	-909.141	181.21	126.6
Barium				
Ba (c)	0.0	0.0	62.8	28.1
Ba^{2+} (aq)	-537.6	-560.7	—	—
BaO (c)	-554	-525	70.4	47.8
BaF$_2$ (c)	-1215	-1165	96.4	71.2
BaCl$_2$ (c)	-859	-810	123.7	75.1

Formula	ΔH_f° kJ mol^{-1}	ΔG_f° kJ mol^{-1}	S° J K^{-1} mol^{-1}	C_p° J K^{-1} mol^{-1}
Barium, continued				
$BaSO_4$ (c)	−1473	−1362	132	101.8
$Ba(NO_3)_2$ (c)	−992.1	−796.7	214	151.4
$BaCO_3$ (c)	−1216	−1138	112	85.4
Beryllium				
Be (c)	0.0	0.0	9.50	16.4
BeO (c)	−609	−580	13.77	25.5
$BeCl_2$ (c, α)	−490	−446	82.7	64.9
(c, β)	−496	−449	75.8	62.4
$BeSO_4$ (c, tetragonal)	−1205.2	−1093.9	77.9	85.7
Bismuth				
Bi (c)	0.0	0.0	56.74	25.5
Bi_2O_3 (c)	−573.9	−493.7	151.5	113.5
$BiCl_3$ (g)	−265.7	−256.1	358.7	79.7
(c)	−379.1	−315.1	177.0	104.6
Boron				
B (c)	0.0	0.0	5.90	11.1
(g)	560	516	153.33	—
B_2O_3 (c)	−1273.5	−1194.4	53.97	62.9
B_2H_6 (g)	36	86.6	232.0	56.9
B_5H_9 (l)	42.7	171.7	184.2	151.1
(g)	73.2	174.9	275.8	96.8
BF_3 (g)	−1136.0	−1119.4	254.3	50.5
BCl_3 (g)	−403.8	−388.7	290.0	62.7
(l)	−427	−387	206	107.1
BBr_3 (g)	−205.6	−232.5	324.1	67.8
(l)	−239.7	−238	229.7	—
$(CH_3)_3N \cdot BH_3$ (c)	−142.5	70.5	187	—
(g)	−84.9	87.0	325	128.0
Bromine				
Br_2 (l)	0.0	0.0	152.21	75.7
(g)	30.91	3.14	245.35	36.0
Br (g)	111.86	82.43	174.90	20.79
Br^- (aq)	−121.5	−104.0	—	—
BrO (g)	125.8	108.2	237.44	32.1
BrF_3 (g)	−255.60	−229.45	292.42	66.61
BrF_5 (g)	−428.8	−350.6	320.08	99.62
Cadmium				
Cd (c, γ)	0.0	0.0	51.8	25.9
(g)	111.9	77.3	167.64	20.79
Cd^{2+} (aq)	−75.9	−77.7	—	—

Formula	ΔH_f° kJ mol^{-1}	ΔG_f° kJ mol^{-1}	S° J K^{-1} mol^{-1}	C_p° J K^{-1} mol^{-1}
Cadmium, continued				
CdO (c)	−258.1	−228	54.8	43.4
CdCl$_2$ (c)	−391.5	−344.0	115.3	74.7
CdCl$_2 \cdot$ H$_2$O (c)	−688.4	−587.06	167.8	—
CdBr$_2$ (c)	−316.2	−296.3	137.2	76.7
CdI$_2$ (c)	−203	−201.4	161.1	80.0
CdS (c)	−161.9	−156.5	64.9	55.2
CdSO$_4$ (c)	−933.38	−822.78	123.04	99.6
Caesium				
Cs (c)	0.0	0.0	85.2	31.0
Cs$^+$ (aq)	−258.0	−291.7	—	—
CsCl (c)	−442.7	−414.2	101.2	52.7
CsBr (c)	−405.7	−391.0	112	51.9
CsI (c)	−348	−342	123	51.9
Calcium				
Ca (c)	0.0	0.0	41.6	25.3
Ca^{2+} (aq)	−541.3	−552.8	—	—
CaO (c)	−635.1	−603.5	38.1	42.8
Ca(OH)$_2$ (c)	−986.1	−898.6	83.39	87.5
CaCl$_2$ (c)	−796	−748	105	72.6
CaSO$_4$ (c, α)	−1425.2	−1313.5	108	100.2
(c, β)	−1420.8	−1309.0	108	99.0
CaC$_2$ (c)	−59.8	−64.9	70.0	62.72
CaCO$_3$ (c, calcite)	−1206.9	−1128.8	92.9	81.9
(c, aragonite)	−1207.2	−1127.8	88.7	81.3
Carbon				
C (c, graphite)	0.0	0.0	5.740	8.527
(c, diamond)	1.88	2.900	2.377	6.115
(g)	716.7	671.27	157.98	20.8
CO (g)	−110.53	−137.15	197.56	29.12
CO$_2$ (g)	−393.51	−394.37	213.68	37.1
CH$_4$ (g)	−74.5	−50.8	186.15	35.31
C$_2$H$_6$ (g)	−84.0	−32.9	229.5	52.6
C$_3$H$_8$ (g)	−104.5	−23.4	269.9	73.6
n−C$_4$H$_{10}$ (g)	−126.5	−17.15	310.1	97.4
n−C$_5$H$_{12}$ (g)	−146.5	−8.37	348.9	120.2
(l)	−173.2	−9.58	263.3	—
C$_5$H$_{12}$ (g, 2 methyl butane)	−153.8	−14.64	343.6	153.8
C$_5$H$_{12}$ (g, 2, 2 dimethyl propane)	−167.4	−15.22	306.4	—
n−C$_6$H$_{14}$ (g)	−167.1	−0.29	388.4	143.1
(l)	−198.6	−4.39	295.9	216

Formula	ΔH_f° kJ mol^{-1}	ΔG_f° kJ mol^{-1}	S° J K^{-1} mol^{-1}	C_p° J K^{-1} mol^{-1}
Carbon, continued				
n$-$C$_7$H$_{16}$ (g)	-187.5	8.03	427.8	166.0
(l)	-224.0	1.00	328.5	—
n$-$C$_8$H$_{18}$ (g)	-208.5	16.40	466.7	189
(l)	-250.0	6.36	361.2	276
n$-$C$_9$H$_{20}$ (g)	-228.4	24.81	505.7	211.7
(l)	-274.9	11.76	393.7	—
n$-$C$_{20}$H$_{42}$ (g)	-455.8	117.3	934.1	463
(l)	-556.6	71.6	749.2	—
C$_6$H$_{12}$ (l, cyclohexane)	-156.3	26.7	204.4	157.7
C$_2$H$_2$ (g)	228.0	209.2	200.8	43.9
C$_2$H$_4$ (g)	52.2	68.1	219.5	43.6
C$_3$H$_6$ (g)	20.2	62.72	266.9	64
C$_6$H$_6$ (g)	82.9	129.7	269.2	81.6
(l)	49.0	124.7	172	132
CH$_3$C$_6$H$_5$ (l)	12.00	114.1	219.6	160
CCl$_3$F (g)	-268	-238	309.8	78.1
(l)	$-301.$	-236.9	225.4	121.5
CCl$_2$F$_2$ (g)	-478	-439	300.7	72.3
CClF$_3$ (g)	-710	-653	285.2	66.9
CF$_4$ (g)	-934.5	-879	261.5	61.1
CCl$_4$ (g)	$-97.$	-60.6	309.7	83.3
(l)	-129.6	-65.3	216.4	131.8
CH$_3$Cl (g)	-82.0	-57.4	234.5	40.8
CH$_2$Cl$_2$ (g)	-95.7	-65.9	270.1	51.0
(l)	-124.1	-67.3	177.8	100
CHCl$_3$ (g)	-105	-70.4	295.6	65.7
(l)	-135.1	-73.7	201.7	113.8
C$_2$H$_5$Cl (g)	-112.1	-60.5	275.9	62.8
C$_2$Cl$_4$ (l)	-49	4.6	267	341
(g)	-9	22.6	341	94.9
C$_2$F$_4$ (g)	-661	-615.9	300	80.5
HCHO (g)	-108.7	-113	218.7	35.4
CH$_3$CHO (g, acetaldehyde)	-165.8	-128.9	250	57
(l, acetaldehyde)	-191.5	-128.2	160	275
HCOOH (l)	-425.0	-361.4	129.0	99.0
CH$_3$COOH (l)	-484.3	-390	159.8	124
CH$_3$OH (g)	-201.6	-162.0	239.7	43.9
(l)	-239.1	-166.4	126.8	81.6
C$_2$H$_5$OH (l)	-277.1	-174.9	160.7	111.5
C$_3$H$_7$OH (g, 1-propanol)	-254.8	-165	—	—
(l, 1-propanol)	-302.7	-173	—	—
COCl$_2$ (g)	-218	-205	283.4	57.7
CS$_2$ (g)	116.7	67.2	237.7	45.4
(l)	89.0	65.3	151.3	75.7

Formula	ΔH_f° kJ mol^{-1}	ΔG_f° kJ mol^{-1}	S° J K^{-1} mol^{-1}	C_p° J K^{-1} mol^{-1}
Carbon, continued				
$CO(NH_2)_2$ (c)	−333.7	−196.8	104.6	93.1
CO_3^{2-} (aq)	−675.2	−528	—	—
HCO_3^- (aq)	−689.9	−587	—	—
Chlorine				
Cl_2 (g)	0.0	0.0	222.965	33.91
Cl (g)	121.290	105.70	165.088	21.84
Cl^- (aq)	−167.08	−131.29	—	—
HCl (g)	−92.3	−95.3	186.79	29.1
ClF_3 (g)	−163	−123	281.5	63.85
Cl_2O (g)	80.3	97.9	266.1	45.40
ClO_2 (g)	103	120	256.7	41.97
Chromium				
Cr (c)	0.0	0.0	23.8	23.4
CrO_4^{2-} (aq)	−881.2	−727.8	—	—
$Cr_2O_7^{2-}$ (aq)	−1490	−1301	—	—
Cr_2O_3 (c)	−1139	−1058	81.2	118.7
$CrCl_2$ (c)	−395	−356	115.3	71.2
$CrCl_3$ (c)	−556	−486	123	91.8
Cobalt				
Co (c, hex)	0.0	0.0	30.0	24.8
(c, fcc)	0.5	0.3	30.7	—
Co^{2+} (aq)	−58	−54	—	—
CoO (c)	−237.9	−214.2	52.97	55.2
Co_3O_4 (c)	−891	−774	102.5	123
$CoCl_2$ (c)	−312.5	−269.9	109.2	78.5
Copper				
Cu (c)	0.0	0.0	33.15	24.4
(g)	338	298	166.29	20.8
Cu^+ (aq)	71.7	50.0	—	—
Cu^{2+} (aq)	65.69	65.6	—	—
Cu_2O (c)	−168.6	−146.0	93.1	63.6
CuO (c)	−157.3	−129.7	42.6	42.3
$CuCl$ (c)	−137.2	−119.9	86.2	48.5
$CuCl_2$ (c)	−220.1	−175.7	108.1	57.8
Cu_2S (c, α)	−79.5	−86.2	120.9	76.1
CuS (c)	−53.1	−53.6	66.5	47.8
$CuSO_4$ (c)	−771	−662	109.2	100
$CuSO_4 \cdot H_2O$ (c)	−1085.8	−918.2	146	134
$CuSO_4 \cdot 3H_2O$ (c)	−1684.3	−1400.2	221	205
$CuSO_4 \cdot 5H_2O$ (c)	−2279.7	−1880.1	300	280

Formula	ΔH_f° kJ mol^{-1}	ΔG_f° kJ mol^{-1}	S° J K^{-1} mol^{-1}	C_p° J K^{-1} mol^{-1}
Fluorine				
F_2 (g)	0.0	0.0	202.685	31.30
F (g)	79.39	62.31	158.640	22.74
F^- (aq)	−335.4	−282	—	—
F^+ (g)	1766.2	—	—	—
HF (g)	−273.3	−275.4	173.67	29.13
F_2O (g)	−23.0	−4.6	247.3	43.30
Gallium				
Ga (c)	0.0	0.0	40.9	25.9
(g)	272	239	168.9	25.4
Ga_2O_3 (c, rhombic)	−1089	−998	85.0	92.1
Germanium				
Ge (c)	0.0	0.0	31.1	23.4
GeO_2 (c)	−580	−521	39.7	52.1
GeH_4 (g)	90.8	113	217.0	45.0
GeF_4 (g)	−1190.2	−1150.0	302	81.8
$GeCl_4$ (l)	−531.8	−462.8	245.6	—
Gold				
Au (c)	0.0	0.0	47.4	25.42
$AuCl_4^-$ (aq)	−322	−235.2	—	—
$Au(CN)_2^-$ (aq)	242	286	—	—
Au_2O_3 (c)	80.75	163.2	—	—
Helium				
He (g)	0.0	0.0	126.039	20.786
He^+ (g)	2378.4	—	—	—
Hydrogen				
H_2 (g)	0.0	0.0	130.570	28.824
H (g)	217.997	203.29	114.604	20.786
H^+ (g)	1536.2	—	—	—
H_2O (g)	−241.81	−228.58	188.72	33.58
(l)	−285.83	−237.19	69.95	75.29
D_2O (g)	−249.20	−234.55	198.23	34.27
(l)	−294.60	−243.49	75.94	84.35
H_2O_2 (g)	−136.3	−105.6	232.6	43.1
(l)	−187.8	−120.4	109.6	89.1
OH^- (aq)	−230.03	−157.34	—	—
Indium				
In (c)	0.0	0.0	57.8	26.7
(g)	236.7	208.7	173.7	20.8
In_2O_3 (c)	−925.8	−830.7	104.2	92

Formula	ΔH_f° kJ mol^{-1}	ΔG_f° kJ mol^{-1}	S° J K^{-1} mol^{-1}	C_p° J K^{-1} mol^{-1}
Iodine				
I_2 (c)	0.0	0.0	116.14	54.4
(g)	62.42	19.36	260.57	36.8
I (g)	106.76	70.2	180.6	20.9
I^- (aq)	−56.9	−51.9	—	—
IO_3^- (aq)	−221	−128	—	—
HI (g)	26.4	1.58	206.48	29.3
Iron				
Fe (c)	0.0	0.0	27.3	25.1
(g)	415	371	180.38	25.7
Fe^{2+} (aq)	−89.1	−78.9	—	—
Fe^{3+} (aq)	−48.5	−4.6	—	—
Fe_2O_3 (c, hematite)	−824	−742	87.4	103.9
Fe_3O_4 (c, magnetite)	−1118	−1015	146	143.4
$FeCl_2$ (c)	−341.6	−302.2	118	76.7
$FeCl_3$ (c)	−399	−334	142	96.7
$FeSO_4$ (c)	−928.4	−820.9	108	100.6
Fe_3C (c, cementite)	25.1	20.1	105	105.9
$FeCO_3$ (c, siderite)	−747.7	−674.0	92.9	82.0
Krypton				
Kr (g)	0.0	0.0	163.97	20.786
Lead				
Pb (c)	0.0	0.0	64.8	26.4
(g)	195.2	162.3	175.27	20.79
Pb^{2+} (aq)	0.92	−24.4	—	—
PbO (c, red)	−219.5	−189.8	67.8	45.8
(c, yellow)	−217.3	−187.9	68.7	45.8
PbO_2 (c)	−277.4	−217.4	68.6	64.6
Pb_3O_4 (c)	−718.4	−601.2	211.3	146.9
PbF_2 (c)	−664.0	−617.1	110.5	—
$PbCl_2$ (c)	−359.4	−314.2	136.0	—
$PbBr_2$ (c)	−279	−261.9	161.5	80.1
PbI_2 (c)	−175.5	−173.6	174.8	77.4
PbS (c)	−100	−98.7	91.2	49.5
$Pb(N_3)_2$ (c, monoclinic)	478.2	624.7	148.1	—
$PbSO_4$ (c)	−919.9	−813.1	148.5	103.21
$PbCO_3$ (c)	−699.1	−625.5	131	87.40
PbC_2O_4 (c)	−851.4	−750.2	146	105.4
Lithium				
Li (c)	0.0	0.0	29.1	23.4
(g)	161	122.2	138.67	20.9

Formula	ΔH_f° kJ mol^{-1}	ΔG_f° kJ mol^{-1}	S° J K^{-1} mol^{-1}	C_p° J K^{-1} mol^{-1}
Lithium, continued				
Li$^+$ (aq)	−278.46	−292.6	—	—
LiH (c)	−90.42	−69.96	24.7	34.7
LiOH (c)	−487.4	−441.4	42.8	49.8
LiF (c)	−618.2	−584.9	35.7	41.8
LiCl (c)	−408.6	−384.3	59.3	50.2
Li$_2$CO$_3$ (c)	−1215.5	−1132.6	90.4	97.5
Magnesium				
Mg (c)	0.0	0.0	32.7	24.9
(g)	147.1	113.1	148.54	20.79
Mg^{2+} (aq)	−467	−455.6	—	—
MgO (c, periclase)	−601.5	−569.2	27.0	37.2
Mg(OH)$_2$ (c)	−924.5	−833.6	63.2	77.0
MgF$_2$ (c)	−1124	−1071	57.2	61.6
MgCl$_2$ (c)	−641.3	−591.8	89.6	71.4
MgCl$_2 \cdot$ H$_2$O (c)	−966.6	−861.8	137	115.3
MgCl$_2 \cdot$ 2H$_2$O (c)	−1279.7	−1118.1	180	159.2
MgCl$_2 \cdot$ 4H$_2$O (c)	−1899.0	−1623.5	264	241.4
MgCl$_2 \cdot$ 6H$_2$O (c)	−2499.0	−2115.0	366	315.0
MgSO$_4$ (c)	−1285	−1171	91.6	96.5
Mg$_2$Si (c)	−77.8	−75.3	75	73.6
Mg(NO$_3$)$_2$ (c)	−790.7	−590	164	141.9
MgCO$_3$ (c, magnesite)	−1096	−1012	65.7	75.52
MgNi$_2$ (c)	−55.2	−54.0	88.7	73.34
Manganese				
Mn (c, α)	0.0	0.0	32.0	26.3
Mn^{2+} (aq)	−220.7	−228	—	—
MnO$_4^-$ (aq)	−541	−447	—	—
KMnO$_4$ (c)	−837	−737	171.7	117.6
MnO (c)	−385.2	−362.9	59.7	45.4
MnO$_2$ (c)	−520.0	−465.2	53.1	54.1
Mn$_2$O$_3$ (c)	−959	−881	110	107.7
Mn$_3$O$_4$ (c)	−1387	−1283	156	139.7
MnCl$_2$ (c)	−481.3	−440.5	118.2	72.9
MnSO$_4$ (c)	−1065.3	−957.4	112	100.5
MnCO$_3$ (c)	−894	−817	85.8	81.5
Mercury				
Hg (l)	0.0	0.0	75.9	27.98
(g)	61.38	31.88	174.86	20.79
Hg^{2+} (aq)	170.16	164.4	—	—
Hg$_2^{2+}$ (aq)	166.82	153.6	—	—
HgO (c, red, orthorhombic)	−90.8	−58.6	70.3	44.1
(c, yellow)	−90.5	−58.4	71.1	—

Formula	ΔH_f° kJ mol^{-1}	ΔG_f° kJ mol^{-1}	S° J K^{-1} mol^{-1}	C_p° J K^{-1} mol^{-1}
Mercury, continued				
Hg_2Cl_2 (c)	−265.5	−210.8	192	101.7
$HgCl_2$ (c)	−224.3	−178.7	146	76.6
$HgCl_4^{2-}$ (aq)	−554	−447	—	—
HgS (c, red)	−58.2	−50.6	82.4	48.4
(c, black)	−53.6	−47.7	88.3	—
Hg_2SO_4 (c)	−743.4	−626.2	200.7	132.0
$(CH_3)_2Hg$ (l)	59.5	140	209	—
(g)	94	146	305	83.3
Molybdenum				
Mo (c)	0.0	0.0	28.7	24.1
MoO_2 (c)	−589	−533	46.3	56.0
MoO_3 (c)	−745	−668.0	77.7	75.0
MoS_2 (c)	−235	−226	62.59	63.6
MoF_6 (l)	−1585.5	−1473.1	259.7	169.8
(g)	−1557.7	−1472.3	350.4	120.6
Neon				
Ne (g)	0.0	0.0	146.21	20.786
Ne^+ (g)	2086.9	—	—	—
Nickel				
Ni (c)	0.0	0.0	29.9	26.1
Ni^{2+} (aq)	−54	−46	—	—
$Ni(NH_3)_6^{2+}$ (aq)	−630	−256	—	—
NiO (c)	−239	−212	38.0	44.3
NiS (c)	−82.0	−79.5	53.0	47.1
$NiCl_2$ (c)	−305.3	−259.06	97.7	71.7
$NiSO_4$ (c)	−872.9	−760	92	138
$NiSO_4 \cdot 6H_2O$ (α, green, tetragonal)	−2682.8	−2225.0	334.5	327.9
$Ni(CO)_4$ (l)	−633.0	−588.3	313	205
(g)	−602.9	−587.3	411	145
Nitrogen				
N_2 (g)	0.0	0.0	191.50	29.12
N (g)	472.68	455.55	153.189	20.79
NO (g)	90.25	86.57	210.65	29.84
NO_2 (g)	33.2	51.30	239.95	37.2
N_2O (g)	82.0	104.2	219.74	38.5
N_2O_4 (g)	9.16	97.82	304.18	77.3
(l)	−19.50	97.45	209.2	142.7
N_2O_5 (g)	11.3	115	355.6	84.5
(c)	−43.1	114	178.7	143.1

Formula	ΔH_f° kJ mol^{-1}	ΔG_f° kJ mol^{-1}	S° J K^{-1} mol^{-1}	C_p° J K^{-1} mol^{-1}
Nitrogen, continued				
NO_3^- (aq)	−207.4	−111.5	—	—
NH_4^+ (aq)	−133.3	−79.5	—	—
NH_3(g)	−45.94	−16.44	192.67	35.06
$(CH_3)_3N$ (l)	−46.0	100.8	208.4	135.2
(g)	−24.3	99.0	287.	—
HNO_3 (l)	−174.1	−80.8	155.60	109.9
NH_4OH (l)	−361.2	−254.1	165.56	154.9
NH_4NO_3 (c)	−365.6	−184.0	151.08	139
NH_4Cl (c)	−314.4	−202.9	94.56	84.1
N_2H_4 (g)	95.4	159.3	238.36	49.6
(l)	50.6	149.2	121.21	98.9
Oxygen				
O_2 (g)	0.0	0.0	205.03	29.35
O_3 (g)	142.7	163.2	238.82	39.2
O (g)	249.170	231.748	160.946	21.9
			—	—
Phosphorus				
P (c, white)	0.0	0.0	41.09	23.84
(c, red)	−17.6	−12.1	22.80	21.3
(g)	316.5	280.13	163.09	20.9
P_2 (g)	144	104	218.01	32.0
P_4 (g)	58.9	24.5	279.9	67.2
P_4O_{10} (c, hexagonal)	−3010	−2724	231.0	211.7
PO_4^{3-} (aq)	−1277	−1019	—	—
PH_3 (g)	5.4	13.4	210.12	37.1
H_3PO_4 (c)	−1279	−1119	110.50	106.1
PCl_3 (g)	−287.0	−267.8	311.67	71.8
(l)	−320	−272	217.1	—
PCl_5 (c)	−443.5	—	—	—
(g)	−374.9	−305.0	364.47	112.8
Potassium				
K (c)	0.0	0.0	64.7	29.3
(g)	89.60	—	160.23	—
K^+ (aq)	−252.2	−282.5	—	—
K_2O (c)	−361.5	−322.2	—	—
KH (g)	125.5	105.0	198	—
KOH (c)	−424.8	—	—	—
KF (c)	−567.3	−537.8	66.57	49.0
KCl (c)	−436.7	−408.61	82.6	51.5
$KClO_3$ (c)	−392.84	−292.65	143.0	100.4
$KClO_4$ (c)	−432.75	−303.2	151	110.2
KBr (c)	−393.8	−380.1	95.9	53.6

Formula	ΔH_f° kJ mol^{-1}	ΔG_f° kJ mol^{-1}	S° J K^{-1} mol^{-1}	C_p° J K^{-1} mol^{-1}
Potassium, continued				
KI (c)	−327.90	−324.4	106.1	55.2
K$_2$SO$_4$ (c)	−1438.0	−1319.7	175.6	130.1
KNO$_3$ (c)	−494.6	−394.6	133.1	96.2
Rubidium				
Rb (c)	0.0	0.0	76.8	30.5
(g)	79.5	—	169.99	—
Rb$^+$ (aq)	−251.1	−283.6	—	—
RbF (c)	−558	−519	—	52.7
RbCl (c)	−435.4	−407.8	95.9	52.4
Selenium				
Se (c, black, hexagonal)	0.0	0.0	42.44	25.4
(g)	227.1	187.1	176.6	20.8
Se$_2$ (g)	146.0	96.2	252	35.4
SeF$_6$ (g)	−1117.1	−1016.7	313.8	110.5
Silicon				
Si (c)	0.0	0.0	18.8	20.1
(g)	450	—	167.87	—
SiO$_2$ (c, quartz)	−910.7	−856.32	41.46	44.4
(c, cristobalite)	−909.48	−855.88	42.68	44.2
SiH$_4$ (g)	34.3	56.9	204.5	42.8
Si$_2$H$_6$ (g)	80.3	127.2	272.5	80.8
SiF$_4$ (g)	−1615.0	−1572.8	282.7	73.6
SiCl$_4$ (l)	−687.0	−619.9	239.7	145
Si(CH$_3$)$_3$Cl (l)	−384	−247	278.2	—
Si(CH$_3$)$_4$ (l)	−272	−100	277.3	204
SiC (c, cubic)	−65.3	−62.8	16.6	26.9
(c, hexagonal)	−62.8	−60.2	16.5	26.7
Silver				
Ag (c)	0.0	0.0	42.6	25.4
(g)	284.9	246.0	172.88	20.79
Ag$^+$(aq)	105.75	77.09	—	—
AgCl$_2^-$ (aq)	−245	−215	—	—
Ag(NH$_3$)$_2^+$ (aq)	−111.3	−17.2	—	—
Ag(CN)$_2^-$ (aq)	270	305	—	—
Ag$_2$O (c)	−31.1	−11.2	121	65.9
AgCl (c)	−127.07	−109.8	96.2	50.8
AgBr (c)	−100.6	−97.1	107.1	52.4
AgI (c)	−62.3	−66.7	115.5	56.8
Ag$_2$S (c, α, orthorhombic)	−32.6	−40.7	144.0	76.5
(c, β)	−29.4	−39.5	150.6	—

Formula	ΔH_f° kJ mol^{-1}	ΔG_f° kJ mol^{-1}	S° J K^{-1} mol^{-1}	C_p° J K^{-1} mol^{-1}
Silver, continued				
Ag_2SO_4 (c)	−715.6	−618.4	200.9	131.6
$AgNO_3$ (c)	−124.3	−33.4	140.6	93.1
Ag_2CO_3 (c)	−505.9	−436.8	167	112.3
Ag_2CrO_4 (c)	−731.7	−641.8	218	142.3
Sodium				
Na (c)	0.0	0.0	51.3	28.2
(g)	108.43	76.6	153.62	20.8
Na^+ (aq)	−240.30	−261.9	—	—
Na_2O (c)	−417.	−376.6	72.8	68.2
Na_2O_2 (c)	−511.7	−451.0	104	—
NaOH (c)	−425.6	−379.7	64.5	59.5
NaF (c)	−573.66	−546.3	51.3	46.0
NaCl (c)	−411.2	−384.3	72.5	49.8
NaBr (c)	−361.1	−349.1	87.2	52.3
NaI (c)	−287.8	−282.4	98.5	—
Na_2SO_4 (c)	−1387.1	−1269.4	149.5	127.3
$Na_2SO_4 \cdot 10H_2O$ (c)	−4328	−3647	592.	587.4
$NaNO_3$ (c)	−467.9	−367.1	116.5	93.1
Na_2CO_3 (c)	−1131.4	−1048.1	136.0	110.5
$Na_2CO_3 \cdot 10H_2O$ (c)	−4083.6	−3426.3	542.2	535.6
$NaHCO_3$ (c)	−947.7	−850.2	102.1	87.6
Strontium				
Sr (c)	0.0	0.0	52.3	26
SrO (c)	−592	−562	54.4	45.0
SrF_2 (c)	−1223	−1172	82.1	70.0
$SrCl_2$ (c)	−829	−781	114.9	75.6
$SrSO_4$ (c)	−1453	−1341	117	—
$SrCO_3$ (c, strontianite)	−1220	−1140	97.1	81.4
$Sr(NO_3)_2$ (c)	−978.2	−780.2	194.6	149.9
Sulphur				
S (c, rhombic)	0.0	0.0	32.05	22.6
(c, monoclinic)	0.3	—	—	—
(g)	277.0	236.5	167.72	23.8
S_2 (g)	128.5	79.33	228.06	32.5
S_8 (g)	102.1	49.8	—	156.5
S^{2-} (aq)	30	79	—	—
H_2S (g)	−20.6	−33.4	205.6	34.3
HS^- (aq)	−16.4	12.4	—	—
SO_4^{2-} (aq)	−909.6	−743.6	—	—
HSO_4^- (aq)	−887	−677	—	—
SO_2 (g)	−296.81	−300.10	248.11	39.8

Formula	ΔH_f° kJ mol^{-1}	ΔG_f° kJ mol^{-1}	S° J K^{-1} mol^{-1}	C_p° J K^{-1} mol^{-1}
Sulphur, continued				
SO_3 (g)	−395.7	−371.1	256.6	50.67
(l)	−441.0	−368.4	95.6	—
H_2SO_4 (l)	−814.0	−690.1	156.9	138.9
SF_6 (g)	−1209.	−1105.4	291.7	97.3
Tellurium				
Te (c)	0.0	0.0	49.71	25.5
TeO_2 (c)	−322.6	−270.3	79.5	—
TeF_6 (g)	−1318	—	—	—
Thallium				
Tl (c)	0.0	0.0	64.2	26.3
(g)	181.2	147.4	180.85	20.8
TlCl (c)	−204.1	−184.9	111.3	50.9
$TlNO_3$ (c)	−243.9	−152.5	160.7	99.5
Tin				
Sn (c, *white*)	0.0	0.0	51.18	27.2
(c, *grey*)	−2.1	4.6	44.1	25.9
(g)	301.2	266.3	168.38	21.3
SnO (c)	−285.9	−257.2	57.2	44.3
SnO_2 (c)	−580.8	−519.7	52.	52.7
$SnCl_4$ (l)	−511.3	−440.2	258.6	165
SnH_4 (g)	163	188	227.6	49.0
Titanium				
Ti (c, α)	0.0	0.0	30.6	25.0
TiO_2 (c, *rutile*)	−994.2	−939.	50.3	55.0
(c, *anatase*)	−940	−884	49.9	55.5
$TiCl_4$ (l)	−804	−737	252.3	145
(g)	−763	−726	353.3	95.4
$TiCl_3$ (c, α)	−721	−654	140	97.2
$TiBr_4$ (c)	−616.7	−589.5	244	131.5
$TiBr_3$ (c)	−548.5	−523.8	177	101.7
TiI_4 (c)	−375.7	−371.5	249	125.6
TiC (c)	−185	−181	24.2	33.6
Tungsten				
W (c)	0.0	0.0	32.6	24.3
WO_2 (c)	−589.7	−533.9	50.54	56.1
WO_3 (c)	−847.9	−764.1	75.90	73.8
WF_6 (l)	−1747.7	−1631.47	251.5	—
(g)	−1721.7	−1632.2	341.0	119

Formula	ΔH_f° kJ mol^{-1}	ΔG_f° kJ mol^{-1}	S° J K^{-1} mol^{-1}	C_p° J K^{-1} mol^{-1}
Uranium				
U(c)	0.0	0.0	50.2	27.6
UO$_2$ (c)	−1085	−1032	77.0	64.0
UO$_3$ (c)	−1224	−1146	96.7	—
U$_3$O$_8$ (c)	−3575	−3370	282.6	—
UF$_6$ (g)	−2112.9	−2029.2	379.7	—
Vanadium				
V(c)	0.0	0.0	28.9	24.9
V$_2$O$_3$(c)	−1228	−1139	98.3	103.2
V$_2$O$_4$ (c)	−1427.2	−1318.4	103	117.0
V$_2$O$_5$ (c)	−1550.6	−1419.6	131	127.7
VO$_2^+$ (aq)	−650	−587	—	—
VO^{2+} (aq)	−487	−446	—	—
VO$_3^-$ (aq)	−888	−784	—	—
HVO$_4^{2-}$ (aq)	−1159	−975	—	—
VOCl$_3$(l)	−735	−669	244	—
(g)	−696	−659.3	344.2	89.9
Xenon				
Xe (g)	0.0	0.0	169.573	20.786
XeF$_4$ (c)	−261	—	—	—
Zinc				
Zn (c)	0.0	0.0	41.6	25.4
(g)	130.4	94.9	160.88	20.8
Zn^{2+} (aq)	−153.39	−147.23	—	—
ZnSO$_4$ (c)	−982.8	−874.5	119.7	117.2
ZnCO$_3$ (c)	−813.0	−731.9	82.4	79.9
ZnO (c)	−350.5	−320.5	43.6	40.3
ZnF$_2$ (c)	−764	−713.4	73.7	65.6
ZnCl$_2$ (c)	−415	−369.4	111.5	71.3
ZnBr$_2$ (c)	−328.7	−312.1	138.5	—
ZnI$_2$ (c)	−208.0	−209.0	161.1	—
ZnS (c, zincblende)	−206.0	−201.3	57.7	46.0
Zirconium				
Zr (c)	0.0	0.0	39.0	25.4
ZrO$_2$ (c, monoclinic)	−1100.6	−1042.8	50.4	56.2
ZrCl$_4$ (c)	−980.5	−890	182	119.8
(g)	−870	−836	368	98.3
ZrF$_4$ (c, monoclinic)	−1911	−1810	105	103.7
(g)	−1674	−1636	319	87.4
ZrSiO$_4$ (c)	−2033	−1919	84.1	98.7

APPENDIX 2

SI UNITS

There has been increasing acceptance by the scientific community, including both pure and applied scientists and engineers, of the system of units approved by the International Union of Pure and Applied Chemistry (IUPAC), Commission on Symbols, Terminology and Units, in 1969, designated officially "Le Système Internationale d'Unités," and briefly, "SI units." Students who have become familiar with what has been called the MKSA system will have used the same basic units for length, mass, time and other quantities. Some basic SI units are shown in the table below and the details of their individual definitions follow the table.

Some Basic SI Quantities and Units

Measured Quantity	Symbol	Basic SI Unit	Symbol
1. length	l	metre	m
2. mass	m	kilogram	kg
3. time	t	second	s
4. electric current	I	ampere	A
5. temperature	T	kelvin	K
6. amount of substance	n	mole	mol

Definitions of basic units:

1. The *metre* is the length equal to 1 650 763.73 wavelengths in vacuum of the radiation corresponding to the transition between the levels $2p_{10}$ and $5d_5$ of the krypton-86 atom.

2. The *kilogram* is the unit of mass; it is equal to the mass of the international prototype of the kilogram.

3. The *second* is the duration of 9 192 631 770 periods of the radiation corresponding to the transition between the two hyperfine levels of the ground state of the caesium-133 atom.

4. The *ampere* is that constant current which, if maintained in two straight parallel conductors of infinite length, of negligible cross-section, and

placed 1 metre apart in vacuum, would produce between these conductors a force equal to 2×10^{-7} newton per metre of length.

5. The *kelvin*, unit of thermodynamic temperature, is the fraction 1/273.16 of the thermodynamic temperature of the triple point of water.

6. The *mole* is the amount of substance of a system which contains as many elementary entities as there are carbon atoms in 0.012 kg of carbon-12. The elementary entities may be atoms, molecules, ions, electrons, other particules, or specified groups of such particles.

From the above basic units others are derived. Only a fraction of these latter are shown below, even of those used in chemistry.

Some Derived SI Quantities and Units

Measured Quantity	Symbol	SI Unit	Symbol
Dimensional:			
area	A	metre^2	m^2
volume	V	metre^3	m^3
specific volume	v	metre^3/kg	m^3 kg^{-1}
density	ϱ	kg/metre^3	kg m^{-3}
Dynamic:			
velocity	v	metre/second	m s^{-1}
acceleration	a	metre/second^2	m s^{-2}
frequency	ν	hertz	s^{-1}
force	F	newton	N = kg a = kg m s^{-2}
pressure	P	pascal	Pa = N m^{-2}
osmotic pressure	π	pascal	Pa = N m^{-2}
Electrical:			
quantity of charge	Q	coulomb	C = A s
electrical potential	V	volt	V = kg m^2 s^{-3} A^{-1}
electromotive force	E	volt	V = J s^{-1} A^{-1}
electric resistance	R	ohm	Ω = V A^{-1}
power	P	watt	W = V A = J s^{-1}
dipole moment	μ	coulomb metre	C.m
Energetic:			
heat	q	joule	J = N m = kg m^2 s^{-2}
work	w	joule	J
internal energy	U	joule	J
enthalpy	H	joule	J
Gibbs' energy	G	joule	J
chemical potential	μ	joule/mole	J mol^{-1}
heat capacity	C	joule/kelvin	J K^{-1}
entropy	S	joule/kelvin	J K^{-1}

The magnitudes of all the units can be extended by powers of ten to suit the quantity measured. For this purpose the following prefixes can be used. Of these, the ones underlined are apt to be used most.

Prefixes for Use with Basic and Derived SI Units

10^1 deca (da)	10^{-1} deci (d)
10^2 hecto (h)	10^{-2} centi (c)
10^3 kilo (k)	10^{-3} milli(m)
10^6 mega (M)	10^{-6} micro (μ)
10^9 giga (G)	10^{-9} nano (n)
10^{12} tera (T)	10^{-12} pico (p)
10^{15} peta (P)	10^{-15} femto (f)
10^{18} exa (E)	10^{-18} atto (a)

Examples:
$$15\,000\,m\ =\ 15\,km$$
$$0.000\,003\,74\,m\ =\ 3.74\,\mu m$$
$$76\,500\,000\,W\ =\ 76.5\,MW$$

Besides the above units, there are units which are part of the metric system, although not of the SI system, and which are well established in scientific and commercial usage. With these units it is difficult to know what is "official." IUPAC has urged that all such units be phased out. On the other hand, most national committees have endorsed their use. In Canada, for example, one buys milk, wine and motor gasoline by the litre, and toothpaste by the millilitre. For most scientists and engineers these units will be of importance. The following units are therefore used in conjunction with IUPAC units throughout this book, just as they are in most countries.

Non-IUPAC units used in National SI Systems

Unit	Symbol	Value
minute	min	$1\ min = 60\ s$
hour	h	$1\ h = 3600\ s$
day	d	$1\ d = 86\,400\ s$
degree (of arc)	°	$1° = (\pi/180)\ rad$
minute (of arc)	′	$1' = (\pi/10\,800)\ rad$
second (of arc)	″	$1'' = (\pi/648\,000)\ rad$
litre	L	$1\ L = 1\ dm^3$
millilitre	mL	$1\ mL = 1\ cm^3 = 10^{-6}m^3$
tonne	t	$1\ t = 10^3\ kg$
degree Celsius	°C	$0°C = 273.15K; 25°C = 298.15K$
bar	bar	$1\ bar = 10^5\ Pa$

Some Conversion Data

length $1 \text{ m} = 10^2 \text{ cm} = 10^3 \text{ mm} = 10^6 \text{ } \mu\text{m} = 10^{10} \text{ Å} = 39.370 \text{ in} = 3.281 \text{ ft}$

   $1 \text{ km} = 0.6214 \text{ statute mile}$

   $1 \text{ in} = 2.54 \text{ cm}$

volume $1 \text{ m}^3 = 10^3 \text{ L} = 35.316 \text{ cu ft} = 220.0 \text{ imp gal} = 35196 \text{ imp fl oz}$

   $= 264.2 \text{ US gal}$

mass $1 \text{ tonne} = 10^3 \text{ kg} = 2204.6 \text{ lb} = 1.1023 \text{ short ton}$

   $1 \text{ amu} = 1.66041 \times 10^{-27} \text{ kg}$

temperature $T_K = T_C + 273.15 \qquad\qquad T_R = T_F + 460.0$

   $T_F = \frac{9}{5} T_C + 32 \qquad\qquad T_R = \frac{9}{5} T_K$

energy $1 \text{ J} = 1 \text{ N m} = 0.2390 \text{ cal}; 1 \text{ cal} = 4.184 \text{ J}; 1 \text{ kcal} = 4.184 \text{ kJ}$

   $1 \text{ electron volt} = 1.6022 \times 10^{-19} \text{ J} = 1.6022 \times 10^{-12} \text{ erg}$

pressure $1 \text{ Pa} = 10^{-5} \text{ bar} = 0.98692 \times 10^{-5} \text{ atm} = 7.3006 \text{ mmHg}$

   $1 \text{ bar} = 10^5 \text{ Pa}; 1 \text{ atm} = 1.01325 \text{ bar} = 14.6974 \text{ psi}$

   $1 \text{ torr} = 1 \text{ mmHg} = 1.316 \times 10^{-3} \text{ atm} = 1.333 \times 10^{-3} \text{ bar}$

A note on the use of SI units in equations

The basic and derived SI units of the first two tables are self consistent within equations. If all but one quantity in an equation are in basic and derived units, the last quantity will be as well. This will not normally be true if use is made of units created by using the prefixes of the third table. For example,

$$PV = nRT$$

$$P = \frac{nRT}{V} = \frac{(\text{mol})(\text{J mol}^{-1} \text{ K}^{-1})(\text{K})}{\text{m}^3}$$

$$= \text{J m}^{-3}$$

$$= \text{N m m}^{-3}$$

$$= \text{N m}^{-2}$$

$$= \text{Pa}$$

GLOSSARY

Absolute zero of temperature—the temperature at which an ideal gas would have zero volume according to Charles' Law. It is not possible to cool any substance to a temperature lower than this.
$0 K = -273.15°C$.

Acid—a substance which affords protons (Brønsted-Lowry) or accepts electron pairs (Lewis).

Acid-base reaction—one in which transfer of solvated hydrogen ions takes place from donor (acid) to acceptor (base), (Brønsted-Lowry); or one in which transfer of electron pairs takes place from donor (base) to acceptor (acid), (Lewis).

Activation energy (see energy of activation).

Activity—a thermodynamic property of any material, which can be approximated in many instances by a concentration or a concentration related term.

Activity coefficient—the ratio of the relative activity of a species to its concentration.

Addition polymerization—that which takes place by the addition of monomer to monomer molecules at double bonds.

Adduct molecule—a compound molecule formed by the addition of one molecule to another.

Adhesion—used to describe the holding together of *different* species (e.g. a liquid drop on a solid surface) as distinct from cohesion, which refers to forces holding together like species.

Adiabatic process—one which is so insulated that no heat is exchanged between system and surroundings.

Adsorption—the attachment of atoms, ions or molecules to a surface.

Allotropes—different physical forms of a particular element in a particular state.

Alpha particle—the positive nucleus of a helium atom.

Amalgam—an alloy of mercury with another metal(s).

Amphiprotic—capable of sometimes donating a proton, sometimes gaining a proton.

Amphoteric—capable of acting sometimes as an acid, sometimes as a base.

Angular momentum—the product of the radius and the linear momentum for a curved path.

Anion—a negatively charged ion.

Annealing—a process in which a solid product is held for an extended period of time just below the melting point in order to allow diffusion processes to promote uniformity of composition and properties.

Anode—the electrode at which oxidation occurs.

Antifreeze—a solution (often of a polyalcohol in water), designed not to freeze solid when used as a coolant under winter or polar conditions.

Aromatic compound—an unsaturated organic compound with a 'resonating' ring structure; (e.g. benzene and naphthalene).

Atactic polymer—one with side groups randomly oriented about the main chain.

Atom—the smallest particle of an element that can participate in chemical reactions.

Atomic number—equal to the number of protons (and hence the charge) in the nucleus of the atom; or, in a neutral atom, to the total number of electrons.

Atomic orbital—a wave function which is a solution to the Schrödinger equation for an electron in an atom.

Aufbau principle—a set of rules for building up the configurations of electrons in atoms.

Avogadro number, N_A—the number of elementary entities in one mole, which is $6.022\,045 \times 10^{23}$.

Azeotrope—a constant boiling mixture that vaporizes without change in composition.

Azeotropic points—points in multi-component phase diagrams where maxima or minima occur.

Band—an energy range containing closely spaced energy levels for the electrons in a solid.

Band gap—an energy range in which there are no energy levels for the electrons in a solid.

Barometer—an instrument used to measure the atmospheric pressure.

Base—a substance which accepts protons (Brønsted-Lowry); or affords electron pairs (Lewis).

Battery—a series of voltaic cells in one package used to furnish electrical energy.

Black body radiation—that emitted from a small hole in a furnace.

Boiling point—the temperature at which a liquid and its vapour are in equilibrium at some specific pressure. The normal boiling point quoted in tables is the temperature at which the vapour pressure of the liquid is equal to the standard pressure, $P°$.

Boltzmann constant—is equal to the gas constant, R, divided by the Avogadro number, N_A.

Bond angle—that between two imaginary lines joining the nuclei of two atoms separately to the nucleus of a third atom.

Bond energy—that energy required to break a particular chemical bond: usually quoted on a molar basis.

Bond length—the distance between the nuclei of the bonded atoms.

Bond order—the number of electron pairs involved in a particular bond.

Bonding pair—a pair of valence shell electrons of an atom which are shared with another atom.

Bravais lattice—one of the 14 possible different lattices which can be constructed in three-dimensional space on the basis of their crystal symmetry.

Brillouin zone—one of a series of zones resulting from the division of k-space.

Brisance—is a measure of the shattering ability of an explosive, determined empirically by the amount of sand crushed by a given charge, fired under carefully set conditions.

Brønsted-Lowry acid—a substance which donates a proton.

Brønsted-Lowry base—a substance which accepts a proton.

Buffer—a solution which resists change in pH on the addition of moderate amounts of acid, base, or solvent.

Buoyancy—the upward force on an object owing to the density of the object being less than the density of the surrounding medium.

Cage effect—a situation in which a solute entity is screened by solvent molecules from other reacting solute entities.

Calcining—the heating of limestone ($CaCO_3$) in a kiln to produce quicklime (CaO) by driving off CO_2; sometimes generalized to mean driving off any gas by heat.

Calorimeter—a device which measures the heat taken in or given out during a chemical reaction under controlled conditions.

Carbonium ion—an organic cation in which the positive charge resides on one of the carbon atoms.

Carnot machine—a hypothetical device by which a complete thermodynamic cyclic process is carried out in four steps.

Catalyst—a substance which increases the rate of a chemical reaction but can be recovered unchanged after the reaction.

Catenation—the ability of certain elements such as carbon to bond their atoms together to form a chain.

Cathode—the electrode at which reduction occurs.

Cement—the product of a mixture of certain clays, limestone and other ingredients which is fired to form a clinker and ground to a powder.

Chain reaction—a reaction or set of reactions which is self-propagating in that the reaction step or steps produce the radical or other active species which initiated the reaction sequence, so that the reaction steps can be repeated many times.

Chemical bond—the phenomenon responsible for holding atoms together with sufficient strength to form a distinct and stable chemical compound.

Chemical equation—a statement made in terms of chemical symbols and formulae to describe a particular chemical reaction.

Chemical formula—a set of symbols listing the elements present in the substance, with the relative numbers of atoms of each element expressed as a set of (usually) whole numbers, written as subscripts to the respective elemental symbols.

Chemical reaction—a process in which chemical change in the nature and composition of some substance(s) occurs.

Chirality—a molecular property of having optical isomers or enantiomers, with non-superimposable mirror images analogous to a pair of hands.

Chlorinity—is the chloride content of a natural water expressed in g of Cl^- per kg of the water.

Cholesteric mesophase—a nematic type of liquid crystal, composed of optically active molecules having a spiral orientation.

Cis—a prefix indicating that two groups are on the same side of the molecule.

Clinker—a hard mass of material formed on firing.

Close packing—the spatial arrangement of spheres which gives the greatest density.

Cohesion (see adhesion)

Colligative properties—are those which depend on the concentration of entities in solution rather than on the nature of the entities.

Colloid—a substance consisting of sub-microscopic particles, small enough to remain suspended in the solvent, but larger than most molecules. (approx. 10^{-9} to 10^{-7}m diameter).

Common ion—one which is the same as one involved in the equilibrium expression.

Complex—an entity formed by coordination in which a metal atom or ion accepts one or more electron pairs from donor ions or molecules.

Compound—a substance containing more than one element in definite proportions by mass, with well-defined physical and chemical properties which differ from those of the component elements.

Compressibility—the fractional volume change produced by unit change in pressure.

Concentration—amount of solute per unit volume.

Concrete—a hardened mixture, set after thoroughly mixing hydrated cement, sand, and gravel or crushed rock.

Condensation—the transfer of a substance from the gas phase to the liquid or solid phase.

Condensation polymerization—that process in which suitable monomers link to one another with the attendant elimination of a small molecule such as H_2O.

Condensed phase—phase in the liquid or solid state.

Condenser—a heat exchanger in which a gas is converted to a liquid.

Conduction band—the upper energy band in which electronic energy levels are found for a polyatomic solid, in which the electrons are relatively mobile.

Congruent melting—that in which the liquid formed has the same composition as the solid melted.

Conjugate acids and bases—acids and their corresponding bases, differing only by a proton, as in, $$HA = H^+ + A^-.$$
acid   base

Conjugation (organic)—the alternation of single and double bonds in a molecule.

Convertor—a primary cell or fuel cell used in the conversion of chemical to electrical energy.

Coordinate bond—a type of covalent bond in which the electron pair is provided by one of the atoms.

Copolymerization—the production of a polymer containing two or more types of monomer.

Coring—a phenomenon in which crystallization under non-equilibrium conditions produces a solid of non-uniform composition.

Corrosion—an undesirable and harmful reaction of a metal with its environment whereby the metal becomes oxidized.

Corrosion inhibitor—a substance used to stifle the reaction at the anode or cathode and thereby inhibit corrosion.

Covalent bonding—that in which the bonded atoms share electrons.

Critical point—the temperature and pressure at which the liquid and vapour states are in equilibrium and have identical properties.

Critical pressure—is the pressure at the critical point.

Critical temperature—is the temperature at the critical point, above which liquid cannot exist.

Critical volume—the volume of a mole of liquid or its vapour at the critical temperature and pressure.

Crosslinking—the bonding of one polymer chain to another making the polymer more hard and rigid.

Crystal—a solid with a regular arrangement of its atoms, ions or molecules.

Crystal lattice—a regular array of points representing the positions of entities (atoms, ions, molecules) in a crystal, all points having identical surroundings.

Crystal system—one of 7 different crystal lattices, classified according to the shape of the unit cell and its symmetry.

Crystallography—the scientific description of crystals.

Current density—the value of the electric current per unit area of conductor.

Cycle—a set of steps which returns a system to the same state which it had initially.

Dative bond (see coordinate bond).

Decomposition—a reaction in which a chemical compound breaks up into two or more simpler compounds or elements.

Dehydrogenation—a reaction in which a compound loses hydrogen.

Density—a property of matter expressing the mass per unit volume.

Desalination—the removal of pure water as product from salt water or of salts from water in order to leave a pure water product.

Detonation velocity—the rate at which the explosion races through the explosive crystal.

Detonator—a substance used in relatively small amount to initiate the explosion of less sensitive explosives.

Dipole moment—in a polar molecule is the product of the charge at one end of a dipole and the distance between the centres of positive and negative charge.

Dissociation—the breakdown of an ionic compound into its ions.

Distil—to evaporate a liquid and collect the vapour by condensation, usually in order to purify the liquid.

Domain—a region where one species prevails.

Doping—the addition of impurity atoms to a pure material in a controlled way to produce an extrinsic semiconductor.

Eclipsed configuration—is a molecular configuration around a C-C single bond in which the set of atoms at one end is directly in line with the set at the other end.

Eh—the redox potential of a natural aqueous system based on the hydrogen scale.

Elastomer—a rubber-like polymer.

Electrode—a conductor at which electrons pass into the ionic solution (cathode); or from the ionic solution (anode).

Electrolysis—a process by which an applied potential difference from an external source causes an electric current to pass through an electrolytic solution, effecting oxidation at one electrode (anode) and reduction at the other (cathode).

Electrolyte—a substance which on solution confers electrical conducting power by the formation of or dissociation into ions.

Electrolytic cell—an electrochemical cell to which a potential difference is applied from an external source in order to produce chemical changes at the electrodes.

Electromotive force, emf—the maximum potential difference developed by an electrochemical cell, measured on open circuit with no appreciable current flow.

Electron—a fundamental subatomic particle, with negative charge about 1.602×10^{-19} C and mass about 9.1×10^{-28} g.

Electron affinity—of a neutral atom is the ionization energy of its singly charged negative ion.

Electron configuration—in an atom is a listing of the number of electrons assigned to each quantum level.

Electronegativity—is the tendency of an atom to attract electrons and acquire partial negative charge, expressed as a number on one of several arbitrary scales.

Electrophile—an electron deficient atom, alone or in an ion or molecule, which bonds readily with an electron rich species.

Element—a substance which cannot be broken up into any other stable substances by chemical means, and which cannot be made as the sole product of a chemical reaction between other substances.

Elementary reaction—is a process which takes place in a single step.

Empirical formula—is the formula for a compound with relative numbers of component atoms expressed as the simplest set of whole numbers.

Enantiomer—an optical isomer, having a non- superimposable mirror image.

Endothermic reaction—one in which heat enters the system from the surroundings when carried out isothermally.

Energy of activation—the energy E in the Arrhenius equation for the rate constant, $k = Ae^{-E/RT}$ interpreted as an energy barrier which reactants must overcome in order to react.

Engine—a device designed to convert heat or chemical energy into work.

Enthalpy, H—is a thermodynamic property of a system equal to the sum of the internal energy and the pressure-volume product, $H \equiv U + PV$; also termed the heat content in older texts.

Enthalpy of formation—of a compound is the enthalpy change for the reaction in which one mole of the compound is formed directly from its elements in their most stable form under standard conditions.

Entropy—is a state function in thermodynamics defined by the differential relation, $dS = dq_{rev}/T$; it is interpreted as a measure of the disorder in a system.

Equation of state—is an equation expressing the relation among pressure, volume, temperature and amount of substance present.

Equilibrium—in chemistry, a condition of balance in which the rate of a process or reaction forward is equal to that in reverse; or the net rate is zero.

Eutectic point—is a minimum melting point of a mixture of two immiscible or partly miscible solids.

Eutrophication—a condition resulting from an overabundance of nutrients, causing excessive plant growth, followed ultimately by an excessive consumption of oxygen on decay.

Evaporator—a heat exchanger in which a liquid is vaporized to a gas.

Exclusion principle (Pauli)—a limitation by which no two electrons in an atom, molecule or solid can have the same set of quantum numbers.

Exothermic reaction—one in which heat leaves the system and enters the surroundings when carried out isothermally.

Explosive—a substance or mixture which reacts very rapidly with sudden release of energy.

Extrinsic semiconductor—material in which the semiconducting properties are imparted by the presence of impurity atoms.

Faraday—the charge equal in magnitude to that of one mole of electrons or one mole of protons; and equal to 96485 C.

Fermi energy—the highest occupied energy level in a solid at zero kelvin.

Fermi surface—that which connects all the states with energy equal to the Fermi energy.

Ferromagnetism—the property possessed by certain elements such as iron, cobalt, and nickel of having very strong natural magnetism, even in the absence of an externally applied magnetic field.

Fibres—are materials formed into shapes in which the length is at least two orders of magnitude greater than the other dimensions.

Flade potential—a potential on an experimental potentiostatic curve at the point where the current density becomes suddenly minimal owing to the onset of the formation of a passivating film.

Fluidity—the ability of a liquid to flow.

Fluorescence—the reemission of radiation at the same (or other) wave length as that received.

Force constant—a proportionality constant between restoring force and displacement from equilibrium; used in describing vibrating springs and vibrating molecules.

Formality—the number of moles of a solute of a particular formula which have been added to and/or can be recovered from a litre of solution; the solute may or may not be present in the configuration shown by the formula. See also molarity.

Free radical—a reactive organic species characterized by the presence of an unpaired electron.

Freezing point—the temperature at which solid and liquid are in equilibrium at $P°$.

Fuel—a substance which is oxidized, usually by air, to produce energy in the form of work or heat.

Fuel cell—an electrochemical cell in which new reactants are fed in continuously, with fuel at the anode and oxidant at the cathode, in order to produce electrical energy.

Functional group—a bonded atom or group which confers characteristic chemical properties onto a host organic molecule.

Galvanic cell—an electrochemical cell which acts as a source of electrical energy by providing a potential difference at its terminals.

Gauge pressure—the measured difference between the absolute pressure and atmospheric pressure.

Geometric isomers—two different arrangements of the same atoms in the same molecule, and with each atom bonded to the same set of atoms but with different geometrical arrangements of the atoms in space; see also structural isomers, optical isomers.

Gibbs energy, G—is a thermodynamic state function defined by $G \equiv H - TS$; formerly called Free Energy.

Half-life—is the time required for half of the starting substance to react.

Hard water—water which contains objectionable dissolved salts.

Heat—is the energy which flows from a hot object to a cooler one.

Heat capacity—of a system is the amount of heat required to raise the temperature of the system by one kelvin.

Heat of combustion—is the enthalpy change of the reaction in which one mole of fuel is completely oxidized by O_2, to give $CO_2(g)$ and H_2O (*l*).

Heating (or cooling) curve—a plot of the temperature of a system as a function of time, while heat is added (or removed) at a uniform rate.

Heat of explosion—is the enthalpy change in an explosive reaction per unit mass of explosive.

Heat pump—a device designed to transfer heat to a hotter body from a cooler one.

Heterogeneous reaction—is one involving substances in two or more phases.

H.E.T.P., height equivalent to a theoretical plate—is the physical height of a distillation column divided by the number of theoretical plates achieved, where each theoretical plate corresponds to a separate vapour/liquid equilibration.

Hole—a positively charged location in the lattice of a p-type semiconductor, resulting from a deficiency of electrons in the valence band.

Homogeneous reaction—is a reaction involving only a single phase.

Homologous series—is a series of closely related organic compounds, each differing from the former by the addition of one methylene group.

Hydrate—a substance having a definite ratio of attached water molecules.

Hydration—the attachment of a definite number of water molecules to an ion or compound.

Hydrolysis—is a reaction in which water is one of the reactants.

Hydrosphere—the total water content of the planet.

Ideal gas—a hypothetical gas which obeys the relation $PV = nRT$ exactly.

Ideal mixture (of gases)—is one which obeys Dalton's law of partial pressures and the ideal gas equation.

Ideal solution—is one in which the properties of the solution are an average of the corresponding molar properties of the two components.

Immiscible—mutually insoluble.

Immunity—a condition wherein a substance is free from injurious attack.

Impurity level—an energy level due to the presence of impurity atoms in an extrinsic semiconductor.

Indicator—a substance which when added in small amount in a reaction, shows by change in colour or other property when the reaction is virtually complete.

Induction period—a time period of slow rate of reaction at the start of a process which needs some initiation.

Inhibitor—a substance which slows the rate of a reaction.

Insulator—a material which at ordinary temperature does not conduct electricity owing to a lack of electrons in the conduction band.

Interatomic distance—the distance between the nuclei of the atoms considered.

Internal energy, U—is a thermodynamic state function expressing the energy stored within a system. The increase in internal energy, ΔU, in a process in a closed system is equal to the sum of the heat added to and the work done on the system, $\Delta U = q + w$.

Intrinsic semiconductor—material in which semiconducting properties are characteristic of the pure material itself.

Inversion—in molecules with non-planar configuration of three bonds about an atom, is a type of motion resembling that of an umbrella turning "inside-out".

Ion—a charged species formed by an atom losing or gaining electrons or by the dissociation of a neutral compound into positive and negative parts.

Ion-exchange—the replacement of one ion species by another of higher concentration.

Ionic strength—a precisely defined algebraic quantity which serves to measure the effect of the charges of ions in solution.

Ionization (of an atom)—is the loss of one or more electrons from the atom to leave a positive ion.

Ionization (in solution)—is the formation of ions in solution by a chemical reaction between solute and solvent.

Ionization energy—is the least amount of energy required to remove an electron from an atom in its ground state.

Isomer—one of a number of compounds with the same molecular formula, but different structures.

Isomorphism—a property of different substances in having the same crystal structure.

Isotactic polymer—is one having the side groups oriented all on the same side of the main chain.

Isothermal process—is one which is maintained at constant temperature as in a thermostat.

Isotopes—atoms of the same element, differing in atomic mass owing to having different numbers of neutrons, but having the same atomic number, that is, the same number of protons.

Kinetics—is the study of reaction rates and mechanisms, and of the factors affecting them.

Knocking—undesirable self-ignition in a motor, rather than controlled combustion initiated by the spark plugs.

Latent heat—is heat absorbed in change of state with no change in temperature.

Lattice energy—is the energy input per mole required to drive the crystal apart into its component ions in the gas phase.

Lewis acid—a substance which accepts an electron pair.

Lewis base—a substance which donates an electron pair.

Ligand—an ion or chemical compound which donates an electron pair by which it is coordinated to a central atom or ion to form a complex ion or coordination compound; ligands are Lewis bases.

Liquid crystals—are molecular liquids in which the orientations of the molecules are ordered but not their positions in space.

Liquid junction potential—is a difference in electric potential which develops between two different electrolyte solutions in contact, owing to the fact that the ions present have different charges and move at different speeds, causing a separation in charge.

Lone pair—a pair of valence electrons of an atom which are not shared with another atom to form a bond.

Lyotropic mesophase—a liquid crystal which is formed as a result of the interaction between a solute and solvent.

Macrophyte—a macroscopic plant.

Manometer—a device for measuring gas pressure, which works by balancing the pressure of the gas against the hydrostatic pressure of a liquid.

Mantle—a zone of the interior of the earth immediately underlying the crust and extending about halfway to the earth's centre.

Mass fraction—of a substance in a system or phase is the mass of that substance present divided by the total mass of the system or phase.

Melting point—see freezing point.

Mesophase—a term applied to liquid crystals to indicate their character intermediate between solid and liquid.

Metabolites—products of various processes occurring within living systems.

Metallurgy—the science and applied science of winning, purifying and adapting metals.

Metathesis—the decomposition of two compounds resulting in the production of two new compounds in which parts of the two original compounds have exchanged places.

Miscible—mutually soluble to give one phase.

Mixture—a system containing two or more substances; 'mechanical mixture' implies the existence of two or more phases whereas the word mixture alone includes solutions.

Molality—of a solution is the amount of solute (in mol) per mass of solvent (in kg).

Molar heat capacity—of a substance is the amount of heat required to raise the temperature of one mole of the substance by one kelvin.

Molar mass—of a substance is the mass of one mole of it.

Molarity—of a solution is the amount of solute present (in mole) per litre of the solution; refers to species actually present. See also formality.

Mole—is the amount of substance which contains as many elementary entities as there are carbon atoms in exactly 12 g of isotopically pure carbon-12.

Mole fraction—of a substance in solution is the amount of it (in mol) divided by the total amount of solute and solvent (in mol).

Molecular formula—for a well-defined molecular substance gives the actual numbers of atoms of each element present in a single molecule of it.

Molecular orbital—a wave function which is a solution to the Schrödinger equation for an electron in a molecule.

Molecularity of a reaction—is the number of entities reacting simultaneously in an elementary reaction.

Molecule—is a group of atoms with no net charge joined together by chemical bonds, and acting physically and chemically as a single unit.

Monomer—the individual molecule which combines with others of its kind to form a larger molecular unit, or polymer.

Natural process—is one which actually occurs without being driven artificially, in a direction towards equilibrium; also called a spontaneous process.

Nematic mesophase—are liquid crystals in which the positions of molecules are completely disordered.

Neutralization—is a reaction between an acid and a base.

Neutron—a fundamental subatomic particle with zero charge and mass about 1.68×10^{-24} g.

Nobility—the relative tendency of an element to resist oxidation or loss of electrons.

n-type semiconductor—an electron-rich semiconductor made by doping the host material with atoms of higher valence than the host.

Nucleophile—an atom which readily coordinates to a positive centre through a non-bonding pair of electrons in its valence shell.

Nucleus—the positively charged central part of an atom, without the electrons, and constituting most of the atomic mass.

Nuclide—an isotope of an element.

Number of components—is the minimum number of different substances needed to specify the composition of the possible phases present in a system.

Optical activity—is the property of causing rotation of polarized light.

Optical isomer—one of two isomers in which all atom-atom distances have an analogue in the superimposable mirror images of each other; see also geometric isomers, structural isomers.

Osmosis—the passing of solvent molecules through a semi-permeable membrane from a region of lower concentration of solute to a region of higher concentration.

Osmotic pressure—the hydrostatic pressure which must be applied on the high solute concentration side to just prevent the osmosis or passage of solvent through a semi-permeable membrane and achieve a balance with no net migration of solvent.

Overall order of reaction—is the sum of the exponents of the concentration terms in the experimental rate law for the reaction.

Oxidant—a substance which oxidizes another substance and is itself reduced.

Oxidation—a process in which a substance increases in oxidation number, or loses electrons; actual combination with oxygen is only one way in which this can occur.

Oxidation state or number—a number assigned to an element to indicate its position on a scale of oxidation levels defined by an arbitrary set of rules.

Paramagnetic—the property of being attracted by a magnetic field.

Partial pressure—of one gas in a mixture of gases is equal to the product of the total pressure and the mole fraction of the one gas.

Passivation—the rendering of a metal inactive by the formation of a protective oxide coating.

pε—for an electrode,

$$p\varepsilon = -\log a_e = \frac{F}{2.303\, RT} \times \varepsilon$$
$$= \frac{\varepsilon}{0.0592} \text{ at } 25^\circ\text{ C}$$

where ε is electrode potential, F is the faraday, R is the gas constant, T is in kelvin.

Period—a horizontal row of elements in the periodic table.

Periodicity—a pattern of behavior in which a repeating sequence of properties of the elements in the periodic table occurs from row to row.

Permittivity—defined as ε_0 in the equation

for Coulomb's law, (for vacuum)

$$F = - \frac{q_1 \cdot q_2}{4\pi\varepsilon_0 r^2}$$

where $\varepsilon_0 = 8.8542\times10^{-12}\,C^2 J^{-1}\,m^{-1}$.

pH—is defined by, $pH = -\log a_{H^+}$, and is approximated by, $pH = -\log [H^+]_r$.

Phase—within a given system, is all of the matter having a particular set of properties, and distinct from other parts of the system.

Photon—a single quantum of radiant energy, $E = h\nu$.

Photosynthesis—a process in plants by which CO_2, under the influence of light of suitable energy, is reduced by a compound such as H_2O to form carbohydrates.

Piston—a disk-shaped part designed to make a snug, sliding closure of gas within a cylinder.

Pitting—is the corrosion of a metal at a particular spot in depth rather than laterally.

Plastic—a polymeric material which can be molded, formed, or extruded into useful shapes when hot.

Plastic crystals—are molecular crystals in which the molecules rotate at temperatures below the melting point.

Pluton—a deep-seated igneous rock formation.

Polar molecule—a molecule in which some separation occurs of the centres of positive and negative charge.

Polarization (electrical)—is the amount by which the potential of an electrode on passage of current differs from the reversible potential when no appreciable current flows.

Polarized light—light in which only one direction of electric vector is present. The electric vector is always perpendicular to the direction of motion, but in ordinary light the electric vector takes all such directions at random.

Pollutant—an undesirable substance either added or developed in the environment.

Polymer—a large molecular unit made by the covalent bonding of identical small units (monomer).

Polymorphism—is the occurrence in a substance of more than one crystal structure at the same temperature and pressure.

Polyprotic acid—is an acid which contains more than one acidic hydrogen atom per formula.

Pressure—is force per unit area.

Primary cell—is an electrochemical cell which when spent is not recharged either chemically or electrically.

Primitive unit cell—is the smallest unit cell for a given lattice, and has only one lattice point.

Proton—is a fundamental subatomic particle with positive charge equal to about $1.602 \times 10^{-19}C$ and mass about 1.67×10^{-24} g.

p-type semiconductor—an electron-poor semiconductor made by doping the host material with atoms of lower valence than the host.

Pyrolysis—is a reaction carried out at high temperature in order to bring about decomposition.

Pyrophoric—having a tendency to catch fire spontaneously on contact with air.

Quantum number—is a number used in quantum mechanics to specify the allowed energy levels in an atom or molecule.

R (gases)—is the gas constant, used in the ideal gas equation, $PV = nRT$, with value $8.314\,33\,J\,K^{-1}\,mol^{-1}$

R (organic)—is used to represent a general organic alkyl or aryl group, e.g. RCl.

Racemic form—is the mixture of equal amounts of the two optical isomers (enantiomers) of a molecular compound; it shows no optical activity.

Rank (of coal)—is a classification of commercial coals on the bases of the moisture content, the content of volatile organic compounds, and the carbon content.

Rate constant—is the proportionality constant in the experimental rate law which expresses the rate of reaction as a function of concentrations of reactants.

Rate law—is the algebraic equation expressing the experimental rate of reaction per unit volume as a function of the concentration of reactants.

Rate of reaction—is the rate at which the amount of a designated reactant (or product) changes with time, as in, $J = \dfrac{dn_A}{dt}$.

Rate of reaction per unit volume—measures the rate at which the concentration of a designated reactant (or product) changes with time, as in, $r = \dfrac{1}{a}\dfrac{d[A]}{dt}$.

where a is the stoichiometric coefficient of A in the chemical reaction.

Reaction mechanism—describes the steps in the path by which a reaction is thought to take place.

Reaction quotient, Q—is the product of the relative activities of the products (each raised to its appropriate power) divided by the product of the relative activities of the reactants (each raised to its appropriate power). When apt, relative concentrations and relative pressures are used in place of relative activities.

Redox reaction—is one in which electrons are transferred from one substance, the reductant, to another, the oxidant.

Reductant—is a substance which reduces another substance and is itself oxidized.

Reduction—is a process in which a substance loses oxygen, decreases in oxidation number, or gains electrons.

Refrigerator—a device designed to transfer heat from a cold body to a hot body.

Relative activity—is the ratio of the activity to a standard activity, that is, $a = \lambda/\lambda°$.

Resonance—is the property of a molecule having a combination of more than one possible Lewis structure at the same time.

Restrainer—is a substance which impedes the reaction at an anode or cathode, and thereby limits corrosion.

Reversible process (thermodynamic sense)—is one in which the state of the system is changed from A to B, but can be returned from B to A in such a way as to leave both the system and its surroundings unaltered.

Reversible reaction (kinetics)—is a reaction in which the backward reaction, as well as the forward one, is significant.

Rigidity—the ability of a material to retain its shape.

Salinity—is the total ionic content of a natural water, expressed in g of solute per kg of the water.

Salt bridge—is the electrolytic connection made between the two electrode compartments to allow electric current to flow by movement of ions. Chemical and electrical potential differences are minimized by using a concentrated solution of a balanced electrolyte such as KCl.

Saturated compound (organic)—is a carbon compound having only single C-C bonds.

Saturated solution—is a solution in which undissolved solute is in equilibrium with solute dissolved in the solvent under given conditions.

Scattering—is the deflection of subatomic particles by collision with atoms.

Scrubbing—removal of gas from solution by passing through an absorbant column.

Selection rules—are those which limit the possible transitions between energy levels.

Semiconductor—material with electrical

conductivity in between those of insulators and metals.

Semi-permeable membrane—is one which allows diffusion of solvent species in preference to solute species.

Sensitivity—is a measure of the ease with which an explosion is initiated by various factors such as heat, spark, or impact.

Sigmoidal—S-shaped.

Single electrode potential—is equal to the measured emf of the cell consisting of the specified electrode and the standard hydrogen electrode. According to an international convention single electrode potentials are expressed as reduction potentials.

Smectic mesophase—a liquid crystal in which the molecules are arranged in layers within which the positions are disordered.

Solder—a low melting alloy of metals used to connect metal parts.

Solubility—is the amount of solute which can dissolve in a given amount of solvent at a given temperature; it is the concentration of a saturated solution.

Solubility product constant—is a thermodynamic constant equal to the product of the relative activities of the participating ions raised to appropriate powers, in a saturated solution of a slightly soluble electrolyte.

Soluble—means capable of being dissolved in a solvent so as to produce only one phase.

Solution—a homogeneous mixture of substances, constituting a single phase.

Sparging—is removal of a gas from solution by flushing with another gas such as nitrogen.

Spectrometer—is an instrument capable of classifying radiation according to accurately measured wave length or frequency.

Spectrophotometer—is an instrument capable of classifying radiation and measuring the intensity at each wave length.

Spectroscope—is an instrument capable of classifying radiation according to wave length, and allowing it to be observed or recorded.

Spectrum—the array or pattern of radiation of different energies transmitted or absorbed, and resolved by either refraction or diffraction according to wave length or frequency.

Spontaneous reaction—is one that, once initiated, proceeds naturally and of its own accord without a supply of energy.

Stability (to explosion)—is the ability of an explosive to remain unchanged over a long period in storage.

Staggered configuration—is a molecular configuration around a C-C single bond in which the set of atoms at one end does not line up with the set at the other end.

State (thermodynamic)—is the condition of a system defined by its properties such as temperature, pressure, and composition.

State (physical)—the physical condition of a system as to aggregation, whether gaseous, liquid, or solid.

State function—is one the value of which depends only on the state of the system.

Steel—an alloy of iron and other metal(s) which does not contain more than 1.5 percent carbon.

Steric factor—an effect determined by the size and position of an atom or group of atoms in space.

Stoichiometry—is the study of chemical equations and particularly the relative mass relations implied by the symbols and formulae used in these equations.

Storage cell—is an electrochemical cell which is reversible in the sense that it can be recharged after use by application of a reverse electrical current.

Strong electrolyte—is one in which the dissociation or ionization to form ions in the solution is complete or virtually so.

Structural formula—one in which the symbols of the elements present are arranged on paper and lines drawn between the symbols to show which atoms are joined by chemical bonds; a structural formula may also indicate the geometry of the atoms in the molecule.

Structural isomers—substances with the same molecular formulae but different structural formulae.

Sublimation—is the conversion of a solid to the vapour state.

Supercooling—is the attainment of a temperature below the normal freezing point of a liquid without solidification.

Surroundings—in thermodynamics, anything outside of the system.

Syndiotactic polymer—is one having chains with side groups arranged alternately on opposite sides of the chain.

Synthesis—is a chemical reaction in which two or more compounds or elements combine to form a desired single compound.

Tangent—is a straight line which touches, but does not intersect, a curved line.

Temperature arrest—is a line on a heating or cooling curve representing a condition where temperature does not change with time.

Thermistor—is a device which utilizes the large change in resistance with temperature of a semi-conductor to monitor temperature.

Thermochemistry—is the study of the heat associated with chemical reactions.

Thermocline—is a water layer in which the temperature gradient with depth is markedly greater than that of the water above or below the layer.

Thermodynamics—is the study of relation-ships among heat, work, energy, and the properties of matter.

Thermoplastic material—can be melted and reformed into a desired shape.

Thermosetting material—on heating sets permanently into a rigid shape.

Thermotropic mesophase—a liquid crystal which is formed on heating a normal crystal and which upon further heating changes to a normal liquid.

Tie line—in a temperature-composition phase diagram, is a horizontal line joining the compositions of two phases in equilibrium at a particular temperature.

Titration—is a determination in which a measured amount of solution of known concentration is added to a definite amount of substance to be determined so that when a recognizable end point is reached, the amount of analyte may be calculated from the amount of titrant added.

Trans—a prefix indicating that two groups are on opposite sides of a molecule.

Triple point—the temperature and pressure at which three phases of a one component system exist in equilibrium.

Trophic level—is a feeding level in a food chain wherein energy, originally derived by plants from the sun, is passed on by higher organisms feeding on lower ones in the chain. Thus plants occupy the first trophic level, herbivores the second, and so on.

Unit cell—is a small representative part of a crystal lattice from which the entire lattice can be generated by repeating the cell in all directions.

Universe (thermodynamic)—is the whole of matter consisting of the system under study and its surroundings.

Unnatural process—is one which is proceeding in a direction away from equilibrium.

Valence—is a number showing the combining power of an element; for example the number of hydrogen atoms combined with one atom of the element.

Valence band—the lower energy band in which electronic energy levels are found in a polyatomic solid, in which the electrons are relatively immobile.

Valence shell—is the outer shell of electrons in an atom.

Vapour pressure—is the pressure of the vapour in equilibrium with liquid at a given temperature.

Viscosity—is the resistance of a liquid to shear and flow.

Voltaic cell—is an electrochemical cell which acts as a source of electrical energy by providing a potential difference at its terminals.

Water pollution—the introduction or development in natural waters of any effect or substance which is deleterious in respect to the use of the water for purposes such as drinking, washing, recreation, irrigation, industrial consumption, or as a natural habitat for aquatic life.

Wave functions—are certain allowed solutions to a wave equation.

Weak electrolyte—is one which is incompletely ionized or dissociated.

Work—is the form of energy transferred when the point of application of a force moves through a distance.

Zero point energy—is the lowest possible vibrational energy that a quantum oscillator can have.

Zone melting—is a technique used to purify metals and alloys in which impurities are removed from the product by successive recrystallizations in a molten zone.

INDEX

INDEX